The History of Italy, from the Commencement of the Wars of the French Revolution

By

Colonel Procter

To CHARLES MILLS, ESQ.

My dear Mills,

Permit me the pleasure of inscribing your name on this work. I need not detail the reasons of private esteem and regard which urge me on this occasion; and no apology will be required for my dedicating this volume to one who has performed so much in literature, and from whom so much more is expected. You have already thrown high romantic interest over the stern features of the Crusades; and you have now found a fairer and more brilliant theme in the history and institutions of Chivalry. Those books will naturally be classed together, and reflect value on each other; and I shall feel proud if my attempt to delineate the revolutions of Italy can be associated with that work, in which you have successfully treated the literature and art of the same interesting country.

Believe me,

My dear Mills,

Very faithfully yours,

G. P.

PREFACE.

IN introducing this volume to the notice of the reader, it is unnecessary to insist upon the general importance of Italian history. Neither need he be reminded of the fact, that our language has hitherto offered no succinct and comprehensive narrative of the prominent vicissitudes in the long tragedy of Italy. I am aware that the deep interest and value of the subject demanded an abler pen: but I may at least derive encouragement from the reflection, that the present work provokes no comparison, and that, as it has been unattempted by others, it will in some measure fill a void in our historical literature.

Of the luminous chapter which Mr. Hallam has devoted to Italy, in his view of the state of Europe during the middle ages, it is impossible to speak without praise. But it is obvious that minuteness of historical details is altogether incompatible with the limits and intention of such a sketch; and the middle ages are only a part of our subject. Besides, Mr. Hallam's elegant province has been rather to allude to facts for general deductions, than to state them in measured narrative; and some previous acquaintance with Italian history is necessary, before the value of his reflections can be appreciated.

For the substratum of his chapter, Mr. Hallam has taken principally M. Sismondi's History of the Italian Republics; and it might appear, at first sight, that a translation of that beautiful work would best familiarize the English reader with a subject, which its accomplished author has treated with equal fidelity and eloquence. But M. Sismondi's design almost wholly excluded the Italian annals of the first five centuries of modern history, and admitted only very imperfect outlines of those of the last three hundred years. His singular minuteness and even his philosophical digressions, however careful and valuable in themselves, must prevent his book from becoming a manual of historical instruction; and the general student may complain, that a single division of his inquiries is expanded into sixteen volumes. If prolixity forbade a translation, incompleteness of design rendered a mere abridgment of M. Sismondi's work equally objectionable. There is little temptation to linger amidst the darkness of the first five hundred years which succeeded the fall of the Western Empire; but, that his journey may be complete, the reader will expect to be conducted, however rapidly, over that gloomy waste, which connects the two splendid periods of Italian greatness. And if, since the second fall of Italy, her annals have been for three centuries languid and her fortunes inglorious, their tale will not be the less eagerly demanded. Yet, beyond the ruin of her independence, M. Sismondi has scarcely felt himself called upon to continue his admirable labours; and he has therefore in a great degree, left the completion of Italian story—an ungrateful task, a melancholy consummation—to inferior spirits.

The English reader, then, would neither have been satisfied with a translation nor an abridgment of M. Sismondi's work; and abandoning the intention of offering either, I have been contented with consulting, not servilely following him. I have admired his talents, I might have relied upon his scrupulous integrity: I have nevertheless often been compelled to differ from him in opinion; and I have sought for the means of judging for myself among the principal authorities from which his own materials were collected. But I am too conscious of the defects of the present work, to expect credit for all the labour which it has cost me; and I can safely advance no other pretensions than conciseness and accuracy.

THE HISTORY OF ITALY.

CHAPTER I. FROM THE FALL OF THE WESTERN EMPIRE TO THE CORONATION OF THE EMPEROR OTHO THE GREAT, a.d. 476-961.

PART I.
Fall of the western empire—Reign of Odoacer king of Italy—Conquest of Italy by the Ostrogoths—Reign of Theodoric the Great—Fall of the Ostrogoth power—Conquest of Italy by Belisarius and Narses—Government of Narses—Invasion of Italy by the Lombards—Kingdom of the Lombards—Stale of Italy after its foundation—Duration and extinction of the Lombard dynasty—Conquest of Lombardy by Charlemagne—His coronation as emperor of the West-Laws of the Lombards—Feudal system—Allodial tenures—Benefices—Fiefs or feuds—Sub-infeudation—State of the feudal aristocracy—Reign of Charlemagne in Italy—His power and character—Successors of Charlemagne—Carlovingian dynasty in Italy—Its extinction—Feudal anarchy in Italy—Berenger I. king of Italy and emperor—His death—Incursions of the Saracens and Hungarians—Effects of their inroads in promoting the freedom of the Italian cities—Hugo, king of Italy—His deposition—His son Lothaire king—His death—Berenger II. king of Italy—Otho the Great king of Italy—Berenger his vassal, deposed—Otho emperor.

THE line which separates the ancient and the modern history of the world can be no other than an imaginary boundary. There is no natural chasm in the train of events, no cessation or interruption in the tide of fate, at which a new æra can be counted distinct from, and unconnected with, the moment that has immediately preceded it. Wherever we assume our station, we must still refer to the past, if we would render the future intelligible. Yet the adoption of some recognised though artificial limit is indispensable; and historians have agreed in dating the commencement of modern history from the Fall of the Western Empire of the Romans. The epoch thus created by common consent is sufficiently convenient for the general annals of Europe; but it is, on many accounts, peculiarly appropriate in its application to the vicissitudes of Italian history. The rise of the feudal system in that country, the establishment of the greatest of her republics, the origin of ecclesiastical power; almost every circumstance which, in succeeding centuries, affected the moral and political condition of the Italians, was either faintly shadowed out or more distinctly visible in the subversion of the western empire.

Of the gigantic fabric of Roman power there had long remained to the western emperors but the name and the precarious possession of Italy, at the mercy of barbarian invaders or mercenaries. But it was not until the end of the fifth century that the final blow was given to the magnificent structure which, however rudely assailed, had gradually fallen rather under the pressure of its own stupendous weight than by the shock of external violence. Odoacer, a leader of the bands of foreign mercenaries in the imperial pay, who formed at once the terror and the defence of Italy, was destined to complete the ruin of ages. His fellow-soldiers were barbarians of various nations: they envied the fortune of their brethren in Gaul, Spain, and Africa, whose victorious arms had acquired an independent and perpetual inheritance; and they insolently required that a third part of the lands of Italy should be immediately divided among them. The audacious demand was resisted by the patrician Orestes, who, having raised his son Augustulus to the imperial purple, governed under his nominal sovereignty; and Odoacer, himself a barbarian of Scythian descent, knew how to found his greatness upon the discontent which the refusal excited. He promised the troops, if they would associate under his orders, to obtain for them by force the lands which had been denied to their petition. He was elected by acclamation to the supreme command; and he speedily accomplished the overthrow of the feeble emperor and his more spirited parent. The patrician Orestes, after an ineffectual struggle, was taken and executed at Pavia; but Augustulus was permitted to preserve an inglorious existence by the resignation of his diadem. The name of the Empire of the West was suppressed by the modesty or prudence of the conqueror, (A.D. 476.) Odoacer reigned only as the king of Italy; and the sovereignty of Rome was transferred, for the first time, to the nations of the north.

The subjection of Italy to an insolent soldiery, and the partition of the third of all its territory among the brutal conquerors, seemed to plunge the degenerate descendants of the Roman name into the lowest abyss of shame and misery; yet it is from this epoch that we may trace the slow revival of those energies which the long and gloomy tyranny of the Cæsars had extinguished in the Italian people. It is impossible to conceive a more melancholy picture of national debasement and universal moral depravity, than is afforded by the last days of the empire. The Roman nobles, utterly sunken in slothful and voluptuous indulgence, were capable of no one manly or generous feeling. Animated neither by the desire of intellectual superiority, nor by the thirst of personal glory, they forsook the civil and military employments of the state, and have left to history no other record of their names than by the spoliation of their enormous and fatal wealth. The very existence of the rest of the nation, if possible more degraded and base, is concealed from our researches in worthless obscurity. The armies were composed only of barbarians, the country was cultivated only by slaves, and we ask in vain for a vestige of the free population. The mixture of the barbarian soldiery of Odoacer with the people whose possessions they had forcibly shared, infused the first principle of re-action and returning life into a diseased and corrupted body. The settlement of the conquerors in the provinces of Italy must be regarded only as the establishment, in a firmer posture, of the foreign mercenaries who had long formed the whole force of the state. The success of Odoacer was gained by no new swarm of barbarians; and the progress of desolation and wretchedness, in a country which had groaned under every extremity of war, pestilence, and famine, was arrested by his prudence, or mitigated by his humanity. His reign was not long; but he only fell to make way for other conquerors; and the native population, far from being exterminated, was again refreshed and invigorated by new accessions of foreign strength. At different intervals we shall find the Goths, the Lombards, and the Franks successively acquiring the dominion of Italy, and each incorporating themselves with their subjects, until the Italian character, thus quickening with the spirit of personal independence, the glorious distinction of these northern people, rose from the lowest depths of humiliation and cowardice to an elevation and dignity of soul which at once fitted it for the enjoyment, and ensured the possession of freedom.

The reign of Odoacer had endured but fourteen years, when he was summoned to defend his throne against Theodoric, king of the Ostrogoths, who prepared, at the suggestion or with the connivance of Zeno, emperor of the East, to lead the whole force of his people from the provinces of the eastern empire to the conquest of Italy. Theodoric, who united in his person all the heroic qualities of uncivilized life, with many of the milder virtues, had succeeded, by the death of his uncles and father, to the hereditary sovereignty of his nation. His youth had been passed at Constantinople, whither he had been sent as a pledge of the alliance which the imbecile Zeno purchased of the barbarians. He had been educated at that capital with care and tenderness; he excelled in warlike exercises; and, if it be doubtful whether he cultivated or neglected the science and arts of Greece, his mind was at least stored with the fruits of observation and intelligence. He had already proved to his subjects, by his exploits, that he had not degenerated from the valour of his ancestors: the whole nation were ready to attend his standard, and the emperor Zeno gladly seized the opportunity of ridding himself of a dangerous ally, by proposing, or consenting, that Theodoric should lead his restless and turbulent followers into Italy. Zeno had maintained a friendly correspondence with Odoacer after the fall of the western empire; but Theodoric nevertheless entered Italy to reign as the ally or lieutenant of the emperor, (A.D. 489.) His march must be considered as the emigration of an entire people, for the families and most precious effects of the Goths were carefully transported with them. Odoacer defended with unshaken courage the crown which his sword had won. He suffered repeated defeats, and lost all Italy, except Ravenna, where he maintained himself; and for three years the contest remained undecided. It was at length terminated by a treaty, which gave equal and undivided authority over Italy to the two leaders, and admitted Theodoric into Ravenna. (A.D. 493.) But, in the midst of the consequent rejoicings, Odoacer was treacherously stabbed by the hand, or at the command, of his rival, his soldiers were every where massacred, and Theodoric reigned, without opposition, from the Alps to the extremity of Calabria.

Notwithstanding the foul act of perfidy which sullied its commencement, the long reign of Theodoric was an era of tranquil felicity for the inhabitants of Italy. Under his vigorous but impartial administration, they found a repose and prosperity to which their wearied country had long been a stranger-. The civil offices of the state were confided to Italians alone; the people enjoyed their dress and language, their laws and customs, their personal freedom, two-thirds of their landed property, and protection from the violence of their barbarian conquerors. Theodoric, with singular moderation, in the pride of victory and flower of his age, renounced the prosecution of farther conquests to devote himself to the duties of civil government. The hostilities in which he was sometimes engaged were speedily terminated by his arms, and his kingdom was preserved from insult by the terror of his name. Agriculture revived under the shadow of peace, navigation was pursued in security, and commerce increased and multiplied beneath his fostering encouragement. It was the policy of Theodoric to maintain the distinction between his Italian and Gothic subjects, by restricting the former to civil, and the latter to military employments. The Goths held their lands as military stipends, which bound them in constant readiness for the public defence; they were spread over the kingdom, in possession of one-third of its soil, and the whole extent of Italy was distributed into the several quarters of a well-regulated camp. In a new and happy climate their numbers multiplied with formidable rapidity, and they could muster two hundred thousand warriors, besides their women and children. While their monarch strove to perpetuate their separation from the Italians, it was his constant endeavour to moderate their barbarian violence, to teach them the duties of civil society, and to confirm them in habits of temperance, obedience, and order. For three-and-thirty years Theodoric watched, with laborious anxiety, over the common happiness of both classes of his subjects. Few sovereigns have in an equal degree merited to be numbered among the benefactors of mankind; yet it is painful to add, that the evening of his life was clouded by popular discontent, soured by ingratitude, and defiled with virtuous blood. The hatred of the Italians was excited by the imposition of taxes which were necessary for the exigencies of the state; and the mind of the king, stung to indignation by their ill-founded murmurs, was filled with suspicions of treason. The murder of his rival, Odoacer, was a stain upon the fair fame of his manhood; and the execution of his minister, the learned and pious Boethius,—the last of the Romans, says a great author, whom Cato or Tully could have acknowledged for their countryman,—and of the innocent and venerable patrician, Symmachus, branded the old age of the monarch with indelible infamy, and embittered his last hours with unavailing remorse.

After the death of Theodoric (A.D. 525), the dominion of the Ostrogoths lasted only twenty-seven years. It was for Italy a period of internal dissensions and foreign invasions, of fearful agitations and bloodshed and horror. Of six princes, whose brief reigns were crowded into this narrow space, no one vacated the throne after the gradual decay of nature's powers: the first perished prematurely by intemperance; the career of royalty of the others was terminated by deposition or violent death. But it is not within my purpose to trace with minuteness every vicissitude in the fortunes of an obscure age and a barbarous people; it will be sufficient to relate the general circumstances which produced the extinction of the Gothic dominion. A change of national character was not the least powerful cause. Notwithstanding the precautions of Theodoric, it was impossible to prevent his followers from losing, in the peaceful bosom of civilized society, some portion of the rude hardihood and valour of barbarian life. Even his successful efforts to humanize their manners and correct their excesses, could not fail to mitigate the violence of their warlike spirit. They had already, during his reign, adopted the fashion of Italian dress, and a period of sixty years must have rapidly effaced the proud distinction between the conquerors, and the people among whom they had every where settled. If mixture with the freemen of the north was calculated to revive the energies of the feeble natives of Italy, Italian example was certain to exercise an equal though opposite and fatal influence upon the simple virtues of the barbarian. The distractions of the Gothic kingdom were insidiously fomented by the arts of Justinian, then emperor of the East; the advantage which Grecian treachery extracted from the disorders of Italy was seconded by the courage and military skill of Belisarius, and afterwards of the eunuch Narses; and the good fortune of Justinian, in possessing such generals, the first of whom he rewarded with the basest ingratitude, gave the temporary possession of Italy to his arms, and shed lustre over the expiring vigour of his empire. Yet under all the evils of intestine disputes, the Gothic kingdom, with a force of two hundred thousand combatants, could not have been twice subjugated by inferior numbers, whose imperfect courage was with difficulty sustained by the talents of their leaders, if the Goths had not already lost the better part of their original spirit. But they still fought with a resolution that merited a happier fate. The details of the conquest of Italy, first by Belisarius, and again, after a general revolt of the Goths, by Narses, belong rather to the eastern empire than to my subject. The contest was long chequered by alternate fortune; but when the two last Gothic sovereigns, Totila and Teias, had successively fallen, as became them, in the field of battle, the total subversion of their monarchy was finally accomplished.

The eunuch Narses, under the title of exarch, administered the government of Italy with wisdom and vigour for about fifteen years. But his virtues were sullied by avarice; his rule became unpopular; complaints of his oppression reached the imperial throne, and he was deprived of his command. The mandate of recall to Constantinople was couched in expressions of insult; and Narses, if the popular belief of his age may be credited, stooping to an unworthy revenge for the ingratitude of the court and the Italians, invited the Lombards, a barbarian nation who had settled in Pannonia, to undertake the invasion and conquest of Italy. This people, whose successful enterprise was to perpetuate their name in the fertile plains of northern Italy, were distinguished, even among the German tribes, for their freedom, their valour, and their ferocity, (A.D. 568.) Their warlike sovereign, Alboin, descended from the Alps with the entire nation, and the whole country, from those mountains to the gates of Ravenna and Rome, rapidly passed under his dominion. The helpless successor of Narses could offer no opposition in the field; the pusillanimous Italians were not ashamed to believe, without a trial, that the barbarians were invincible, and the city of Pavia was the only place which attempted serious resistance to the invaders. The siege lasted above three years, and, when famine opened the gates, Alboin spared the inhabitants, and established among them the capital of the new kingdom of LOMBARDY. His reign was glorious, but he did not live to complete the subjugation of Italy. An independent people had already formed an impregnable fastness in the lagunes of Venice; Rome, under its bishops, who had even then conceived in part their schemes of ambition, continued faithful to the eastern emperors, less from attachment to them, than from terror and hatred of the Lombards; and the province of Ravenna, the Pentapolis of Romagna, and the maritime cities of southern Italy, remained in the hands of the Greeks, and under the supremacy of the imperial exarchs. The kingdom of the Lombards, therefore, embraced only the northern divisions of Italy; but a prince of their nation, subject no more than in name to the monarchy, penetrated with his followers into the centre of those provinces which now form the Neapolitan dominions, and there established the Lombard duchy of Benevento.

The power of the Lombards lasted with considerable splendour for two hundred and six years. Like other rude states, their monarchy was in principle elective; their freedom was often barbarian licence; and crime and disorder throw an occasional stain over the pages of their history: but the succession of their sovereigns was marked with ability and virtue, and the troubled series of their annals was adorned with fair intervals of peace, order, and internal happiness. The effects of prosperity and wealth, and the influence of Italian climate and example, rapidly civilized their manners, humanized their characters, and weakened their hardihood. The founder of their monarchy, Alboin, was gifted with all the qualities, good and evil, which form the character of a barbarian and a conqueror. He was murdered, after a reign of only four years, at the instigation of his queen, Rosamond. (A.D. 573.) Her father had fallen in battle against the Lombards before her forced union with their king; and her brutal lord, during the intoxication of a feast in his palace near Verona, obliged her to drink from a goblet which had been formed of the skull of her parent. She vowed to wipe out the insult in his blood; and the indulgence of an adulterous passion was superadded to the desire of vengeance. The premature death of Alboin arrested the progress of the Lombard arms. Clepho, a noble chieftain, was elected to the kingly office; and a second tragedy closed his mortal career in less than two years, (A.D. 574.) The royal dignity was suspended in anarchy during the minority of his son, Autharis; but his valour and talents restored it with manhood in his person, (A.D. 584.) He successfully defended his kingdom from the arms of the Merovingian sovereigns of France, and confirmed and extended the power of his nation, (A.D. 591.) From the death of Autharis to the overthrow of the Lombard greatness by Charlemagne, nineteen princes successively reigned in the capital of Pavia; but their history will no farther interest the reader than as it is connected with the fortunes of Italy. The provinces which had remained to the Greeks from the original conquest of Alboin, still resisted the efforts of his successors; and, for nearly two centuries, the exarchs of Ravenna shared the dominion of Italy with the monarchs of Lombardy. Under the shadow of a mighty name, the Greek empire had long concealed the extent of its decline. But the charm was at last broken; and the conquest of Ravenna, by the Lombard king Astolpho (A.D. 752), put a final period to the power and the office of the exarchs. All Italy now appeared prostrate at the feet of Astolpho, and the fall of Rome might have completed the glory of his reign; but though the Greek power had sunken for ever, the Lombard kingdom, left without a competitor, had lost its own energy in awaiting the occasion for its display. When the pope in person implored the protection of Pepin, who, succeeding to the power of his father, Charles Martel, had erected his throne on the ruin of the Merovingian dynasty of France, the degenerate Lombards were no longer equal to a struggle with the courageous Franks, (A.D. 755.) A French army crossed the Alps under their gallant monarch, to deliver the church from the oppression of Astolpho; and the Lombard, after a weak resistance, was compelled to restore the territory of Romagna, and to yield the exarchate of Ravenna to the Holy See. After this disgraceful reverse, the monarchy of the Lombards survived about twenty years in languor and decay, until it fell before the irresistible power of Charlemagne. To that mighty conqueror, Desiderio, the last of the Lombard princes, resigned his sceptre and his capital. The friendship of the victor and the papal see was cemented over the ruin of the Lombard dynasty, and in the church of St. Peter at Rome Charlemagne received from the hands of pope Leo III. the crown, the symbol of the restoration of the empire of the West, (A.D. 800.)

The monarchy of the Lombards was, as has been already mentioned, elective. The great assembly of the nation was held in the palace or on the open plains of Pavia; and was composed of the *dukes*, or military governors of provinces, the great officers of state, the public functionaries, and, in fine, of all the freemen of the kingdom. At these assemblies the laws of the Lombards were established by the mutual consent of the sovereign and the people; and they have been esteemed the least imperfect of the barbaric codes. Seventy-six years after the Lombards came into Italy, their laws were solemnly ratified, some new provisions suitable to the silent changes of time were introduced, and the whole were promulgated by king Rotharis as the general act of the nation. Such crimes as threatened the life of the sovereign or the safety of the state were adjudged worthy of death; but the principle of pecuniary compensation extended through the rest of the code; and the price of blood and of an opprobrious word was measured with the same scrupulous diligence. We must not look in these constitutions, or in any code of the barbarian nations, for express acknowledgments of the rights of the people, the prerogatives of the aristocracy, or the limitations imposed upon the royal authority. All these existed independently of the laws; but the circumstance which characterized a free people was the regulation of punishments for each offence, with a precision which might appear ridiculous in our eyes, if we could forget that, in a rude and turbulent age, it formed the security of individuals against all arbitrary inflictions.

The circumstances which attended the establishment of the Lombard monarchy render the epoch of its power one of the most important and interesting events in Italian history; and it will be difficult to comprehend the peculiarities that marked the condition of Italy for several succeeding ages, without pausing in this place to take a rapid survey of the changes which originated in the conquests of Alboin. The continual hostilities which were exercised between the barbarian chieftains and the cities and provinces acknowledging the Greek dominion, infused reviving energy and independence into the Italian subjects of the eastern empire; and the weakness of a government which could afford them but feeble protection from the invaders, while it entailed on the native population the necessity of exertion to save them from the hated yoke of the Lombard, taught them to aspire to that freedom which could only be preserved by their own swords. Even before the fall of the exarchate, the allegiance of its scattered dependencies had evaporated into a name, and after the viceroys of the eastern empire had ceased to rule in Ravenna, the maritime cities of the south asserted and enjoyed the full measure of republican independence. At the close of this chapter it will be our business to revert briefly to the history of these cities, and to trace the rising fortunes of Venice. The aspect of other parts of Italy, under the Lombard monarchy, merits more immediate attention. It exhibits the origin and growth of the feudal system.

When the army of freemen who followed the standard of the Lombard conqueror had achieved the subjugation of northern Italy, the lands of the new kingdom were parcelled out among the victors; who, leaving the natives to cultivate them in a state of servitude, seized a third of the produce. Every soldier thus received a share of land; and though the division was undoubtedly unequal, the scale on which the distribution was regulated has entirely escaped every effort of modern research. There is no reason to believe in the existence of any privileges of hereditary nobility among the Lombards before the æra of their Italian invasion, and it can only be conjectured that the principal leaders of their army acquired a proportion of the spoil commensurate with the rank or estimation to which their military virtues had raised them among their fellow soldiers. The lands so partitioned out, in whatever proportions, were all termed *allodial*: they were subjected to no burthen, except that of the public defence, and passed to all the children equally, or, on their failure, to the nearest kindred. But besides the lands distributed among the nation, others were reserved to the crown for the support of its dignity, and the exercise of its munificence; and of these, the larger portion soon came to be granted out to favoured subjects and to provincial governors, under the title of *benefices* (beneficia). These gifts, which were originally for life, but gradually became hereditary, were saddled with the obligation of military service to the sovereign, who, on his part, was bound to his vassal by the corresponding duties of protection. When the Lombards had established themselves in their new possessions, they gave to their generals the government of cities and the provinces surrounding them, with the title of *dukes* (duces): the allodial proprietors were in readiness to serve under them for the public defence; and the whole conquering population preserved the form and the subordination of a military body. It was upon these great officers, the dukes, the marquises, or margraves, entrusted with the protection of the marches or frontiers, and (afterwards) the counts or governors of towns, that the royal bounty was for the most part bestowed in the shape of benefices; and when, through the weakness of the crown, these gifts were converted by violence or usage into hereditary possessions, the titles of the offices to which they had been originally attached descended with them. In this manner was formed the great hereditary aristocracy of royal feudatories, who held their lands as immediate vassals of the crown, and were bound to their sovereign by the mutual obligation of service and protection.

It was a natural consequence of hereditary benefices, which were afterwards more generally known by the term of *feuds*, that the great proprietors should carve out portions of their demesnes, to be held of themselves, by a similar tenure; and this custom of *sub-infeudation* became in the ninth and tenth centuries universal. It created a subordinate class of nobility, styled *vavassores*, a word expressing their double allegiance, both to their own lord and the superior of whom he held, and completed the chain of feudal aristocracy. The oath of fidelity which the great feudatory had taken, the homage which he paid, and the military service which he owed to his sovereign, were all exacted by himself from his vassals. These latter, from the castles which they every where built on their fiefs, were known by the appellation of *châtelains* as well as vavassores: they enjoyed the military services of inferior feudal tenants, and the labour of the villeins and serfs on their estates, who formed the mass of the peasant population, and were held in abject dependence and slavery.

While the royal donation of benefices was planting the foundations, and the custom of sub-infeuding was extending the ramifications of the feudal system, the condition of the allodial proprietors, who had formed the original strength of all the barbarian kingdoms, was fast assimilating to the same dependance upon a superior lord which distinguished later tenures. Allodial seems so much more desirable than feudal property, that it would appear at first sight extraordinary that the transition from the one sort of tenure to the other should have been, as it generally was, the voluntary act of the possessor. But amidst the rapine and violence, the private wars and public disorders which marked the times, the insulated allodialist found no protection or safety. Without law to redress his injuries, without power in the crown to support his rights, he was ever exposed to the tyranny of the rapacious governors and overbearing lords of his district, and he had no course left but to compromise with oppression, and subject himself, in return for protection, to a feudal superior. In Finance the allodial land almost all became feudal in little more than a century from the period before us; and, if the change was not so general, or cannot be so extensively traced, at least, in Italy, there can be no doubt of its prevalence. Where allodial estates were large, the possessors would naturally strengthen themselves by sub-infeuding them among their tenants, upon condition of military service: where they were small, they themselves needed the protection of the nearest châtelain; and in both cases, the supremacy of the great feudatory of the province would be necessary to complete their security. But it may be suspected that the process was far from being, in all instances, voluntary. The allodialist was often, perhaps, compelled to recognize himself the vassal of a great lord, and thus to confess an original feudal tenure which had never existed.

Under the feudal system generally, and particularly in as far as it prevailed in Italy, territorial property thus belonged only, in reality, to the gentlemen, the lower class of nobility, or châtelains. They were surrounded by their military retainers, and by the serfs of the glebe, whom they had originally enslaved, and from whom they took a third of the produce of the land. The towns were abandoned by a class which comprised the most considerable citizens; and the country bristled with their fortresses. Living on their demesnes like petty sovereigns, they felt neither the wish of cultivating their minds to shine in society, nor the necessity of dazzling, by their splendour, inferiors who were already in abject submission. War and the chase were their only pleasures, and their luxury knew no other objects. The education of the gentleman taught him no more than to tame the fiery spirit of the war-horse, to manage with address the buckler and heavy lance, and to endure without fatigue the weight of the most ponderous cuirass. It was neither required of him to speak with elegance nor to write with correctness. The vulgar tongue had already begun to assume a character entirely distinct from the Latin, while the Latin still formed the only written language. All the contracts of gentlemen of this period, of which a great number have been preserved, are drawn up by notaries in the most barbarous latinity, and at the foot of the act, the vender, the purchaser, and the witnesses, often all of them gentlemen, were able to make no other signature than a cross, which the notary declares to be the mark of the contracting parties. The nobility were as ignorant of the arts as of the sciences. They laboured to make their castles impregnable, but not to adorn their architecture, or render them agreeable abodes. Some of these substantial but gloomy edifices have withstood the attacks both of time and of enemies, and frown over the traveller at this hour from the summits of inaccessible rocks, or the entrance of narrow defiles.

While the whole country was in the hands of the rude lords of these dungeons, the authority of the dukes, their superiors, reposed only on a fiction of property, on an imaginary right to demesnes and provinces of which these great feudatories possessed, in reality, no portion. But still, the same system formed the security of the duke and the vavassore; it equally sanctioned the obedience of the great vassal and his inferior; and, for several centuries, the dukes enjoyed the aggregate of power which the united force of their châtelains could produce. In ascending the feudal scale, the king should have possessed over the dukes the same authority which they exercised over their vavassores. But if the right of property of the great feudatories over their provinces was but a fiction of the law, that of the sovereign over his kingdom was a still fainter shadow of reality; and since the stability of power rested on a territorial basis, the authority of the vavassores among their inferiors was necessarily arbitrary, that of the dukes but precarious, and that of the kings almost a nullity.

Such was the feudal system in its origin among the Lombards. It was a mixture of barbarism and liberty, discipline and independence, singularly calculated to instil into each man the consciousness of personal dignity, the energy which developes public virtues, and the pride by which they are maintained. The slavery of the peasants was, doubtless, the odious part of this system; but it should not be forgotten, that it was established at an æra when even a more absolute and debasing servitude formed part of the system and of the manners of all civilised states; that the Roman slave, who cultivated the soil, might consider the change a happy one which rendered him the serf of the glebe, and that vassalage was the degree by which the lower orders of the people were raised from the servitude of antiquity to modern enfranchisement. In the attempt that has been made to convey some idea of institutions which held a paramount influence over the state of Italian society from the eighth to the twelfth century, it has been sometimes necessary to anticipate the exact course of time, and always impossible, within so narrow a compass, to trace more than the general features of the subject. But no other place has appeared altogether so proper for introducing the preceding remarks; and an elaborate treatise, which should embrace all the peculiarities of the feudal system, would have been beyond the aim, and foreign to the purpose, of the present undertaking. It will be sufficient if what has been said shall have rendered the political state of the fiefs, into which Italy was divided for three centuries after the Carlovingian conquest, intelligible to the reader in his passage through the few next pages.

The overthrow of the Lombard dynasty by Charlemagne and his Franks was regarded by the Italians as a new invasion of barbarians. Yet it does not appear that the conquests of the new emperor of the West disturbed, to any general extent, the settlement of territorial fiefs. The great feudatories and their vassals transferred their allegiance to his power, almost all Italy submitted to his authority, and the imposing title of emperor covered his pretensions with veneration and splendour. His vast dominions were held together solely by the force of his genius, and the watchful activity of his government. He was master of France, part of Spain, Italy, Germany, and Hungary; and, during his life, all these discordant parts of his empire were firmly cemented and wisely consolidated by the mere bond of his personal talents. He is, certainly, one of the most extraordinary and greatest characters in history. His private life was deformed by licentious amours: he was unsparing of blood, though not constitutionally cruel; and his successes in Germany were defiled by atrocious butcheries: yet his vices were relieved, though they were not palliated, by frugality and temperance; and his barbarous ferocity was strangely contrasted with elevated views of national and intellectual improvement. In a life of restless military activity, he found leisure to reform the coinage, and regulate the legal standard of money in his realms; he gathered about him the learned of all countries; founded schools and accumulated libraries; he encouraged commerce; and he meditated the union of the Roman and barbarian codes into one great system of jurisprudence. If he derived much of his renown from a contrast with the rude characters who preceded him, and the imbecility of his immediate successors; if it enhanced the brilliance and grandeur of his appearance, that he stood alone, as it has been beautifully expressed, "like a beacon upon a waste, or a rock in the broad ocean;" his great qualities still blaze with unfading light, and his memory still towers in magnificence above all ordinary fame.

The successors of Charlemagne were unable to wield his mighty sceptre, and sank under the burthen of his colossal power. It was fortunate for humanity that the mediocrity of their talents, and the repeated divisions of their enormous patrimony, prevented the confirmation of an universal monarchy, which, in its perpetuity, would have degraded Europe to an equality with China, and condemned it to a state between ignorance and civilization, without energy or power, without glory or virtue. Charlemagne himself divided his empire among his sons, and, by a happy error, commenced the preparation for its fall. During his life he had associated his son Pepin with him in the sovereignty of Italy (A.D. 781); but Pepin died before his father (A.D. 812), leaving a natural son, Bernard, who succeeded under the emperor to the kingdom of his parent. He enjoyed but a brief career in his new dignity; for, on the decease of Charlemagne (A.D. 814), he attempted an unsuccessful rebellion against the youngest and only surviving son and successor of the emperor, Louis the Pious, who was induced to put him to death, with a severity foreign to his gentle nature, and for which he afterwards violently reproached himself. Louis immediately re-united the kingdom of Italy to the other dominions of Charlemagne, and commenced a reign of error and misfortune. He partitioned his empire among three sons, and experienced in return the most unnatural ingratitude; and though the fault of his character lay rather in a softness of disposition, than in any defect of courage and intellect, he passed an inglorious and troubled life, in continual struggles with his undutiful children. But the history of the Carlovingian family belongs rather to all Europe than to Italy; and I may rejoice, with a great authority, that my subject releases me from the necessity of tracing their fortunes through those disgraceful wars between father and sons, and between brother and brother, which engross the memoirs of their house. After the death of Charlemagne, his descendants preserved for sixty-four years only the vast monarchy which he had founded; and in that period six Carlovingian sovereigns reigned in succession over Italy. After several shameful and miserable reigns, the last of these princes, Charles the Fat, in whose person the empire had nearly re-united, was deposed in a diet. The great imperial feudatories, the dukes, the bishops, and the counts or governors of cities, all seized the fragments of his broken authority, and a consummation was put to the period of greatest feudal anarchy which has been recorded in the annals of Europe. (A.D. 888.) Italy, however, was less unhappy during this period than the other dominions of the Carlovingian dynasty. The kingdom was governed, for twenty-six years, by Louis II., a virtuous prince, who wanted neither ability nor courage; and it was during his reign that the example of French valour revived the love of arms, and re-established the reputation of the warriors of Lombardy; that the fields began again to teem with inhabitants, and cities to recover the population which preceding invasions and distresses had almost exterminated.

For above sixty years after the deposition of Charles the Fat, Italy was convulsed to its centre by intestine wars, and horribly ravaged by the predatory incursions of foreign enemies. Native princes aspired to the feudal crown, and the lesser nobles were ever arrayed against each other in support of rival candidates, or in resistance to the reigning sovereign. Meanwhile, the piratical Saracens from the sea coasts, and the merciless Hungarians from the north-eastern frontiers, spread themselves like a devouring pestilence over the land, and left frightful traces of their impetuous and unresisted course in the conflagration of the open country, and the massacre of its inhabitants. But the revolutions of the throne, and the sufferings of the people amidst these turbulent and disastrous scenes, brought the energies of the Italian character, for the first time, into play, determined the bent of the national spirit, and developed that desire of republican liberty which we shall, in the next chapter, observe predominant in the cities of Lombardy.

Under the Carlovingian family, the number of the Lombard duchies, which had originally been thirty, had, by accident or violence, by family alliances or the law of the strongest, become much diminished; more than one of the great fiefs sometimes falling under the power of the same feudatory; and, on the contrary, a great fief being often divided among several counts, or lesser proprietors. Hence, at the deposition of Charles the Fat, there were but five or six great lords in condition to command the nation and dispute the crown. The great Lombard duchy of Benevento, which had stood almost distinct from the kingdom, had been the most powerful of Italian fiefs; but it was now in decay, and its princes were not in a situation to aim at the throne. The dukes, or marquises—for these titles were of equal dignity and indifferent application—of Friuli, Spoleto, Ivrea, Susa, and Tuscany, were the leading feudal potentates of the kingdom. The last of these, however, Adalbert, count of Lucca and marquis of Tuscany, abstained in prudence from dangerously aspiring to the diadem of Italy. Possessing the beautiful province of Tuscany, which nature has separated by a chain of mountains from the rest of Italy, as though she had designed it for an independent state, he and his successors continued to govern it for a century and a half with considerable happiness, and their court passed for the most brilliant and sumptuous among those of the great feudatories. The marquis of Ivrea was master of Piedmont; but both he and the lord of Susa might veil their pretensions before the splendour of the princes of Friuli and Spoleto; and the kingdom was agitated for years by the rivalry of these puissant chiefs. Berenger, marquis of Friuli, was the Lombard representative of the ancient ducal family of that province, and, moreover, by his mother, the grandson of the emperor Louis the Pious. Guido, duke of Spoleto, of Frankish origin, was also allied to the royal family of Charlemagne. Motives of personal hatred were added to ambition in the struggle between Berenger and Guido: both pleaded royal descent, both solicited the crown from the states of Italy, and, by turns conquering and defeated, both purchased the favour of the electors, at each revolution, by new concessions. The crown was thus despoiled of all its prerogatives without acquiring steady partisans by the sacrifice; and, in these and subsequent civil wars, the feudatories always embraced the part of the vanquished, or of some new candidate for royalty, because the conqueror had presumed to challenge their obedience. Berenger was, however, altogether more successful than any of his rivals; for though Guido and his son both bore, in succession, the title of king of Italy, and even of emperor, he broke the power of their house; and though Louis, king of Provence, and Rodolph, king of Burgundy, were afterwards supported by the Italian nobles against him in competition for the throne, he kept his seat and resisted their pretensions. He reigned for thirty-six years as king of Italy, and for the last nine of his life with the dignity of emperor. Active and courageous, humane and honorable, he was a prince of considerable talents and virtue, and his life was at last sacrificed to the indulgence of a generous, but misplaced, confidence. The archbishop of Milan and several lords, all of whom he had loaded with benefits, entered into a plot against him, and engaged a noble Veronese, named Flambert, whose son the emperor had held at the baptismal font, to assassinate him. Berenger, having discovered the conspiracy, summoned Flambert into his presence, reminded him of the kindnesses which he had received at his hands, and of the vows of attachment which he had poured forth in return; pointed out the little fruit which he could hope to gather from his meditated guilt; and, presenting him with a golden cup, added, "Let this goblet be the pledge of my oblivion of your crime and of your repentance. Take it, and do not forget that your emperor is also the sponsor of your child." The same night, instead of shutting himself up in the security of his fortified palace, Berenger, to show that he had discarded all suspicion, slept unattended in a summer-house in his gardens. But in the morning, as he was going to mass, Flambert, accompanied by an armed retinue, met him, and, approaching as if to embrace him, basely stabbed him with his poniard, (A.D. 924.) History has failed to explain the motives of this revolting act of ingratitude and treachery, and has only related the retributive vengeance which instantaneously overtook it. Milo, count of Verona, rushed to the aid of the emperor, and, though too late to defend him, sacrificed the traitor and his associates on the spot.

It was principally during the reign of Berenger that the incursions of the Hungarians and Saracens added a frightful scourge to the horrors of civil discord. The latter of these people had conquered the Island of Sicily from the Greeks about half a century before, and established themselves in the south of Italy, whence they carried their ravages into the heart of the kingdom, while other bands of their Mussulman brethren, landing from the shores of Spain, fortified themselves on the northern coast, and devastated Piedmont. These destroyers, and the yet more sanguinary Hungarians, who first penetrated into Italy through the march of Treviso, in the year 900, carried on their warfare in the same manner. Their armies were composed exclusively of light horse, who scoured the country in small squadrons, without caring to secure a retreat, or to attempt permanent conquests. The rapidity of their flight gave them immeasurable advantages over the heavy cavalry of the feudal chieftains. These vassals of the crown were formidable only against their sovereign, and ever powerless before a foreign enemy. The sluggish infantry of the cities was equally unable to contend in the open plains with plunderers whose object was only to accumulate booty and avoid an encounter. Neither the sovereign nor his feudatories lost any portion of their dominions; they counted the same number as before of subject cities and castles, but all around them was devastation and misery.

But the course of human suffering is often attended by a healing power. The Hungarian and Saracen inroads had a powerful and beneficial influence upon the freedom of the Italian communities. Before these invasions the towns had been open and without fortifications; but in the general confusion and distress, the cities were left by the great feudatories to their own means of defence. They were reduced to the necessity of erecting walls for their protection from these freebooters, to train their burghers to the use of arms, to enrol them into a regular militia, and, finally, to commission their own magistrates to command them. The inferior orders of the people were forced into action, and taught at once to guard their homes and to understand their rights.

The generous qualities of a hero had been unavailing against licentious violence and perfidy; the Italians were now to be taught by an oppressor to feel the necessity of a free constitution. Two years after the death of Berenger, the nation fell under the yoke of a remorseless tyrant. Hugo, count or duke of Provence, was elected to the Italian throne (A.D. 926); and by alternate fraud and violence, by fomenting the jealousies of the nobles, and rendering them a prey to each other, and by oppressing them all in their turns, he removed every bar to his ambition, and established a cruel and despotic authority. He had despoiled all the great vassals of their fiefs, with the solitary exception of Berenger, marquis of Ivrea, grandson of the emperor of that name, and had resolved to make that young prince, although his relative, the last victim of his sanguinary oppression. An order was already issued to deprive Berenger and his consort of their eyes; and they with difficulty escaped to the court of Otho, king of Germany. That sovereign, who has deservedly been surnamed the Great, afforded an asylum to the fugitives (A.D. 940); and though he gave no other assistance to Berenger, suffered him to assemble the Italian malcontents in the German dominions, and to prepare his schemes of vengeance against Hugo, (A.D. 945.) After a lapse of five years, Berenger entered Italy with a few followers, and soon found himself at the head of a powerful army, against which Hugo was unable to contend. The marquis of Ivrea, therefore, assembled the states of the kingdom to obtain their suffrages in favour of pretensions which he now put forth for the crown, and against those of Hugo; but the nobles, feeling the power to be once more in their hands, endeavoured to preserve the balance between the rivals, by deposing Hugo, electing his son Lothaire to the throne, and confiding the general administration of the kingdom to Berenger. (A.D. 945.) It was not probable, however, that such a partition of authority could be maintained. The ambition of Berenger was far from being satisfied; he saw that Lothaire had not, like his father, incurred the hatred of the people; that his queen Adelaide was adored by the Italians; and that there was too much reason to fear that the confidence of the nation would be daily more fully bestowed upon the son of Hugo, and more openly withdrawn from him. (A.D. 950.) The young king died, and Berenger is accused, by a contemporary chronicler, of having resorted to poison to remove the object of his suspicion and dread. He subsequently demanded for his son the hand of the royal widow, and Adelaide endured harsh and menacing treatment by her resistance to the proposal. But the time was past for attempting to strengthen the throne of Italy by crimes: Berenger had himself taught the nation that there existed beyond the Alps an avenger for the vices of the Lombard sovereigns. The people had witnessed his coronation with dissatisfaction, the clergy were touched with the piety of Adelaide, and the nobles dreaded to find a despot in a king without rivals. With one consent all orders of the state addressed themselves to Otho the Great, and entreated him to deliver Italy from the very king whom they had received from the asylum of his court as their liberator.

Otho was not unwilling to accede to their prayer. He entered Italy, set queen Adelaide at liberty, afterwards espoused her, and, advancing to Pavia without resistance, received in that city the crown of Italy, (A.D. 951.) But the affairs of Germany demanded his return before he could settle his new possessions, and he suffered Berenger to hold his kingdom of him as a fief. Some years after, however, the tranquillity of Germany again permitted Otho to direct his views towards Italy; and he found the reason or the pretext for interference in the numerous complaints against Berenger which the pope and the Italian nobles addressed to him. He descended from the Alps a second time, deposed Berenger, and imprisoned him for life, and received at the hands of pope John XII. the imperial dignity, which had been suspended for nearly forty years. (A.D. 961.)

PART II.
Rise and growth of ecclesiastical and papal power—Influence of the clergy over the barbarian conquerors of Italy—Their wealth and power—Origin of the popedom—Pontificate of Gregory I.—State of Rome from the fifth to the tenth century—Separation of the Latin and Greek churches—Donations of Pepin and Charlemagne to the holy see—Disorders of the papacy in the ninth and tenth centuries—Southern Italy—Rise of the republics of Naples, Gaeta, and Amalfi—History of those states to the tenth century—Republic of Venice—Its geographical position—Origin and primitive constitution of the republic—Its first war—Change in the form of government—First appointment of a doge—War of Pepin, son of Charlemagne, against the Venetians—Their victory—Building of Venice—Naval wars of the republic in the ninth and tenth centuries—Capture of the Venetian Brides by the pirates of Istria.

AT the great epoch in Italian history, which united the crown of Lombardy to the empire of Germany, I have paused to consider detached parts of my subject which I have hitherto declined to notice, that the thread of the narrative might not be unnecessarily broken. It is an inherent difficulty in pursuing the current of the Italian annals, that instead of flowing in one great and uninterrupted channel, it breaks out into a multiplicity of smaller streams, whose devious and often mingled courses the eye can with difficulty mark. In the progress of these volumes we shall find Italy divided into as many independent republics and principalities as there are monarchies at this day in the whole western quarter of the globe; and as all these small states have their separate histories, our transitions must be nearly as frequent, and almost as unconnected as they would be if the general history of Europe, and not that of Italy, were the object. To obviate as far as is practicable the inconvenience and obscurity thus arising from the very nature of the work, I have proposed to render the affairs of those governments, which for the time took the lead in Italian politics, the prominent matter of attention in every chapter, and afterwards to bring down the insulated history of less conspicuous states to the same period. I shall thus hope to bind the fragments of the subject together without much violation of chronological order or lucid narration. Proceeding upon this principle, I have hitherto held in view the kingdom of Lombardy only; and I am now, before I pass to the second chapter, to attempt a rapid sketch of the growth of ecclesiastical power, and of the rise of the republics of Naples, Amalfi, and Venice, during the period of which I have treated, that is, from the end of the fifth century to the coronation of Otho the Great.

When the barbarous nations of the north overthrew the power of Rome, they found the clergy endowed in every country of the empire with considerable possessions, and as the rude invaders were themselves rapidly converted to Christianity, the lavish donations of a new piety were added to the former wealth of the church. The devotion of the barbarians, as it was less enlightened, was more munificent than that of the subjects of the empire. They brought from their forests, though they had changed their faith, the elementary principles of all barbarous idolatry; a superstitious reverence for the priesthood, a credulity that invited imposture, and a confidence that offences might be expiated by offerings to the altar. The crafty churchmen of those ages knew full well how to profit by the simplicity and religious fears of the northern conquerors. Donations of lands to the bishops, and in still more ample proportion to the monastic foundations, poured in from every side; provinces were bequeathed to different sees; to die without allotting a portion of worldly wealth to pious uses, was accounted almost like suicide; and monarchs, powerful lords, and petty barons, all felt the necessity of atoning for the disorders and crimes of their past lives by plundering their heirs in favour of the church. In this manner, before the entrance of Otho the Great into Italy, the most prosperous of its cities, and the most fertile of its districts, had passed into the hands of the episcopal and monastic clergy, who thus uniting temporal power with the paramount influence upon the laity, which the prejudices of a blind superstition ensured to them, exercised a double tyranny over conscience and property. The spiritual duties of their orders were scandalously forgotten in the rapacious pursuit of worldly authority and possessions, and the holy purity and sacred truths of Christianity were shamefully violated or perverted by the practices and arts of its professors.

But while the clergy were prosecuting a system of encroachments upon the laity, a new scheme was secretly forming within the bosom of the church, to subject both it and the temporal governments of Europe to an ecclesiastical monarch. The power of the popes was of very gradual and silent progression. We may agree with Ariosto in placing in the moon the donation of Constantine to the Roman see: but the Constitution of the same monarch, in 321, is the foundation of the wealth of the church. Religious pastors had, indeed, before accepted the liberality of their flocks, but a legal sanction was now given to their holding property of every description, and whether acquired by gift or testamentary disposition. Before the seat of the Roman empire was changed, the church was divided into three patriarchates—Rome, Alexandria, and Antioch. The bishoprics of Constantinople and Jerusalem were afterwards raised to the patriarchal rank.

From classical and religious prejudices the bishops of Rome were especially venerated. Rome, too, being often neglected by the emperors of the East, was left to its own defence. The bishops, by their learning and talents, gained political ascendancy. For awhile they exercised their power with moderation, and it was a common saying that it was better to be governed by the crozier of a bishop than the sceptre of a king; but presumption grew with increase of authority, and the bishops at length became temporal as well as spiritual tyrants. Before the end of the sixth century, the popes or bishops of Rome had so far succeeded in reducing the clergy of Italy to subjection, that their confirmation was necessary to the validity of episcopal elections. But the papal authority had made no decisive progress in any country of the West but Italy, until the pontificate of Gregory I., in the beginning of the seventh century. Ambition and enthusiasm were some of his qualities, and I may pass over both his sanctity and his love of ignorance, to notice that he was honourably distinguished by his paternal government of Rome. He maintained unceasing correspondence with the barbarian sovereigns of the West, and the hierarchy of the church; and in his pretensions, the divine authority and office of the successors of St. Peter were first clearly defined, and as strangely acknowledged by the ignorant nations to whom they were addressed.

For one hundred and twenty years after the death of Gregory, the power of the papacy received no remarkable accession, although the lapse of time was confirming its authority. But the schism produced by the controversy on image-worship, which separated the Latin from the Greek church in the eighth century, gave the next great impulse to the grandeur of the popedom, and gifted it with independent temporal authority over the city of Rome.

The condition of that once mighty and fallen capital of the world had been affected, until the invasion of the Lombards, by the same vicissitudes as the rest of Italy. Under the great Theodoric, its citizens had enjoyed the repose and happiness which were common to his kingdom; in the wars of his successors with the generals of Justinian, they had undergone every extremity of woe, for the city was five times taken and recovered by the Goths and the Greeks, before Narses had achieved the reduction of Italy, and established an imperial prefect in the capitol. It is unaccountable by what means Rome escaped from the yoke of the Lombards: but they never obtained possession of it, and the Italian fugitives who swelled its population from the provinces, perhaps, gave it strength to resist the conquerors. The Lombards were either Arians, or still buried in paganism; their heresies rendered resistance to them a struggle of religion; and the popes animated the defence of the citizens, and encouraged their fidelity to the eastern emperors. The pontiffs of this period, who were generally Romans by birth, and chosen by the clergy, senate, and people, appear to have merited their elevation by their virtues; and deserted by the feeble court of Constantinople, the Romans withdrew their respect and confidence from the emperors, to repose their obedience on nearer protectors.

The disputes which agitated Christendom respecting the worship of images, at length put a termination to the nominal authority of the eastern empire over Rome. The Latin church was attached to this superstitious practice: the Greek emperor, Leo the Iconoclast, (image-breaker,) issued his edict for the destruction of these objects of veneration; and pope Gregory II. (one of the brightest characters of modern history) authorized the Romans to refuse obedience to his command, to renounce the imperial authority, and to establish the forms of an independent republic, of which the real power devolved on the papacy. (A.D. 726.) This was a remarkable æra in the history of pontifical power, and the fall of the Lombard dynasty produced a second and yet more memorable one. Assuming the monstrous right of sanctioning the usurpation of the French throne by the Carlovingian family, the popes received in return the assistance of Pepin and of Charlemagne, against the oppression of the Lombards, (A.D. 754.) The donations which these monarchs bestowed upon the popedom, from the fruits of their Italian conquests, nominally comprised the exarchate, and the Pentapolis of Romagna; and though the execution of the present by Charlemagne was evasive and partial, the holy see was enriched by him with many considerable fiefs and substantial temporalities.

It appears that these new possessions, which were sub-infeuded by the popes to military vassals, were a temptation for men of very different character to aspire to the papal chair, from those who had previously occupied it; and the annals of the Roman Catholic church are from this period sullied with the debasing and atrocious crimes of its chiefs, (A.D. 849.) One pope, Leo IV., who courageously defended Rome against a Saracen inroad, and who was the protector of his flock, merits to be excepted from the general infamy. But I have no inclination to follow my authorities through details of the enormous and scandalous vices which characterized the popes of the ninth and tenth centuries. Amidst a series of revolutions and crimes, six popes were deposed, two murdered, one mutilated; and for many years the supreme pontiffs were bestowed on the church by two women of rank and power, but of wanton and vicious character; Theodora and her daughter Marozia. The city was held by their lovers, commanded by the fortified houses of their dependants, and given over to the most terrible disorders. In this confusion, and in the darkness of the tenth century, which no contemporary historian has dispelled, the institutions of Rome seem to have been decidedly republican. The city was free from external dependence, and Hugo, the tyrant of Italy, who had endeavoured to plant his authority within its walls, by a disgraceful marriage with Marozia, was expelled by Alberic, her son by a former husband. Alberic had prevailed by the assistance of the people, and he afterwards governed as their patrician or consul. He was able at his death to bequeath his power to his son Octavian, who, willing to unite the spiritual and temporal authority once more, and in his own person, was consecrated pope under the title of John XII.; and it was from his hands that Otho the Great received the imperial crown.

Like Rome, Naples and the other cities of the south shared the common lot of the rest of Italy, from the suppression of the western empire to the conquests of Belisarius and Narses; and when the kingdom of the Lombards was founded in northern and central Italy, parts of the southern provinces were still preserved, with the Roman duchy and the exarchate of Ravenna, to the sceptre of the Greek emperors. But the establishment of the great Lombard principality of Benevento (in the heart of the present Neapolitan dominions) interrupted the communication between their remaining Italian possessions, and separated Ravenna and Rome from each other, and from their maritime dependencies in Campania, Apulia, and Calabria. This separation produced the rise and independence of three republics, Naples, Gaeta, and Amalfi. The Lombard principality of Benevento occupied all the interior of southern Italy: its sovereigns, owing but a nominal obedience to the kingdom of their nation, were powerful, active, and enterprising; and their efforts were unceasing for several centuries to subjugate the territory which the Greek emperors still held in their vicinity. But all their attempts were unavailing, and many favourable circumstances combined to aid the maritime districts in successful opposition to them. The Greeks were masters of the sea; the emperors had caused the principal cities on the coast, whose sites were naturally advantageous, to be skilfully fortified; and the very inability of the court of Constantinople to afford the inhabitants troops to defend the works, was in itself a source of strength. For the people, left to their resources, and perceiving the security of their situation, were at no difficulty to guard their walls. In the repulse of frequent attacks they grew hardy, confident, and intelligent: they formed a militia; they elected their own civil magistrates and military officers; and the Greek emperors viewed without opposition, the progress among them of a spirit of freedom, which, however at variance with the despotic institutions of the rest of the empire, could alone prevent them from being wrested from it by the strong arm of the Lombard. The exarchs, as the imperial lieutenants in Italy, named the governors, or dukes, of the principal maritime towns, and exercised the shadow of sovereignty over them until the fall of Ravenna, after which the emperors themselves assumed the appointments.

In the sixth century, the Greeks had preserved some of the principal cities in Lucania and the Calabrias, and they subsequently, as the Lombard energies declined, even extended their power in those provinces. But they also possessed, on the south-western coast, in Campania, two small maritime districts—the duchies, as they were called, of Gaeta and Naples; and these two little provinces alone merit our particular attention. The city of Gaeta, the capital of the first duchy, which extended between the Cæcuban and Massican mountains, so celebrated by Horace, was by situation nearly impregnable; for it stood on a rocky peninsula, connected with the continent by a low tongue of land. The duchy of Naples, farther south, comprehended a small territory round that city, and the neighbouring promontory of Sorrento, on which stood the town of Amalfi. And these three cities of Gaeta, Naples, and Amalfi, devoting themselves to commerce, and favoured by their maritime position and strength, rapidly acquired wealth, naval power, and republican liberty. Farther separated from the empire than the shores of Calabria and Lucania, they consummated a more decided and brilliant independence than the other Greek cities. Choosing their own magistrates and imposing their own taxes, the citizens, at last, in the tenth century, began to elect the dukes, whom they had, until then, received from the eastern emperors. They were involved in perpetual hostilities with the princes of Benevento, who often penetrated to the foot of their walls: but their dependant villagers found a secure refuge in their castles. The citizens themselves, from behind their lofty battlements, defied the efforts of their besiegers; and as, before the invention of artillery, the means of defence, when aided by courage, were ever superior to those of attack, the assaults of the Lombards were constantly repulsed. Once only the little republic of Amalfi was betrayed by internal discord into the hands of Sicard, prince of Benevento; but so untameable was the spirit of the Amalfitans, that, though their conqueror removed them all to his city of Salerno, they rose on his death in a body, returned to their ruined habitations, rebuilt their fortifications, and revived the prosperity of Amalfi with increased lustre, (A.D. 839.)

The restoration of the republic of Amalfi was followed by a revolution in the principality of Benevento, which proved the ruin of the Lombard grandeur in southern Italy. Sicard, the oppressor of the Amalfitans, had incurred the hatred of all orders of his subjects; and he fell by the hands of conspirators. He had imprisoned his own brother, Siconolf, at

Tarento, where he still remained at the period of this murder: and the citizens of Benevento, the Lombard capital, raised the treasurer, Radelchis, to the ducal throne. But the inhabitants of Salerno, adhering to the rights of Siconolf, combined with the Amalfitans to attempt his release, and for this purpose planned a secret enterprise. Some trading vessels, filled with merchants of Amalfi and Salerno, entered the harbour of Tarento, and the passengers, spreading themselves over the town in the evening, demanded aloud through the streets, after the manner of the times, hospitality for the night. Some of them were offered a lodging, as they had hoped, by the gaolers of Siconolf, who told them, that they had a spare apartment at their service, and should be satisfied if they repaid the kindness by a small present on the morrow. The merchants entered, desired their hosts to purchase provisions for them, invited them to share their cheer, and, during the repast, plied them with wine until they were incapable of guarding their charge, who escaped with his deliverers to Salerno.

The double election of Siconolf and Radelchis, at Salerno and Benevento, was the cause of long and bloody civil wars, which terminated in the partition of the principality, and the decay and eventual fall of the Lombard power. In their struggle, the rival princes each had recourse to the dangerous assistance of opposite sects of the Saracens, from Spain and Africa. Another musulman army had already conquered Sicily from the Greeks (A.D. 831); and, while the Christians were wasting their strength in discord, the infidels ravaged southern Italy, and established themselves in several of its cities, (A.D. 846.) They even besieged Gaeta; but the republics of Naples and Amalfi succoured that city; and the combined fleets of the three states, under the duke of Naples, afterwards contributed to the defeat of the Saracens by pope Leo IV. (A.D. 849.) Some years after, the emperor, Louis II., was drawn into southern Italy by the prayers of the Lombards of the Beneventine duchy for protection against the Saracens, (A.D. 866.) Uniting his arms to those of the eastern empire, he succeeded in expelling the infidels from most of their continental acquisitions; and, on the ruin of the

Carlovingian family, the fleets of Constantinople, with a transient vigour, pursued the advantage, drove the Saracens from all their conquests in Italy (though they still preserved Sicily), and established a new Greek province, of which Bari was the capital. An officer, afterwards termed *catapan*, resided there, and directed the general administration of the possessions which the eastern empire now held in southern Italy.

The republics of Campania were the only powers, except the Greek empire, who possessed any fleets in the Mediterranean at this period. Their vessels—fitted alike for war and commerce—defended the territory, and yearly augmented the riches of Naples, Gaeta, and Amalfi. The last of these cities, after the recovery of its liberty, rapidly increased in population and wealth, and began to cover the seas with its gallies, and to possess itself of all the commerce of the East. Its citizens acquired a brilliant reputation for courage and wisdom; and, in the extinction of the freedom and existence of their little state, which we shall hereafter take occasion to notice, they have left to our times three legacies that entitle their memory to veneration. It was a citizen of Amalfi, Flavio Gisia, or Gioia, who invented the mariners compass, or introduced it into the West; it was in Amalfi that the copy of the Pandects was found, which revived throughout Europe the study and practice of the laws of Justinian; and it was, lastly, the maritime code of Amalfi which served as a commentary on the rights of nations, and as the foundation of the subsequent jurisprudence of commerce and of the ocean.

From observing the ephemeral splendour of Amalfi, we turn to contemplate the dawn of the lung glories of Venice. The origin of this celebrated republic must be dated even before the commencement of modern history; and its extinction has been among the great political vicissitudes of our own times. For so lengthened an existence, Venice was in a great measure indebted to its peculiar geographical position. All the streams which descend from the southern declivities of the Alps, find their outlet in the Adriatic, and empty themselves into the sea near the head of that gulf, along an extent of about ninety miles. This length of coast is fronted, at from twenty to thirty miles distance from the shore, by a parallel line of several slips of land, with narrow openings between them; and the intermediate great basin, filled up by the gravelly and slimy deposits of the Alpine rivers, and studded with some hundreds of islets, is in no place covered by more than two or three feet of water; except where the rivers, breaking through it to find their way to the sea, by the openings in the external islands, have ploughed it into deep intersections, or natural canals, by the rapidity of their currents. The great shoals are termed the *Lagunes* of Venice; and, on the interior islets which rise from their surface, was the seat of the republic. Inaccessible from the continent by shallows, over which only the light gondola can skim, the islets are of difficult and dangerous approach from the sea; for nothing but the experience of native pilots can guide a vessel through the narrow openings of the exterior land, and amongst the perplexing intricacies of the channels. But, improved by the aid of art, these canals are capable of admitting the largest friendly vessels to the wharfs of Venice; and are equally advantageous to the inhabitants for commerce and defence.

The Venetian islands were, probably, inhabited from the earliest ages, for the convenience afforded by their position for fishing and for the collection of salt, which accumulates almost naturally in the lagunes. And when the Gothic invasion, under Alaric, struck terror into the people of Italy, some of the inhabitants of the neighbouring continent fled for shelter from the barbarians to this maritime fastness, where, in the year 421, they built the little town of Rialto—the modern Venice. Thirty years later, the horrible devastation of the Huns, under Attila, drove the nobles and citizens from the flames of Aquileia and other places to the same refuge; and the towns of Grado, Caorlo, Palestrina, and Malamocco, rose among the islets. In this manner a new state sprang up amidst the lagunes, and, protected from all hostile approach, acquired a secure and silent independence. The emigrants from the continent, whose ruined fortunes had reduced them to a common equality, mingling with the fishermen of the islands, and compelled to labour for a subsistence, grew industrious and active: invited by their situation to commerce, and inured by their occupations to the sea, they became enterprizing and courageous. Their light barks engrossed all the traffic of the neighbouring shores; and, in the distractions of the continent, the little ports of the lagunes were the only mercantile entrepôts of the coast. The rude constitution of the new state was, probably, that of a federative republic; for it would appear, by the earliest authentic documents which we possess of its condition, that it was governed by tribunes, of whom the people of each principal islet chose one, and who, administering the magistracy of their respective towns, met to deliberate upon the common interests of the whole republic. For all essential purposes, their state was in the exercise of freedom from its earliest establishment. To the hated barbarians, who successively ravaged Italy until the fall of the western empire, the Venetians acknowledged and paid no obedience; but there is evidence that they lived in amity with the government of the great Theodoric, and even submitted, in some measure, to receive his commands. And, much as the point has been disputed by the pride of their modern descendants, the Venetians certainly appear to have considered themselves subject, in a large sense, without violation of internal independence, to the eastern empire for several centuries after the conquest of Italy by Narses, whom they materially aided. They were interested in resistance to the Lombard princes, and might naturally be led, by the memory of former allegiance to Rome, to transfer a nominal obedience to the court of Constantinople.

In the history of nations calamity is more prominent than happiness, and I proceed to observe, that the first national war in which the Venetians engaged, was produced by the necessity of protecting their commerce. The Sclavonians of the opposite coasts of Dalmatia, succeeding to the country and the manners of the ancient Illyrians, had betaken themselves to piracy; and the small trading vessels of the Venetians were particularly exposed to their depredations. The courage of the republicans was now equal to a struggle with the barbarians of the north; and the hardihood and energies which they had acquired by a seafaring life were successfully proved against the marauders. They boldly crossed over to seek them in their own ports, and commenced a series of enterprises, which ended, before the close of the tenth century, in their conquest of all maritime Dalmatia.

While the republic was in this long period making trial of its strength, the form of its government underwent a remarkable change, and the extinction of its independence was almost effected by a foreign enemy. The tribunes of the islands had, by their ambition and frequent discords, occasioned a general disgust at the form of their administration. An authority so divided was, perhaps too, found inadequate to the conduct of the increasing powers of the state, and it was determined to replace the tribunes by a duke, or *doge* in their dialect. He was chosen for life by a general assembly, the exact composition of which is no where clearly marked, (A.D. 697.) His powers were restrained for some centuries by no limitations, but the existence of general assemblies preserved the balance of the republic. Paolo-Luca Anafesto was the first of these new sovereign magistrates, and under his government the resources of Venice were augmented, the Sclavonians were defeated, and the Lombards compelled to acknowledge the independent rights of the republic. But some of his successors abused their authority, and lost their lives in popular commotions; and the annals of the republic present for a long period, a train of obscure revolutions and disorders which would ill-repay our investigation. While these were in progress, the dynasty of the Lombards had been overthrown by Charlemagne, and the Venetians were yet torn by internal dissensions, when Pepin, the son of the emperor, who governed Italy under him, took advantage of their divisions to attempt the subjugation of the republic. He equipped a powerful fleet and army, succeeded in entering the Lagune, burnt several of its towns, and even captured Malamocco, then the capital of the republic. But Angelo Participazio, a citizen of distinction, preserved the fortunes of his country, (A.D. 809.) He animated his fellow-citizens to a continued resistance, and he had persuaded them to evacuate Malamocco, and remove their riches to Rialto, the position of which was more inaccessible, and in the centre of the Lagune. The fleet of Pepin attempting to pursue them, was entangled in the shoals, and utterly defeated, and he retired in disgrace to Ravenna. In a subsequent peace between the Carlovingian and eastern empires, Venice was included as a dependancy of the Greek power.

The gratitude of the Venetians raised Angelo Participazio to the ducal throne, which he had merited by his virtues; and during his glorious reign of eighteen years. Rialto became the lasting capital of the state. Sixty islets which surrounded it were joined to that town by bridges, and were shortly covered with new habitations. The ducal palace was raised on the site which it still occupies, and the new city of VENICE took the general appellation of the republic. Twenty years afterwards the body of St. Mark was transported from Alexandria to the new city: the saint became the patron of the state; his lion was blazoned on the standard of the republic, and stamped on its coin; and his name was identified with the pride and the power of Venice.

During the ninth, and the first sixty years of the tenth centuries,—from the government of Angelo Participazio, to the coming into Italy of Otho the Great,—the Venetian affairs, with brief intervals of repose, were wholly occupied with civil commotions and naval wars. The doges of the republic were often murdered; its fleets were sometimes defeated; but, under every adverse circumstance, the commercial activity, the wealth, and the power of the state were still rapidly increasing. In the ninth century the Venetians, in concert with the Greeks, encountered, though with indifferent success, the navies of the Saracens; but the Narentines, and other pirates of Dalmatia, were their constant enemies, and were frequently chastised by the arms of the republic. The Venetian wealth invited attacks from all the freebooters of the seas, and an enterprise undertaken by some of them who had established themselves on the coast of Istria deserves, from its singularity and the vengeance of the republic, to be recorded in this place. According to an ancient custom, the nuptials of the nobles and principal citizens of Venice were always celebrated on the same day of the year and in the same church, (A.D. 944.) The eve of the purification was consecrated to this public festival, and the state annually increased the general joy of the occasion by endowing twelve maidens with marriage portions. In the morning, gondolas elegantly ornamented assembled from all quarters of the city at the episcopal church of Olivolo. The affianced pairs disembarked amidst the sound of music; their relations and friends in their most splendid habiliments swelled their retinue; the rich presents made to the brides, their jewels and ornaments, were proudly borne for display; and the body of the people unarmed, and thoughtless of danger, followed the glad procession. The Istrian pirates, acquainted with the existence of this annual festival, had the boldness to prepare an ambush for the nuptial train in the city itself. They secretly arrived over night at an uninhabited islet near the church of Olivolo, and lay hidden behind it with their barks until the procession had entered the church, when darting from their concealment they rushed into the sacred edifice through all its doors, tore the shrieking brides from the arms of their defenceless lovers, possessed themselves of the jewels which had been displayed in the festal pomp, and immediately put to sea with their fair captives and their booty. But a deadly revenge overtook them. The doge, Pietro Candiano III., had been present at the ceremony: he shared in the fury and indignation of the affianced youths: they flew to arms, and throwing themselves under his conduct into their vessels, came up with the spoilers in the lagunes of Caorlo. A frightful massacre ensued: not a life among the pirates was spared, and the victors returned in triumph with their brides to the church of Olivolo. A procession of the maidens of Venice revived for many centuries the recollection of this deliverance on the eve of the purification. But the doge was not satisfied with the punishment which he had inflicted on the Istriots. He entered vigorously upon the resolution of clearing the Adriatic of all the pirates who infested it: he conquered part of

Dalmatia, and he transmitted to his successors, with the ducal crown, the duty of consummating his design.

CHAPTER II. FROM THE CORONATION OF THE EMPEROR OTHO THE GREAT, TO THE PEACE OF CONSTANCE, a.d. 961-1183.

PART I.

Reigns of Otho the Great, Otho II., and Otho III.—Continued disorders of the papacy—Rome under the consul Crescentius—Probable state of the Lombard cities during these three reigns—The crown of Lombardy disputed between Ardoin marquis of Ivrea, and Henry II. king of Germany—Reign of the emperor Conrad II. in Italy—Circumstances which introduced the great struggle between the empire and the papacy for ecclesiastical investitures—Reign of the emperor Henry III.—Scandalous state of the papacy—Reformations—Reign of the emperor Henry IV.—Pontificate of Gregory VII.—Character of the famous Countess Matilda—Contest between Henry and Gregory—Death of Gregory—The struggle with Henry continued by his successors—Deposition and death of Henry IV.—Reign of the emperor Henry V.—Prosecution of the dispute for ecclesiastical investitures—Concordat of Worms—Termination of the contest between the papacy and empire—Independence of the Lombard cities—Their mutual animosities and oppressions of each other—Death of the emperor Henry V.—Disputed succession to the empire—State of the papacy—Reigns of the emperors Lothaire and Conrad III.—Accession of Frederic Barbarossa to the imperial crown—His character and ambitious designs—Entrance of Frederic into Italy—Wars between the emperor and the Milanese—Blockade and submission of Milan—Arbitrary conduct of Frederic—Revolt of the Milanese—Second blockade and destruction of Milan—Subsequent tyranny of Frederic over the cities of Lombardy—Resistance of the cities, and general league against Frederic—Rebuilding of Milan—Battle of Lagnano—Establishment of the independence of Lombardy—Peace of Constance.

DURING a reign of twelve years the emperor Otho the Great administered the government of Italy with vigour and prudence. The reputation of signal victories which he had gained over the Hungarians, the great power which he wielded as the common sovereign of Germany and Italy, and, more than all, the force of his personal character, ensured respect and obedience to his authority. His skilful policy cemented the dominion which he had acquired by the sword; the cities of Lombardy were attached to his rule by the blessings of peace which the kingdom enjoyed under his firm and tranquil administration; and the great Italian fiefs were dextrously weakened by his practice of separating districts from their jurisdiction under inferior marquises and rural counts. He was engaged in a long war with the Greeks in southern Italy, which terminated amicably by an alliance between the two imperial families; but his relations with the popedom form the most remarkable events in his reign, of which contemporary historians have left any traces.

Though pope John XII. had invited Otho into Italy, he soon perceived that he had only prepared chains for himself by seeking the aid of so formidable a champion. The year after the emperor's coronation he declared against him, and in favour of Berenger; but Otho marched to Rome and put him to flight. A council was assembled under the imperial authority in that city to judge the pope, the disorders of whose life were equally notorious and shameful; he was deposed, and Leo VIII. was consecrated in his place. But a large faction in Rome were partisans of the family of Alberic, of which John XII. was the representative; the citizens in general were ill-disposed to obey the commands of a foreign sovereign, and Otho had no sooner retired from the city than his pope was expelled. John returned to Rome, and died before the emperor could depose him again, and the Romans elected Benedict V. to succeed him. But when Otho, at the head of his army, restored Leo VIII. in triumph to the papal chair, Benedict threw himself at the feet of his competitor, confessed that he was an usurper, and was exiled to Germany. Otho had thus deposed two popes, and on the death of Leo his will conferred the keys of St. Peter on John XIII. But the Romans still struggled against the yoke, and the presence of the emperor was once more necessary to restore the pope of his choice to the seat from whence the factious hatred, or independent spirit of the citizens, had driven him. Otho was then in Germany, but he crossed the Alps again; punished this rebellion, as he doubtless considered it, with cruel severity, by the execution or exile of all the republican magistracy of Rome, and experienced no farther resistance from the inhabitants of that city during the few remaining years of his life, which he terminated near Magdeburgh, in Germany, (A.D. 973.)

Otho the Great had associated his son, the second of his name, with himself in the empire during his life; but, after his decease, Otho II. was detained in Germany by a civil war, until the year 980, when he passed into Italy. His reign was less glorious than that of his father, for he was unsuccessful in the war which he renewed with the Greeks in southern Italy, and he found no leisure to interfere in the affairs of the popedom. After his death, the long minority of his son, Otho III., whom he had left an infant, was spent amidst civil wars in Germany; but the young monarch had no sooner attained manhood, than he entered Italy, and asserted the imperial authority. During his whole infancy the disorders of the papacy had continually increased. Perhaps no period of the pontifical history is altogether stained with deeper crime, than that which is contemporary with the reigns of the three Othos. The atrocious and scandalous characters of several succeeding popes had inspired the citizens of Rome with contempt and hatred of their authority, and animated the democratic spirit of a turbulent populace. They had again established a republican government, under the consul Crescentius, even in the reign of the second Otho, and, during the minority of his son, the temporal sovereignty of the popes was annihilated. But when Otho III. entered Italy, the posture of circumstances was reversed. He raised one of his relatives to the papal throne, by the title of Gregory V.; and the expulsion of this pontiff by Crescentius and the popular party, drew down the imperial vengeance. Otho besieged and took the city, and crushed all resistance in the people by the execution of their consul, whom he had treacherously inveigled into his hands by promises of safety, (A.D. 998.) Crescentius has sometimes been represented as a factious demagogue, sometimes as a patriot hero; but the annals of Rome at this period are so thickly shrouded in darkness, that it is impossible to determine on the real merits of his character. The perfidious manner of his death, at least, reflects infamy on Otho, who did not long survive him. He died in the flower of his age, and is said to have fallen by poison, which was administered to him by the injured widow of Crescentius. As he left no children, the imperial line of Saxony terminated in his person, (A.D. 1002.)

The dearth of historical records, and the meagre character of the few chronicles of the times, have entirely veiled from later researches a far more interesting subject of inquiry than the internal condition of Rome at this epoch. If we could clearly discern the state of the cities of Lombardy under the house of Saxony, a period of forty-one years, we should probably find them making rapid strides towards that republican freedom which they had certainly acquired at the end of the eleventh century. A philosophic historian has attributed to the first Otho the systematic design of elevating the Lombard cities, by charter, into free municipal communities, as a counterpoise to the power of the feudal nobility, of whose obedience he might reasonably be distrustful. But no evidence has been preserved of the fact, nor are there any archives of these cities extant of earlier date than the twelfth century; and it is therefore unsafe to follow a supposition which nothing remains to substantiate. There were, however, causes in action, which, without resorting to hypothesis, may in a great measure account for the subsequent emancipation of the Lombard cities. We have referred to the erection of their walls against the Hungarian invasions, which preceded the reigns of the Othos, and to the practice, which was undoubtedly adopted by the first of those monarchs, of diminishing the extent of the great fiefs. By the former circumstance the cities acquired the means of defence; by the latter, the power of the feudatories was so much subdivided, that the count, or governor of a town, scarcely ruled beyond the precincts of its walls, and remained amongst the citizens without rural vassals, and therefore with no more than a nominal authority over the numerous inhabitants. Very many too of the oppidan signories were assigned to bishops, naturally less warlike than lay chieftains, and indebted in some measure to the citizens themselves for their election to their sees. With arms in their hands, the consciousness of their own strength and the weakness of their temporal and ecclesiastical lords, could not fail to inspire the citizens with ideas of independence. The three Othos passed twenty-five years out of Italy: their successors were less powerful, their reigns more disturbed, and the intervals of their absence from Lombardy yet longer and more frequent. A sovereignty so often interrupted could not be strongly exerted, and nothing remained to control the growth of municipal liberty.

The death of Otho III. without children, terminated the engagement by which Italy had bound herself to the emperors of the Saxon line. Her obedience was not equally due to every sovereign whom the princes of Germany might place on their throne; and, therefore, while the latter made choice of the duke of Bavaria for their king, by the title of Henry II., a diet of the lay and ecclesiastical lords of Italy assembled at Pavia (A.D. 1002), and bestowed the crown of Lombardy upon Ardoin, marquis of Ivrea. But such was already the rivalry between Milan and Pavia, that it was sufficient for the election of Ardoin to have taken place in the latter city, to disaffect the Milanese to his authority. Arnolph, their archbishop, too, had been absent from the assembly at Pavia; and, supported by his citizens, he protested against an election, to which, as first ecclesiastical prince of Italy, he had given no assent. He convoked a new diet at Roncaglia, near Milan; and, in concert with many of the Italian nobles who were hostile to Ardoin, elected Henry II. to the Lombard throne, (A.D. 1004.) That monarch, entering Italy, and possessing himself of Pavia, was there crowned by the archbishop of Milan, and obliged Ardoin to retire into his patrimonial fiefs.

On the day of Henry's coronation, his German followers (A.D. 1004), in the drunken riot of the occasion, having insulted some of the citizens of Pavia, were driven out of the town: the king was besieged in his palace; and his army, which was encamped under the walls, could only penetrate through the barricadoed streets to his succour, by setting fire to the houses. The superb capital of Lombardy was reduced to ashes; a frightful massacre ensued; and when the surviving inhabitants, on the retirement of their enemies, rebuilt the town, a fresh motive was added to that hatred of the German nation which a large proportion of the Italians entertained. But the intrusion of these foreigner was scarcely felt during the subsequent reign of Henry. He passed little of his time in Italy. Ardoin still asserted his pretensions; and the contest between the rivals was maintained rather by the mutual hostility of their adherents than by their personal exertions. After an interval, however, of ten years, Henry, in a second expedition into Italy, received the imperial crown at Rome (A.D. 1014); and by the support which he gave to pope Benedict VIII. checked the republican spirit of the citizens, whom we find now governed by a son of Crescentius, with the title of patrician. The emperor appears to have encountered no opposition on his march from Ardoin, who shortly afterwards resigned the pomp of royalty (A.D. 1015), and retired into a monastery, thinking, that between the business and the close of life some space should intervene.

On the death of Henry (A.D. 1024), the Italians were again inclined to free themselves from their connexion with Germany. But neither Robert, king of France, nor the duke of Guienne, to both of whom they offered the crown of Lombardy, were disposed to involve themselves in the pursuit of a disputed honour: and Eribert, archbishop of Milan, who had conducted these intrigues, and other Lombard lords, made a merit of necessity, and, repairing to Conrad II., (the Salic) duke of Franconia, the successor of Henry on the German throne, tendered him the sovereignty of Italy, which he was ready to claim as a dependency upon his crown. Neither Conrad nor his successors were ever regularly elected to reign over Italy, but we may date from this era that subjection of the kingdom to the Germanic electoral body, which became an unquestioned right.

The reign of Conrad II. is remarkable only in Italian history for the civil wars which broke out between the vavassores and their feudal superiors, and between the former again and their lower vassals; and for the ineffectual efforts of the emperor to restore tranquillity by a famous edict which regulated the feudal law of Italy. In one of these internal struggles (A.D. 1035), the vavassores who held of the archbishop of Milan, rose in arms against his oppression: the citizens supported their prelate; the war was carried on even in the streets of the city; and the nobility were, at length, expelled from its walls. These and similar contests throughout Lombardy continued without intermission. The emperor, opposing himself to the ecclesiastical lords and their cities, vainly strove to put a period to the struggles by his arms; and it was not until just before his death that a pacification was effected. The vavassores were compelled to abrogate the most obnoxious of their feudal privileges in favour both of their military vassals and their serfs; and they began, from this period, to feel the necessity of putting themselves under the protection, and to share the citizenship, of the great towns in their vicinity.

We have now arrived at the real commencement of that memorable period which is distinguished by the struggle between the empire and the papacy, for ecclesiastical investitures; a struggle which, during the reigns of the two emperors of the house of Franconia who succeeded Conrad the Salic and his son Henry III., engrosses the history of Italy, and which terminated, as the course of subsequent events most clearly proved, in reversing the possession of power, and in reducing the emperors to a humiliating bondage to papal tyranny. During the reign, indeed, of Henry III. who, on the death of his father Conrad, was recognized as king of Germany and Italy, the struggle neither began nor could be foreseen; but it was certainly prepared by the reforms which he effected in the state of the papacy. It was some years before he had leisure to take possession of the crowns of Lombardy and the empire; but when he, at length, entered Italy, he found the holy see in shameful disorder, (A.D. 1046.) Three popes, all of whom had purchased their elections by infamous simony, claimed, at once, the obedience of the church, and divided the possession of the city. The emperor, with the support of his army, obliged the citizens to renounce the right of election which they had so scandalously abused; procured the deposition of the three rival pontiffs by the decision of a council, and filled the chair of St. Peter by his own presentation. The new pope, Clement II., conceded to him, for the future, an explicit right of nomination, as the only means of raising the church from the abyss of depravity into which she had fallen; and Henry, piously acting against the dictates of a selfish policy, in the sequel appointed three successors to Clement, of characters to reform the manners of the clergy, and to purify the morals of the holy see. The consequences of these measures were not experienced by Henry himself; but on his death, and during the minority of his son Henry IV., they soon became visible.

The last of the popes appointed by Henry III., had been recommended to him by the monk Hildebrand, by far the most conspicuous personage of the eleventh century. This extraordinary man was distinguished by dauntless courage, immeasurable ambition, and stem unconquerable energies. In the hardening solitude of the cloister, he had utterly estranged himself from all the kindly affections of our nature, and discarded from his heart every feeling of humanity or conscience, which has commonly power to turn men aside from the relentless execution of iniquitous projects. Unshackled by personal ties, and standing aloof from the ordinary relations of life, his ambition assumed the colouring of pious duty to the church, and his exertions the merit of resolutely upholding ecclesiastical rights. He found the papacy subjected to the imperial authority; he determined to elevate it above all temporal power; and he succeeded. The subsequent grandeur of the popedom is plainly attributable to the views which he opened and the purpose which he developed. The impulse given by his character to ecclesiastical pretensions continued after his death, and was prolonged until it had established the absolute supremacy of the popes over all the temporal monarchs of Europe. Even before the death of Henry III., Hildebrand, who originally filled an inferior office in the Roman church, had, by his singular qualities, acquired a paramount influence in ecclesiastical affairs. By his lofty views of aggrandisement for the church, he excited the enthusiastic hopes of the Italian clergy; he gained an unbounded ascendancy over their minds; and he was regarded as their chosen leader, and the hope of their common cause. We are not told how he acquired an almost equal sway over the senate and people of Rome, but it is certain that, upon one occasion, they empowered him singly to nominate a pope on their part. For twenty years before his own elevation to the tiara, Hildebrand, the ruling spirit of the papal councils, the tutor and director of the pontiffs, was regarded as something greater than the popes themselves. And it might surprise us that he did not sooner place himself in their chair, if it were not natural to suppose, that the clear judgment which regulated his ambition, equally taught him the fitting moments for its self-denial and indulgence.

The reformation of the clergy was wisely seen by Hildebrand to be necessarily the first step towards the meditated superiority of the spiritual order. He felt that the respect of a superstitious age, the best foundation for this superiority, would be most readily secured to the priesthood, by the reputation of austerity. By the act of the popes, he, notwithstanding much opposition, rigorously enforced upon the secular clergy the celibacy enjoined by the canons of the Romish church, but which hitherto had been little regarded. (A.D. 1058.) By thus cutting off the ecclesiastical body from the affections of domestic life, he not only acquired for them the veneration of the ignorant laity, who in those times had a strange respect for monastic virtues, but rendered them independent of all other feelings than devotion to the common interests of the church. The next and bolder measure of Hildebrand, was directed against the simoniacal purchase of ecclesiastical benefices, which certainly had reached a disgraceful height. The practice was denounced as infamous, and forbidden on pain of excommunication.

The passage was easy from the decree which forbade the purchase of a church benefice from a lay lord, to that which extended the same prohibition to the acceptance of investiture, upon any terms, from the hands of the laity, (A.D. 1059.) Both the inferior clergy and the bishops, had originally, in the early ages of the church, been elected by the people of their respective parishes and sees. But, when monarchs and great feudal lords piously bestowed endowments of land on the church, they naturally reserved to themselves and their successors the right of presentation to the ecclesiastical benefices which they created. As these grants seemed to partake of the nature of fiefs, they required similar formalities—investiture by the lord, and an oath of fealty by the tenant. The church had fairly forfeited part of her independence in return for ample endowments and temporal power: nor could any claim be more reasonable, than that the investiture of spiritual as well as lay fiefs should be received from the feudal superior. The worth of a benefice was estimated by the rapacious churchman according to the value of its temporalities; and the patron in whose gift these were placed became the real elector. The right of nomination thus passing from the people, devolved, in effect, upon monarchs and feudal lords, who exercised the prerogative for more than two centuries without opposition or scandal; and invested the new bishops with the ring and crozier, as visible symbols suited to the spirit of feudal institutions. The abolition of this practice of lay investiture was an essential part of the scheme which Hildebrand had formed for emancipating the spiritual, and subjugating the temporal powers. The notorious bribery which was frequent in lay presentations, afforded him a plausible reason for abolishing them; and under his influence, the papal denunciations were thundered against their continuance.

The edict against lay investitures was not immediately applied to the election of the popes themselves; but Hildebrand obtained (A.D. 1059) a celebrated decree of pope Nicholas II., which was intended as a preparation for this extension of the principle. By this remarkable instrument, the form of papal elections was established much on the foundation which has continued to this day. The choice of the supreme pontiff was vested in the cardinals, with the subsequent concurrence of the laity of Rome; and the new pope was finally to be presented for confirmation to the emperor. Not only were the citizens of Rome thus excluded thenceforward from their effectual participation in papal elections, but the emperors were deprived of their ancient legal prerogative of nomination to the holy see, to receive in exchange an empty and precarious right of approval.

The long minority of Henry IV. had been judiciously chosen for this series of papal encroachments. But the moment was at length arrived at which the relative strength of the empire and the papacy was to be put to the trial. Henry IV. reached his manhood; and, precisely at the same period, Hildebrand entered the lists against him as the recognised head of the church, whose councils he had long directed. On the death of pope Alexander II., against whom the German court and their party in Italy had vainly set up an anti-pope, Honorius II., Hildebrand was elected to the vacant chair of St. Peter, by the title of Gregory VII. (A.D. 1073.) Henry was too proud and too valiant to submit to the disgraceful yoke which Gregory had prepared for the imperial authority; but his character singularly disqualified him for the encounter with an adversary at once so cool, so wily, and so resolute. The temper of the young monarch was generous and noble, but his education had been faulty; he surrendered himself with little restraint to the impetuosity and excess of youthful passions, and disgusted his German subjects by arbitrary and despotic conduct. Gregory tampered with their disaffection, and craftily used the advantage which the disorders of Germany afforded to his views. But his strength might have been unequal to an open contention with the empire, if he had not been supported by the fanatical superstition and heroic courage of a woman. Matilda, countess of Tuscany, had just at this epoch united in her person the inheritance of that, and other great fiefs and provinces, which had accrued by marriages to her house. Her vast possessions gave her extraordinary power at this juncture, and she blindly and zealously devoted its exclusive exercise to the service of the church. Joining the excessive weakness and trembling credulity of female superstition to a masculine energy of character in other respects, she was a fitting associate or instrument for Gregory. Her fanaticism or ambition was as great and as exclusive as his own, but it differed from his ruling passion in this, that her devotion was to a cause which could yield her no temporal return, his to a throne which he had only laboured to plant on high, that he might seat himself on it above the powers of the world. Wedding herself to the maintenance of ecclesiastical rights, Matilda had no place in her heart for softer feelings; she separated from two husbands successively, because they did not share her absurd attachment to the papacy; she adhered, with unshaken fortitude, through all vicissitudes to Gregory and his successors; and finally, she bequeathed, at her death, all the possessions of which she was entitled to dispose, to the holy see for the supposed salvation of her soul. (A.D. 1115.)

Fortified by the allegiance and resources of this religious amazon, Gregory began by excommunicating some of Henry's ministers on pretence of simony, and remonstrated with the emperor because they were not immediately dismissed. He next renewed the papal edicts against lay investitures, and finally, as the consummation of insolence, cited Henry himself to appear at Rome, and vindicate himself from the charges of his rebellious subjects. Such insults filled the inexperienced and passionate monarch with violent indignation. He assembled a number of his prelates and other vassals at Worms, and procured a sentence that Gregory should no longer be recognised as legitimate pope. (A.D. 1076.) But the time was past for such strong and decisive measures, and the relations of power between the empire and papacy were now reversed. Gregory solemnly excommunicated Henry, and in turn released his subjects from their oaths of allegiance. Disaffection and superstition combined against the emperor; the German prelates fled from his side at the sound of the excommunication; he was deserted as a person tainted with some horrible infection, and his malcontent subjects transferred their obedience to the duke of Swabia. In this reverse of fortune the courage of Henry forsook him, and he had recourse to the miserable and ignominious expedient of submitting to the pope, and crossing the Alps in the depth of winter to solicit absolution, (A.D. 1077.) Bare-footed, and clothed only in a woollen shirt, he abjectly stationed himself in the outer court of the cattle of Canossa, near Reggio, where Gregory then resided with the countess Matilda, and remained for three whole days thus exposed to the severity of the season, before he could obtain admission into the presence of the pope, and receive absolution at his hands. But this base humiliation, instead of conciliating his enemies, only procured for him universal contempt. His friends were indignant at his abjectness, the pope was not the less resolved on his ruin, and Henry was roused by the conflicting dangers of his position to a more manly spirit. He broke off his treaty with Gregory, and resolved to fall, if to fall was inevitable, as the defender, not the betrayer, of the imperial rights. Fortune smiled upon his recovered intrepidity. The insolence of the pope excited indignation both in Germany and in Italy; in the former country the duke of Swabia was defeated and slain, in the latter the troops of Matilda were routed by the imperialists, and the emperor received his crown at Rome from the anti-pope Guibert, whom he had raised to the papal throne, (A.D. 1084.) Gregory, in misfortune and flight, still supported himself by the unshrinking pride of his nature; he was compelled to seek a refuge among the Normans of Naples, and he died in exile; but he repeated with his last breath the excommunications which he had hurled against Henry, the anti-pope, and their common adherents. (A.D. 1085.)

The death of so formidable and inveterate an antagonist produced little respite for Henry in his struggle with the church. The successors of Gregory, Urban II., and Paschal II., prosecuted his views, and as strenuously supported the great contest for ecclesiastical independence. They raised enemies to Henry in the bosom of his family, supported his sons in unnatural rebellions, and drew upon him the fanatical hostility of the leaders of the first crusade on their passage through Italy. For twenty years the unhappy emperor was persecuted by the unrelenting hatred of the pontiffs, wearied with incessant hostilities, and loaded with anguish by the infamous revolt of his children. He was at length treacherously deposed by the parricidal hands of his second son, Henry, and died in old age and misery, broken-hearted and destitute. (A.D. 1106.)

Both pope Paschal II., who had remorselessly instigated Henry V. to criminal violence towards his father, and the young emperor himself, who had unnaturally upheld the cause of the church against his parent, reaped the just fruits of their iniquity. Paschal was betrayed and imprisoned by the prince who had been his guilty confederate; and Henry, on his part, was long troubled and finally humiliated by the ecclesiastical power for whose alliance he had violated every filial duty.

For above fifteen years of his reign he was arrayed in open opposition to the church in the struggle for the right of ecclesiastical investiture; and successive popes still maintained against him a strenuous opposition to this prerogative. As he was stronger in the support of his German vassals than his father had been, the pontiffs were never able to proceed to similar extremities with him, and a long and injurious contest was protracted without any decisive success. At length, in the pontificate of Calixtus II., both parties had become utterly exhausted and weary of this ruinous struggle, and a treaty was concluded at Worms, which set at rest the question of ecclesiastical investiture. (A.D. 1122.) The compromise which effected a pacification was so simple an expedient, that it might at first sight astonish us that it was not sooner adopted, since it appeared at the time equally to satisfy both the opponents. The emperor resigned the spiritual, the pope his claim to the temporal prerogative of investitures. The former recognised the liberty of episcopal elections, and renounced all pretence of investing bishops with the ring and crozier; the latter agreed that elections should always be made in presence of the emperor or his officers, and that the new bishop should then receive the temporalities of his see from the feudal sovereign by the type of the sceptre. The compact wore the appearance of equity; but it was only the exhaustion of long and destructive wars which had reduced the partizans either of the church or the empire to a reasonable moderation. Yet we may rather make allowances for the tenacity with which the emperors clung to the rights of centuries, than for the fierce and unholy ambition which actuated the pontiffs to the support of novel and intolerable pretensions; and the emperors might with justice fear to make any concessions to such audacious and overbearing antagonists. Even while the success seemed, in the issue of the contest, to be equally balanced, the emperors had lost a valuable part of their former prerogative, the popes had acquired a degree of power corresponding to that of which they had deprived the empire, and the progress of subsequent events proved that the victory had remained with the church.

Before the close of the great contest about ecclesiastical investitures, the towns of northern Italy had silently perfected the formation of their free constitutions, and Lombardy contained almost as many republics as there were cities within its limits. Debarred from all acquaintance with the progress of these states towards independence during the long wars between the empire and papacy, we must be contented to describe their political condition as it existed in the first part of the twelfth century. At that period the new republics had succeeded in overpowering nearly the whole of the rural nobility in their vicinity; and it is asserted by a contemporary chronicler, that before the middle of the century there was scarcely any feudal nobleman to be found who had not submitted to some city. It was the object of the civic communities at once to break the independence and to conciliate the affection of the nobles, and it was, therefore, an invariable provision in the treaties which admitted them to the rights of citizenship, that they should reside for some months in the year within the walls which contained the strength of the republic. Thus deprived of the authority which they had enjoyed in their castles, the nobility gave a new direction to their ambition, and aspired to the highest offices in the government to which they were attached. The respect which the prejudices of mankind have ever conceded to high birth and fortune, obtained for the nobles the object which they coveted, and in all the Lombard republics the principal dignities of the magistracy were long entrusted to the superior families. It may, however, be presumed, that the haughty spirit of the feudal aristocracy could with difficulty endure the assumption of equality in a class of men upon whose condition they had been habituated to look with contempt; while on the other hand, the burghers, in the insolence of rising importance, were not likely to use their success with moderation, still less to brook any outrage of the rights of a free democracy. On one occasion in particular (A.D. 1041), at Milan, a casual insult, offered in the streets by one of the nobles to a plebeian, was the cause of a furious commotion, in which the fortified residences of the nobles within the walls were demolished in one day by the citizens, and their order a second time expelled from the city. But the inhabitants depended for food upon the surrounding country, which the banished nobles held with their retainers. The nobles on their part had already found themselves too weak to support a contest with the citizens, and both factions were prudent enough to discover, that their common interests were identified with the safety of the state, (A.D. 1044.) A pacification was effected, and the nobles resumed their abode in the city, and their share in its government.

The supreme administration of affairs in the Lombard republics, both in peace and in war, was entrusted to consuls, of whom there were usually two, though in some instances more. At once the judges and generals of the state, they were elected annually by the votes of the citizens, and it was their business to convoke the general assemblies of the republic upon extraordinary occasions. But as these bodies were too numerous for the convenient dispatch of current affairs, two councils were chosen by the people to assist and control their magistrates. The smaller and more select of these, that of the credenza or secrecy, regulated financial concerns, guided the external relations of the republic, and watched over the conduct of the consuls; the other, the senate or great council, permanently represented the sovereign people. Every law or measure of national importance necessarily received the approval of the council of credenza, and of the senate, before it could be submitted to 'the general assembly of the people, which, at the 'sound of the great bell of the city, met in some public place to ratify or annul the proposition.

The military system of the republics was assimilated to the forms of their civil government. The consuls commanded the levies, and the people chose their own officers of inferior rank. The cities of Lombardy were divided, usually according to their number of gates, into several quarters; each of these had its standard, and gonfalonier or ensign bearer, under whose direction the inhabitants, whenever an enemy threatened, rushed in arms to their proper gate and to the neighbouring ramparts, with the defence of which they were specially charged. Every citizen was bound to serve the state, the artisans on foot, the gentlemen on horseback. The former were arrayed in bands of infantry according to the quarter which they inhabited; the latter were enrolled into troops of cavalry, of which each city boasted one or more. Of the infantry, chosen portions in every quarter were armed, lightly with the crossbow, heavily, with the iron helmet, the lance, and the buckler; but the mass of the citizens had no other trust than their swords. The mounted nobles, armed cap-a-pie, fought with the lance and in hauberks, or coats of twisted mail.

But a singular invention marked at once the rudeness and the wisdom of the tactics which regulated the free militia of Lombardy. This was the carroccio, or great standard car of the state; it is said to have been first used by Eribert, archbishop of Milan, in the war of 1035, in which the citizens supported him against the rural nobility, and it soon came to be introduced into the array of all the republics. It was a car upon four wheels, painted red, and so heavy that it was drawn by four pairs of oxen, with splendid trappings of scarlet. In the centre, raised upon a mast, which was crowned by a golden orb, floated the banner of the republic, and beneath it, the Saviour extended on the cross appeared to pour benediction on the surrounding host. Two platforms occupied the car in front and behind the mast, the first filled with a few of the most valiant soldiers of the army, the chosen guard of the standard, the latter with a band of martial music. Feelings of religion and of military glory were strangely associated with the carroccio. It was an imitation of the Jewish ark of the covenant, and it was from its platform that a chaplain administered the holy offices of Christianity to the army. It thus became sacred in the eyes of the citizens, and to suffer it to fall into the hands of an enemy entailed intolerable disgrace. The thickest of the battle ever encircled the carroccio; it guided the advance, the duty of its defence gave order and a rallying point in retreat, and it was in every situation calculated to remedy the absence of discipline and the unskilfulness of military movement which belonged to that age. It afforded a common centre, a principle of weight and depth and solidity, to the untrained infantry of the citizens, and enabled them to resist without difficulty the impetuous charges of the feudal chivalry. In this respect the carroccio was a most sagacious expedient, and completely answered the purpose of its inventor, in rendering the cavalry of the feudal nobles powerless against the thick masses of the burghers; and if the movements of the car were incompatible with celerity of operations, this defect could be little appreciated where to move without confusion at all had been previously unknown. To march straightforward towards an enemy, and to fight, were the only tactics; the ranged battle, or the predatory incursion to carry off the harvests of a foe, the only business of a campaign.

The confidence which the Lombard citizens acquired in the field, was wrought to a tone of insolent defiance from the security which they enjoyed within the walls of their towns. Until after the invention of gunpowder, the means of defence for fortified places were greatly superior to those of attack. The moveable towers, penthouses, battering rams, and machines for throwing stones and darts, usual in ancient sieges, continued with little change to form the only resources of the middle ages in the assault of fortresses; and these cumbrous engines of offence were advantageously opposed by the thick and lofty walls, flanked by towers, and fronted by a broad and deep moat, which composed the defences of cities. Within these strong bulwarks and impassable trenches, and in the midst of well peopled streets, the industrious citizens of Lombardy dwelt secure from the licence of freebooters, and the oppression of feudal tyrants. Their crafts became respectable and even honourable; they grew wealthy and numerous; and many of their cities attained a larger population than the capitals of any of the European kingdoms of the age.

Pavia and Milan had long been the greatest among these cities, and with the increase of riches and power their early rivalry darkened into inveterate hatred. Pavia, seated at the confluence of the Tesino and the Po, seemed to hold the keys of the Lombard waters, and her barks, laden with the produce of the fruitful plains through which these rivers flow, descended into the Adriatic, and exchanged their raw freights for the manufactures and the merchandize of Venice. The population and riches of Pavia swelled the pride which she inherited as the ancient capital of the Lombard kings, and the site of their palaces; but in numerical strength and in real importance, she was still second to Milan. That city had, perhaps, preserved a large population from the times of the Roman empire: the surrounding country is luxuriantly fertile; the climate is pure and healthful; but these advantages were equally enjoyed by other Lombard cities, and it must have been from some unexplained cause that Milan outstripped them all in the number and riches, the warlike spirit, and the profitable industry of her inhabitants. The city of Cremona was next in consequence to these two great rival capitals, and Lodi, Crema, Como, Tortona, Brescia, Novara, Bergamo, and farther off, Modena, Parma, Verona, Reggio, Placentia, Ferrara, and Bologna, were among the considerable cities which were invigorated by the genius of freedom.

But, unhappily, the conduct pursued by these republics in their external relations was not always of a character to merit that interest in their fate which the spirit that breathed through their free institutions is so powerfully calculated to excite. With that restless desire of tyrannizing over weaker neighbours from which a democracy is seldom exempt, they played over again, as has been truly observed, the tragedy of ancient Greece, with all its circumstances of inveterate hatred, unjust ambition, and atrocious retaliation, though with less consummate actors upon the scene. The Milanese, who were, at no very distant period, themselves to taste of the dregs of misery, were unrelenting oppressors of the smaller republics, at the opening of the twelfth century, (A.D. 1111.) After a war of four years, they took the city of Lodi by assault, razed it to the ground, and distributing the surviving inhabitants into six open villages, exercised over them a galling and cruel tyranny. Seven years afterwards they commenced a more difficult war with the little city of Como, the siege of which, repeated during ten successive summers, terminated, after an heroic resistance on the part of the inhabitants, in their subjection, though on lenient terms, to the conquering republic, (A.D. 1128.) But though Milan was odiously preeminent in her career of tyranny, others of the more powerful republics were not free from the same reproach. Cremona, in the last year of the eleventh century, attacked and subjugated the city of Crema; and Pavia, some years later, was successful in the work of oppression against Tortona. These and other tyrannical enterprises had filled all Lombardy with various animosities and implacable hatreds. At the period when the emperor Henry V. (A.D. 1125) closed his life, shortly after the peace of Worms, most of the Lombard cities were leagued with Milan in the war against the independence of Como; but in the year following the surrender of that town, the attempt of Crema to throw off the Cremonese yoke had separated Lombardy into two great factions, or leagues, of nearly equal forces, (A.D. 1129.) Milan, into whose arms Crema had thrown herself, extended protection to that little state, and was supported by several republics; while Pavia, Placentia, Novara, and Brescia were arrayed on the other side as the allies of Cremona.

The local causes of contention between these well-balanced powers were swallowed up, in the disputes which arose for the succession to the empire, on the death of Henry V., who left no children to inherit his dignity. Germany was divided between the rival pretensions of the houses of Saxony and Swabia. Lothaire, duke of Saxony, was proclaimed emperor by the German diet (A.D. 1125); but the two brothers of the house of Swabia, nephews of Henry V., opposed their claims to his elevation; and one of them, Conrad, duke of Franconia, assuming the royal title (A.D. 1128), passed into Italy, and with the support of the Milanese, received the crown of Lombardy in their city. But his power was unequal to his ambition; and when Lothaire entered Italy in his turn (A.D. 1132), with so feeble an army that he excited the ridicule of the Italians, Conrad was obliged to retire into Germany with humiliation, before even his scanty array. Lothaire received the imperial crown at Rome from Honorius II., by whom he was supported; but, contrary to the established custom, his coronation took place in the church of St. John, in the Lateran, for an anti-pope ruled in the Vatican; and the new emperor, after the ceremony, hastily abandoned Rome and Italy.

There is no circumstance more striking in the history of the popedom, than the alternations of weakness and strength which its annals exhibit. When circumstances favoured the pretensions of papal arrogance, or when the tiara graced the brows of a master spirit, we are certain to find new assumptions of authority, and fresh advances successfully established towards ecclesiastical dominion over the universe: when schisms disturbed the church, or men of weak character filled the chair of St. Peter, we are astonished at the decline of pontifical rule. But these powerless intervals were moments of slumber, not of decay; and when the talents of the reigning pope or the progress of events admitted the developement of papal ambition, we invariably discover, that the energies of the church have merely been dormant, and that they have not retrograded from the highest point that they had formerly gained. On the death of Paschal II., who, with his predecessor, had emulated the pride and prosecuted the views of Gregory VII., the hostile influence of two powerful Roman families in the conclave of cardinals produced double elections, and a long and scandalous schism in the papacy. The citizens of Rome availed themselves of the disorders of the times, to re-establish their republican independence and their importance, which the vigorous reign of Gregory and his successors had formerly destroyed. In their opposition to the popes they were instigated by the exhortations of a republican monk, Arnold of Brescia, who, with a singular spirit for one of his order, devoted his remarkable eloquence, and the weight of irreproachable morals and orthodox faith, to expose the vices of the clergy. Whatever were his motives, he satisfied the conviction of his hearers when he inveighed against the dangerous consequences of the union of temporal and ecclesiastical power in the popedom. The Roman republic was restored under his direction; the popes were compelled to recognize its authority; and Arnold of Brescia, after suffering persecution and exile, became the real master of Rome. (A.D. 1145.)

After the first expedition of the emperor Lothaire into Italy, several years elapsed before he again crossed the Alps. In this interval, his rival, Conrad, though he had received the crown of Lombardy, submitted to his authority (A.D. 1136); and Lothaire at length descended into Italy again, with a more respectable force than had formerly accompanied him. His presence had a momentary influence upon the affairs of the church and of Naples, but scarcely any upon the general aspect of Italy. He died, after a short and glorious campaign, on his return to Germany; and was succeeded, in the following year (A.D. 1137), by Conrad III., the same prince who had formerly contended with him for the imperial crown; and whose reign of fourteen years is altogether unconnected with Italian history, since, during the whole of the period, he neither appeared in the kingdom nor exercised the slightest influence over its affairs. He left an infant son; but the German diet, setting aside the claims of the minor by the advice of the dying emperor himself, elected for his successor his nephew, Frederic Barbarossa, duke of Swabia, then in the flower of his age, and the most powerful prince of Germany, (A.D. 1152.) Equally allied to the two princely families whose rivalry had long distracted Germany, Frederic concentrated in his person the conflicting affections and interests of their factions, and wielded the whole feudal strength of the kingdom. His elevation to the throne of Germany introduced a new era of splendour and power for the imperial dignity; but it also opens the most glorious and interesting epoch in the chequered story of Italian independence.

In Frederic Barbarossa the Italians were destined to find a very different sovereign from their last emperors, who had rarely appeared in Italy, and with forces quite inadequate to the maintenance of their authority. The talents of Frederic were of the highest order, and he was active, enterprising, and valiant; but these favourable qualities were disgraced by a severe and arbitrary temper, a systematic inflexible cruelty, and a haughty conceit that his imperial rights entitled him, as the successor of Augustus, to the despotic dominion of the earth. The conqueror and the tyrant have never wanted their apologists among men who are dazzled by the vanity of warlike renown, and awed by the contemplation of stupendous power; but to the calm eye of philosophy, the character of Frederic Barbarossa, as of all who, like him, have harassed nations and outraged humanity, will appear only as a fitting object for the unmingled detestation of mankind. Covetous of power, greedy of military glory, and enjoying the undivided obedience of numerous and warlike nobles, Frederic looked upon Italy as a fair field for his grasping ambition and formidable array. Immediately after his accession, he summoned all the vassals of the German crown to be in readiness, within two years, to attend him on an expedition into Italy; and he concluded an alliance with pope Eugene II., who promised to place the imperial crown on his head, and whom in return he undertook to deliver from the thraldom of the Roman republic.

But it was towards the free communities of Lombardy that the impatience and resentment of Frederic were most strongly directed. To his absolute pretensions, the independence of those cities was mere rebellion, which it behoved him to crush; their successful efforts to govern themselves, an intolerable usurpation of the rights of his crown, which his dignity required him to uphold. In this temper he unhappily found too much reason, in the conduct of some of the Lombard cities towards each other, for his interference and common oppression of them all. Forty-two years had now elapsed since the Milanese had completed the destruction of Lodi, and scattered its citizens into villages; the generation of the conquerors and of the oppressed had alike passed away, and liberty might be known only to the sons of the Lodese by the lamentations of their parents. But the spirit of a free people is an undying inheritance; and the inhabitants of Lodi had continued to cherish in their defenceless villages the fond memory of ruined independence, and the bitter sense of present humiliation. Two of them happening accidentally to be at Constance when Frederic held a diet there, in the year after his accession (A.D. 1153), threw themselves at the feet of the emperor, and implored him, as the ultimate source of justice, to redress the wrongs of their country. The designs of Frederic sufficiently disposed him to lend a favourable ear to their prayer; and he immediately dispatched an order to the Milanese to re-establish the people of Lodi in their ancient privileges, and to renounce the jurisdiction over them which they had arrogated to themselves. But such was the terror inspired by the Milanese power, that when the imperial messenger arrived in Italy, the magistrates of Lodi disclaimed the complaints of their countrymen, and the people were overwhelmed by a horrible dread of summary vengeance from the formidable republic, against which the remote assistance of Frederic appeared no protection. By the Milanese themselves, the order to set the people of Lodi at liberty was received with violent indignation and contempt; and the imperial envoy escaped with difficulty from the fury of the populace. But the consuls of Milan, learning the approaching entrance of the emperor into Italy, were unwilling to provoke his anger by any attack upon the people of Lodi; and they even, with the other Lombard cities, sent to him the presents which it was customary to offer on the accession of a new sovereign.

Meanwhile Frederic, passing the Alps, entered Italy through the Trentine valley, at the head of all his German vassals, and with a more brilliant and powerful army than any of his predecessors had ever led into Lombardy. (A.D. 1154.) Advancing to the neighbourhood of Placentia, he opened the ancient feudal assembly of the states of the kingdom on the plain of Roncaglia, on the Po. Here complaints of the ambition of Milan poured in from various quarters. The consuls of Lodi now repeated the supplications which they had formerly disavowed; those of Como had similar intreaties to prefer, for protection against the Milanese tyranny; and the deputies of Pavia, Cremona, and Novara, from inveterate hatred to Milan, were ranged in support of the same cause. But the consuls of Milan were ready to reply to the charges of their enemies, and they were seconded, in the angry discussion which was carried on before the emperor, by the delegates of Crema, Brescia, Tortona, Placentia, and other cities.

The party of Pavia was evidently the weaker; and the insidious policy of Frederic, therefore, impelled him to throw his sword into their scale. Milan stood in no need of his aid; but she once subdued, her opponents were too feeble to withstand him. He at first, however, dissembled, and commanded both the leagues, who had already commenced desultory hostilities, to lay down their arms, and await his decision at Novara. Breaking up the diet, he began his march through the Milanese territory towards that place; and making it a cause of offence against the consuls of the republic, who conducted him on his route, that the supply of provisions was insufficient for his wasteful army, he rejected all their submissive efforts to avert his displeasure, and gave over the country to fire and rapine. The people of Milan now saw that the tyrant was inexorable, and they began to prepare for a vigorous resistance; they strengthened the works of their capital, collected supplies, and confirmed their alliance with the cities of their party. The storm soon burst upon the confederacy. Frederic, after passing into the territory of Turin and Vercelli, and receiving those cities, though they governed themselves as republics, into his favour, returned towards Pavia, and on his march satiated his vengeance against the city of Asti, and the little town of Chieri, which had dared to espouse the cause of independence. Their citizens, distrusting the strength of their defences, fled at his approach; and Frederic, reducing their deserted habitations to ashes, drew near to Tortona, and ordered that republic to renounce the alliance of Milan for that of Pavia. But the magistrates of this little state replied with a noble spirit, that they were not used to desert their allies in the hour of adversity: and the numerous army of Frederic sat down before their walls, (A.D. 1155.)

The lower part of the city was little susceptible of defence, and the emperor soon made himself master of it; but the upper town, elevated on a rocky hill, was strong by situation and art. The Milanese threw two hundred of their best citizens into the place, induced some of the rural nobility of Liguria to share in the defence, and for two months enabled the people of Tortona, with these aids, to defy the imperial power. The emperor pressed the siege with skill and obstinacy; and his machines—the balistæ of the ancients—threw such masses of rock into the city, that upon one occasion three of the principal inhabitants were buried under the fall of a single piece. But despair lent incredible strength to the besieged; their engineers countermined the subterranean approaches of the assailants under the only tower which was not placed on a rock, and suffocated the enemy in their own galleries. The sallies of the citizens were frequent and terrible; and Frederic vainly endeavoured to awe them into surrender, by erecting gibbets before the walls, and, with execrable barbarity, hanging the few prisoners who fell into his hands in the defence of their liberties. The horrors of thirst at last accomplished that which the sword could not effect. The besiegers succeeded in poisoning with sulphur the only fountain—it was without the walls—to which the sallies of the heroic burghers could afford them access; and, after sixty-two days of incessant combats, they capitulated for their lives and personal freedom. Their town was razed to the ground, and the citizens of Milan afforded them an hospitable refuge.

After this victory Frederic made his triumphal entry into Pavia, and there received the crown of Lombardy. But instead of pursuing his success against Milan, his ambition was dazzled by the desire of wearing his imperial crown; and he marched towards Rome to accept it from pope Adrian IV., who, on the death of Eugene III., and after the short reign of his successor, Anastasius IV., had ascended the papal chair. Barbarossa carried into Rome his hatred of popular liberty; the citizens trembled before his sword, and their eloquent adviser, Arnold of Brescia, was betrayed into his hands. Frederic consigned the unhappy monk to the inhuman vengeance of the pope, and he was burnt alive at Rome, by the sentence of a council which had unjustly condemned him for heresy. After this tragedy the pope and the emperor met to cement their blood-stained alliance; and such was now the measure of pontifical arrogance, that Adrian obliged the haughty emperor to hold his stirrup while he descended from his mule, before he would bestow upon him the kiss of peace. After receiving the imperial diadem, and punishing the Romans for a popular insurrection, Frederic was compelled to disband the greatest part of his army at Ancona, for his German vassals were impatient to return by different routes to their country; and, with his remaining followers, traversing Romagna, and the Mantuan and Veronese territory, he himself re-entered Germany by Trent and Balzano, after an absence of one year.

The army of Frederic had no sooner quitted Lombardy for Rome, than the Milanese rebuilt Tortona at their own expence, and by the voluntary labour of their citizens. They then, taking advantage of the emperor's return to Germany, proceeded to punish those who, equally interested with themselves in the liberties of Italy, had made common cause with the foreign oppressor, (A.D. 1157.) They defeated the people of Pavia and Novara, and the marquis of Montferrat, and by their successes completely re-established the reputation of their arms. With less justifiable violence they expelled the injured citizens of Lodi from their dwellings; they strengthened their own walls and rural castles; they formed closer relations of mutual defence with their allies; and Frederic soon learnt that his presence in Italy could alone prevent the whole of Lombardy from being drawn into a confederacy against him. He convoked all the German vassals of the empire for a second expedition beyond the Alps; and after an absence of two years, descended from the mountains again, with the flower of the German nobility and an immense army. (A.D. 1158.) When his numbers were augmented by the feudal array of the Italian nobles, and the contingents of the cities, almost all of whom contributed their militia, either willingly or from the terror of his overwhelming force, he had assembled fifteen thousand cavalry and one hundred thousand infantry.

The whole of this mighty power was directed against Milan, and the people of that city prepared with resolution for the siege which awaited them. The circuit of their walls was immense, a broad and deep fosse swept round the bulwarks; and Frederic found that to attack them with the battering-ram and moveable tower would be in vain. Against the numerous inhabitants, famine might be rendered more effectual than these engines of destruction. The Milanese, in the expectation that the emperor would not be able to complete the investment of so great a city on all sides, had neglected to lay in sufficient supplies; and when Frederic, by the skilful disposition of his blockade, had disappointed their hopes and repulsed their sallies, the immense population became a prey first to hunger, and then to disease and despair. They yielded to want and pestilence rather than to the arms of Frederic, and obtained favourable conditions. They were compelled to renounce their authority over the people of Como and Lodi, to build a palace for the emperor, to pay him a large ransom, and to abjure their regalian rights; but the possession of their territory was confirmed to them. Their allies were included in the capitulation; they were allowed to maintain their confederacy, and to choose their own consuls; and the imperial army was restricted from entering their walls.

These terms were not in themselves under all circumstances severe; but it was soon perceived how much faith might be placed upon their observance. In a diet which Frederic held at Roncaglia, after the capitulation of Milan, the nobles and the clergy of Italy vied with each other in exalting the imperial prerogatives; the juris-consults of Bologna, where the civil law was now studied, lent him all the aid of the despotic principles which they could deduce from the codes of Justinian, and the rights of the empire were so defined, as utterly to destroy the independence of the cities. These regalian rights, as they were termed, were held to belong to the emperors alone, from whom they had been gradually usurped; and instead of the general supremacy, with the enjoyment of supplies of provision whenever the sovereign entered Italy, which the cities had always conceded to the imperial authority, the absolute possession of all the revenues and appurtenances of government was now grasped by its prerogative, and only remitted for a pecuniary stipulation. A more intolerable innovation was next introduced; an imperial magistrate, with the title, which afterwards became famous in Italian history, of podestá, was placed in each city, ostensibly to execute justice in appeals to the imperial authority, but in reality to overawe the republican consuls. Frederic soon proceeded farther, and abolishing altogether the popular magistracies, threw the whole judicial power into the hands of his own officers.

It was this last outrage which stung the people of Milan to madness, (A.D. 1159.) The faithless tyrant had already violated the terms of his treaty with them, seized part of their territory, robbed them of their proper jurisdiction, subjected their allies; and they now resolved rather to make one desperate struggle for independence, than tamely to witness the gradual and total subversion of their freedom. After the submission of Milan, and on the approach of winter, many of the great German feudatories had returned to their homes, and Frederic had led the remainder of his followers into Romagna, to establish the imperial pretensions over its cities and fiefs. Circumstances, therefore, favoured the Milanese: they rose in arms, and Frederic, too weak at the moment to form the siege of their city, contented himself with putting them under the ban of the empire. But Lombardy was prostrate in subjection; only the Brescians and the little state of Crema dared to share the fortunes of Milan; and Frederic, reinforced from Germany, and supported by the cities inimical to Milan, was everywhere successful. He invested Crema, and took it by capitulation, after an obstinate defence of six months, which recalled many of the circumstances of the siege of Tortona, with even more atrocious cruelty on the part of Frederic; for he exposed his hostages and prisoners to the darts of their besieged friends, by fastening their bodies on the exterior of the moveable towers which he directed against the walls.

Notwithstanding the fate of Crema, the Milanese maintained their struggle for independence with unshaken courage, and for two years they successfully resisted all the efforts of their haughty adversary. At first the force of Frederic was weakened by the necessity of disbanding his army, as his vassals were, as usual, soon tired of service, and anxious to revisit their country; and the contest was then reduced so nearly to a parity of strength, that the Milanese fought a ranged battle against him at Cassano with signal success, (A.D. 1160.) Advancing with deliberate firmness to the attack with their carroccio, they utterly routed one wing of the imperialists, and though in the other quarter of the field, the personal bravery of Frederic broke through all obstacles, so that the sacred car fell for a moment into his hands, and its standard was torn down, a second charge of the republicans obtained the victory, and compelled Frederic to abandon the field. This and other partial successes buoyed up the hopes of the Milanese. But when, after the first year, the emperor was again joined by a fresh feudal army of Germans, their cause wore a different aspect, and grew daily more desperate. Their harvests were utterly destroyed, their plains were devastated; and while a hundred thousand men blockaded their city, a calamitous fire which broke out within the walls, destroyed their granaries, and left them without food in the depth of winter. Harassed with perpetual fatigues, worn out by famine, by reverses, and by despair, the wretched citizens were finally reduced to surrender at discretion. The victor at first preserved a sullen silence on the fate which he intended for them, and excited deceitful hopes by a delay of three weeks in the expression of his pleasure. But at length the people of Milan were commanded to quit their habitations, and to retire beyond the circuit of their walls; they obeyed with trembling submission, and Milan was a solitude. The imperialists then entered the deserted streets; the citizens of Pavia and Cremona, of Lodi and Como, were ordered to glut their hatred of Milan in the respective quarters of the city which were allotted to them; and for six days they laboured with malignant industry in levelling the ramparts and houses with the ground, (A.D. 1162.) On the seventh the vengeance of Barbarossa had been accomplished: Milan was a pile of ruins, and her children were scattered in misery and servitude over their plains.

The destruction of Milan appeared to consummate the grandeur of the imperial dominion. No power remained to oppose the despotic pretensions of Frederic; the liberties of Lombardy were completely overthrown, and the tyrant, casting off the mask, and abandoning himself to the indulgence of his arbitrary temper, alike subjected his faithful adherents, and the states which he had crushed, to a merciless and onerous yoke. Even in many of the cities which had assisted him, he abolished the republican magistracy, and substituted his podestá; his officers every where exercised the most despotic authority, and extorted immense contributions; and the unhappy Milanese in particular, in the villages into which they had been distributed, were the victims of intolerable exactions and tyranny. The imperial lieutenant, the archbishop elect of Cologne, who governed in Italy on Frederic's return to Germany (A.D. 1162), emulated the disposition of his master, and ruled over Lombardy with a sceptre of iron. We are assured, that under his authority the podestás raised the contributions of their cities to six times the amount which had ever before been demanded of them. It was without effect that, on the entrance of Frederic into Italy in the following year, the Italians carried their remonstrances and supplications to the foot of his throne. They were received with indiscriminate displeasure, or heard only to be met by empty promises of enquiry into the conduct of ministers who had acted with a spirit so congenial to his own. But the fire of liberty had not been utterly extinguished in Lombardy. The cruel internal animosities, the dark and vindictive hatreds which had convulsed the bosom of Italian society, were calmed by the general misery, and converted into indignation and shame by the common degradation of states which had once been free. A salutary but too transient oblivion of former jealousies was produced by detestation of the universal tyrant; and, with the single exception of Pavia, the cities of Lombardy were animated by an unconquerable resolution to recover that independence which all had lost either by violence or treachery.

The cities of the Veronese March, hitherto almost strangers to the wars of Lombardy, were the first to confederate, and their success gave a happy promise to their compatriots (A.D. 1164), for Frederic was repulsed from their district, and compelled to seek reinforcements in

Germany; upon the militia of his subject cities he dared not rely. His absence, and the subsequent employment which was given to his arms in central Italy, by his support of an anti-pope against Alexander III. (the successor of Adrian IV.) and the king of Sicily, afforded opportunities for Verona and the confederate cities of Eastern Lombardy to spread their coalition, (A.D. 1167.) Cremona, formerly the faithful ally of the emperor, Brescia, and other towns joined their cause; the people of Milan were taken under their protection, and the first act of the new alliance was to rebuild the walls of the ruined city, and collect its natives within them from their defenceless villages. Milan revived as a powerful republic, Lodi was compelled to join the insurrection, and the two clusters of cities on the east and west of the Adige united in the famous Lombard League. An obligation of mutual assistance for twenty years, the recovery of their elective magistracies, and of their rights of peace and war, and the restoration of all the regalian privileges which had been extorted from them at the diet of Roncaglia, were the condition and the objects of the league.

It was cemented at a fortunate crisis. The emperor had imprudently embroiled himself with the church and the king of Sicily, by his ineffectual attempts to oppose a rival to Alexander III. On leading a new army into Italy he suspended the punishment which he intended for the Lombards, to conduct his force against Rome, where the citizens had declared for Alexander. He vigorously pushed the siege of that city, but the hour of retribution for a life of execrable ambition had at length arrived. His great army fell a prey to the autumnal fever of the *maremma* (A.D. 1167), which visits the vicinity of that city, the flower of his German nobility were cut off by the ravages of this pestilence, and he was compelled to abandon his enterprise, and to continue a disgraceful retreat to the Alps.

Six years had passed before Frederic could again lead his forces into Italy; and two years more, in which he sacrificed another army to the murderous influence of climate, were consumed in indecisive hostilities with the Lombard league, before his unbending spirit would receive the lessons of misfortune and chastisement. At length was fought that memorable battle which was to confirm the independence of Lombardy, and to put the finishing stroke to the humiliation of her oppressor.

It was in the spring of the year A.D. 1176 that Frederic, having received large reinforcements from Germany, and collected all the troops which he could previously bring into the field, advanced for the last time into the territory of Milan, at the head of a formidable army. The Milanese, on their part, had not neglected to avail themselves of the cessation of hostilities during the winter, to prepare for the struggle of the campaign. They had formed two bodies of chosen cavalry; the one a devoted band of nine hundred men, who had sworn to die for their country rather than to yield ground to the enemy; the other, of three hundred youths of the first families of the republic, who were bound by a similar oath to the defence of the sacred carroccio. The rest of the citizens were divided into six great masses of infantry under the banners of their several quarters in the city. When intelligence was received of the approach of Frederic, the republic had not yet received the expected succours from all her confederates. The militia of Placentia, with a handful of the chosen troops of Verona, Brescia, Vercelli, and Novara, were the only allied force which had effected their junction. But the Milanese boldly led out the carroccio from their gates, and advanced to encounter the imperial army on the plain of Legnano, within less than fifteen miles of their capital. As the two armies approached, a skirmish of cavalry soon brought on a general engagement; and the German chivalry, led by the emperor in person, made a furious charge upon the carroccio. As they came on at the gallop, the Milanese threw themselves on their knees, commended the purity of their sacred cause to God, St. Peter, and St. Ambrose, and then, rising and unfurling their banners, bravely advanced to meet the assailants. But so impetuous and tremendous was the onset of the German chivalry, that the chosen guard of the carroccio was borne down before them and broken by the weight of the shock, and the sacred car itself, as its defenders wavered, became in imminent peril. At that moment of trial, the devoted squadron of the Milanese raised their voices to heaven, with the solemn and enthusiastic repetition of their vow to conquer or perish, threw themselves with resistless desperation upon the enemy, and decided the glorious fortunes of their country. The imperial standard was trampled in the dust, and Frederic, who fought with a courage worthy of a better cause, in the foremost ranks of his nobles, was thrown from his horse. The column which his example had animated fled on his fall, and the Milanese infantry steadily advancing, the rout in the imperial army soon became general. The swords of the Milanese were dyed with a terrific vengeance. For eight miles the plain was covered with the slaughter of the fugitives; and of those among them who escaped the pursuit, the greater number were drowned in the waters of the Tesino.

Frederic had not been killed, as was supposed for some time by his followers, but after being several days missing, he appeared at Pavia alone, humiliated, and in the disguise in which he had contrived to escape after the battle. Two and twenty years had elapsed since his first expedition into Italy; and, during that time, in the vain struggle against freedom, he had led seven great armies to their destruction, by pestilence or the sword: he had shed torrents of blood, razed cities to their foundations, and sickened humanity with his atrocities. Yet, so precarious is power when raised on injustice and oppression, so unextinguishable the spirit and so elastic the courage which can animate a people in the cause of independence, that, in the zenith of his greatness, and when he appeared most completely to have succeeded in the establishment of despotism, Frederic was plunged by his insatiable ambition and relentless temper from one misfortune into another; defied, baffled, and ignominiously put to flight by the people on whose necks he had fixed the yoke, and whose heart-rending supplications for mercy he had sternly and inexorably resisted.

After the battle of Legnano, Frederic could scarcely hope to raise a fresh army, still less to succeed in his pretensions against the free cities of Lombardy. His mortified pride still rendered him unwilling to acknowledge their independence, but he opened negotiations with pope Alexander III. and was reconciled to the church; and he was then persuaded by the mediation of the Venetian republic to consent to a truce for six years with the cities of Lombardy, the stipulations of which were all favourable to the league. During its continuance, the emperor won over Cremona and other cities to his party, an unhappy proof of reviving animosities between the Italian states; but at its expiration the anxiety of Frederic to associate his son with him in his crowns of Germany and Italy, to which the renewal of hostilities would have presented serious obstacles, induced him to sacrifice his pride, and to conclude at Constance a final pacification with the Lombard republics, (A.D. 1183.) By this memorable treaty, he consented to all that those states had contended for. The general supremacy which they had never denied to the imperial authority, and the customary tribute of provisions during the emperor's residence in Italy, were freely preserved: but the election of magistrates, the power of levying war and raising fortresses, all the regalian rights to which the republics had ever laid claim, were solemnly confirmed to them, and the real independence of Lombardy was triumphantly effected.

PART II.
Southern Italy—State of the Greek and Lombard possessions in the tenth century—The Normans—First appearance of their pilgrims in Italy—Their exploits and settlement at Aversa, near Naples, and conquest of Apulia—War of pope Leo IX. against the Normans—His defeat and captivity—Robert Guiscard, duke of Apulia and Calabria—Norman conquest of Sicily—Roger I., great count of Sicily—Successors of Robert Guiscard—Extinction of the direct line of his family—Roger II., great count of Sicily and duke of Calabria and Apulia—Subjugation of the Campanian republics—Ruin of Amalfi—Submission of Gaeta and Naples—Roger II., king of the two Sicilies, by papal investiture—His death—William I., the Bad, and William II., the Good, kings of the Sicilies—Republics of Venice, Pisa, and Genoa—General advance of the power and Wealth of Venice—Acquisition of Dalmatia by the republic—Changes in the Venetian constitution—Establishment of the great council, and of the little council and senate—Severe restrictions on the powers of the Doges—Form of ducal elections—Pisa—Her early commerce and enterprises—Her conquest of Sardinia and the Balearic Isles—Genoa—Connexion of her early history with that of Pisa—Her conquest of Corsica—Constitution of the Pisan and Genoese republics—Furious wars between the two states—Part taken by Venice, Pisa, and Genoa, in the Crusades—Consequent Wealth of these republics.

WHEN the first Otho raised himself to the imperial throne, the greater part of Southern Italy was still possessed, as we have seen it seventy years before, by the Greeks, under their provincial governor at Bari. The free republics of Naples, Gaeta, and Amalfi, flourished in untarnished independence: but the great Lombard duchy of Benevento, broken up into lesser principalities, had fallen from its ancient splendour, and declined in energy and strength. Otho the Great determined to subject alike the Greeks and the Lombards to his Italian crown: but the efforts of a long war were unavailing, and the contest was terminated by a treaty of marriage between the son of Otho and the daughter of an eastern emperor, (A.D. 970.)

Otho II. renewed the pretensions of his father to the sovereignty of Southern Italy; and his alliance with the imperial line of Constantinople was an additional pretext for claiming the Greek province as the dower of his empress. But the eastern emperors resisted his demand, and Otho led a powerful army towards the south to enforce their acquiescence. Pandolph of the Iron Head, one of the Lombard princes, had succeeded at this epoch in re-uniting the duchy of Benevento under a single chief, and Otho was fortified by his alliance. The Greeks, trembling at the approach of Otho, hired the services of a body of Saracens from Sicily; and, with the aid of these enemies of their faith, ventured to encounter the emperor at Basantello, in Calabria, (A.D. 983.) The first attack of the Germans was vigorous, and put the pusillanimous Greeks to flight; but their musulman auxiliaries, who formed their reserve, threw themselves in unbroken order upon the conquerors, at the moment when the latter had lost their ranks in the ardour of pursuit, and reversed the fate of the day. The infidels made a frightful massacre, in which Pandolph lost his life, and the emperor escaped with difficulty from their hands. He, however, died shortly after this unfortunate expedition; and the Greek province, with Naples and its sister republics, was secured by the long minority of his son, from farther attacks. The death of Pandolph, too, had been followed by the partition of the Beneventine duchy into numerous petty principalities;

and the weakness of their chieftains enabled the Greeks to extend the limits of their Italian possessions.

From this period to the middle of the eleventh century, the history of Southern Italy is enveloped in obscurity and confusion, perplexed with endless petty wars and revolutions, and tinged with the fabulous exaggeration of romantic and almost incredible achievements. Divided between the Lombard chieftains, the maritime republics, and the Greeks—who, after the display of some exertion, but without real strength, had relapsed into weakness and sloth—the south of Italy was delivered over to all sorts of internal disorders, and became an unresisting prey to the Saracen corsairs of Sicily. But a singular revolution put a period both to these devastating inroads and to the dominion of the Greeks and Lombards. The Normans, a famous piratical people of Scandinavia, after inflicting dreadful ravages on the coasts of Europe, had, in the first part of the tenth century, permanently established themselves in the French province which has ever since been named after them. Reposing in their new dominions from the wanderings and rapine of a life of piracy, they embraced Christianity, and carried into their devotion to a new faith all their ancient ardour for strange and perilous enterprises. The pious duty of visiting the shrines of saints and martyrs, and, above all, of kneeling on the sacred places of Palestine, recommended itself to them, as gratifying their spirit of curiosity and passion for adventure. Traversing France and Italy to embark on the Mediterranean for the Holy Land, the Norman pilgrims, in small but well-armed companies, were prepared, on their toilsome and dangerous route, either to crave hospitality in the blessed name of the cross, or to force their way at the point of the lance.

In one of the first years of the eleventh century, about forty of these martial devotees were at Salerno, on their return from the holy sepulchre, when that city was insulted by a fleet of the Sicilian Saracens, with an imperious demand for contributions. The Lombards, who, under the enervating influence of a delicious climate, had utterly lost the courage of their forefathers, would basely have yielded to the summons; but the handful of Norman pilgrims, in astonishment at their cowardice, intrepidly sallied from the gates of Salerno, charged the infidels, and so inspired the degenerate inhabitants by their example, that the invaders were driven to their vessels with immense slaughter. This achievement introduced into Italy the reputation of the Norman prowess; the pilgrims on their return home, inflamed the enterprising spirit and the cupidity of their countrymen, by reports of the fertility of these southern regions, and the effeminacy of its possessors; and new adventurers were attracted to the rich and promising field which opened to their ambition. A knight, named Drengot, was the first to emigrate from Normandy with his family and retainers; and on the arrival of his band in Apulia, they found immediate employment in the domestic quarrels of the Greeks. Their first success, however, was indifferent; but they passed into the service of the Lombard princes of Salerno and Capua; their strength was yearly increased by new swarms of soldiers and pilgrims, and their swords obtained for them a settlement at Aversa, near Naples (A.D. 1029), which the gratitude of that republic, for their services against a prince of Capua, afterwards raised into a permanent fief under count Rainulf, the surviving brother of Drengot.

The next remarkable exploit of the Normans was in the service of the Greeks. In one of those moments of transient energy which relieve the sluggish annals of the eastern empire, the catapan Maniaces led an expedition from his province to attempt the conquest of Sicily from the Saracens. He took into his pay on this occasion three hundred Norman cavaliers, of whom the commanders, or at least the most distinguished knights, were the three eldest sons of a Norman châtelain, Tancred of Hauteville. Aspiring above the narrow fortunes of their house, they had arrived in Italy to share in the enterprizes of their countrymen; and of their nine brothers seven, encouraged by their example and sharing in their spirit, successively quitted the paternal castle for the same destination, leaving the other two to guard their father's age and perpetuate his race.

The valour of the Normans at first signally promoted the success of Maniaces in his Sicilian expedition; and, aided by their intrepidity, he made considerable conquests in the island. But he rewarded their splendid services with injustice and ingratitude, and denied them their share of the spoil. The fearless and avaricious adventurers were by no means of a temper to bear with injurious treatment; but they dissembled their resentment until they could, without suspicion, repass the straits and join their brethren at Aversa, who shared in their indignation, (A.D. 1041.) There, in concert with count Rainulf and his followers, they formed the audacious resolution of revenging themselves upon the Greeks, by the conquest of their possessions on the Italian continent. With the aid of Rainulf, they could muster no more than seven hundred horse and five hundred foot; and it may seem incredible that the overthrow of the Greek power, in a great province, should have been attempted and achieved by their insignificant numbers. But the orientals were cowardly and inactive, and their dissensions increased the superiority of the northern hardihood and prudence. The Normans gained in succession three great victories (A.D. 1042), and speedily subdued Apulia, and divided its possession amongst twelve counts, whose fiefs formed a feudal republic.

In these new demesnes the Norman counts bestowed a general supremacy upon one of their number, William of the Iron Arm, the eldest of the brothers of Hauteville. But the authority of this renowned warrior was little more than nominal; the counts pursued a career of rapine and violence; and even the shrines and convents, which had received the devotions of the Norman pilgrims, were now violated by their spoliations. Their excesses and tyranny excited general indignation, and pope Leo IX. formed an enterprise for the punishment of their sacrilege and the destruction of their power. The emperor Henry III. lent him some German cavalry, the Lombards and Greeks joined the cause of religion, and the pope imprudently forsook his sacred character to lead a numerous but undisciplined host. The Normans undauntedly faced the storm. William of the Iron Arm and his next brother were dead; but Humphrey, the third, was their worthy successor in the supreme command. Robert Guiscard, too, the fourth of their house, had now arrived from Normandy with a reinforcement of adventurers; and the count of Aversa joined his countrymen in their common danger. In the battle of Civitella the pope was completely defeated, and fell into the hands of enemies (A.D. 1053), who, instead of triumphing in their victory, prostrated themselves in the dust before him, and implored his absolution for the guilt of having defended themselves against him. Leo, a pious and simple-minded ecclesiastic, was penetrated by their submission, and readily extended his pardon to a people at once so devout and so valiant. He was thoroughly reconciled to them, and granted to their prayers the investiture, as a fief of the holy see, not only of the lands which they already possessed, but of such also as they might thenceforward conquer in Southern Italy and Sicily.

The Normans had now leisure to extend their power. Robert Guiscard, who was pre-eminent in the valour and wisdom of a rude age, undertook the conquest of Calabria; and, on the death of his brother Humphrey, obtained from his compeers the election to the headship of Apulia, (A.D. 1057.) But his ambition was not yet satisfied: for twenty years he persevered, with scanty numbers, in the scheme of subjugating the dominions both of the Greeks and Lombard princes, and in confirming his authority over his haughty and turbulent Norman barons. These chiefs with difficulty recognized a sovereign in one whom they had known as their equal, and like themselves an adventurer. But Robert triumphed over their jealousies and the weakness of the common enemy. He accomplished the reduction of almost all the country which composes the present kingdom of Naples; and, extinguishing the long dominion of the Beneventine Lombards and of the eastern empire in Italy, finally received from pope Nicholas II. The confirmation of the titles which he had assumed of duke of Calabria and Apulia. The republics of Campania alone preserved a doubtful independence, and compromised for their privileges by electing him as their duke.

While Robert Guiscard was perfecting his dominion on the continent, his younger brother Roger engaged in the astonishing design of conquering the large and beautiful island of Sicily from the Saracens with a few Norman volunteers. An air of romantic extravagance breathes over all the enterprises of the Normans in Italy; and even if we discard the incredible tales which the legends and chronicles of the times have preserved of the valour and corporeal strength of these northern warriors, enough will remain in the authentic results of their expeditions to stagger the reason and warm the imagination with attractive visions of chivalrous achievement. The war against the infidels of Sicily might wear a character of yet greater elevation and heroism than the contest in Italy, by the admixture of religious inspiration, and the more extraordinary disproportion of force. We are assured that three hundred Christian knights were the greatest number which Roger could for many years bring into the field; and that one hundred and thirty-six routed a prodigious host of Saracens at the battle of Ceramio. If we adopt the plausible supposition, that each of these knights was attended by five or six followers, who, as was at least afterwards customary, were not included in the muster of noble cavaliers, we shall still be at a loss how to regulate our belief of the Norman victories. But the Saracens were embroiled in internal discord, and their island was broken up into numerous petty states; we may, therefore, attribute to their dissensions a great part of the success which the chroniclers of the Normans have assigned to their good swords alone. Roger had, however, embarked in an arduous and laborious undertaking, which it required the unbending perseverance and patient valour of thirty years to accomplish. His followers, or rather companions, could not be retained under his standard when the enjoyment of their booty demanded a season of repose, or the caprice of independence tempted to other adventure. But at length all Sicily bowed to his sway; Norman barons were infeuded over its surface, and Roger, with the title of great count, held the island as a fief of his brother's duchy, (A.D. **1090**.)

The remainder of the life of Robert Guiscard, after the completion of his conquests in Italy, was passed in the same restless and fiery spirit of enterprise which belonged to his nation and his family. It is not within our purpose to follow him through his expeditions into Greece, which he twice invaded with the magnificent design of overthrowing the eastern empire: his career was splendid, and though his strength was unequal to his views, he defeated the eastern emperor in person at the great battle of Durazzo. (A.D. 1081.) Compelled to return to Italy by the affairs of his duchy, Robert supported Gregory VII. against the empire in the struggle for investitures. In the reverses of his last years, Gregory owed his deliverance from the hands of the emperor Henry IV. to the Norman duke, who advanced to Rome, burnt half the city, raised the siege of the castle of St. Angelo where Gregory had been shut up by the imperialists, and afforded the pope an asylum in his dominions. This was the last exploit of Robert, and he died in the same year, as he was preparing his second expedition against the eastern empire, (A.D. 1085.)

On the death of Robert his dominions were disputed between Bohemond his eldest, and Roger his second son. Bohemond, born of an obscure marriage which Robert had dissolved in his prosperity, was illegitimized and deprived of his inheritance by his father's testament; but he asserted his right by arras, and a civil war ensued between the brothers, until the first crusade opened new prospects of glory and conquest to Bohemond. Accompanied by his cousin Tancred, the high-minded and generous hero of Tasso, he left Italy for ever, and subsequently established in the east the Latin principality of Antioch. The reigns of the immediate descendants of Robert Guiscard—of his son Roger, thus left in peaceful possession of his duchy, and of his grandson William—present no great event to deserve our attention; but on the death of the latter without children (A.D. 1127), the extinction of the direct line from Robert Guiscard threw the whole inheritance of the family of Hauteville into the hands of Roger II., the son of the conqueror of Sicily, who united the coronet of that isle with the ducal crown of Calabria and Apulia.

The reign of Roger II. is memorable for the total subjugation of the Campanian republics, and for the elevation of the Norman ruler of southern Italy and Sicily to the kingly crown by papal investiture. Whether the courage of the citizens of Amalfi, now the great emporium of eastern merchandize, had declined with the growth of wealth and luxury, or whether the Normans were more formidable enemies than the Lombards, their republic would seem to have exhibited little vigour against the assaults of Roger, who, on their refusal to renounce to him all their privileges, attacked their little state with his whole force, and reduced it to subjection. The calamities of two subsequent assaults by foreign enemies were superadded to the Norman oppression. The Pisans, who viewed a commercial rival with jealousy and hatred, sacked Amalfi once while its force was absent on compulsory service with Roger against Naples, and, in a second attack two years afterwards, completed the ruin of a city which had boasted of fifty thousand inhabitants, and the traffic of Asia. (A.D. 1137.) The fall of Gaeta is passed over by historians in silence; but the city of Naples was reserved for less disastrous fortunes than its sister republics. Its inhabitants at first resolutely defended their liberties against Roger; they were aided by pope Innocent II. and the Pisans; and the emperor Lothaire, in his second expedition into Italy (A.D. 1137), siding with Innocent against Roger, triumphantly raised the siege of the city, and overran the continental dependencies of Sicily. But the resistance of Naples ceased with Lothaire's return to Germany; the Pisans forsook the cause, and Roger, immediately recovering his territories, received the submission and respected the municipal institutions of the future capital of southern Italy, (A.D. 1138.)

The league of the Pisans, of Innocent II., and of his protector Lothaire, against Roger had been occasioned by his alliance with the anti-pope Anaclet. The pride of the Sicilian sovereign had not been contented with his titles of duke and great count: he had aspired to the name of king, and obtained the regal crown from the anti-pope as the reward of his adherence to him. Roger had at first conveyed Anaclet in triumph to Rome, but his rival, Innocent, was supported by the emperor, and relieved by the death of the anti-pope. Still pursuing his hostility against Roger after the death of Lothaire, and rashly venturing his person in the field, the pope fell, as Leo IX. had done formerly, into the hands of the Norman; like that pope, was reconciled with the conqueror, and confirmed to him the title of king, and the investiture of the Two Sicilies, (A.D. 1139.) By a singular train of accidents the misfortunes of two of the weakest of the pontiffs, Leo. IX. and Innocent II., had thus enriched the tiara with one of its most valuable jewels. The see of Rome could claim the right of investiture over the conquests of the Normans by no better pretensions than the questionable donation of some of the emperors. But the conquerors were eager to consecrate the work of their swords by the protection of the church; and from this period the crowns of Naples and Sicily acknowledged for six hundred years the feudal superiority of the popedom. The remainder of the reign of Roger was on the whole visited with glory and success; (A.D. 1153) but his last years were saddened by the loss of his elder sons, and after his death, one son only, William, who succeeded him, and a posthumous daughter, Constance, remained of his offspring. The latter was fated to transfer the inheritance of her family to a line of German emperors, as we shall observe in the next chapter; and the reign of her brother offers nothing to arrest our observation. He merited by his personal vices his surname of "The Bad," but he was destitute neither of courage nor ability. During his reign, however, and that of his son, the second William, whose virtues were rewarded with the opposite title of "The Good," the kingdom of the Two Sicilies somewhat declined from the prosperity and power to which Roger II. had elevated it; but it underwent no material vicissitudes in its relation with Italian history.

During the two centuries which intervened between the age of the Othos and the peace of Constance, the riches and power of the Venetian republic were constantly augmenting. But the growth of commercial activity and wealth is so gradual and silent, that it can be told only in its results; and the naval wars, which exercised the strength and increased the reputation of the republic, are too numerous to be detailed with minuteness, too indistinct in their immediate consequences, and too similar in their events to deserve the attention of the reader. The pirates of the Adriatic, the Saracens, the Normans of Naples, and even the Greeks, to whose empire their republic had once offered at least a respectful deference, were successively combated by the fleets of the Venetians. The course of the republic in these maritime contests alternated between victory and defeat, but her intrinsic energies remained the same under all foreign and even domestic vicissitudes; and whether misfortune clouded her arms, or faction, pestilence, and conflagration raged in her streets, the spirit and perseverance of her citizens still rose superior to every reverse. The progress of Venetian grandeur might be checked for a time, but it was never permanently impeded.

With the general concerns of Italy, Venice had meanwhile little connection. She was sometimes, indeed, agitated by jealousies and broils with the continental cities in her immediate vicinity, and these disputes were terminated by appeals to arms in which her citizens were usually victorious. But such petty hostilities were of little moment, and the formation of the league of Lombardy was the only occasion in these ages on which Venice can be said to have taken an active part in Italian affairs. Yet even here she was an interested if not a faithless ally. She entered into the Lombard league against Frederic Barbarossa because the continuance of his formidable and arbitrary power might threaten her own independence; but her alliance with the free cities did not prevent her from assisting the emperor in an unsuccessful attack upon Ancona (A.D. 1174); because the oppression of a city which pretended to some trade gratified her commercial ambition, and forwarded her schemes for engrossing the navigation of the Adriatic.

In the history of Venice, then, during the two centuries which occupy this chapter, we shall find only three great circumstances for our notice:

the subjugation of Dalmatia to her government, the changes effected in her constitution, and the influence of the crusades upon her wealth and prosperity. We have already had occasion to speak of the wars of Venice with the barbarian pirates of the eastern coasts of the Adriatic, and of the advantages which were gained over them by the doge Pietro Candiano III. After his death, however, the disorders of the republic suspended for some time the prosecution of his successes (A.D. 997); but just at the close of the tenth century the republic was again governed by a man of ability and courage, and enabled by a fortunate concurrence of events to complete the security of her seas and extend the limits of her dominion. When the Sclavonians wrested the country of Illyria from the eastern empire, and founded the kingdoms of Croatia and Dalmatia, many of the fortified cities on the coasts had successfully resisted the conquerors, and, being deserted by the court of Constantinople, had acquired a republican independence, much in the same manner as Naples. But they were surrounded by the barbarians, and constantly harassed by their incursions and piracies. After several centuries of suffering, some of these little states were at length induced by the depredations of the Sclavonians of Narenta, the most powerful of the pirates, to unite in a league against that city, and to place the republic of Venice at the head of the confederation. The doge Piero Urseolo II., sailing from the lagunes with the most formidable fleet that the republic had ever put to sea, received the homage and contingent of such of the Dalmatian cities as had confederated, and persuaded or compelled by arms all the others to enter the same league. He then led his accumulated forces against the barbarians, and reduced them to such a condition, as for ever after incapacitated them from a renewal of their piracies. But the alliance of the strong and the weak is always a dangerous association, and the Dalmatian cities which had invited the aid of the doge shortly found that they had only acquired a master. They were, whether by their own consent or otherwise, taken completely under the authority of Venice, and their citizens no longer permitted to enjoy any share in their government. Podestás, chosen from the highest Venetian families, were sent to all the cities to replace the native magistrates with absolute command; and a large extent of the Dalmatian coast being thus subjected to the Venetians, they caused their doge to assume the title of duke of Venice and Dalmatia. But it was long before these conquests were ensured to the republic. The kings of Hungary were redoubtable neighbours, and ever ready to foster rebellion in the Venetian province. The city of Zara in particular revolted with foreign aid more than once, but the fortunes of Venice as often prevailed, and maritime Dalmatia was fated to remain for several centuries the appendage of her sceptre.

The Venetians had, for above four hundred years, experienced the evils of a form of government which was regulated by no specific limitations, before they attempted to fix the bounds and control the exercise of the sovereign authority. General assemblies were found to be in practice tumultuary and incapable of business: in effect not the people, but contending factions, prevailed in turn in the nomination of the doges. These magistrates, once elected, were restrained by no legal provisions, and punishable by no process but the blind fury of a mob. It was a natural consequence of this absence of all constitutional order, that Venice was torn and distracted by the rancorous hostility of party, and that her doges were murdered by the unreasonable and ferocious populace almost as often as any calamity befel the state. From the ambition, too, of her sovereign magistrates, the republic had every thing to dread, and, considering that their authority was unshackled, we may wonder how the state was preserved from hereditary obedience to a ducal family. The doges indeed did frequently associate their sons in the dignity, and the antiquity of this custom was, in the eleventh century, already beginning to give it the air of a right, when the first amelioration was effected in the republican constitution. The audacious attempt of a member of the family of Urseolo to seat himself, without even the form of popular suffrage, on the throne which several of his illustrious house had occupied with honour, awakened the jealousy of the Venetians, and produced a fundamental law of the state, that the reigning doge should never associate a son in the government, (A.D. 1082.) It was likewise provided, that he should not determine on affairs of government without the consent of two counsellors who were given to him. He was required also on extraordinary occasions not to act without the approbation of some of the principal citizens, whom however he might himself select, to advise him. These latter, termed pregadi, "the requested," from being solicited by the doge to render him their assistance, were the foundation of the Venetian senate of after-times.

One hundred and forty years were suffered to elapse before any further alteration was attempted in the Venetian constitution; and it was at length in the anarchy which followed the murder of a doge, that the council of justice, the only permanent deliberative body of the state, persuaded the people to adopt a political system, which at once offered security against the exercise of arbitrary power by the doges, and obviated the inconvenience of the general and tumultuary assemblies of the people. We are not informed by what skilful address the council of justice prevailed upon the people to consent to an innovation, which in a great measure deprived the democracy of its influence; but from this period may certainly be dated the foundation of the oligarchical government of Venice. Without entirely abolishing the general assemblies of the nation, which were still to be convened upon extraordinary occasions, it was decreed, that the supreme powers of the state should thenceforward be seated, conjointly with the doge, in a representative council of four hundred and eighty members. But the election of this great council, as it was termed, was not to be vested immediately in the people, (A.D. 1172.) The citizens of each of the six districts of Venice annually chose two tribunes; and every one of these twelve magistrates nominated forty members of the representative body. The natural weight of birth and wealth filled the great council almost exclusively with men of the first families of Venice; and though the general assemblies of the people continued sometimes to meet and exercise certain functions for nearly two centuries longer, their real authority had already expired. We shall hereafter trace the steps by which the aristocratic order perfected their unresisted acquisition of sovereignty.

But the great council was still too large an assembly for the steady and secret dispatch of affairs, or the effectual control of the doge. Two lesser bodies were therefore deputed from its number: the one of six members formed the little council of the doge, composed with him the signiory or visible representative of the state, and discharged all the duties of executive administration. Except in conjunction with these counsellors, the doge was bound by his inaugural oath to transact no business with foreign states. The other deputed body was the senate or assembly of pregadi, who, from being originally chosen at the pleasure of the doge, now came to be nominated instead, to the number of sixty, by the great council. They were gifted with such authority as rendered them in effect within a smaller compass the depositaries of all the sovereignty which lay in the great council itself. The legislative functions remained indeed with the latter body, but the right of imposing taxes and of making peace and war was vested in the senate. It is however doubtful, whether the pregadi were thus transformed, in their mode of nomination and their character, into a necessary part of the Venetian government quite as soon as the great council commenced its existence, and a celebrated native historian has dated the change fifty years later.

The establishment of the great council and the enactments which proceeded from that body had effected a remarkable revolution; and the unlimited prerogative of the doges was at once reduced to a powerless dignity. But the precautions of the aristocracy were carried even farther, (A.D. 1179.) The administration of criminal justice was formally placed in a council called "the forty," beyond the control of the first magistrate; and the terms of his initiative oath were a virtual renunciation not only of all substantial authority, but even of personal liberty. The form of the ducal election, primarily seated in the whole of the great council, was reduced to such a mixture of ballot and free nomination among the members, as totally prevented any scheme for the aggrandizement of particular families or parties by the choice of improper persons for the dogeship. This wholesome jealousy of undue bias in the balloted electors was at subsequent periods carried to such a height, that a curious complication of chances entirely prevented its being foreseen on what members of the great council the duty of appointing a doge could by probability fall.

The settlement of the Venetian constitution prepared the republic for her brilliant career of commercial and political grandeur; and a new source of wealth and power had meanwhile been unfolding itself to her cupidity and ambition. No circumstance contributed more effectually to her subsequent prosperity than the religious wars of the Europeans for the recovery of the Holy Land from the Muhammedan infidels. But, as the influence of the crusades was felt with equal advantage by two other maritime republics of Italy which had in the eleventh and twelfth centuries been gradually rising in importance, some account of the origin of these states may be appropriately introduced in this place; and we shall consider in one view the share which Venice, Pisa, and Genoa occupied in these celebrated expeditions to the scenes of human redemption.

Long after the free states of Lombardy had begun to govern themselves, the cities of Tuscany for the most part acknowledged obedience to imperial governors. The history of Florence and the other inland towns of the province is however very obscure, until we discern the earliest symptoms of their partial independence in the divisions excited in Italy, by the wars between the Lombard cities and pope Alexander III. on the one part, and the emperor Frederic Barbarossa on the other. In these wars Sienna, Pistoia, Lucca, and the rural nobility of Tuscany sided with the empire, and Florence, as well as the republic of Pisa, with the church. But no great event marked the progress of hostilities in Tuscany; and of the annals of the Tuscan cities in these ages, those of Pisa alone demand our observation. Even her early records are few and scanty. She began, however, to be eminent as a commercial city before the close of the tenth century, and her galleys were perhaps the first which dared to encounter the Saracen corsairs who ravaged the western coasts of Italy. Her situation, in the midst of a fertile district, at the mouth of the Arno, afforded for the light barks of the times, a harbour equally sheltered by its shoals from tempests and hostile approach; and the Pisans, devoting themselves to commerce, and habituated to naval encounters with the Saracens, began to cover the Mediterranean with their fleets. As mariners they were famous for intrepidity, and as their strength increased with their traffic, they successfully undertook two remarkable conquests. From the Moors, who had long held Sardinia, they wrested that island; and the musulman sovereign, after a protracted and gallant struggle, became their captive, and ended his days in the dungeons of Pisa. The conquerors parcelled out his kingdom into four great fiefs, and bestowed them upon the same number of noble Pisan families by whom principally the expedition had been fitted out. Sixty-five years after the loss of Sardinia the infidels had again to mourn at the prowess of these republicans. The Balearic Isles, which composed a Saracen monarchy, were reduced in a single campaign (A.D. 1115): one musulman prince perished in the field, the capture of a second swelled the pride of the victors, and immense treasures were brought from Majorca to their city.

While Pisa was thus growing in power, a neighbouring and rival republic was pursuing a similar career of commerce and enterprise. Surrounded by rocky and barren mountains whose surface is utterly destitute of verdure, Genoa has received from nature but a single gift: a safe and capacious harbour. With this solitary advantage her citizens, applying themselves, like the Pisans, to commerce, and acquiring possession of the maritime territory of Liguria east and west of their capital, claimed to govern themselves like other Italian cities, and rose to a similar grandeur with Pisa. The foreign history of the two republics is completely interwoven. Allies against the infidels, and rivals in commerce, they first assisted each other in mutual victories, and then quarrelled over the spoil. It was with the aid of Genoa that Pisa conquered Sardinia, and the former republic at the same time reduced the island of Corsica under its own dominion. This proved a more durable though a less brilliant conquest than the Pisan acquisition. But the fortunes of Genoa altogether were fated to be more lasting, though in the outset less splendid, than the glories of Pisa.

No chronicle has transmitted to our days any account of the particular form of the Pisan constitution; but it appears that the government was consular: we learn the original structure of the Genoese republic from the pen of one of its magistrates of the twelfth century. Consuls, chosen at first for three or four years, but afterwards annually, and varying in number from four to six, were the supreme directors of the state. They were usually of noble family, and elected in a general parliament of their fellow-citizens. In like manner each of the quarters of the city annually chose one of the seven judges of the republic, and an occasional appointment of a select council by the general assembly provided for the correction of the laws. This simple constitution probably long answered every purpose of freedom and internal peace; and to the end of the twelfth century, the popular assemblies of Genoa seem with honourable singularity to have been disturbed by no criminal excesses, (A.D. 1169.) Once only the rivalry of two noble families split the citizens into factions and threatened civil war; but the venerable archbishop, labouring with a spirit which rarely belonged to the churchmen of the age, exerted the weight of his sacred vocation in effecting a reconciliation between the contending parties.

It was not until the beginning of the twelfth century that the jealousy between Pisa and Genoa broke out into open warfare. But by their vicinity and commercial emulation, their equality of strength and clashing interests, they had long been secret enemies; and it is strange how their natural rivalry and hatred were smothered for above one hundred years. When the flame was once kindled, it burnt with fierce and almost incessant activity. The attempt of one pope to subject the churches of Corsica to the Pisan archbishop produced the first conflict, and it raged without intermission for fourteen years, until the mediation of another pontiff calmed the irritation which the partiality of his predecessor had excited. He removed the cause of dispute by giving Genoa an archbishop, and transferring the Corsican clergy to his jurisdiction. If we may credit the statement of the Genoese chronicler, that, in the first year of this war, his republic attacked Pisa with a fleet of eighty galleys, attended by four large vessels with battering engines, and manned by twenty-two thousand combatants, of whom a fourth were armed with the casque and cuirass, we shall form a magnificent idea of the power of these maritime cities; since Pisa resisted so immense an armament, and balanced the indecisive event of the war. It was immediately, too, after this lengthened and arduous struggle that Pisa, with unimpaired strength, accomplished the ruin of Amalfi, as we have already seen. (A.D. 1137.) But no long interval of forbearance could prevail between the Genoese and Pisans, who constantly encountered each other in their voyages, and mingled the prosecution of their bitter animosities with the peaceful occupations of trade. In their commercial expeditions to the East, their fleets frequently engaged each other with fury, and one memorable war was produced by the conflict of their colonies at Constantinople, (A.D. 1162.) It terminated like former hostilities without material advantage to either state.

On the waters of the Levant, both Genoa and Pisa had, long before this contest, found a third combatant in the rivalry of Venice. The three republics had alike engaged in the crusades, and the transport of the soldiers of the cross to the shores of Asia, became for them all an important and lucrative employment. Their vessels returned to port laden with the produce of these eastern climes, and the services which they rendered to the crusaders procured for their states most valuable privileges of traffic in all the cities which were conquered from the infidels on the Syrian coasts. During the possession of Palestine by the Christians, Venice, Pisa, and Genoa were thus the channels through which the produce of the East was conveyed to the people of Europe. The wealth of Venice in particular was prodigiously increased by the remuneration which she exacted as the price of her exertions in carrying the crusading hosts to the scenes of their enterprises, and provisioning them on their voyages. In the first crusade she employed two hundred vessels in this manner, and the religious object of the expedition did not prevent her fleet from attacking that of Pisa, though occupied in the same purpose. Alternately sharing in the efforts of the crusaders against the common enemy, extorting from their allies every selfish advantage, and constantly endeavouring the destruction of each other, the three republics prosecuted a singular career of religious fanaticism, commercial avarice, and deadly animosities. But they all found the same profit in their Asiatic enterprises; and while the rest of Europe poured out her best blood and resources in the barren pursuit of an imaginary duty, the maritime republics of Italy were alone enriched and invigorated amidst the general exhaustion.

CHAPTER III. FROM THE PEACE OF CONSTANCE TO THE EXTINCTION OF THE HOUSE OF SWABIA, a.d. 1183-1268.

PART I.
State of the Lombard cities after the peace of Constance—Last years of Frederic Barbarossa—Reign of the emperor Henry VI.—Affairs of Naples and Sicily—Acquisition of those countries by Henry VI.—His cruelties and death—Aspect of Italy at the close of the twelfth century—Occurrences in the Trevisan March—Rise of the families of Romano and Este—Factions of the Guelfs and Ghibelins—Pontificate of Innocent III.—His exercise of arbitrary authority over temporal princes—Ambitious schemes of Innocent in Italy—League of Tuscany—Interregnum in the empire—Otho IV.—His contest with Innocent III.—Continued wars between the Lombard cities—The emperor Frederic II.—State of his kingdom of the Sicilies—Crusade of Frederic—Excommunication against him—Return of Frederic to Europe—Papal intrigues—Renewal of the league of Lombardy—Singular power of a Dominican friar—War between the emperor and the Lombard league—Extinction of freedom in the Trevisan March—Papal persecution of Frederic II.—Council of Lyons—Sentence of deposition against the emperor—Unshaken power, death, and character of Frederic II.

THE freedom which the cities of Lombardy had so gloriously asserted, and which the terms of the peace of Constance promised to perpetuate, was clouded by their internal distractions, and too shortly extinguished by their selfish jealousies and vicious factions. Even while our admiration of their unconquerable resistance to oppression is warm and recent, we are presented with the revolting picture of vindictive and inextinguishable hatreds. The Italian character in the middle ages was unhappily overcast by the darker passions of the human heart, and the energy and strength of purpose which, otherwise, might have qualified the national mind for a long career of virtuous grandeur, were prostituted to the gratification of implacable revenge and flagitious ambition.

The same spirit which had humbled the power of Frederic Barbarossa might have cemented the numerous states of Lombardy in a permanent and invincible confederation, if the deadly hostility by which the cities were animated against each other had not far outweighed every patriotic and honourable feeling. The elements of the Lombard league had been scattered even before the consummation of its object, and they could never again be wholly collected. United in no one common bond of safety, the cities were left without protection against foreign enemies or domestic traitors, and in little more than half a century they had all, in well merited slavery to tyrants, reaped the bitter punishment of their general disunion. The same lasting hostility between the aristocratic and plebeian orders, which had existed in the commonwealths of antiquity, agitated the Lombard republics; and this fatal discord being almost always in action, produced, or was varied only by, multiplied factions which were generated with appalling facility. The noxious vices, which were cherished in the corrupted soil of private life by the intensity of individual passion, composed a fruitful hotbed of political crime. Motives of personal revenge, or even the caprices of accident, were at any time sufficient for the excitement of sanguinary public feuds, or the indulgence of shameful injustice and atrocious proscription. It is a striking proof of the reciprocal suspicion of partiality and violence which filled the citizens of the Italian republics, that they dared not entrust the administration of justice to the hands of their townsmen. Immediately after the peace of Constance, all the cities adopted the custom of electing a judicial magistrate out of the pale of their own society.

The podestá, as this officer was termed, was always a nobleman of some one of the neighbouring cities, and usually a man of distinguished character. He was jealously cut off from all society and friendship among the citizens, but he enjoyed a dictatorial authority in the execution of justice, and the body of the people bound themselves to second him by arms against the turbulent and powerful offenders who habitually set his decrees at defiance. His power in the state was in some measure shared by the consuls and committees of trust (credenza); but he was frequently the general as well as the judge of the republic, and whatever might have been the necessity which prompted this concentration of authority in one individual, it is not improbable that the practice of confiding all the executive administration ^to a podestá, had a pernicious influence in preparing the public mind for submission to a single will.

The gradual overthrow of the liberties of the Lombards, which commenced very soon after the peace of Constance, was wholly the work of their own parricidal hands. Frederic Barbarossa, so long their oppressor, would appear from this epoch sincerely to have abandoned his projects against them. Convinced by experience that the hope of subjugating them was utterly vain, he gave a new direction to his ambition, and was invited by the state of the Sicilies to attempt the addition of that kingdom to the Swabian dominions. The probability that William II. would die without issue, rendered his aunt Constance the presumptive heiress to his throne, and the emperor succeeded in effecting a marriage between that princess and his eldest son Henry, (A.D. 1186.) His future claims upon the inheritance of his daughter-in-law might be promoted by the friendship or opposed by the hostility of the Lombard republics, and Frederic earnestly laboured to conciliate the affection and compose the differences of those states. But he did not live to require their assistance, and was fated to terminate his existence in other scenes. All Europe was afflicted at this epoch with the intelligence that Jerusalem had fallen before the power of Saladin (A.D. 1187): the pope proclaimed a new crusade, and the emperor, though in advanced years, engaged with all the courage of his youth in an expedition to Palestine for the recovery of the holy sepulchre. He led a numerous army into the East, and was victoriously traversing the plains of Armenia when he was drowned at the passage of an insignificant stream, (A.D. 1189.)

The death of Barbarossa was followed in the same year by that of William II. of Sicily, and Henry VI., the son of the emperor, who had for the last five years of his father's life worn the crowns of Germany and Italy, now succeeded both to the imperial diadem, and through his wife Constance, to legitimate pretensions over the kingdom of the Two Sicilies. But the Norman barons detested the prospect of subjection to a foreign monarch, and their aversion was not diminished by the character of Henry. He had inherited the courage, but possessed neither the talents which had shed lustre over the criminal ambition of his parent, nor the magnanimity of which Barbarossa was sometimes capable. Even the cruelty, which had disgraced the conqueror of Milan and Crema, was mercy when compared with the inherent ferocity of his son.

Though Constance was the only legitimate descendant of the royal Norman line, the Sicilians found in Tancred, the natural son of one of her brothers, a worthy inheritor of the courage and virtues of the Rogers; and disdaining the German yoke, the nobles of the Two Sicilies placed him by acclamation on their throne. He successfully defended both Sicily and Naples against the power of Henry (A.D. 1190), and the new emperor, after losing by pestilence the greater part of an army which he led against him, was compelled to a precipitate retreat from the Neapolitan dominions. His empress fell into the hands of Tancred, but he generously restored her without ransom or conditions to her husband, and during the brief residue of his life was disturbed by no further attacks. His reign was too short for the happiness of his subjects; and after seeing his eldest son perish in his arms in the flower of his youth, he himself sank into a premature grave, (A.D. 1194.) The indulgence which he had shown to the wife of his cruel rival was repaid to his own widow and children by shocking barbarity. The helpless boy who succeeded to his crown was unable to defend it; his nobles, left without a leader, submitted on the approach of Henry, and the emperor possessed himself of the Two Sicilies.

The unhappy family of Tancred, surrendering themselves upon promise of favourable treatment, were sent into Germany by the savage conqueror, who detained them in a long captivity, and deprived the youthful king of his eyes. The emperor followed up this atrocity by the exercise of remorseless oppression and devilish vengeance against his new subjects. Sicily was drained of her treasures, which were conveyed to Germany; and, of the barons who had supported the cause of Tancred, some were hanged, others were burned alive, and the remainder escaped only with the loss of their eyes. The exhortations of the pope were unavailing to stop this series of horrors; the prayers of

Constance were equally vain in obtaining mercy for the subjects of her fathers, and the indignant princess suffered herself to be numbered with conspirators against the inhuman tyranny of her husband. The sudden death of this monster (A.D. 1197), while engaged in the siege of a revolted castle, brought deliverance to suffering humanity; Constance herself, who on his decease assumed the reins of government for her infant son, survived him but a year; and the orphan child, who succeeded to the hereditary dominions of the houses of Swabia and Sicily by the title of Frederic II., was left at the age of four years destitute of protection, and surrounded by rivals.

During the reign of Henry VI. and the early minority of Frederic II., it is difficult to offer any distinct and connected view of the condition of Italy. The whole country was convulsed by the internal feuds of contending factions in the different republics, and filled with the violence of petty warfare; but no great and determinate object affords consistency to these confused and various struggles, or exhibits them in a combined and intelligible shape. The chronicles, too, of the Lombard cities at this juncture are either silent, or barren of important information, and some occurrences in the Trevisan March—the ancient Venetia—may alone claim our attention. These are interesting as connected with the rise of two famous Italian families, and the clearest contemporary records are fortunately those which respect them.

The Trevisan March is a mountainous district abounding in situations of strength, and the nobility of the province, occupying these with their castles, had not been generally reduced, like the châtelains of the plains on the upper Po, into subjection to the neighbouring cities. They were therefore a formidable body; and at once preserving their rural fiefs, and making choice of that residence in the cities which with the Lombard nobles was compulsory, the influence of power and high birth threw all the offices of the magistracy into their hands. Even where the Italian nobility had been compelled to become citizens of the republics, the abodes which they erected within the walls were castles rather than houses. Built of massive stone and strengthened by towers, they were rendered capable of enduring the assaults to which the turbulent violence of their tenants and the vicissitudes of faction often exposed them. But in the cities of the Trevisan March, in Verona, Padua, Vicenza, and Treviso, the nobles secured their voluntary residence within the walls by the construction of regular fortresses, which might set at defiance every burst of popular commotion. Huge gates and barriers of iron defended the entrance to these strongholds; their solid walls were manned by numerous bands of faithful retainers; and if the external bulwarks should be forced, a square donjon tower or keep in the interior, afforded a sure retreat for the lord and his followers. The insolence of power which was begotten by impunity, filled the cities of the March with rivalry and bloodshed between the great families, and their rural fiefs were the perpetual scenes of open hostility.

Among the nobility of the Trevisan March, the most distinguished towards the close of the twelfth century were the families of Romano and Este. The former were descended from Eccelino, a German knight, who had accompanied the emperor Conrad II. into Italy, and received from his master the fiefs of Romano and Onaro in recompense for his services. The rise of the family which he thus founded was fortunate and rapid: the lords of Romano successively enlarged the acquisitions of their ancestor, and under his namesake Eccelino, the Stammerer (known in history as Eccclino I.), their patrimony had already grown into a formidable principality.

The narrative of one enterprise undertaken by this Eccelino da Romano may be appropriately introduced, as illustrating both the aggrandizement of his family and the manners of his age. He was united by the ties of marriage and amity with Tisolino of the Campo San Pietro, a noble Paduan, and was acquainted by his friend with his design of marrying his son to Cecilia the orphan heiress of Manfred Ricco, signer of Abano. The lord of Romano was seduced, by the advantage which so wealthy an alliance might afford to his own house, to betray the confidence of Tisolino, and he secretly plotted to obtain the hand of the lady for his own son Eccelino II. By corrupting her guardians he got the heiress into his own hands, and carrying her to his castle of Bassano, celebrated her nuptials with his son. This act of treachery filled the family of Campo San Pietro with violent indignation, and instigated Gerard, the son of Tisolino, who had been the destined husband of Cecilia, to a horrible revenge. As the bride, with a more brilliant than warlike train, passed into the Paduan territory to visit her demesnes, she was seized by Gerard, borne off to his castle, and there brutally dishonoured, (A.D. 1190.) The wretched victim, on being suffered to return to Bassano, did not attempt to conceal the outrage: she was divorced, and her husband married again, but both her estates and those of the second wife of Eccelino II. swelled the power of the lords of Romano. They swore an eternal hatred to the family of San Pietro, and the deadly feud between the two houses, which was perpetuated for many generations, could be satisfied only by blood.

While Eccelino II. was augmenting his greatness, and embroiling the republics of upper Venetia which bordered on his estates, in destructive wars by alliance with or hostility to his cause, the increasing power of the house of Este was the signal for tumults and disorders in the central part of the province. The possessions of this ancient family were situated between Padua, Verona, Vicenza, and Ferrara, and their ambition was fatal to the repose of all these states. A fortunate union with an heiress of Ferrara established Obizzo, marquis of Este, in that city, and placed him at the head of a faction within its walls, (A.D. 1180.) In this, like the subsequent marriage of Eccelino, another noble house had been supplanted by treachery: furious commotions were excited between the rivals, and during a civil war, which raged within the walls of Ferrara for nearly forty years, the hostile factions were ten times alternately expelled from the city. But the power of the marquises of Este continued to increase, and at the close of the twelfth century they divided the possession of sovereign influence in the Trevisan March with Eccelino da Romano II. By their descent from the German line of the Guelfs they were the natural enemies of the Swabian emperors: the lords of Romano were, on the other hand, attached to those monarchs by the memory of benefits; and the two families headed the Guelf and Ghibelin parties of Venetia.

These terms of Guelf and Ghibelin, of ominous sound to an Italian ear, were received from Germany, where they had long been the war-cry in the quarrels of the houses of Bavaria and Swabia; but they were not introduced into Italy, until the first years of the thirteenth century. The former was the family name of the dukes of Bavaria, from whom, as is well known, the present royal line of Great Britain claims its descent: the latter is derived from Wibelung, a Franconian town, the birthplace of the emperor Conrad II., who was the progenitor through females of the Swabian emperors. The Ghibelins were therefore the adherents of these sovereigns, the Guelfs their opponents; and, in the struggles between the emperors and the popes, the friends of the church readily assumed the title of Guelfs. But when these names, the seeds of bitter animosities, were once sown in the rank soil of Italian faction, their fruits might be recognised only for their poisonous qualities. Parties were at first Guelf or Ghibelin by their attachment to the papacy or the empire, but afterwards by no other principle than that of mutual and unintelligible hatred.

From the peace of Constance to the death of Frederic I., and during the whole reign of Henry VI., the lustre of the papacy was dimmed before the star of those monarchs. But the weakness of the minor, Frederic II., and an interregnum in the empire, offered a favourable occasion for the assertion of the papal authority; and just at this epoch arose a pontiff, the greatest, except Gregory VII., of all those who at successive periods knew, how to revive and to increase the slumbering energies of the church. In the same year which terminated the life of Henry VI., Innocent III. was raised to the tiara at the early age of thirty-seven. Uniting the courage and ambition of a Roman noble, with reputed sanctity as a churchman, he not only succeeded in elevating the ecclesiastical pretensions of Gregory VII. to a stupendous height, but aspired to seize upon a temporal state for the papacy in the centre of Italy. And though he did not entirely perfect this scheme, and three centuries more were to pass before the secure consolidation of the temporal dominions of the Roman church, Innocent III. was the real founder of the structure which has lasted to our times.

The monstrous assumption of arbitrary dominion over all the temporal powers of the world, which Innocent audaciously maintained, scarcely belongs to Italian history. Wielding the thunders of excommunication and interdict with the skill of a consummate politician, he augmented the terrors of these ecclesiastical arms by the address with which he selected the moment for their exercise; and his celebrated triumph over the most pusillanimous of our English kings, sinks into contempt before his subjection of the other sovereigns of Europe. Our John was a heartless coward, but Philip Augustus of France, and the monarchs of Arragon, Portugal, and Denmark, were not used to tremble before less dreaded enemies than Innocent.

It is curious to observe how the power of the greatest popes was strengthened by distance. The superstitious veneration which was entertained for the chiefs of Christendom was ever most feeble nearest to its source; and a long familiarity with the weakness and crimes of the pontiffs left little room for fear and respect in the Italian mind. While Innocent III. lorded it over transalpine despots, he was necessitated to resort to petty intrigues for the extension of his slender authority in Italy. The immense possessions, bequeathed by the famous countess Matilda to the Holy See, had hitherto been withheld by the Swabian emperors, and Henry VI. had bestowed in fief upon his different German captains the March of Ancona, the duchies of Romagna and Spoleto, and the marquisate of Tuscany, all of which were supposed to be included in the donation of the countess. The tyranny of the German chieftains had excited unqualified hatred, and their weakness, after the death of their monarch, provoked universal resistance to their sway. Innocent easily wrested the March of Ancona and the duchies of Spoleto and Romagna from their feeble grasp; but so sensible was he of his own want of strength, that he prudently granted the former fief to the marquis of Este, and confirmed the municipal independence of the cities of Spoleto and Romagna, with a general reservation of the papal supremacy. But over the more powerful cities of Tuscany, which had enjoyed a republican independence under the lieutenants of the emperors, he could not hope to claim even a nominal sovereignty, and, as it was his interest by whatever means to prevent the revival of the imperial power, he contented himself with achieving a general Guelphic league of all the Tuscan republics, except Pisa, for the preservation of their common rights, (A.D. 1197.) Of this association he was placed at the head, and it was declared to be expressly established for the honour of the apostolic see. The cities engaged themselves to protect the church, and to acknowledge no emperor without the approbation of the pope. By the testament of the empress Constance, Innocent acquired even a greater advantage. The young orphan, Frederic, was placed under his protection as the feudal superior of the crown of the Two Sicilies, and the authority in that kingdom thus passed into his hands.

The intrigues of Innocent for the subversion of the imperial power were not confined within the Alps. On the death of Henry VI., the German electors, disregarding the claims of his infant son, were divided between two competitors, Philip of Swabia and Otho the Guelf. Philip was of a house always inimical to the church; the family of the latter had ever been obedient to the popes; and Innocent therefore espoused his cause, which was for many years the weakest. But the death of Philip finally placed Otho, the fourth of his name, on the German throne; and for once the papacy and the empire were in amity. But the interests of the two powers were too opposite to permit this harmony to last; and when Otho IV., entering Italy, had received the imperial diadem from Innocent (A.D. 1209), the new emperor refused to alienate the fiefs of the countess Matilda from his crown. Innocent now stirred up opposition to the prince whom he had so long protected; the marquis of Este and other Guelfs remained faithful to the church even against a Guelf emperor; and, at least in name, the politics of the Italian factions were reversed. The interest of the reader would be little excited in the obscure vicissitudes of the wars which ensued. The successful resource of the pope was to convert his young pupil, Frederic II., whom he had hitherto neglected, into a rival for his former ally. He caused the youthful monarch to pass into Germany, where he found a powerful party in the rebellious subjects of Otho; and the emperor, after some successes, was compelled to abandon Italy for the defence of his German dominions, (A.D. 1212.)

Innocent III. had now reached the pinnacle of grandeur: his worldly and inordinate ambition had been crowned with brilliant success, and, if we could forget the assumed sanctity of his office, his greediness of power might not excite severer reprehension than the similar passion of temporal sovereigns. But his character is darkened by the spirit of unrelenting persecution, and the establishment of the Inquisition will cover his memory with everlasting infamy. The close of his life was passed in enforcing the horrible massacres of the Paulician heretics, and he died at Perugia (A.D. 1216), after a reign of eighteen years, while the south of France was yet deluged with the blood of the Albigenses.

At the period of Innocent's death, Frederic II. still disputed the possession of the imperial crown with Otho IV. Germany was the field on which the rivals personally engaged, but all Italy was filled with discord in support of their opposite pretensions. The flames of war were every where lighted up, and under the appellation of Guelfs and Ghibelins, and in the struggle between the papal and imperial interests, the Italian factions enjoyed a feasible pretence for the indulgence of their rancorous animosities. It therefore mattered not that the nature of the contest reversed the denomination and the principles of parties. When the pope and the adherents of the church supported the cause of Frederic, the Guelfs upheld the natural chief of the Ghibelins, and that, too, against a Guelf emperor: when the Milanese assisted the pretensions of Otho IV., they forgot their jealousy of the imperial prerogatives and their Guelf principle of attachment to the church, in hereditary hatred to the house of Swabia. They formed a league with

Crema, Placentia, Lodi, and other cities, and were furiously opposed by Pavia, Cremona, and the rest of the Ghibelin Lombard republics. In this contest, almost all the cities claim by their chronicles to have been victorious, and it may therefore be conjectured that success was pretty equally balanced. Pavia, however, was oppressed by the superiority of Milan, which with flourishing manufactures and a fertile territory, had, since the era of its rebuilding in the war against Barbarossa, yearly increased in population, riches, and warlike strength. The Milanese devastated the territory of Pavia, and compelled that state to renounce its ancient party, and to become the subject-ally of their republic, (A.D. 1217.) But, on the other hand, this triumph of Milan was clouded by a partial reverse. At the obstinate battle of Ghibello, the Cremonese, in concert with the forces of other cities of the Ghibelin league, inflicted a memorable defeat upon the Milanese and their partisans, (A.D. 1218.)

It is a singular proof of the influence of free institutions in almost all the cities, that, until the subversion of the Lombard liberties, neither internal discord, nor these fierce wars between the republican leagues, prevented the rapid growth of population and wealth. The citizens were frequently compelled, by the pressure of their superabundant numbers, to increase the circuit of their walls; and we should be wholly at a loss to account for their surprising prosperity in the midst of so many disorders and commotions, if we failed to consider the immense advantages which, so long as a vestige of liberty remained, were enjoyed by their free and industrious artisans over the oppressed and unprotected peasantry of the country.

Otho IV. maintained an unfortunate contest in Germany with Frederic II. for several years: but his death at last left that young monarch without a competitor for the imperial crown, (A.D. 1218.) The church had hitherto played Frederic off as an useful engine against the power of Otho; but he had no sooner prevailed in the struggle, than he became himself an object of suspicion and dread. Honorius III., the successor of Innocent, demurred for some time to confer on him the imperial crown which that pope had promised; and he extorted from the new emperor a vow, that he would undertake the deliverance of the Holy Land from the Saracens, before he would finally perform the ceremony, (A.D. 1220.)

But the situation of the kingdom of the Sicilies furnished ample employment for the attention of Frederic, and several years were occupied in repairing the evils which a long anarchy had entailed on those countries. Ever since the death of William the Bad, the Neapolitan provinces had been almost always a prey to civil wars. Every town or castle was possessed by some baron, and the royal authority was nearly extinguished by the ambition of the feudal chieftains. But, by the admixture of vigour and treachery, Frederic, who was not very scrupulous in the measures which he pursued, succeeded in breaking the force of the aristocracy, and in restoring subordination and peace. The condition of Sicily had been yet more desperate than that of the continent. The remains of its Saracen population had been driven to revolt by the oppression of the Christian barons of the island, and had invited the assistance of their piratical brethren from Africa. But Frederic defeated the rebels in several encounters, and, completing their subjection at different periods, removed them from the island to the province of Naples, where he settled them in the fertile plains of the Capitanate and in the lovely valley of Nocéra. These musulmans in their new colonies proved the most faithful of his subjects, and supplied him with excellent troops in his Italian wars. To the city of Naples, Frederic was a real benefactor. He built a magnificent palace within its walls, founded its university, and established the grandeur of this beautiful capital.

Frederic had probably never intended to fulfil his engagement of delivering the Holy Land from the hands of the infidels. But while he was engaged in regulating the affairs of his own dominions, the situation of the Christians in Palestine was becoming hourly more hopeless; and the violent indignation of Honorius was excited by his neglect to redeem the pledge which he had given before his coronation. The pope vainly urged him, both with entreaties and threats, and finally laboured to enlist his ambition in the cause, by obtaining for him the hand of Violante, daughter of John de Brienne, titular king of Jerusalem, who consented to transfer his nominal crown to his future son in law. Frederic accordingly espoused the princess (A.D. 1225), and from this period not only dispatched succours to Palestine, but prepared to follow himself with a fleet and army. Two years were passed in the equipment of this force; crusaders assembled from England, Germany, and Italy, to await the sailing of the expedition; and the emperor at length embarked at Brundusium. (A.D. 1227.) But the burning climate of Apulia and Calabria had produced a destructive epidemic among the northern foreigners; the contagion carried off immense numbers of them, the remnant were dispirited, and Frederic, being himself attacked by the pestilence, was compelled to disembark and postpone the crusade.

The intelligence of this delay filled Gregory IX., who had just succeeded to Honorius, with disappointment and fury, and he immediately thundered an excommunication against the emperor. Frederic, on his part, contented himself with defending his conduct by circular letters to the princes of Christendom, and proving his sincerity by the activity of his preparations for the sacred expedition which he still meditated. In the following summer he sailed for Palestine, though with a diminished army, and arriving at St. Jean d'Acre, commenced his operations. But the arrogant pope viewed it as a new offence, that he had presumed to enter on so holy an enterprise under the sentence of an excommunication, and, reiterating his fulminations, he not only thwarted the progress of the imperial arms in Palestine by the intrigues of his ministers, but preached a crusade against Frederic, and sent John de Brienne with an army of papal partizans to ravage the Neapolitan dominions. Notwithstanding the hostility and artifices of the pope, the energy and prudence of Frederic gained more for the Christians of Palestine than any prince had effected since the foundation of the Latin kingdoms. His arms obtained from the weakness of the Saracens the cession of Jerusalem; and in that city he placed on his own head the crown of his new kingdom, with which no priest could be induced to invest him. (A.D. 1229.)

His hasty return to Europe after this ceremony struck terror into his enemies. The papal army disbanded at his approach, the senate and people of Rome espoused his cause against their pontiff, and Gregory was compelled to conclude a hollow reconciliation with the man whom he detested. (A.D. 1230.) The tranquil obedience of Germany and of the Two Sicilies, rendered Frederic a formidable enemy; his Saracen subjects, whom he had seated almost at the gates of Rome, were not likely to be restrained by conscientious scruples from attacking the head of the church at the command of their master; and among the inhabitants of the ecclesiastical capital itself, and of all the Italian provinces, there were numerous imperial adherents. The situation of Gregory was therefore extremely critical, but he found a formidable support in northern Italy, and he dissembled no longer than was necessary for the maturity of his plots against Frederic. The inveterate hostility which the Milanese cherished towards the Swabian family had produced from them, some years before, a refusal to invest the emperor with the ancient Lombard crown, which they preserved at Monza; and their fears of his vengeance for this insult had occasioned the revival of the whole league of Lombardy against the empire. While the emperor was preparing for his expedition to Palestine, the Milanese induced the Guelf cities of Lombardy to renew the terms of the association in which the ambition of Barbarossa had united them sixty years before (A.D. 1226); and the confederation was joined by Turin, Vercelli, the republics of the Trevisan March, and Bologna; which last city had now grown powerful by increased population, and eminent by the fame of its celebrated university. The league of Lombardy was included by the pope in his short-lived pacification with the empire.

While the papal intrigues were cherishing the seeds of war, a singular spectacle of an opposite nature was exhibited in northern Italy. Some members of the newly established order of Dominician friars employed all the powers of eloquence over a half civilized age in exhortations of universal peace; and the preaching of one of these brethren had an astonishing but transient influence upon the ardent temperament of the Italian people. At Bologna, Padua, Verona, and the surrounding cities, Giovanni di Vicenza began, three years after the pacification of 1230, to denounce the iniquity of war, and to inculcate the general forgiveness of injuries. He was heard with veneration and humility. At his voice the feuds of generations were hushed, vows of reconciliation were poured forth by the bitterest enemies, and he was entreated by contending cities and factions to reform their governments and compose their differences. So absolute became his influence, that a general assembly was convened on the plain of Paquara upon the banks of the Adige, for the establishment of perpetual peace; and the Guelf and Ghibelin cities and castles of Lombardy were emptied of their population at the summons of the preacher. By this immense concourse an universal amnesty and oblivion of mutual wrongs was declared at his suggestion, and Giovanni became the arbitrary master of political consciences. But he had not virtue and disinterestedness to support the office which he had assumed, if indeed it had ever been possible to support it. He aspired at becoming the temporal as well as the spiritual director of his flock; he grossly abused his authority, and the people of Vicenza, awaking from the dreams of enthusiasm, shook off his strange yoke, and consigned the pseudo-apostle of peace to a captivity, from whence he escaped only with the entire loss of his ephemeral reputation, (A.D. 1233.)

In less than two years after this extraordinary ebullition of religious sentiment, the whole of Lombardy was in arms. Henry, the son of the emperor by his first marriage, had revolted against him in Germany (A.D. 1234); the pope is accused of having encouraged this unnatural rebellion; and the Lombard league had promised the young prince their support. But the appearance of Fredcric in Germany was sufficient to confirm the fidelity of his nobles; his son was compelled to sue for mercy, and the relentless severity of the offended parent, or the repeated machinations of Henry, doomed him to an imprisonment for life. The conduct of the Lombard league might justly excite the anger of Frederic, and his desire of vengeance was fomented by the passions of the Ghibelin party. In the Trevisan March the family of Romano were still the chiefs of this faction. Eccelino II. had retired into a monastery, but his power had devolved upon his two sons, Alberic and Eccelino III. The latter, the scourge of his age and country, had with the aid of a Ghibelin faction in Verona established himself in the sovereignty of that city (A.D. 1236); and Cremona and other Lombard republics of the same party formed an alliance with him against the Guelf league. The return of the emperor to Italy at the head of his German cavalry was the signal for hostilities. Eccelino and the Ghibelins united under the imperial standard, the Guelf cities were firm in their association, and for years the fairest portion of Italy was filled with bloodshed and rapine.

The first Lombard league against Frederic Barbarossa had been ennobled by every principle which could actuate a suffering and courageous people, and the purity of their cause had been rewarded by a glorious triumph. The second Lombard league was different in its character and results. It had been provoked by no injuries, and was dictated rather by selfish ambition than the generous spirit of freedom: the contest was not for liberty, but the indulgence of party hatred; not of the oppressed against the oppressor, but of two rancorous and equally culpable factions. The interests of the church and of the empire were the pretence, the animosity of the Guelfs and Ghibelins the real spring of action.

Except in their pernicious influence upon the liberties of the cities, these long wars are marked by few vicissitudes of interest. In 1208 Ferrara, or rather the Guelf faction which then preponderated within that city, had set a fatal example to the rest of Italy by choosing the marquis Azzo VI. of Este for the signer or lord of the republic: by the similar triumph of the opposite party in Verona, Eccelino III. da Romano, under the new title of captain of the people, now enjoyed supreme authority within its walls; and in the first years of the Lombard war, after these ominous precedents, a second city of importance fell under his dominion. Padua had been distinguished in the Trevisan March by attachment to the Guelf cause; but the revolution of factions threw her government into the hands of some of the nobles who were Ghibelin, and these men, after making vain stipulations for their liberties, declared the adherence of the republic to the imperial party, and allowed Eccelino, as the lieutenant of Frederic, to enter the place. That active and treacherous partizan had no sooner passed the gates than, under pretence of guarding the Ghibelin interests, he established his own despotic authority, and Padua groaned for many years beneath a horrible tyranny. By different arts Eccelino entrapped into his grasp the most illustrious citizens even among the Ghibelin party, and threw them into the dungeons of his own castles. Many of the Paduan nobles fled from the city, and their houses were immediately razed; others were dragged to the scaffold by the jealous tyrant; and many of the burghers of humbler fortunes were inhumanly consigned to the flames on the mere suspicion of attachment to freedom. While Ferrara had voluntarily surrendered her rights to the house of Este, and Verona and Padua were subject to Eccelino, Treviso was governed by his brother Alberic da Romano, and Vicenza, being surprised by the imperial troops in the first campaign, had equally lost her freedom. The liberties of the Trevisan March had thus faded for ever, and from this epoch the cities of the province might change their masters, but they never recovered their independence.

The degradation of the Lombard republics was longer deferred than the slavery of the Trevisan cities; and their ruin more silently prepared by the spirit of partizanship which, in the conflict of "rival factions, habituated every citizen in ready obedience to a Guelf or Ghibelin chief. The events of the war between the Lombard league and the empire were, when taken together, wholly indecisive. After the success of Frederic against Vicenza, the affairs of Germany demanded his presence, and Eccelino was entrusted with the direction of his Italian interests; but in the following year the emperor recrossed the Alps with two thousand German cavalry, and being joined by ten thousand of his

Neapolitan Saracens, and the forces of the Ghibelin party, won a great battle, at Corte-Nuova in Lombardy, over the Milanese and the troops of the other Guelf cities, (A.D. 1237.) The podestá of Milan fell into the power of the conqueror, and Frederic also numbered the carroccio of that republic among the trophies of his brilliant victory; but the result afforded him few solid advantages, and was balanced in the next summer by his unsuccessful siege of Brescia, a city of the league, which was long and courageously defended against him, until he was finally compelled to abandon the enterprise.

While the progress of the war in Lombardy was thus chequered by alternate fortune, a more formidable enemy than any of the republican states had openly declared against the emperor. Gregory IX. renovated the courage of the Guelf league of Lombardy by avowing himself its protector; and he soon after this act took occasion to excommunicate Frederic, (A.D. 1239.) The spiritual censures of the pontiff might be regarded by the emperor with contempt or indifference in their personal application to himself; but they were of eminent disservice to his cause. His zealous partizans, whose understandings were strong or whose passions had been violently heated in the conflict, were indeed unshaken by the artillery of the church, but with the superstitious and the lukewarm the case was far otherwise. The anathemas of Gregory palsied the timid, determined the wavering, and encouraged the disaffected. The subjects of the emperor were absolved from their allegiance and encouraged to revolt, and in the following year the pope even declared a crusade against him for the defence of the church, as if he had been the common enemy of Christendom. But Frederic took a summary vengeance on the disciples of fanaticism by putting to death every prisoner who bore the cross, and the sacred emblem was no longer prostituted in so unholy a service. But the implacable Gregory was not the less resolved on the ruin of his enemy. He convoked a general council to meet in the Lateran, and Frederic foresaw that, if the authority of the pope over the assembled prelates should obtain from the united voice of the church a confirmation of the ecclesiastical sentence against him, defection would be multiplied in his party. He therefore employed all the vessels which he could equip in the Sicilies to oppose the passage of the French clergy by sea to Rome. Genoa, on the other hand, sent her fleet to transport those prelates who embarked for the Italian shores, but Pisa united her naval force to the imperial galleys to intercept their voyage. Near the little island of Meloria, the future scene of a more interesting combat, the hostile squadrons came to an encounter, and the Genoese were utterly defeated, (A.D. 1241.) So immense a quantity of specie fell into the hands of the victors, that it is said to have been shared between the imperialists and the Pisans by a wooden measure; and the captive prelates being conveyed to Pisa, were loaded, by a curious contradiction of respect and rigour, with silver chains.

The mortification with which this disaster overwhelmed the aged pontiff was supposed to have hastened the close of his days. He died within a few months; and two years elapsed before the intrigues of the conclave would suffer that assembly to agree in the choice of a successor. But when the new pope, Innocent IV., had assumed the tiara, the emperor found that his victory had only suspended, not suppressed, the rancorous hostility of the church. Innocent secretly repairing to Genoa, passed from thence into France, and summoning a general council at Lyons, which was attended by the bishops of England, France, and Spain, with a few of those of Germany and Italy, solemnly proposed the resolution that Frederic should be deprived of his crowns, (A.D. 1245.) The emperor condescended to defend himself by his ambassadors; but the council were subservient to the pope, and Innocent, in presence of one hundred and forty bishops, but without collecting their suffrages, deprived the emperor of all his dignities, and absolved his subjects from their oaths of allegiance.

This has been justly termed the most pompous act of usurpation in the records of the Romish church: since the tacit approbation of a general council seemed to realize all the audacious vaunts of the papal dominion over the powers of the earth which had distinguished the pontificates of Gregory VII. and Innocent III. After his first burst of just indignation at this unprincipled persecution, the emperor, oppressed with grief and alarm at the defection of many of his friends, submitted to the vain humiliation of soliciting the pardon of Innocent. But the papal tyrant was inexorable, and Frederic, roused to the natural vigour of his character, soon placed himself in an attitude to defy both his ancient enemies and his revolted adherents. The event proved that neither the intrigues of Innocent, and the countenance which he at least gave to atrocious projects for the assassination of the emperor, nor yet the support which his decrees had received from an obsequious council, possessed power to endanger the throne of Frederic II. For the five remaining years of that monarch's reign, the struggle between the papal and imperial parties, or rather between Guelf and Ghibelin interests, was obstinately maintained; and Frederic closed a troubled and eventful life without any memorable reverse of fortune. He died of dysentery, at his castle of Ferentino in the Capitanate of Naples, in the fifty-sixth year of his age, after a turbulent reign of thirty-one years over the empire, thirty-eight over Germany, and fifty-two as king of the Sicilies, (A.D. 1250.)

Frederic II. was endowed with many noble and eminent qualities: his talents were unquestionably of the highest order; he was valiant and active, munificent and courteous. His own mental acquirements and tastes were far from contemptible: he was thoroughly acquainted with the philosophy (such as it was) of his times, and was a zealous patron of learned men, and an enlightened encourager of institutions for the revival of letters. He spoke various languages, and, himself a poet, was one of the earliest cultivators of that melodious corruption of the Latin which first became in his days the written language of Italy. In the internal government of his dominions he showed himself a wise and just monarch; and if his administration was rigorous, it was also equable and prudent. Such was the fair side of his character: but the demoralizing influence of education, and of the atrocious scenes into which he was thrown, cast darker shades over a high-minded and generous nature. His private life was sullied by licentious pleasures; his conduct in the Lombard wars was sometimes stained by the cruel spirit of his age, and the reproach of excessive dissimulation cannot be removed from many of his actions. But he had unhappily been nursed in the faithless policy of the Roman see; he was profoundly acquainted with the treacherous designs of the pontiff's, and the corruption of early example might dictate the employment, in self-defence, of the same, weapons which were unhesitatingly used for his destruction.

His vices may be explained, though they cannot be palliated, by the superior wickedness of his papal tutors and adversaries.

PART II.
Conrad IV., son of Frederic II.—His reign over the Sicilies, and death—Papal invasion of the Sicilies—Internal state of Rome—The senator Brancaleone—Cruelties of Eccelino da Romano—Crusade against Eccelino—Fall and death of the tyrant—Fall of the Lombard republics—Changes in the military art—Manfred, king of the Sicilies—Projects of the popes against him—Invasion of the Sicilies by Charles of Anjou—Battle of Grandella—Death of Manfred—Charles of Anjou, king of the Sicilies—Enterprise and execution of Conradin—Extinction of the house of Swabia.

INNOCENT IV., in the asylum which he had chosen for himself at Lyons, welcomed the intelligence of the death of Frederic II. with open rejoicings, and immediately prepared to avail himself of the total change in the posture of affairs which that event had occasioned. He returned to Italy, and visiting in succession all the great Guelf cities of Lombardy, was every where received with splendid state, and greeted with the triumphal acclamations of his party. The Ghibelins, on the other hand, were overwhelmed with consternation at the loss of their heroic chief; and, in the first moment of depression, they almost universally solicited peace. The appearance, however, in Italy of the representative of the Swabian family, revived their drooping courage. This was Conrad IV., the eldest of the two surviving legitimate sons of Frederic, who had been crowned king of Germany during his father's lifetime, and for several years entrusted with the government of that country; and who, being appointed by the emperor's will his successor in all the dominions of his house, crossed the Alps with a numerous army to assert his Italian rights, while Innocent IV. was yet making his progress through Lombardy. (A.D. 1251.)

Though Conrad was strengthened, on his arrival in the Trevisan March, by the support of Eccelino da Romano and the Ghibelins, the confederated Guelfs in northern and central Italy were so powerful, that he judged it most prudent to avoid a contest with them, and to proceed at once by water from the head of the Adriatic gulf to the coasts of Naples. Innocent, pretending that by the deposition of Frederic II. the Sicilies had reverted as a forfeited fief to the papal see, had on the emperor's death declared his intention of placing that kingdom under his immediate government. The dread of incurring the sentences of excommunication and interdict, by resistance to the papal pretensions, and the machinations of the mendicant friars—the devoted militia of the pontiffs—had occasioned a dangerous revolt in the Neapolitan dominions, against the Swabian government. The capital and most of the great towns rose in open rebellion, and the insurrection became nearly general. But the courage and active talents of the youthful Manfred, prince of Tarento, one of the illegitimate sons of Frederic II., who was regent of the kingdom for his brother Conrad, quickly reduced most of the revolted provinces and cities to obedience; and the debarkation of the new king and his army was almost immediately followed by the complete establishment of his authority, (A.D. 1253.)

The pope now discovered that the unassisted powers of the church, however formidable, were insufficient for the conquest and preservation of the kingdom of the Sicilies; and since he could not hope to retain their crown as an immediate appendage of the Roman see, he sought to bestow it upon some prince who would hold the gift as a faithful vassal of the papacy. To this policy of Innocent IV. may be traced the introduction of a French dynasty into Naples, and the origin of those cruel wars which were to devastate Italy for successive centuries with the contentions of foreigners.

The first views of Innocent were directed to the English court; and Richard earl of Cornwall, the brother, and Edmond the son, of our

Henry III., were both the objects of negotiations; which were diverted by the offer of Charles, count of Provence and Anjou, brother of Louis IX. of France, to place his person and the resources of his great inheritance at the disposal of the church, in exchange for the Sicilian diadem. But just at this period, the sudden death of Conrad, at the early age of twenty-six years, revived the hopes of Innocent, that the Sicilies might yet be annexed to the popedom; and he immediately broke off his intrigues for foreign aid. (A.D. 1254.) Conrad had left an infant son, Conradin, in Germany; and it appeared easy to the father of Christendom to seize the inheritance of the orphan. This child was the sole legitimate survivor of the family of Frederic II., but there remained in Manfred a worthy inheritor of the unyielding valour and splendid abilities of that monarch.

While the papal partizans excited commotions in the Sicilies, Innocent himself assembled an army among the Guelf republics of Lombardy and Tuscany, and advanced into the Neapolitan provinces. Manfred, who had been induced to assume the reins of government for his infant nephew, could at first offer no resistance to the invader, and adopted the ineffectual policy of professing to regard him as the protector of Conradin; but when the pope required all the barons of the kingdom to take an oath of allegiance to the holy see, and at once exacted the same fealty from Manfred, and deprived him of a part of his fiefs to enrich one of his own creatures; that prince perceived that no alternative remained between the surrender of his rights and those of his house and a courageous resistance. He withdrew from the destruction which threatened him, to seek an asylum among the Saracens at Luceria, the faithful subjects of his father. He was received with transports of affection; the German soldiery of Conrad ranged themselves under his standard; his force daily increased, and he was soon in a condition to oblige the papal army to seek a shelter within the walls of Naples.

While the spirit of the Swabian adherents was animated by his success, and the popular affection and confidence were gained by his talents and chivalrous gallantry, the death of Innocent at Naples at this critical juncture struck a panic into the Guelf party. The papal forces were every where defeated, the friends of Manfred declared themselves in all quarters, Naples and Capua opened their gates to him, and in less than two years after the decease of Innocent IV., the whole kingdom of the Sicilies was cleared of enemies, and placed under his tranquil government as regent for the infant Conradin.

The pontificate of Innocent IV. was a splendid era of ecclesiastical power; but while the Swabian princes were combated and oppressed by the ambition and relentless hatred of that pope, his authority was openly set at defiance in the seat of the papacy itself. The turbulent independence of Rome, under the greatest pontiffs of the thirteenth century, presented a curious contradiction to the gigantic tyranny which they exercised beyond the limits of their see. Notwithstanding the cruel fate of Arnold of Brescia, the republican constitution, which had been established under his auspices in the middle of the twelfth century, long continued unshaken. Rome was divided into thirteen quarters, termed *Rioni*; the citizens in each of these subdivisions annually named ten delegates; and the electoral body thus composed appointed a senate of fifty-six members. In these representatives of the Roman people—sometimes, perhaps, under the presidency of a patrician or prefect—the government of the city was vested for nearly half a century. But in Rome, as in the other great cities of Italy, the feeble administration of a numerous and often divided assembly, was utterly incompetent to restrain the lawless and turbulent spirit of the age. The Roman populace were at once fickle and bloodthirsty, and the nobles were even more tyrannical and licentious than the aristocracy of the Trevisan March. The ruined monuments of the ancient grandeur of Rome were converted by the barons into formidable strongholds, from which, in the prosecution of their feuds, or in enterprises of public robbery, they audaciously sallied forth to fill the city with bloodshed and rapine.

The same causes which had induced the citizens of the other republics, soon after the peace of Constance, to seek relief, in the dictatorial authority of a foreign magistrate, from the frightful disorders to which they were constantly exposed, actuated the Romans: and in 1192, they superseded the functions of their senate by the appointment of a single senator, who differed only from a podestá in name. A distinguished individual of some Italian city was animally selected for this arduous office of government, and established in the palace which the senate had occupied in the capitol. The same spirit of independence which forbade the Romans to subject their senate to the control of the popes, was preserved under the new administration; and, though the vigorous and artful character of Innocent III. obtained during his reign a general recognition of the temporal superiority of the popedom, the senator was the efficient representative of the Roman republic. The immediate successors of Innocent III. did not enjoy even the moderate influence which he had acquired; and Gregory IX. could with difficulty procure an exemption for his ecclesiastical officers and court from the jurisdiction of the senator.

The temporary removal of Innocent IV. to Lyons, seemed to destroy even the appearance of papal influence within the walls of Rome, and the horrible excesses of the Roman nobles became at this period so intolerable, that no other resource remained to the miserable citizens, than to confide the absolute disposal of their lives and fortunes to some foreign magistrate of undoubted integrity and impartial rigour. They selected for their senator a Bolognese noble, the famous Brancaleone d'Andalo, whose administration has been celebrated by the pen of one of the greatest of our historians. The character of Brancaleone was perfectly adapted to the office, which he only accepted (A.D. 1253) after requiring that thirty Roman hostages of distinction should remain at Bologna, as his security against the notorious inconstancy of the people whom he was called to govern. His courage and firmness were unbounded; as a magistrate he was active, just, and upright; and the inflexible severity of his' temper was both strengthened and regulated by the honourable anxiety of a virtuous reputation. The most powerful offenders were not spared by his vigorous arm. No crime against the public peace escaped his vigilance. At the head of the citizens he attacked the fortresses of the nobles who habitually outraged the civil authority, and in the course of his government one hundred and forty of these domestic citadels were razed, and many of their proprietors previously hanged on their own towers. By such tremendous examples the public order and happiness of Rome were completely established; the arms of the republic were successfully employed in the field in reducing to obedience the surrounding territory; and even Innocent IV., on his return to Italy, and before his expedition against Naples, was compelled by the threats and at the command of the Roman people, to remove from his residence in one of the neighbouring towns within the walls of his proper see; where he was, however, honourably received by Brancaleone.

The eminent services of the great senator were rewarded with ingratitude by the people, who were unworthy of the blessings which his firmness had procured for them: a revolt was excited against him by the arts of the nobles whose tyranny he had destroyed, and of pope Alexander IV., the successor of Innocent, who could not pardon the humiliation of the see. Brancaleone was deposed and imprisoned, and his life would have been sacrificed to the vengeance of his enemies, if the Bolognese had not retained their hostages, and in the cause of their illustrious citizen withstood the terrors of a papal interdict. He was released from confinement, and the Romans, enjoying full leisure in the renewal of disorders to reproach themselves with their conduct towards him, besought his return to their city with repentant entreaties. For the short residue of his life, his government was vigorous and fortunate; the pope was compelled to submission; and, though the enemies of order and of the senatorial authority were executed with too revengeful a spirit, the citizens deplored the death of their protector with well-merited tributes to his memory. (A.D. 1258.)

The pontificate of Alexander IV. was distinguished by a more justifiable and honourable, if not a more disinterested project, than the persecution of Brancaleone. On the death of Frederic II., Eccelino III. da Romano cemented his horrible tyranny over Verona, Padua, and other cities of the Trevisan March, into an absolute and independent sovereignty. Secure in the power which no superior remained to control, he rioted in the indulgence of the cruelty in which he was atrociously pre-eminent. There is scarcely another example in European history of the endurance of mankind under so long and sanguinary a career of government; nor of a character of such unmingled and wanton ferocity as his. Power seemed in him to be no otherwise an object than as it might minister to the gratification of his master passion of demoniacal atrocity. Insensible to the attractions of woman, the sexes were equally his victims, and age and infancy alike the sport of torture and murder. His crimes would be incredible, if they were not remarkably well authenticated by the agreement of all contemporary writers, and they excited universal horror even in an age when inhumanity towards enemies was almost too common to be a reproach. By day and by night, in the cities under his sway, the air rang with the agonizing shrieks of the wretched sufferers who were expiring under the dreadful variety of torture. All that was distinguished in the Trevisan March for public virtue, for birth, station, or wealth, even for private qualities or personal beauty, fell under the suspicion and hatred of the gloomy tyrant. A silent and fearful submission reigned through his dominions; resistance to his numerous satellites was hopeless, and flight impossible.

In the second year of his pontificate, Alexander IV. animated the indignation of mankind by preaching a crusade against this enemy of the human race. (A.D. 1255.) The cause was truly a sacred one, and it had been well if worldly hostility had never been worse directed under the sanction of religion. Yet, such was the selfishness of Italian faction, that the war was at first undertaken only by Guelf animosity, and the monster found puissant allies in the Ghibelin name. Under the command of the papal legate, the Guelf cities of northern and central Italy united their forces with those of the marquis of Este, and other nobles of the same party in the Trevisan March; and the whole of the Paduan exiles, with many of the Venetians, assuming the cross, swelled the numbers of the army.

Eccelino, strengthened by Ghibelin aid, was equal to his enemies in numerical force, and infinitely superior in activity and skill. The legate proved himself wretchedly incompetent in the conduct of the war; but a fortunate accident in the first campaign gave the possession of Padua to the crusaders (A.D. 1256), in the absence of Eccelino, who was ravaging the Mantuan territory with fire and sword. The numerous and crowded prisons of Padua were thrown open, and among the miserable captives, many of whom had been mutilated by torture, were found aged persons of both sexes and delicate young females, all bowed down with privation and suffering: but it was at the appearance of crowds of helpless children, whom the fiend had deprived of their eyes, that horror and pity most agitated the shuddering spectators. Eccelino had not yet inflicted the last calamity of his reign on the unhappy Paduans. Eleven thousand of the flower of the citizens were serving in his army when the city was taken: they composed a third of his troops, and he could place no dependence upon their fidelity. Dexterously therefore disarming them in succession, he threw the whole number into prisons, and, when famine and massacre and the sword of the executioner had done their office, no more than two hundred of the victims survived.

Notwithstanding the loss of Padua, the power and abilities of Eccelino enabled him with the aid of his allies to support the war for two years, and finally even to rout and disperse the crusading army. (A.D. 1258.) This victory was followed by the subjection of Brescia, where the Ghibelin faction acquiring the ascendancy opened their gates to Eccelino. But this was the last material success of the tyrant, and his fall was prepared by that perfidy in his nature which he could not refrain from indulging, even towards his friends. The Ghibelin nobles who had hitherto supported him, endured with shame the reproach of his enormities, and the discovery of his treacherous designs against themselves, soon after the capture of Brescia, completed their disgust and alienation. They united with the Guelf confederation by a treaty, in which the contracting parties solemnly swore, that no consideration should turn them aside from the destruction of the inhuman and faithless Eccelino.

Their purpose was shortly consummated. Eccelino made vigorous efforts in the field, but his enemies were now every where superior, and near Cassano their armies enclosed the monster in the toils. Defection began to spread in his ranks, and forsaken by his myrmidons, furious with desperation, and covered with wounds, he fell into the hands of the confederates. In captivity he preserved an obdurate silence; he repulsed all surgical aid, tore open his wounds, and died in a few days, after a reign of blood and terror which had lasted without intermission for twenty-four years. (A.D. 1259.) The death of Eccelino seemed an imperfect expiation for so many crimes: his brother, Alberic da Romano, shared several features of his character, and the confederates sternly resolved to spare no individual of so detested a race. Not only Alberic, but his wife, six sons, and two daughters, were all mercilessly pursued and executed; for it was in the barbarous spirit of Italian hatred to confound the innocent with the guilty.

In the internal discords of the Lombard cities, the rise of factions, the struggle between the noble and plebeian orders, and the habit of submission to the government of a single magistrate, we have endeavoured to trace the decline of that generous spirit of freedom, which renders these republics the most interesting objects in early Italian history. We are now arrived at the period of their fall. In the Trevisan March, the destruction of the family of Romano only occasioned a transition of the yoke, and gave place for the dominion of other noble houses, of which those of Este at Ferrara, and Della Scala at Verona, were the most distinguished. In the cities of Lombardy about the same epoch, a despotic authority was in like manner yielded to *signores* or lords, and the possession of sovereignty in that great province was almost exclusively divided between the families Della Torre and of Pelavicino. At Milan the dissensions between the nobles and plebeians had attained an irreconcileable violence, and produced a furious civil war (A.D. 1257), in which the ambition of Martino della Torre placed him, though a noble, at the head of the popular party. After some fluctuations of success, the aristocracy were expelled and completely worsted, and Martino reigned over the state as lord and captain of the people. (A.D. 1259.)

The empty forms of a republic might still be retained, but when once the blind favour of the democracy had chosen an aspiring and talented leader for their protection, they were easily induced to renew the distinction in his family. Five of the Torriani were successively entrusted with the supreme and unlimited direction of affairs; their fortune was enjoyed with moderation; and the people gradually forgot their independence in continued obedience to an absolute chief. The example of the greatest state of Lombardy was followed by smaller communities: the democracies of Lodi, Novara, Como, Vercelli, and Bergamo, had all in a few years sought protection from their nobles under the dominion of the Torriani. The marquis of Pelavicino, the head of the Ghibelin faction of Cremona, had, as such, long enjoyed in effect the signiory of that city; and his alliance with Martino della Torre and his first successor, though it was not lasting, enabled him to extend his influence over almost every part of Lombardy which was not possessed by the lords of Milan.

A gradual and silent change in the mode of warfare, which had been perfected before the middle of the thirteenth century, has been sometimes cited as one of the causes which hastened the overthrow of the Lombard liberties. It might, perhaps, be more correctly numbered among the circumstances which, after that overthrow had been accomplished, perpetuated the work of slavery. In the Italian wars of the eleventh and twelfth centuries, the armies of the free states were principally composed of infantry. Every citizen was habituated to the use of arms, and the burgher militia was a general levy of the brave and hardy population. The nobles fought on horseback, but their numbers were comparatively small, and neither their offensive weapons nor their imperfect armour differed much from those of the foot-soldier. And even the feudal levies of Germany, employed by Frederic Barbarossa in his Lombard wars, were for the most part of infantry and similarly equipped. The pride of nobility, and the effects of an education and life exclusively devoted to military exercises, of course rendered the high-born knight more martial in character, and more skilful in the management of arms, than the industrious artisan; but the ruder courage of freemen did not yield before the spirit of more practised warriors, and as long as the armour of the knight and of the burgher foot-soldier was similar, the superiority of the noble chivalry was not severely felt.

But when, in the course of the twelfth century, such improvements had been introduced in the quality of defensive armour as rendered the mounted knight almost invulnerable in every part of his frame, he aspect of war was altogether changed. The well-tempered coat of mail—a double net work of iron rings, or a covering of iron scales sown on leather—enclosed the whole body. The steel helmet with its barred visor, protected the head and face; and the throat, breast, arms, and legs, were farther guarded by the gorget, cuirass, brasses, and cuisses of solid steel. Not only the warrior himself, but his destrier or war-horse was clothed in iron; and the foot-soldier could no longer contend for an instant with the knight whose armour of proof resisted the sword and turned aside the shaft of the cross-bow, whose horse was equally protected from missiles, and whose long and weighty lance inflicted death before a combatant less heavily armed could close with him. A body of five hundred gens-d'armerie or *lances*, as the mounted gentlemen were termed, might, in firm and compact order, charge without danger any number, however immense, of footmen whose weapons could not penetrate their armour, and who wanted discipline to oppose the weight of the phalanx to their hostile shock. The republican citizens found themselves perfectly defenceless as often as they attempted to encounter the chivalry of the nobles in the field, and no change of equipment could remove their inferiority; since the practice of enduring without fatigue the ponderous burthen of knightly armour, the skilful management of the war-horse, and the exercise of the unwieldy lance, were all alike foreign to their industrious and peaceful habits, and could be acquired only by men whose sole occupation and pleasure were war.

In the middle of the thirteenth century, experience had thrown the burgher infantry into contempt; armies came to be numbered only by the force of their mounted lancers; cavalry could be no otherwise successfully opposed than by cavalry; and the Lombard states, feeling the weakness of their native militia, whose courage could not preserve them from unresisted slaughter, were compelled to take into pay bodies of lancers composed of gentlemen, who under some great noble served for extravagant stipends. The liberties of the republics had already expired before this practice was adopted; but when the defence of the state was once placed in a foreign cavalry, and the citizens had withdrawn from the use of weapons which they found ineffectual, it was easy for a tyrant to uphold his reign by the lances of hired adventurers, and to perpetuate the yoke on a people who had abandoned the practice of arms and the public defence to rapacious and insolent mercenaries.

During the pontificate of Alexander IV., the kingdom of the Sicilies had been entirely freed from the papal invasion by the talents of Manfred; and though that heroic prince at first governed only as regent for his infant nephew, he was seduced by ambition to assume the crown on the circulation of a rumour of the death of Conradin, which he had probably himself set afloat, (A.D. 1258.) As soon as his coronation was known in Germany, the widow of Conrad IV. remonstrated by her ambassadors, in the name of her son, against this usurpation. Manfred refused to descend from the throne which his arm had conquered from the popes, and on which the affection of his subjects had placed him; but, having no male offspring, he publicly declared that he reserved the succession of his dominions for Conradin. The German guardians of the young prince were compelled to accept the compact, and the new king was no farther disturbed by the pretensions of his nephew. But he was still pursued by the hostility of the popedom. On the death of Alexander IV., who survived the consummation of the crusade against Eccelino da Romano only two years, his successor Urban IV. adopted the policy and displayed the vigour of Innocent IV. Animated by that hatred and fear of the Swabian house which had become an heirloom of the papacy, Urban renewed the negotiation with Charles, count of Anjou and Provence, which Innocent had broken off. Upon condition of feudal allegiance and payment of an annual tribute to the holy see, Urban bestowed upon Charles the investiture of the kingdom of the Sicilies, which the disobedience and crimes of Frederic II. and his sons were declared to have forfeited. It was the custom with the popes to prostitute upon all occasions the sacred cause of religion to the interests of their see; and Urban converted the intended war against Manfred into a crusade, in which great numbers of the restless nobility of France embarked.

Manfred prepared for the storm that menaced him with the resolution and ability which belonged to his character. He strengthened his connexion with the Italian Ghibelins, harassed the papal adherents, and endeavoured to assemble a sufficient force in Lombardy in conjunction with his ally, the marquis of Pelavicino, to close the passage into Italy against the French, while the Pisans held the seas with their galleys in his cause. The impetuosity of Charles of Anjou induced him, attended by a thousand cavaliers, to hazard the voyage from Marseilles to Rome with a small fleet, while his army was assembling in France; and he was fortunate enough to elude the republican squadron in a storm, (A.D. 1265.) He disembarked at the head of his slender force, and entered Rome, where he was some months after joined by his formidable army, which had defeated Pelavicino and cleared a route through Lombardy.

In the midst of these preparations for war, Urban IV. had died in the year before the arrival in Italy of Charles; but Clement IV., who succeeded him, pursued his designs, and Charles was solemnly crowned king of the Sicilies in the church of the Lateran. After this ceremony he advanced with his army to the Neapolitan frontiers, where Manfred, who neglected no duty of the king, the general, and the patriot, had concentrated all his forces to resist the invaders. But he was ill seconded by the fickle people of southern Italy, and in the hour of his need was too generally betrayed by the cowardice and treachery which, from that age even to our own times, have clung as a foul stain to the Neapolitan character. It was on the plain of Grandella near Benevento, that Manfred resolved by a single battle to avert the consequences of disaffection, and to determine the fate of his kingdom. His cavaliers, the nerve of armies, three thousand six hundred in number, were divided into three bodies; the first, the remains of the German chivalry of his father and brother; the second, composed of the same nation and of Lombard and Tuscan Ghibelins; the third and most numerous, which he commanded in person, of Saracens and Neapolitans. Charles of Anjou ranged his gens-d'armes, about six thousand strong, French, Provençals, and Italian Guelfs, in four lines. The battle was begun by the Saracen archers of Manfred, who, crossing a river which separated the armies, made dreadful havoc by their thick flights of arrows among the numerous and feeble infantry of Charles. But a division of the French chivalry moved forward to support the foot, the papal legate poured benedictions on them as they advanced, and raising their national war-cry of *Montjoie St. Denis!* they impetuously overthrew the Saracen archers. The German cavalry now came on in turn, rushed upon the French with loud shouts of *Swabia! Swabia!* and the encounter between the hostile chivalry was long and obstinately maintained. Only two divisions of the cavalry of Manfred had yet engaged against the whole gens-d'armerie of the invaders, and still the advantage was with the smaller force, when the French, contrary to the laws of chivalry, were commanded to strike at the horses of their opponents. Numbers of the Germans were dismounted, a common exhaustion had overpowered the combatants, and Manfred led his fresh reserve to succour his party, and to seize the victory by a vigorous charge upon the wearied French. But at this crisis most of the Neapolitan barons basely fled, the tide of battle was reversed, the rout among the Germans became general, and the heroic Manfred, rushing into the thickest of the fight, met the death which he sought.

With the fall of Manfred his whole kingdom submitted to the victor, and the Neapolitans soon discovered that they had shamefully abandoned their gallant prince but to fall under a merited and frightful yoke. Many of the most distinguished adherents of Manfred were barbarously executed, and his wife and daughters terminated their existence in prison. The country near the field of battle was first delivered over in cold blood to pillage and under, and the whole kingdom afterwards groaned under the extortions and violence of foreigners.

The battle of Grandella was not only fatal to the fortunes and life of Manfred, but it proved also the signal for the depression of the Ghibelin cause throughout Italy. Assisted by Charles, the Guelfs were every where successful; but while the rapacious insolence and ferocity of the French envenomed popular hatred in the Sicilies, the republic of Pisa, ever the faithful ally of the Swabian house, the marquis of Pelavicino (expelled by the Guelfs from his authority in Lombardy), and other Ghibelins, united with the ancient Neapolitan partizans of Manfred in inviting the youthful Conradin, with assurances of a joyful reception, to claim his rights by the sword, and to deliver his inheritance of the Sicilies from the odious grasp of the Angevin conqueror.

Conradin, the last scion of an illustrious stock, was then only seventeen years of age. Centering in his person all the pretensions, and inheriting all the daring courage of the Swabian house, he rashly conceived that the moment had arrived to avenge the wrongs of his family, and to seat himself on the throne of his ancestors, (A.D. 1268.) Two years after the fatal battle of Grandella, he crossed the Alps from Germany at the head of the flower of the young nobility of his country; and being escorted as far as Verona by the forces of the princes of

Bavaria and Tyrol, his relatives, was immediately joined by the Italian Ghibelins. Passing triumphantly through northern and central Italy, while the Neapolitans and Sicilians had broken out into open insurrection in his favour, he reached the confines of the kingdom of Naples with an army of five thousand gens-d'armes; and penetrating through the Abruzzos, found the Angevin king posted with a veteran force of smaller number on the plain of Tagliacozzo. Charles was indebted to the wily counsel of an old French baron for a stratagem which, by the cruel sacrifice of a portion of his troops, gave him a complete victory. Dividing his army into three bodies, he drew out two of them before the enemy as if they had been his whole array, and entrusted the command to a nobleman, Henry of Cosenza, who, resembling him in person, was drest in the royal insignia. Charles himself with the third body of his bravest cavaliers, lay concealed in a small valley. The young and impetuous Conradin fell into the snare. Reconnoitring the small force before him, and reckoning on an easy triumph, he at once led his whole chivalry to the charge. The gens-d'armerie of Cosenza were overwhelmed by superior numbers, Henry himself was slain, and the Germans, taking the corpse for that of the king, imagined the field their own. But their ranks were no sooner broken in the ardour of pursuit and plunder, than Charles led his reserve from their ambush, fresh and in compact order. Their charge was irresistible; the Germans, fatigued, dispersed, and astonished, were unable to regain their formation; their numbers only swelled the massacre, and the day was utterly lost. Conradin was borne by the barons who surrounded him from the scene of destruction, but only to be betrayed into the hands of the victor by the treachery of a noble in whose castle he had sought a shelter.

Charles of Anjou had now full leisure to display the inherent cruelty of his nature. Neither the laws of honourable warfare, nor any sentiment of generous pity, could move him to spare the unhappy boy, who had become his prisoner in the brave effort to recover his legitimate inheritance. He resolved, after the mockery of a trial, to purchase the security of his own title, by the public execution of a prince who could owe him no fealty, and of whose rights he was himself, on the contrary, the usurper. The young victim deported himself on the scaffold with a spirit worthy of his race. One touching burst of agony escaped him; but it was for his parent, not for himself. "Oh my mother!" was his exclamation, "dreadful will be the grief that awaits thee for my fate." Then turning to the defenceless multitude of his subjects, who could only weep round his scaffold, he cast his glove among them as the gauntlet of future vengeance, and bowed his neck to the executioner. Thus perished the last of the Swabian line.

PART III.
Republic of Florence—Natural advantages and commercial prosperity of the city—First dissensions at Florence—Establishment of the popular constitution—Expulsion of the Ghibelin nobles—Civil war—Battle of the Arbia—Revengeful spirit and tyranny of the Ghibelin conquerors—Deliverance of Florence—Settlement of the constitution Maritime Italian republics—Venice—Her share of the Latin conquest of the eastern empire—Splendid acquisitions of the republic—Extension of Venetian commerce—Affairs of the Venetian colonies—Connexion of the republic with the Latin empire of the East—Pisa—Genoa—Her internal distractions—Furious naval wars between the Genoese and Venetians.

THE rise of the greatest republic of Italy, except the maritime free states, is contained within the period embraced in the present chapter. Florence, like the rest of Tuscany, was longer subject to imperial lieutenants than the cities of Lombardy; but her republican independence was perfected in the middle of the twelfth century, and, before the peace of Constance, the nobles of the surrounding territory had been reduced to subjection by the arms of her citizens. She had sometimes, too, engaged in petty warfare with neighbouring cities, but the first occasion on which she challenged observation and opened the dawn of her eminence, was by appearing as the principal city of the Guelf league of 1197. Situation and accident conspired in elevating Florence to the first rank among Italian cities. Her skies are cloudless, her climate is pure and healthful, and the country about her walls is the loveliest portion of Tuscany. An amphitheatre of swelling uplands, rising beside the chain of the Apennines, is overspread with vineyards and olive grounds which produce the most exquisite wines and oil of

Italy; and the mountains which tower in the distance are covered with productive forests of chestnuts, the food of the peasantry, and give birth to limpid and fertilizing streams. Among these, the classic Arno, bathing the walls of the fair city, and flowing into the Mediterranean through vales of the most luxuriant richness, affords an outlet, when its bed is filled in the rainy season, for the transport of superabundant harvests. The Florentines were thus invited by nature to agricultural industry; but they applied themselves also to commerce. By some fortunate chance, the art of manufacturing woollen cloths was very early cultivated in their city, though the exact period and circumstances of its introduction are unknown. The advantage was diligently improved; the excellence of the Florentine cloths was already established in the thirteenth century, and continued unrivalled throughout Europe for three hundred years; and this branch of trade, together with that in silks, of slower growth if not of later establishment, filled the city with prodigious wealth and population.

We shall find the spirit of freedom to have been more durable in its existence, and happier in its influence, at Florence than in any of the inland republics of Italy. The discovery of an adequate cause for this distinction is a problem which has scarcely been resolved. The character of the people will hardly account for their superior fortunes. They were not braver, more virtuous, nor less factious than the Lombards; and, on the contrary, they had rather a larger share of inconstant liveliness and desire of change than was common in the Italian temperament. Neither will the security of their situation in an upland province explain, as has been sometimes pretended, their escape from the tyranny which reigned in the Lombard plains, since that tyranny was common to the hilly March of Treviso. And, in as far as the changes in the military art, to which we have referred, were hostile to the cause of liberty, the Florentines possessed no advantage over their neighbours; they were neither more warlike, nor more exempt from the frequent necessity of repairing the weakness of their burgher infantry by taking bodies of mercenary cavalry into pay. But perhaps, although I am not aware that it has been much dwelt upon, the real cause of the preservation of liberty at Florence was, the activity of the commercial spirit—the offspring and guardian of free institutions. The influx of riches created an order of wealthy and powerful merchants, unknown in other inland republics, and whose interests were identified with the rights of the commonalty. They were at first the natural leaders of the lower citizens in their struggles against the ancient nobles, who had been compelled, as in other Italian cities, to dwell within the walls; and the triumph of the people was afterwards perfected and secured by the elevation of a class of hereditary plebeian grandees (popolani grandi) who formed a counterpoise to the power of the original nobility; and were themselves long an essential portion of the democracy.

Until the beginning of the thirteenth century, Florence was governed by consuls and a senate of popular choice, but she then fell, like other cities, into the fashion of entrusting her government to a foreign podestá. Though she had engaged in the Tuscan league, her repose was little disturbed by the contest between the papacy and the empire; and tranquillity appears to have reigned within her walls, until a feud between two noble families plunged her in the long and unhappy distraction of Guelf and Ghibelin hatred, (A.D. 1215.) A vain and elegant young man, the chief of the noble house of Buondelmonti, who had been affianced to a lady the relative of a second powerful family, the Uberti, was blinded by the superior charms of another fair to forget his plighted faith, and solicit the hand of his new beauty. His marriage was regarded by the Uberti and their friends as an insult which could only be washed out in his blood, and they cruelly murdered him as he rode in a gala dress on his white palfrey through the city. The fierce passions of private life were usually the source of Italian calamity. Florence was filled with the deadly quarrel which these reciprocal injuries had produced between the two houses; and the feud was multiplied by the hostility of their partizans. The Buondelmonti were attached to the church, the Uberti to the empire; their animosity raised the cry of faction throughout the nobility; and, for thirty-three years, the city was stained with almost uninterrupted bloodshed before either party had fully prevailed. At length, on Candlemas-eve, in the year 1248, the Ghibelin nobles, with the assistance of some German cavalry, lent to them by Frederic II., succeeded by a vigorous effort in expelling their Guelf adversaries from the city; and gave the first example, which fatally recoiled on themselves, of razing the massive palaces of their enemies.

The triumph of the Ghibelin nobles was very transient. On the expulsion of the Guelfs they seized the government of the city under imperial protection, and oppressed the citizens with aristocratic insolence. The people, frugal, industrious, and independent, were little disposed to submit to their tyranny; they were besides generally attached to the church; and little more than two years had elapsed, when they were excited to resistance by some of the wealthy burghers. Assembling in arms, they hastily decreed the formation of a popular constitution (A.D. 1250); they deposed the podestá, and elected a capitano del popolo; and dividing themselves into twenty companies of militia, each under a leader, according to the divisions of the city in which they dwelt, they easily compelled the Ghibelin nobility to submit to the revolution. A council of twelve ancients, elected every two months in the six quarters of Florence, was entrusted, together with the captain of the people and a new podestá, with the signiory of the republic. This simple constitution was formed just before the death of Frederic II., and the intelligence of the decease of the great chief of Ghibelinism in the same year was no sooner received, than the Florentines completed their work by recalling the Guelf nobles, and obliging the Ghibelins to live in peace with them. The arms of the republic were now vigorously employed, and generally with success, in the cause of the church. The Ghibelin cities of Tuscany were every where humbled; Pistoia was for a time entirely subjected; Sienna and Volterra were forced to adopt a Guelf government; and even the powerful republic of Pisa was reduced to sue for peace, (A.D. 1255.) It was in the midst of this brilliant prosperity, that the Florentines first struck their gold coin, the florin, which, by its purity, acquired deserved celebrity in the commercial transactions of the middle ages.

This fortunate epoch in the Florentine annals had lasted only eight years, when the discovery of a conspiracy among the Ghibelin nobles to re-establish their tyranny obliged the people to assist the podestá, in expelling them from the city by force of arms. (A.D. 1258.) The exiles had recourse for aid to Manfred, king of the Sicilies, as the natural protector of their faction, and received from that monarch, after some delay, a body of eight hundred German cavaliers with infantry; while the republic of Sienna, now again under Ghibelin administration, afforded them an asylum and united its army in their cause. The desperate fortunes of the exiles made them desire an immediate and decisive action; but the Siennese were more cautious, and the Florentines had but to avoid a battle to ensure the dissolution of the force of their enemies, as the cavalry of Manfred were only paid for three months. But the exiles prepared a treacherous design against their countrymen which was completely successful. Under pretence of desiring to regain the favour of the republic, they offered, if the Florentine army would advance to Sienna, to open one of their gates to them. The council of ancients credulously entered into the negotiation, and induced the people to take the field. Summoning all their Guelf confederates of Tuscany to provide their contingents, the Florentines and their allies advanced to the river Arbia, a few miles from Sienna, with a force altogether of three thousand horse and thirty thousand infantry. (A.D. 1260.) But instead of finding that city betrayed to them, their exiles, the German cavalry, and the whole Ghibelin army of Sienna and her allies, unexpectedly sallied from the gates to attack them, and, though very inferior in numbers, succeeded by the surprise, and by treason in the Florentine ranks, in entirely routing them with dreadful slaughter. The lower people of Florence seized with terror, and perhaps left defenceless by the destruction of their army, abandoned all hope of resistance to the conquerors. The principal Guelf families among the nobles and burghers retired to the friendly state of Lucca; and, on the appearance of her victorious exiles, Florence immediately surrendered. What followed may illustrate the rancour of Italian hatred. The Pisans and Siennese, knowing the firm attachment of the Florentine people to the Guelf cause, proposed in a general Ghibelin diet the destruction and razing of the city, as the only security for the opposite party in Tuscany; and the vengeance of the Ghibelin exiles of Florence eagerly supported the vote for the ruin of the country from which they had been expelled.

It was only the voice of a single patriot which averted the doom of Florence. Farinata degl'Uberti was the most distinguished leader among the Florentine Ghibelins, and his talents and exertion had been the soul of their cause; but he indignantly resisted the proposition in which his party had concurred, and Florence was indebted to the virtuous influence of his personal character, and to the force of his passionate eloquence, for protection against the fury of her unnatural sons. The Ghibelins of Florence could only maintain the arbitrary government which they now re-established, by foreign aid; and as long as Manfred reigned, a strong body of his lancers garrisoned the city under count Guido Novello. The exiled Guelfs, on the other hand, joined the standard of Charles of Anjou on his entrance into Italy, and fought in his army with remarkable valour at the battle of Grandella. That victory of the Guelf party, with happier results in Tuscany than in the Sicilies, brought deliverance to Florence, (A.D. 1266.) When intelligence of the event reached the city, the joy of the people was openly expressed, and count Guido, finding that efforts to conciliate their affection came now too late, and intimidated by their revolt, withdrew with his gens-d'armerie and the native Ghibelins. The citizens immediately fortified themselves against the return of their oppressors; the policy of Charles of Anjou induced him to dispatch a body of cavaliers to their assistance; and, under his protection, with the dignity which was no more than nominal of signer, the republican government was restored in full vigour.

The establishment of the constitution of 1266 is a remarkable era in Florentine history. It was attended by three circumstances which exercised a lasting influence upon the character of the republic; the erection of the *arts*, or companies of the citizens engaged in commerce, into political bodies; the unresisted exclusion of the nobles from power; and the formation of an organized Guelf society or party, an imperium in imperio, a miniature republic within the republic itself. The commercial citizens had for half a century been classed, according to their occupations, into greater and minor arts; the former, seven in number, were the lawyers, merchants of foreign cloth, bankers, woollen manufacturers, physicians and druggists, silk manufacturers, and furriers; the latter, at this period of five descriptions, but which in the issue extended to fourteen, were retailers of cloth, butchers, shoemakers, smiths, masons, and other inferior tradesmen. The seven greater arts were now erected by law into corporations, whose existence was essential to the constitution; and had each a council of its own, a judicial magistrate, and a captain or standard bearer (gonfaloniere), around whose banner the company assembled whenever the peace or safety of the city was endangered. The minor arts were not incorporated until later periods.

For the discharge of the executive administration, the council of ancients was restored under a different name; and twelve Buonuomini (good men), chosen in the six quarters of Florence, composed the visible signiory. But they could determine on no measure of importance without the successive approbation of four larger councils of citizens, from the two first of which the nobles were excluded, while the chiefs of the greater arts sat in three of them by virtue of their office. About five hundred citizens of all degrees had thus immediate voices in every deliberation of common interest, and though the general parliament of the people was seldom convened, the ultimate sovereignty of the democracy was a recognised and efficient principle.

The exile and proscription of the Ghibelins were followed by the confiscation of their estates; and the remains of their property, after satisfying the losses suffered by the Guelfs during their government, was divided between the state and the new corporation which, with a signiory and two councils of its own, was instituted to watch over Guelf interests, and prosecute suspected Ghibelins. The primary object of this powerful and wealthy body is explained by the relentless spirit which, in the Italian republics, ever pursued an outlawed and unhappy faction; but we shall find the Guelf society in the sequel engaged in schemes of ambition which were foreign to its original purpose.

From the epoch of the peace of Constance to the end of the twelfth century, the history of Venice is occupied by no occurrence which deserves to be recorded. But the first years of the thirteenth century are the most brilliant and glorious in the long annals of the republic. They are filled with the details of a romantic and memorable enterprise: the equipment of a prodigious naval armament, the fearless pursuit of a distant and gigantic adventure, the conquest of an ancient empire, the division of the spoil, and the consummation of commercial grandeur. The diversion of the fourth crusade from its original destination to the walls of Constantinople, and the siege and capture of the eastern capital by the barons of France and the Venetians have been related, at least twice, in our language with so much accuracy and elegance, that if my limits permitted, and my subject required me to attempt the same narration, I could hope to add no interesting fact, and should despair of arresting attention to that which had been already so admirably told. But my plan forbids me to introduce at length this splendid episode; and the particulars of the Latin expedition belong rather to the Decline and Fall of the Roman Empire, or the History of the Crusades, than to that of Italy, or even more strictly of Venice. Referring the reader to other pages for the story of the fourth crusade, it will be my business to confine myself to its attendant circumstances as they illustrate the resources and character of the republic, and to its important consequences upon her power and greatness.

In the year 1198, pope Innocent III., by the preaching of Fulk of Neuilly, a French priest, had stirred up the greatest nobles of that kingdom to undertake a crusade for the deliverance of the Holy Sepulchre. Baldwin, count of Flanders, enrolled himself in the same cause, and Boniface, marquis of Montferrat, accepted the command of the confederates. They were warned by the sad experience of former crusades not to attempt the passage to Asia by land; and the maritime states of Italy were the only powers which could furnish shipping for the transport of a numerous army. The barons therefore sent a deputation to Venice to entreat the alliance and negotiate for the assistance of the republic, (A.D. 1201.)

Henry Dandalo, who, at the extraordinary age of ninety-three, and in almost total blindness, still preserved the vigorous talents and heroism of youth, had been for nine years doge of Venice. He received the illustrious ambassadors with distinction; and after the object of their mission had been regularly laid before the councils of the state, announced to them in the name of the republic the conditions upon which a treaty would be concluded. As the aristocracy had not yet perfected the entire exclusion of the people from a voice in public affairs, the magnitude of the business demanded the solemn assent of the citizens, and a general assembly was convened in the square of St. Mark. There, before a multitude of more than ten thousand persons, the proud nobles of France threw themselves upon their knees to implore the assistance of the commercial republicans in redeeming the sepulchre of Christ. Their tears and eloquence prevailed; the terms of alliance had been left to the dictation of the doge and his counsellors; and for 85,000 marks of silver, less than 200,000*l.* of our money, and not an unreasonable demand, the republic engaged to transport 4500 knights with their horses and arms, 9000 esquires, and 20,000 infantry, to any part of the coasts of the East which the service of God might require, to provision them for nine months, and to escort and aid them with a fleet of fifty galleys; but with the farther conditions that the money should be paid before embarkation, and that whatever conquests might be made, should be equally shared between the barons and the republic.

The Venetians demanded a year of preparation; and before that period had expired, both their fidelity to the engagement and the extent of their resources were conspicuously displayed. Barracks for the troops, stabling for the horses, and abundance of provisions had been prepared for the rendezvous of the crusaders; and 120 palanders, or large flat-bottomed vessels for the conveyance of the horses, 240 sail of transports for the men, and 70 store-ships, laden with provisions and warlike engines, were all in readiness for the expedition, while a formidable squadron of 50 galleys was destined to convoy the fleet, and to co-operate with the land forces.

But all the crusaders were not equally true to their faith: many whose ardour had cooled shamefully deserted their vows; others had taken ship for Palestine in Flanders, at Marseilles, and at other Mediterranean ports; and when the army had mustered at Venice, their numbers fell very short of expectation, and they were utterly unable to defray the stipulated cost of the enterprise. Though their noble leaders made a generous sacrifice of their valuables, above 30,000 marks were yet wanted to complete the full payment, and the republic, with true mercantile caution, refused to permit the sailing of the fleet until the amount of the deficiency should have been lodged in their treasury. The timid and the lukewarm already rejoiced that the crusade must be abandoned, when Dandalo suggested an equivalent for the remainder of the debt, by the condition that payment should be deferred if the barons would assist the republic in reducing the city of Zara, which had again revolted, before they pursued the ulterior objects of their voyage.

The citizens of Zara had committed themselves to the sovereignty of the king of Hungary, and the pope forbade the crusaders to attack the Christian subjects of a monarch who had himself assumed the cross. But the desire of honourably discharging their obligations prevailed with the French barons over the fear of papal displeasure, and, after some scruples, the army embarked for Zara. (A.D. 1202.) The aged doge having obtained permission from the republic to take the cross and lead the fleet, many of the citizens followed his example in ranging themselves under the sacred banner, and the veteran hero sailed with the expedition of nearly five hundred vessels, the most magnificent armament, perhaps, which had ever covered the bosom of the Adriatic. Though Zara was deemed in that age one of the strongest cities in the world, the inhabitants were terrified or compelled into a surrender after a siege of only five days: their lives were spared, but their houses were pillaged, and their defences razed to the ground.

After this conquest it was determined, as the season was far advanced, that the army should winter at Zara, and pursue the objects of their sacred expedition in the following spring. It was during this period of repose, which was not undisturbed by broils between the French soldiers and the Venetian mariners, that an entirely new destination was given to the armament. In one of those revolutions so frequent and natural in the palaces of despots, Isaac Angelus, emperor of the East, himself an usurper, was deprived at once of his diadem and eyes, and consigned to a prison by his own brother Alexius. The youthful son of Isaac, named also Alexius, was spared from the same fate to wait on the person of his uncle, but he found means to escape from his tyranny. He arrived in Italy while the crusaders were assembling at Venice, and their powerful array inspired him with the hope of recovering his father's throne by their aid. (A.D. 1203.) At Zara he renewed in person the offers, which he had already made by his ambassadors at Venice, to induce the confederates to direct their arms against the usurpation of his uncle. He tempted both their avarice and their religious zeal by the promise that their success should be rewarded by a payment of 200,000 marks, the subjection of the Greek church to the papal authority, and the co-operation of the forces of the eastern empire in the deliverance of Palestine. Most of the French barons were influenced by these magnificent proposals, but a division was produced among the crusaders by the interference of the pope. The emperor Alexius had ingratiated himself into his favour, and Innocent, trusting that the religious allegiance of the Greek empire to the Roman see would become the price of keeping the usurper on the throne, took him under his protection, and prohibited the crusaders on pain of excommunication from deferring the performance of their vows for any other object.

The superstitious French already reproached themselves that they had once disobeyed the injunctions of the pontiff by attacking Zara; many of the most eminent barons chose rather to separate from the army than to incur the guilt of a second offence; and the cause of young Alexius would have been hopeless if the doge and the Venetians had been equally moved by the dread of spiritual censures. But Venice, though preserving a respectful demeanour towards the Holy See, had already adopted a firm and enlightened policy which repelled the encroachments of papal tyranny. Before the expedition quitted Venice, the doge had refused to admit the control of the papal legate over the conduct of the crusade; and the reduction of Zara was an earnest how lightly the republic would regard the authority of innocent, whenever it should be opposed to her passions or interests. Against the Greek empire she had more than one cause of animosity; and motives of vengeance and commercial ambition were mingled in the ostensible design of succouring the youthful and unfortunate Alexius.

When, in the decay of all national energy, the slothful Greeks had abandoned even the commerce of their own dominions to foreigners, the Venetians had formed advantageous establishments for trade in the capital and provinces of the eastern empire, and in return for the favours which they enjoyed, had long afforded the assistance of their fleets to the emperors. But during the last half of the twelfth century, these friendly relations had been frequently interrupted. The enterprising republicans betrayed their arrogance and contempt towards the degenerate and feeble Greeks; their insolence provoked hatred and injury, and every vicissitude of revolution or popular tumult in the eastern empire was the signal for the plunder and mal-treatment of the Venetian merchants, either by the systematic exactions of the imperial officers, or the irregular violence of the cowardly populace. The arms of the republic or the dread of her vengeance generally, indeed, obtained subsequent indemnification for the losses of her citizens; but repeated broils cherished mutual antipathy, and when the Pisans availed themselves of the dislike of the Greeks towards their rivals to supplant them in their commercial relations with the empire, the exasperation of the Venetians reached its height. By assisting young Alexius, their republic would avenge its wrongs, and regain its commercial advantages in the East.

The politic Dandalo was not slow to discern the favourable prospect which opened to his country: his patriotic ambition was not shackled by any superstitious veneration for the papal authority, and his talents were successfully exerted in overcoming the religious scruples of the French barons. Though the army was weakened by many desertions, the host of the crusaders finally resolved, notwithstanding the fulminations of Innocent, to undertake an expedition which, besides holding out such splendid invitations to their cupidity, might plausibly be represented as an advantageous preparation for the subsequent deliverance of Palestine. The recovery of Jerusalem would be promoted by their possession of Constantinople; and the doge exultingly steered the armament against the seat of the eastern empire.

I have declined the arduous and unnecessary task of describing the first siege of the Grecian capital by the crusaders; the revolution which restored the captive emperor Isaac to his throne, and associated young Alexius in the imperial purple; the hatred of their conquered subjects; the deposition and death of the father and son; the vengeance of the Latins against the new usurper and the contemptible nation; the second siege and capture of Constantinople (A.D. 1204); and the disgraceful fall of the once mighty empire of the East before a few thousand French warriors and Venetian seamen. In the brief course of a year one of the most astonishing enterprises in the history of warfare had been fearlessly achieved, and no other labour remained to the victors than to share their enormous accumulation of booty, to elect from their ranks a new head to the empire, and to determine the partition of their conquests. The solemn choice of the confederates bestowed the diadem of the East on Baldwin count of Flanders; but no more than a fourth of the capital and empire was allotted to the support of his dignity and power, and the remainder was equally divided between the French barons and the Venetian republic.

The talents and heroism of the venerable Dandalo had won for the doges of Venice the splendid and accurate title of Dukes of three-eighths of the Roman Empire; he died at Constantinople almost immediately after the Latin conquest, full of years and glory; and bequeathed to the republic the difficult office of governing a greater extent of dominion than had ever fallen to the inhabitants of a single city. All the islands of the Ionian, and most of those in the Ægean seas, great part of the shores of continental Greece, many of the ports in the Propontis, or sea of Marmora, the city of Adrianople, and one-fourth of the eastern capital itself were all embraced in her allotment, and the large and valuable island of Candia was added to her possessions by purchase from the marquis of Montferrat to whom it had been assigned. But the prudence of her senate awakened Venice to a just sense of her own want of intrinsic strength to preserve these immense dependencies; and it was wisely resolved to retain only under the public government of the state the colony at Constantinople, with the island of Candia and those in the Ionian sea. The subjects of the republic were not required to imitate the forbearance of the senate, and many of the great Venetian families were encouraged, or at least permitted, to found principalities among the ruins of the eastern empire, with a reservation of feudal allegiance to their country. In this manner most of the islands of the Ægean Archipelago were granted in fief to ten noble houses of Venice, and continued for several centuries subject to their insular princes.

From the Latin conquest of Constantinople to the close of the period to which the present chapter is devoted, the affairs of Venice continued to be almost entirely separated from those of Italy in general. Her attention was exclusively devoted to the care of a vast commerce, the anxious charge of foreign and disaffected subjects, the support of the Latin empire of the East, and the prosecution of sanguinary maritime warfare with the republic of Genoa. Some notice is demanded for all these subjects, but none of them need detain us long. By far the most solid advantage which accrued to the republic from the expedition of Dandalo was the immense extension of her commerce. From the Adriatic to the Euxine, a continued chain of sea-ports had fallen into the possession of Latin nobles, who were bound by ties of friendship and interest to her citizens. Her fleets were the common carriers for their commercial wants, and Constantinople itself her great depot for the trade of eastern Europe. The activity of her merchants was equal to the measure of the advantages which they enjoyed, and her wealth and splendour were now honourably perfected by their industrious enterprise. In another direction the island of Candia was the arm which connected their trade with the shores of Egypt and Syria; but that desirable possession was endangered during the whole of the thirteenth century by frequent revolts.

When the senate resolved to establish their government over Candia and the Ionian islands, a strong squadron of galleys easily reduced them to subjection; garrisons were placed in their fortresses, and it became the policy of the state to colonize their shores with Venetian citizens. But the numerous population of Candia submitted with reluctance to a foreign yoke, and all the resources of Venice were long demanded to crush their frequent and alarming insurrections. We may suspect that the disaffection of the Candiotes had too often its origin and excuse in the oppression of Venetian governors; for we find that the same spirit of revolt prevailed in the Dalmatian maritime possessions of Venice, and that the odious sway of the republic was only maintained in her numerous dependencies by the vigour of her arms.

After the first moment of conquest and terror, the weakness of the Latin empire of Constantinople was palpably betrayed to the numerous Greeks. Unwarlike and cowardly as they were, the shame of submission to the detested Latins was animated into resistance when, by the dispersion of the French barons over the provinces, their scanty force was lost among the native population. A spark of hope and independence was kindled among a nation of slaves by the weakness and divisions of their conquerors; and almost immediately after the capture of Constantinople, several small states were saved and formed from the wrecks of the empire by Grecian leaders, whose personal qualities gave a better title to the obedience of their countrymen than hereditary pretensions. One of these states was established at Nice on the Asiatic side of the Bosphorus, and attracted from the opposite shores all the better spirits of Constantinople and the European provinces, whose patriotism or religious zeal spurned the yoke of the stranger, and the supremacy of the Latin church. The Greeks were gradually nerved by adversity, their new empire silently grew in strength and extent, and re-crossing the Bosphorus, they successively wrested from the Latins the neighbouring provinces of Europe.

The power of the handful of warriors who had seized the eastern empire, could never be adequate to its preservation. Their prayers for assistance from western Europe were met with coldness and neglect; they were disunited among themselves; and the Latin empire, whose sole force was a few turbulent barons, the compeers rather than the vassals of their feeble princes, was destitute of all foreign aid, except such as Venice could spare from her own more immediate necessities and interests. The maritime strength of the great colony, which the republic had established in her quarter of Constantinople, was long the chief support of the Latin throne, and the fleets of the parent state were sometimes added to the force of the colonists. But the occasional efforts of the republic could not prevent the extinction of a power which the reviving energies of the Greeks had limited to the walls of Constantinople. During the absence of the small Latin force with the Venetian fleet on an imprudent expedition, the capital was surprised; Baldwin II., the poor phantom of imperial dignity, sought refuge with the descendants of the Latins in the returning galleys of the republic, and Michael Palæologus, the sovereign of Nice, restored the eastern empire of the Greeks, fifty-seven years after its overthrow by the crusaders, (A.D. 1261.)

The consequences of this great revolution were not so disastrous to the trade of Venice, or to her colony at Constantinople, as might have been apprehended from the intimate connexion of the republic with the Latin empire, and her long career of injurious hostility towards the Greeks. The Venetian magistrates, and the greater portion of their countrymen, had fled with Baldwin, but many others had remained in the city; and though Palæologus prosecuted the war against their republic, and dispossessed the Venetian feudatories of some islands in the Ægean, he prudently abstained from depriving his capital of the industry of the Italians. Though the Genoese had been his allies, and the Venetians his bitterest enemies, he extended an impartial protection to the merchants of the two states and of Pisa. A separate quarter was allotted in Constantinople to each of these three maritime people: they were permitted to govern themselves by their own magistrates, and three little Italian republics were embraced within the walls of the eastern capital.

The furious naval wars, which broke out in the thirteenth century between Genoa and Venice, give a connexion to the affairs of the two states, and may introduce a brief notice in this place of the prominent circumstances in the Genoese fortunes during the period before us. From the peace of Constance to the extinction of the Swabian family, the condition of the third maritime republic, Pisa, unlike that of the other two, was closely interwoven with the common politics of Italy, and presents no fact for observation which we have not already thrown into the general stream of Italian history. We have remarked, that, in the wars of Frederic Barbarossa, Pisa espoused the cause of the church; but her attachment was transferred, and her fidelity secured to the empire, by the confirmation of regalian rights and the sovereignty over an extensive territory, which the emperor Henry VI. bestowed upon her (A.D. 1192); and, ever after her alliance with that monarch, she continued, by unchangeable inclination and principle, Ghibelin. The queen of that part in Tuscany, her affection never swerved from the house of Swabia. We have seen her squadrons guarding the seas for

Frederic II. and for Manfred, and her armies upholding the Ghibelin name in her province; and her exhortations and aid inspired and attended the ill-fated expedition of Conradin. Still the rival and perpetual foe of Genoa, she forgot her commercial jealousy of the Venetians in this more inveterate hostility, and flourishing in undiminished prosperity, sided with the latter people against a common enemy.

The long domestic tranquillity which had reigned at Genoa, with only one interruption, to the beginning of the thirteenth century, was then destroyed by the ambition of the aristocracy, and the hostility with which their usurpations were naturally regarded by the lower people. The greater part of the nobles, enrolling themselves into eight associations or companies, had silently acquired such an influence in the state that they were at length suffered to form a council, by a deputation of one member from each body; which, under the nominal supremacy of a foreign podestá, arrogated to itself all the sovereign powers, and filled the republic with magistrates of its own nomination and exclusively of noble birth. Four great families, the Doria, the Spinola, the Fieschi, and the Grimaldi, were conspicuous in an oligarchy that was not only hateful to the plebeians, but to the portion of the nobility which was not enrolled in the eight companies. The ineffectual struggles of the people agitated Genoa with the usual convulsions of Italian faction, and were near producing the same disastrous consequences over which Lombardy had for centuries to mourn. There were not wanting men among the nobility to forsake the cause of their order, and to flatter the passions of the democracy, for purposes of selfish ambition. Several of these noble demagogues placed themselves, at different periods in the thirteenth century, at the head of the populace; and one, more famous than the rest, Guilelmo Boccanegra, reigned for five years as captain of the people, until his undisguised tyranny alienated the citizens, and induced them to escape from more alarming evils by restoring the noble government. Yet the people were still restless and dissatisfied; the state was harassed by continual troubles; and the general rights of all orders would have been sacrificed to an individual, if the republic had not possessed two fortunate safe-guards in the rivalry of her nobles, and in the more generous spirit of independence which animated her commercial citizens.

These internal distractions did not paralyze the energies of Genoa in her foreign relations; and the vigour of the republic was never more strikingly displayed than when her bosom was torn by faction. At the period of the Latin conquest of Constantinople, the aggrandizement of Venice had excited the jealousy and enterprise of the Genoese, and they endeavoured to seize on a share of the spoils of the eastern empire. But the fleet which they dispatched for this purpose against the isles of the Ægean, was encountered and completely defeated by the Venetian admiral Trevisani; and they were compelled to desist from further attempts. (A.D. 1205.)

The animosity created by this contest rankled for half a century, before the two republics measured their strength in a more obstinate and protracted struggle; and the petty occasion which was at last the signal for an open rupture, betrayed the depth of the hatred which they mutually cherished. In the city of Acre—one of the few places on the coasts of Palestine which the Christians still possessed—the commercial residents of Genoa and Venice quarrelled about the possession of the single church which was allotted to them in common. (A.D. 1258.) The Genoese excluded their rivals, fortified the building, pillaged the magazines of the Venetians, and expelled them from the city. The haughty queen of the Adriatic immediately equipped a fleet to avenge the affront: sailing to Acre, and burning the vessels of their rivals in that harbour, her troops landed, took the disputed church by storm, and drove the Genoese in their turn from the city.

After these mutual injuries the fleets of the two republics met on their proper element. In the first encounter, which was only the prelude to more dreadful combats, the Venetians were victorious; the two states armed with the utmost rapidity; and, in the course of the same summer, they had each dispatched a formidable squadron to the Syrian coast. Off the port of Tyre, the Venetian force of forty-nine galleys and four heavy ships, under Andrea Zeno, the son of the reigning doge, discovered the Genoese admiral, Guilelmo Boccanegra, with four large ships also and forty galleys; and the fleets, after passing the night in observing each other, engaged with fury at sun-rise. The Genoese line was broken at the commencement of the action, and, after a desperate conflict, their squadron was completely defeated with the loss of twenty galleys, and the slaughter of above two thousand men. The houses and property of their countrymen at Tyre were immediately destroyed, and their whole colony in that town made prisoners. But Genoa was still undismayed; a second fleet was equipped, and the war continued with increased obstinacy.

Each state now fortified itself by a foreign alliance, (A.D. 1261.) While Venice obtained the aid of Pisa, the Genoese allied themselves, notwithstanding the prejudices of the Latin world and the excommunications of the pope, with the Greeks; acquired possession of the island of Scio; and, on the capture of Constantinople, were gratified by Palæologus with the destruction of the palace and exchange of the Venetian colony. The policy of the emperor, however, forbade his allies from the persecution of their rivals in the eastern capital; their arrogance and numbers even excited his suspicions; and, removing them from the city, he fixed the seat of the Genoese colony in the suburb of Galata, on the opposite side of the port. A truce between the emperor and Venice shortly left the Genoese to encounter the Venetians single handed; and in five great battles the flag of St. Mark still waved triumphantly. In one victory, off Trapani on the Sicilian coast, which was marked by a horrible carnage, not a single Genoese vessel escaped. Yet, such was the untameable and heroic pride of Genoa that, during eleven years of maritime disaster, no word of submission or peace was ever breathed in her councils; and it was only by the intervention of Louis IX. of France, who needed the assistance of both republics for the transport of his last and fatal expedition against the infidels, that—in the year after the extinction of the Swabian house—a truce was effected between the combatants, (A.D. 1269.) Not a single advantage rested with either party: Venice might indeed recount her series of splendid and barren victories, but the enormous waste of blood and of treasure had fallen equally on her rival and herself.

CHAPTER IV. FROM THE EXTINCTION OF THE HOUSE OF SWABIA, TO THE MIDDLE OF THE FOURTEENTH CENTURY. a.d. 1268-1350

PART I.
State of Italy after the extinction of the Swabian family—Cruelty, ambition, and power of Charles of Anjou—Pontificate of Gregory X.—His ineffectual efforts to reconcile the Italian factions—Troubles at Genoa and in other quarters—Story of Imilda de Lambertazzi—Papal jealousy excited by Charles of Anjou—Rodolph of Hapsburg emperor—Nicholas III.—His policy—Cession of Romagna, &c., to the holy see—Affairs of Sicily, Giovanni di Procida—The Sicilian Vespers—General revolt of the island from Charles of Anjou—Naval defeat of Charles—Peter of Aragon king of Sicily also—Last years, humiliation, and death of Charles—Affairs of Lombardy, rise of the Visconti—Tuscany—Grandeur of Pisa—War between Pisa and Genoa—Battle of Meloria, and extinction of the naval power of Pisa—Story of count Ugolino—Affairs of Pisa after his death—Florence—Creation of the priors of arts—Lawless spirit of the nobles—Enactments against them, ordinances of justice, &c.—Factions of the Black and White Guelfs—Fall of the latter party—Banishment of Dante.

WITH the extinction of the house of Swabia, the great divisions of Italian faction had entirely lost their original signification and ostensible purposes. The triumph of the church was complete. No enemy remained to excite the fears and intrigues of the papacy; the imperial standard no longer floated over Italy, the imperial dignity itself was for many years suspended; and while the Guelf star ruled the ascendant from the Alps to Calabria, the Ghibelin name was almost every where a term of proscription. Yet these war cries of faction, so far from being hushed by the decision of the contest, were only repeated with deeper execrations. The relentless spirit of hatred which had been cherished for successive generations, was inherent in the national character; a senseless word, or an accidental emblem, was a sufficient excuse for the indulgence of the most odious passions; and without one honourable motive or intelligible design, the best feelings and energies of an ardent and intellectual people were extinguished and consumed in struggles which could terminate only in degradation and weakness.

From the middle of the thirteenth century, the unhappy divisions of faction which raged without principle or object, had the effect of depriving Italian history of all general and determinate connexion. For above two hundred years, we shall be at a loss to discover among the numerous states of Italy any moment of common action and union, on which it is possible to rest as an epoch in her annals: we are thrown on a wide and tempestuous sea of endless revolution, and bloodshed, and crime; and yet these are not the storms of barbarism. The refulgence of intellectual light, the revival of poetry and literature, the dawn and noonday of immortal art, play over the troubled scene in strange contrast with its gloomy horrors; with the atrocities of implacable factions, the din of unceasing wars, the appalling silence of domestic tragedy.

In the absence of any natural division which I can give to this long period, I shall conduct the present chapter to the middle of the fourteenth century. The general features which it will present are the fortunes of southern Italy as influenced by the Angevin dynasty of Naples, the removal of the papacy to Avignon, the transformation of the republics of Lombardy into hereditary principalities, the decline of Pisa, the grandeur of Florence, the rivalry of Genoa and Venice, and the changes in the constitution of both those great maritime commonwealths.

By the defeat of Conradin, Charles of Anjou appeared to have consummated his power over his new kingdom of the Sicilies. No rival seemed left to dispute its possession; for though a surviving daughter of Manfred, Constance, was married to the king of Aragon, the pretensions which she might convey to her husband, a sovereign of small power, at the extremity of Europe, were little calculated to raise apprehension. Not contented with the judicial murder of Conradin—an act which excited at the time, as it has done through subsequent ages, general and unqualified abhorrence—Charles satiated his cruelty upon the miserable adherents of the young prince. On the same scaffold on which he had died, Frederic duke of Austria, and several Ghibelin chiefs, were successively led to execution; the revolted barons of Calabria, and all the Sicilian nobles of the same party, who fell into the hands of the French on the suppression of the insurrection in that island, shared a similar fate. The vengeance of the conquerors descended to meaner victims; and besides the massacre of whole troops of Ghibelins at Rome and other places on the continent, the Sicilians were mercilessly butchered wherever they were found in arms. The desire of vengeance with which these cruelties might inspire the islanders, was sharpened by the continued exactions and insults of the French. A deep and silent hatred of their foreign oppressors filled all ranks of the Sicilians, and slowly prepared the way for the horrible explosion which followed.

For many years, however, no reverse shaded the criminal excesses of the new king of the Sicilies; his power, on the contrary, was continually increasing, and he confidently aspired to the same authority over all Italy which the emperors had formerly enjoyed. Florence and her Guelfs had bestowed on him a nominal signiory, and a more substantial advantage was gained by the fall of the marquis Pelavicino, the chief of the Ghibelins of Lombardy, who was again expelled from all the cities which he had governed, to die in exile. The pope had already invested Charles with the office of papal vicar-general in Tuscany; and this new title, by which Clement IV. pretended to constitute him imperial lieutenant during the interregnum of the empire, gave him the supremacy over the Guelf party in that province. Almost all Lombardy was now under Guelf authority; and in a diet of that party, many of the cities chose the king of the Sicilies for their signor, while others more prudently declared that they would have him for a friend, not a master, (A.D. 1269.) He would probably not have contented himself with this relation, if his views had been confined to Italy. But he had designs upon the Greek empire; and he was, besides, diverted from the pursuit of ambition in Italy, by the influence which his brother Louis IX. possessed over him. He was persuaded by that pious monarch to accompany him to Africa, in his last crusade; and his ability lightened the disastrous issue of the expedition, (A.D. 1270.)

Pope Clement IV. had survived the execution of Conradin only a month; and the cardinals, after his death, suffered nearly three years to elapse before they gave another head to the church. At length, after the return of Charles of Anjou from Africa, their choice fell upon an ecclesiastic who held the simple station of archdeacon in Palestine. A long residence in that distant country had separated the new pontiff, who assumed the name of Gregory X., from the factious politics of the Italian church, and engrossed his mind with the sole project of delivering the Holy Land from the infidels. Attaching little importance to the quarrel between the Guelfs and Ghibelins, which was now left without a reasonable motive, he earnestly employed himself, on his appearance in Italy in the year after his election, in labouring to compose the deep-seated animosities of those parties, and to unite the powers of Europe in a general crusade. His policy produced the singular spectacle of a pope acting with sincerity as the common father of Christendom. But his impartial design of restoring tranquillity to Italy, was frustrated by the usual passions of faction, and by the selfish ambition of the Angevin king.

Gregory began the work of pacification in Tuscany, where he found the Ghibelins in subjection or exile. Sienna had been forced by Florence to give the helm to the Guelfs, and to expel their adversaries; even Pisa had been compelled to receive back her Guelf exiles, after an unsuccessful campaign against Charles of Anjou; and the persecuted Ghibelins of other cities, and of Florence especially, burned with exasperation against their oppressors. Attended by Charles, Gregory held a general assembly of the Florentine people on the banks of the Arno; and summoning before him the principal men of both parties, commanded the restoration of the Ghibelins to their homes and property, and the conclusion of a domestic peace both at Florence and in the other Tuscan cities. His authority was respectfully acknowledged; the Ghibelins returned among their fellow-citizens, and Gregory pronounced a sentence of excommunication against the first who should disturb the public happiness. But Charles of Anjou was influenced by far other feelings than the venerable pontiff. He considered such a pacification fatal to his ambitious views; and he did not hesitate to make the Ghibelins of Florence understand, that his partizans had orders to put them all to death, if they did not immediately quit the city. The character of the tyrant gave full weight to his menace. The Ghibelins hastily withdrew, after communicating their danger to the pope; and the indignation of Gregory against Charles and the Florentine Guelfs, was vented in a sentence of interdict which he thundered over the city.

While the Ghibelins were thus persecuted in Tuscany, the opposite party shared a similar fate at Genoa; and the influence of Gregory was equally unavailing to pacify the factions in that city. Two of the four great families, the Spinola and Doria, gaining the favour of the people by their promotion of some democratical changes in the constitution, raised themselves to the government of the republic, and drove their rivals, the Grimaldi and Fieschi, into banishment. Charles of Anjou had plundered some Genoese merchants; and this was sufficient both to induce the successful party to unite their republic with the Ghibelin cause, and to force the exiles into the arms of the Guelfs. (A.D. 1273.) As usual, a furious war was the consequence; but it produced no great event: and though Charles directed the whole Guelf power of Tuscany against the Genoese, while an army of his Provençals invaded Liguria from the western frontier, the republicans defended their territory with courage and success. This was for some years almost the only occasion on which fortune attended the Ghibelin standard.

It need scarcely be told, that the same spirit of discord which thwarted the peaceful exhortations of Gregory in Tuscany and Liguria, prevailed in other provinces; and the reader may be spared the fatigue of numerous transitions through the more obscure and less important vicissitudes of this stormy period. Yet one tragedy, which in its consequences deluged the principal city of Romagna with blood, will not be perused without interest. The noble families of the Gieremei and Lambertazzi of Bologna, the chiefs of the Guelf and Ghibelin factions of their city, had long been opposed in deadly animosity, when Bonifazio Gieremei and Imilda, the daughter of Orlando de' Lambertazzi, forgot the enmity of their houses in the indulgence of a mutual and ardent passion. In one of their secret interviews in the palace of the Lambertazzi, the lovers were betrayed to the brothers of Imilda; she fled at their approach, but they rushed upon Bonifazio, immediately dispatched him with their poisoned daggers, and dragged his body to a deserted court. The unhappy girl, returning to the chamber, discovered his cruel fate by the stains of blood, and traced the corpse to the spot where it had been thrown. It was yet warm, and with mingled agony and hope she endeavoured to suck the venom from its wounds. But she only imbibed the poison into her own veins; and the ill-fated pair were found stretched lifeless together. This sad catastrophe inflamed the hatred of the two houses to desperation; their respective factions in the city espoused their quarrel; they flew to arms; and for forty days the streets and palaces of Bologna were the scenes of a general and furious contest, which terminated in favour of the Guelfs. The Lambertazzi and all their Ghibelin associates were driven from the city; their houses were razed, and twelve thousand citizens were involved in a common sentence of banishment. But the exiles, retiring to the smaller towns of Romagna, were still formidable by their numbers; and offering a rallying point to almost all the Ghibelins of Italy, were joined by so great a force, that, concentrating under count Guide di Montefeltro, they twice defeated the Guelfs, and filled Bologna with consternation, (A.D. 1276.) The reigning faction in that city adopted the usual resource of the times: they chose rather to sacrifice their liberties to a stranger than to submit to the vengeance of their fellow citizens; and imploring the protection of Charles of Anjou, they accepted from his hands the orders of a foreign governor and the protection of a garrison.

In selecting Charles of Anjou for their champion, the popes had vested him with powers which now threatened the independence of the church itself and of all Italy. In whatever quarter Gregory X. directed his exertions for the establishment of peace, he still found the ambitious policy of the Angevin monarch employed in counteracting his labours, and in keeping alive the principles of dissension. This conduct of Charles was sufficient to excite the irritation and jealousy of the pope, and it was probably with the intention of restraining him by the establishment of a rival, that Gregory exhorted the German electors to give an efficient head to the empire, which, since the death of Frederic II., had not been preserved from a state of absolute interregnum by the double nomination of feeble pretenders. The electors, following the advice of the pontiff, bestowed the imperial sceptre upon Rodolph, count of Hapsburg, the founder of the present reigning house of Austria; and their choice was immediately approved by the pope, after receiving a promise from the new emperor to respect ecclesiastical privileges, to confirm the pretensions of the holy see over its temporal domains, and to leave Charles of Anjou undisturbed in the possession of the Sicilies. (A.D. 1273.) That monarch, therefore, was still protected by the church, but the revival of the imperial authority was sufficiently unfavourable to his schemes of universal dominion in Italy. The slender power of Rodolph, whose family have survived to our times to rivet a yoke of iron on the necks of the Italians, was, however, unequal to the assertion of the same supremacy which the Swabian dynasty had exercised beyond the Alps, and he prudently abstained from hazarding his limited resources on the dangerous theatre of Italian politics. Yet Gregory had succeeded in discovering an expedient for holding the Angevin king in awe; and he was on the eve of accomplishing the plan nearest his heart, by engaging the emperor Rudolph and the greatest sovereigns of Europe in a crusade to Palestine, when he was seized with a sudden illness which terminated his life at the most glorious moment of his pontificate, (A.D. 1276.)

After the death of Gregory X., and the brief reigns of three other popes, who successively closed their mortal career within the space of twelve months, the chair of St. Peter was filled by Nicholas III., whose pontificate is a remarkable era in the history of the temporal monarchy of the holy see. This pontiff, treading in the footsteps of Gregory X., though with less disinterested motives, displayed all the arts of a consummate politician in turning the hostile pretensions of Rodolph and of Charles into engines for the aggrandizement of the papacy. The continued authority to which Charles pretended in Tuscany and Lombardy as vicar-general provoked the complaints of Rodolph; and the preparations of the new emperor to conduct an army into Italy excited the fears of the king of the Sicilies. Nicholas assumed the office of mediator between them, and in that capacity obliged Charles to cede to the emperor the alarming authority which he had usurped beyond the frontiers of Naples. But while he enforced this cession of power, which could no longer be dangerous when in the hands of a distant sovereign, he extorted from Rodolph, as the price of his interference, the absolute renunciation of the imperial rights over the March of Ancona, Romagna—the old exarchate of Ravenna—and all other fiefs which the charters and testaments of the early emperors and of the countess Matilda had ever bestowed on the papacy, (A.D. 1278.) By this act the states of the church acquired the same extent in central Italy which they possess at this day: but the papal authority was limited to the imposition of the same oaths of supremacy which the independent nobles and cities of this great territory had formerly taken to the empire. The popes, therefore, for two centuries longer stood only in the place of the emperors, and their general sovereignty did not interfere with internal government.

The successful policy of Nicholas III. was not confined to these measures; and his efforts to reconcile the contending factions at Florence, Sienna, Bologna, and other cities of Tuscany and Romagna, were at least for a time more efficacious than those of Gregory X. had proved. During his life the power of Charles of Anjou was confined to his immediate states; but the death of the great pontiff destroyed the equilibrium, (A.D. 1280.) Charles hastening to Viterbo, where the cardinals had assembled in conclave, succeeded by intimidation and violence in seating one of his own creatures, Martin IV., on the papal throne. With the connivance of this pontiff, the tyrant, by fomenting the troubles of Italy, had rapidly recovered his influence, and was even busily preparing for the transmarine expedition which he meditated against the Greek empire, when he was suddenly awakened from dreams of eastern conquest by a terrific revolt, which the patriotic vengeance, the indefatigable activity, and the deep-laid machinations of one man had been silently maturing in his own dominions.

Giovanni di Procida, a Neapolitan noble, the faithful adherent and confidential friend of Frederic II. and of Manfred, had ranged himself in the cause of his country or party under the standard of Conradin, and escaped, after the disastrous fate of that prince, to the court of Aragon; where he was received by Constance and her husband Peter, with the favour which his loyalty to her unfortunate house might justly demand. But under the lapse of years, and even in this honourable and wealthy security, he could neither forget the tragical death of Manfred and of Conradin, nor the wrongs of his countrymen. His hatred of their foreign oppressors was redoubled, and his hopes of vengeance stimulated, by the intelligence which he constantly received from the Two Sicilies of the relentless and wanton tyranny of the conquerors, and the smothered indignation of the people; and he represented to the Aragonese king the favourable occasion which was before him for the assertion of his wife's claim to the throne of her father, Manfred.

The ambition of Peter was tempted by the prospect of acquiring the crown of the Sicilies; but, though his possession of the maritime countries of Catalonia and Valencia favoured the equipment of a naval armament, the resources of his small kingdom were unequal to a contest with so powerful a monarch as Charles of Anjou; he was destitute of funds to defray the cost of a foreign expedition; and he dreaded to incur the papal displeasure by attacking the great feudatory of the holy see. Procida, whose zeal was undaunted by obstacles and dangers, undertook the arduous and seemingly impracticable office of surmounting all these impediments. Converting the large possessions which he enjoyed by the bounty of Peter and Constance into money to expend in their service, he disguised himself as a Franciscan friar, and resolved to pass into the Sicilies to ascertain by personal observation the temper of his countrymen, and to animate their hatred of their inhuman masters. In this dangerous mission, he found the numerous and warlike followers of Charles too firmly seated in the provinces of the continent to admit the hope of successful insurrection; but in Sicily the prospect was more encouraging, (A.D. 1279.) In the cities and on the coasts, the French governors and licentious soldiery exercised a stem oppression which they aggravated by every species of outrage and cruelty; but they were not sufficiently numerous to occupy the interior of the island, into which they only occasionally penetrated with their extortions and insults. The native barons and peasantry still, therefore, held in their mountains the remains and the love of independence; their courage was animated by the eloquence of Procida, and the expectation which he held out of foreign assistance; and so deep and universal was the abhorrence with which the French had inspired all classes of the islanders, that from the shores to the centre of Sicily, a wide-spreading conspiracy was organized with impenetrable secrecy.

From the future scene of action, the unwearied Procida was borne on the wings of patriotism or vengeance to the court of Constantinople, with intelligence of the immense preparations which Charles of Anjou was making in the Italian ports for the invasion of the eastern empire. He impressed on the emperor, Michael Palæologus, the policy of diverting the arms of the Angevin king from Greece, by exciting rebellion in his own states; and he received the promise of a large subsidy to provide arms for the Sicilians, and to defray the expenses of Aragonese succours. But Palæologus, who had reconciled the Greek empire to the holy see, insisted that the consent of the pope should first be obtained; and Procida, still in the garb of a friar, hastened to Rome with an imperial ambassador. Nicholas III., the secret enemy of Charles, gladly listened to the project; and the skilful mover of these complicated intrigues at last returned in triumph to Spain, with a papal deed which transferred the investiture of the Sicilies to queen Constance. But he had scarcely landed, when the sudden death of Nicholas threatened the subversion of all his labours. The king of Aragon dreaded the hostility of the new pope Martin IV., the creature of Charles; he wavered; and Procida flew to Constantinople again to expedite the subsidy which might confirm his resolution, (A.D. 1281.) Palæologus had now no longer any terms to keep with the papacy. Martin IV. had already excommunicated him for relapsing into the Greek heresy, and converted the projected expedition of Charles into a crusade against his empire; he therefore cheerfully entrusted Procida with 25,000 ounces of gold for the secret diversion of the storm. The money was well expended for his purpose; it renovated the confidence of Peter, and he equipped an Aragonese fleet and army of 10,000 men, and sailed to the African coast under pretence of attacking the Saracens, there to await the course of events, while Procida crossed over into Sicily, and traversing the island in different directions and under various disguises, ripened the execution of his plots. Although the ramifications of the conspiracy had, during two years, embraced the opposite extremities of Europe, the secret had been preserved with universal fidelity; and it was at last an accidental outrage which provoked its appalling disclosure.

On Easter Monday, in the year 1282, the citizens of Palermo were moving in procession according to an annual custom, to hear the vesper service at the church of Montreal, three miles from their capital, when a young maiden of rank and beauty was brutally insulted in the crowd by a French soldier. The wretch was instantly sacrificed to the fury of the spectators, and pierced with his own sword; the Sicilians had been disarmed by their tyrants, but the moment of frightful retribution had arrived; the long stifled cry of vengeance was raised; the few French in the procession were overpowered and murdered, and the people rushing back to the city, while the church bells were yet tolling for vespers, possessed themselves of weapons, and began an indiscriminate slaughter of the foreigners. Not a Frenchman in Palermo escaped; four thousand perished on that first evening; the example was imitated in other places of the island, and the work of death did not cease until eight thousand French had been included in the horrible massacre of the Sicilian Vespers.

This sudden tragedy had no sooner commenced, than Procida and his conspirators seized the occasion, and all Sicily burst into the flames of insurrection. Where the lives of the French were spared, they were driven out of the island, and in less than a month the national deliverance had been effected, and an invitation dispatched to Peter of Aragon to assume and defend the sovereignty of the kingdom.

Charles of Anjou might perhaps still have recovered the possession of Sicily, if the ferocity of his temper had not wrought the spirit of the people to desperation. Unprepared for resistance, terrified at his great power, and finding that Peter, did not immediately arrive to their assistance, they had scarcely expelled their oppressors before they besought the clemency of Charles, and offered to return to obedience upon condition that their revolt should be pardoned, and their liberties respected. But the tyrant would listen to no accommodation, and vowed an unsparing revenge. Assembling the forces which he had prepared for the Greek war, he crossed into the island with five thousand gens-d'armes and a quantity of infantry, and laid siege to Messina. The people of that city, hopeless of mercy, made an obstinate defence, and the crafty Peter, after delaying until events had assured him of the constancy and resolution of his new subjects, at length came to their assistance. His squadron, fitted solely for war, was better armed than the fleet of half equipped galleys and transports into which Charles, expecting to find no enemy on the seas, had hastily thrown his troops; and the hardy Catalan sailors of Peter were commanded, too, by Roger di Loria, like Procida, a noble Neapolitan refugee, who became the most famous admiral of his times. The haughty Charles was compelled to decline a combat under such disadvantages, and to save his army by a precipitate retreat from being cut off from the continent and starved in the island. He had just come to raise the siege of Messina and to carry off his land forces, when Di Loria appeared off the port; captured twenty-nine of the French galleys; pursued the remainder of their fleet to the Calabrese shore, where Charles had landed his troops, and there burnt the whole number before the eyes of the baffled tyrant. This exploit of Di Loria sealed the deliverance of Sicily, and firmly established Peter of Aragon, who had already received the insular crown from the barons at Palermo, in the possession of his new kingdom.

Charles of Anjou had hitherto triumphantly advanced in a career of flagitious cruelty and inordinate ambition. He had unjustly won the kingdom of the Sicilies, and stained his conquest, in the field and on the scaffold, with torrents of blood; he had founded and exercised a tyrannical influence over all Italy by the proscription of the whole Ghibelin party, and with his formidable powers, the subversion of the eastern empire seemed an easy consummation of greatness. But his pride was now to be levelled with the dust, and the reverses and humiliation of his last years might offer to mankind an imperfect retribution for a previous life of successful crime. The destruction of his fleet was a fatal blow. With the command of the seas he lost the means of employing his great army in the Sicilian or Greek war, and this first disaster was followed by a long series of misfortunes and political errors. He suffered Peter of Aragon to amuse him, and to gain time for strengthening himself in Sicily, by futile and protracted overtures for the decision of their respective claims by a single combat; his eldest son was provoked in his absence to a rash engagement off the Neapolitan coast, and taken prisoner by Roger di Loria; and when he had himself at length equipped a great naval armament in the harbours of his Provençal dominions, his confidence in his own fortunes was gone. He consumed in irresolution and in vain efforts to obtain the release of his son, the time which should have been employed in vigorous action, until, deluded by his enemies with hollow negotiations, and overwhelmed with disappointment and shame at the downfall of his grandeur, his health broke under the conflict of inward agony, and he sank into the grave only three years after the revolt of Sicily, (A.D. 1285.)

While the Sicilians were preparing to cast off the yoke which they had so long endured, another revolution was in progress at the opposite extremity of Italy. The people of Milan and of great part of Lombardy elevated the noble house of the Visconti to sovereign power on the ruin of the Torriani; but a change of masters produced no revival of freedom, and the descendants of the heroes of Legnano, after having sacrificed a glorious inheritance before the madness of faction, surrendered themselves a second time to the power of hereditary lords without an effort, perhaps even without a wish, for the recovery of republican liberty. During the sovereignty of Martino della Torre, the first signer of Milan, pope Urban IV., who was incensed at his alliance with the Ghibelin Pelavicino, had availed himself of a disputed election to the archiepiscopal see of the city in the year 1263, to set aside the pretensions of a member of the Torriani family, and to nominate in his place Otho Visconti, a Milanese canon of high birth. The injurious treatment with which Martino resented the partiality of the pope by plundering his favourite, drove the new archbishop to range himself with the party of the defeated and banished nobles. The chief of a faction rather than the father of his flock, Visconti maintained in exile a civil war against Martino and his successors for eleven years with unvaried ill fortune and unshaken resolution. But the noble outlaws whom he commanded were still formidable enemies; betaking themselves to mercenary service, as was common in their desperate circumstances, they had formed a well disciplined band of gens-d'armerie; and the archbishop, swelling their numbers with other adventurers, was at length enabled to approach towards Milan, (A.D. 1277.) Napoleon della Torre, the reigning signor, advanced from the city, also with his cavalry, to encounter him; but, despising an enemy whom he had so often defeated, he suffered himself to be surprised in the night, and was captured with several of his relatives, while others of his house were slain in the rout. This calamity extinguished the fortunes of the Torriani. The maintenance of a mercenary cavalry and the expenses of a long contest with the exiles, had compelled Napoleon to impose heavy taxes on the Milanese; their affections were alienated, they rose in arms on the news of his captivity, and electing the archbishop Otho for their signor, they joyfully welcomed his return to their city with the noble exiles his partizans.

From this period Otho Visconti reigned at Milan with uninterrupted prosperity until the termination of his life. It does not appear that he abused the absolute powers with which the people had invested him; but his ambition was displayed in his projects for securing to his family the hereditary possession of sovereignty. Destining his nephew Matteo Visconti to succeed him, he first induced the people of Milan, ten years after his own accession (A.D. 1287), to invest him with the title of captain of the people, and afterwards obtained for him the same dignity at Novara and Vercelli. At a later period his influence procured for Matteo from Adolphus of Nassau, emperor elect, the office of imperial vicar-general in Lombardy, and with it a claim to universal supremacy in the province, over great part of which the archbishop himself possessed more substantial authority. Thus, when Otho closed a long and eventful life at the age of eighty-eight years, and in the full vigour of intellect, his policy had laid the foundations for the permanent grandeur of his house, and Matteo Visconti assumed without opposition the signiory of Milan and other cities of inferior importance, (A.D. 1295.)

There is little in these vicissitudes of despotism to engage the attention of the reader, and I gladly turn to survey the condition of the Tuscan republics at the same period. In the decline of the Ghibelin cause after the defeat of Conradin, Pisa, whose strength lay on the field of waters, was unable to maintain alone a contest by land against Charles of Anjou, the Florentines, and other Tuscan Guelfs. (A.D. 1276.) She therefore cheaply purchased peace by receiving her own Guelf exiles back within her walls, and confiding to them a principal share in the government. The virtuous policy of Gregory X. had already reconciled the republic with the church; she was at peace with her ancient rival Genoa; and the Guelf nobles who returned from banishment, while their revenues augmented the public wealth, enjoyed their restoration to the bosom of their country in moderation and tranquillity. Thus released from foreign and undisturbed by domestic enemies, Pisa, so far from suffering humiliation or loss of power by the forced pacification to which she had submitted, flourished with an astonishing increase of prosperity and wealth. The public security produced so rapid and immense an extension of commerce, that, in the few years which immediately preceded her fatal war against Genoa, her revenues had doubled their former amount. The epoch of her meridian splendour, and of the sudden and total extinction of her maritime grandeur, is all contained within the narrow compass of three summers, (A.D. 1281.) In the year before the Genoese war, her power had attained its greatest height; she possessed wealthy colonies at Constantinople and Acre, which carried on a great trade with the Greeks and Saracens; she was mistress of Sardinia, Elba, and great part of Corsica; and from all these foreign possessions, enormous wealth flowed both into the coffers of the state and of her private citizens. Among these Pisa numbered many lords who, in their fortunes and titles, in the extent of their insular fiefs, and the pomp of their retinues, might rival the power and the magnificence of princes.

This happy condition of the republic contained the germs of destruction. The general influx of riches, and the rapid accumulation of the national resources, cherished restless pride and overweening ambition; and in this spirit the Pisans were ill disposed to preserve any friendly relations with their old enemies and perpetual rivals the Genoese. The pursuit of the same commerce in the Levant, the clashing interests of their colonies on the shores of the Greek empire and of Syria, and their common pretensions to the sovereignty of Corsica, all kept alive the long jealousy and hatred of the two republics; but their last and decisive struggle was provoked by the wanton aggressions of Pisa. She protected the piratical enterprises of a Corsican noble against the vengeance of Genoa; her colonists at Acre instigated the people of that city to pillage and expel the Genoese residents, and her vessels insolently seized a Genoese galley on its homeward passage from Sicily. Satisfaction for these outrages was in vain demanded by the injured state, and both republics eagerly appealed to arms.

The first two years of the memorable contest which ensued were consumed in partial encounters, (A.D. 1282.) So nice was the equality of strength, and so serious the mutual conviction that national honour and maritime dominion were irretrievably staked on the quarrel, that both Pisa and Genoa cautiously avoided its decision until they could concentrate all their forces for one gigantic effort. Their scattered seamen were gradually collected from the distant pursuit of commerce, their fleets were sedulously exercised in desultory operations, and while all their merchant vessels were embargoed in their ports for the public service, above one hundred new galleys were constructed by both parties. But while the great issue of the struggle still hung in suspense, several disasters were omens of the fading fortunes of Pisa. In the first year she lost in a furious hurricane above half of a squadron which had ravaged the Ligurian coast; the next naval campaign afforded no counterpoise to this misfortune, and yielded no advantage in return for a vast expenditure; and early in the third summer she experienced a double reverse. An expedition on its passage to Sardinia with troops and treasure fell into the hands of the Genoese, and the squadron of twenty-four galleys which convoyed it was totally defeated, after an obstinate engagement, in which four of the number were sunk and eight captured, with fifteen hundred men.

These misfortunes only inflamed the Pisans with wounded pride and the desire of a signal vengeance. The treasures of the state were nearly exhausted, but the patriotism of the great families repaired the deficiency. They equipped at their own expense some one, some two, others more wealthy, five and six galleys, and one house even armed eleven. In this manner, by the public resources and individual sacrifices, an immense fleet of one hundred and three galleys was formed; and yet the Genoese could oppose it with superior numbers. The armed galley of those ages carried from two to three hundred men, and above fifty thousand Pisans and Genoese were therefore to contend on the waters for the mastery: an incredible force for two cities with only a slender maritime territory, if the facts were not perfectly authenticated.

The Pisan fleet was no sooner equipped than it put to sea, and appearing before Genoa, insulted that city by a discharge of arrows tipt with silver. (A.D. 1284.) This curious bravado failed in provoking the Genoese, whose preparations were not fully completed, to sally from their port; but the Pisans had only returned to the Arno a very few days when they were followed by their enemies, who stationed themselves off the mouth of the river, near the little isle of Meloria, with above one hundred and thirty galleys. The Genoese admiral, Oberto Doria, concealing thirty galleys behind the island, offered the Pisans battle with an apparent equality of numbers. The challenge was joyfully accepted, the Pisans descended the Arno, and the two mighty armaments closed, galley to galley, in a general and furious conflict. Every excitement of honour and courage, of hatred and despair, swelled the relentless carnage of that day; but there are few circumstances for relation in these naval combats, and the horror of one great scene of various and indiscriminate slaughter must be imagined rather than described. The battle long raged without perceptible advantage to either party, until the hidden reserve of the Genoese shot from behind the isle of Meloria, and bore down upon the fight. The vessel of the Pisan admiral, and a second galley which displayed the great standard of the republic, were overpowered by this reinforcement and captured; and at that fatal moment, the too famous count Ugolino gave the signal of flight to the division which he commanded. The naval glories of Pisa sank for ever: five thousand of her bravest citizens had perished, eleven thousand more were conducted to a lingering captivity, and it became the common saying of Tuscany, that thenceforth he who would see Pisa must visit her at Genoa.

Count Ugolino della Gherardesca, on whose name and story the greatest of Italian bards has bestowed a fearful immortality, was the chief of one of the most distinguished families of Pisa, and had long borne a conspicuous part in the factions of the republic. Though his house had always been attached to the dominant party in the state, he had given his sister in marriage to the representative of the Visconti family, the leader of the Pisan Guelfs. This alliance, which appears to have been dictated by projects of selfish aggrandizement, rendered count Ugolino justly suspected by all orders of his countrymen. His former friends of the Ghibelin faction viewed it as a desertion of their cause; the Guelfs received their new associate with the distrust and repugnance engendered by long animosity, and the most virtuous citizens of the state regarded the unnatural union of the two great houses with apprehension and jealousy. These feelings, and the prevalence of Ghibelin influence among the people, occasioned, in 1274, the banishment of the Guelf party and the imprisonment of Ugolino, who was only released to share their exile in the following year, and to assist in their parricidal efforts against the city of their birth.

The pacification of 1276 restored count Ugolino, with the Guelfs, to his political station in Pisa; and, though his odious alliance with the enemies of his party and of his country was not easily forgiven by his fellow-citizens, he gradually recovered the former influence which his high rank and possessions had obtained for him in the state. He was associated with the podestá and another noble in the command of the Pisan squadron, and his flight from the disastrous scene of Meloria is attributed by the chroniclers of the republic to the treacherous design of enfeebling his country, that he might raise a tyranny upon her ruin. This accusation is, perhaps, scarcely borne out by the recorded circumstances of the battle, nor is it easy to reconcile the confused and perplexing narrative of the subsequent conduct of Ugolino. Yet we may collect from the general mass of evidence, that the bad ambition of this man was directed to the subversion of the Pisan liberties; that if he did not promote the first disasters of his country, he traitorously converted them into engines for the security of his power; and that, by alternately intriguing with the opposite factions, and by opposing difficulties to the ransom of the Pisan captives at Genoa, whose return he dreaded, he laboured to perpetuate his arbitrary authority.

The defeat of Meloria presented a tempting occasion to the Guelf cities of Tuscany to complete the humiliation and ruin of the only

Ghibelin state of their province. Florence, Lucca, Sienna, Pistoia, all ungenerously coalesced with the avowed purpose of razing the walls of Pisa. Forgetting the Ghibelin principles of Genoa, they allied themselves with her against the more immediate object of their hatred, and engaged to besiege Pisa by land, while the Genoese galleys should blockade the Arno. The unhappy Pisans could discover no better method of averting the destruction which threatened them, than by confiding the dictatorial administration of their affairs to count Ugolino, whose Guelf connexions might conciliate their foes, and whose arts had probably instigated the hostility of that faction. The dangerous alternative relieved them from foreign conquest; the new ruler of Pisa, by address, by bribery, by the shameful sacrifice of the castles and territory of the republic, succeeded in dissolving the Guelf league (A.D. 1285); and for years after the state was subjected to his sway. But he at length fell; and the unworthy minister of retribution was the archbishop Ruggieri degl' Ubaldini, the associate of his iniquitous projects, whom he had refused to reward with a share of his ill-gotten power. In concert with the principal Ghibelin families, the archbishop exasperated the people by unveiling the treacherous policy of Ugolino. The tyrant was attacked in his palace, overpowered, and thrown into prison with his two youngest sons and two of his grand-children. After suffering the count and these four youthful victims to remain for some months in the usual state of confinement, the inhuman archbishop caused the key of their prison to be thrown into the Arno, and the Pisans left them to perish by hunger, (A.D. 1288.) In his last agonies, says the historian Villani, the count was heard from without confessing his guilt, but no priest was allowed to approach the "tower of Famine." The crimes of Ugolino might have demanded expiation on the scaffold, but the atrocity of his punishment has deservedly branded his enemies with eternal infamy, and the horror and pity of mankind may still echo the stern reproach with which the indignant numbers of Dante apostrophized "the modern Thebes"—the murderess of his guiltless offspring.

The fall of Ugolino threw the administration of Pisa entirely into the hands of the Ghibelins, and occasioned an immediate coalition of all the Guelf states of Tuscany against her. Since the death of Charles of Anjou, Florence had become the acknowledged queen of this party in the province, while the city of Arezzo under her bishop had declared for the opposite faction. This martial prelate at first raised the Ghibelin cause by his successes against the Siennese, but he was shortly defeated and slain by the Florentines at the battle of Campaldino, the most sanguinary encounter which had been fought in Tuscany since the engagement on the Arbia. (A.D. 1289.) After this event, the Pisans had to contend unassisted against the whole Guelf power; but notwithstanding the dreadful reverses which they had suffered, they maintained the war with heroic resolution. Choosing for their general count Guido di Montefeltro, one of the most celebrated captains of the age, they succeeded in a few years under his prudent and vigorous conduct in recovering, by force or stratagem, all the castles which Ugolino had yielded to their enemies; and they at last procured peace from the Guelf league upon honourable terms. (A.D. 1293.) They again restored their Guelf exiles to their rights, and granted the Florentines an immunity from duties in their port; but they preserved the ancient limits of their territory. It was six years later, however, before they could obtain tolerable conditions from their proud victors the Genoese (A.D. 1299); and when the pacification released the surviving captives of Meloria from a miserable imprisonment of fifteen years in the dungeons of Genoa, they had wasted from eleven to less than one thousand persons.

Notwithstanding the courage of the Pisans, they were less indebted to their own arms for their successes against the Guelf league, than to the domestic troubles which engrossed the attention of the Florentines. The provisions of the accommodation which Nicholas III. had effected between the Guelfs and Ghibelins of the republic, had admitted the latter to a share in the signiory; and Florence was for a short time governed by fourteen buonomini, of whom six were Ghibelins. But this division of power contained in itself the principles of discord; the executive council was constantly the scene of dissensions; and the weaker party were once more and finally expelled. It would seem that this revolution was made the occasion, by the commercial orders, for strengthening the democratical character of the constitution, at the expense of the nobles. Some of the latter order had found their way into the council of buonomini; but the executive power was now transferred exclusively to a signiory of six members, to be chosen for the six quarters of the city, one from each of the greater arts, except that of the lawyers, whose judicial occupations already gave them an essential share in the public authority, (A.D. 1282.) This form of supreme magistrature lasted to the extinction of the republic, and may therefore deserve our particular attention. The six priors of the arts and of liberty, as they were termed, were elected every two months, and obliged to reside, during their period of office, in the palace of the state; which they were forbidden to quit, and where they were maintained, at a common table, by the public funds. The priors going out of office, jointly with the chiefs and councils of the seven greater arts, and with assistants named by themselves (arroti), chose their successors. But we shall find this form of election modified at a later period.

Though the nobles were not yet restricted from entering the companies of arts, and though many of their order, enrolling themselves in these commercial bodies, ranked among the principal merchants of Florence, the majority of the ancient aristocracy were now wholly excluded from public office; and the members of government could only arrive at their dignity by virtue of a commercial and democratic station. But though the noble families could offer no direct opposition to the popular enactments, which thus deprived them of all share in the government, they revenged themselves by outraging the public peace, and by habitually setting the laws at defiance. With insolent confidence in the aid of their numerous relatives, in the services of their domestics and various retainers, and in the strength of their castellated houses, the individuals of almost all the great families held the authority of the magistracy in open contempt. The peace of the city was constantly disturbed by the bloody feuds which divided the nobility among themselves; and they agreed only in oppressing the lower citizens. The latter had no protection from their outrages and assassinations. If the civic magistrates attempted to bring a noble criminal to justice, his whole family rose to rescue and protect him, and seldom failed to wreak their vengeance upon his accusers. The citizens were compelled to endure every injury from an order of men who were above the laws, and against whom no witness dared appear; or if the people attempted to support their magistrates, the whole city was filled with uproar and slaughter.

The insolence and tyranny of the nobility at length excited the violent indignation of an individual of their own order, who had associated himself in one of the commercial companies. During his short period of office as a prior, Giano della Bella seized the moment when the people were assembled in parliament, to suggest and carry some remarkable enactments for reducing the nobles to obedience to the laws. The most effectual and praiseworthy of these was the creation of a gonfalonier of justice, with a permanent guard of one thousand citizens, which was shortly increased to four times that number. The duty of this officer—the sword of the civil power—was to execute the commands of the magistracy and the sentences of the law. His guard was selected from the different divisions of the city, and distributed into companies; the commanders of which—termed also gonfaloniers—were resolved upon particular occasions into a college or corporate body, which shared in the public deliberations. When the gonfalonier of justice hung out his gonfalon or banner from the windows of the public palace, the commanders of companies immediately repaired to him with their followers; and he marched at the head of this national militia against the powerful or refractory offender. The gonfalonier of justice was at first subordinate to the signiory of priors; but the importance of his functions shortly occasioned his elevation to an equality with that body, and terminated in placing him at their head. Like them, he was elected every two months, and resided in the public palace; with them he completed the signiory; and he was, in effect, the first magistrate of the state.

While this new institution was framed to curb the lawless spirit of the nobility, a less justifiable measure was adopted by the popular party against that class: they were declared incapable of ever holding the office of priors, or of enrolling themselves in the companies of arts, (A.D. 1292.) Thirty-seven of the greatest families of Florence were incapacitated by name from these rights of citizenship, and entered on the list of nobles or grandi. Thus, by a singular provision, the title of nobility was coupled with an exclusion from the enjoyment of public honours, and became not only an useless incumbrance, but a punishment. At the instigation of Giano della Bella, it was provided by the same decree, that, to guard against the intimidation of special witnesses, the voice of public report, attested by two respectable persons, should be received as sufficient evidence against any nobleman.

It has been often and truly observed, that these *Ordinances of Justice,* as they were styled, which deprived the nobility of political rights, were scandalously unjust; and that the last especially, was a violation of those immutable principles of equity which forbid us, on any reasons of expediency, to risk the sacrifice of innocent blood. In arming the executive power against the insubordination of the great families, Giano della Bella had been fully justified; and it does not appear that his zeal for the liberties of the lower people was sullied by any sinister views of personal aggrandizement; but his prejudice and animosity against the nobles were wrought to this persecuting spirit by the natural obstinacy and violence of his disposition. This defect of character occasioned his destruction. Many of the rich burgesses were jealous of his influence with the common people, and availed themselves of the imprudent severity with which he persisted in reforming some abuses of internal regulation among the companies of arts, to excite dangerous enemies against him. Deserted by the fickle citizens, he was driven, in little more than two years, into the exile in which he died. (A.D. 1294.) His banishment, says Villani, caused a considerable change in the administration of the state; the artisans and lower people lost their influence, and the government remained in the hands of the rich citizens. But the enactments which he had suggested against the ancient aristocracy remained in full operation, and became the lasting charter of the republic.

The exile of Giano della Bella procured little repose for his ungrateful country. Florence was still increasing in extent and opulence; and this is the era at which, in the pride of architectural embellishment, she followed the example of Pisa—the first Italian city which ennobled the use of commercial wealth by the magnificence of her public structures. The ancient palace of the signiory, the Palazzo Vecchio, and more than one pious edifice, remain to attest the riches and grandeur of Florence at the period before us; yet the prosperity which is indicated by these splendid works, continued to be alloyed by all the evils of faction. The spirit of the nobles yet remained to be broken by ages of proscription; and it was, above all, the elevation of the commercial aristocracy which they could least patiently endure. One of these new families, the Cerchi, which had amassed an enormous fortune by trade, eclipsed the ancient lustre of the great and noble house of Donati; and a law suit had already inflamed the rivalry between them, when accident afforded a pretext for political hostility. In the little Tuscan state of Pistoia, a private quarrel, between two branches of the principal Guelf family of the Cancellieri, had been attended with even more horrible atrocities than were usual in Italian feuds. The enmity of these relatives, to whose common descent some caprice had given the distinction of Neri and Bianchi (black and white), was shared by numerous partizans; and the magistrates of Pistoia could only stop the effusion of blood in their streets, by committing the government of their republic to the temporary custody of the leading Guelf state of their province. The signiory of Florence impartially assumed the friendly office of restoring order in Pistoia, and removed the chiefs of both factions to their own city, in the hope of thus reconciling them. (A.D. 1300.) But this imprudent measure only introduced the contagion within their own walls. When the strangers arrived at Florence, the Donati bestowed their hospitality upon the Neri, the Cerchi upon the Bianchi. The rival hosts, who wanted only an excuse for open hostility, eagerly embraced the quarrel of their guests; the example spread with fatal rapidity, and all Florence was speedily divided into the virulent factions of the Black and White Guelfs, of which Corso Donati and Vieri de' Cerchi were the leaders.

Though the White Guelfs showed in the sequel a disposition to coalesce with the Ghibelins, it cannot be discovered that any question of political rights was mixed up with the intestine hostility which now raged throughout Florence, or that the great parties which owed their origin to this insufficient cause of division, proposed any intelligible object beyond the gratification of that factious spirit which was so congenial to the Italian temperament. The principles of public virtue could as little justify the White as the Black Guelfs; and the latter prevailed in the contest only because their leader, Corso Donati, a bold, turbulent, designing man, was beyond all comparison superior in the arts of command and intrigue to his feeble rival Cerchi. At first the White Guelfs had the advantage, and contrived to banish their adversaries; but they excited the enmity of pope Boniface VIII., by refusing to accept his mediation; and the pontiff, who had enlisted a French prince (Charles of Valois, the brother of Philip the Fair) in the service of the church, with the intention of employing him in the Sicilian wars, now dispatched him with his gens-d'armerie to restore peace at Florence, under the new title of Pacificator of Tuscany. If Cerchi and the principal men among the White Guelfs had possessed energy and hardihood to break at once with the pope, they might easily have prevented the entrance of Charles into their city; but they hesitated, suffered him to introduce his gens-d'armerie into Florence, and were ruined. Charles, disregarding his solemn promises, betrayed one of the gates to Corso Donati and the Black exiles, imprisoned the chiefs of the Whites, and suffered their palaces to be burnt, their property to be pillaged and confiscated, and several of their persons to be assassinated. After permitting, during five months, every disorder to the victorious party, and enriching himself with a share of the heavy fines which they extorted, Valois quitted Florence and Tuscany, pursued by the execrations of the province which he had entered to pacify. But before his departure, six hundred of the principal White Guelfs whose destruction he had effected, were finally proscribed and driven into exile. (A.D. 1302.) One interesting circumstance in this revolution has deserved to survive the long oblivion of ages. Among the White Guelfs who were included in the sentence of banishment and proscription, was Dante, or more properly. Durante Alighieri, who had held the office of prior while that party acquired ascendancy in the state. It was during a lingering and cruel exile, which lasted unto his death, that he composed or completed his vision of Hell, Purgatory, and Paradise, the Divina Commedia, one of the most sublime and original works of human genius. Seeking a refuge at the courts of the Della Scala, lords of Verona, and other Ghibelin chieftains, he tasted all the bitterness of dependence and poverty; and, pouring out in terrific invective and political satire the indignation of a lofty and imaginative spirit which had darkened in adversity, he filled the awful scenes of his great poem with the personages of contemporary history, and branded the crimes and dissensions of his age in numbers that will live for ever.

PART II.
Affairs of the pontificate—Boniface VIII.—Continued wars for the possession of Sicily—Charles II. of Naples—Frederic, king of Sicily—Miserable end of Boniface VIII.—Translation of the popedom to Avignon—Condition of Lombardy at the beginning of the fourteenth century—Frequent revolutions—Numerous petty signors or tyrants—Power and reverses of Matteo Visconti—Growth of respect in Italy for the imperial authority—The emperor Henry VII. in Italy—Submission of Lombardy to his authority—New troubles in that province—Guelf league formed by Florence against the emperor—Critical situation, activity, and death of Henry VII.—Robert, king of Naples—His projects of universal sovereignty over Italy—Wars between the Guelfs and Ghibelins in Tuscany—Rise of Castruccio Castracani, prince of Lucca—Hostilities in Lombardy—Successes of the Ghibelins—Siege of Genoa—Grandeur of Matteo Visconti—His death—Successes of Castruccio Castracani—Danger of Florence and the Tuscan Guelfs—The emperor Louis IV. of Bavaria in Italy—Brilliant fortunes and death of Castruccio—Rise of the house of Gonzaga at Mantua.

UNTIL the interference of Boniface VIII. in the Florentine troubles, I have not had occasion for some time to speak of the affairs of the pontificate, or scarcely to mention even the name of a pope. From the death of Martin IV., which occurred immediately after that of Charles of Anjou, until the accession of Boniface, ten years later, there is not, indeed, much in the papal history to require observation. The intermediate period, which was filled with the reigns of pontiffs whose rapid succession deprived the holy see of its usual influence in Italian politics, is remarkable only for the power which the noble Roman family of Colonna acquired by the favour of Nicholas IV. But the intriguing and active character of Boniface VIII. renewed the ascendancy of the papacy. This pope owed his seat, on the willing abdication of his predecessor, Celestinus V. (a poor fanatic, whom he afterwards persecuted to the grave), to the friendship of Charles II., king of Naples; and the support with which he repaid that monarch closely interweaves the affairs of his pontificate with those of the Two Sicilies.

During the contest between Charles of Anjou and Peter of Aragon, Philip III. of France, siding with his relative, had invaded the kingdom of Aragon, which Martin IV., by a sentence of deposition against Peter, had assumed the right of transferring to Charles of Valois, second son of the French monarch. Peter had thus to fight for the crown of Sicily within his native dominions, but he successfully defended himself; and on his death, which was embraced in the same year with that of Charles of Anjou, of Philip, and of Martin, he bequeathed Aragon to Alphonso his eldest, and Sicily to James his second son. The general war languished for three years after the death of all these potentates, until a pacification was effected under the arbitration of our first English Edward, (A.D. 1288.) Charles II. of Anjou, who had remained in captivity since his defeat by Roger di Loria, was released, to assume his father's crown of Naples; but he made a formal cession of the throne of Sicily to James of Aragon, and promised to obtain a similar renunciation from Charles of Valois of his imaginary claims upon the kingdom of Aragon.

Charles II. was no sooner at liberty than he violated all the conditions of the treaty; and pope Nicholas IV. at once placed the crown of the Two Sicilies on his head, and absolved him from the oaths by which he had sealed the pacification. Charles of Valois, too, refused to renounce his pretensions over Aragon, and the war immediately recommenced in all quarters. Attacked at once by the French, by the fulminations of the church, and by the king of Castile, who entered the league against him, Alphonso was unable to defend his inheritance, and could not be expected to sacrifice it to his brother's interest. He concluded a peace with his enemies, by which he promised to recall all the subjects of Aragon from the Sicilian service, and to exhort his brother to renounce the insular crown, (A.D. 1295.) On these conditions, Charles of Valois was to abandon his pretensions, and the church, on receipt of a tribute, to restore the Aragonese king to her bosom. But Alphonso died immediately afterwards, and James, quitting Sicily, and leaving the administration of the island in the hands of his third brother Frederic, assumed the crown of Aragon.

The first service which Boniface VIII. rendered to his patron Charles II. of Naples, was to induce the new king of Aragon to conclude a shameful treaty, by which he not only confirmed the renunciation of Sicily, but engaged, if the Sicilians should continue to assert their independence, to aid in conquering the island for the Angevin monarch. In return for these infamous conditions Charles II. bestowed his daughter on James, and the father of Christendom rewarded him with the investiture of Sardinia and Corsica, which, as belonging to the Pisans and Genoese, were not his to grant. But the Sicilians had too lively a remembrance of French tyranny, and cherished the love of freedom too warmly, to submit to the Angevin king, or tamely to suffer their rights to be bartered by the royal conspirators. The venerable Procida was still the adviser of the Sicilian barons, when, solemnly abjuring their allegiance to the man who had basely deserted them, they placed the crown of Sicily on the head of his brother Frederic. (A.D. 1296.) The long wars which the ambition of the popes and of the house of Anjou had already occasioned for the possession of the island were now kindled anew, and cruelly ravaged both the Sicilies, continental and insular, for several years. Frederic, who proved himself an able and courageous monarch, at first carried his arms into Calabria, and, together with the invincible admiral of Sicily, Roger di Loria, gained several victories over the Angevin party. But successive misfortunes soon began to thicken around him: upon some disgust Di Loria deserted his service; his own brother James, as champion of the church, led an army into Sicily against him, and overran half the island; and, when the Aragonese sovereign, struck with tardy remorse for this cruel and ungenerous attack, at last withdrew his army, and refused to be the instrument of his brother's ruin, Boniface VIII. enticed Charles of Valois from the distant wars of Flanders to another invasion of Sicily, (A.D. 1299.) But the patient valour and the solid talents of Frederic and the constancy of the Sicilians triumphed over every adverse vicissitude. Too weak to hazard a general engagement with the formidable army which Valois had led into Sicily from Naples, Frederic harassed the enemy with continual skirmishes, interrupted their supplies and communications, and left the climate to do the rest. Its ravages were so great that the French prince was compelled to evacuate the island; and Charles II. and the pope, at length despairing of their cause, concluded a peace with Frederic, and guaranteed to him for life the insular crown with the title of king of Trinacria, upon condition that he should hold it as a fief of the holy see, to be restored after his death to the house of Anjou: an engagement which it was easy to foresee would never be fulfilled, (A.D. 1302.)

Boniface VIII. survived this pacification only one year; and was visited in the miserable termination of his life with a just punishment for a career of pride and worldly ambition. The disaffection which two cardinals of the Colonna family betrayed in the sacred college had induced him to persecute their whole house, and to expel them by treachery and by arms from all their domains. Philip the Fair of France—a monster of inhumanity, whose subsequent proscription of the

Templars has doomed his memory to eternal opprobrium—afforded an asylum to the Colonna from enmity to Boniface; and this act widened the breach which several subjects of altercation had already occasioned between him and the pope, notwithstanding the attachment of the latter to the kindred house of Anjou. After some outrageous proceedings on both sides, Philip prepared a signal vengeance against the pontiff. He secretly dispatched a French knight with one of the Colonna and some followers into Italy to seize the person of Boniface, and probably to assassinate him. The conspirators, arriving near Annagni, where Boniface resided, and being joined by the partizans of the Colonna, surprised the papal palace, which they held for three days. But while their leaders hesitated in irresolution on the fate of their captive, and their followers were pillaging his immense treasures, they were attacked and driven from the palace by the papal adherents. The pope was thus rescued, but only committed his person to the protection of the Orsini, the rivals of the Colonna, to find himself still a prisoner. Indignation at the first outrage, acting upon an aged frame and a haughty temper, had destroyed his health and unsettled his reason; and the fresh aggravation of insult threw him into a paroxysm of rage and insanity in which he died. (A.D. 1303.) Charles II. of Naples, a less unamiable character, terminated his days more happily. The last years of his reign were laudably devoted to repair the evils of a long war; and he closed his life in tranquillity; leaving his rival, Frederic of Sicily, to survive him for many years, and to renew the same contest with his son. (A.D. 1309.)

After the violent end of Boniface VIII., the papal chair was possessed, for a short time only, by Benedict XI.; for this pontiff, a man of talents and virtue, had no sooner attempted to free himself from the thraldom in which the cardinals and Roman nobles designed to retain him, and evinced a disposition to resent the outrage which the king of France had offered to the holy see in the person of Boniface, than he was carried off by poison. (A.D. 1304.) Philip the Fair, whose character has thrown probability on the accusation, is stated by a contemporary writer to have bribed two cardinals to the commission of this crime: he certainly reaped every advantage from its success. The death of Benedict was immediately followed by an event which long rendered him the real mover of the mighty engine of papal authority: I mean the removal of the popedom to Lyons and afterwards to Avignon. This remarkable occurrence in ecclesiastical history, had probably been in a great measure prepared by the long and intimate connexion of the holy see with the house of Anjou. The influence of the Angevin princes had introduced into the sacred college many cardinals who were Frenchmen by birth; and on the death of Benedict there was a strong French party in the conclave entirely devoted to Philip. The interest of the Colonna was thrown into the same scale, but the opposite faction were notwithstanding so nearly equal in numbers, that, after a long struggle, in which neither could command a sufficient majority for the cardinal of their choice, it was solemnly agreed that the tiara should be bestowed on some foreign prelate out of the pale of the college, that one party should name three individuals, and that the other should select a pope from among them. The anti-French party, preferring the right of primary nomination, carefully chose three prelates, all of them French, yet all declared and violent enemies of their sovereign. Yet this answered the object of Philip; his partizans immediately dispatched to him the list, at the head of which was the archbishop of Bordeaux, and the king, hastening into Gascony, and convincing this enemy in a secret interview that he could seat him in the chair of St. Peter, easily purchased his friendship and gratitude. The archbishop readily swore to the conditions required by the king as the price of his elevation, and the creatures of Philip were then instructed to declare him elected. The anti-French party anticipated a leader in the new pope, who assumed the title of Clement V., but they were thunderstruck when they found him the tool of Philip. Whether terrified by the fate of his predecessors, or influenced by the French king, Clement resolved never to cross the Alps, and astonished Christendom by a summons to the cardinals to attend his coronation at Lyons, (A.D. 1305.) They could not refuse obedience, the ceremony was performed in that city, and thus commenced a separation of the papal court from the proper capital of its see which was to endure for sixty years: an era distinguished for its scandalous disorders even in the polluted annals of the popedom. The reign of Clement V. was a worthy opening for this disgraceful period. At the expense of every other duty, that pope evinced better faith to his patron than might have been expected from the iniquitous nature of their connexion, for he strictly fulfilled all the conditions of their simoniacal bargain. He absolved the king from all censure for his conduct towards Boniface VIII.; he filled the college of cardinals with his creatures; he suffered him to plunder his clergy; and he finally sanctioned and promoted the horrible persecution which the avarice and cruelty of Philip directed against the innocent knights of the Temple. (A.D. 1307.)

In relating generally the transition of the Lombard cities from a republican independence to the government of signers or lords, I have purposely abstained from distracting the reader with innumerable and worthless details of the petty wars which occupied these obscure tyrants, or the petty revolutions which precipitated them from power, only to elevate rivals who pursued the same career, and usually shared the same fate. From the real extinction of liberty in Lombardy in the middle of the thirteenth century, to the period before us, I have no farther solicited attention to this part of Italy than to notice the contest between two rival families for the sovereignty of Milan; and the mode in which the capital of Lombardy passed from one master to another may convey a sufficient idea of the alternate changes of fortune which befel less celebrated usurpers and inferior cities.

There was a striking similarity in the history of most of the numerous despotisms of northern Italy. The turbulent and artful demagogue, flattering the passions of the multitude, or putting himself forward as the chief of a faction, first raised himself by the affection of the people or the preponderance of his party to the Sovereign command. The solemn decree of the council of government or of the assembled citizens, was in every instance carefully obtained to sanction his elevation. The signiory of the state was assigned to him, sometimes for life, sometimes for a limited period only. All the forms of a republic were still preserved, its magistrates, its councils, its popular assemblies, and the sovereignty of the people was acknowledged with outward respect, while their real liberties were utterly destroyed. Thus the progress of the signor gradually accelerated from a cautious and measured exercise of authority to the undisguised assertion of unlimited and hereditary power, and from the temperate and conciliating use of that power to the wantonness and atrocities of a cruel despotism. But neither the protection of mercenary troops nor the uncertain fidelity of interested adherents could give security to the seat of the tyrant; the open hostility of exiled enemies constantly threatened his destruction; secret treachery among his party or even his relatives watched the ready moment of popular hatred to hurl him from his throne. Sometimes the gates were betrayed to the banished leader of a faction who cleared the streets and rode the city, as it was termed, with his gens-d'armerie; sometimes domestic treason excited a sedition within the walls; and the cry of the conspirators was still the same, "Popolo! Popolo!" for the people!—the watchword of democracy. The citizens rose at the prostituted signal of liberty to shake off the intolerable yoke of the tyrant, and immediately to surrender their happiness and freedom to another and often a more ferocious master.

About the beginning of the fourteenth century there were almost as many signers in northern Italy, as there had been free cities. Alberto Scotto ruled over Placentia, Albuino della Scala over Verona, Ricciardo di Camino at Rovigo, Maffeo de' Maggi at Brescia; the lords of Correggio were masters of Parma, the Passerini of Mantua, the Ghiberti of Modena and Reggio, the Polenta of Ravenna, the Brusati of Novara; while the house of Cavalcabo governed at Cremona, and that of Este at Ferrara, though in the vicissitudes of Italian politics that city was shortly to be wrested from them for a few years. Bologna and Padua alone were free; but the latter republic at length fell under the tyranny of the Carrara. In Piedmont two sovereigns of hereditary dominions had, late in the thirteenth century, acquired possession of many of the free cities; these were the counts of Savoy and the marquises Montferrat; but both these ancient and princely houses experienced the same reverses as were common to more ephemeral tyrants. Falling into the hands of the citizens who had risen against their despotic authority, both Boniface of Savoy in 1263, and William of Montferrat in 1292, were inclosed in cages of iron, and ended their days in captivity.

Very few of these Lombard usurpers were destined to found a lasting grandeur for their families; and their power was eclipsed, at the opening of the fourteenth century, by the superior and more extensive domination of Matteo Visconti, the lord of Milan. Since his succession to his uncle the archbishop Otho, Matteo had pursued a course of unceasing ambition and prosperity; he had acquired possession of the province of Montferrat, and his matrimonial connexion with Albuino della Scala and the marquis Azzo VIII. of Este seemed to connect his security with theirs. But the jealous animosity of Alberto Scotto proved more dangerous to him than these alliances were beneficial. The people of Milan were weary of his tyranny, and Alberto, forming a league among the Lombard signers of the second order in favour of the exiled Torriani, succeeded in exciting a rebellion among the Milanese, and in effecting the downfall of Matteo. Expelled from the capital of Lombardy, the chief of the Visconti gave place to the rival family della Torre, who resumed their power after twenty years of proscription; and the Milanese, concealing their slavery under the flimsy veil of popular suffrage, surrendered themselves to the will of Guido della Torre. (A.D. 1302.)

Such continued the state of Lombardy, when the intelligence of the meditated entrance of an emperor into Italy engaged the anxious attention and enlivened the projects of all parties. For nearly sixty years no German prince had descended from the Alps to assert the imperial authority in Italy; and immediately after the extinction of the Swabian family, the Ghibelins, the natural adherents of the empire, had been almost everywhere overpowered and proscribed. Yet in the long period which had elapsed since the death of Frederic II., and notwithstanding the triumph of the Guelf party, the imperial prerogatives were so far from having fallen into oblivion, or grown into contempt among the Italians, that the mere influence of a singular change in public opinion had elevated them in imagination above all former pretensions, and swept away the barriers which the resistance of ages had raised against their exercise. The revival of ancient letters in all the Italian universities had silently produced this strange revolution. An extravagant respect for antiquity was the characteristic of all the learned Italians of the time; but the lawyers and jurisconsults in particular were blinded with veneration for the Pandects and Code of Justinian, their favourite studies. The arbitrary principles of the Roman civil law were universally disseminated and implicitly recognised; the despotic rights of the Roman emperors had been proclaimed in the spirit of their decrees, and the conclusion was easy which transferred the exclusive and unlimited supremacy of the Cæsars to sovereigns who, though elected by a few foreign princes, were supposed to inherit their dominion over the world. Thus the German emperors gained infinitely more in their absence from Italy than the courage, the ability, and the great power of Frederic Barbarossa, the Italian possessions, the numerous partizans, and even the virtues of his grandson, had ever been able to extort from their subjects.

This theory of the duty of passive obedience was most prevalent in Italy when Henry count of Luxembourg, whose election to the imperial throne had been confirmed by Clement V., prepared to require it in practice, (A.D. 1308.) The hereditary possessions of Henry VII., a prince whose superior talents and courage were accompanied by several amiable qualities, were too small to admit of his exerting much real authority over the German princes, though he obtained the crown of Bohemia for his son, and he prudently resolved to seek a more promising scene of ambition and glory in Italy. At the head of a few German cavalry, he crossed the Alps, two years after his election, and his appearance in Lombardy immediately created a striking though transient change in the aspect of almost all Italy, (A.D. 1310.) His court became instantly crowded with the ambassadors of the different states, and with exiles from every quarter; while almost all the Lombard signors attended him in person in the hope of gaining, by devotion and service, his confirmation of their dignities. Henry received the whole of these envoys and suitors with the same affability and favour, and without the slightest distinction of party, and publicly announced his intention of pacifying the factions of Italy. But he declared to the Lombard signors that their powers were illegal and must be surrendered; and these usurpers, aware that the hatred with which they had generally inspired their countrymen would second the intentions of the emperor, endeavoured to resign their pretensions with a good grace. They were rewarded for their submission by Henry with fiefs and titles of nobility; the Guelf and Ghibelin exiles were indiscriminately restored to their homes; and imperial vicars were quietly admitted to govern all the cities. In two instances only was any hesitation evinced to receive the commands of the emperor. Guido della Torre, the lord of Milan, at first displayed some disposition to resist; but the approach of Henry was hailed with open rejoicings by the Milanese, and their tyrant, alarmed at the prospect of defection, made his submission; his rivals the Visconti returned to the city in the capacity of private citizens, and the Torriani remained within the walls in the same condition. The refusal of Albuino della Scala to admit the Guelfs into Verona was more successful; and either the remoteness and strength of that city, or favour towards a zealous partizan of the empire, made Henry overlook a solitary act of disobedience. The deputies of all the cities of northern Italy, except Venice and Genoa, flocked to Milan to swear fealty to the emperor, and he received in that city the iron crown of Lombardy.

The tranquillity which Henry VII. had laboured to effect in Lombardy by the deposition of the petty tyrants of that great province, and by a laudable impartiality between the Guelfs and Ghibelins, was too shortly disturbed by the consequences of his own necessities, (A.D. 1311.) His poverty and the rapacity of the German adventurers who had attended his standard, and whose services he had no means of repaying, obliged him to demand large contributions that disgusted the people, and everywhere converted the acclamations with which they had welcomed their deliverer into murmurs and open discontent. The dissensions, too, to which Italy had so long been a prey, were incurable by any effort of conciliation. The Torriani and Guelf faction of Milan were the first to instigate the populace to an insurrection against the emperor; and all the Lombard cities where the same party preponderated imitated their example. By the aid of the Visconti and the Ghibelins the sedition at Milan was quelled; the Torriani and their adherents were expelled; and thus the power of Matteo Visconti was in fact re-established. But it was only by force of arms that the Guelfs in the rest of Lombardy were temporarily subdued, and Brescia in particular cost Henry a long siege before it surrendered. The fair fame of the emperor was clouded in these transactions by more than one act of injustice and cruelty, and he had no sooner quitted Lombardy than the Guelf cities revolted again, while he found central Italy filled with enemies.

The resolution which the emperor had expressed on entering Italy to pacify her factions had armed the greatest portion of Tuscany against him. The Florentines had already prepared to acknowledge his authority, when the prejudices which favoured the imperial pretensions were overborne by hatred of the exiles whose restoration must be the consequence of submission to his orders. They immediately bestirred themselves to form a Guelf league against him, and extended the ramifications of their policy throughout the peninsula, and even beyond its limits. Thus the signiory of a mercantile republic, always varying in its members, yet still unchanging in its designs, conceived, perhaps for the first time, that idea of the balance of power which has become the regulating principle of European politics. Florence was the centre and the great mover of a Guelf confederation which embraced not only the

Tuscan cities of her party, but those of Lombardy also, the Orsini and their faction in Rome, and Robert king of Naples, while the influence of France and of the papal court of Avignon was obtained for the same cause. On the other hand, Frederic king of Sicily, the republic of Pisa, the Colonna at Rome, Cane della Scala, now the lord of Verona, the Visconti at Milan, and the Ghibelin cities of Lombardy sided with the emperor. Evincing that defect of military valour which was ever afterwards strangely combined with a courageous spirit of independence, Florence mainly depended in this war for her security upon bands of those mercenaries whom we shall hereafter find under the too celebrated name of *condottieri*, the lasting scourge of Italy; and she solemnly bestowed a temporary dictatorship upon Robert of Naples in the anticipation of his assistance, (A.D. 1312.) Yet, when the emperor was at her gates, her firmness continued undaunted, and Henry was compelled to turn aside from her walls.

The emperor, who had entered Italy in the hope of asserting an unlimited authority, which was favoured by the spirit of the age, and as it would appear, with the intention of exercising his power to promote the public happiness, now found himself involved in a dangerous contest, from which his small resources could scarcely extricate him with honour. The greater part of Italy had already leagued against him, and the doubtful adherence of a few Ghibelin cities and lords was hardly a counterpoise against the union and strength of his enemies. The energy of his personal character, however, well fitted him for the encounter with difficult and even adverse circumstances. He obtained some considerable succours from Germany, roused his Italian partizans to vigorous exertions, and in the year following his appearance before Florence had assembled a formidable army. A general war was now kindled throughout Italy, and every prognostic indicated the maturity of a long and desperate struggle, when his sudden death completely changed the posture of Italian affairs. (A.D. 1313.)

While the unexpected death of Henry VII. deprived the Ghibelin party of its leader, and long wars between rival candidates for the succession to the German throne placed the imperial authority over Italy in abeyance, Robert king of Naples, the chief of the Guelf party, the possessor of Provence, and the favourite of the church, began to aspire to the general sovereignty of Italy. He had succeeded to the crowns of Naples and Provence on the death of his father Charles II., in opposition to the recognized laws of inheritance, (A.D. 1309.) His elder brother Charles Martel, by his marriage with the heiress of Hungary, had been called to the throne of that kingdom, and had died before his father. His son Carobert, the reigning king of Hungary, on the death of his grandfather Charles II. asserted his just rights to all the dominions of that monarch; but Robert, hastening to Avignon, whither Clement V. had now removed his court, obtained from the pope, as feudal superior of the royal fief of Naples, a sentence which set aside the claims of his nephew in his own favour. The king of Hungary did not seriously attempt to oppose this decision, and Robert, a prince of wisdom and address, though devoid of military talents, soon extended his ambitious views beyond the kingdom over which he reigned undisturbed. Naturally inimical to the imperial pretensions, we have seen him joining the Guelf league against Henry VII., and the death of that emperor left him every opportunity both to attempt the subjugation of the Ghibelin states, and to convert his alliance with the Guelfs into the relation of sovereign and subject. He would probably have realized his schemes of aggrandizement to their fullest extent, if the extraordinary talents and energetic character of several of the leaders who started up at this crisis from the Ghibelin ranks, had not retrieved the state of disorganization and weakness into which that faction was thrown on the death of the emperor.

It was in Tuscany that the storm first broke over the Ghibelins after the loss of their imperial chief, and that the first ray of success unexpectedly beamed on their cause. Florence and the other Guelf cities of the province were no sooner delivered from the fear of Henry VII., than they prepared to wreak their vengeance against Pisa for the succours which she had furnished to the emperor. But that republic, in consternation at her danger, had taken into pay a thousand German cavalry, the only part of the imperial army which could be prevailed upon to remain in Italy, and had chosen for her general Uguccione della Faggiuola, a celebrated Ghibelin captain. The ability of this commander, and the confidence with which he inspired the Pisans, turned the tide of fortune, and rendered the republic formidable to her enemies; who displayed on the contrary an absolute want of energy and skill in the use of their great superiority of resources. Uguccione was everywhere victorious; and the Florentines, who were dismayed at his successes, and king Robert, who wanted to gain time to attack the Ghibelins in other quarters, proposed peace to the Pisans. The offer was on the point of acceptance, when Uguccione, foreseeing the loss of occupation to himself, raised a sedition in Pisa to oppose the pacification, overawed the council of government, and acquired for a time a tyrannical influence over the state. The vigour of his arms reduced the Guelf people of Lucca to sue for peace; they were compelled to restore their Ghibelin exiles; and then Uguccione, fomenting the dissensions which were thus created within the walls, easily subjected one of the most wealthy and flourishing cities of Tuscany to his sword, (A.D. 1314.)

The loss of so valuable an ally as Lucca alarmed the Florentines and the whole Guelf party, and actuated them to serious exertion. King Robert sent two of his brothers into Tuscany with a body of gens-d'armerie; the Florentines and all the Tuscan Guelfs uniting their forces to this succour formed a large army; and the confederates advanced to relieve the castle of Montecatini which Uguccione was besieging. After concentrating all the Ghibelin strength in that part of Italy, this great captain could muster only twenty-five hundred heavily armed cavaliers, while the Guelfs numbered above three thousand; and though the historians of that age seldom care to enumerate the amount of an infantry which was despised, we find that Uguccione could oppose only twenty to above fifty thousand men of that arm. Yet he gained a memorable victory near Montecatini, in which both a brother and a nephew of the king of Naples were numbered with the slain, (A.D. 1315.) This triumph rendered Uguccione more formidable than ever; but his tyranny became insupportable both to the Pisans and Lucchese, and a conspiracy was formed in concert in both cities; while his terrible presence repressed insurrection in Lucca, the same spirit broke out in Pisa; while he hastened his return to the latter capital, the Lucchese rose behind him; and excluded from both places and deserted by his troops, he retired to the court of the Scala at Verona, (A.D. 1316.) So Pisa recovered her liberty, but Lucca was less fortunate or wise, for her citizens only transferred the power which Uguccione had usurped to the chief of the Ghibelins, Castruccio Castracani degl' Interminelli, one of the most celebrated names in Italian history.

This extraordinary man, who was destined to triumph through a brilliant career of successful ambition, had early in life shared the common fate of exile with the White Guelfs or Ghibelins of Lucca. Passing ten years of banishment in England, France, and the Ghibelin cities of Lombardy, he had served a long apprenticeship to arms under the best generals of the age. His valour and military talents, which were of the highest order, were seconded by the arts of profound dissimulation and unscrupulous policy; and he had no sooner returned to Lucca with the Ghibelin exiles, who were restored by the terms of the peace with Pisa, than he became the first citizen of the state. His skill and courage mainly contributed to the subsequent victory of Montecatini, and endeared him to the Lucchese; his influence and intrigues excited the jealousy of Uguccione, and caused his imprisonment; and the insurrection which delivered Lucca from that chief, liberated Castruccio from chains and impending death to sovereign command. Chosen annual captain of the people at three successive elections, he at length demanded and obtained the suffrages of the senate and citizens for his elevation to the dignity of signer, (A.D. 1320.) By a rigid public economy, and by animating the military spirit of the peasantry who inhabited the mountainous district of Lucca, he had already husbanded the resources of that commercial city, formed numerous bands of excellent troops, and exalted the power and reputation of his state. Passionately beloved by his soldiery, whose affections he knew how to gain, while he strictly enforced their obedience, and respected and feared by the people, whom he governed without oppression, his acquisition of the signiory was but the preparation for future grandeur. Under his government Lucca enjoyed repose for some years; for she had, together with Pisa, concluded a peace, immediately after the fall of Uguccione, both with Florence, and with Robert king of Naples. This monarch, after the disastrous issue of the battle of Montecatini, had found sufficient employment for his arms in other parts of Italy to increase his desire for the suspension of hostilities in Tuscany.

During these transactions in Tuscany, the Lombard plains were still desolated by incessant and unsparing warfare. The efforts of the Neapolitan king were mainly directed to crush Matteo Visconti and the Ghibelins in this part of Italy; and immediately after the death of Henry VII. he poured his forces from Provence, in concert with the Lombard Guelfs, into the Milanese territory. But though the confederates gained a battle in the first campaign it produced little fruits; the following summer passed without any decisive event; and, in the third, the Ghibelins obtained a signal advantage by the utter defeat and ruin of the Guelfs of Pavia. (A.D. 1315.) That city fell into the hands of Matteo Visconti, and a general consternation seized the Guelf cities. Tortona and Alexandria submitted to the conqueror, who already held Como, Bergamo, and Placentia, and the Ghibelin party were almost everywhere triumphant in Lombardy; while Cane della Scala, the lord of Verona, was equally successful against the Guelfs in the Trevisan March.

In this prosperous state of the Ghibelin interests the domestic feuds of Genoa attracted the tide of war to her gates. The ambitious rivalry of her four great families of the Grimaldi, the Fieschi, the Spinola, and the Doria, had long agitated the bosom of the republic; and at the period before us the two former, who headed the Guelf party, had, after various convulsions, gained possession of the government. The Spinola and Doria, retiring from the city, fortified themselves in the smaller towns of the Genoese territory, and immediately invited the Ghibelin chiefs of Lombardy to their aid. The lords of Milan and Verona promptly complied with the demand, and, joined by the exiles, a Ghibelin army, under Marco, the son of Matteo Visconti, advanced into Liguria, and laid siege to the capital. The rulers of Genoa could then resort in their terror to no other protection than that of the Neapolitan king. Robert, conscious of the importance of preserving the republic from subjection to his enemies, hastened by sea to its defence, and obtained the absolute cession of the Genoese liberties into his hands for ten years as the price of his services. The presence of the king and the magnitude of the object soon rendered the siege of Genoa the focus of Italian hostility. The combatants were mutually reinforced from all the Guelf and Ghibelin states, and a numerous gens-d'armerie was thus concentrated in the Ligurian mountains, though the nature of the country prevented that force from acting. The assembled Guelfs, however, were more numerous than their assailants; and, after the possession of the suburbs and outworks of Genoa had been obstinately contested during ten months, the Ghibelins were compelled to raise the siege. But Robert had scarcely quitted the city to pass into Provence, when the exiles with aid from Lombardy again approached Genoa, and during four years continued a war of posts in its vicinity. But neither the Lombard signors nor Robert engaged in this fruitless contest, and Lombardy again became the great theatre of warfare.

While the first siege of Genoa was yet in progress, the Ghibelin princes had assembled a general diet of their party, to give consistency to their alliance; and forming a solemn league, they placed at its head Cane della Scala, whose talents and generous qualities had procured for him the surname of the Great. But Matteo Visconti was, in fact, the leading sovereign of northern Italy. This wily chieftain had profited by the experience of former reverses, to conciliate the affections of the Milanese, and to avoid the arrogance which had precipitated him from power. A cautious and consummate actor in the treacherous politics of the age, he was even more dangerous in negotiation than in arms; and while great part of Lombardy was subjected to his vigorous and temperate sway, his four sons, who were all numbered among the best captains of Italy, rendered him implicit obedience, and contributed by their activity and talents to the grandeur of their house. Not all the machinations and efforts of Robert king of Naples, nor of his creature pope John XXII., could shake the power of Matteo Visconti. Clement V. had died in 1314, and John XXII., who succeeded him after a vacancy in the papal see which lasted two years, and who had conceived a blind hatred of Matteo Visconti, not only pursued him with the fulminations of the church and the arms of her adherents, but instigated two invasions of Lombardy, from France and Germany, for the sole purpose of effecting his destruction. At the persuasion of the pope, Philip of Valois, son of that Charles who had formerly appeared in Italy with so much discredit, undertook a similar expedition under papal auspices, (A.D. 1320.) But he had scarcely entered Lombardy, when Galeazzo and Marco Visconti enclosed his army between the Tesino and the Po, and partly by the dread of famine, partly by tempting his avarice with large presents, induced him to a dishonourable evacuation of Italy. After this failure the pope engaged Frederic of Austria, one of the candidates for the imperial throne, to purchase his favour by a like diversion in support of the Guelf cause, (A.D. 1322.) But Visconti had the art to convince Frederic, that the ruin of a Ghibelin chieftain would ill advance his future interests in Italy; and the German prince recalled his troops. Matteo, who had attained a great age, survived his escape from this last danger no more than a month. After passing many years of his life in contempt of spiritual censures, and triumphing over the temporal hostility of the papal party, he viewed his approaching end with terror, and died while endeavouring to reconcile himself with the church.

The reinforcements which Florence and the Tuscan Guelfs sent to Philip of Valois, in his expedition against the Ghibelins of Lombardy, afforded Castruccio Castracani an excuse for recommencing hostilities in Tuscany. He had not suffered several years of peace to elapse without profiting by them to augment his resources and discipline his soldiery; and under pretence of punishing the Florentines for their infraction of neutrality, he broke into their territory with fire and sword, and possessed himself of several of their castles. But his views in the prosecution of this war were directed to more important acquisitions; and notwithstanding his alliance with Pisa, he took advantage of his having an army in the field to make a treacherous attempt to surprise that city, while her noble and popular factions were combating each other within the walls. This act of base ingratitude towards a state which had rendered him valuable assistance against his enemies met with no success, for the Pisans, forgetting their dissensions at his approach, easily held their gates against him. Though the perfidy of Castruccio determined Pisa to renounce his alliance, the war still continued in Tuscany for three years, without any decided advantage. During that period, however, the Ghibelin leader was weaving his toils about the little Guelf city of Pistoia, a member of the Florentine alliance; and he was at length admitted into the place by the treason of a demagogue who sold the signiory to him. (A.D. 1325.)

This acquisition, which was highly dangerous to Florence, produced such alarm in that republic, that she called out her whole native force for the more vigorous prosecution of the war; and so great were her population and resources, that besides fifteen hundred French cavalry in her pay, and one thousand Florentine gentlemen, who mounted and served at their own cost as men at arms, she maintained fifteen thousand native infantry; her Guelf allies contributed fifteen hundred men at arms. On the other hand, though Castruccio at last took a body of a thousand gens-d'armerie into his pay under Azzo Visconti, he was still very inferior in numbers, but his talents more than compensated for the disparity of force. During the whole campaign he evinced the skill of a consummate general, and had already filled his enemies with apprehension, when both armies drew out to decide the event of the war, near the castle of Altopascio. The Florentine cavalry, their Guelf allies, and their mercenaries, fled almost at the first charge; and though the republican infantry made as vigorous a resistance as was possible against the gens-d'armerie of Castruccio, he gained a complete victory. The Florentine general, many French captains, and a great number of persons of distinction, were taken prisoners; the whole Florentine territory was ravaged and plundered; and the conqueror carried his insults to the gates of the capital. Then returning to Lucca with an immense booty, he made his triumphal entry into that city with his captives and the carroccio of Florence, which had fallen into his hands.

In the ruin which threatened the Guelf party in Tuscany, the Florentines had recourse to king Robert of Naples with entreaties for aid. This monarch, after remaining in Provence for several years in apparent insensibility to the continued misfortunes of his allies, had now returned by sea to Naples; but he would only yield assistance to Florence upon condition that his absolute command over the republic, which had expired in 1321, should be renewed for ten years in favour of his son Charles, duke of Calabria, with the annexation of a large revenue. The Florentines, after cautiously stipulating for the preservation of their liberties, acceded to these conditions, and Charles arrived in Tuscany with a body of two thousand men at arms. (A.D. 1326.) His presence placed Florence in security against Castruccio, but instead of attacking that chieftain, he employed himself solely in extending his own authority over the lesser Guelf cities. While he was thus occupied a new storm threatened the Guelf party, and the approach of the emperor Louis IV. of Bavaria animated the Ghibelins to increased efforts for completing the ruin of their opponents.

After a long contest for the crown of Henry VII., Louis of Bavaria had triumphed over his rival Frederic of Austria, and taken him prisoner at the sanguinary battle of Muhldorf in 1322. Having since passed five years in confirming his authority in Germany, Louis was now tempted by ambition and cupidity to undertake an expedition into Italy. (A.D. 1327.) On his arrival in Lombardy the affairs of that great province demanded his first attention. Crossing the Alps with only a few German horse, he was immediately joined by all the Ghibelin princes, and received the Lombard crown at Milan. But though he had entered Italy as the leader of the Ghibelins, his first act after this ceremony was to depose the greatest chieftain of the faction, and to inflict one more reverse upon the house of Visconti. The history of that family for the few preceding years will afford a necessary explanation of this vicissitude.

Notwithstanding the great power of Matteo Visconti, his eldest son Galeazzo did not find the inheritance which he had bequeathed an easy acquisition, (A.D. 1322.) By the disaffection of the Milanese and the infidelity of the German condottieri of Matteo, Galeazzo was even for a short time expelled from Milan; and when the mercenaries by declaring again for him established his power, his destruction was threatened by a formidable Guelf army which, under a papal legate, laid siege to Milan. From this danger he was delivered by Louis of Bavaria, who, sending his ambassadors for the first time into Italy, took Galeazzo under his protection, and commanded the other Ghibelin lords in the imperial name to relieve the Milanese signer. The legate was compelled to withdraw his army, and from that period Galeazzo gradually regained the power which his father had acquired. But the protection which the emperor had afforded him so exasperated pope John XXII. that he not only excommunicated Louis, but declared him incapable of ever holding the imperial sceptre. The continued animosity between his protector and the pope, did not, however, prevent Galeazzo Visconti from endeavouring to reconcile himself with the court of Avignon. The discovery of his secret negotiations for this purpose was assigned by Louis on his arrival at Milan as a reason for depriving him of his states. Corrupting the leaders of the mercenaries in the Milanese service, the emperor threw Galeazzo with his brothers and sons into prison; and establishing at Milan the vain image of a republic under an imperial lieutenant, he extorted enormous contributions from the citizens.

It does not appear that this deposition of the greatest Ghibelin lord of Italy occasioned any displeasure in the other chieftains, and Louis, after obtaining a large grant of money from them, proceeded with the troops which they afforded him into Tuscany on his march to Rome, where he intended to receive the imperial crown. He was welcomed with joy by the signor of Lucca, and the superior genius of Castruccio at once acquired the entire ascendant over the weaker mind of Louis. Against the united forces of the emperor and of Castruccio, the duke of Calabria and his Guelf army cautiously maintained themselves on the defensive; but the passage of Louis through Tuscany was attended with disastrous consequences to the most famous Ghibelin city of that province. Since the fatal war of Meloria, Pisa had in effect ceased to be a maritime state; her galleys no longer appeared on the waters, her foreign commerce rapidly dwindled into extinction; and of the dependencies of her naval power the great island of Sardinia alone remained to her. Directing her attention exclusively to continental affairs, and cheerfully making every sacrifice to the cause which she had espoused for ages, she was still the greatest and almost the only support of the Ghibelin interests in Tuscany, when Castruccio formed his treacherous design upon her liberty. She had then adopted a cautious neutrality, and it was at this dangerous crisis in her fortunes that she was called upon to defend the last remnant of her maritime grandeur. Though Boniface VIII. had unjustly attached the investiture of Sardinia to the Aragonese crown, James of Aragon made no attempt against that island; but his son Alphonso now invaded it with a formidable armament, and after some brave but ineffectual efforts, which only exhausted her remaining resources, Pisa was compelled, in 1325, to abandon it to his government. In the decay of her fortunes the republic had more reason than ever to dread the projects of Castruccio, and his alliance with the emperor. After vainly endeavouring to purchase exemption from the presence of Louis, she closed her gates against his forces, united as they were with those of her enemy. But her resistance was ineffectual, and after enduring a month's siege, her governors were compelled by popular clamour to submit to the emperor. She thus fell in reality into the hands of Castruccio, who shortly established his absolute authority over her capital and territory.

After extorting a heavy contribution from the Pisans, and rewarding the services of Castruccio by erecting the state of Lucca into an imperial duchy in his favour, the rapacious emperor pursued his march to Rome. There he consumed in the frivolous ceremony of his coronation, and in the vain endeavour to establish an antipope, the time which he might have employed, with the forces at his command, and in conjunction with Frederic king of Sicily, in crushing for ever the power of Robert of Naples and of all the Guelfs of Italy who depended on that monarch. But while he slumbered, his great adherent Castruccio was recalled by the hostility of the Florentines into Tuscany, where he drove his enemies as usual from the field. Prince of Lucca and of an extensive territory which boasted three hundred castles, and signor of Pisa, Castruccio Castracani had now attained an elevation which seemed to threaten, at no distant period, the total subjugation of all Italy. Still in the prime of life, and in the full enjoyment of bodily and mental vigour, no schemes of future grandeur might appear too arduous to the extraordinary man who had already from a humble outset effected so much; but in the midst of this brilliant prosperity he was suddenly hurried to the grave by a violent fever. His death had an immediate influence upon the condition of all Tuscany. Florence breathed again from impending oppression, Pisa recovered her freedom, and Lucca sank from ephemeral splendour into lasting obscurity. (A.D. 1328.)

By the death of Castruccio, the emperor had lost his best counsellor and firmest support, and he soon ceased to be formidable to the Guelfs. His subsequent operations were only calculated to fill Italy with the remembrance of his ingratitude and shameful avarice. Hastily returning into Tuscany, he plundered the infant orphans of Castruccio of their inheritance to sell Lucca to a new signor, and to impose ruinous contributions upon the Pisans, before his return into Lombardy delivered them from tyranny. While these and preceding acts of extortion and cruelty rendered Louis hateful and even despicable in the eyes of his own party, the mutiny of a body of his German mercenaries left him nearly powerless; and he had retained little influence and less respect in Italy, when the intelligence of new troubles in his German dominions obliged him to abandon Lombardy and recross the Alps, to defend his imperial crown, (A.D. 1330.)

The first proceeding of Louis in Lombardy had been to ruin the Visconti, and to drain their states of money; almost his last act in the province was to make the restoration of this family to power a new source of profit. At the solicitation of Castruccio he had released Galeazzo and his relatives from the dungeons of Milan, and the once powerful lord of that and seven other great cities died miserably, a poor soldier in the pay of the prince of Lucca, a short time before the death of Castruccio himself. To his son Azzo, Louis restored the signiory of Milan upon condition that a large sum of money should be raised in his lordship, and paid to the emperor. Thus the Visconti began once again to recover their grandeur. The restoration of Azzo was immediately followed by a shocking tragedy in the palace of the tyrant. His uncle Marco Visconti, the most warlike of the sons of Matteo, returning from his exile to Milan, was so warmly greeted with the acclamations of the people as to awaken the jealous apprehension of the signor. Inviting Marco and his other relatives to a sumptuous banquet, Azzo drew his uncle at its conclusion into a private apartment, and there gave the signal to assassins, who rushed on him, strangled him, and cast his body from the windows of the palace into the public square.

Just at the epoch of the restoration of Azzo Visconti to the signiory of Milan, Lombardy was the scene of another vicissitude which may deserve our notice from the durability of its effects. The family of the Passerini had governed Mantua with absolute and unresisted authority for forty years, when the brutal arrogance of the son of the reigning signor produced the ruin of his house. One of three young men of the noble family of Gonzaga, who were his relatives and associates in debauchery, having excited his jealousy in an affair of licentious gallantry, he swore in the insolence of his anger to take a horrible revenge upon the wife of his rival. The threat excited the indignation and alarm of the three brothers; they immediately conspired against its author and his whole house, and obtaining some men at arms, rode the city, and called upon the citizens to throw off the yoke of the Passerini who had loaded them with taxes. The call was obeyed; the signor of Mantua was killed in the fray, and his son was thrown into prison, and there murdered by a young nobleman whose father he had consigned to death in the same dungeon. The three young Gonzaga proclaimed their father signor of Mantua, and thus founded a dynasty which was destined to preserve its power to the commencement of the eighteenth century.

PART III.
Domestic affairs of Florence—Changes in her constitution—Sudden power acquired in Italy by John, king of Bohemia—League excited by Florence against him—Success of the confederates—Abandonment of Italy by the king of Bohemia—Treachery and power of Mastino della Scala, lord of Verona—League formed by Florence and Venice against him—His humiliation—Prosperity of Florence—War with Pisa—Discontent at Florence—Arrival of the duke of Athens in the city—His elevation to power—Subversion of the republic—Florence under the tyranny of the duke of Athens—Numerous conspiracies against him—Fall of the tyrant—Restoration of freedom—Affairs of Naples and Sicily—Last years and death of Robert king of Naples—Joanna queen of Naples—Murder of her husband Andrew—Louis king of Hungary, the avenger of his brother Andrew—His conquest of Naples—Subsequent war and pacification between Joanna and Louis—Re-establishment of Joanna in her kingdom—State of Rome during the absence of the popes at Avignon—Private wars and crimes of the nobles—Cola di Rienzi—Excites the citizens to a successful insurrection—His government as tribune of the people—Good effects of the revolution—Extraordinary reputation of Rienzi—Enthusiasm of Petrarch—Errors and fall of the tribune—His subsequent fortunes, second administration, and violent death—General dearth in Europe in the middle of the fourteenth century, followed by the great pestilence—Frightful ravages of the latter in Italy—Republics of Genoa and Venice—Their rivalry—Sovereignty over the Adriatic asserted by Venice—Annual ceremony of wedding the Adriatic—Wars between Genoa and Venice—Changes in the Venetian constitution—Closing of the great council—Final establishment of the oligarchy—Conspiracies against its usurpations—Institution of the council of ten—Its despotic powers—Increased vigour of the republic under its direction—Its mysterious tyranny over Venice—Domestic fortunes of Genoa—Creation of the first doge.

IN noticing the prominent vicissitudes which rapidly succeeded each other during the long and furious wars of the age before us, I have avoided a partial reference to the internal condition of Florence. But while she was acting the conspicuous part which we have seen in the general politics of Italy, she was gradually adopting some farther modifications of her constitution which I have reserved to exhibit at a single view. In the quarrel of the Black and White Guelfs at the beginning of the century, the triumph of the former faction might appear to revive the influence of the ancient nobility, who, with their leader Corso Donati, were most conspicuous in these troubles. But though all the efforts of the White exiles were ineffectual to obtain by solicitation and conspiracy their readmission to the rights of citizenship, Corso Donati found that the ascendancy of his party did not produce for him the tyrannical power at which he aimed. The noble families of the Black faction, instead of serving his ends, displayed so great a jealousy of his authority that he broke off his connexion with them in disgust, and endeavoured to excite new disorders by the intrigues which he directed against his former associates. Rearing himself in defiance to the signiory, and assuming a bold and dangerous demeanour which justly challenged suspicion, he was accused by the priors in 1308 of aspiring at a tyranny. He replied to the charge by fortifying himself with his retainers in his palace; and the gonfalonier of justice, his militia, and the citizens, who cheerfully obeyed the call of their governors, immediately proceeded to attack his residence. After an ineffectual resistance he fled, was taken, and anticipated a public execution by destroying himself.

After the fall of this ambitious noble, Florence was still encompassed with dangers from the enterprises of restless and desperate exiles, and the hostility of neighbouring states. Yet the ardent spirit of independence and the activity which animated her citizens successfully protected their own liberties even in the midst of defeats, and rendered the republic in some measure the guardian of the balance of power in Italy. We have seen her, however, more than once necessitated by the pressure of foreign war to adopt the most hazardous of all measures, that of suspending the public rights under a temporary dictatorship. Neither the precautionary stipulation that the signor should alter no part of the republican constitution, nor the sanctity of the oaths by which he was bound, could divest this expedient of the most perilous tendency. In consigning the signiory to king Robert, the Florentines might deem his power the less alarming, as the prosecution of foreign hostilities left him little leisure for attempting to perpetuate a despotic authority in their city; but they had more reason to apprehend the designs of his son Charles, duke of Calabria, who, even while Castruccio threatened their frontiers, employed himself in strengthening his own power in Tuscany instead of defending their territory. The death of Castruccio freed the Florentines from the necessity of foreign aid, and, just at this epoch, the republic was fortunately relieved from the presence of a signor, who was no longer useful and might be dangerous, by the sudden death of the duke of Calabria.

The first use which the Florentines made of the revival of their political rights after this event, was to perfect some changes in their constitution, which they had commenced five years before. The renewal of the principal offices of magistracy every second month had constantly filled the city with intrigues and ferment. It was therefore resolved in a parliament of the people, held in the year 1323, to adopt a singular plan of election, that both obviated the quick recurrence of this evil, and flattered the ambition of a democracy, at once intelligent and jealous, and vain of their sovereignty. This was to admit all citizens of respectable character to the magistracy by rotation. (A.D. 1328.) By the scheme which was now digested, five public bodies, the reigning signiory of priors, the gonfaloniers of militia, the captains of the Guelf society, the twelve buonomini, and the consuls of arts, separately made out lists of all citizens, above thirty years of age and of Guelf origin, whom they deemed deserving of public trust. And to prevent the omission of any respectable name by these electoral colleges of distinct interests, a sixth body of other deputies from the different quarters of the city also prepared a similar list. Then all the lists thus formed were united into one, and the six colleges, in number altogether ninety-seven persons, meeting, proceeded to ballot upon every name. Sixty-eight suffrages were necessary to place an individual upon either of the reformed lists from whence the priors, the buonomini, the consuls of arts, and the gonfaloniers, were to be taken respectively at every renewal of the magistracies. As none of these could be held for more than two or four months, several hundred citizens were summoned in rotation within two years to take their share in the government. All the names on the reformed lists were written on separate tickets, placed in bags, and drawn out as they were wanted, by lot, to fill the vacant magistracies. But, at the end of every two years, fresh names were added by the same process as before to those which remained undrawn. At the same time with these enactments, the four great legislative councils of the state were abolished and replaced by two new bodies; the first of three hundred members, entirely plebeian, and termed consiglio di popolo; the second, or consiglio di commune, composed of two hundred and fifty persons, of whom one half might be noble. Both these councils were changed every four months.

The tranquillity which Florence and all Tuscany might have hoped to enjoy, after the death of Castruccio Castracani and the return of the emperor Louis into Germany, was almost immediately disturbed by the strange elevation of a new and unexpected sovereign. John, king of Bohemia, son of the emperor Henry VII., a prince of singular character, had for several years borne a distinguished part in the affairs of Germany. By his chivalrous qualities, his noble figure and dignified eloquence, and by the disinterestedness with which he devoted himself to reconcile the German factions, he had acquired an extraordinary reputation for generosity and self-denial. The personal glory of becoming the pacificator of Europe appeared to be his sole ambition; and for this he abandoned the care of his own states to traverse the continent with the rapidity of a courier. He happened to be on the confines of Italy when the Brescians, moved by the report of his virtues, sent an embassy to offer him for life the signiory of their town. Gladly entering on a new field of employment, he accepted the offer; and numerous other Italian cities immediately imitated the example of Brescia.

It is a remarkable proof of the restlessness of the people, and of the general disgust with which the fleeting reigns of their own petty tyrants and the struggles of faction had inspired them, that in a few months nearly the half of northern and central Italy had implored the eccentric monarch to become its master, (A.D. 1331.) In Lombardy, Bergamo, Cremona, Pavia, Vercelli, and Novara invited tranquillity under his government; and even Azzo Visconti, the puissant lord of Milan, was induced or compelled to offer him his signiory and to rule as his vicar. Thus, too, the rulers of Parma, Modena, and Reggio opened their gates to him; and the same spirit spreading into Tuscany, the new Ghibelin signor of Lucca, who was attacked by the Florentines, eagerly surrendered his authority to the pacific conqueror. John every where reconciled the opposite factions, and charmed Italy with the fame of his virtues. The Florentines alone were proof against the general enthusiasm; they saw only in John a foreign prince and a dangerous neighbour; the son of their old enemy Henry VII., and the ally of Louis of Bavaria; an object of suspicion and of dread. They immediately put in motion against him that active and extensive policy which distinguished them from the other Italian states; and their efforts were seconded by the alarm with which Azzo Visconti and Mastino della Scala awoke to a sense of their danger. While the king of Bohemia, leaving his son to maintain his new power with a body of gens-d'armerie, was raising fresh forces in Finance, Italy was surprised by a league between the old king of Naples and the Florentine republic, and their ancient enemies the Ghibelin princes, (A.D. 1332.) The partition of the dominions so suddenly acquired by the stranger prince was the object of the confederates, and the restoration of the former equilibrium the pretext of the compact. Cremona was to fall to Azzo Visconti, Parma to the lord of Verona, Modena to the marquis of Este, Reggio to the signor of Mantua, and, finally, Lucca to the Florentines.

It was to no purpose that John of Bohemia shortly entered Italy, attended by the flower of the French chivalry, (A.D. 1333.) After some uninteresting hostilities, the confederates proved too strong for him; and with a reverse of fortune as rapid as his success, he saw new enemies gathering daily around him, while the cities which had invited him to govern them, either revolted or submitted to his sovereignty with impatience and disaffection. Finding the aspect of Italian affairs no longer favourable to his influence, he at once resolved, with characteristic levity, to abandon the country altogether. But he first collected all the money of which he could drain the cities under his sway, by contributions and by the sale of their signiories to the different chiefs of parties. Then sending his German cavalry under his son into Bohemia, and himself returning to figure in the tournaments of Paris, he finally quitted Italy, after having for three years exercised an influence over its politics to which the situation of his own dominions could in no respect contribute.

The departure of the king of Bohemia removed every obstacle to the success of the Ghibelin and Florentine confederates; the signors to whom he had sold his authority finding resistance unavailing, successively surrendered their cities upon the best conditions which they could obtain; and thus all the acquisitions contemplated by the allies fell into their hands, (A.D. 1335.) The lord of Milan secured Cremona and other cities; the marquis of Este and the signor of Mantua acquired Modena and Reggio respectively; and Mastino della Scala established his power over Parma. Florence only, whose exertions had animated the confederates, whose contingents had been constantly furnished to their armies, and whose impartial intervention had alone restricted them from robbing each other of their spoils, Florence was herself defrauded of her share of the general conquests. The lord of Verona, having obtained possession of Lucca by negotiation with its signor, refused to deliver up the city to the Florentines, to whom it had been allotted by the treaty of partition; and the republicans discovered too late, that they had wasted their resources merely to aggrandize a formidable neighbour.

Mastino della Scala, lord of Verona, had, jointly with a brother, who was wholly absorbed in pleasures, succeeded his uncle, the great Cane, in 1329, in the possession of the whole Trevisan March. Inheriting the talents and ambition, without the virtues, of Cane, Mastino had already, by the acquisition of Parma, extended his states from the north-eastern frontiers of Italy to the confines of Tuscany; and the possession of the strong city of Lucca now gave him a secure footing in this province. He shortly made it appear to what purpose he meant to apply this new advantage. Under the plea of re-establishing the Ghibelin interests, but in reality to forward his own schemes of dominion, he began to fill all Tuscany with his machinations. Florence was neither slow to discover her danger, nor to resent the treachery of her faithless ally. But after herself contributing, by the part which she had taken in the late war, to elevate the power of Mastino, she found it not easy to put a rein upon his pride and ambition. From Azzo Visconti and the Ghibelin signors of Lombardy, his natural allies, she could hope for no aid; and though the Guelf cities of Tuscany and the king of Naples were engaged to her by their old connexion, neither these little republics nor Robert, whose activity was chilled by age, were likely to afford her a vigorous assistance. Alone, notwithstanding her population and wealth, she was scarcely able to cope with an enemy who, by his personal talents, his large possessions, and the splendid revenues which they yielded to him, had become the first native prince of Italy. The commercial citizens of Florence, however, displaying a spirit equal to the emergency, and cheerfully opening their coffers for the public service, shortly placed the treasury in a condition to meet every demand; and the interests of a state hitherto almost as much a stranger to the politics as to the factions of Italy, were fortunately involved in similar hostility to the projects of the Veronese prince.

By restricting the Venetian citizens from the manufacture of salt on the Trevisan coast which bordered on their lagunes, and by subjecting their vessels to heavy duties in navigating the Po, Mastino della Scala had given serious offence to the queen of the Adriatic. The haughty and prudent republic could neither brook the novel pretensions, nor be indifferent to the increasing power, of her designing neighbour; and she listened with pleasure to the overtures by which Florence secretly tempted her to unite in humbling the object of their common jealousy. The Tuscan state liberally engaged to defray half the charges of an army which should be employed against Mastino della Scala in the Trevisan March, and to resign to Venice the sole possession of such conquests as might be made in that quarter; only reserving for herself the acquisition of Lucca, which she was to obtain by attacking Mastino in Tuscany, entirely with her own resources. Upon these terms an alliance was signed between the two republics, and the lord of Verona had soon abundant reason to repent of the pride and treachery by which he had provoked their formidable union, (A.D. 1336.) While a large army, which they jointly took into pay, entered the Trevisan March under Piero de' Rossi, the most chivalrous and virtuous noble of the age, the skilful negotiations of the Florentines seduced the lords of Milan and Mantua, and the marquis of Este, to forsake the alliance of Mastino, and to unite in stripping him of his territories. Nor were the Florentines contented with drawing down the hostility of the Lombard powers upon their enemy, their indefatigable policy even extended to the frontiers of Germany, and engaged the duke of Carinthia to pour an army into his dominions.

Mastino della Scala was utterly powerless against the host of enemies which the vengeance of Florence had excited against him. During three campaigns he was unable to oppose the league in the field, and was compelled to witness the successive loss of many of his principal cities, (A.D. 1337.) His brother Albert was surprised and made prisoner in Padua, by the treachery of the family of Carrara, who acquired the sovereignty of that city; Feltro was captured by the duke of Carinthia; Brescia revolted, and fell with other places to Azzo Visconti; and though the republics sustained a heavy loss in the death of their celebrated captain Piero de' Rossi, who was killed at the siege of a petty castle, the fortunes of the Scala became so desperate that peace could alone save their house from total destruction. In this hopeless condition, Mastino artfully addressed himself to the Venetians, and, by satisfying all their demands, detached them from the general interests of the coalition, (A.D. 1338.) By a separate treaty which their republic concluded with him, and which was then only communicated to the Florentines for their acceptance, Mastino ceded to Venice Treviso, with other fortresses and possessions, and the right of free navigation on the Po; he agreed at the same time to yield Bassano and an extension of territory to the new lord of Padua, and to confirm the sovereignty of Brescia to Azzo Visconti; but for the Florentine republic no farther advantage was stipulated than the enjoyment of a few castles which they had already conquered in Tuscany. Upon these conditions Albert della Scala was liberated from prison.

Thus Florence was a second time abandoned by a league which had been formed solely by her exertions, and whose successes had been purchased in a great measure at her charge. Too confident in the result of the war, and desirous of sparing a city and territory which she considered must eventually fall to her as the reward of her sacrifices to the common cause of her allies, she had abstained from any vigorous attack upon Lucca, and suffered the prize to slip from her grasp. Though in the first moment of indignation at this treachery the Florentines hesitated whether they should not still continue the war with Mastino unassisted, the heavy debt which they had contracted, and two appalling checks which their commerce sustained at this epoch, determined them in favour of more pacific counsels. The wars of the times between England and France had involved Florence in both these misfortunes. From two of her commercial houses, the Bardi and Peruzzi, Edward III. had borrowed immense sums, which so much exceeded his means of repayment as to produce the failure of these bankers, and with it the ruin of many of their fellow-citizens. And while the necessities or bad faith of one monarch entailed this disaster on the republic, his rival, Philip de Valois, with a more open violation of justice, replenished his exhausted funds by seizing the effects of all her merchants in his dominions under the pretext of their usurious transactions. Under the heavy pressure of the temporary distresses which these losses occasioned, Florence unwillingly acceded to the terms of the general pacification with the lord of Verona.

For about three years after the termination of the war against Mastino della Scala, Florence and all Tuscany were at peace; and even this short interval of repose was sufficient to recruit the strength of the republic and to revive her schemes of ambition. The vast commerce which her citizens maintained, notwithstanding the inland position of the city, with every foreign country of the civilized world, poured astonishing riches into the state, and quickly repaired the waste of the greatest expenditure. From one extremity of Europe to the other, her bankers and merchants pursued their transactions in every city. In the magazines of Venice and Antwerp, in the markets of London and Paris, in the vessels which traded on the Mediterranean and the ocean, in the convoys which traversed Italy, Germany, and France, Florentine manufactures and Florentine property were still to be found. Thus notwithstanding every misfortune and loss, perpetual and increasing wealth flowed into the coffers of her enterprising citizens, and invigorated the resources of her free community. Not that tranquillity and public happiness reigned undisturbed in her streets. A frightful pestilence, which was in the middle of the century to ravage all Europe simultaneously or in quick succession, first broke out in the city during this short period of pacification, and carried off 16,000 persons; and its horrors had scarcely subsided when they were followed by the miseries of civil discord. Since the establishment of the ordinances of justice, the administration of affairs had principally rested in the hands of the higher classes of the plebeian citizens; and this wealthy oligarchy, which was little less the object of dislike to the lower people than to the old nobility, maintained its power with difficulty against the popular disaffection, and the conspiracies of nobles who were debarred of all share in the government, and perpetually galled by the arrogance of their successful rivals. Yet such was the vitality of public energy which was inspired by a prosperous commerce and a free constitution, that in the midst of internal dissensions the republic was in a condition, three years after the peace with the lord of Verona, to undertake the purchase of the city of which she had twice failed to obtain the acquisition by her warlike confederacies.

In the decline of his power Mastino della Scala had still retained the sovereignty of Parma until it was wrested from him, through the usual process of a conspiracy, by one of his own relatives who rode the city and established himself as its signor. (A.D. 1341.) This loss interrupted the communication between his original dominions and Tuscany; and determined him to sell the sovereignty of Lucca either to the Florentines or the Pisans. The former people first closed with his offer, and agreed to pay 250,000 florins for an assumed right, of which the purchase and the sale were equally iniquitous. The Pisans, who had recovered something of their ancient vigour, could not regard the prospect of further aggrandizement to a state, whose preponderance already threatened their safety, without the greatest uneasiness and jealousy. They no sooner learnt the conclusion of the bargain, than they assembled all their militia, and marched to the siege of Lucca. Their old influence with the Ghibelin party seemed at once to revive. The chieftains and cities of that faction in Tuscany and Romagna leagued with them; the Ghibelin princes of Lombardy, including the signor of Milan, sent them assistance; and Florence, at first unprepared for this new war, was compelled to assemble an army to secure her purchase. But though she was now aided by Mastino, who put her in possession of Lucca and supplied some auxiliaries, she not only failed, through the incapacity of her generals, to oblige the Ghibelins to raise the siege of that city, but sustained a total defeat under its walls; which the operations of the next campaign did not retrieve.

Florence was now on the eve of more intolerable misfortune and disgrace than the unsuccessful or unskilful conduct of a foreign war.

(A.D. 1342.) While the public discontent, which had been excited by the failures of two campaigns before Lucca, was at its height, Walter de Brienne, titular duke of Athens, who had served the state under the signiory of Charles of Calabria as lieutenant of that prince, arrived at Florence on his road to Naples; and the favour which he was known to enjoy with king Robert immediately determined the rulers of the republic to invest him with some command in their army, in the hope of inducing that monarch to fulfil his standing engagements of succour. The duke, joining their forces, distinguished himself in some skirmishes, but the Florentine general, instead of supporting him, and improving an occasion of destroying the Ghibelin army, unaccountably retreated before it, and the garrison of Lucca, thus abandoned to its fate, and having exhausted its provisions, capitulated after a siege of twelve months, and delivered the city to the Pisans.

Amidst the violent indignation which broke out at Florence on the inglorious return of the army, the voice of the people was loud in contrasting the courage and activity of the duke of Athens, with the incapacity or cowardice of their own general. The discontent of the citizens became so alarming that the reigning oligarchy, to satisfy them and promote their own views, were glad to invest the duke both with the civil authority of captain of justice and the supreme military command. He was already the object of regard to two parties in the state, alike dangerous for the public liberty. These were the ancient nobility, and the new aristocracy of wealthy citizens—the popolani grandi. The former, excluded from political rights, and possessing no interests in common with those of freedom, were willing to purchase a share of power at any price; the latter, obnoxious both to the nobles and people, were eager to preserve at all hazards the oligarchical influence which they had contrived to exercise over the biennial elections of priors, and with it the exclusive direction of the state. Perpetually reproached with domestic misgovernment and foreign disasters, and generally suspected of peculation, this party, to put a stronger curb upon the spirit of the nobility whom they principally feared, had several times within the last six years procured the nomination of a foreign magistrate of almost unlimited criminal jurisdiction; and had each time converted the temporary authority of this judge into an engine of grievous oppression for their enemies. They now intrigued to make a similar use of the duke of Athens, while on the other hand the nobles projected their own restoration to power by devoting themselves to the service of the same prince. The ruling oligarchy secretly excited the new captain of justice to a rigorous severity of administration, which they designed to turn against the nobles. But though the duke in the outset dissembled and appeared to fall into their measures, he shortly convinced them that he had no intention to play any secondary part. The first capital sentences which he pronounced were directed against four leading persons of their own oligarchy. The punishment of two of them, whom he condemned to death for peculation, was commuted for ruinous fines; but the two others, charged with military offences, were beheaded. One of these great commoners was Giovanni de' Medici—an ancestor of that celebrated family who were destined in the sequel to hold 80 brilliant and, for the cause of liberty, so fatal a career in the annals of Florence. His surrender of Lucca, of which he had been governor, was made the pretext—as far as it would appear, an unjust one—for his execution.

These sentences, whether iniquitous or otherwise, gratified the jealous hatred of the nobles against the wealthy commoners, and were even more agreeable to the lower people, who are always pleased with the humiliation of their superiors. While the oligarchy by this severity were filled with terror at the power which they had themselves elevated, the duke sedulously cultivated the favour of the nobles by promising to restore them to power, and won the affection of the populace by base familiarity and adulation. These opposite classes, thus seduced by his arts, and uniting in the common desire of satiating their detestation of the reigning party, blindly seconded the bad ambition of a foreign adventurer. In a general parliament of the sovereign people, it was resolved by the clamorous voice of the multitude to bestow on the duke of Athens the signiory of Florence for life; and though the more virtuous citizens, as well as the oligarchy, regarded the measure with horror, the idol of the hour was installed by the armed nobles and the riotous populace in the palace of the priors. The standard of the republic was dragged through the mud, and publicly burnt with the book of the ordinances of justice; the arms of the state were thrown down from the public buildings to be replaced by those of the new signor; and Walter de Brienne remained lord of Florence.

Until this disgraceful epoch, Florence had never, amidst all the virulence of faction, and under every vicissitude of fortune, renounced her republican freedom. Even when circumstances had induced her to consult her safety under the occasional dictatorship of the princes of Anjou, she had tempered the evil, great as it was, with studied precaution. The maintenance of her permanent institutions had always been guarded by the solemn imposition of oaths, and with the watchfulness of a wholesome jealousy. But she had now fallen from her pride of place; and there might appear every reason to expect that the next generation would see her sons numbered with the degenerate slaves of the tyrants of Italy. Fortunately, however, for her happiness and fame, the duke of Athens was utterly deficient in that treacherous moderation by which the first signors of Lombardy had riveted the chains of their victims. He at once took into his pay all the French adventurers whom he could assemble from other parts of Italy, and having thus organized a formidable body of cavalry, he immediately began to treat the Florentines like a conquered people. To avoid the chance of encountering any reverse which might weaken his power over the city, he concluded a dishonourable peace with the Pisans, to whom he abandoned the possession of Lucca, while all the cities which had been more or less subject to Florence seized the moment of her disgrace to cast off the yoke. Within her walls the shame of this loss of national honour, and the undisguised tyranny of the duke, roused all classes of the citizens from their short-lived infatuation. The nobles, instead of being raised to power, found themselves the sport of the caprice and contempt of an insolent master, who filled the offices of magistracy from the dregs of the populace; the wealthy plebeians were oppressed with onerous taxes, and even the lower artizans, an order whom the duke desired to court, were disgusted by the abrogation of their corporate laws. Meantime the horrible and incessant executions and tortures by which the tyrant sought to strike affright into the people, excited their horror and commiseration for the sufferers; and an accidental dearth of provisions completed the general discontent and misery. The usurpation of the duke of Athens had endured little more than ten months when it became altogether intolerable. Numerous conspiracies, each totally unconnected with the others, and the three greatest of which comprehended almost all the old nobility and popolani grandi, were separately organized for the restoration of liberty. The imprudence of a soldier who had been gained over to the public cause awakened the suspicion of the duke, aware as he was of the general hatred against him. Several individuals were in consequence arrested and put to the torture, and all the members of the different conspiracies, fearing their own secret discovered, immediately armed. At this juncture some obscure plebeians raised the cry of revolution in the streets, and in an instant all Florence arose. Such of the duke's soldiery as were detached throughout the city were at once overpowered and slaughtered; the streets were quickly barricaded to prevent the main body of the foreign gens-d'armerie from riding the city; and these troops were first hemmed in within the square before the palace of the tyrant, and then compelled to abandon their horses and seek shelter in the palace itself from the showers of missiles which were directed against them from the house-tops. The fallen tyrant was thus reduced to extremities (A.D. 1343); and though, by the intervention of the bishop of Florence, himself a conspirator in the glorious cause, his own life was spared, he was compelled solemnly to abdicate the signiory, to depart for ever from the city, and to surrender the guilty ministers of his cruelties to be torn in pieces by the infuriated and merciless populace.

The first care of the Florentines on the restoration of freedom was to re-establish their republican institutions. But the important services which the nobility had performed in the general deliverance, demanded the public gratitude, and they were at first cheerfully admitted, in equal numbers with the commoners, into the signiory of priors. This harmony was unhappily but of short duration. The nobles were scarcely relieved from the long restraint which had been imposed upon them by the ordinances of justice, when they began to insult and oppress the lower citizens, and even to fill the city with their assassinations and outrages. But the people knew their power; the general indignation against the nobility was roused into action by the Medici and other wealthy commoners, and after a short but furious struggle in the streets, the ancient aristocracy were entirely defeated, their fortified palaces forced and burnt, and their most obnoxious members driven from the city, only two months after the expulsion of the duke of Athens. The ordinances of justice were then restored in full vigour; but in absolutely excluding the general body of nobles from political rights, the republic made an equitable distinction in behalf of individuals who had not disturbed the public peace. Five hundred and thirty nobles were erased by an act of favour from the list of the proscribed aristocracy, and raised to the privileges of commoners; a singular elevation, for such it was, since, without the power of really affecting nobility of descent, it superadded qualification for all the offices of state to hereditary honour.

After this new triumph of the people, the constitution underwent some trifling modifications. The priors were increased from six to eight, and chosen, two each, from the four quarters into which the city was divided; and instead of being selected from the greater arts only, the signiory composed of these eight magistrates with the gonfaloniers of justice, were to be taken equally from the three orders of the great commoners, the second class of citizens, and the artizans. The gonfaloniers of companies (now reduced to sixteen) and twelve buonomini were to form, with the signiory, a deliberative body for the discussion of every proposition before it should be presented for the legislative enactment of the great councils. But the gonfaloniers of companies and the buonomini were only the advisers of the signiory, since every measure necessarily originated with the latter body. Under this modified constitution Florence at length enjoyed internal repose for many years.

While tranquillity was beaming anew upon Florence, the prospect in southern Italy was overclouded by the death of king Robert of Naples. Though the designing interference of this monarch in the factions of the times, and his ambitious schemes of universal supremacy over the peninsula, have frequently introduced his name into the preceding pages, I have hitherto scarcely had occasion to notice the condition of his own kingdom. During the wars which he instigated in other quarters in the earlier part of his long reign to forward his greediness of dominion, Naples was seldom the theatre of action; and the coasts and frontiers of that kingdom were undisturbed to the close of his life, except by the occasional revival of the ancient contest of his house with Frederic king of Sicily. The periods of Robert's absence from his kingdom, and his hostilities with the emperor Henry VII., and with his successor Louis of Bavaria, were eagerly and unscrupulously seized by the Sicilian prince to invade the Neapolitan dominions, and Robert as often employed the first moment of relief from the pressure of other enemies to carry his arms into Sicily: but I shall not detain the reader with the story of these desultory and uninteresting wars, for their course was sullied by sanguinary and atrocious circumstances, and they produced not the only legitimate object of contest, a firm and enduring peace. But Frederic chose the moment of some of the distractions in which the politics of Italy involved his rival, to proclaim his son Peter heir to his crown, contrary to the conditions of his treaty in 1303 with Charles II. of Naples; and he induced the barons, the clergy, and the cities of Sicily to swear allegiance to their future monarch. Accordingly on the death of Frederic at an advanced age, and after a warlike reign of above forty years (A.D. 1337), the memory of his virtues and talents secured the affection of his subjects towards his son, and established

Peter II. on the throne. This prince, unlike his father in all kingly qualities, wore the crown of Sicily only five years, and it devolved on his decease to his infant son Louis. Both on the death of Frederic and of Peter, the king of Naples renewed his enterprises against Sicily; but neither the factious divisions of the Sicilian nobility, nor the feeble character of Peter and the weakness of a subsequent minority, enabled Robert to triumph over the independent spirit of the islanders; and oppressed by years and domestic cares, he at length renounced his projects, and left the descendants of Frederic in unopposed possession of Sicily.

The last years of Robert formed a gloomy reverse to the fortune and vigour of his earlier reign. In the inactivity of old age he lost all his influence in the general politics of Italy, and the administration of his own dominions fell into confusion and disorder. The death of his only son, while exercising the signiory of Florence, in 1.328, deprived his throne of its natural support; and as the duke of Calabria left only two infant daughters, the old monarch might justly tremble for the future security of these helpless children. He laboured to avert the fatal consequences of a disputed succession by inducing his nephew Carobert, king of Hungary, whose rights he had originally usurped, to betroth his second son Andrew at the age of only seven years to Joanna, the eldest of his infant grand-children; and the young prince was removed to the court at Naples to receive his education as its future sovereign.

This union which, to the erring eye of human foresight, might seem to have been planned with singular wisdom, was destined to scatter the seeds of civil war and calamity for above a century and a half. As Andrew advanced towards manhood, he displayed a sullen and vicious temper; his habits were low and brutal, his capacity weak, and his manners barbarous. Acquiring none of the elegance of the court in which he had been educated, then the most brilliant, although the most corrupt, in Europe, he associated only with rude Hungarians, whose gross propensities accorded with his taste. The old king reading his character, apprehended the consequences of entrusting the rights of his grand-daughter to his generosity; and one of his last acts was to assemble the states of the kingdom, and to impose on them an oath of allegiance to their future queen, Joanna. At the same time, changing his original purpose, and excluding Andrew from a joint succession to his throne, he limited the future sovereignty of his kingdom to Joanna alone. Finally, by his last testament at the approach of dissolution, he bequeathed his dominions to that princess with remainder to her younger sister, established a regency, declared that her administration should not commence until the completion of her twenty-fifth year, and restricted Andrew to a matrimonial crown and the reversion of the principality of Salerno if his consort should die without issue. After these precautions Robert prepared for his end, and terminated a reign of thirty-three years at the age of eighty, (A.D. 1343.) This sovereign, the friend and patron of Petrarch and Boccaccio, and the protector of letters, was extravagantly eulogized by the learned of his times as a prodigy of wisdom and virtue; and the severity of later criticism, subjecting his memory to the usual fate of an over-rated reputation, has, on the contrary, dwelt only on his pedantry, his avarice, and the errors which marked the internal administration of his kingdom. Yet an impartial estimate of his character will raise it far above mediocrity. He was certainly learned himself in no ordinary degree for that age, and an encourager of learning in others, a skilful and active politician, and judging him by the fair standard of contemporary sovereigns, not a bad king. Many of his laws, at least, breathe the spirit of wisdom and justice, and the measures by which he strove to regulate the succession to his throne, however unhappy in their results, were evidences of no common ability and prudence.

Joanna was but sixteen years of age when she succeeded to the throne of her grandfather, and her husband Andrew was only two years her senior. Young, beautiful, and inexperienced, the mistress of a brilliant court, the splendour of which was enhanced by the presence of numerous princes of the blood (sons of Robert's brothers), Joanna found but too many temptations to plunge into a career of thoughtless and dissipated, perhaps of criminal gaiety. The aversion that she had acquired for her husband was increased by the jealousy of power which he evinced, and sedulously fomented by her advisers and confidants, who desired to exclude Andrew from the direction of affairs, that, by immersing the queen in pleasures, they might themselves govern in her name. Andrew, on the contrary, was surrounded and ruled by Hungarians, and particularly by an artful and ambitious friar, his preceptor, who openly aspired to govern the kingdom in his name. By such men he was taught, for their own selfish ends, to despise a matrimonial crown and a shadow of authority, while his own descent from the elder brother of king Robert gave him a better hereditary claim to the throne than his wife could derive from that monarch. He was therefore encouraged to solicit the papal court of Avignon to sanction his pretensions by authorizing his immediate coronation. In this design he had every prospect of success, and daily expecting a papal bull to legalize the ceremony, he already began to discover his resentment against his enemies by threats of vengeance, and to betray his doubts of the fidelity of his youthful queen, who was, indeed, generally suspected of an intrigue with her cousin, prince Louis of Tarento. The projects and menaces of Andrew were communicated to Joanna by her courtiers, and among these the principal favourite was a female of low birth, Philippa the Catanian, who had been elevated by the royal family of Naples to wealth and distinction, and was the confidante of the queen's most intimate secrets. By this woman, her family, and associates, a conspiracy was immediately formed against Andrew, of which it appears to me difficult to believe her ignorant.

Under the pretext of a hunting party, the court was carried to the neighbourhood of Aversa, and after the amusement, the king and queen, with a train principally composed of the conspirators, repaired for the night to the solitary convent of San Pietro, not far from that town. After supping gaily together, the royal pair withdrew to the chamber prepared for them; but just as Andrew was retiring to rest with the queen, one of the conspirators came to the door of the chamber, and stated that a messenger had arrived from Naples with despatches of the utmost importance. The victim rose unsuspiciously at the summons; but he had no sooner passed the door of his apartment than it was closed against him by the female attendants of the queen, and he was seized by the conspirators who were waiting for him in the corridor, (A.D. 1345.) He was overpowered after a desperate resistance, in which he drew blood from several of the assassins. Stopping his mouth with their gloves, they dragged him towards an adjoining window, and believing that a ring which his mother had given to him was a talisman against death by the sword or poison, they fastened a silken cord about his neck, and pushed him out of the window which was near the ground. Some of their associates, who were in readiness in the gardens below, then pulled him down by the legs as he hung, and completed the work of strangulation. It was probably the intention of the murderers to have buried the body in the convent garden, but Isolda, a faithful Hungarian woman who had nursed the infancy of Andrew, and watched over his manhood with undiminished solicitude, was roused by his cries, and rushing into his apartment, found the queen there alone, seated by the nuptial couch with her face buried in her hands. The reply of Joanna to her agonized enquiry after her master increased the alarm of this woman; she ran with a flambeau to a window, and from thence saw by its light the corpse of the unhappy prince extended on the grass, with the fatal cord still round his neck. Concealment was no longer possible, the assassins fled at the appearance of Isolda, and her shrieks immediately spread the alarm through the convent, and from thence to the neighbouring town.

Amidst the general indignation and horror which this foul tragedy excited, Joanna returned to Naples with the body of her murdered husband, which was there privately interred, and fear and gloomy suspicion pervaded the voluptuous court which, but a few days before, had echoed only to the voice of pleasure. The Neapolitan princes, whose hands were not dyed in the conspiracy, fortified their palaces as though their own lives were endangered, and Charles duke of Durazzo, another of them who had married the queen's sister, and who did not escape suspicion of having been concerned in the conspiracy, instigated the populace to avenge the murder of the king, probably with the hope of ascending the throne by the deposition of Joanna. The queen on her part, with Louis of Tarento, now her avowed lover, also assembled her partizans, and every thing threatened a furious civil war. But the intelligence of the fate of Andrew had in the mean time reached the court of Avignon, and Clement VI., the reigning pontiff considering himself called upon, as feudal superior of the Neapolitan crown, to punish the authors of the atrocity, directed a commission to Bertrand del Bazzo, grand justiciary of the kingdom of Naples, to institute a process for the discovery of the murderers, without respect of persons, or regard to human dignities, (A.D. 1346.) Joanna was powerless against this mandate: the seneschal of the royal household, having been first arrested on suspicion and put to the torture, disclosed his accomplices, and the justiciary, attended by the populace of the capital bearing a standard on which the murder of Andrew was depicted, presented himself before the queen's fortified palace to demand the persons of the conspirators. After an ineffectual attempt to resist, Joanna was compelled to deliver up the accused, who were her most devoted servants, and among them Philippa, her special and infamous confidante; and these miserable wretches, of whose guilt there appeared no doubt, after being made to suffer the most frightful tortures, were burnt alive. But it was remarked that, contrary to usage in these execrable proceedings by torture, the public were entirely excluded from hearing the confessions of the criminals.

But this secrecy could neither remove the conviction which the world entertained of the guilt of Joanna, nor shield her from the indignation of an avenger. It was in vain that she wrote to Louis, king of Hungary, the elder brother of Andrew, who had succeeded his father Carobert on the throne of that kingdom some years before, to exculpate herself from the crime with which she was publicly charged. Louis only replied by sternly pronouncing his reasons for believing her guilty; and immediately prepared both to revenge the cruel fate of his brother, and to assert his own hereditary claim to the throne, which he declared that Joanna had forfeited by her crimes. But Louis was unavoidably detained in his own kingdom for above a year before he could undertake an expedition into Italy, which would really appear to have been conceived less in the spirit of ambition than of just and natural indignation at the murder of his brother; and in the mean time Joanna strengthened the evidence against her innocence by an indecent marriage with her lover, Louis of Tarento, who was believed to have been engaged in the plot against Andrew, and whose mother had afforded an asylum to some of the conspirators, who fled before they were accused. At length the king of Hungary passed into northern Italy with a small force and a well-filled treasury; levied an army of condottieri, and entered the kingdom of Naples, where he was universally welcomed by the nobility and people, (A.D. 1347.) The queen and her new husband fled to Provence, but Charles of Durazzo and the other princes her cousins, repairing to the camp of the Hungarian monarch, acknowledged him for their sovereign, and the whole kingdom gladly submitted to his authority.

Passing through Aversa on his march, Louis desired to visit the convent which had been the scene of his brother's murder, and attended by the Neapolitan princes, proceeded to the fatal balcony from which Andrew had been thrown. The sight of this place might awaken emotions of grief and fury; and Louis suddenly turning to Charles of Durazzo in a transport of passion, denounced him as a wicked traitor whose insidious intrigues had occasioned the death of Andrew. "Thou shalt die," exclaimed he, "here, even on the spot where he perished." The ferocious Hungarians immediately fell upon Durazzo, dragged him by the hair to the window, and threw him from it to despatch him on the ground on which the corpse of Andrew had been discovered. It is difficult to understand whether Durazzo was really implicated in the murder of Andrew, nor does it appear that any evidence was ever adduced of his immediate guilt. His activity in urging the punishment of the conspirators might even furnish an argument for his innocence, if his own station, both as the nearest male heir to the crown (except the king of Hungary), and as the husband of the queen's sister and destined successor, did not explain his eagerness to procure the exposure and deposition of Joanna. And in the perplexity in which the mysterious story of Andrew's murder is throughout enveloped, the just and honourable character of Louis will scarcely warrant any other presumption than that a discovery of the guilty intrigues of Durazzo had wrought him to the infliction of this summary vengeance, rash and violent, and altogether unjustifiable as it was.

Louis did not long preserve his new kingdom. Leaving garrisons in its strong places, he returned to Hungary, and the government of his generals became almost immediately disagreeable to the fickle Neapolitans, (A.D. 1348.) Pope Clement VI., too, could not without dissatisfaction see the kingdom of Naples transferred to a powerful sovereign, who was not very likely to prove an obedient vassal to the holy see. Receiving the queen in a solemn audience, in which she pleaded her cause in person, he declared his conviction of her innocence; and Joanna and her husband, encouraged by the disaffection of the Neapolitans against their foreign governors, and fortified by papal countenance, returned from Provence, and taking a body of condottieri into pay, wrested great part of the kingdom from the Hungarians. After three years of indecisive warfare, in which the mercenary troops on both sides committed shocking atrocities, Louis, who had made a second expedition into southern Italy, became weary of hostilities to which there appeared no end; and he listened at last to terms of accommodation. Joanna engaged again to submit the investigation of her guilt or innocence to the pope, and to resign her crown to the king of Hungary, if his holiness should pronounce sentence against her; but if the issue of the enquiry should be favourable to her, Louis agreed to withdraw his troops. A solemn process was accordingly instituted at the court of Avignon, of which it was easy to foretell the result. Yet so evident appeared the guilt of the queen, that her ambassadors could adopt no better defence, than by the deposition of witnesses that sorcery had been practised upon her, and the conclusion that, if her participation in the conspiracy were proved, she must still stand absolved, as having yielded only to the resistless powers of hell. Upon this strange and ridiculous plea the pope and his cardinals, who were eager to find a pretext for her acquittal, abolished the accusation, and pronounced her cleared of offence. The king of Hungary submitted with good faith to the decision, and even refused by his ambassadors to receive an immense sum, which the pope awarded to him as a remuneration for the charges of the war, declaring that he had not undertaken it to amass money, but to revenge the murder of his brother. (A.D. 1351.)

Although the popes continued, from their distant and luxurious retreat of Avignon, to assert and exercise a paramount authority over the affairs of Naples, a foreign residence considerably weakened their influence over the rest of Italy. There had been, perhaps, in the general tenor of their policy, little reasonable cause for the discontent and regret which we find that their absence occasioned among the Italians. They had much more frequently proved themselves the disturbers than the protectors of public happiness in the peninsula; and it is not easy to discover how the removal of the pontificate could be injuriously felt in any city or state except Rome. But the ancient seat of the papal court had certainly sufficient occasion to deplore the change. Besides the splendour and wealth which remained to that fallen capital from the presence of the ecclesiastical chiefs of Europe, some degree of order was usually preserved, so long as a sovereign pontiff dwelt within the walls; and though the crimes and violence of the nobles, and the excesses of a vicious population, could not always be restrained, and were even often excited by the conduct of the popes, all regard for the office and authority of the successors of St. Peter was seldom entirely abandoned.

The measure of respect and obedience which the popes exacted in Rome might naturally be regulated by their personal characters. Some even successfully claimed the right to appoint the senator, the temporal ruler of the city; or at least, to require a general oath of supremacy from that magistrate. And when the weakness of the reigning pontiff prevented his effectual interference in the maintenance of tranquillity, the arm of civil justice was never wholly and altogether powerless. But the holy see was no sooner transferred to Avignon than Rome fell into a frightful and universal anarchy. The nobles, among whom the great rival families of the Colonna and Orsini were most conspicuous, carried on their atrocious feuds with impunity, and in daring insult to all municipal authority. Too barbarous to appreciate the majestic relics of ancient power and beauty, the sole glory of their city; too insensible to have respected, if they had known their value, they were invited by the massive grandeur of the old monuments to profane them with rapine and bloodshed. Converting many of these venerable edifices into fortresses, it was from the impregnable shelter which they afforded that the nobles sallied with their retainers, to prosecute their sanguinary quarrels, or to violate the city with public robberies and offences of the darkest iniquity. Unable from their poverty to maintain bands of regular soldiery, they gave a refuge in these strongholds to banditti and men of desperate lives, who repaid the protection which enabled them to set all laws at defiance, by garrisoning the fortresses and executing the criminal projects of their patrons. It was in vain that the shadow of republican institutions was still preserved amidst the oppression, and spoliations, and murders in which the nobles audaciously revelled. The civic council was impotent; the supreme senator was usually himself a noble, who protected only his own followers, and punished only his personal enemies. Thus, just before the period at which this chapter is to terminate, the insolent excesses of the nobles had reduced the citizens of Rome to the lowest depths of abasement and misery, when the enthusiasm of one man, unassisted by the influence of high station and powerful adherents, imagined it possible, not only to establish peaceful government in Rome, but to recover for the eternal city her ancient dominion over the earth. The first part of his design failed solely by his own want of judgment; without this capital defect in his character, the second could never have been conceived.

Cola di Rienzi, the son of an innkeeper and washerwoman of Rome, had by the care of his parents received an education far above his station. The study of the best classical writers had early inflamed his mind with romantic admiration for antiquity, and inspired him with sorrow and shame at the modern degradation of his country. Gifted by nature with astonishing powers of eloquence, and animated by a generous desire to rekindle in the breasts of his fellow-citizens the spirit of their republican ancestors, his learning could not teach him, and his inexperience of mankind prevented him from discovering, that the time for restoring the pristine majesty of Rome was for ever fled. By some accident, or by the reputation which his genius and eloquence had already procured for him, he was appointed a member of the deputation which the nobles, the clergy, and the citizens of Rome despatched to Avignon in 1342 to supplicate the new pope Clement VI. to re-establish the holy see in its original seat. The mission failed of success, but the talents of Rienzi, who took the lead in opening its purpose, attracted the notice of Clement, and procured his appointment to the lucrative office of notary of the apostolical chamber. For several years after his return to Rome Rienzi was distinguished by the unusual integrity with which he performed the duties of this situation; and he was unceasingly occupied at the same time in rousing the spirit of the citizens to attempt their deliverance from the insolent tyranny of the nobles, and the general calamities which oppressed them. By allegorical pictures of the shipwrecked state, by ironical devices of their own shame, by the explanation of the monuments of extinguished grandeur, he laboured to arrest the attention of the ignorant multitude; by harangues, by satire, by resistless exhortations, he animated their passions and excited their hopes. The nobles regarded his efforts with stupid indifference or contempt; until at last, in the temporary absence of the chief of the Colonna, Rienzi induced the most respectable and higher classes of the citizens to enter into a conspiracy for the restoration of what he emphatically termed the good estate, (A.D. 1347.) After a night passed in prayer, he issued at their head from one of the churches, armed, and with allegorical standards of liberty, justice, and peace; repaired in procession to the capitol, while assembling multitudes gradually swelled his train, and proclaimed the establishment of the good estate, amidst the glad acclamations of an immense concourse of citizens.

This extraordinary revolution was at first completely successful; the astonished nobles, utterly unprepared for such an explosion of the popular strength, were compelled to submit to its violence; and the presence of the papal legate, who had been artfully associated in the ceremony, lent the apparent sanction of the pope to the insurrection. Rienzi was placed at the head of the good estate, with the modest title of tribune, but with unlimited powers; and a militia of horse and foot was organized in the different quarters of Rome to support his authority. The first effects of these measures seemed to realize all the prophecies which Rienzi had attached to the establishment of the good estate. Tranquillity reigned in the city; some severe and just though arbitrary examples of punishment awed the boldest and most exalted offenders; the neighbouring country was subjected to the Roman republic; the roads and the banks and mouth of the Tiber were cleared of robbers and pirates; and the tribune was universally regarded as a new founder of Rome.

Nor was the glory of Rienzi confined to the narrow sphere of the civic territory. Though the court of Avignon could not view so strange a revolution without alarm and displeasure, the deference which Rienzi at first professed for the papal authority either calmed the inquietude or produced the dissimulation of Clement VI. Throughout most of the Italian states the envoys of the tribune were welcomed with extravagant enthusiasm, as if he had already regenerated Rome and consummated the restoration of the ancient glories of her empire. An unbounded veneration for antiquity, which had been constantly increasing since the revival of classical learning, was the cause of this excitation of national feeling. It was nourished and disseminated by numerous men of letters, with whom Italy was now filled, and the charge was most loudly proclaimed by him whose mind was oftener tuned to a gentle theme. The lover of Laura had contracted a friendship for Rienzi and an admiration of his eloquence and spirit, during his embassy to Avignon. Like the tribune, Petrarch cherished the monstrous belief that Rome had an unextinguishable right to her ancient dominion over the universe, and a deep conviction of the practicability of restoring its exercise. He drew exulting presages of the durability of the late revolution; and its first consequences might almost justify this illusion of the great classical enthusiast. Most of the Italian republics sent ambassadors to Rome on the ostentatious summons of Rienzi, to felicitate him on his success, and to deliberate with him on the good estate of Europe; and even many princes were not deterred from courting the friendship of a man who openly elevated the pretensions of the Holy Roman Republic, as he now styled her, above the other powers of the world. Though the other tyrants of Italy treated his letters with contempt, the lord of Milan sought his alliance; the emperor Louis of Bavaria appealed to him to reconcile his differences with the pope; and the king of Hungary and Joanna of Naples offered to submit their quarrel to his decision.

The mind of the tribune was not strong enough to support this wonderful exaltation; and the dreams of ideal virtue which had warmed his early fancy and stimulated his exertions, were forgotten in his prosperity, or abandoned for the indulgence of a selfish and inordinate vanity. Assuming the luxurious expense and unseemly state of a monarch, he dissipated the revenues of the city in idle pomp, and disgusted the citizens by his prodigality and affectation. He adopted the most vain and extravagant titles; and, with more serious imprudence, provoked the enmity and excommunication of the pope by arrogating to himself the sovereignty of the world, and summoning its ecclesiastical chief to his tribunals. He first exasperated the Roman nobles by his capricious tyranny, and then excited their contempt by his sudden repentance. They were tempted to rebel openly, and the discovery that the tribune was deficient in personal courage, increased their boldness, and completed the general conviction of his incapacity for the station to which he had pretended. As enemies multiplied around him, the people forgot his good qualities, and the real benefits which he had conferred on them, to remember only his extravagance and folly: his eloquence could no longer intoxicate them, his summons could no more assemble them in arms for his support; and after an administration of only seven months, no voice opposed his proffered abdication. Resigning his short-lived authority he privately withdrew from Rome, and the city relapsed again into its former condition of anarchy and wretchedness.

The subsequent fortunes of this celebrated man, whose character has been aptly designated as half fantastic, half heroic, will excite the curiosity of the reader, and I shall relate them in this place, although in the order of time they may be considered to belong rather to the following chapter. After wandering for several years in distress through the cities of Italy, Germany, and Bohemia, he was at length shamefully delivered up by the emperor Charles IV. to the pope, and conducted to the prisons of Avignon. He would scarcely have escaped a sentence of death, if Innocent VI., who had just been seated in the chair of St. Peter, had not deemed it his interest to confide to him the government of Rome. The people of that capital, during years of tumult and disorder, had learnt to sigh for the repose of the good estate and the return of their magistrate. But Rienzi entered Rome again in 1354 under the title, not of tribune, but of senator;—not as the independent chief of the republic by popular election, but as the slave of the pope.

His character had not improved in adversity and exile; he had contracted habits of intemperance, his resolution had not been fortified by danger, his early enthusiasm and virtues had been exchanged for suspicion and cruelty. He was at first received by the Romans with unbounded joy, but his government soon became odious and contemptible; a sedition was excited against him; he was wounded in attempting to gain a hearing from the populace; and, after betraying an unworthy pusillanimity, was taken in attempting to escape from the city, and dragged to execution. Still the multitude hesitated in consigning to an ignominious death the once venerated champion of their liberties, the guardian of their happiness: he was about to profit by the general pause and silence to address them, and his eloquence might yet have touched their compassion and gratitude, when a ruffian near him, dreading the influence of the appeal if he should be suffered to make it, plunged a dagger into his breast. He fell; and the rekindled fury of his enemies pierced his body with innumerable wounds.

Throughout the first half of the fourteenth century, we have seen Italy incessantly afflicted with all the evils of sanguinary wars, furious intestine commotions, and endless revolutions; and we have now arrived at a period of new and more frightful calamities, whose overwhelming and withering influence for a time silenced even the din of arms and the yells of faction. In the autumn of the year 1345 excessive rains, which prevailed not only in Italy but in France and other countries, either interrupted the sowing of the grain or rotted the seed in the ground; so that, in the following season of harvest, the earth barely yielded a sixth part of its produce of any description. An appalling scarcity began to manifest itself in Italy after the harvests of 1346; and, in the succeeding winter and spring, an universal famine raged throughout the land. In Florence alone the general misery was such that, before the summer, above ninety thousand persons were dependant upon the state for the issue of their daily food, and the wretchedness of the lower orders elsewhere must have been yet greater. For the government of that enlightened republic displayed a foresight and paternal care of its subjects, which were almost unknown to the age. Prodigious exertions were made to alleviate the sufferings of the people, and to obtain corn from all the coasts of the Mediterranean where the wealth of the state enabled her to buy it up. Although a part of this supply was intercepted in the Arno by the distress of the Pisans, the signiory, with a real and uncommon spirit of humanity, turned no stranger from their gates; and while the richer citizens maintained their immediate dependants, the government fed the immense multitude who must otherwise have perished.

But the scanty and unwholesome provisions which were every where eagerly devoured, occasioned an alarming increase of disease, and a destructive epidemic was already spreading over Italy, when, in the year 1348, the plague, after devastating the East, was introduced from the Levant by some Genoese vessels. The effects of the preceding scarcity, which had been felt almost all over Europe, favoured the progress of this dreadful scourge among a squalid and debilitated population; the infection was conveyed with horrid rapidity from one country to another, and before the termination of the year 1350, it was computed to have swept away, from one extremity of Europe to the other, three-fifths of the human race.

Of the ravages of this horrible contagion, which appears not to have differed in character from the plague of our times, we have numerous accounts in the contemporary Italian writers, and from their narratives of the great pestilence (a distinction of fearful import) a picture of human destruction might be composed for which this age of the world has happily no parallel. Whole families every where perished together, or were spared only in part by the dissolution of the best feelings and affections of our nature. They who were yet unstricken shunned and fled from the dearest relatives; fathers, even mothers, deserted their offspring; children abandoned the death-bed of their parents; husband and wife, brother and sister, forsook each other in the last hour of agony. The dead were so numerous that it was impossible to perform the solemn rites of religion, and their bodies were frequently indebted for a hasty burial only to the fear of the survivors that the air would become fatally corrupted. In the cities the ordinary business of life was wholly suspended, in the country the farms were left without labourers, and the ripe crops wasted upon the straw. The restraints of law, and the rights of property were loosened and disregarded; the common sympathies of humanity were extinguished, and in hideous contrast to the reign of death, the prevalent belief that fear and melancholy prepared the body for infection, induced many persons of both sexes to drown the sense of danger in revelry and debauch. Every law of God and man was forgotten.

Of the numbers who perished in Italy in the year 1348, it would not be easy to form an estimate, for none of the statistical calculations of that age can be depended upon. But we may gain some idea of the mortality from the comparison of different relations. Florence is declared by her historian to have lost three inhabitants out of five, and Boccaccio states that 100,000 persons were carried off; we are told that 80,000 died at Sienna (an incredible number), 60,000 at Naples, 40,000 at Genoa, seven in ten at Pisa, and that at Trapani in Sicily not a soul survived. The imagination sinks under the accumulated woe which can be measured only by such tremendous results; yet we shall hereafter find that the madness of ambition and crime which engrosses the pages of Italian history was calmed but during the moment of these awful visitations, and that the great pestilence had no sooner ceased than it was succeeded by the usual afflictions of war and faction.

During the period reviewed in the foregoing chapter, from the extinction of the house of Swabia to the middle of the fourteenth century, we have found the affairs of Genoa and of Venice more than once interwoven with the general politics of Italy. We have seen the dissensions of the great Genoese nobles, under the cloak of zeal for the Guelf and Ghibelin interests, attract all the powers of Italy to the siege and defence of their city; we have observed the active part taken by Venice, in conjunction with Florence and other states, in the war against Mastino della Scala. But notwithstanding this occasional connexion of the great maritime republics with the ramifications of Italian politics, their history in the period before us still continues detached and distinct from that of the peninsula, and there are several inducements in their furious naval wars with each other, and in the remarkable and opposite changes which were effected in their constitutions, both to bring their annals under the same point of view, and to separate them from those of Italy in general.

It would have been contrary to the experienced course of human passions if, after the galleys of Venice and Genoa had once met in hostile array, there had been any durable peace and friendship between two republics so equal in power and wealth, so eager in mercantile competition, so jealous of maritime and commercial dominion, so haughty and unyielding in spirit. But after the pacification or truce which was produced by their common exhaustion in 1269, the republics maintained towards each other a posture of distrust and suspicion for above twenty years without resorting to arms; and during that period Venice even permitted her rival to crush the naval power of Pisa forever in the war of Meloria, without availing herself of so favourable an occasion to aid the weaker state against her more formidable opponent. Venice had afterwards sufficient cause to regret the refusal which she returned to the solicitations of the Pisans for assistance, and to discover the false policy of having suffered the moment to pass for humiliating a common enemy. But it would appear as if she were engrossed at this crisis in establishing the right to which she arrogantly pretended of the exclusive navigation of the Adriatic, (A.D. 1275.) She asserted her absolute dominion over its waters by imposing a tribute on all vessels which entered the gulf, and even requiring them to repair to Venice for payment of duties on their cargoes before they proceeded to their destined ports. The Italian states which bordered on the Adriatic, and had at least an equal claim with the republic to navigate its surface, naturally resisted this tyrannical pretension, but the arms of Venice easily chastised a feeble opposition which was supported by no maritime strength, and from this period the exclusive sovereignty of the republic over the Adriatic was universally recognised by foreign powers.

It was as a type of this sovereignty that the doge of Venice annually observed the famous ceremony of wedding the Adriatic. It may be true that pope Alexander III., in gratitude for the refuge which he had found in the city, just before the peace of Constance, from the hostility of Frederic Barbarossa, presented a ring to the doge with the declaration, that by that token the sea should be subjected to him and his successors as a bride to her spouse; but the appropriateness, perhaps the origin, of the custom may be dated from the epoch before us. On the annual return of the feast of the Ascension, the doge, attended by all the Venetian nobility and foreign ambassadors, was rowed in the gilded vessel of state, the Bucentaur, to the outside of the port, and there solemnly pronounced his espousal with, and dominion over the sea, by dropping a consecrated ring into the waves.

When the smothered animosity between Venice and Genoa was kindled into a flame by the accidental encounter of some of their merchant vessels off Cyprus (A.D. 1293), the extraordinary wealth and power which the rival republics had derived from an immense commerce were proudly displayed in the magnitude of their armaments. Every season of indecisive operations increased their efforts, until, in the third year of the war, the Genoese put to sea with a fleet of one hundred and sixty galleys, manned by more than thirty thousand combatants. The Venetian fleet was of equal force; but during that year and the next the hostile squadrons alternately sought each other without meeting, and the Venetians then detached sixty galleys to destroy the Grecian colony of Pera. This place was unfortified, and though the inhabitants found a hospitable refuge in Constantinople, the Venetians consumed their houses and property to ashes. The Genoese establishments in the Black Sea shared the same fate. This destruction however proved in the event more serviceable than injurious to the Genoese. The friendship of the eastern emperor permitted them to guard against a similar surprise by fortifying the seat of their colony, and Pera was shortly encompassed with works of such strength as rendered this suburb of Constantinople not only a secure depot for the commerce of the Euxine, but a citadel from whence the republicans learnt to overawe and insult with impunity the capital of the East. The Genoese were not slow in avenging the conflagration of their colony. Their fleet, entering the Adriatic under Lamba Doria, encountered the naval power of Venice near the island of Corzola, and gained a memorable victory, (A.D. 1298.) The doge Andrea Dandolo fell into their hands, and preferred self-destruction to the ignominy of being led captive to Genoa; but seven thousand prisoners graced the triumph of Doria. Of the Venetian squadron sixty-six galleys were burnt and eighteen captured. But this battle, in which the combatants were nearly of equal numbers, was not won without a desperate struggle, and an immense slaughter on both sides. The conquerors were hardly less weakened than the vanquished by their loss on this occasion and their preceding exertions, and a peace was shortly concluded which, as usual, without any decided advantage, left both republics in common exhaustion, (A.D. 1299.)

This pacification was frequently broken during the first half of the fourteenth century by the mutual hatred which the Genoese and Venetians constantly cherished; but their desultory hostilities were attended with no interesting circumstances or very serious consequences, until some commercial disputes in the Black Sea gave rise, about the year 1350, to a more determined contest, which will be related in the following chapter. For great part of the period, which I may thus dismiss in a few words, Genoa was convulsed to her centre by the civil wars in which her Guelf and Ghibelin nobles contended for the supremacy. But Venice was more fortunate in the employment which she gave to her arms; and we have seen that in the only important operations wherein she engaged off her own element, her interference in the affairs of Italy was followed by the cession which Mastino della Scala made to her of Treviso and its district, (A.D. 1338.) This was her first acquisition of territory on the main land of Italy, beyond the immediate shore of the lagune.

The constitutional changes at Venice and Genoa, which terminated in the opposite results of oligarchy and democracy, are more deserving of our attention than the progress of foreign hostilities between these republics. I have endeavoured in an earlier part of this volume to trace the course of gradual and silent innovation by which the great council of Venice became not only vested with the appointment of the executive government, but usurped to itself the nomination and control of the electors who were to renew its own body. The rights of the people had thus lapsed into the hands of their representatives almost without their perceiving the loss; and the nobles who, by the usual influence of high birth, had always obtained the great majority of seats in the legislative body, were in fact the sovereign citizens of the state. As they were neither supported like the feudal aristocracy by numerous bands of armed vassals, nor accustomed to a life of licentious impunity, they never exasperated the lower people by the tyranny and insolence which made the nobles hateful in other Italian states. They possessed no rural castles, they had no retainers to garrison fortresses in the heart of the city, and their defenceless palaces were only distinguished by superior magnificence from the houses of the citizens among whom they peacefully dwelt. But the moderation which was thus forced upon them was in its consequences infinitely more dangerous to the freedom of the commons, than the intolerable excesses of such a nobility as that of Florence. The Venetian people were not provoked by personal indignities to discover the progress of aristocratical encroachment, until ages of insensible usurpation and unsuspicious submission had riveted their chains. When the popular jealousy was at length awakened, an hereditary aristocracy had in effect been created; and it was manifested that the firm and vigorous government which this order had engrossed, was more than a match for the people who had so long been habituated to its sway.

On the death of a doge in 1289, while the committee of the great council, which had been formed by the admixture of ballot and suffrage in the usual manner, were deliberating on the choice of a successor, the people assembled in the place of St. Mark, and proclaimed Jacopo Tiepolo, a man of ancient lineage and irreproachable virtue, doge of Venice by their own election. But this nobleman was firmly attached to the aristocratic party, and immediately withdrew from the city to avoid the proffered dignity; and the committee of the great council, after suffering the popular ferment to subside, elevated Pietro Gradenigo to the vacant dignity. This choice was peculiarly odious to the people from the violent character of Gradenigo, and the intemperate zeal which he had always evinced in favour of the aristocracy. Yet, notwithstanding the hatred of the commons towards him, no opposition was made to his reign; and he even successfully commenced and perfected the series of enactments which, in three-and-twenty years, completed the triumph and perpetuated the tyranny of the oligarchy.

It was, while the public attention was occupied in the war against Genoa, that the doge carried in the legislative body that celebrated decree which has since been distinguished as the closing of the great council (serrar del consiglio). (A.D. 1297.) As the selection of members for the great council had generally devolved either on persons who had sat before, or at least on individuals of the same families, the useless ceremony of annual nomination was abolished by this law; the council of justice or "forty" balloted upon the name of each member who already sat, and whoever gained twelve approving suffrages out of forty preserved his seat. Vacancies by death or rejection were supplied by a similar ballot, from a list of eligible citizens which was annually prepared by three chosen counsellors. The artful construction of this decree prevented its full tendency from being discovered, since it appeared to leave the prospect of admission open by successive vacancies to all citizens of merit. But subsequent enactments within three years forbade the three counsellors from inserting any citizen on their list, whose ancestors had not sat in the great council; and at length the exclusive aristocracy of birth which these laws had established was freed from all elective restraint, (A.D. 1319.) By the crowning statute of hereditary rights, every Venetian noble whose paternal ancestors had sat in the great council became himself entitled to the same dignity on completing his twenty-fifth year. "On proof of these qualifications of descent and age, his name was inscribed in the golden book of nobility, and he assumed his seat in the great council, whose numbers were no longer limited.

These usurpations were not accomplished without discontent, and resistance, and effusion of blood. Insidiously as they were prosecuted by

Gradenigo, the people were no longer blinded to the servitude to which they had been reduced, and their indignation was shared by the wealthy commoners and even by some men of ancient birth, who found themselves, by the operation of the first laws which followed the closing of the great council, deprived of participation in its dignities. Two remarkable conspiracies were organized for the overthrow of the oligarchy while these innovations were in progress, (A.D. 1300.) The first, which was headed by three commoners, was discovered by the vigilance of Gradenigo before its explosion, and its leaders executed within a few hours; the second, which was formed ten years later, was of a more formidable nature. Boemond Tiepolo, the son of the nobleman who had formerly rejected the popular favour, and the chiefs of two other of the most ancient families of Venice, who had all causes of animosity against the doge, were the principal conspirators: they associated themselves with the people and with the nobles who had been excluded from the great council, in a plot to assassinate Gradenigo and restore the old forms of election. (A.D. 1310.) So well concealed was their project, that the doge had only reason for suspicion on the evening before its execution, by the intelligence of an unusual assemblage at the palace of Tiepolo. But Gradenigo passed the night in active preparations for defence, and when the conspirators, after raising the populace, marched at day-light to the place of St. Mark from different quarters, they found it barricaded and occupied by the doge and the partizans of the oligarchy. The peculiar construction of the city opposed every obstacle to the attack of the insurgents: they were repulsed with loss, some of their leaders were slain, and, on the arrival of troops from the garrisons of the neighbouring islets, the victory of the government became complete. Tiepolo escaped, but several of his principal associates were beheaded, and the rest sentenced to exile.

The terror with which this conspiracy inspired the oligarchy even after the immediate danger was past, gave rise to the establishment of the most singular and odious part of the Venetian government, (A.D. 1310.) To observe the movements of the conspirators, who after their flight or banishment still hovered on the shores of the neighbouring continent, and to watch over the machinations of the numerous malcontents in the city, the great council erected ten of its members into a secret tribunal of despotic though temporary authority; and this institution, which was originally intended only for these special purposes, became at once an integral and most formidable portion of the executive administration. Its existence, after a few successive renewals, was confirmed by a statute of annual election; it was associated with the doge and signiory of six; and the consolidated body was vested with unlimited and dictatorial power over the doge himself, the senate of sixty, the great council, and all the magistracy of the state. The famous council of ten therefore was in reality composed of sixteen members besides the doge, who was president for life. The ten black counsellors, as they were termed from the colour of their gown of office, were chosen annually by for different deliberations of the great council; but the six members of the signiory, who were known by their robes as the red counsellors, were renewed, half at a time, every four months.

The creation of the council of ten certainly strengthened the executive government of Venice, and gifted it with a vigour and constancy of purpose which could never have distinguished the foreign or domestic policy of so numerous a body as the great council or even the senate. The entire control of affairs abroad and at home passed into its hands. From the era of its establishment the conduct of the republic towards other states was for several centuries marked by a vigilance and firmness in the execution of her projects, by an impenetrable secrecy and a shameless perfidy, which rendered her at once formidable and hateful. But it was in the gloomy tranquillity which reigned in the populous streets of Venice, while every other republican city of Italy was disturbed by the incessant ebullition of popular feeling, that the mysterious tyranny of the council of ten wore its appalling distinction. No dignity was a protection against its resistless authority, no spot was sacred from its inquisitorial intrusion. The nobles themselves who yearly created it, were the trembling slaves of its immeasurable jurisdiction; the rights of the highest and the lowest citizen were alike prostrate before it. The innocent and the guilty were equally exposed to the stroke of an invisible power, whose jealousy never slumbered, whose presence was universal, whose proceedings were veiled in profound and fearful obscurity. Individuals disappeared from society and were heard of no more: to breathe an inquiry after their fate was a dangerous imprudence, and even in itself an act of guilt. Before the council of ten the informer was never confronted with the accused; the victim was frequently denied a hearing, and hurried to death or condemned to linger for life in the dungeons of state: his offence and its punishment untried and unknown. The detestable influence of a secret police pervaded the city; the sweet privacy of domestic life, the confidence of familiar discourse, were violated by an atrocious system of vigilance which penetrated into the bosom of families. Scarcely a whisper of discontent escaped the ear of the hired spy; private conspiracies against the government were immediately detected; and popular assemblages and revolt were impracticable in a city so intersected with innumerable canals.

To such a state of servitude had the aristocracy of Venice reduced themselves and the people, in the effort to guard the privileges of hereditary descent: privileges which were held only on terms that might seem to render life itself as worthless as it was insecure. Yet though, at the annual elections of the council of ten, the nobles had only to withhold their suffrages from its destined members to suppress this execrable tyranny at once, it was still renewed until the extinction of the republic. The hope of sharing in its functions reconciled the nobles to its continuance; the increasing grandeur of the state under its government gratified an unworthy ambition with lucrative employments; and when, in later times, some disposition was shown in the great council to suffer an institution to expire which had become yearly more oppressive, a conviction that centuries of degradation had rendered its power essential to the existence of the vicious state ensured its perpetuity.

I have been obliged to relate at some length the course of these usurpations, which slowly converted the ancient freedom of Venice into an oligarchical tyranny: the single revolution by which the Genoese people threw off the yoke of a nobility, whose civil wars had been so long fatal to the public happiness, may be told in fewer words. After the expulsion of two of the four great families and the siege of Genoa in 1318, the Doria and Spinola had established themselves with the Ghibelins their followers at the sea-port of Savona, in the territory of the republic. From thence they not only waged for several years a destructive civil war by sea and land against the Fieschi and Grimaldi, who with the Guelf party were dominant in the capital, but acted in all respects as if they had founded at Savona a distinct and rival commonwealth to oppress their country. It required seventeen years of incessant and furious contests to convince the people of the folly and iniquity of the fruitless strife in which they were involved by the quarrels of these turbulent families: an accommodation was then effected between the adverse parties, and the strength of the republic was once more united within the capital, (A.D. 1331.) But the result of this pacification was far from producing contentment among the people. They found that the whole powers of government were still usurped by the leading nobles, and that as the Spinola and the Doria, the Fieschi and the Grimaldi, alternately prevailed in the struggles of faction, they engrossed all the great functions of magistracy and of military and naval command for the members of their own houses, to the exclusion of the rest of the citizens. All the troubles of the state for nearly a century might be traced to their ambition and rivalry; and when they dared to abolish the office of abbot of the people—a magistrate who appears to have been created, like the tribunes of Rome, for the protection of the plebeians against the aristocracy—it became evident that they designed to elevate an oligarchical tyranny on the necks of their countrymen. The temper of the Genoese had not been prepared, by a slow and insidious policy, for the tame endurance of such a yoke; and some discontent which broke out among their seamen swelled to a general popular insurrection. The first object of the people was only the restoration of their magistrate; and the government, which was then in the hands of the Doria and Spinola, was compelled to accede to their demand. But while a general assembly of the nobles and people awaited the result of the election, which was entrusted to twenty plebeians, an artisan suddenly directed the favour of the impatient crowd to Simon Boccanigra, a nobleman whose unblemished and temperate character had endeared him to the citizens. It was immediately declared by acclamation that Boccanigra should be abbot; but he reminded the people that his birth disqualified him from holding a plebeian office; and a mingled cry was then raised that he should be signer or doge. The former of these titles was associated only with tyranny, the latter with the limited powers of a republican chief; and the voices of the great majority of the people proclaimed Simon Boccanigra the first doge of the Genoese republic, (A.D. 1339.) A council of popular election limited his authority, the tyranny of the old oligarchy was overthrown, and, for several years, Boccanigra, who made an impartial and glorious use of his power, administered the domestic and foreign government of the republic with vigour and success. Thus almost at the same epoch which confirmed the servitude of the Venetians, the commons of Genoa triumphantly vindicated their political rights; and, in the continued struggle between these maritime rivals, the bold spirit of a free democracy might seem to ensure an easy victory over an enslaved and degraded people. Yet so uncertain is the course of human fortune, so superior the influence of situation and accident to the fairest promise of national character, that we shall hereafter observe the meridian splendour of Venice coeval with the decline of the glory and independence of Genoa.

CHAPTER V. FROM THE MIDDLE TO THE END OF THE FOURTEENTH CENTURY, a.d. 1350-1400.

PART I.

Political state of Italy at the middle of the fourteenth century—Military system—Exclusive employment of foreign mercenaries—Companies of adventure—Invention of gunpowder and cannon—Affairs of Genoa and Venice—Their commerce in the Black Sea.—Furious war between the republics—Great naval battle in the Bosphorus—Battle of Loiéra—Total defeat of the Genoese fleet—Genoa surrenders her liberty to the lord of Milan, and continues the war with Venice—Destruction of the Venetian squadron at Sapienza—Termination of the war—Marin Falieri, doge of Venice—Conspires against the oligarchy, and is beheaded—Unfortunate war of Venice with the king of Hungary—Loss of Dalmatia—Affairs of Tuscany—War between Florence and the lord of Milan—Siege of Scarperia—Peace between Florence and Milan—The Great Company of Adventure levy tribute in Tuscany—War among the Lombard signers—The emperor Charles IV. in Italy—Continued war in Lombardy—Fortunes of Pavia—Crimes of the Visconti—Prosperity of Tuscany—War between Florence and Pisa—The White or English Company of Adventure—Sir John Hawkwood.

IN passing through the quick series of wars and revolutions which crowd the annals of Italy during the first half of the fourteenth century, it has been impossible to avoid altogether the confusion and perplexity with which so many unconnected details and rapid transitions must necessarily fill the mind of the reader. Before we resume our passage, in the present chapter, through the remaining half of the century, it may not, therefore, be useless to pause for an instant at the point to which we have already conducted our subject, and to collect the scattered results at which we have arrived, into a brief and general summary of the condition of Italy in the middle of the fourteenth century. Of the two great powers whose rivalry had so long desolated Italy with contending factions, neither possessed any longer its pristine influence. The personal talents and activity of Henry VII. had for a moment, in the beginning of the century, swelled the form of imperial pretensions into the substance of authority; but after his short expedition and sudden death, the extravagant respect of the learned Italians for the prerogatives of the successors of Augustus, was almost the only "vestige of their sovereignty. After Henry VII., Louis of Bavaria had indeed appeared in Italy; but the long absence of former emperors, which left their rights over the peninsula in abeyance, was far less injurious to their power than the disgust and contempt which followed that avaricious and ungrateful monarch in his return to Germany.

The removal of the seat of the popedom beyond the Alps, the servile devotion of the pontiffs of Avignon to the sovereigns of France, the selection of natives of that country almost exclusively to fill the papal chair and the sacred college, and the scandalous debaucheries and corruptions of the papal court, which even exceeded all former reproach, had altogether conspired to alienate the minds of the Italians from a foreign and vicious church. Clement V., who had transported the Roman see to France, John XXII., Benedict XII., and Clement VI., had all rested in voluntary exile from the ancient capital of Christendom; and the last of these pontiffs, who still reigned at the period before us, continued by the dissoluteness of his own life to augment the shame of the papacy. While various causes had thus weakened the influence of the imperial and papal chiefs, the third power which the popes had elevated to champion their cause, and which had aspired to supersede the empire in its general sovereignty over Italy, had now fallen into utter decay. Under the feeble and disgraceful administration of Joanna, the kingdom of Naples was so far from maintaining the preponderance which it had possessed under the two Charleses, and during great part of the reign of Robert, that its existence was almost forgotten in the political balance; and so slight was the connexion between the Two Sicilies and the rest of Italy for fifty years from this epoch, that I shall without inconvenience detach the meagre narrative of their affairs from the general course of the present chapter.

While Italy was thus freed from the control of the papacy, the empire, and the Angevin dynasty of Naples, the principalities or tyrannies which had been founded upon the ruins of freedom in northern Italy, and the few republics which had still preserved their existence, were left without any common enemy to dread, and without rival chiefs to animate and envenom the atrocious spirit of faction. The incessant revolutions of the last hundred years had extinguished many obscure states and petty tyrants, and proportionately lessened the difficulty of surveying the political geography and aspect of Italy. The whole of its great northern province of Lombardy, from the Alps to the line at which the peninsula is narrowed by the gulfs of Genoa and Venice, was possessed, after the subversion of inferior signors, by the five princely houses of the Visconti of Milan, the Scala of Verona, the Carrara of Padua, the Gonzaga of Mantua, and the marquises of Este at Ferrara and Modena. The counts of Savoy and marquises of Montferrat, whose domains bordered on the western dependencies of the Visconti, might perhaps be numbered among the Lombard potentates; but though these sovereigns had sometimes acquired an authority over the cities of Piedmont, their history has little interesting connexion in these ages with Italian politics.

From the southern extremities of Lombardy to the northern frontiers of Naples, we may consider central Italy as divided generally by the chain of the Apennines into Tuscany westward and Romagna on the east; Rome and the old patrimony of the church intervening between the former province and Naples. As Lombardy was the peculiar throne of tyranny, so was Tuscany the great theatre of liberty; the commonwealths of Florence and Pisa, and the minor republics of Sienna, Perugia, Arezzo, &c., covered its surface. The province of Romagna, notwithstanding the formal cession which the emperor Rodolph had made of its sovereignty to the Roman see, acknowledged little obedience to the popes of Avignon; for the most part subject to petty tyrants, there is little in the obscurity of its condition and annals to challenge our interest. Rome and its surrounding territory, after the fall of Rienzi, will scarcely invite greater attention. Such, then, glancing the eye to the narrow maritime domains of Genoa and Venice, is a rapid survey of the political divisions of Italy in the middle of the fourteenth century; I am sensible that it is not minutely accurate, but it is at least sufficiently so for the general purpose of history. A few observations upon the condition and views of the different states, may serve to elucidate the character of subsequent transactions.

Of the five Lombard principalities, that of Milan was infinitely the most powerful. The slothful Gonzaga never made any considerable increase to the Mantuan territory; the dominion of the Carrara over Padua was recent; the princes of Este, sunken in debauchery and crime, had degenerated from the ancient activity of their house; and Mastino della Scala, who, until his humiliation by the Venetians and Florentines in 1338, had been so formidable in Italy, dying at this epoch, the state of Verona fell, under his execrable successors, into insignificance. The united forces of these four houses were unequal to a struggle with the lords of Milan. Since the restoration of Azzo Visconti, in 1329, to the power of which Louis of Bavaria had ungratefully deprived his father, no occasion has presented itself for my noticing the fortunes of his house. But though the private character of Azzo was sullied by the treacherous assassination of his uncle Marco, his public administration was just and temperate; and during a reign of ten years, he not only extended his dominion by wresting numerous Lombard cities from lesser signors, but gained the universal affection of his subjects. On his death, at an early age, without issue, in 1339, his uncles Luchino and Giovanni, the surviving sons of the great Matteo, succeeded jointly to his power. Inheriting the talents and ambition which had hitherto distinguished all their house, without possessing the same public virtues as Azzo, the brothel's, by their activity, their lust of dominion, their ferocious cruelty, and perfidious intrigues, excited the alarm and suspicion of all the Italian states. Giovanni, who had been bred to the church, resigned the government to Luchino, to accept the archbishopric of Milan; but on the death of his brother, who was poisoned by his wife in 1349, he united in his person the spiritual and temporal command of the state which now comprehended sixteen of the great cities of Lombardy, with all the central parts of the province. The dreadful ravages of the pestilence for a short time paralyzed the efforts of ambition and defence; but from the accession of the archbishop Giovanni, the faithless enterprises of the Visconti, and the well-founded terror with which their continued aggrandizement was regarded, were the great springs of Italian action to the close of the century.

The independence of the Tuscan and maritime republics was particularly endangered by the machinations of so alarming a tyranny, and there were many circumstances in their situation which increased their general peril. Sienna, Perugia, and Arezzo, were a prey to virulent factions. Florence, who, under the tyranny of the duke of Athens, had lost all her former acquisitions of territory, had scarcely recovered from the yoke of that detestable adventurer, when she was still further weakened by the successive calamities of famine and pestilence. Pisa, no longer a maritime republic, and, since her defeat at Meloria, directing the current of her strength exclusively towards the politics of Tuscany, had become the most warlike state in the province, and obtained the sovereignty over Lucca in the last war with Florence. But the continual factions which agitated her bosom, the devastations of the late pestilence, and the repugnance with which the numerous people of Lucca submitted to her sway, combined to render the position of Pisa critical and dangerous. The Tuscan states, thus exposed by their weaknesses or internal dissensions, had every thing to dread from the unprincipled and insidious enterprises of the Visconti; the two maritime republics, bent only on the indulgence of their mutual animosity, which some commercial differences in the Euxine had revived in its deadliest spirit, and reckless of other dangers than each anticipated in the aggrandizement of the other, separated themselves altogether from continental affairs, to prosecute their own sanguinary quarrel.

A remarkable change in the style of warfare, which had become general in Italy since the beginning of the century, is too important in its connexion with the political aspect of the peninsula to be passed over without notice in this place. The successive expeditions of Henry VII., of Louis of Bavaria, and of John of Bohemia, had filled Italy with numerous bands of German cavalry, who, on the retirement of their sovereigns, were easily tempted to remain in a rich and beautiful country, where their services were eagerly demanded and extravagantly paid. The revolution in the military art, which in the preceding century established the resistless superiority of a mounted gens-d'armerie over the burgher infantry, had habituated every state to confide its security to bodies of mercenary cavalry; and the Lombard tyrants in particular, who founded their power upon these forces, were quick in discovering the advantage of employing foreign adventurers, who were connected with their disaffected subjects by no ties of country or community of language. Their example was soon universally followed; native cavalry fell into strange disrepute; and the Italians, without having been conquered in the field, unaccountably surrendered the decision of their quarrels, and the superiority in courage and military skill, to mercenaries of other countries. When this custom of employing foreign troops was once introduced, new swarms of adventurers were continually attracted from beyond the Alps to reap the rich harvest of pay and booty which was spread before them. In a country so perpetually agitated by wars among its numerous states, they found constant occupation, and, what they loved more, unbridled license. Ranging themselves under the standards of chosen leaders, the condottieri, or captains of mercenary bands, they passed in bodies of various strength from one service to another, as their terms of engagement expired, or the temptation of higher pay invited; their chieftains and themselves alike indifferent to the cause which they supported, alike faithless, rapacious, and insolent. Upon every trifling disgust they were ready to go over to the enemy; their avarice and treachery were rarely proof against seduction, and though their regular pay was five or six times greater in the money of the age than that of modern armies, they exacted a large gratuity for every success. As they were usually opposed by troops of the same description, whom they regarded rather as comrades than enemies, they fought with little earnestness, and designedly protracted their languid operations to ensure the continuance of their emoluments. But while they occasioned each other little loss, they afflicted the country which was the theatre of contest with every horror of warfare; they pillaged, they burnt, they violated and massacred with devilish ferocity.

Such were the ordinary evils which attended the employment of the foreign condottieri and their followers in the quarrels of Italy. But some years before the middle of the fourteenth century, these mercenaries had adopted a new system of action which deprived the weary country of all hope of relief from their ravages, short as it usually was, which occasional pacifications had before afforded. This was the formation of companies of adventure, by the union of numerous bands of the foreign mercenaries, who, when not in the service of any particular power, made war under some general leader on their own account, invading the dominions of one state after another, pillaging and laying waste the country, or exacting enormous contributions as the price of their forbearance. Before this custom had been reduced into a regular system, the formidable demeanour of the German bands who mutinied against Louis of Bavaria in 1328, and the conduct of the mercenaries of the same nation who were disbanded by Venice and Florence ten years later, after the war against Mastino della Scala, had given an appalling presage of what Italy had to dread from such troops. Upon the last occasion, one of the Visconti who had quarrelled with Azzo, induced these mercenaries to second his desire of vengeance against the chief of his family, by offering to lead them to the plunder of Milan. They formed themselves into an independent army under the title of the company of St. George; and though they were overpowered and defeated by the troops of Azzo, the fury and desperation with which they fought when thus armed against society, contrasted with the want of vigour which characterized their service when employed for others, excited the attention and alarm of every Italian government. It was only four years after this that, on the close of the war in 1343 between Florence and Pisa, a German adventurer, Werner, who is known in Italian history as the duke Guarnieri, persuaded a body of above two thousand of his mounted countrymen, who were disbanded by the Pisan republic, to remain united under his orders, and to subject states indiscriminately to tribute or military execution. This ruffian, whose hand was against all mankind, indulged his followers in the commission of every atrocity; he declared himself, by an inscription which was blazoned on his corslet, "the enemy of God, of pity, and of mercy," and he levied contributions or inflicted desolation on most of the lesser states of Italy, until his followers were desirous of retiring into Germany to dissipate their accumulated booty. Appearing again with other condottieri in the Neapolitan wars between Joanna and Louis of Hungary, serving both these sovereigns in turn, and forming a second company of adventure with which he ravaged the papal states, Guarnieri merits altogether the odious distinction of having founded that atrocious scheme of general depredation, which succeeding captains prosecuted on a greater scale and with more systematic deliberation.

It has been truly observed, that there is less difference between the tactics of antiquity and those of our times, than between either and the warlike operations of the middle ages. The military principles of the ancients were founded like our own on the employment of infantry, the real strength of armies whenever war has risen into a science. But in the Italian contests of the fourteenth and fifteenth centuries, though the personal service of the feudal array had fallen into disuse, the old chivalry was only replaced by a heavily armed and stipendiary cavalry, which continued to form the nerve of every army. Successive improvements were effected in the defensive arms of this force, until the cavalier was completely incased in impervious steel, and his horse in a great measure covered with the same harness. This perfection of defence had its striking disadvantages. It paralysed all activity of movement. An army of cuirassiers was incapable of performing a long march by the weight of armour; a river, a morass, a mere ditch, or a garden wall, was sufficient to arrest the course of such heavy cavalry; operations in mountainous countries were impracticable; and since the slightest intrenchment presented insuperable obstacles to an assailant, a battle was only possible even on a plain, when both armies equally desired it; an unfrequent contingency, because the encounter which one combatant sought, it must usually have been the interest of the other to avoid.

The appalling inhumanity with which the condottieri ravaged the theatre of war, was in some measure lightened in its effects by the protection which a simple wall offered against them. Italy was filled with petty village fortresses or castles, in which, on the approach of danger, the inhabitants secured themselves and their property. Behind their ramparts the peasantry might defy the assaults of an unwieldy cavalry, and oppose a desperate and successful resistance to the most merciless of enemies, who were unassisted by battering machines or cannon. The tremendous engines of attack, to which all the ingenuity of modern science has failed in opposing any permanent defences, had indeed been already introduced, but the rudeness of their original construction, their tardy fire, and uncertain aim, and the difficulty of transporting them before the expedient of mounting them on suitable carriages was adopted, were all unfavourable to their power and general use. Whatever were the means by which the composition of gunpowder first became known to the nations of Europe, or the exact era at which this discovery was followed by the invention of cannon and afterwards of small arms, at least two hundred years from the period before us were destined to elapse, before the employment of these implements of destruction had effected that great revolution in the military art, which has altered the moral and political condition of the universe.

Passing from this general view of the political state and military system of Italy to resume the course of our narrative, the furious contest which was rising between the maritime republics will first engage our attention. The commercial rivalry of these states in their distant establishments, ever the fruitful source of bloodshed between them, was as usual the origin of their quarrel. Before the progress of navigation had opened the passage to India round the Cape of Good Hope, and rendered the Baltic the outlet of northern commerce, the ports of the Black Sea were the main conduits through which the productions of the East and North flowed into the bosom of Europe. The spices and precious merchandize of India were brought overland in caravans to the southern shores of the Euxine; the timber, the naval stores, the furs, all the raw commodities of Russia, were floated down the rivers which discharge themselves into that vast basin at its opposite side. The Genoese and Venetians, the great carriers of the Mediterranean, had established numerous factories round the whole circuit of the Black Sea, to gather the rich produce of this immense traffic; and the colonies of the former people flourished with a splendour which rivalled that of their capital. By their great fortress of Pera they now held the key of the Bosphorus; by purchase from the Tartars they had obtained possession of the site of Caffa in the Crimea, and rendered the town which they built there the populous and impregnable seat of a prosperous trade; and in common with the Venetians and Florentines, they held important establishments in the Tartarian city of Tana at the mouth of the Don. A private quarrel in the year 1349 between an Italian and a Tartar in this place, in which the latter was murdered, provoked the vengeance of the khan, and induced him to expel all the Italian merchants from the city. The Genoese opened an asylum to them at Caffa, and the barbarian, forgetting in his fury the advantage which accrued to himself and his subjects from their commerce with the Latins, resolved to drive them altogether from the country. But the strength of Caffa easily resisted the assaults of his undisciplined hordes; his own coasts were ravaged by the warlike traders; and the total cessation of traffic deprived his subjects of a market for their produce, and of the commodities for which they had been accustomed to exchange it. The Genoese, blockading the mouth of the Don, determined to grant the khan no peace until he should be reduced to permit the erection of a fortified colony for the Latins at Tana; but the Venetians, weary of exclusion from a profitable intercourse, deserted the common cause, reconciled themselves with the barbarian, and violated the blockade. Their vessels in attempting to enter the Don were seized and condemned as prizes by the Genoese, and they immediately armed to revenge the injury and maintain the interests of their commerce. A strong squadron was dispatched from Venice to the scene of contention, and encountering a smaller Genoese force on the voyage, which was also bound for Caffa, captured several galleys.

The war having thus commenced, both republics eagerly prepared for more serious hostilities. (A.D. 1350.) The factions of Genoa were fortunately hushed at the moment in temporary calm, and she could put forth her whole force in the contest; but Venice had not recovered from the depopulation of the Great Pestilence, and was unable to furnish crews for her empty galleys. But she found an useful ally in the king of Aragon, Peter IV., who had himself a cause of quarrel with Genoa. When Sardinia passed from the Pisan to the Aragonese dominion, several Genoese families had still retained fiefs in the island of which Peter was endeavouring at this juncture to deprive them; and their republic had supported them against him. He therefore readily entered into an alliance with Venice, declared war against her rival, and engaged to man a portion of the Venetian galleys with his Catalan subjects, who were still numbered among the best sailors of the Mediterranean. The insolent defiance with which the Genoese colonists of Pera conducted themselves towards the eastern empire, drew upon their republic the hostility of a third and more feeble enemy. Two years before this the colonists had forcibly occupied some commanding ground near their suburb which they wished to fortify, and braved the impotent efforts of the emperor to chastise their presumption. After defeating his galleys and blockading the port of Constantinople, a temporary accommodation left them masters of the heights which they had usurped; and it now seemed their object to exhaust the contemptible patience of the Greeks by aggravated insults. From the ramparts of Pera one of their balistic engines hurled a mass of rock into the midst of Constantinople: the remonstrance of the emperor produced only an ironical excuse; and next day the Genoese, by a repetition of the outrage, satisfied themselves that the imperial capital was within the range of their machines. The emperor then closed with the proposals of the Venetians, who were pressing him to enter into a league with them against the Genoese; but, in the language of a great historian, the weight of the Roman empire was scarcely felt in the balance between these opulent and powerful republics.

The principal efforts of both parties were directed to the eastern seas. (A.D. 1351.) An armament of sixty-four galleys which was dispatched from Genoa under Paganino Doria, after insulting the Adriatic, swept the Archipelago and blockaded the enemy's squadron on that station; until a fleet of fifty Venetian galleys, half of which had been manned at Barcelona, arrived in the same quarter. On their approach Doria steered towards the Hellespont, and Niccolo Pisani, the Venetian admiral, assuming the supreme command of all the Venetian and Catalan armament, prepared to winter in Greece. But such was the impatience of both parties for an encounter, that, before the end of January, the hostile squadrons again put to sea, and directed their course towards the Bosphorus. The season was still stormy and dangerous, when Doria, who had first reached Constantinople, stationed himself off the mouth of that port to dispute its entrance against his rival, (A.D. 1352.) But a violent wind and current setting into the harbour forced the Genoese to seek a shelter for his fleet under the Asiatic shore, and Pisani triumphantly anchored beneath the walls of the eastern capital. The emperor could only reinforce him with eight galleys, but with this addition of numbers, Pisani, though the weather was hourly becoming worse, immediately issued again from the port to attack the Genoese. The combined squadron numbered seventy-five galleys, Venetian, Catalan, and Greek: the Genoese had only sixty-four, but their vessels were larger. Doria had not been able to form his scattered line, when Pisani bore down upon him, but his pilots were perfectly acquainted with the navigation of the Bosphorus, and the whole fleet, obeying his signal, safely ran in among the rocks and shallows of the Asiatic shore. In gallantly attempting to follow them, the Catalans, who were ignorant of the intricacies of the channels, lost many of their vessels; but, notwithstanding this disaster, the fleets engaged with desperate courage. The storm had now increased with frightful violence, the clouds blackened over the heads of the combatants until the fleets were shrouded in darkness, and the wild waves rolled appallingly over the breakers which every where surrounded them. Yet amidst the deafening clamour and horrors of the scene, the battle continued to rage with undiminished fury, and though the Greek galleys fled at the close of day, the event remained undecided. During a long and stormy night, the struggle was alternately interrupted by the tempest, and resumed as often as the glimmering and flitting lights of the hostile galleys disclosed them to each other, and it was not until morning broke over the fleets and the hurricane calmed, that the extent of their mutual loss was ascertained. The sea was covered with wrecks and carnage: the Genoese had lost in all thirteen galleys, but they had captured double that number with eighteen hundred men, and the remains of the Venetian and Catalan fleet sought safety in a Grecian port. The Catalans, who had performed prodigies of valour, had to lament the death of their admiral: many distinguished Venetians had also fallen; and the slain of the allies exceeded two thousand. The Genoese bought their victory dearly, if it be true that, of their nobility alone, above seven hundred perished in the fight.

After refitting his squadron at Pera, Doria prepared to blockade Pisani in his harbour, but the Venetian succeeded in passing through the victorious squadron in a strong gale, and, quitting the Grecian seas, conducted his remaining force without further loss to Venice. Doria, left without an opponent, easily reduced the pusillanimous Greeks to sign a separate peace with Genoa, by which they agreed to close all their ports against the Venetians and Catalans; and he then returned with glory to Genoa. But the reverse which the Venetians had sustained in no degree damped their resolution; and, in concert with the Catalans, they equipped a new armament in the following year, and achieved a brilliant victory, which effaced the reproach of their defeat in the Bosphorus. The allied fleet, still under Pisani, which effected a junction off Sardinia, amounted to seventy galleys; besides three of the large round vessels termed *cocche*, which were employed in those ages, each manned by four hundred Catalans. The Genoese, ignorant that the union of these formidable powers had already taken place, put their squadron to sea in the hope of fighting them in detail. They were now commanded by a Grimaldi: for it is observable that, notwithstanding the revolution which had deprived the four great families of their influence at home, the republic almost invariably entrusted some individual among them with the supreme naval command. When Grimaldi, with only fifty-two galleys, fell in with the enemy near Loidra on the Sardinian coast, he discovered the superiority of their united force too late to avoid a combat. The day was calm; the Genoese trusted that the three great vessels, whose motion depended on the wind alone, would be unable to move; and courageously lashing all their galleys together, except a few to protect the wings of their line, they slowly rowed towards the enemy, (A.D. 1353.) The allies followed their example, and the two mighty masses were closing, when a breeze suddenly sprang up and filled the sails of the *cocche* which were lying becalmed. These great vessels then steered towards the Genoese flank, and at once determined the event of the day. After an obstinate defence, in which they lost two thousand men, the Genoese were utterly defeated. Part of their fleet, casting off from the line, fled under Grimaldi himself; but thirty galleys with three thousand five hundred men, the flower of the republic, surrendered to the victors.

The arrival of Grimaldi at Genoa filled the city with mourning and despair. The national calamity was aggravated by the mutual reproaches and dissensions which it occasioned among the citizens; and this people, who passed for the freest and proudest of the universe, suffered themselves to be so overwhelmed with consternation and fury, that they could imagine no safety and meditate no vengeance but under a foreign master. With strange infatuation they deposed their doge, and voluntarily offered their necks to the yoke of the lord of Milan. The wily Visconti gladly accepted the signiory of Genoa. A Milanese governor and garrison were received into the city, and Visconti immediately supplied the senate with money to equip a new fleet: as if his gold could recompense the Genoese for the loss of their freedom. He also vainly endeavoured to induce the Venetians to terminate a war, from the prosecution of which he could derive no advantage. But the virulent hostility of the Venetians was yet unsatisfied, they declared war against the new signor of Genoa himself, and both parties redoubled their efforts to prosecute the struggle with vigour. The Genoese with the aid of Visconti equipping a squadron of thirty-three galleys, placed their force under Paganino Doria. This great admiral, to whom they were already indebted for their victory in the Bosphorus, after appearing in the Adriatic and striking terror into Venice, who was left defenceless by the absence of her fleet off Sardinia, sailed for the Grecian seas; whither Pisani, who yet commanded the Venetians, shortly followed him with thirty-five galleys. The two admirals vainly sought each other, until Pisani had put into the port of Sapienza in the Morea to refit, when Doria appeared off its entrance and offered him battle. Pisani had sent up part of his fleet to careen at the head of the harbour, which was very long, while he guarded its narrow mouth with the rest of his galleys; and remaining in this strong position notwithstanding the taunts of the Genoese, he determined not to fight until his whole fleet should have completed their repairs. The fortunate temerity of young Doria, the nephew of the Genoese admiral, gave a fatal issue to this resolution, (A.D. 1354.) The youth boldly steered his galley between the extremity of the Venetian line and the shore, and entered the harbour; twelve other vessels one by one followed in his wake; and Pisani, confident that they were rushing into destruction between the two divisions of his fleet, suffered them to pass unopposed. But they were no sooner within the harbour than young Doria led them up at once to the distant head of the port, and impetuously attacked the Venetian crews, whose galleys were moored to the shore, when they least expected it. They were seized with a panic, made but a feeble resistance, and their whole division were captured or destroyed. Young Doria then returned to the mouth of the port to attack Pisani from within, while his uncle assaulted him in front: their success was complete; after a frightful carnage the Venetian admiral surrendered with his whole squadron; and the Genoese found that, although four thousand Venetians had been slain, they had taken nearly six thousand prisoners of every quality. This contest terminated the war. The navy of Venice, who had already exhausted her strength in prodigious efforts, was nearly extinguished by the loss of a whole squadron and ten thousand of her chosen seamen, (A.D. 1355.) Reduced by so heavy a calamity to sue for peace, she purchased it by the payment of 200,000 gold florins to Genoa for the charges of the war, and by engaging to renounce the commerce of Tana.

The eagerness of the Venetian senate for the restoration of tranquillity, even upon terms which were little agreeable to the pride of the republic, might be occasioned in part by the imminent danger which the oligarchy had encountered but a few months before from a conspiracy, headed by no less a personage than the doge himself. Marin Falieri, a nobleman who had honourably filled many of the principal offices of state, had been raised in the preceding year to the ducal throne at the age of seventy-six. He was married to a young and beautiful woman; but the demon of jealousy violated his repose. At a masqued ball in the ducal palace during the first carnival after his accession, he observed some sighs and glances of love between a young nobleman, Michel Steno, and one of the ladies of the duchess's train, and immediately commanded the gallant to quit the assembly. Steno, under the momentary irritation excited by this insult, indulged his pique, as he passed through the adjoining council chamber, by writing on the ducal throne two lines which reflected on the honour of the doge and the purity of his wife. This pasquinade, of which Steno was easily discovered to be the author, filled the old doge with uncontrollable indignation. He viewed it as an insult of offensive and deadly poignancy, and endeavoured to make it a crime of state; but the council of ten contented itself with leaving the cause to the decision of the forty of justice, of which council Steno was himself a member, and he was sentenced only to a short imprisonment. This lenity so exasperated the irascible and jealous dotard against the whole aristocracy, that, availing himself of the discontent of several plebeians who had been personally insulted by the arrogant nobles, he engaged them in a conspiracy to raise the city and massacre the whole oligarchical order. The general existence of a plot was discovered; the manner in which the doge treated the information excited the suspicion of the council of ten; they privately arrested several of the accused, and put them to the torture; and they then learned from their confessions that Falieri himself was implicated. The sequel is characteristic of the decision and vigour of that stern and mysterious tribunal. After taking instant and effectual measures for the security of the city, the ten summoned twenty of the principal nobles to assist their deliberations at so momentous a crisis. They secured the person of their chief magistrate, confronted him with his accomplices, heard his avowal of guilt, and condemned him to die. He was privately beheaded before them on the great staircase of the ducal palace, the spot where the doges were wont to take their initiatory oath of fidelity to the republic. One of the ten, the reeking sword of justice in his hand, immediately presented himself at the balcony to the people, and proclaimed aloud that "justice had been executed on a great offender;" and, at the same moment, the gates of the palace were thrown open, and the populace admitted to view the head of Falieri weltering in its gore. Between the detection of the conspiracy, and the consummation of this tragedy, there had elapsed only two days, and the election of a new doge was peaceably conducted under the usual forms.

In the year after the decapitation of Falieri, the Venetians were involved in a dangerous and unfortunate war with the king of Hungary. (A.D. 1356.) Louis (he who formerly appeared in Italy as the avenger of his brother Andrew) had maintained but few relations of amity with the republic. Distinguished for his active courage, his superior talents, and his generous temper, though these noble qualities were in some degree marred by an inconstancy of purpose, he had raised his kingdom to an eminence of power and splendour unparalleled in its history. He regarded the maritime province of Dalmatia as a natural part of his inheritance, and the Dalmatians themselves had long shown their attachment to the Hungarians, and their hatred of the Venetian yoke. In the frequent insurrections of the people of Zara, and other cities on the same coast, they had always appealed to the sovereignty of the Hungarian kings, and Louis had himself on a former occasion vainly endeavoured to protect their revolt. He had lately shown his animosity towards Venice by declaring war against her at the instigation of Genoa; and though this measure had not at the time been followed by any important consequences, he now found himself in a condition to make a formal demand of the cession of Dalmatia. Upon the refusal of the Venetian senate to submit to his pretensions, he attacked the republic with prodigious numbers, both in the district of Treviso and in Dalmatia. His armies were composed entirely of a feudal light cavalry, furnished only with the bow and the sword, and with no other defensive harness than quilted doublets, which resisted the stroke of the sabre, and the point of the arrow and lance. After appearing in the first campaign at the head of fifty thousand of these vassals, who in their Scythian mode of warfare covered the face of the Trevisan district, and left it a desert; Louis finding the republic inflexible, maintained the war by incessant invasions in smaller numbers, which ruined the Venetian territory, and kept Treviso in continued blockade. In these incursions he was secretly aided by the lord of Padua, who, though in alliance with Venice, supplied him with provisions: an injury which that vindictive republic never forgave to the house of Carrara. The Venetians were, from the nature of their resources, peculiarly unequal to the support of such a warfare; all the cities of Dalmatia fell into the hands of the Hungarian by open revolt, or secret treason; and the republic, humbled by so many reverses, sued for peace, and left the terms to the generosity of her enemy. Louis was worthy of the confidence; he exacted neither money, nor the cession of the Trevisan district, in which he had taken many castles; but, adhering to his original demand, obliged the

Venetians to renounce the sovereignty of Dalmatia, and their doge to expunge that pretension from the roll of his dignities. Upon these terms peace was concluded, and the chiefs of the republic, who had so long affixed to their office the proud designation of dukes of Dalmatia, and of three-eighths of the Roman empire, were, for a while, reduced to the more modest title of doges of Venice, (A.D. 1358.)

The first serious troubles which arose in Tuscany after the ravages of the Great Pestilence had subsided, were occasioned by the ambitious enterprises of the lord of Milan. The archbishop Giovanni Visconti had scarcely assumed the sovereignty of that state, on the death of his brother Luchino, when his machinations excited the alarm of the Florentine republic. Two brothers of the family of Pepoli, who had succeeded to the signiory of Bologna, with difficulty maintained their power against the papal lieutenant in Romagna; and Visconti, availing himself of their danger, concluded a secret treaty with them, by which they basely sold the rights of their fellow-citizens, and gave him possession of the place, (A.D. 1351.)

This acquisition, by which the archbishop extended his power to the confines of Tuscany, and the alliance which he formed with the petty signers of Romagna, filled the Florentines with well-grounded apprehensions of so active and perfidious a neighbour. Ever the watchful guardians of the political balance in Italy, they were conscious of being the particular object of hostility to a tyrant who aimed at the wide extension of his dominion; and, though their safety was identified with the common cause of independence, they stood alone in the disposition to resist him. The Lombard princes, who had every thing to dread from the preponderance of his power, were either his allies, or too debauched and feeble to offer opposition to his aggrandizement; Pisa was friendly to him from her Ghibelin predilections; and the Guelf republics of Tuscany, Sienna, Perugia, and Arezzo, trusting to the poor security of their remoteness from the immediate scene of danger, refused to make exertion or sacrifice to avert it. While clouds were gathering into a storm against her, Florence therefore found herself without other aid than that of the neighbouring little states of Prato and Pistoia, which enjoyed a doubtful independence under her protection, and, rather her subjects than her allies, required the employment of force to prevent their factions from delivering them to the Ghibelin party.

Though the Milanese troops hovered on the frontiers of Tuscany, and Visconti assembled a diet of the Ghibelin chieftains at his capital, he was profuse in assurances of his desire for the maintenance of peace; and he even lulled the suspicions of the magistracy of Florence until his forces broke through the passes of the Apennines, and attempted to surprise Pistoia. A small body of volunteers from Florence threw themselves into the town in time to secure its preservation; but the crafty Visconti having thus thrown off the mask, his Ghibelin allies poured from all quarters into Tuscany. The lords of Lombardy and Romagna hastened to furnish their contingents to his army; the Ghibelin chieftains who had always retained independent domains in the fastnesses of the Apennines, joined his standard with their vassals; and his general found himself at the head of five thousand cuirassiers, two thousand lighter horse, and six thousand foot, and extended his ravages to the gates of Florence. To this overwhelming force the republic could oppose no resistance in the field: she had no army on foot, and her government had scarcely any mercenaries in pay; but the passive courage which always so curiously distinguished her unwarlike population in the contests of these ages, preserved her in this hour of imminent peril. The peasantry threw themselves as usual into the fortified villages which bristled the country, the citizens manned the walls of the capital, and the public confidence remained unshaken. The neutrality of Pisa, too, removed one great cause of anxiety; for the rulers of that state, for once preferring the dictates of sound policy to the virulence of factious animosity, refused to join the Ghibelin lords, their allies, against the Guelf protectress of Italian liberty.

After devastating the open territory of Florence, the numerous forces of Visconti and his confederates soon ceased to be really formidable. All the provisions of the country which had not been destroyed were secured within the rural fortresses; and such was the firm countenance of the peasantry behind these defences, that every petty castle required a regular siege to reduce it. The invaders thus began to be straitened for food; they could no longer subsist in the plain of Florence, and withdrawing from it by the valley of Marina, they undertook the siege of the little town of Scarperia. Here the superiority of the defensive art over the assaults of an army whose only real strength was in heavy cavalry, was conspicuously displayed. Scarperia was but indifferently fortified, and yet the Florentine garrison, of no more than five hundred men, preserved their post with successful valour against the whole Ghibelin army.

The Florentines meanwhile gained time to levy forces and take bands of mercenaries into their service; the republic of Sienna afforded them a tardy succour of troops; and the armed peasantry harassed the enemy, and intercepted the convoys of food which he drew from Lombardy. But so much terror did the power of Visconti at this time excite in Italy, that no chieftain of reputation could be found among the condottieri to provoke the enmity of the Milanese lord by accepting the command of the republican forces; and the Florentines, without a leader of experience, dared not therefore hazard a battle for the relief of Scarperia, which began to be reduced to extremity. But two native captains—the one a Medici—bravely undertook to reinforce the garrison with a handful of men, and under the cover of night dextrously passed through the camp of the besiegers into the place. Their seasonable arrival inspired the garrison with new strength and spirit; and the Milanese general, who had hoped to exhaust and overwhelm them by reiterated attacks and the incessant discharge of masses of rock and showers of missiles from his engines, was thenceforth disappointed in every effort. He caused all the machines employed in sieges to be constructed, but his moveable wooden towers and his battering rams were burnt in a sally: he thrice attempted to carry the walls by open escalade and by surprise, but he was as often repulsed with slaughter in these general assaults; and at length, after his army had endured severe privations from scarcity of food and the unhealthiness of the season, incurred heavy loss and disgrace, and consumed two months in the ineffectual siege of this petty fortress, he withdrew from before it, and evacuated the Florentine territory.

While the whole power of Visconti was thus broken against the walls of Scarperia, Florence assumed an attitude of pride and security. She accumulated new levies of mercenaries, she strengthened all her fortresses, and the other Guelf republics of Tuscany concluded a defensive alliance with her. On the resumption of hostilities, therefore, in the following spring, she was no longer in the same unprepared state as in the preceding year; and Visconti, instead of again invading Tuscany with a single great army, distributed his forces on numerous points, and instigated the Ghibelin chieftains of the Apennines to pour their vassals into the lands of the Guelf republics from various quarters, (A.D. 1352.) But after some partial successes, these invasions were every where repulsed, and the republics concluded a desultory but glorious campaign by driving the invaders from their territories.

The Florentines, however, not contented with rousing the Guelf strength of Tuscany against so insidious and formidable an enemy as Visconti, had meanwhile laid a new train for crushing his power, by inviting Charles IV. of Bohemia, then king of the Romans, into Italy. They represented to that monarch that the continued ascendancy of the lord of Milan must be fatal to the remains of the imperial authority in the peninsula, they solicited him to aid them in humbling the ambition of Visconti, and they offered to support him with all their forces and treasure, on his appearance to claim the crowns of Lombardy and the empire. Charles immediately entered into a treaty with them; and the alarm with which these negotiations inspired the archbishop, although they produced no other result, together with the continued ill success of the Ghibelin arms, and the apprehensions which he entertained at the moment of papal hostility, induced him to make pacific overtures to the Tuscan republics. His proposals were accepted, and under the mediation of Pisa a peace was concluded at Sarzana, which guaranteed to both parties the possessions which they had held when the war commenced, (A.D. 1353.)

The repose which this pacification procured for Tuscany had lasted only a few months, when the formation of a new and more formidable company of adventure than had hitherto appeared in Italy renewed the evils of warfare under their most frightful aspect. This army of robbers was drawn together by a Provençal gentleman, Montreal of Albano, a knight of St. John of Jerusalem, who had served with distinction in the Neapolitan wars of Louis of Hungary. Having attracted many of the German condottieri under his standard by the promise of regular pay for their bands, as well as the unbridled licence usual with such companies of adventure, he commenced his ravages in Romagna; and, after devastating that province with fire and sword and extorting contributions, approached the frontiers of Tuscany. His successful career of rapine was a dangerous invitation to the cupidity of all the foreign mercenaries of Italy, and his force had accumulated with such fearful rapidity, that in less than twelve months the Great Company, as it was called, consisted of seven thousand cuirassiers, with above twenty thousand ruffian followers of all descriptions. Montreal had the art, while he indulged this execrable multitude in the commission of every atrocity against the inhabitants of the country, to give regularity to their enterprises, and even to maintain rigorous discipline and order in their camp. (A.D. 1354.) When he approached Tuscany, the Guelf republics showed a disposition to league for their common defence; but he seduced Perugia into a base desertion of the cause by offering her a neutrality; Sienna next purchased exemption from the ravages of the company by a heavy contribution; and Montreal then entered the Florentine territory. That republic was unfortunately at the moment governed by priors of no ability; and after suffering the company to plunder the country without attempting resistance, they paid a large and ignominious tribute for the promise of two years' deliverance from the presence of these organized freebooters. Pisa shared in the disgraceful treaty; and Montreal then drew off his forces into Lombardy, which now presented a new theatre of action for his followers.

We have seen how the acquisition of the signiory of Genoa by the lord of Milan involved him in hostility with Venice; and very shortly after he had concluded the peace of Sarzana with the Tuscan states, the negotiations of that republic lit up the flames of war in Lombardy. The lords of Mantua, Verona, and Padua, and the marquis of Este, had all continual causes of complaint against Visconti, who carried his treacherous intrigues into every city under their dominion. But though the whole of these princes dreaded the power and machinations of the archbishop, they dared not singly provoke his open vengeance, and they were too much divided among themselves, and too mutually suspicious, to combine with each other. Venice, however, laboured incessantly to reconcile their differences, and arm them against her enemy and theirs; and she at length succeeded in uniting them in a league with her to attack the Milanese lord. It was this confederacy which summoned the great company to Lombardy to enter into their pay; and after ineffectually urging Florence to break the peace of Sarzana and join them, they applied, as she had done, to Charles IV., and invited him into Italy. At the same time Visconti, to frustrate their design, equally courted the friendship of the emperor elect; and Charles, who found himself thus alternately the object of solicitation from the republics of Tuscany, from Venice, and from all the Lombard princes, and who was besides on good terms with the papal court of Avignon, saw every obstacle removed which former emperors had experienced in their Italian expeditions. He therefore crossed the Alps (A.D. 1354); but all the powers of Italy, who had negotiated in turn with him to direct his power against their enemies, heard with astonishment that this successor of Augustus was attended only by a small and unarmed train of three hundred cavaliers. Charles, a mean-spirited and avaricious prince, had in truth no other views in undertaking this journey, than to receive the imperial crown, and to extort as much money as possible from the Italian states. The results of his expedition were as insignificant as his purposes, and I may, therefore, pass with rapidity over the circumstances which attended his enterprise.

Before the arrival of Charles in Lombardy, the archbishop Giovanni Visconti was no more, and the three sons of one of his deceased brothers, Matteo, Bernabo, and Galeazzo, had succeeded without opposition to the sovereign power which he bequeathed jointly among them. The brothers divided the Milanese dominions in such manner, that while each had a third as his proper appanage, the capital and the sovereign power rested in common with all. The death of the archbishop produced no peace in Lombardy; and Charles IV., who observed a strict neutrality, and exerted his mediation between the Visconti and the confederated signors, could only induce the contending parties to sign a truce. The Visconti, after making an ostentatious display of their forces, in contemptuous contrast with his slender escort, suffered him to receive the iron crown of Lombardy in their capital, and he then passed into Tuscany.

The appearance of the new emperor in this province was regarded by the Florentines with alarm and jealousy, though they had but lately desired his presence, (A.D. 1355.) Notwithstanding his weakness, the respect which the imperial name still excited in Italy rendered him a dangerous visitor for the Guelf republics. Pisa received him with honour, and in that city the Ghibelin chieftains of the Apennines, together with all the partizans of the same faction in Tuscany, crowded around him, and instigated him to revenge on Florence the hostility which she had formerly shown to his family; to his grandfather the emperor Henry VII., and his father John of Bohemia. On the other hand, the Guelf communities who had undertaken to be guided by Florence in their demeanour towards him, forsook their engagement, and surrendered to this new master the signiory of their republics.

The circumstances which followed are worthy of notice, as they illustrate the feelings of the free citizens of Florence. The rulers of that state were sensible of the danger of the crisis, if Charles should gratify the passions of the Ghibelins by declaring against their republic; and that monarch, whose only object was money, increased their alarm to induce them to purchase his protection. He required of the Florentines a large sum, as the price of the repeal of an imperial sentence of condemnation, which Henry VII. had passed against their city; and engaged, for one hundred thousand florins of gold, to take them into favour, and to confirm their liberties and privileges. But in his treaty with them, he assumed a lofty style of sovereignty; he obliged their deputies to do homage and swear obedience to him; and declaring that he restored Florence to the rank of an imperial city, he constituted the magistrates whom the people should thenceforth elect, perpetual vicars of the empire. The leading men of Florence, who saw that these pretensions were no more than nominal, easily reconciled themselves to a submission which was rendered prudent by existing circumstances; but the high-spirited democracy, more tenacious about words, could with difficulty be induced to ratify stipulations that seemed to admit the renunciation of their sovereignty. The treaty with Charles was seven times presented for confirmation to the council of the people, and as often rejected, before the influence and persuasion of the magistracy and principal citizens could bring the popular assembly to a more prudent line of conduct; and when their efforts at last succeeded, the proclamation of the treaty was heard by the people with silent gloom, as if some heavy disgrace or misfortune had overwhelmed the state.

    Shortly after this, Charles IV. being now joined by a splendid and warlike train of the feudal nobility of Germany, who had followed him into Italy according to the laws of the empire to attend his coronation, proceeded to Rome escorted by a brilliant army of German and Italian nobles, and received the imperial diadem in that city. After this ceremony, his attendant chivalry immediately dispersed, the Italians to their homes, and the Germans to recross the Alps, and the emperor returned without forces into Tuscany. Without embarrassing the attention of the reader with transactions of little importance or interest, I shall only observe that the remainder of his residence in Italy served but to betray his weakness, and expose the defects of his character. The people of Sienna threw off the yoke which he attempted to fix on them, and expelled his lieutenant; he excited general indignation among the Pisans (who had manifested towards him all their ancient attachment to the empire) by his abortive treachery in endeavouring, contrary to the faith of his treaty with them, to free the people of Lucca from their yoke that he might fill his own coffers; and when he quitted Tuscany, he experienced studied disrespect from the Visconti in his passage through their states, and finally crossed the Alps followed by general contempt and detestation.

After the return of Charles IV. into Germany, Lombardy, on the expiration of the truce which he had effected between the Visconti and the other confederated princes, still continued the scene of warfare. The marquis of Montferrat, who had long been the ally of the Visconti, deserted them and joined the league of their enemies on some personal cause of offence; the family of Beccaria, who governed Pavia under Milanese protection, revolted and embraced the same party; several other cities followed this example; and the great company, now under a German, count Lando, entered the service of the confederates. But the war, which was principally carried on with foreign mercenaries on both sides, proceeded with little vigour, and had no other result than to enrich these adventurers at ruinous expense to the tyrants who paid them, and to the unhappy country in which they served. The condottieri under opposite standards, with proverbial bad faith towards their respective employers, were almost always in an understanding with each other, and purposely avoided decisive encounters to prolong the contest and multiply their gains.

After three years of fruitless warfare, therefore, both the Visconti and their enemies became weary of its continuance, and a pacification was concluded upon equitable terms, (A.D. 1358.) But the league of the Lombard allies was no sooner thus dissolved, than the perfidious lords of Milan resolved to wreak their vengeance upon Pavia for her revolt, though they had formally recognised the independence of the people of that city by the conditions of the peace. On the other hand, the marquis of Montferrat refused to deliver up the city of Asti to Galeazzo Visconti as he had promised, and hostilities were resumed; but with this difference, that the Milanese signors were now at liberty, by the neutrality of the other Lombard princes, to direct their whole power against the marquis and Pavia. I need only remark of the former, that he supported the unequal conflict with difficulty for several years; but the fortunes of Pavia deserve and shall receive more particular notice.

The people of that city had been roused to the reformation of morals and the assertion of freedom by the preaching of a monk of irreproachable character, Fra Jacopo de' Bussolari, who inveighed with powerful eloquence against the corruption of their manners, and the shame of their subjection to dissolute tyrants. He had inspired the citizens with energy and valour; he had led them in successful enterprises against their Milanese enemies, and induced them to re-establish their ancient republic, and to throw off the yoke of the Beccaria. That family, who had long exercised the signiory, on being thus shorn of their power, reconciled themselves in secret with the Visconti; and, being exiled from the city for their treason, aided those tyrants with their rural retainers. Deserted by the powers of the league after the late pacification, and finding the marquis of Montferrat no longer able to assist them, the unfortunate people of Pavia were utterly unable to contend with the Milanese power; and Fra Jacopo at length himself advised their submission, and, without stipulating for his own safety, negotiated a treaty which guaranteed their municipal liberties under the sovereignty of the Visconti. (A.D. 1359.) But when Galeazzo was once admitted into Pavia, he perfidiously violated the engagement, subjected the citizens to a frightful tyranny, and consigned the virtuous monk to a prison, in which he miserably terminated his existence.

Of the three joint lords of Milan, the eldest brother Matteo had survived his accession to power but a short time. Sunken in the lowest abyss of sensuality and crime, he had abandoned the cares of government, and was surrounded only by the dishonoured wives and daughters of his subjects, whom he had forcibly torn from the bosom of their families. A gentleman of Milan was sent for, and commanded by this monster, on pain of death, to bring to the palace and consign to infamy his young and beautiful wife. The outraged husband implored the protection of the brothers of Matteo; and they, though they equalled him in depravity of heart, dreading lest his unmeasured excesses should drive their common subjects to desperation, hesitated not to remove him by poison. The unnatural guilt of these fratricides was if possible deepened by the cruelties of their subsequent reign. Galeazzo, himself a perfidious and remorseless tyrant, was excelled in wanton ferocity by Bernabo. They jointly laboured to strike universal terror into their enemies by the systematic atrocities which they exercised upon those who fell into their hands. After the conclusion of the war in Lombardy, they selected numerous victims at Pavia and other cities which had attempted revolt; and a contemporary historian has preserved a copy of a public law of Bernabo, which regulated the sufferings of these state offenders. By this execrable enactment, the provisions of which should at once have armed society against the fiend who could dictate them, the Milanese tribunals were directed to protract all capital punishments, during forty days of various and lingering tortures:—but I shall pass to a fairer theme.

For several years after the expedition of the emperor Charles IV., the Tuscan states enjoyed a season of prosperity and comparative repose, which was less seriously interrupted than usual in this turbulent age by internal troubles and open hostilities. During this period Florence, in particular, acquired well-merited honour. She terminated by her mediation a war between the Guelf republics of Sienna and Perugia; and when the Great Company, in 1368 and the following year, again appeared in this part of Italy, and subjected the other powers to a repetition of disgraceful contribution, she alone resolutely determined to put a period to the shame of submission to these enemies of society, and to refuse all compromise with their demands. But though the Italian governments I had hitherto wanted courage to defy this army of robbers, their exactions and audacity had raised general indignation;

and even the Ghibelin princes of Lombardy, all of whom they had outraged and betrayed in turn, furnished auxiliaries to the Guelf republic against them. The army which Florence thus assembled was, it is true, principally composed also of foreign mercenaries: but the company, awed by the firm countenance of the republic, shunned an engagement, and at last made a disorderly retreat; and Florence not only protected her territory, but humbled the insolence of the condottieri, and had the glory of teaching other states, that protection against their depredations was to be found, not in tribute, but resistance.

At this favourable epoch, too, the security of the Tuscan republics was increased by the subjection of many of the feudal nobles of the Apennines who had hitherto preserved the independence of their fiefs; and, partly by liberal purchases, partly by force, Florence, Sienna, and Perugia all aggrandized themselves by acquiring the territory of these predatory chieftains. Amidst this prosperity, the domestic repose of all the Guelf republics and of Pisa was not, indeed, undisturbed, and, almost at the same moment, dangerous conspiracies were discovered in each; but these were timely frustrated, and Tuscany had seldom been so tranquil, when rising animosity between Florence and Pisa began to darken the political horizon, and finally to overspread the province with a new storm of war.

The guilt of the original aggression which destroyed the harmony that had for many years prevailed between the two states, rested solely with Pisa. Her government had passed into the hands of the most violent of her Ghibelin citizens, who studiously sought in secret to provoke a rupture, which the signiory of Florence for some time as carefully endeavoured to avert. After wantonly instigating some of their disbanded mercenaries to seize a Florentine castle, the Pisan rulers laid a duty upon all merchandize which entered their harbour; and contrary to the terms of a former treaty by which the Florentines, who carried on their foreign commerce through this channel, enjoyed freedom from all such impositions, they refused to exempt them from the tax. Finding remonstrance useless, and still resolved if possible to avoid recourse to hostilities, the Florentine signiory adopted an effectual measure for punishing the arrogance of their enemies. They commanded all their subjects to close their mercantile business at Pisa and withdraw from that city; and by treaty with Sienna transferred the seat of their maritime trade to the small port of Telamone belonging to that republic, (A.D. 1356.)

The commerce of Pisa was thus annihilated at a single blow, for all the foreign merchants who resorted thither solely for the Florentine markets, were obliged to change the destination of their vessels to Telamone. The total stagnation of employment, and the consequent ruin which threatened the Pisan artisans, filled that city with clamour; and the government then endeavoured to appease the popular ferment by conciliating the Florentines, and offering to abolish their imposts. But this high-spirited and wealthy people were in their turn inexorable; and a singular contest ensued. The Pisans, arming some galleys, cruized off the Tuscan coast, and used force to oblige the merchant vessels, which were bound for Telamone, to land their cargoes at Pisa free of all duties; and the Florentines, rather than submit to receive their imports in this manner, brought their merchandize at increased expense by land from Venice, from Avignon, and even from Flanders. But such was the spirit which animated a republic that possessed not an inch of maritime territory, that she resolved to inspire respect for her flag even on the seas. She hired armed galleys in Provence, at Genoa, and at Naples; and, with the small squadron which she thus formed, attacked a rival who had once aspired to the dominion of the waters. But Pisa had long ceased to be a naval power, her strength was directed to the acquisition of continental territory, and so feeble had she become on the waves, that the few vessels in Florentine pay ravaged her coasts and insulted her harbours with impunity. (A.D. 1362.)

Meanwhile, after repeated injuries on both sides, the smothered animosity between the two republics had broken out into an open contest by land; and, for three years, their territories were alternately laid waste by desultory operations of various success. The forces employed by each party were as usual composed chiefly of foreign cavalry, and Pisa had at one time above six thousand of these mercenary cuirassiers in her pay. The reader would be little interested in the detail of predatory incursions and ridiculous bravades which occupied the rival republics, and were only suspended by the appearance in Tuscany of the plague. After showing itself first in Flanders, this terrific scourge spread over Europe at the epoch before us with a raging mortality, second only in horror to that of the Great Pestilence of 1348. Its ravages in Tuscany increased the pressure of a war which weakened the hostile states without any decided preponderance of fortune. The advantage however upon the whole rested finally with Florence; and when the two republics had at length become weary of ruinous hostilities, and mutually desirous of peace, the Pisans engaged, by the pacification which was concluded between them, to pay 100,000 florins in ten years to Florence for the charges of the war, and to confirm the exemption of Florentine merchandize from all duties in their port. (A.D. 1364.) Upon these terms Florence agreed to make Pisa again the emporium of her maritime commerce. Tranquillity was thus restored to Tuscany; but just at the moment when Pisa was relieved from the danger of foreign hostility, she fell a prey to the ambition of one of her own citizens, and afforded another example of those strange and sudden revolutions which were so common in Italian states. Giovanni dell' Agnello, a merchant of obscure family, secretly aided by Bernabo Visconti, and supported by the foreign mercenaries of the republic, overthrew her liberties, and assumed, first the dignity of doge, and afterwards, the more despotic title and authority of signer.

 One circumstance in the war between Pisa and Florence may possess some attraction for the British reader. Among the foreign condottieri who served in these campaigns, by far the most celebrated captain was an Englishman; and the palm of martial excellence is conceded by our contemporary writers to the bands of our nation who followed his standard. After the peace of Bretigni, which our Edward III. and John of France concluded in 1358, their disbanded soldiery had formed themselves into companies of adventure, several of which, after horribly ravaging the exhausted provinces of northern France, carried their devastations into Provence; and from thence one of them, the White, or English Company, passed into the service of the marquis of Montferrat, who was still at war with the Visconti. But with the characteristic inconstancy of such adventurers, the company shortly delivered the marquis from their onerous maintenance, by entering the Pisan pay on the expiration of their engagement with him. They had been trained in the wars of Edward III., and the Italian historians speak with admiration both of their valour and of their ability in surprises and stratagems,—the partizan warfare of the times. Their cavalry introduced two new military practices into Italy: the custom of reckoning their numbers by lances, and of dismounting to combat on foot Each lance, as it was termed, was, at least at this time, composed of three cavaliers, who were bound to each other in a species of association; and as the White Company mustered a thousand lances, besides two thousand infantry, their whole force was five thousand men. Their cavaliers made little other use of their horses than to bear them in their heavy armour to the field of battle, where they usually dismounted and formed an impenetrable and resistless phalanx; and in this close order, with their ponderous lances lowered at the charge, and each held by two men, they slowly advanced with loud cheers towards their enemy. Their defensive arms were of the mixed character of plate and mail, which was still retained in England and France, after the full casing of steel had been adopted in Italy. Over their mail-coats of interlaced chain they wore cuirasses of iron; their brasses, their cuisses, and boots, were of the same material; and their array shone with dazzling splendour, for each cavalier was attended by a page whose constant occupation was to burnish his armour.

These hardy English bands, habituated to their own bracing climate, braved with indifference the utmost rigour of an Italian winter; the severity of no season was a protection against their enterprises; and the light scaling ladders, which they carried in detached pieces, facilitated the war of surprises wherein they excelled. The talents of their leader added to the reputation which these qualities of soldiership obtained for them. This eminent captain, who is called by the Italians *Acuto*, or *Auguto*, was Sir John Hawkwood, an adventurer of mean extraction, for he is said to have been originally a tailor, who had been knighted by Edward III. for his distinguished services in the French wars. The Pisans entrusted him with the supreme command of their forces in the contest with Florence; and from this period we shall find him passing the long remainder of his life in the incessant troubles of Italy, and deservedly regarded as the most accomplished commander of his times.

PART II.
Affairs of the pontificate—Conquest of Romagna by the holy see—Scandal of the papal residence at Avignon—Pope Urban V.—Restoration of the seat of the popedom to Rome—Alliance between the emperor Charles IV. and Urban V.—League against the Visconti—Arrival of Charles IV. in Italy—His disgraceful conduct in Lombardy and Tuscany—His sale of freedom to Lucca—Revival of that republic—Grandeur of Urban V.—New wars provoked by the Visconti—Return of the pope to Avignon—His death—War between Florence and the Church—Revolt of Romagna—Arrival of pope Gregory XI. at Rome—His death—Election of a new pope—Violence of the Roman populace—Urban VI. chosen by the conclave—His offensive conduct to the cardinals—Their secession—They annul the election of Urban VI., and substitute Clement VII.—Question on the validity of Urban's title—The great schism of the West—Domestic affairs of Florence—Factions of the Ricci and Albizzi—The Guelf corporation—Tyranny of that oligarchy—The Albizzi, chiefs of the Guelf aristocracy—The Ricci, leaders of the democratical party—Insurrection of the democratical faction—Fall of the Guelf aristocracy—Sedition of the Ciompi—Florence in the hands of a mob—Anarchy in the republic—Patriotism of Michel di Lando—Restoration of order Triumph of the democratical faction—Administration of its leaders—Their judicial murders, tyranny, and fall—Restoration of the Guelf oligarchy to power—Affairs of Venice—Rupture of the republic with Genoa—Powerful league against Venice—War of Chiozza—Naval operations—Total defeat of the Venetian fleet—The entrance into the lagunes of Venice forced by the Genoese fleet—Capture of Chiozza—Extremity of Venice—Courageous spirit of the senate and people—Their energetic exertions to equip a fleet, and skilful operations—The Genoese blockaded in the lagune—Increase of the Venetian force and confidence—Surrender of the Genoese fleet—Continuation of the war—Peace of Turin.

DURING the long and voluntary exile of the popes at Avignon, the intimate connexion which had formerly subsisted between the affairs of the papacy and the complicated politics of Italy had been almost entirely destroyed; and, in endeavouring to clear the path of the reader through the tangled mazes of my subject, I have scarcely found occasion to arrest his progress through the transactions of the last sixty years by any notice of papal history. But at the point which we have now reached in our course, two circumstances revived the influence of the popes in Italy, and will necessarily claim our attention: I mean the total subjugation of Romagna to the church, and the temporary restoration of the pontificate to its original seat.

The province of Romagna was, as has been noticed in another part of this history, subject to petty signers; and, notwithstanding the solemn cession of the imperial rights of sovereignty which Rodolph of Hapsburg had made to the church, it acknowledged little obedience to the pontiffs of Avignon. But Clement VI., in 1350, commissioned his legate in Italy to bring all the cities of Romagna, by force or intrigue, under the authority of the church, and supplied him with a body of mercenary troops and a large sum of money for the different purposes of force and persuasion. The enterprise was not of easy accomplishment; for the inhabitants of the papal states were, of all the Italians, the only people who had retained their warlike character; and their chieftains, the Malatesti, lords of Rimini, the Ordelaffi of Forli, the Pollenta of Ravenna, the Manfredi of Faenza, and other noble families, instead of confiding the defence of their little states, like the Lombard princes, to German mercenaries, habitually led their own forces, composed of the gentlemen and peasantry of their mountain demesnes. They were themselves a race of skilful and active captains; war was their constant occupation, and, when not engaged in hostilities among themselves, they were usually to be found in the service of the more powerful princes and republics. Their reputation for bad faith was as remarkable as their ability and valour; and, in ages when the contempt of all moral obligations had become too generally the reproach of the Italian character, the Romagnol perfidy was proverbial in the peninsula.

The scheme of Clement VI. for subjugating these chieftains failed of success; for his lieutenant, by a treacherous attempt to wrest Bologna, the only great city of Romagna, from the Pepoli, induced those tyrants, as we have seen, to sell their power to the archbishop Giovanni Visconti, and involved himself in a dangerous war with the Milanese lord. The avarice of the papal court left the legate without the means of maintaining this contest. Clement vainly thundered his spiritual censures against the archbishop; and Visconti, partly by bribes to the mistress and courtiers of the pope, and partly by the menace of visiting Avignon with an army, obtained the cession of the sovereignty of Bologna, to be held by him as a fief of the church. But, on the death of Clement, in 1352, the projects which he had formed of bringing Romagna under the obedience of the holy see were renewed by his successor Innocent VI., and finally accomplished by the unassisted talents and activity of one man.

This extraordinary person was the cardinal Egidio Albornoz, a noble Spaniard, who had learnt the trade of a skilful general in the religious wars of his own country against the Moors, and improved his capacity for dissimulation and artifice in the intrigues of the papal court. He entered Italy as papal legate in 1353, almost without forces or treasure; and pursuing his designs with vigour and singular address for more than twelve years, finished by completely humbling the tyrants of Romagna, and reducing them into abject submission to the church. He was equal to any of these Romagnol chieftains in the field; he excelled them all in their own perfidious policy. By adroitly tampering with their cupidity and fomenting their mutual jealousies and hatred, he armed them against each other; and conquering them in succession with their own weapons, he wrested the little cities of the province from their sway to place them under papal governors. His crowning acquisition was the city of Bologna. The Milanese lieutenant who governed there had revolted in 1355 from the Visconti, and, joining the league of the Lombard princes against their house, had maintained himself in the signiory of the city by this alliance. The Visconti had acknowledged his independence by the peace of 1358, but they attacked him with overwhelming force two years afterwards; and Albornoz took advantage of the extremity to which he was reduced to obtain from him the surrender of Bologna to the holy see in exchange for a papal fief. A new war between the Visconti and the church was the consequence of this treaty: but the cardinal engaged the affections of the Bolognese in the contest by granting them a municipal government; he was served by the subjugated chieftains of Romagna with unusual fidelity; he excited a fresh league of the Lombard princes against the signers of Milan; and these puissant lords were, after various hostilities, the issue of which was unfavourable to them, rejoiced to terminate the war by the cession of Bologna to the pope. The same treaty restored peace to Lombardy, and consummated the quiet subjugation of Romagna to the papal authority. (A.D. 1364.)

I have referred, in the beginning of this chapter, to the circumstances in the residence of the popes at Avignon, which, more than their mere absence from the ancient capital of their see, conspired to estrange the minds of the Italians from their influence: their servile dependence upon the kings of France, the selection of subjects of those monarchs almost exclusively to fill the papal chair and the sacred college, and the shameful dissoluteness and profligacy of the papal court. The scandal of these corruptions in the church was felt not only in Italy but throughout Europe; and indignant Christendom pointed to Avignon as the Babylon of the west. Since clerical preferment was the reward of intrigues and bribery, that city was crowded with the most abandoned adventurers of France and Italy; and the manners of its court and its people were a faithful copy of the worst vices of these nations. The restoration of the papal throne to Rome was therefore the object of ardent wishes to all who were alive to the honour of the church; and the feelings of the age in this respect may be gathered from other contemporary evidence, as well as from the celebrated letters of eloquent remonstrance and entreaty which Petrarch boldly addressed to the pontiffs and published to Europe. In Italy, indeed, the worldly ambition and pride, the public crimes and personal vices of successive popes, had for several hundred years been gradually working their pernicious effects upon the cause of religion; and before the energy of thought and acuteness of observation which distinguished the national mind in the fourteenth century, the disorders and impostures of the papacy were bared to contempt and derision. The enthusiastic spirit of devotion which had animated the Goths, the Lombards, the Franks, and the Normans, the blind submission which these northern barbarians paid to the priesthood, had been slowly and silently converted by their intellectual descendants into insensibility and indifference to spiritual truths.

A residence at Avignon possessed many attractions for the papal court. To the pontiffs and the great majority of their cardinals, France was the native country; Avignon itself, after its purchase from Joanna of Naples as countess of Provence, had been decorated with their splendid palaces; and in its quiet streets their silken repose was neither interrupted by the tyranny of a Roman nobility, nor disturbed by the insurrections of a turbulent populace. It is therefore probable that, notwithstanding the discontent of Europe, Avignon would have retained the papal court permanently within its walls, if they could have continued to ensure to the pontiffs an inviolable sanctuary. But, as we have seen, Provence, after the north of France had been devastated by the English wars, became a prey to companies of adventure, formed of the soldiery which the peace of Bretigni had disbanded. The wealth of Avignon was a tempting lure for these armies of plunderers; and on several occasions during the pontificate of Innocent VI. the luxurious prelates of his court were startled from their slumbers by the approach of danger. Sometimes the walls of Avignon were defended against the companies of adventure by the arms of the citizens, oftener was immunity from pillage purchased by the gold of the pope; and on the death of Innocent in 1362, his successor, Urban V., though also a Frenchman by birth, was disposed, by the quick repetition of these alarms, to listen more earnestly than his predecessors had done to the wishes of Christendom. At the moment of his election, he declared his resolution to re-establish the holy see at Rome, and evinced his sincerity by the preparations which he made for the purpose.

Some years, however, elapsed before Urban could carry his design into effect; but at length he departed from Avignon with his cardinals, who all followed him, however reluctantly, with the exception of five; and they refused to quit Provence, (A.D. 1367.) The intelligence of the pope's intention had every where been welcomed with delight; the galleys of Venice, Genoa, and Pisa, and of Joanna of Naples, escorted him in his voyage from the Rhone to the Tiber; and on his landing in the papal states, the people of Rome, in the full and fresh feelings of joy and gratitude, or in weariness of the intestine disputes which as usual agitated them, laid the offer of the signiory of their city at his feet. Urban sustained a heavy loss shortly after his arrival in Italy, in the death of Albornoz; but the cardinal left the ecclesiastical states to his master in the obedience to which he had reduced them.

Urban V., some time before his arrival in Italy, had concerted measures with the emperor Charles IV., the ostensible object of which was the deliverance of the peninsula from the bands of foreign mercenaries who had inflicted so many evils upon her. But the real design of the pope was to humble the Visconti, the ancient enemies of the papacy, and that of Charles to repeat the extortions by which he had, in his former expedition, amassed so considerable a treasure. It was the last service which Albornoz rendered to the pope, to conclude for him an alliance with all the enemies of the Milanese lords. This league embraced the emperor, the king of Hungary, the queen of Naples, and the signers of Padua, Ferrara, and Mantua. The power of the Visconti, notwithstanding the shifting vicissitudes of the perpetual wars in which their ambitious schemes had involved them, remained unshaken; the splendour of their house had been augmented by two matrimonial alliances with the royal lines of England and France; and the brothers prepared to repel or avert the assaults of their numerous foes with their accustomed activity and skill. Though they took Hawkwood with the English company into their pay, their forces were however very inferior to those of their enemies, when Charles IV. had entered Lombardy from Germany with a considerable army, and had been joined by the contingents of the Italian league. (A.D. 1368.) But Hawkwood arrested the advance of the imperialists and their confederates for some time in the Mantuan territory, by cutting the dykes of the Adige and inundating their camp; and meanwhile Bernabo Visconti, who well knew the avarice of Charles, employed yet more effectual means for paralyzing the efforts of his enemies. By large presents he bribed the emperor to negotiate a peace, and to send back the greater part of his army into Germany.

Italy responded to the proclamation of this shameful treaty by one universal cry of surprise and indignation. Fifty thousand men had been assembled by the league for the deliverance of the peninsula from the machinations of the Visconti, and the ravages of the companies of adventure; and this great coalition had been frustrated solely by the rapacity of its chief. But Charles, indifferent to reproach so long as he added to his treasures, passed with undiminished assurance into Tuscany with the remaining body of his cavalry. He was invited into this province by his ruling passion. During the subjection of their city to Pisa, many of the Guelf exiles of Lucca had established themselves in France, and accumulated riches by commerce. To obtain the restoration of freedom for their birth-place, they offered Charles the full indulgence of his pecuniary desires; and he promised himself an exorbitant reward from their sacrifices to affectionate patriotism. The situation of Pisa favoured his views. Giovanni Agnello, the new signer of that city, depended for the continuance of an usurpation which was detested by the Pisans, upon the protection of the emperor; and Charles constituted him imperial vicar over Pisa, upon condition that Lucca should be surrendered into his own hands. The very ceremony which was to publish the prostituted dignity of Agnello, proved fatal to his ambition. During his solemn installation as imperial vicar, which took place at Lucca where the emperor had established his residence, his leg was broken by the fall of the temporary gallery on which he stood; and the Pisans, while their tyrant was confined to his couch, rose in arms, restored their republic, and compelled him to abdicate the signiory.

During his residence in Tuscany, Charles IV. played over again nearly the same part of rapacity and meanness, of treachery and impotence, which he had acted in his former visit. From Lucca he was imprudently invited by the people of Sienna, notwithstanding their experience of his character in his preceding expedition, to mediate between their contending factions; and he then, fomenting instead of allaying the troubles of the city, thought only of seizing the signiory that he might sell it to the pope. After some perfidious intrigues, he had personally repaired to Sienna and assembled within its walls nearly three thousand cuirassiers, partly his own forces, partly those of the pope. But the Siennese, awakening to a sense of their danger, did not hesitate to attack this imposing force in their streets; and so furious and desperate was their onset, that, after a bloody combat of several hours, the whole of the imperial cavalry were dismounted or put to flight; above a thousand of them were slain or grievously wounded; and the emperor, detected and baffled in his disgraceful schemes, and utterly defeated by the indignant citizens and abandoned by his followers, was compelled to surrender at discretion. The people used their victory with moderation: they only required that he should acknowledge their rights, quit their city, and trouble them no more; and they even paid him a contribution which he had the effrontery to demand, as soon as he regained his composure, in compensation for the insults which the imperial dignity had sustained by their triumph. He was, in truth, neither abashed by his disgrace, nor prevented by it from the continued pursuit of his design to extort money from all the Tuscan cities. Against Florence he revived some obsolete claims of the empire; he attempted, in concert with the defeated partizans of Agnello, to possess himself of Pisa; and, when his gens-d'armerie had been disgracefully repulsed in this enterprise, he employed them in insulting the Florentine and Pisan territories. By these vexations and hostilities he gained his object: the two republics, who would have better consulted their dignity by an appeal to arms, preferred to rid themselves peaceably of his pretensions and assaults by money; and he obtained 50,000 florins from each as the price of his leaving them undisturbed.

The conduct of Charles IV. in Tuscany had put the finishing stroke to the degradation of the imperial authority; but, amidst the general contempt and obloquy which he provoked, he found means to leave, in one city at least, the memory of benefits alone. Yet the only action which he performed that might have been truly glorious if it had been disinterested, was converted by the stain of his characteristic avarice into a transaction of mere mercenary traffic. He resolved before he quitted Tuscany to restore freedom to Lucca: but he determined also to drain the last florin from her citizens for the ransom of their independence. During fifty-six years of servitude—from the usurpation of Uguccione délla Faggiuola, throughout the tyranny of Castruccio Castracani and the Pisans, and to the surrender of her government to Charles IV. by Agnello—Lucca had lost her population, her manufactures, her riches, and great part of her territory; but her citizens had still inherited the passion of their fathers for freedom, and cherished the ardent hope of its revival. For this they had sighed in their homes, or destined the fruits of their industry in exile; for this those of the number who had amassed wealth in foreign lands were ready to sacrifice their blood and their treasure. Notwithstanding the extravagant price which the sordid emperor set upon the deliverance of their country, they cheerfully yielded to his extortions; and accompanied an enormous payment of 300,000 florins of gold, with a sincerity of joy and unmerited gratitude, that might have overwhelmed him with shame, if to shame he had ever been accessible, (A.D. 1369.) He quitted Tuscany, and returned into Germany before they could raise the whole of the stipulated amount: but they at length completed it by loans from the Florentines and others of their allies: the imperial lieutenant to whom they had been consigned in pledge then surrendered the keys of the city to their magistrates; and the republic of Lucca once more revived. (A.D. 1370.) As their ancient laws had fallen into oblivion, the citizens modelled their constitution after that of

Florence; they instituted an annual festival to celebrate the recovery of their independence and to commemorate their obligations to Charles IV.; and they decreed that, as long as the freedom of Lucca should endure, their coin should be impressed with the effigy of that monarch.

If Urban V., in restoring the seat of the holy see to Rome, had designed to elevate the pride and the power of the church, he had no reason to regret his resolution. The papal states were tranquil under his sway; he enjoyed the affection of Italy; and the two emperors of the East and West had repaired to Rome to prostrate themselves before his throne. John Palæologus, whose empire was crumbling before the might of the sultan Amurath, quitted Constantinople to throw himself at the feet of the Roman pontiff, and to pour out those solicitations for the aid of western Europe which were ineffectually repeated by his successors until the fall of the Greek monarchy; and Charles IV., who had deservedly incurred the displeasure of Urban by his desertion of the league against the Visconti, reconciled himself with the church, during a short visit which he made to Rome, by every abject humiliation. But Charles had no sooner returned into Germany, than Urban found his repose endangered by the insolence of the Milanese lords, whose pride had risen with the dissolution of the Italian league. They stirred up another war in the peninsula by encouraging the revolt of the little town of San Miniato against the Florentines; and Urban, who saw in the Visconti the perpetual disturbers of Italy, availed himself of the indignation of Florence to form a new league against them, of which he placed himself at the head. Several of the Lombard princes, and the republics of Pisa and Lucca, joined the confederacy; but it produced little effect. Hawkwood, still the general of Bernabo Visconti, inflicted a signal defeat upon the Florentine army at Cascina in Tuscany, and made a bold but unsuccessful attempt to carry Pisa by surprise in conjunction with the deposed doge Agnello; and although the army which he commanded, as well as the forces of the Visconti in Lombardy, were afterwards obliged to retire before the troops of the confederacy, the war languished in indecision. Amidst these troubles, the pope sighed for the repose of Avignon, and at length quitted Italy to return to that city. But he had scarcely arrived in Provence, when he breathed his last; and the intelligence of his death induced the league to conclude a peace with the Milanese lords, (A.D. 1370.)

The restless perfidy of the Visconti as usual prevented the continuance of his pacification; and soon after the election of the new pope Gregory XI. at Avignon, their attacks upon the allies of the church in Lombardy produced a fresh war. In this, however, Florence, and the Tuscan republics, who were now decidedly led by her counsels, took no share; and the Visconti were successful at all points against the papal and Lombard confederates: until they imprudently discharged Hawkwood and his company, who passed into the service of the church, surprised the Milanese army, and changed the fortune of the contest. After this the affairs of the Visconti continued to decline; a pestilence and famine ravaged Lombardy; and a truce was produced by the general exhaustion of the combatants, (A.D. 1374.)

It was during this brief interval of repose that a new turn was given to affairs by the treachery of the papal legate who commanded for Gregory in Italy. While Florence was oppressed by the pestilence and dearth, which prevailed in Tuscany, as well as the Lombard states, the crafty and unprincipled churchman imagined that, by increasing the distress of the city, he might excite its populace to revolt against the signiory, and reduce the enfeebled republic under the papal yoke. He therefore, pretending to discharge Hawkwood and his company from his pay, secretly ordered that adventurer to enter Tuscany, and burn the Florentine harvests to aggravate the famine. The ingratitude of the legate towards their state, which had ever been the faithful ally of the church, filled the people of Florence with the deepest indignation; and though their Guelf prejudices, unconnected indeed as these were with any superstitious feeling, at first revolted at the project of entering into a war against the ancient chief of their national faction, the bitter sense of unmerited injury finally prevailed in their councils, (A.D. 1375.) To render their operations more vigorous, they confided all the executive power of the republic to a new magistracy of eight, who were termed the signors of the war. These commissioners formed a league with the republics of Sienna, Lucca, Arezzo, and Pisa, to attack the legate: they resolved to rouse all Romagna to the assertion of freedom against the tyranny of French ecclesiastics; and, in the depth of their resentment against the church, they even entered into an alliance with Bernabo Visconti, a tyrant with whom they had hitherto shunned all connexion as the natural enemy of their free commonwealth. But, though they well knew his perfidious character, they were also aware of his hostility to the Roman see, and they trusted to the bond of self-interest which they imagined would unite their cause with his own.

The vigour with which the talents of the new signers of the war inspired the Florentine league had the most disastrous consequences for the papal power. The sway of the French legates, who were set over Romagna by the court of Avignon, was universally odious; and when the Florentines displayed their standards in that province, with the simple and emphatic motto of 'LIBERTY' emblazoned on them in letters of gold, every city and castle hailed the invitation. It was to no purpose that Hawkwood with execrable cruelty endeavoured to strike terror into the disaffected by a diabolical massacre at Forli, the inhabitants of which he suspected of the intention to revolt: the insurrection spread in every direction, and, in less than twelve months, in all the ecclesiastical states Rimini and its castles were the only places which had not hoisted the banner of freedom, (A.D. 1376.) Gregory XI., in consternation at this train of reverses, had first recourse to spiritual arms; but he vainly endeavoured to alarm the consciences of the Florentines by striking their city with an interdict, and their rulers with excommunication; and he then redoubled his efforts in the field. Taking into his service the company of the Bretons, the last and most ferocious of the bands formed after the English wars, which still remained in France, he dispatched two new cardinals into Italy with these reinforcements. They numbered two thousand lances, or six thousand cuirassiers, with four thousand foot; and their appearance in Lombardy induced the Visconti to desert the Florentine league, and make their separate peace. The war was then carried into Romagna with frightful inhumanity: wherever the Bretons entered by assault they spared not even children at the breast; and these, and similar atrocities, during the whole war, were instigated by men who wore the garb of religion, and styled themselves the servants of the Almighty. One of the papal legates, the cardinal of Geneva, afterwards anti-pope under the title of Clement VII., personally encouraged and directed a massacre at Cesena, which had surrendered to him upon the solemn faith of a capitulation. Five thousand souls, men, women, and children, perished in this butchery; in which the Bretons seized infants by the feet and dashed out their brains, against the stones.

These inhuman tragedies filled the Florentines and their allies with more indignation than fear. They gained over Hawkwood into their service on the expiration of his engagement with the pope; and they prosecuted the war with unabated resolution and activity. Meanwhile, circumstances had convinced Gregory XI. that his presence in Italy could alone avert the total ruin of the papal affairs. He therefore had quitted Avignon, and arrived at Rome; from whence he directed his endeavours to effect a pacification with the confederates, (A.D. 1377.) He was first successful in detaching Bologna from the league; but solely upon condition that this city, which had shared in the general revolt of Romagna, should continue to govern itself as a republic under the nominal supremacy of a papal vicar. The Tuscan republics were then induced by this and other desertions to open negotiations for peace; but while they were treating under the guidance of Florence, the conferences were suddenly suspended by the death of the pope (A.D. 1378); and the extraordinary events which arose in the church changed all the relations of the popedom with the Italian powers.

At the period of Gregory's death, the sacred college was composed of twenty-three cardinals; but of these seven were absent: six had remained at Avignon when the late pope quitted that city, and the seventh was legate in Tuscany. Sixteen cardinals therefore entered the conclave at Rome in the usual manner, to give a successor to Gregory XI.; and, of these, one was a Spaniard, eleven were French, and only four Italians. Above two-thirds of the electoral body were thus foreigners; their dislike of an Italian residence was well known; and the people of Rome might justly apprehend their choice of another French pontiff, a fresh secession to Avignon, and a long renewal of the disorders and calamities which the absence of the popes had entailed upon their city. The dread of these consequences filled the capital with ferment and uproar. Since the death of Rienzi, Rome had relapsed into her former state of distraction; and we find her successively oppressed by the tyrannical nobility, governed by an obscure demagogue, and eager to surrender her freedom to the popes on their appearance within her walls. But, at the period before us, she was ruled by a republican signiory of thirteen *bannerets*; and these magistrates sent a deputation from their body to demand an audience of the assembled cardinals, and to echo the public voice of the city, which had been already declared with alarming earnestness. The sacred college answered to these envoys, by the mouth of their dean or president, that they were astonished at the presumption of the Roman magistracy in attempting to influence an election which must be determined neither by respect nor fear, by favour nor popular clamour, but by the suggestions of the Holy Spirit.

The bannerets withdrew, little satisfied with this reply; and the discontent of the populace burst forth with redoubled violence. They had previously broken into the Vatican, as the cardinals were entering the conclave, to proclaim their wishes; the palace had been with difficulty cleared of the intruders; and the mob now assembled round it in immense numbers, and demanded with appalling menaces a Roman or at least an Italian pope. Amidst this storm of popular tumult, the conclave proceeded with the election; and finally, with only one dissentient voice, gave their suffrages in favour of the archbishop of Bari, a Neapolitan, and not a member of the sacred college. This choice satisfied the citizens, and, in a few days, tranquillity having been restored, the new pope was crowned with the usual ceremonies, in which all the members of the late conclave took their share. For several weeks the cardinals voluntarily continued their obedience to him; they announced him to their absent brethren at Avignon as the object of their choice; and all the acknowledgments that were customary on the accession of a pontiff were freely rendered to Urban VI. by the sacred college, the citizens of the capital, and the people generally, where the intelligence of his undisputed election had penetrated.

But the quiet possession of the chair of St. Peter, which had thus been given to Urban, was soon shaken by his own violent and arbitrary temper. He had been indebted for his elevation to the character which he had acquired for learning and piety; but the event proved that the cardinals could with difficulty have made a more unfortunate election, and they shortly found that they had given themselves not merely a master, but a capricious and passionate tyrant. He filled them with disgust and alarm by the want of moderation and prudence with which he declared his intention of reforming their manners; he loaded them with opprobrious language and personal insults, and he united the whole French party against him by publicly announcing his resolution to confine his residence to Italy, and to make so numerous a creation of Italian cardinals, that foreigners should no longer possess a majority in the sacred college.

The consequences of this offensive conduct of Urban were displayed as soon as the cardinals, obtaining permission one after another to retire from Rome, under pretence of establishing themselves in the summer residence which had been appointed for them in the neighbouring town of Agnani, had assembled at that place, while the pope still remained in the capital. Here they had leisure to interchange the expression of their general discontent, and to concert their schemes of common vengeance. Their resolution was hastened by an unreasonable order which Urban sent to them to join him at Tivoli, where he now determined to pass the summer, notwithstanding the expense of their preparations at Agnani. They refused obedience; the cardinal of Geneva summoned to their protection the company of the Bretons which he had led into Italy, and retiring to Fondi, they there solemnly annulled the election of Urban, upon the plea that the menaces of the Roman populace had compelled it. Declaring the chair of St. Peter still vacant, they then entered anew into conclave, and chose for the legitimate pope the cardinal of Geneva, who assumed the title of Clement VII. In these proceedings the few Italian cardinals took no part; but neither did they any longer acknowledge the authority of Urban. Divided between their hatred of him, and their reluctance to assent to measures which might again transport the seat of the popedom beyond the Alps, they observed a neutrality, and withdrew from the theatre of contest. But as the foreign prelates had composed above two-thirds of the conclave, they formed, without the Italians, the majority on which the legitimacy of Urban's pretensions must rest, and maintained their right to annul a nomination which they ascribed to violence.

The validity of the election of Urban VI. is a question which has scarcely to this day received the formal decision of the Romish church; nor is it one to deserve our serious attention. I may, however, remark that it has been much agitated. On the one hand, it has been asserted that all the probabilities are against the voluntary choice of an Italian by the great majority of French cardinals, who ardently desired a return to Avignon; nor can it be denied in addition to this inference, that a considerable degree of intimidation was produced in the conclave by the threats of the Roman populace, since the cardinals had every reason to dread that their lives would be sacrificed to the fury of the mob, if they elected a transalpine subject. But there is evidence on the other side that the French party was itself divided into two provincial factions, each of which courted the suffrages of the few Italians in the college; and of one of these factions Urban had been the creature. It is, moreover, certain that, for several weeks after the election, during which the sacred college were freed from restraint, no attempt was made to invalidate the legitimacy of the pope, or to enter a protest against the compulsory violence which the conclave had suffered; and that, on the contrary, when the cardinals might with safety have withdrawn their allegiance from Urban, they announced their choice of him to their absent colleagues, and continued to obey him, as all former pontiffs had been obeyed, until his own conduct provoked their resistance. We may therefore at least conclude with very little doubt that, if that pontiff had not outraged the pride and selfishness of his constituents, their protest would never have disturbed the tranquillity of the church. This is the sole point of interest to determine; and I shall only add, that the church of Rome has given a tacit preference to the cause of Urban by numbering that pope and the successors of his party in the roll of ordinal legitimacy, while it excludes the memory of their adversaries from the same honours.

The mere merits of the contest between two parties which equally deserve our contempt are almost beneath inquiry: the fruits of their quarrel are of another character. These were no less than the division of the religious obedience of Europe for above forty years: the Great Schism of the West. France and Spain, with the queen of Naples, espoused the cause of the French cardinals, and acknowledged Clement VII.; Italy gladly adhered to an Italian pope, and England, Germany, Hungary, and Portugal likewise sided with Urban VI. But between two men, neither of whom were personally calculated to inspire the Christian world with respect, the pontifical authority dwindled into a shadow. Joanna of Naples was the only sovereign who took an immediate part in the struggle between the rival pontiffs: Clement retired first to her capital and subsequently to Avignon, where a papal court was once more established; Urban, who created nineteen new cardinals, all of them Italians, remained at Rome. In tracing the isolated revolutions of Naples, at the close of this chapter, we shall have occasion to refer to his subsequent conduct; but over the rest of Italy his authority was too little felt to influence the general affairs of the peninsula; and I need only state, that immediately after his accession, he hastened to reconcile the church with Florence and her allies, and to conclude the pacification which his predecessor had meditated. The conditions were more favourable to the republic than those proposed by Gregory XI.; but she strangely consented, notwithstanding her victories, to atone for the scandal of her just resentment at ecclesiastical perfidy, by pecuniary sacrifices.

After the expulsion of the duke of Athens from Florence, in 1343, the internal tranquillity of that republic had been, for above fifteen years, undisturbed by a single ebullition of discontent, and twenty years more had passed without any very serious interruption to the repose of the city. Periods of national happiness are usually least fertile in incident; and the domestic annals of Florence, during the first of these epochs, have failed in attracting our attention, merely because they are unstained by crime and unchequered by calamity. But the same year which produced the Great Schism of the West is memorable in Florentine history for a series of troubles and popular commotions which fearfully endangered the existence of freedom, and shook the agitated state to its centre. The origin of these disorders must be sought in the new character gradually given to the constitution of the republic by some political transactions during the last twenty years, which were themselves no more than the fruits of a contest between two powerful and adverse families. These were the Ricci and the Albizzi, both of the order of popolani grandi, the great commoners or plebeian aristocracy, which had risen to power on the ruins of the old nobility. Some accidental and private cause of offence between these wealthy and arrogant houses had rankled into deadly animosity; they had found a ready theatre of rivalry in the political arena, and in the year 1357, one of them, to work the ruin of the other, set an engine in motion, the tremendous powers of which had existed in the state for nearly a century, without being fully manifested or dangerously wielded in action.

In describing the settlement of the Florentine constitution, I have noticed the establishment of a powerful corporation within the republic to prosecute suspected Ghibelins, and guard the general interests of the national faction; and I have stated, that this Guelf society was endowed for such purposes with a part of the confiscated property of the Ghibelins, and provided with a regular executive magistracy and councils of its own. But Ghibelinism had been so completely crushed in Florence by proscription and exile, that there remained little call for the exertions of the Guelf society; and that body plays no conspicuous part in the guidance of the state until after the fall of the duke of Athens. The signal triumph which democratical principles had gained by that revolution appears to have produced the first symptoms of jealousy from the Guelf society, from the offices of which the old nobility had, by a curious anomaly, never been excluded, as they were from all other situations of public trust. Besides the democratical influence of the species of lottery which regulated the succession of government at Florence, a specific law, called the *divieto*, had the effect of increasing the preponderance of the lower citizens in the direction of affairs. This statute provided that two individuals of the same name should not hold office together; and thus its exclusive tendency militated solely against the more ancient and respectable houses, whose members were extremely numerous, pretty much according to the duration of their wealth and prosperity, while new and obscure families scarcely knew their relatives, and seldom bore a common sirname. The operation of the divieto, too, was the more destructive to the power of the great commoners, as all above one member of a family whose names were drawn at the same renewal of magistracies, lost their turn wholly, until the bags were replenished at the biennial ballot.

The Guelf society, in which the old nobility and the popolani grandi enjoyed a paramount influence, were naturally adverse to the democratical spirit of the divieto and of the lottery itself, by which persons of low condition, and sometimes of Ghibelin origin, came into office. The cause of Ghibelinism, as it was that of the perfidious tyrants of Lombardy, and of their partizans generally throughout the peninsula, was hostile to freedom, while the Guelf states, and Florence especially, were the champions of Italian liberty. It was therefore easy for the

Guelf society to sound the alarm in the republic, that Ghibelinism was raising its head; and in 1347 they obtained the enactment of a law by which every person whose family had been Ghibelin since the commencement of the century, or who was not himself of unsuspected Guelf principles, was pronounced ineligible for offices of trust. They in this way obtained their real object, that of in some measure counteracting the effect of the divieto, by depriving a part of the democracy in turn of a share in the government by the exclusion of those citizens who could not establish their Guelf origin.

The law of 1347 does not appear, however, to have been very vigorously put in force during the succeeding ten years; and the power of the Guelf society yet remained in abeyance, when it was converted, in 1357, by the ambitious feuds of the Albizzi and Ricci, first into an instrument of mutual oppression, and afterwards of universal tyranny over the state. The Albizzi were reputed descendants of a Ghibelin family of Arezzo; and Uguccione de' Ricci, the chief of the rival house, had sufficient influence, notwithstanding considerable opposition, to carry a law against Ghibelinism, which was aimed at the Albizzi, and revived and strengthened the earlier enactment. It was now decreed that any reputed Ghibelin who accepted office should be punished, at the pleasure of the executive magistrate, with fine or imprisonment, or even loss of life. The iniquity of this ordinance was the greater, as no better evidence was required for condemnation than common fame attested by six witnesses; the captains of the Guelf party were themselves entrusted with the judicial cognizance of such accusations; and a citizen once convicted before them became ever after incapable of exercising magistracy. But the application of the law was widely different from that contemplated by its mover. The Albizzi and their friends, far from themselves suffering its penalties, succeeded, by the Ultimate alliance which they formed with the old nobility, in engrossing the direction of the Guelf corporation; and these powerful commoners, so connected with the ancient aristocracy, began to exercise an alarming tyranny over the partizans of their enemies, although they did not venture to attack the Ricci themselves.

Though the moderate Guelfs were displeased with the rigour of the new law, they could only effect some modification of it, by which the captains of the corporation were directed to warn or admonish (ammonire) suspected Ghibelins beforehand against accepting office, instead of awaiting their appointment and then inflicting punishment. But this expedient for preventing condemnation only anticipated its injustice, and enlarged the tyrannical functions of the corporation. No individual dared to resist so formidable an oligarchy, for, if he disregarded their admonition, he was at once treated as a convicted Ghibelin. In this manner above two hundred of the enemies of the Albizzi were at different times excluded from political rights. But the Ricci by intrigue subsequently acquired in their turn a similar influence over the captains of the Guelf society, and gave a counter direction to the system of exclusion; and thus, as the rival houses alternately prevailed in the corporation, the whole power of the state passed by intimidation or violence into the hands of an oligarchy of great families.

The tyranny of this Guelf party soon became odious at Florence. For the kind of proscription which they exercised, under the pretext of crushing Ghibelinism, was in fact carried on only against individuals who were obnoxious to themselves. Their admonitions were constantly addressed to persons whose connexions and principles were thoroughly Guelf; but the loss of political rights was not the less dependant upon the mere arbitrary pleasure of the leaders of the corporation. The numbers of persons who were unjustly deprived of the privileges of citizenship continually increased, and composed a regular body of malcontents. But these ammoniti (the admonished) were not equal, numerous as they were, to a contest with the Guelf oligarchy, who carried on their attacks under the shield of law, and counted on their side the superior discipline of secrecy and union, and the sanction of the authority which their party had arrogated in the state.

The abortive conspiracy which was detected in 1360 was formed by the ammoniti, and embraced many men of distinguished name, who, in their indignation against the authors of an oppressive proscription, were not deterred from endangering the general liberty of Florence by summoning foreign aid for their vengeance. Some of the leaders of this plot were put to death, but the forbearance which the ruling faction displayed towards others who were less prominent, in a great degree reconciled all parties to their sway. The ability, courage, and virtuous policy with which the Guelf oligarchy meanwhile directed the foreign affairs of the republic, doubtless had the same tendency, and almost redeemed the injustice of their domestic administration. The dignity of the state had never been so honourably sustained as during the period when their party were the real governors of Florence. The repulse of the Great Company, the moderation and wisdom which preceded, and the vigour which conducted the war with Pisa, were all brilliant proofs of their sound judgment and political talents; and it was under their skilful guidance that the counsels of Florence acquired a tacit supremacy over the other republics of Tuscany.

For above ten years after the detection of the conspiracy of the ammoniti, we hear of little opposition to the sway of the oligarchy; but in 1371 the open enmity between the Albizzi and Ricci and their respective adherents had reached its height; and the proceedings to which the rival houses by turns instigated the Guelf society, as they prevailed in its councils, roused the general indignation of the people, and kept the city in a ferment. The existing signiory of the state chanced to be neutral between these great families, and obtained a law which, to prevent them from disturbing the tranquillity of the republic, equally excluded the members of both from magistracy for five years. This measure was successful for a time in checking the rival ambition of these great commoners; and the Guelf corporation itself soon afterwards declined in influence, when the republic was provoked into her war with the church by the perfidy of the papal legate. The leaders of that society could not stem the torrent of popular fury against the ingratitude of the church; but they were averse from a rupture with the pope, in which it seemed a contradiction and a sacrifice of consistency for Guelfs to engage; and thus the direction of affairs fell into other hands. The eight commissioners of the war were all of the party opposed to the corporation; the success of their government was viewed with extreme jealousy by that body; and two regular and powerful factions were thus created in the administration of the republic and of the Guelf society. The Albizzi, with the old nobility and the majority of the popolani grandi, constituted the Guelf oligarchy or aristocratic party, whose original object it had been to keep the lower citizens out of office: the faction of the Ricci, with the great commoners in their interest, identified themselves with the democracy, ostensibly from indignation at the exclusive policy of the oligarchy, but in reality from the spirit of selfish ambition. The former chief of the Ricci, Uguccione, was dead; but, besides this family, the Alberti, the Medici, and other distinguished plebeian nobles, ranged themselves with the lower people; and Giorgio Scali and Tomaso Strozzi succeeded Uguccione de' Ricci as leaders of the party.

The close of the war against the church appeared to the Guelf oligarchy a favourable occasion for recovering the authority of which they had been deprived by a contest so much at variance with the ancient prejudices of their faction. They therefore began, even before the peace with Urban VI was signed, to renew their admonitions, and, in a few months, excluded eighty citizens from office. Thus, as Sismondi observes, they made it an unpardonable offence against individuals that their ancestors, a century or two back, had borne arms against the church, in opposition to which both they themselves and their republic were at the moment arrayed in open hostility. These arbitrary measures determined the democratical faction by one vigorous effort to break the chains which the Guelf corporation were bent upon forging anew for their fellow citizens; and they were certainly justified by every principle of liberty, and seconded by the general voice of the people, in their resolution to resist the reviving oppression of so ambitious an oligarchy.

In studying the domestic history of free states, we shall seldom be safe in surrendering our entire approbation to the motives and conduct of any party or confederated order of men; and, in the fierce contention of factions which perpetually agitated the Italian republics, we should be especially liable to error if, in pursuit of any imaginary consistency of opinion, we suffered our partialities to be thrown into either scale. In the memorable struggle which arose in the Florentine republic on the occasion before us, it has been sometimes the fashion to represent the democratical party as the virtuous champions of freedom, because their opponents may justly be stigmatized with the reproach of labouring to establish an oligarchical tyranny. Yet it was rather the accident of rivalry among the great commoners than any real superiority in the purity of their designs, which ranged the Ricci and their friends with the lower people in opposition to the Albizzi and the Guelf corporation. The ambitious quarrel of these factions was, in truth, only for power; and there are many circumstances in the proceedings of the democratical leaders that will forbid us from attributing to them the integrity of purpose which can alone ennoble the conflict for political rights. Yet, however we may question their designs, the cause which they espoused was at least the better one; and the projects of the Guelf oligarchy had merited the alarm and suspicion which' they excited, when Salvestro de' Medici, a man of intrepid character, whose Guelf descent and principles were too generally known to afford the oligarchy a pretence for excluding him from office, became gonfalonier of justice by the usual process of the lottery.

In concert with Tomaso Strozzi, Giorgio Scali, and Benedetto Alberti, the new magistrate determined, by virtue of his official functions, to propose a law which should revive the ordinances of justice against the nobility, restrict the authority of the captains of the Guelf corporation, and revise the admonitions which they had issued. His propositions were violently opposed in the signorial college, in which every law necessarily originated, by the Guelf interest; and he then boldly appealed to the assembled council of the people. This action was the signal for all the insurrectionary movements which followed: his address produced a tumultuary effect in the council; Benedetto Alberti roused the citizens collected without to arms by the watchword of "Popolo!" "for the people;" and in that moment the oligarchy, so long the terror of their opponents, wavered before the declaration of the popular will. (A.D. 1378.) They yielded to the motion of Salvestro, and his propositions were riotously carried into a law.

With this concession the people appeared at first satisfied; and tranquillity was for the moment restored. But the popular ferment was far from being in reality allayed; the shops and private houses of Florence were closed and barricaded; and everything announced that an alarming crisis was at hand. Of the twenty-one trading arts, which contained at once the mercantile and political divisions of the city, the seven greater and more wealthy, in which the popolani grandi were enrolled, were generally attached to the Guelf oligarchy; the fourteen lesser, formed of the mechanics and retail traders, naturally belonged, on the contrary, to the democratical party; and between these two descriptions of citizens lay all the jealousy and furious animosity of party spirit. The lesser arts were resolved to render the republic a pure democracy: in the course of the few days which succeeded the passing of the law of Salvestro de' Medici, they repeatedly assembled in arms under their respective banners; they compelled the signiory to summon a general committee of the magistracy to reform the republic; and they attacked and destroyed the houses of the Guelf leaders, and obliged many of those chiefs to fly from the city. The signiory attempted at first to soothe the insurgents by temporising measures; but the passions of the multitude had been too violently excited to leave them contented with anything short of a full assent to their demands. At the instigation of the ammoniti, they required that this proscribed class should be immediately restored to their complete rights; that the authority of the Guelf corporation should be limited, and its magistracy taken out of the hands of the faction which had engrossed it; and that several of the most obnoxious of that oligarchy should be outlawed. All these conditions were submitted to, and order seemed at length re-established in the city.

But the success with which the lesser arts had dictated laws to the republic was a dangerous example to the numerous classes of the population of Florence, who were yet lower in the scale of society. There were several kinds of artizans in the city who were not included in the organization of the arts, and were consequently deprived of political privileges. These workmen were held in dependance by the different arts for which they laboured: as, for example, the woollen manufactures, which were estimated to employ thirty thousand persons, were placed under the government of the great art of the drapers; and in this manner the carders of wool, the dyers, weavers, and similar craftsmen, instead of forming corporations in themselves, were all subject to the tribunals of their employers, against whose oppression they, perhaps justly, complained that they could, when aggrieved, obtain no redress. They were, therefore, full of discontent, and resolved to imitate the conduct of the lesser arts, who had gained by insurrection whatever they desired. A secret and fearful conspiracy spread among them, and embraced also the lowest dregs of the populace, the *ciompi*, as they were called, who had been set in action by the intrigues of Salvestro de' Medici and other demagogues in the late troubles, and had already whetted their appetite for pillage.

Though the signiory discovered the existence of a combination among the lower populace on the evening before the meditated rising, the whole of the more respectable citizens of Florence seemed with one accord to abandon the line of their duty and of the public safety at this momentous crisis. The government, as the republic was at peace, had only a few score of cuirassiers in pay; the gonfaloniers of companies with their militia, instead of obeying the summons of the priors to assemble around the palace of the signiory, thought only of remaining in their several quarters to guard their own property from pillage; and thus by the cowardice, or lethargy, or connivance of the incorporated citizens, the dregs of the populace were suffered to gather in arms, and to grow in audacity by the impunity which they enjoyed. The flame of insurrection spread with frightful rapidity; the mob became terrible by their immense numbers and the blind fury which animated them; and the whole city was delivered up at their will to fire and pillage. The houses of all the better citizens who were obnoxious to them were reduced to ashes, and their property plundered or destroyed; and every miscreant who had private malice to gratify, led a troop of incendiaries to the quarter where he desired to glut his vengeance. Amidst this scene of wild uproar and general rapine, the caprice of the wayward mob took a strange character. They insisted upon conferring knighthood upon all their favourites among the leaders of the democratical party, who had first instigated the resistance of the people against the oligarchy; and in the revolution of their phrenzy they even added others, whose houses they had but just demolished, to the number. Above sixty of the principal citizens of Florence, trembling for their lives, were compelled to receive the honours of chivalry from a ferocious rabble, who, if they had betrayed the least signs of reluctance, would have torn them to pieces with as little hesitation as they bestowed this curious mark of their approbation.

During these excesses, which lasted for three days, all government in Florence was at an end. On the first morning, the signiory vainly attempted to treat with the insurgents, and the house of the gonfalonier of justice was burnt; on the following day, the populace attacked and carried the palace of the podestá by assault; and they then condescended to signify to the signiory their propositions for the reform of the republic. These conditions were at first confined to the establishment of three new arts, two for the mechanics dependent on the drapers, and one for the lowest populace; it being provided at the same time that two of the eight priors should be chosen from these new companies; and that all civil actions for debts under fifty florins should be forbidden for ten years, with some minor stipulations. But the demands of the insurgents rose in extravagance with the concessions of the signiory; the usual forms of assembling the councils for confirming their proposals into laws could not be dispatched, to keep pace with their impatience; and, on the third day, the mob assembled about the palace of the signiory in greater numbers and with more appalling violence than ever. They ordered the priors to abdicate their station, on pain of being massacred with all their families; they compelled them to fly; the gates of the public palace were then thrown open; the populace entered; and the work of anarchy was completed.

At that moment, which seemed to consummate the ruin of the republic, Florence was saved by an accidental caprice of the rabble, and by the singular character of one of the rioters. When the multitude rushed into the public palace, the standard of justice, which had been wrested from the charge of the gonfalonier on the first day of the insurrection, happened to be in the hands of a wool comber, one Michel di Lando. This man, bare-footed and ragged, preceded the populace, and, ascending the great staircase to the audience hall of the priors, turned round to the people and cried aloud to them that the palace and the city itself were their own, and demanded to know their sovereign will. The thoughtless mob, seeing the gonfalon in his hand, at once shouted their acclamations that he should himself be gonfalonier and reform the state at his pleasure. This unwashed artificer was thus raised by the breath of the fickle multitude to be absolute lord of Florence; and might perhaps, from the same hour, have established a tyranny more despotic and ruinous than that attempted by the duke of Athens. But, although he had borne an obscure part in the insurrection, Michel di Lando sincerely loved his country, and was, moreover, notwithstanding his abject station, fortunately gifted with sound judgment and undaunted courage. He resolutely set about the re-establishment of order; and, while the populace were momentarily calmed, he decreed that the signiory of nine, the gonfalonier and eight priors, should thenceforward be taken in equal proportions from the greater arts, the lesser arts, and the lower people. With this intention, the bags, from which the magistracy was to be drawn for the following two years, were replenished by the usual process of election and ballot.

The leaders of the democratical party who had originally animated the people to resist the Guelf oligarchy, though they were not the authors of the sedition of the ciompi, now thought to reap the fruits of the revolution. The eight commissioners of war, who belonged to their faction, had alone of all the late government remained in the palace; and, fancying themselves masters of the state, began to elect new priors. But Lando, who knew how to maintain his authority, sent them a peremptory order, which they dared not resist, to abdicate. He then, with the signiory, which was elected according to his scheme, took vigorous measures for the preservation of order; he obliged the populace by menaces of punishment to resume their usual occupations; and tranquillity once more reigned in Florence. But when the ciompi had recovered the first astonishment into which they were thrown by the measures of their chosen leader, they were far from being satisfied with the cessation of anarchy and the sudden termination of the licence in which they had revelled. Their indignation against Lando was unbounded, and their evil spirit was shown by fresh indications of revolt. But the gonfalonier was unshaken in his purpose: he collected a large body of mounted citizens, who possessed a stake in the commonwealth and cheerfully supported his government; and when the seditious mob rose again in arms, he fearlessly met them, charged and routed them in the streets, and, not without considerable slaughter, utterly quelled their dangerous insurrection. Having thus triumphantly preserved the public liberty which had lain prostrate at his feet, he proved the purity of his intentions and established his title to the gratitude of his country, by retiring from office in the proper rotation of the magistracy:—a memorable example of true patriotism in a station of life in which temptation is strongest, and disinterestedness most difficult of exercise.

In the successive insurrections of the lesser arts and of the ciompi, the aristocratical faction had been completely overpowered, and many of its leaders, exiled, fined, or ennobled to deprive them of political rights; and when the revolt of the ciompi was in turn suppressed, the democratical party, or that of the lesser arts, immediately preponderated. When the companies of the arts were assembled in the public square, at the first drawing of magistrates which succeeded the retirement of Lando, the incorporated citizens received the three priors who had been selected according to the late regulations, jointly from the new arts and the ciompi, with open contempt. They hooted them from the spot, they declared unanimously that they would not suffer persons of such base condition to sit in the signiory, and, as the spirit of the lower populace had been utterly crushed by the chastisement which they had undergone, the constitution was again changed without opposition. It was resolved that the nine members of the signiory should in future be taken, four from the greater arts and five from the lesser, which now were sixteen in number. The triumph of the lesser arts over the ciompi raised to the surface the chiefs of the old democratical party; and thus the men, by whom the late troubles had been originally excited, were left at their close in possession of the power at which they had aimed. Giorgio Scali, Tomaso Strozzi, Salvestro de' Medici, and Benedetto Alberti, all great commoners who had been driven by hatred of their adversaries in the aristocratical party to embrace the cause of the people, were the leaders of the faction which, with the support of the lesser arts, now became supreme in the state.

The new government which these men moved at their pleasure was detested by both extremes of the population: by the ciompi and the aristocratical party. But strong in the affections of the lesser arts, whose numerous militia were at their command, the rulers of the state might treat the machinations of the lower populace with contempt and defiance; and when their discontent broke out it was punished with vigorous severity. The aristocracy by their wealth and station were far more dangerous; and the demagogues who swayed the republic did not scruple to employ an iniquitous procedure for effecting the destruction of those leaders of the aristocratical faction whom proscription had hitherto spared, (A.D. 1379.) Under pretence of a conspiracy, Piero Albizzi and several of the most distinguished citizens in Florence of his party were arrested; but no evidence was produced of their guilt, and the podestá refused to condemn them. Benedetto Alberti, who in general integrity was very superior to his colleagues, was led by his blind hatred of the aristocratical party to follow up an atrocious vengeance against them, which has left a foul stain upon his memory. He declared to the podestá, in the name of his fellow-citizens, that, if judgment were not immediately executed upon the prisoners, the people would take the cause into their own hands; the populace threatened the judge himself, on his resisting this interference, with instant death if he suffered the noble malefactors to escape: and the devoted victims were finally dragged to the scaffold with the prostituted forms of justice.

These infamous measures seemed to strengthen the power of the demagogues; and for nearly three years they continued to direct the councils of the state. But as their security increased, they became overbearing and insolent towards all their fellow-citizens; and they continued to oppress their enemies by the odious employment of stipendiary informers. The tide of popularity set against them, and in favour of the fallen Guelfs; Tomaso Strozzi and Giorgio Scali persisted, notwithstanding, in their headlong career of audacity; and Benedetto Alberti dissolved his connexion with tyrants more arrogant, more despotic, and more dangerous to freedom, than the oligarchy to which they had succeeded. While the public dissatisfaction was at its height, a last outrage of Scali and Strozzi against the majesty of the republic, in rescuing one of their perjured spies from the hands of justice, roused the spirit of the existing signiory, and inflamed the resentment of the people. Alberti himself counselled their punishment: Strozzi fled, but Scali was arrested and lost his head on the scaffold. (A.D. 1382.)

The punishment of this demagogue proved the signal for the ruin of all his party: the friends of the Guelf oligarchy began to stir in the city, and to avail themselves of the revulsion of popular feeling; in a few days afterwards the streets were suddenly filled with armed men; and at the sound of their cries of "Live the Guelfs!" all the ancient attachment of the citizens to that name, identified though it had become with the cause of the oligarchy, at once revived. The old nobility, the Albizzi, and the popolani grandi, their adherents, were suffered to possess themselves of the city without opposition; to name a committee of an hundred citizens to reform the state; and so to re-establish, after three years of depression, the supremacy of the Guelf corporation and of the oligarchy by which it had been governed. The committee of dictatorship or *balia*, as such an assembly was called at Florence, immediately commenced their office of reform. Besides restoring all its ancient functions and power to the Guelf corporation, the balia decreed that the two new arts created for the lower trades should be abolished; and that the lesser arts generally, now reduced to their former number of fourteen, should supply only a third, instead of more than one-half of the public magistracy.

The new government displayed the usual passions of an Italian faction. They exiled the chiefs of several illustrious houses, who had supported the democratical cause; they passed the same sentence on Michel di Lando, the saviour of his country, whose services and virtues merited the gratitude and applause of every friend of order; and after persecuting Benedetto Alberti in various ways for some years, they at length banished him also. But notwithstanding these acts of violence, the Guelf aristocracy had acquired moderation and prudence by the experience of former errors; they reversed all the sentences passed against the partizans of their own faction, but, at the same time, they annulled the admonitions which they had themselves put in force against their enemies; and, secure in their wealth and in the ancient respect which attached to their families and their faction, they continued, under the direction of the great house of the Albizzi, to enjoy for nearly fifty years a leading influence in the government of the Florentine republic.

While Florence, in the brief space of four years, was passing through the arduous ordeal of so many domestic revolutions, another Italian republic stood on the very brink of destruction. The ruin which had menaced the Tuscan state was contained in her own bosom: the imminent danger that threatened the existence of Venice arose from the alarming confederation of foreign enemies.

After the inglorious peace of 1358, many years had passed without any interesting occurrence in the Venetian annals. The state was, however, harassed by a formidable rebellion in Candia (A.D. 1363), which had its origin, not among the indigenous and subjugated population of that island, but with the descendants of the noble colonists of Venice, who had found themselves deprived, by the closing of the great council, of those privileges in the parent city which their ancestors had enjoyed. They were even more disaffected to the Venetian government than the rest of the Candiotes. They excited the whole island to revolt; they established an independent government; and it was only after a contest of several years, and with the aid of a numerous body of mercenary troops, that Venice succeeded in chastising the insurrection of this important colony. At length, after the devastation of the island, and the cruel punishment of all the movers of the rebellion, the despotic administration of Venice was securely re-established, and every germ of independence so completely eradicated from among the colonists, that this was the last effort of the Candiotes to throw off the yoke. (A.D. 1367.)

While Venice was with difficulty reducing her revolted subjects to obedience, her repose was troubled from a quarter from whence, if personal gratitude were ever numbered among political virtues, she might have expected fidelity and support. Francesco da Carrara had forgotten that his house were indebted for the lordship of Padua, and all their consequent grandeur to the Venetian republic. In her war with the king of Hungary he had supplied the troops of that monarch with provisions; and he strengthened the recollection which the indignant republic cherished of this ungrateful conduct by a continuance of insult and injury. He attempted to enlarge the Paduan territory by encroaching on the Venetian frontier in the Trevisan March; from his states, which bordered on the lagune, he carried his machinations and conspiracies against the oligarchy of Venice into the heart of their capital itself; and when the vigilance of the council of ten had detected and punished his emissaries, the senate resolved to take signal vengeance for his open aggressions and secret treachery, (A.D. 1372.) They therefore declared war against him, invaded the Paduan state, and routed his troops; and though the king of Hungary, bearing in mind the good offices which Carrara had formerly rendered to him against the Venetians, dispatched an army to his aid, and turned the scale of success for a time in his favour, the republican arms finally prevailed. The Hungarian general was defeated and made prisoner, his soldiers refused to fight again until he should be ransomed, and Carrara was thus forced to sue for peace, (A.D. 1373.) It was only granted by the Venetian senate upon the most galling conditions; for, besides submitting the demarcation of his frontiers to the will of the conquerors, the lord of Padua was compelled to pay large contributions; and to send his son in his name to Venice, to kneel before the doge, and in that posture to solicit pardon for his aggressions, and swear fealty to the republic.

Francesco da Carrara had probably been actuated in his projects against the Venetians only by the ordinary motives of unprincipled ambition; but the humiliation which had proved the only fruit of his schemes inspired him with profound detestation of that people, and animated him with the concealed resolution of future revenge. It was not many years before an occasion presented itself for the indulgence of his purpose. The inveterate animosity which had prevailed for ages between Venice and Genoa might slumber in exhaustion or repose, but was never extinguished; and the spirit of warlike rivalry, the petty jealousies of trade, and the conflicting interests of their colonies in the east, were ever in action to foster the mutual hatred of the two republics, and to kindle the flames of war. The last contest between these maritime states had originated in their commercial disputes in the Euxine, and it was still in the eastern seas that the new and more memorable struggle arose, in which the lord of Padua bore a prominent share.

While the arms of the Turks were rapidly dismembering the Greek empire, and the incessant revolutions of Constantinople were hastening the fall of the feeble monarchy, the Genoese and Venetians were constantly at hand to foment the intrigues of the imperial palace, and to grasp with selfish ambition at the ruins of the Christian dominion. The continental possessions of the eastern empire were now almost embraced within the walls of the capital; but, of the few islands which had not been wrested from it, that of Tenedos, which commanded the Propontis and the channel of the Hellespont, attracted the cupidity of both the Italian republics. The Genoese obtained the cession of it as the price of assisting an usurper against his father (A.D. 1376); the opposite party anticipated them by delivering it into the hands of the Venetians, who determined to preserve so important an acquisition; and the Genoese then, under the plea of their alliance with the usurper, assisted him in an ineffectual attempt to dislodge their garrison.

The indirect hostilities which thus commenced for the possession of Tenedos between the Genoese and Venetians, soon afterwards assumed a more decided character. At the coronation of Pierre de Lusignan, king of Cyprus, in 1373, a dispute for precedence had arisen between these ambitious republicans who held powerful establishments in that island. The Cypriot court favoured the pride of the Venetians; the Genoese resisted the preference, and repaired to the royal banquet in arms to support their pretensions; they were overpowered, and thrown out of the windows of the palace; and their insolence so excited the fury of the Cypriots, that it produced a general massacre of their countrymen in the island. The republic of Genoa was not slow to avenge the murder of her citizens: a formidable armament was immediately fitted out and dispatched to Cyprus; the whole island was conquered; and after exercising a summary vengeance upon the principal instigators of the massacre, the Genoese obliged Lusignan to become their tributary, and left a garrison in his capital. The Cypriot king submitted to their yoke with impatience, until he observed the rising quarrel between the maritime republics for the possession of Tenedos. He then sought the alliance of Venice, himself rose in arms, and engaged Bernabo Visconti, to whose daughter he was betrothed, to expend her dowry in attacking the Genoese in Liguria.

The Genoese attributed all the wars in which they now found themselves engaged in Tenedos, in Cyprus, and in Liguria, to the hatred and jealousy of the Venetians. They resolved to retaliate on their rivals by the formation of a league among the enemies of Venice, and with this intention they applied to the lord of Padua. Carrara needed little solicitation to forward their views; and, by his exertions, the most formidable coalition which had ever endangered the independence of Venice was rapidly organized. Besides Genoa and the lord of Padua, Louis king of Hungary, Joanna queen of Naples, the brothers Della Scala, reigning signers of Verona, the duke of Austria, and the patriarch of Aquileia—who imitated his predecessors, the eternal enemies of Venice—had all their various causes of offence against the republic, and eagerly confederated for her destruction. (A.D. 1378.) To oppose them she was left with no other ally than the lord of Milan, who had attacked Genoa at the instigation of the king of Cyprus, and whose object it was not to succour Venice, but to seize a favourable occasion for making conquests in Liguria and the Veronese dominions. Thus on the consummation of the Genoese league, hostilities immediately burst forth from one extremity of Lombardy to the other. While two Milanese armies severally entered Liguria and the Veronese state, the troops of Hungary, Padua, and Aquileia, on the other hand, invaded from opposite points both the district of Treviso and the *Dogado*, or narrow territory of Venice which bordered on her lagunes. All these operations, which were as usual carried on principally with mercenary troops, were generally indecisive, and present few details that deserve to be recorded. Merely observing, therefore, that the confederates, to whom Venice could scarcely oppose an adequate resistance, overran her territory on the main land to the edge of the lagunes, and straitened her within those waters, I shall turn from the notice of continental hostilities, to relate the events of the maritime struggle between Genoa and Venice, which have given to this memorable contest the name of the war of Chiozza.

It was in the Tuscan seas, off the promontory of Antium, on which the ancients had elevated a temple to Fortune, that the fleets of Genoa and Venice encountered each other for the first time in this war. But the forces of the hostile squadrons did not correspond with the power which we have seen the two republics display in former contests. Their numerous mariners, who were scattered over the seas in commercial occupations, could not during the first year be recalled for the service of their states: fewer vessels were armed than had been usual, and these were distributed into small expeditions. The Genoese stationed their admiral, Fiesco, on the coast of Tuscany, with only ten galleys for the protection of their trade: the armament which the Venetians dispatched to the same quarter consisted of fourteen sail under Vettor Pisani, the most illustrious and able of their commanders. The two squadrons engaged with the fierce and courageous spirit which had ever distinguished the wars of their republics; the event was decided only by superiority of numbers; and Pisani, capturing five galleys, obtained a complete victory. A small Venetian force, which had been sent to Cyprus, also gained a partial advantage over the Genoese, and burnt several of their vessels in the port of Famagosta, but the principal attention of both parties was shortly attracted from all other objects to the waters of the Adriatic.

The remains of the fleet which Pisani had defeated, instead of attempting to fly for refuge to their own ports, boldly steered southward, and doubling the capes of Italy directed their course to the Adriatic, where Luciano Doria, great admiral of Genoa, by degrees accumulated a fleet of twenty-two galleys, and menaced the security of Venice. The senate of that republic recalled Pisani to the defence of the gulf; but though the fleet under his orders had now been augmented to twenty-five galleys, besides a small force which he had detached to operate a diversion in other quarters under Carlo Zeno, he could not avail himself of his trifling superiority to force the Genoese to an action. Doria had numerous points of support in the harbours of the king of Hungary; and while the Genoese admiral ravaged the Istrian dominions of Venice on the one hand, and his adversary on the other captured some maritime towns of Dalmatia, the remainder of the summer passed without any encounter between their fleets.

On the approach of winter, the Venetian senate, to prevent Doria from commanding the navigation of the gulf, obliged their admiral to keep the sea with his squadron, notwithstanding his urgent representations of its exhausted state. During this long and fatal cruise in the severe season, a destructive epidemic which broke out in the Venetian galleys, carried off immense numbers of the seamen; and Pisani had at length been compelled to seek repose for his enfeebled squadron in the Istrian port of Pola, when the Genoese fleet of twenty-two galleys appeared in the offing. The Venetian sailors were driven to desperation by the hardships of their lengthened service; they were eager to terminate their sufferings by bringing the enemy to action; and Pisani, hastily completing his crew with the landsmen of Pola, was unwillingly induced to yield to the clamours of his followers, and to lead them against the Genoese. Yet his anticipation of the result did not prevent him from discharging all the duties of a valiant and experienced admiral. He furiously attacked the Genoese, and their admiral fell in the onset: but Luciano Doria was only one of a race of heroes; and his brother, immediately assuming the command, animated his followers to revenge and victory. In courage they were equal to the Venetians; in numbers and in skill they were superior to a mixture of landsmen and sailors enfeebled by disease. Pisani was utterly defeated: he could save only seven galleys, and he had no sooner taken refuge with them in Venice, than he was consigned by the senate to a dungeon, as if their error had been his crime. (A.D. 1379.)

While Venice was filled with consternation at this defeat, the Genoese squadron was augmented by a strong reinforcement to forty-eight galleys; and Piero Doria, another of the same noble family as the late admiral, arriving from Genoa to succeed him, immediately prepared to complete the destruction of the rival republic. After concerting his measures with the lord of Padua, he appeared off the long line of narrow islands which separate the Venetian lagune from the Adriatic. These strips of land are intersected by six openings which were navigable for the armed vessels of the times, and formed so many entrances into the lagune. All of these the senate had caused to be hastily closed by triple chains, booms, and other defences, behind which were moored heavy vessels planted with artillery. Doria, after some hesitation, resolved to force the most southerly, except one, of the six passages. Just within this opening, among a group of the interior islets of the lagune, like those upon which Venice itself is built, stands the town of Chiozza, twenty-five miles south of the capital. A deep canal, cut through the shallows of the lagune, forms the only passage for large vessels from Chiozza to Venice and the outlets to the sea farther north; but besides the opening immediately opposite to the town, the channel of Brondolo, still more southward, affords another communication between Chiozza and the Adriatic.

When Doria resolved to penetrate into the lagune through the strongly fortified opening before Chiozza, it was agreed that Francesco da Carrara should co-operate with him from the Brenta, which flows into the lagune, by descending that river with a numerous flotilla, following the deep channels which its waters had delved through the shallows towards the outlet of Chiozza, and assaulting the passage in rear while the Genoese gave their onset from without. Success attended this combined operation. The small Venetian force which occupied the floating defences of the pass, thus placed between two superior attacks, could oppose but a brief resistance, though their struggle was vigorous, and the Genoese fleet rode triumphantly within the lagune and formed the siege of Chiozza. The Venetians had thrown a garrison of three thousand men into the place, and these troops, aided by the burghers, made a gallant and obstinate defence; but the united forces of the

Genoese and of Carrara, who posted part of his army to prosecute the siege on the neighbouring island of Brondolo, with which Chiozza was connected by a bridge, were by land and sea twenty-four thousand strong; and after a series of furious conflicts, in which the besiegers lost in six days almost as many men as the whole numbers of the garrison, they finally entered the town by storm. Four thousand prisoners fell into their hands, and the banner of St. George floated from the towers of Chiozza above the reversed lion of St. Mark.

Such was the consternation which the capture of this advanced post of the capital excited at Venice, that the doge was reduced to sue for peace. His ambassadors took with them some Genoese prisoners who were released as a propitiatory offering to Doria, and a sheet of blank paper, on which the admiral and the lord of Padua were desired to dictate their pleasure to the republic with no other reservation than her freedom. Carrara was anxious to terminate the war at so favourable a moment; but the Genoese admiral seeing the ancient and detested rival of his country prostrate before him, was steeled against mercy by national hatred, the desire of vengeance, and the confidence of victory. Summoning the ambassadors to a public audience before him and Carrara, he thus addressed him: "I declare unto you before God, ye Venetian lords, that ye shall have no peace from the lord of Padua nor from our republic, until first we have put a curb in the mouths of those wild horses that stand on your place of St. Mark. When we have them bridled to our hands, they shall be tame enough. Take back your Genoese prisoners, for I shall be with you at Venice in a few days to release both them and their companions from your dungeons."

When this insulting answer was reported at Venice, the senate prepared for the defence of the republic with the energy which was characteristic of their counsels, and they succeeded in animating the people with a spirit that seconded their own. But when the popular enthusiasm was roused, there was but one man in Venice on whom the general confidence and affection of her mariners and citizens could repose. The multitude bore in mind the successful services of Vettor

Pisani, and thought only of his misfortunes to remember the injustice of the disgrace and imprisonment in which he languished. The whole city simultaneously rose to demand the release of the only man who seemed capable of delivering the sinking state; the public palace was besieged with loud acclamations of "Live Vettor Pisani, our admiral!" and the senate, abandoning in this season of peril the inflexible firmness of their ordinary policy, yielded to the popular voice, and drew Pisani from his prison to bestow on him the office of high-admiral. The hero nobly forgot his personal injuries in the danger of his country; he rendered a prompt and modest obedience to the senate, and under his intrepid and able conduct the fortunes of Venice revived. The inaction of Doria favoured his exertions to rally and collect the disorganized strength of the republic. For above two months the Genoese admiral remained in possession of Chiozza, and within sight of Venice, without attempting any enterprise against the city. It is not easy to account for this apparent supineness except by the probability that, while the difficulties of the navigation deterred Doria from hazarding his galleys among the intricacies and shallows of the lagune, he confidently relied upon starving the Venetians into a surrender. They were cut off from intercourse with the neighbouring continent of Italy, Dalmatia, and Istria, by the Paduan and Hungarian troops, and the Genoese obstructed the approach of supplies from the sea. But instead of tamely awaiting the approach of famine, the Venetians in the midst of their privations were working out their deliverance under the guidance of Pisani by labour and patriotic sacrifices. The first care of their great commander was to occupy the deep and narrow channel which led from Chiozza to Venice with large round vessels or floating batteries armed with heavy artillery; for the use of ordnance had now become general. All the other canals and passages which communicated between Venice and the sea were similarly guarded; and after these precautions had been effectually taken, the Venetians proceeded to equip a new fleet. Their docks contained only a few dismantled galleys, but others were rapidly constructed; contributions of all kinds were eagerly made by the patriotism of individuals; in the exhaustion of the national funds and the ruin of commerce, private plate was melted and offered to the state, and the senate stimulated the emulation of the citizens by promising to ennoble thirty plebeian families who should most distinguish themselves in zeal and devotion to the state. In this manner a fleet of thirty-four galleys was fitted out; but the want of seamen compelled Pisani to man them in a great part with artizans and other landsmen, and some time was passed in exercising their motley crews in the canals of Venice before the admiral could venture to lead them against the veteran seamen of Genoa.

At length the moment arrived at which the Venetians dared in their turn to become the assailants. Doria had laid part of his galleys up to give repose to his sailors during the winter, and observing with alarm the increasing strength of an enemy whom he had despised, he concentrated his whole force about Chiozza. At this juncture, in a December night, the doge Canterini, a brave old man who had passed his seventieth year, carried the standard of Venice on board the ducal galley, and assuming in person the principal command of the fleet, which was accompanied by a numerous flotilla of light barks, led the armament out of the lagune opposite to Venice, and steering down the gulf, suddenly appeared at the mouth of the passage of Chiozza, through which Doria had originally forced his way into the lagune. The Genoese little suspected that his design was to enclose them in the station which they had victoriously assumed, when he pushed one of the large round vessels, which we have seen employed in former contests under the name of cocche, into the narrow channel of Chiozza, and anchored her there to block up the strait. The Genoese galleys came out to attack her, overpowered her crew, and imprudently set her on fire. She burnt to the water's edge and went to the bottom on the spot; and the Venctians, then deriving more profit from this accident than they had anticipated from their first design, advanced with boat-loads of stones, and sinking these successively upon her, completely choked up the channel. After this exploit of the doge, there yet remained to the

Genoese two outlets from Chiozza; they might either advance towards Venice along the principal canal of the lagune which communicated with some of the northerly passages into the open sea, or regain the Adriatic in the opposite direction by retiring through the port of Brondolo, the most southerly of the six openings. But Pisani at once closed the canal against them by sinking loads of stones in the same manner as had been done before Chiozza; and while the Genoese, still apparently unconscious of their danger, made no effort to put to sea through the pass of Brondolo, the Venetian admiral again issued from the lagune, and boldly sailing to the only point of egress which was yet open to the enemy, posted his inferior fleet in so able a manner at the mouth of the port of Brondolo, that the Genoese could neither issue from it, nor form their line of battle in the narrow channel to attack him.

The position of the combatants was thus completely reversed, and the Genoese found themselves enclosed in the toils. But still as their ally, the lord of Padua, held the neighbouring continent, it was not easy for the Venetians to reduce them by famine, and their great superiority of force utterly forbade an assault upon them. Farther, although the manner in which Pisani had skilfully disposed his fleet prevented the Genoese from issuing or forming to engage, his own situation was one of great peril and risk. Part of his galleys were compelled to lie under the fire of the enemy's batteries; the first gale or even squall which should blow him for a few hours off the port of Brondolo must immediately give release to the besieged squadron; and if the Genoese could once regain the open sea, the advantage of numbers and seamanship was entirely on their side. The Venetian crews were discouraged by the insecurity and hardships of their station, they were exhausted with the incessant and wearisome duty of keeping the sea to guard the blockade, and utterly averse from passing the whole winter in this harassing service. Yet if Pisani quitted his commanding posture at the strait of Brondolo, and allowed the Genoese to come out, Venice, which was even now provisioned with much difficulty, must be again cut off from supplies and famished into surrender. To rekindle the expiring courage of his followers, and shame them from deserting him, the old doge took a solemn oath before the assembled armament, that he would never return to Venice till the banner of St. Mark should again wave over Chiozza. Pisani and all the leading Venetians laboured with equal earnestness to encourage the soldiery and mariners, by cheering them with the hope of speedy relief from the return of the squadron which had been detached on a cruise into other seas before the defeat of Pisani at Polo.

Carlo Zeno, who in courage, and skill, and patriotism, was almost worthy to be ranked with that great admiral, had when he quitted the Adriatic only eight galleys under his orders; but with this force, after making some valuable captures of Genoese merchant vessels off Sicily, and proceeding from thence to carry insult and terror into the coasts of Genoa, he had quitted the Italian seas, and steered for Greece and the Levant. There, among the Venetian colonies, his squadron was gradually augmented to eighteen galleys, and he was about to bring home the merchant fleets of Venice, which with their rich cargoes awaited convoy in the Syrian ports, when one of the light barks which had been dispatched to him through the fleet of the besiegers to announce the danger of his country, and to declare the orders of the signiory for his recall, at length succeeded in reaching him.

While the squadron of Pisani lay off Brondolo, every eye anxiously sought the horizon of the Adriatic for the expected succours, of which no intelligence had yet been received. But successive days passed in disappointment; the patience of the Venetians was utterly worn out; and the doge was induced to promise them that he would raise the blockade of Chiozza, if the long-hoped for reinforcement did not arrive by the first of January, 1380. To this crisis there wanted at the time only forty-eight hours, before Venice must be besieged in her turn, and the senate were already deliberating whether they should not transfer the seat of their republic to Candia, when, on the very morning of the first of January a squadron was discerned in the offing, (A.D. 1380.)

Eighteen galleys were counted as they drew near, well armed and stored with provisions; and the cheers that rang through the fleets of Venice proclaimed the arrival of Carlo Zeno.

From that hour abundance reigned in the markets of Venice, the courage of the seamen and troops revived, and the united squadrons of Pisano and Zeno outnumbered the enemy. By the vigorous attacks which the Venetians now commenced, the Genoese were gradually, from being enclosed in the lagune, confined within Chiozza itself, and their communications with the continent intercepted. Famine then began to threaten them; but they continued to defend themselves with obstinate courage for several months in anxious expectation of relief. But when a second fleet, which their republic dispatched to their aid, at last appeared off the lagune, the entrances were so completely closed and strongly fortified, that the new expedition could neither force a passage to succour Chiozza, nor bring the Venetians, who remained cautiously within the lagune, to an encounter. The besieged Genoese made one desperate and ingenious attempt to effect a passage through their enemies and to join their countrymen, but it was frustrated; and then, perishing with famine, and entirely cut off from hope of rescue, even in sight of the fleet which had vainly sought to release them, the remains of the proud armament which had denied mercy to Venice, were finally compelled to surrender at discretion. Only nineteen galleys out of forty-eight were still in good condition; and in ten months which had elapsed since their capture of Chiozza, the fourteen thousand seamen and soldiers which had manned the fleet were diminished in equal proportion.

The surrender of Chiozza saved Venice, but did not terminate the war; and while that republic, her resources consumed, her treasury empty, her commerce stagnant, her revenues and dominions in Istria and Italy in the hands of enemies, was reduced to the last stage of distress and exhaustion by the prodigious efforts which she had made, the fresh Genoese fleet, nine-and-thirty galleys strong, still rode the Adriatic. She therefore earnestly desired peace; and the rival republic, in the loss or captivity of the flower of her seamen, had equal reason to deplore the indulgence of national animosity. But it was not until the following year that the demands of the Genoese league were reduced within the limits of the sacrifices which Venice was contented to make. At length, under the mediation of the count of Savoy, terms were mutually adjusted; and by the peace of Turin, Venice recovered the repose for which she sighed. (A.D. 1381.) But she was compelled to abandon her territorial acquisitions on the Italian continent, and could only console herself that, by having already ceded Treviso to the duke of Austria, she had prevented it from passing to her most inveterate enemy, Francesco da Carrara. But in favour of that lord she cancelled all the conditions of the treaty of 1372; to the king of Hungary she engaged to pay contributions and confirmed the relinquishment of her possessions on the opposite coasts; and, finally, to Genoa she conceded the abandonment of the isle of Tenedos, the original cause of dispute. The dominion of Venice, except over her transmarine colonies, was now confined to the circuit of the lagune; while Genoa, however imperfect the recompense for so many sufferings, in some measure held the palm of victory. Yet we shall find Venice reviving, after the exhaustion of this war of Chiozza, to a brilliant pre-eminence of power and commercial prosperity; and Genoa, on the contrary, silently wasting into debility, as if excess of exertion had fatally strained the secret springs of her vigour and strength.

PART III.
Affairs of Lombardy—Gian Galeazzo Visconti, lord of Milan—War between the signors of Verona and Padua—Interference of Gian Galeazzo in their quarrel—His overthrow of the house of Scala—His projects against the house of Carrara—Conquest and partition of their states—Alarming power of Gian Galeazzo—His ambitious designs in Tuscany—War between Florence and the lord of Milan and their allies—Fortunes of Francesco Novello da Carrara—His re-establishment in the lordship of Padua—Prosecution of the war between Florence and the lord of Milan—Defeat of the count d'Armagnac, the ally of Florence—Skilful retreat of Hawkwood—Peace of Genoa—Perfidious character and intrigues of Gian Galeazzo Visconti—Erection of Milan into an imperial duchy—New war between Florence and the duke of Milan, terminated by a truce—Successful machinations of Gian Galeazzo—Pisa subjected to his yoke—The signiory of Sienna and Perugia surrendered to him—Decline of the spirit of freedom—Italy in danger of tailing under the universal tyranny of the duke of Milan—Revolutions of Genoa—Rise of the commercial aristocracy—Recovery of the republic from the Milanese yoke—Struggles of

faction—Incessant revolutions, and exhaustion of the republic—Surrender of the state to the protection of Charles VI. of France—Affairs of Naples—Continuation of the reign of Joanna—Condition of Sicily—Charles of Durazzo adopted by Joanna for her successor—His rupture with her, and enterprise against her throne in concert with Urban VI.—Adoption of the duke of Anjou by Joanna—Conquest of Naples by Charles of Durazzo—Murder of Joanna—Expedition of Louis of Anjou into Naples—His failure and death—Reign of Charles III.—His attempt to seize the crown of Hungary, and murder—Civil wars in Naples between the parties of Anjou and Durazzo—Louis II. of Anjou—Ladislaus, son of Charles III.—His character, and success against his rival—His final establishment on the throne.

THE power of the Visconti, which had for many years worn a formidable aspect in northern Italy, had not however been attended by the full effects of its alarming preponderance, so long as the possessions of that house were shared between the two brothers, Galeazzo and Bernabo. But, shortly after the termination of the war of Chiozza, the whole of the Milanese dominions were united under a single chief, who concentrated in his person all the odious and dangerous qualities of his family, and gave ample cause to the other states of the peninsula to apprehend the establishment of one wide-spreading and general tyranny. This was Gian Galeazzo, the son of Galeazzo, who, by the death of that lord in 1378, had inherited his portion of central Lombardy, and fixed his court at Pavia, while his uncle Bernabo resided at Milan.

The ties of kindred were as little valued by these perfidious usurpers as any other bonds of humanity; and the first efforts of Bernabo, on his brother's decease, were directed against the life and reign of his nephew. But Gian Galeazzo was more than a match for him in duplicity. While he warily guarded himself against the plots of Bernabo without seeming to penetrate them, he affected to be exclusively engrossed in devotional exercises and personal fears. Travelling about with a retinue of priests, he was incessantly telling his beads, and visiting the different saintly shrines of Lombardy; and his coward terrors were displayed in the number of guards who constantly surrounded him, and denied access to his presence. He thus gained his object of inspiring his uncle with a sovereign contempt for his imbecility; and as he passed near Milan on a pretended pilgrimage, with a numerous escort, Bernabo and two of his sons came out to meet him without suspicion. The hypocrite received them with affectionate embraces; but suddenly turning to two of his captains, gave them an order in German, then the universal military language of Italy, to arrest his three relatives. Their soldiers immediately seized the bridle of the mule on which Bernabo rode; his sword was cut from his side; and he was dragged off the spot from his attendants with his sons, vainly imploring his nephew not to prove a traitor to his own blood. Milan at once opened her gates to Gian Galeazzo, and the captive signor was confined with his sons in one of her castles; where, in the course of a few months, poison was at three several times administered to Bernabo in his food, and at last terminated his flagitious existence. His crimes had rendered him so detested that neither his subjects nor allies showed any inclination to avert or avenge his fate; and his nephew, throwing off the mask of devotion, reigned unopposed lord of the whole Milanese dependencies, (A.D. 1385.)

The ambition of Gian Galeazzo, thus already steeped in unnatural crime, was not likely to be satisfied even with these great possessions: and a war, which was excited by Venice between the houses of Carrara and Scala, shortly opened a new field for his perfidious intrigues. The implacable hatred of the Venetians towards Francesco da Carrara had been strengthened by their sufferings in the war of Chiozza: and the purchase of Treviso and its district, which the lord of Padua effected from the duke of Austria some time after the termination of that contest, aggravated their long jealousy of so enterprising a neighbour. The enfeebled condition of their republic prevented them from openly provoking a new struggle with him; but they in secret instigated Antonio della Scala, a bastard of the house of Verona, who, sharing the power of his legitimate brother, had caused him to be assassinated that he might reign alone, to declare war against Carrara, in revenge for the horror which that lord had publicly expressed at his guilt, (A.D. 1386.) But notwithstanding the pecuniary aid of Venice, the Veronese signor was unsuccessful in the struggle; and, after two great defeats of his mercenary troops in successive campaigns by those of Carrara, he was reduced to listen to the overtures of the lord of Milan.

Gian Galeazzo, from the commencement of hostilities between the combatants, had awaited the moment of their common exhaustion to offer succors to each that he might despoil them both: but such was their mutual dread of his character that they had in turn rejected his proffered aid, until the distresses of Scala left him no other resource than to escape more imminent danger by accepting his alliance; and Carrara, who had vainly sought peace, was then compelled to anticipate his purpose, and to sign a treaty with Gian Galeazzo for the partition of the Veronese dominions, (A.D. 1387.) This act was fatal to both the rivals. Antonio della Scala was utterly unequal to resist the coalition of the Milanese and Paduan signors; he was rapidly stripped of all his possessions, and compelled to seek refuge at Venice with his treasures; and a single campaign accomplished the ruin of the house of Scala, which had reigned at Verona for above one hundred and twenty years, and more than once aspired to an universal supremacy over the peninsula. But it was farthest from the intention of Visconti that Carrara should share in the spoil. He knew the hatred which the Venetians bore to that lord; and after having enabled him to overthrow Scala, whom they had secretly aided but dare not openly protect, the crafty and perfidious tyrant at once proposed to them to dispossess the signor of Padua in turn of his dominions, and offered to enter into a league with their republic, to accomplish the ruin of their detested enemy, and the partition of his states.

The skilful policy which usually actuated the Venetian senate might have suggested to them that Visconti, established on the shore of their lagune, must prove infinitely a more dangerous neighbour than Carrara. In the lust of dominion, in faithless machinations, the lord of Padua could scarcely equal Gian Galeazzo: in power he was confessedly inferior and less to be dreaded. Yet the senate, listening only to the dictates of ambition and vengeance, eagerly accepted the proffered alliance of the Milanese lord, and signed a treaty with him, into which the marquis of Este and the lord of Mantua were admitted, for the partition of the Paduan states, (A.D. 1388.) The old lord of Carrara, thus assailed by a coalition of enemies of whom the least was alone his equal in force, was at once reduced to the extremity of distress; for his subjects of Padua, oppressed by the accumulated burthens of successive wars, were clamorous and disaffected, and eager for any revolution. In the general ruin which thus menaced his house, some of his counsellors suggested, as the only expedient for averting its consummation, his abdication of the signiory of Padua in favour of his son, Francesco Novello da Carrara. They represented to him that the enmity which the Venetians bore to him personally could not extend to this young man, that the hearts of the Paduans were with him, and that he would find new resources in her devotion. The old signor listened to their advice; he publicly went through the vain ceremony of resigning his authority into the hands of the citizens of Padua, as if they had still been free to choose his successor; Francesco Novello was declared lord of the state in his stead; and he himself immediately withdrew to Treviso, of which he determined to retain the sovereignty.

But this arrangement failed in diverting the enemies of the Carrara from their purpose; and, on the very day on which the elder Francesco retired to Treviso, the heralds of Gian Galeazzo brought a defiance and a declaration of war to his son. The states both of Padua and Treviso were immediately invaded from all points by the troops of the league; panic and treason spread through the cities, the castles, and the camps of the Carrara; and neither father nor son could discover any other mode of escape from the merciless hands of the Venetians, their deadliest foes, than by surrendering the keys of their capitals and fortresses to Jacopo del Verme, the general of Gian Galeazzo, and obtaining a safe conduct for themselves to proceed to Pavia, and implore the generosity of the conqueror. Thus the viper (il biscione) the armorial bearing of the Visconti, a term which is figuratively used by contemporary chroniclers as the emblem of their power, erected his crest on the shores of the Adriatic. The standards of Gian Galeazzo, which floated over the walls of Padua and her dependant fortresses, might be discerned from the towers of Venice; and when the Paduan deputies knelt in homage before the lord of Milan, he boastfully promised them that, if God only gave him five years of life, he would make the proud senators of Venice their equals, and put an end to the alarm which that amphibious republic had so long occasioned to their city.

While the machinations and arms of Gian Galeazzo had thus dispossessed the houses of Scala and Carrara in succession of their inheritance, his treacherous projects had not been confined to the extension of his dominions in eastern Lombardy. He had already sought another field for his intrigues among the Tuscan states, and had only suspended the prosecution of his designs in that quarter, that he might receive no interruption in the conquest of the Veronese and Paduan lordships. But, in almost all the Tuscan cities, his emissaries were incessantly occupied in exciting troubles by which he might profit for the establishment of his power; and the eternal enmities and dissensions, which filled the republics of that province, afforded him but too many occasions for weaving his toils among them. Florence, ever the enemy of the tyrants of Italy, was as usual the particular object of his hostility, and watchful in observing his motions. Some disputes, which arose between her and Sienna, impelled the people of the latter city to offer their signiory to the lord of Milan for the blind gratification of their animosity; and though the tyrant dissembled for some time, and even concluded an amicable treaty with the Florentines, the continuance of his faithless enterprises at length determined their rulers to prefer open warfare with him to an insidious peace. In this resolution they were imitated by Bologna; and, in less than two years after the fall of the Carrara, a general war was kindled in Tuscany, (A.D. 1390.) Besides the support of his Lombard allies, the marquis of Este, and Gonzaga lord of Mantua, Visconti had drawn into his party the Tuscan republics of Sienna and Perugia, and all the petty Ghibelin signers of the same province and of Romagna; and the confederates brought into the field in the first campaign fifteen thousand cuirassiers and six thousand foot. The allied republics could not oppose to them nearly the same force; but Florence placed Sir John Hawkwood at the head of an army of two thousand lances, or six thousand cavalry, and Bologna supported a thousand lances. Against this inferior force, however, the numerous array of Visconti and his confederates gained no decisive success. The assailants were scattered round a large circuit of frontier; no great battle was fought; and the war languished in a few incursions and surprises of petty castles, when the attention of both parties was suddenly diverted to the Trevisan March, by the bold enterprise of one man, who by his courage and talents, by the energy of his character, and above all by his hatred of Visconti, proved himself a most efficient ally to Florence.

This was Francesco Novello da Carrara, whom Gian Galeazzo had deprived of his father's territories and his own. That tyrant, after violating the safe conduct of the Carrara to his presence, that he might avoid seeing them, had imprisoned the father; and having at first amused the son through his ministers with the promise of the signiory of Lodi, finally assigned to him in exchange for his ample states the ruined fortalice of Cortazon near Asti. At this fief, however, Francesco occupied himself in his fallen fortunes, like a simple châtelain, in rebuilding his castle, until his oppressor drove him even from this retreat. The city of Asti had been ceded by Visconti to the duke of Orleans, who had married his daughter; and the lieutenant who commanded for the duke in the place, conceiving an affection for Carrara, gave him intelligence that Visconti had stationed a band of assassins to waylay and murder him between the city and his castle. He counselled an immediate flight, and Francesco followed his advice. The friendly governor undertook to transport his children and treasure to Florence; and under his escort the persecuted chieftain himself suddenly quitted his castle with his wife and a few faithful servants, announcing his intention to make a pilgrimage to a shrine at Vienne in Dauphiny. From thence he proceeded to Avignon to entreat the counsel and aid of the anti-pope; and then embarked at Marseilles to return to Italy by sea. But the dark machinations of Visconti still pursued him; his course was dogged by the emissaries of the tyrant; he was repeatedly driven on shore by tempests and by the sufferings of his wife, a lady of the house of Este, who was far advanced in her pregnancy; and at every spot where the travellers attempted to land from their felucca, the myrmidons of Gian Galeazzo beset their path and menaced their lives. It was not until the fugitive signer and his wife had passed through a long series of romantic and touching adventures, that they at length reached a hospitable asylum beyond the power of their remorseless enemy in the free city of Florence, and found that, by the faithful friendship of the governor of Asti, their family and riches were already sheltered in the same haven.

His mind relieved by the safety of his family, Carrara left Florence to pursue his plans of vengeance against his oppressor, and to encounter a repetition of the dangers which he had escaped. Alternately encouraged and disappointed, as the counsels of Florence wavered between war and peace with Visconti, he wandered in successive journeys between Italy and Dalmatia and Germany, until the Florentines had finally resolved on hostilities; and then, having levied forces among some Hungarian chieftains, who were connected by marriage and friendship with his family, and purchased the aid of the duke of Bavaria, who engaged to lead a large army into Italy, he at length suddenly appeared in arras on the Paduan frontiers. His success was rapid and brilliant: the former subjects of his house, already weary of the grievous yoke of the lord of Milan, welcomed him with acclamations, and every where revolted in his favour; the Venetians, awaking to alarm at the power of Visconti, favoured him under cover of a strict neutrality; the Milanese generals were compelled to shut themselves up in Padua; and Francesco besieging them there, finally entered the city by surprise, and re-established himself in his capital and in the whole of its dependant territory.

The success of Carrara, and the vain efforts which Gian Galeazzo made to recover the Paduan country, operated as a diversion in favour of the Florentines and Bolognese, by removing the principal theatre of hostilities from their territory to eastern Lombardy, or the Trevisan March; and though the duke of Bavaria failed in his engagements, and disgracefully suffered himself to be bribed by Visconti, Carrara and his allies succeeded by their incursions into the Modenese state in forcing the marquis of Este to abandon the Milanese alliance. But the languid progress of the war seemed to promise no decisive event; and the Florentines determined by one vigorous effort to bring it if possible to an honourable conclusion. They therefore addressed themselves to the count d'Armagnac, a French prince of high martial reputation, whose family connexions rendered him unfriendly to Gian Galeazzo. (A.D. 1391.) The sister of d'Armagnac had married a son of Bernabo Visconti; and the prince was eagerly besought by this brother-in-law to aid him in avenging his father's murder and recovering his inheritance from Gian Galeazzo. Thus solicited, and tempted by the large subsidies and offers of Florence, d'Armagnac agreed to enter Lombardy with a force of fifteen thousand gens-d'armerie. It was proposed by the council of ten commissioners to whom the management of the war was committed at Florence, that, while the count thus entered the Milanese dominions from France, the troops of their own republic, with those of Bologna and Padua, should invade them simultaneously from the eastward or opposite frontier. Hawkwood was therefore dispatched with his bands from Tuscany to Padua to assume the chief command of the confederates; and having there assembled fourteen hundred lances in Florentine, six hundred in Bolognese, and two hundred in Paduan pay,—in all 6600 cuirassiers—with 1200 cross-bowmen, and a great body of other infantry, the veteran captain advanced into the states of Visconti, and successively crossing the Adige, the Mincio, and the Oglio, penetrated triumphantly within fifteen miles of Milan, from which the Adda alone remained to separate him.

But here he was suddenly arrested by the intelligence that the rashness and presumption of d'Armagnac had entailed utter destruction on the numerous and gallant army, which he had selected from the flower of the French chivalry. Gian Galeazzo, who was hopeless of arresting the advance of the count in the field, had opposed to him the ablest of his generals, Jacopo del Verme, but with a very inferior force of 6000 cuirassiers and 4000 foot. The Milanese leader had shut himself up in Alessandria; and d'Armagnac, instead of turning aside to effect the junction with Hawkwood which had been concerted, proceeded with an utter but misplaced contempt for the Italian chivalry to carry his bravades to the gates of Alessandria with the elite of his followers, leaving the mass of his army some miles in rear. A corresponding body of the Milanese gens-d'armerie sallied out to meet his challenge: but the French chivalry had no sooner bravely dismounted to fight in phalanx on foot, than their adversaries caracoling round them, drew them off from the spot where their horses were left; and when, harassed by desultory assaults, wearied with marching under the enormous weight of their armour, and overpowered by the dust and the scorching heat of a noon-day sun, their strength had been completely exhausted, Jacopo del Verme placed a second body of his cavalry, which had secretly issued from another gate, between them and their horses, and finally inclosing them with his forces, either slaughtered or captured the whole number, including their leader. The French army, thus left in their camp and deprived of their captains, were seized with a panic; and dispersing, were either massacred by the peasantry who occupied all the passes, or compelled to surrender to the Milanese troops, their pursuers.

These disasters placed Hawkwood in the most imminent peril. He was in the heart of an enemy's country: before him were the whole forces of Milan, victorious and now far superior in numbers, which approached to overpower him, and, in his rear, were three great rivers which he could not hope to pass with impunity in their presence. But the confidence which he felt in the resources of his own genius in no degree abandoned him. After remaining inactive behind his intrenchments, as if paralyzed by terror, until the Milanese, their temerity and carelessness increasing as he tamely received their insults, were thrown off their guard; he suddenly fell upon them with so much impetuosity that he routed them and captured twelve hundred horse. Having thus gained his object of inspiring his enemy with respect, and deterring him from too close a pursuit, Hawkwood commenced a masterly retreat, and had repassed both the Oglio and Mincio before a single trooper of Gian Galeazzo dared appear on their banks. But he had yet the rapid Adige to cross, and the difficulty was the greater as the enemy had already fortified themselves on the dykes, which confine the waters of that river to its bed. The Lombard plains are almost every where on a lower level than that of the streams which intersect them, and are only preserved from continual inundations by artificial embankments, between which the impetuous torrents that descend from the melting of Alpine snows are securely conducted to the sea. But when these dykes are burst or cut, the adjacent plains are at once flooded. Hawkwood, on reaching the range of low land which is known as the Veronese valley, found the Adige, the Po, and the Polesino before him on the north, the south, and the west, and Jacopo del Verme hanging on his rear; and in this situation, the enemy suddenly cut the dykes of the Adige, and let the river loose from its bed upon him. The lower ground about the Florentine camp was at once inundated. As far as the eye could stretch, the country in every direction but one was converted into a vast lake of hourly increasing depth; the waters even menaced the rising spot on which the army lay; provisions began to fail; and Jacopo del Verme, his whole force guarding the only outlet, sent, by a trumpet, a fox enclosed in a cage to the English captain. Hawkwood received the taunting present with dry composure, and bade the messenger tell his general, that his fox appeared nothing sad, and doubtless knew by what door he would quit his cage.

A leader of less courageous enterprise and skilful resource than Hawkwood might have despaired of bursting from the toils; but the wily veteran knew both how to inspire his troops with unlimited confidence in his guidance, and to avail himself of their devotion. Leaving his tents standing, he silently and boldly led his cavalry before day-light into the inundated plain towards the Adige; and, with the waters already at the horses' girths, marched the whole of the same day and the following night beside the dykes of that river, until he found a spot where its bed had been left dry by the escape of the waters; and crossing it at length gave repose to his wearied troops on the Paduan frontiers. Part of his infantry had perished, and he had lost many men and horses in the mud, and in canals and ditches, the danger of which could not be distinguished amidst the general inundation; but the army of the league was saved, and Jacopo del Verme dared not pursue its hazardous retreat.

The subsequent operations of Hawkwood were marked with equal ability, but their event was indecisive; and there appears to me nothing worth recounting in this war after his celebrated and skilful retreat. By the mediation of Genoa, a peace was concluded in the following year, (A.D. 1392.) Its provisions left Francesco Novello da Carrara in quiet possession of the lordship of Padua which he had so gallantly recovered; but Treviso had remained, since the partition treaty with Visconti, with the Venetians, and the old signer, his father, shortly died in the prisons of the lord of Milan, before the adjustment of his ransom could be effected, Gian Galeazzo and the Florentines mutually engaged to abstain from interference, he in the affairs of Tuscany, and they in those of Lombardy. But in negotiating this treaty, the remaining conditions of which were unimportant, the Florentines reposed no trust in their faithless enemy; and when the arbiters of the peace spoke of sureties for its maintenance, "Our surety," said a Florentine commissioner, "shall be in the sword, for the lord of Milan has put our forces to proof, and we have tried his."

The Florentines had full reason to keep an eye of suspicion and alarm upon the movements of Visconti; and they had leisure to perceive, in the course of the few following years, that even a state of avowed hostility, with an enemy so perfidious and restless, was less pregnant with danger than a hollow and faithless peace. Personally unwarlike and pusillanimous, Gian Galeazzo seldom ventured to pass the circuit of his strongly fortified palace at Pavia; but by his numerous agents and emissaries his intrigues dived into the inmost counsels of every state, and his machinations against the general independence of the peninsula were incessant and too extensively successful. The immense revenues, which he exacted from his subjects, were spent in strengthening his mischievous power; almost all the most celebrated condottieri and their bands were attached to his service; and, as he allowed them a constant half-pay, they were still at his command, even while he appeared to give them a formal discharge. He thus turned them loose to subsist by the plunder and ravaging of other states, and left them to rob and exhaust those during peace, against whom he meditated more overt attacks. No oaths or solemn treaties bound him; no crime deterred him; neither remorse nor compunction turned him from the pursuit of the most flagitious enterprises. In the midst of every disappointment and difficulty, he could still command the same calm dissimulation, the same unshaken constancy of purpose; and though his cautious timidity sometimes prevented him from reaping the full measure of opportunity, a watchfulness that never slumbered, and a plausibility of profession which no exposure could shame, rendered him supreme in duplicity even among the wily politicians of Italy. Therefore it was that his negotiations and plots were infinitely more to be dreaded than his arms; and though the Florentines perfectly understood his character, and had alone the courage to offer an habitual resistance to his arts, they were not the less exposed to the effects of his perfidy.

The fall of Pisa under the dominion of a creature of Visconti offered the first new cause of alarm to the Florentines. Notwithstanding the engagement into which the tyrant had entered not to interfere in the affairs of Tuscany, he secretly instigated the treason of Jacopo d'Appiano, a man of base extraction, who had been raised to the office of chancellor of the Pisan republic by the friendship of Piero Gambacorti, the chief of the ruling faction. Gambacorti, a citizen of moderation and virtue, had long governed that republic by the annual renewal of his office of captain general; but though his own disinterestedness and simplicity of manners endeared him to the people, the pride and insolence of his family excited universal disgust, and filled the citizens with the apprehension of an hereditary tyranny. But Gambacorti himself might have preserved his credit with his countrymen to the natural close of a long and honourable life, if he had not reposed confidence in an ungrateful traitor. Appiano, with the connivance of the lord of Milan, secretly assembled numerous armed ruffians from various quarters, excited a furious sedition in the city under pretence of revenging a private quarrel, and basely assassinating his benefactor in the tumult, seized the reins of government. Gian Galeazzo immediately dispatched troops to his support, and under their protection Appiano firmly established himself in the signiory. Before this revolution Visconti had already shown his continued hostility against Florence, by instigating several bodies of disbanded mercenaries, who had formed companies of adventure, to attack the territory of the republic; but the firm countenance of the state repressed these incursions. About the same time, too, he carried his intrigues into the reigning families of Ferrara and Mantua. In the first of these houses he encouraged a disputed succession, in the hope of profiting by a civil war; and, in the second, he persuaded Francesco Gonzaga, by a devilish plot, of the infidelity of his lady, the daughter of Bernabo Visconti, whose enmity he dreaded as the murderer of her father. The lord of Mantua put his guiltless wife to death; and, when he discovered her innocence too late, and was stung by remorse and fired with indignation against the fiend who had deceived him, Gian Galeazzo, finding his alliance lost, was the first to accuse him of the murder of his lady, and thenceforth took every occasion to injure him without an open violation of peace. In the midst of this course of ambition and crime, the power and dignity of the tyrant received a new increase. By the payment of 100,000 florins, he induced the feeble Wenceslaus, who now reigned in Germany as king of the

Romans and emperor elect, to raise Milan and its dependencies into an imperial duchy, and to bestow on him the solemn investiture of this fief. (A.D. 1395.) Thus he in some measure seemed to acquire a recognized right over his dominions, and to remove the long stain of usurpation which had humbled his ancestors and himself before the legitimate dynasties of Europe. Such had been the gradual progress of the overwhelming tyranny of his house, that the cities which were now embraced in the imperial duchy of Milan, were precisely those which, two centuries before, had comprised the league of Lombardy, and triumphantly conquered their freedom from Frederic Barbarossa.

The few years of feverish anxiety, which the Florentine government had passed since their last war, were shortly to terminate in another struggle with the new duke of Milan. Notwithstanding the little fruit derived by the republic from a treaty of alliance which she negotiated with the king of France, she had already prepared for a renewal of her contest with Gian Galeazzo, when a treacherous attempt of some of the condottieri, whom he had formerly disbanded, but who were notoriously under his influence, to seize upon the little city of San Miniato, the subject-ally of Florence, hastened their resolution, and even denied them the option of peace, (A.D. 1397.) For Alberic di Barbiano, the chief of these condottieri, on the failure of the enterprise against San Miniato, united the troops of the duke of Milan in the Siennese and Pisan territories to his bands, and thus forming an army of above ten thousand cuirassiers, began to act openly against Florence as the general of Gian Galeazzo, though without any declaration of war. At the same time two other Milanese armies, on the distant side of Lombardy, broke into the Mantuan territory and ravaged it, also without the usual prelude of honourable hostilities. The war now became general in the Mantuan district. The Florentines, besides defending themselves, sent succours to Gonzaga; the marquis Nicholas III. of Este and the lord of Padua openly assisted him; and Carrara, notwithstanding the ancient quarrel of the Venetians with his father, having succeeded by friendly and submissive overtures, soon after his restoration, in reconciling himself with them, the aid of their republic was indirectly given in concert with his. With the support of all these auxiliaries, Francesco Gonzaga gained a great battle against the Milanese troops near the castle of Governolo. But Venice, though she was alarmed at the increasing power of the duke of Milan, and had now committed herself with him, was still fearful of declaring openly against him, and anxiously sought to re-establish the peace of Lombardy. She therefore offered her mediation to the belligerents; but so interminable were the frauds and deceptions of Gian Galeazzo, that, after eight months of negotiation, all hopes of a definitive peace were renounced, and the good offices of Venice could produce no more than a truce for ten years under her guarantee, (A.D. 1398.)

This imperfect pacification only afforded Gian Galeazzo the greater opportunity and leisure to extend his intrigues. His support of Jacopo d'Appiano, the tyrant of Pisa, and his insidious alliance with Sienna against Florence, had given him an alarming influence over both those states; and this he now found means to convert into an absolute sovereignty. During the life of Jacopo d'Appiano, who was at a very advanced age when he usurped the signiory of Pisa, Gian Galeazzo had already made one treacherous effort to gain possession of the Pisan castles by means of the troops whom he had sent to the support of his creature; and when Appiano discovered and defeated this project, he impudently disclaimed all knowledge of it, and bade the Pisan signor punish the Milanese general and soldiery, and their accomplices in the city, who had fallen into his hands; as if they had acted without his knowledge or approbation. By this artful conduct the duke lulled the suspicions of his dependant, and the death of Jacopo shortly enabled him to seize on the signiory of Pisa by a treaty with the feeble son of that usurper. Finding himself unequal to the preservation of his father's power, Gerardo d'Appiano sold the republic to Gian Galeazzo for 200,000 florins and the signiory of Piombino and the Island of Elba, possessions which the family of Appiano were destined to hold for two centuries. Several thousand of the ducal troops were suddenly admitted into Pisa; the chains of the fallen republic were riveted; and her citizens, hopeless of successful resistance, were compelled to receive a Milanese governor, (A.D. 1399.) Thus successful in enslaving one of the principal republics of Tuscany, the perfidious duke seemed to draw the minor states of the province into the vortex of his despotism, as if by the exercise of some mysterious and potent spell over their counsels. In the same year which planted his standards at Pisa, the Ubertini and other Ghibelin feudatories who held petty mountain fiefs delivered themselves over to his sovereignty; and afterwards the republics of Sienna and Perugia, ravaged by the continued incursions of condottieri, torn by their own factions, and filled with his emissaries, voluntarily called him in for their lord, declared their signiory hereditary in his family, and exchanged their uneasy freedom for his powerful protection and despotic authority. Thus the Florentines found Gian Galeazzo extending his conquests all around their territory. On the side of the Tuscan plains, the viper of Milan was crested on the towers of Pisa, Sienna, and Perugia, cities that had lately been free as their own: from the mountains that overhung their frontier a new storm was gathering in the hostility of the Ghibelin chieftains of the Apennines, who had chosen the Milanese duke for their sovereign. Entirely encompassed by enemies, the Florentines might justly tremble for their own independence, in the defence of which they vainly looked around for assistance.

But the moral desolation in which they were left was even more appalling than the palpable danger of their territorial position. The spirit of freedom seemed to approach its extinction throughout Italy. Of all the inland republics of the peninsula, none besides their own remained to pretend to freedom but Lucca and Bologna; and both these cities were a prey to violent commotions and intrigues, which but too surely portended the establishment of tyrannies in each. In fact, in less than two years after the subjection of Pisa to Gian Galeazzo, both Lucca and Bologna had submitted to domestic tyrants. Of the maritime republics, Genoa had already, as we shall presently find, surrendered herself to a foreign sovereign; and Venice, inactive in the security of her lagunes, and not daring to rouse herself to stem the progress of the Milanese power, abandoned Italy to her fate. The prostration of the peninsula before one universal tyranny in the person of Gian Galeazzo seemed at hand; and amidst the gloomy forebodings which his overwhelming power was calculated to excite, and the horrors of the pestilence which had just re-commenced its cruel ravages, the fourteenth century closed over Italy.

To lessen as much as possible the distractions necessarily entailed on the reader by the numerous transitions in our subject, I have hitherto almost entirely abstained from noticing the domestic history of Genoa during the period embraced in the present chapter; and I have been enabled to reserve the internal affairs of this maritime republic for a brief and separate notice, because they have little connexion with the general history of Italy. The revolution of 1339, which produced the first appointment of doge at Genoa, had a farther and even more important influence upon the subsequent condition of the state. By the exclusion from authority of the old nobility, it paved the way, as a similar vicissitude had done at Florence, for the elevation of a plebeian and commercial aristocracy. An order of wealthy commoners arose, who in dignity and physical strength, in the extent of their property and the number of their retainers, and even in the martial spirit of their characters, and the deadly feuds which divided them, emulated the power and the pride of the ancient families. (A.D. 1350-1400.) Thus the new houses of Adorno and Guarco, of Montalto and Fregoso, moved in a distinct and parallel course with the Grimaldi and Fieschi, the Spinola and Doria. Eagerly seizing an occasion for hatred of each other in the distinction of Guelfs and Ghibelins, these merchant-nobles agreed only in common animosity against the old aristocracy. A sufficient idea of the different position of these two orders in the state may be gathered from observing the sources of their power. The old aristocracy were supported by their vassals, the peasantry of the fiefs in the Ligurian mountains which they held with their castles: the merchant-nobles numbered their retainers among the seamen and artificers of the capital. Personally engaged in the active business of their commerce, they embarked in their own vessels, which were fitted at once for war and trade; the numerous members of the same family often commanded each his galley, and lived among his mariners; and thus thousands of sailors and workmen were maintained in the pay of the same house, and bound by the common ties of affection and interest to their employers. In a free and maritime state, the relation between patron and client constituted a formidable bond of union, and rendered the commercial orders more than a match for the rural proprietors and their followers.

We have seen how the Genoese were reduced after their defeat by the Venetians, in the naval battle of Loiera, in 1353, to consign the signiory of their republic to the archbishop Giovanni Visconti, lord of Milan. But as soon as the pressure of the Venetian war had ceased, the high-spirited people indignantly supported the onerous yoke of Milan, to which their blind hatred and momentary dread of their maritime rivals had induced them rashly to submit; and, after impatiently enduring the government of the Visconti for about three years, they rose in arms, expelled the Milanese governor and garrison, and recalled their doge Simone Boccanigra, the same whom they had originally raised to that dignity in 1339. (A.D. 1356.) From this period Boccanigra exercised his limited and temperate authority for the public honour and happiness to the close of his life. (A.D. 1363.) But on his death, which was not without suspicion of having been caused by poison at a banquet given by the state to the king of Cyprus, a popular commotion arose, and occasioned the tumultuary election of Gabriello Adorno for his successor.

Thus commenced a long and obstinate struggle between the two parties, at the head of which the new families of wealthy commoners had placed themselves. It was the preponderance of the Guelf faction which raised Adorno to the ducal throne; and two years later, after a violent contest, the Ghibelins with their leader, Leonardo di Montalto, were expelled from the city, and immediately waged a civil war against their country. (A.D. 1365.) Pope Urban VI. temporarily appeased these furious dissensions; but they shortly broke forth again with redoubled virulence; and Gabriello Adorno had only retained his seat for seven years, when a popular insurrection hurled him from power and placed on his throne Domeneco Fregoso, who had succeeded Montalto in the direction of the Ghibelin party. Both Adorno and Fregoso governed the state in turn with talent and vigour equal to their ambition; but both shared the same fate, (A.D. 1378) Fregoso was deposed by the tumultuous voice of the people; and the usual oscillation of parties gave the ducal chair to the faction opposed to that of the last doge, and seated in it Nicola di Guarco, one of the leaders of the Guelfs. It was under the dogeship of Guarco that the war of Chiozza was so gloriously maintained; and his patriotic zeal to augment the public force induced him to recall the ancient nobility to power, and to unite them in the cause of their country by entrusting the fleets and armies of the republic to their conduct. The courage and devotion of the old aristocracy justified his confidence; but the war was no sooner terminated than the long jealousy of the plebeians against the ancient houses awakened afresh; an alarming sedition was begun by the butchers of Genoa; and after the usual process of insurrection the nobles were again excluded from power, and the doge himself obliged to consult his safety by flight.

In their common animosity against the old nobility, the Guelf and Ghibelin parties, into which the great commoners and the people were divided, had momentarily forgotten their own factious quarrel, and united in effecting this revolution. Antoniotto Adorno, who had inherited his father's influence with the Guelfs, and Leonardo Montalto and Pietro Fregoso who swayed the Ghibelins, had coalesced to overthrow the doge; but the ambitious rivalry of these leaders immediately revived with their success, and the state narrowly escaped a civil war in the struggle of Adorno and Montalto for the ducal dignity. The latter prevailed, but closed his magistracy and his life in the following year; and Adorno was then chosen to succeed him by the unanimous suffrages of the people. From this epoch the revolutions of Genoa became so frequent and numerous that it is impossible—and would be utterly useless if it were otherwise—for us to attempt to trace their course. The deep exhaustion in which the republic had been left by the war of Chiozza was fatally visible in the apathy and decay of her influence in foreign affairs, but seemed only to aggravate her paroxysms of internal violence, and to multiply the incurable factions which consumed her. The four great houses of the old nobility were almost always in arms against the public peace at their rural fiefs; the great commoners with their clients kept the capital in a ferment by their bitter animosities, and found it, under the senseless distinction of the Guelf and Ghibelin name, but too easy to influence the passions of the people; and, besides these turbulent rivals, a new and lower party among the commercial citizens, that of the middle estate as it was called, reared its baleful head. Four times, amidst the shock of these contending factions, was Antoniotto Adorno alternately elevated to the ducal throne and expelled from his seat; and ten times in four years were the doges changed by the violence and shifting affections of the wayward and capricious people. Only one consummation of ill was wanting to the public afflictions,—the insidious interference of a foreign tyrant; and, while Gian Galeazzo Visconti reigned in the peninsula, that evil was ever impending, to exercise its fatal influence upon the disorders of the state. The perfidious ruler of Milan called himself the friend of Adorno, and assisted him in his alternations of adversity. But his succours were even more dangerous than his enmity; his real design was to reduce Genoa to the extremity of weakness, that he might recover the authority which his great-uncle the archbishop of Milan had acquired over her; and Adorno discovered immediately after his last restoration to the ducal throne, which was effected by Milanese aid, that Gian Galeazzo was already actively intriguing with his enemies to dethrone him.

This exposure of the baseness of his ally seems at once to have extinguished or purified the hitherto inordinate ambition of Adorno;

and conscious that the republic was already too much enfeebled to resist the dangerous machinations of the tyrant, he voluntarily determined to lay down his own power, that he might at least secure to her the option of a master. Charles VI., then king of France, was too powerful in appearance for Visconti to hazard a rupture with him, and yet too feeble in character for Genoa to apprehend his usurpation of a more absolute authority than she was contented to entrust to him. He was therefore a desirable, because not personally a dangerous protector; and Adorno concluded a treaty with the French king, by which the signiory of Genoa was consigned to that monarch with every careful reservation of her internal freedom, (A.D. 1396.) The doge descended to a private station, in which he soon after died; a French vicar was admitted into the capital; and French garrisons were permitted in several of the dependant fortresses. But the Genoese were too impatient and fickle to endure this compact, formed as it was to guard, without injuring, their freedom; the French lieutenants were strangers to constitutional forms; and, after only two years of tranquillity, new troubles broke out. A furious insurrection ended only in increasing the power of Charles; and after Genoa had suffered so severely in the struggle, that thirty of her most sumptuous palaces were demolished, and the property of individuals in the city destroyed to the value of a million of florins, the party which supported the authority of the French finally prevailed, (A.D. 1398.)

For many years after the pacification which Joanna, queen of Naples, succeeded in effecting in 1351 with Louis, king of Hungary, there is little either in her history or that of her kingdom to demand our attention. Her second husband, Louis of Tarento, shared her power with the royal title; but, after displaying in the outset some appearance of vigour and activity of character, he neglected the charge of his kingdom to plunge into a career of dissipation and sensuality which brought his life to a premature close. Louis and his queen had been invited by one of the factions which desolated Sicily to undertake an expedition into that island; and the disorders and weakness which attended the minority of its sovereign of the Aragonese dynasty, might have afforded an easy occasion of re-uniting its crown to that of Naples. But the opportunity was lost either by the voluptuous indolence of Louis, or the troubles excited in the Neapolitan states by the princes of the blood, his relatives, of the houses of Durazzo and Tarento, whom the king of Hungary released from captivity in his dominions soon after his peace with Joanna. The distractions entailed on Naples by the private wars of these princes with each other, and by their rebellions against the crown, were aggravated by the ravages of the great company of adventure; and the feeble husband of Joanna, instead of repulsing these freebooters by arms, disgracefully purchased their retreat by heavy contributions. In the same year with his death, the queen married for the third time. (A.D. 1362.) The new object of her choice was James, prince of Majorca, who obtained her hand upon condition that he should neither assume the title of king, nor interfere in the administration of her government; but this union was scarcely more fortunate for Joanna than those which had preceded it. Shortly after his marriage, James received intelligence that his father, the king of Majorca, had been treacherously seized and murdered by the king of Aragon; and he immediately left Naples for Spain to attempt to revenge his death and recover his inheritance. He was taken prisoner in the wars of the Spanish peninsula; and it was to no purpose that Joanna paid an immense sum for his ransom. He only returned to Naples to collect supplies for a second expedition against Aragon, in the course of which he died. (A.D. 1365.)

Joanna passed several years in her third widowhood in tranquillity, which was undisturbed by any remarkable event: but the succession of her kingdom occupied her with a new source of inquietude. Her own children had died in infancy; and, of the numerous males of the royal family of Naples, a series of deaths had left only one: a second Charles of Durazzo, nephew of the former prince whom we have known under the same name. According to the principles of hereditary right, however, Louis king of Hungary had certainly a prior claim to the Neapolitan crown to Joanna herself; and the nieces of the queen, daughters of her sister, were also more nearly allied to her throne than Charles of Durazzo. But Joanna seems to have acted in consonance with the loosely defined opinions of the age, in considering or adopting Charles as her presumptive heir; and she gave him the hand of Margaret, one of her nieces. These measures produced the most disastrous results for her. Charles of Durazzo had been invited by the old king of Hungary to reside at his court; in that warlike school, among a brave and hardy nobility, he had learned to despise the luxurious effeminacy of his native country; and he had probably been inspired by Louis and his Hungarians, who had not forgotten the fate of their prince Andrew, with their ancient aversion for Joanna. Deprived of the presence and support of her destined successor, whose ability and courage might have upheld the throne which he was to inherit, and oppressed by new disorders in her kingdom, Joanna, at the age of forty-nine years, took for her protector and fourth husband, Otho of Brunswick, a German prince of amiable character, who had long resided in Italy as the guardian of the young marquis of Montferrat. (A.D. 1376.) This marriage—by which the queen, however, did not raise Otho to the royal dignity—alarmed and offended Charles of Durazzo; and the part which Joanna shortly afterwards took in the great schism of the church, afforded him an opportunity of openly declaring against her.

In the secession of the cardinals after the election of Urban VI., the queen had permitted them to elect Clement VII. in her dominions; she had promised the anti-pope succour; and had granted him an asylum in her capital, until he was terrified by the disaffection of the people into a flight from thence to Avignon. Urban VI. was impelled by these hostile acts to display all the natural violence of his temper against Joanna; he pronounced a sentence of deposition against her (A.D. 1380); and, aware of her breach with Charles of Durazzo, he offered that prince the investiture of her kingdom. Durazzo gladly closed with his proposal; and Joanna, who was almost defenceless against the rebellion of Charles and the machinations of Urban, looked anxiously round for foreign assistance. By making choice of a French prince for her successor, she hoped to obtain the protection of France and the services of the chivalrous nobility of that country; and revoking her adoption of Durazzo, she transferred it by letters patent to Louis, duke of Anjou, the eldest uncle of Charles VI. and regent for that monarch in his minority. Meanwhile Charles of Durazzo was assembling an army against her. The old king of Hungary afforded him powerful aid; and his alliance with Urban VI. disposed the people of Naples, whose prejudices sided with the Italian against the French pope, to favour his enterprise. After exacting from Durazzo the promise of a principality for his nephew in the Neapolitan dominions. Urban solemnly bestowed the crown of the Sicilies upon him at Rome with the title of Charles III. (A.D. 1381); and, this ceremony concluded, the pretender immediately passed the frontiers of Naples with a powerful army. The Neapolitans, either from cowardice, or disaffection, or both, made no resistance to his advance, and even welcomed his approach; the queen possessed neither an army nor the funds for levying mercenary forces; and Otho of Brunswick, who performed the part of an able and valiant soldier, was deserted by his few followers and taken prisoner. His ill-fated consort was then compelled to surrender to the victor in her capital.

Having seized the kingdom and secured the person of the queen, Durazzo endeavoured to complete the work of the sword by requiring her to execute a solemn deed of abdication in his favour. But in her extremity, and with the certainty of death before her,' Joanna displayed a heroism worthy of her descent from a long line of illustrious ancestors. She pretended compliance with the demands of Durazzo, and he accordingly introduced some Provençal barons to her prison to hear her transfer their allegiance to his person; but they were no sooner admitted than she solemnly enjoined them never to acknowledge for their lord the ungrateful robber who from a queen had made her a captive slave; if ever it should be told them that she had constituted him her heir to believe it not; and to hold any deed that might be shown to that effect as forged or enforced upon her. She added her will that they should own for their lord, Louis of Anjou, whom she appointed her successor and champion to revenge the treason and violence committed against her; and she bade them take no more thought for her, but to perform her funeral obsequies, and to pray for her soul. She was shortly afterwards put to death in prison by command of Durazzo: in what manner is differently related, (A.D. 1382.) The common story is that she was smothered with a pillow; but there seems strong reason for believing the account of the secretary of Urban VI., who was at Naples at the time, that four Hungarian soldiers were secretly introduced into the castle of Muro where she was confined, and, entering its chapel while she was kneeling before the altar, strangled her with a silken cord.

The quarter from whence Joanna had sought protection in her distress, proved too remote to avert her fate. But, though Louis duke of Anjou, her adopted son, had been unable to appear in Italy in time for her relief, he prepared nevertheless to avenge her murder and possess himself of her bequests. His authority was acknowledged without opposition in the Provençal dominions of the unhappy queen; but the kingdom of Naples was now entirely subject to Charles III., and the French prince resolved to wrest it from him by force of arms. He descended into Italy with a fine army, composed of the ardent chivalry of France, and amounting at the most moderate computation to 15,000 men-at-arms, besides their followers, while many contemporary writers rate it at four times that force, (A.D. 1382.) On the entrance of Louis into the Abruzzos, he was immediately joined by those among the Neapolitan nobles who had been attached to the late queen, or were moved to indignation and pity by her murder. The usual inconstancy of the feudal barons gave him other adherents, who forsook Charles III. upon various causes of disgust; and altogether the Sanseverini—the most powerful family among the Neapolitan chieftains—with a large proportion of the nobility, raised the Angevin standards. Thus commenced the pretensions of the second line of Anjou to the Neapolitan crown, and the long contest for its possession which was to cost so much bloodshed to the kingdom. The splendid armament, however, which Louis had led from France by some unaccountable mischance failed of assuring him success; no battle was fought; Charles III. cautiously remained on the defensive; and so silently did the French forces waste by the effects of climate and scarcity, that when Louis himself died, about two years after his entrance into the kingdom, his army dispersed of itself.

As long as Louis of Anjou lived, Charles III. carefully maintained his relations of amity with Urban VI., who had established his residence at Naples; but the king was no sooner released from apprehension by the death of his rival, than he resolved no longer to submit to the arrogant bearing and insolent violence of the pontiff. He also refused to observe his promise of investing the nephew of Urban with a Neapolitan principality; and the quarrel between these former confederates proceeded to such extremities, that the troops of Charles at last besieged the pope in the castle of Nocera, whither he had retired. Urban then threw himself into the arms of the Angevin party, and was delivered from his besiegers by the forces of some barons of that faction; but he immediately escaped to Genoa, and his flight itself rescued Charles from the dangerous vicinity of such an enemy. In the weakness of the Angevin party, Charles with the vigour which marked his character might easily have crushed that faction for ever, if his insatiable ambition had not lured him into Hungary, in pursuit of the crown of that kingdom, before he had finally secured the tranquillity of the throne on which he was already seated. The aged Louis of Hungary had died in the same year with the murder of Joanna, leaving no other child than a youthful daughter under the guardianship of his widow; and the government of the queen-mother and of Nicholas Gara, her favourite, became so obnoxious to a part of the Hungarian nobility, that they invited Charles III., the last male relative of their late sovereign, and who had won their affections during his long residence among them, to receive the crown of their country. Notwithstanding his obligations to his benefactor Louis, Charles did not hesitate treacherously to despoil his orphan daughter, (A.D. 1385.) He passed into Hungary with the ostensible purpose of protecting the two queens, and pacifying the kingdom; and thus admitted into their counsels without suspicion, he obliged them to abdicate in his favour, and succeeded in obtaining the unanimous suffrages of the nobles for his own elevation to the throne. But the royal mother and daughter had only opposed to Charles a dissimulation equal to his own: they meditated a ferocious vengeance for his perfidy, and inviting him to an amicable and private interview in their palace, into which assassins had secretly been introduced, they suddenly caused him to be murdered before their eyes. (A.D. 1386.)

The death of Charles III. involved the kingdom of Naples in the most ruinous anarchy; and delivered it for many years a prey to all the disorders of a long minority and a disputed throne. Charles had left two children, Ladislaus, a boy of ten years old, and a daughter, Joanna; and his widow Margaret acted as regent for her son. On the other hand, the Sanseverini and other baronial families, rallying the Angevin party, proclaimed the young son of the late duke of Anjou king,—also under the guardianship of his mother, Maria—by the title of Louis II. Thus Naples was disturbed by the rival pretensions of two boys, placed beneath the guidance of ambitious and intriguing mothers, and severally protected by two popes, who excommunicated each other, and laboured to crush the minors whom they respectively opposed, only that they might establish their own authority over the party which they supported. Amidst the general confusion, all the barons of the kingdom rose in arms and enjoyed a license for the commission of every crime, under pretence of upholding the cause of the sovereign, to whom they chose at the moment to declare their shifting allegiance. We shall find little temptation to linger over the vicissitudes of so perplexed and uninteresting a contest. For several years the Angevin party seemed to maintain the ascendancy. Louis II. was withheld in Provence from the scene of danger by his mother; but the barons who had raised his standard, forcing Margaret of Durazzo and the adherents of her son to retire to Gaeta, possessed themselves of the capital and great part of the kingdom. When Louis II., therefore, was at length suffered by his mother to appear at Naples, attended by a powerful fleet and a numerous train of the warlike nobles of France, (A.D. 1390,) he disembarked at the capital amidst the acclamations of his people, and would probably have overpowered the party of Durazzo with ease, if, as he advanced towards manhood, he had displayed any energy of character. But he proved very unequal, by his indolence and love of pleasure, to contend with the son of Charles III.

Educated in the midst of alarms and danger, and surrounded from his infancy by civil wars and conspiracies, Ladislaus had early been exercised in courageous enterprise, and trained to intrigue and dissimulation. At the age of sixteen, his mother Margaret committed him to the barons of her party to make his first essay in arms; and from this period he was ever at the head of his troops, and engaged in promoting his interests by perfidious negotiations; while his rival was immersed in voluptuous pleasures. A fortunate marriage, which his mother had effected for him with Constance di Clermont, the heiress of the most opulent noble of Sicily, increased his resources by an immense dowry; and while he made an able use of these riches, the new Italian pope, Boniface IX., the successor of Urban VI., recognized him for the legitimate son and vassal of the church, because Louis was supported by the Avignon pontiff. This decision gained him many partizans; the people, besides, saw in him the only descendant of their ancient monarchs; his talents and valour hourly advanced his success; and at last the Sanseverini and all the barons of the Angevin party, following the tide of fortune, went over to his standards, and opened to him the gates of Naples, (A.D. 1399.)

Louis, who was absent with his French forces at Tarento, despairing of the successful prosecution of the contest, indulged the natural inactivity of his temper; and collecting his native followers, he retired by sea to his Provencal dominions, and finally abandoned the kingdom of Naples. Ladislaus, having thus triumphed over his sluggish antagonist, had leisure to consolidate his stern authority over the licentious and turbulent feudal aristocracy of his kingdom. His energetic talents, and ambitious, fearless spirit, perfectly qualified him for his station; and he soon made it manifest that he designed to rule his disorderly nobles with a sceptre of iron. Regardless of good faith, of mercy, and even of the dictates of gratitude, where these interfered with his ambition, he persecuted, he ruined, he put to death the barons of the Angevin party, notwithstanding their voluntary submission to his authority. He thus crushed the Sanseverini and other great families, whose power might make them dangerous; and having rooted out the seeds of all resistance to his sway in his own dominions, he prepared to direct his vigorous ambition to schemes of foreign conquest.

CHAPTER VI. FROM THE BEGINNING TO THE MIDDLE OF THE FIFTEENTH CENTURY, a.d. 1400-1450.

PART I.
State of Italy at the opening of the fifteenth century—Overwhelming power of Gian Galeazzo, duke of Milan—Continued resistance of Florence to his projects—Expedition of the emperor Robert—Revolution in the military system of Italy—School of Italian generals—Discomfiture of the German chivalry—Evacuation of Lombardy by the emperor—Danger of Florence—Death of Gian Galeazzo—Dismemberment of the Milanese states—Restoration of the political balance in Italy—Conquests of Francesco da Carrara, lord of Padua—Hatred and jealousy of the Venetians towards him—Their last war against him—Gallant defence of Carrara—Fall of Padua to the Venetians—Murder of Francesco da Carrara and his sons in the prisons of Venice—Extinction of the houses of Carrara and Scala—The possessions of Venice extended to the Adige—Florence—Her iniquitous purchase of the signiory of Pisa—Resistance of the Pisans—Blockade of their city—Sufferings and fortitude of the inhabitants—Subjugation of Pisa by Florence—Papal affairs—Progress of the great schism—Successors of Urban VI.: Boniface IX., Innocent VII., Gregory XII.—Eager desire of Europe for the re-union of the church—Benedict XIII., the successor of Clement VII., at Avignon—His efforts to prolong the schism—Mutual evasions of Gregory XII. and Benedict XIII.—Council of Pisa—Deposition of Gregory XII. and Benedict XIII.—Election of Alexander V.—Resistance of the deposed pontiffs—The schism rendered more desperate—Ladislaus, king of Naples—Insidiously interferes in the affairs of Rome, and occupies that capital and the papal territory—His ambitious designs—War of Florence against him—Successes of the republic—Ladislaus driven from Rome—New expedition of Louis II. of Anjou against Naples—Battle of Rocca Secca—Defeat and danger of Ladislaus—His final triumph over Louis, and peace with his enemies—His treachery, sack of Rome, and new conquest of the papal states—Power of Ladislaus—Italy in danger of his universal tyranny—His death—Scandal excited in Europe by the continuance of the great schism—Infamous reputation of Pope John XXIII., the successor of Alexander V.—The emperor Sigismund—His laudable efforts to give peace to the church—Council of Constance—Deposition of John XXIII.—Resignation of Gregory XII.—Deposition of Benedict XIII.—Election of Martin V.—Termination of the great schism of the church—Affairs of Lombardy—Continued anarchy in that province after the death of Gian Galeazzo—Giovanni Maria, duke of Milan—His atrocities and assassination—Filippo Maria, duke of Milan—Revival of the Milanese power—Cruel ingratitude of Filippo Maria to his duchess—His acquisition of the signiory of Genoa, and conquests in Lombardy—Encounter between the Milanese and Swiss—Battle of Arbedo—Grandeur of Filippo Maria.

THE fifteenth century dawned heavily on the only Italian state which still enjoyed or merited the possession of freedom. Without allies and almost without hope, while the spirit of liberty was every where expiring around her, Florence found herself the solitary champion of independence against the crafty and perfidious tyrant, who was eagerly watching the moment for her destruction. Already master of almost all Lombardy, the duke Gian Galeazzo of Milan had now entangled the republics of Tuscany in his snares; the preponderance of his power was hourly becoming more overwhelming and terrific; and having entirely encompassed Florence with fiefs and cities subjected to his dominion, he only awaited the first favourable occasion for undermining by fraud or razing by violence that last stronghold of Italian democracy. The Ghibelin chieftains of the Apennines, the republics of. Pisa, Perugia, and Sienna, had all been inveigled, as if by a species of fascination, into the circle of his tyranny; and these powers, which even by their dissensions had hitherto preserved and balanced the safety of Tuscany, could now in their union under one master contribute only to the completion of the general slavery. Lucca, except Florence, was the sole Tuscan city in any degree independent of Gian Galeazzo; but she had just fallen under a domestic tyrant, Paolo Guinigi, who cultivated the alliance and protection of the duke. (A.D. 1401.)

The condition of Italy generally was as little calculated to animate the courage of the Florentines, as that of their own province. The selfish oligarchy of Venice, in imaginary security within their lagunes, would make no effort to check the projects of the duke of Milan; Genoa herself no longer free, was the subject of France; and, of the three signors of eastern Lombardy, Gonzaga lord of Mantua and the marquis of Este had sedulously reconciled themselves with the Milanese duke. In the interest of the Florentines there remained only the lord of Padua, less an ally from whom succours could be expected, than a faithful dependant who might himself need their protection. While such was the condition of Tuscany and northern Italy, the remainder of the peninsula presented an equally unpromising aspect. In the long train of disorders and civil wars from which Naples was but just emerging under young Ladislaus, that kingdom had almost ceased to be numbered in the political combinations of Italy. The papal power, too, had been reduced to a shadow by the great schism of the church; the ecclesiastical province of Romagna was as usual broken up into petty tyrannies; and its principal city, Bologna—the only interesting spot in this obscure division of the peninsula—was no longer the powerful republic who had lately ranged herself by the side of Florence against Milan. In the first year of the new century the fatal violence of faction threw Bologna into the power of one of her citizens who established himself in the signiory. This was Giovanni Bentivoglio, a name indebted to this revolution for the origin of its celebrity in Italy in later limes. For it was part of the unhappy destiny of this country, that the greatness of her sons seemed to flow from the wounds which they inflicted on her bosom.

Even the consternation which filled Florence at the intelligence that, to crown all the defection which the cause of freedom had sustained, her ancient ally Bologna had passed away under a master from her republican government, could not subdue the resolution of the people and their rulers. They saw by the secret machinations of the duke of Milan, and even by his open aggression upon their frontiers, that the maintenance of peace with him was still impossible. They therefore laboured to prevent the new signor of Bologna from falling under his influence, by themselves concluding an alliance foreign to their principles with Bentivoglio; and they extended their negotiations to discover beyond the Alps a source of aid which was denied to them in Italy. The situation of the empire at this moment favoured their views. The electoral body had deposed the feeble Wenceslaus, and substituted in his place Robert elector-palatine. The German princes considered the creation of the duchy of Milan by Wenceslaus as an alienation of an imperial province; and, in raising Robert to the throne, they made it an article of their compact with him, that he should annul the investiture which his predecessor had sold to Gian Galeazzo. The Florentines therefore found little difficulty in inducing the new emperor to attack the duke of Milan; and a treaty was concluded between Robert and the wealthy republic by which he undertook, on receipt of large subsidies, to invade Lombardy and to strip Gian Galeazzo of his dominions. As the war was declared in the name of the empire, the whole force of the German confederation was summoned to swell the expedition. The preparations which the duke of Milan made for his defence were proportioned to the magnitude of the impending struggle. He levied an extraordinary contribution on his states; and with the immense resources which he thus collected, and by his personal influence with the condottieri, he assembled under his banners all the most famous captains of Italy with their bands. In this manner he drew together an army of about 13,000 cuirassiers, with 12,000 infantry. The emperor Robert on his part, though the contingents of the German feudatories did not amount to above half of their stipulated force, mustered 15,000 cuirassiers besides infantry; and entering Italy with this army, he was immediately joined by the lord of Padua. (A.D. 1401.)

This invasion which was attended with such imposing circumstances, and which appeared to anxious expectation destined to change the political condition of the peninsula, by a strange caprice of fortune produced only a single skirmish. But this partial affair of arms had in itself consequences which, however unlooked for, and contrary to vulgar anticipation, held no unimportant influence upon the subsequent fate of Italy for nearly one hundred years. I have formerly noticed the infatuation by which the Italians of the fourteenth century voluntarily yielded to strangers a superiority in martial reputation; and we have seen the long course of degradation and shame which was inflicted on their country by the exclusive employment of foreign mercenaries, and the unresisted ravages of foreign companies of adventure. Thus, although a few native captains and soldiers of fortune were still to be found thinly scattered among those mercenary bands which fought the battles of the Italian states, the profession of arms was almost wholly abandoned to German, French, and English adventurers, led by captains of their own nations. But before the death of Sir John Hawkwood, the most celebrated and the last of the foreign condottieri, a revolution had silently been prepared in the military system of Italy. In the year 1379, Alberic di Barbiano, a petty Romagnol chieftain, formed under the auspices of St. George a band, composed exclusively of Italians, which successively passed under his orders into the stipendiary service of the different states of the peninsula. This company of St. George, which was ably disciplined by Barbiano, soon became distinguished for valour and military skill, and formed the favourite school into which the adventurous youth of the peninsula entered to learn the qualities of soldiership. Barbiano was himself an accomplished captain, but his fame has been eclipsed by that of more celebrated leaders, who emulated his example, or were formed in the school of St. George. Among his contemporaries, Jacopo del Verme, the faithful general of the duke of Milan, Carlo and Pandolfo Malatesti of Rimini, Ottobon Terzo, Facino Cane, and other Italian captains who had trained bodies of their countrymen, rivalled or surpassed him in reputation; and after his death we shall find the two most famous generals educated in the school of St. George, separating the military adventurers of Italy into opposite factions by a rivalry which continued through more than a single generation.

Notwithstanding the revival of military spirit among the Italians, a lingering prejudice that the native bands were unequal to resist the shock of Transalpine heavy cavalry still pervaded the peninsula, when the emperor Robert descended into the Milanese dominions with the gens-d'armerie of Germany. The army of Gian Galeazzo was composed entirely of Italians; and the timid duke gave a positive order to Jacopo del Verme, who commanded in chief for him amidst a galaxy of the ablest captains of Italy, to avoid the dangerous encounter with the German cuirassiers, and to protract the war by throwing his forces into the strong places of Lombardy. But Jacopo and his brother leaders had a more correct sentiment of their own talents and of the qualities of their bands. The German discipline had remained unchanged and unimproved for a century: the Italians, in resuming the career of arms and in exercising their ingenuity against each other, had exhausted all the resources of that inventive and intelligent spirit which belonged to their nation. They had wrought many advantageous alterations in the tactics, such as they were, of their age; their offensive weapons were wielded with new dexterity, their armour was tempered to perfection, their horses were trained, bridled, and bitted with superior skill; and while armies were only masses of heavy cavalry, excellence in these minutiae was sufficient to determine the balance of victory. Jacopo del Verme fearlessly threw his squadrons into contact with the German chivalry, and in the first skirmish near Brescia the invaders were routed. The duke of Austria and the burgrave of Nuremburg were unhorsed and captured, and the affair would have drawn on the discomfiture of the whole imperial army, if the lord of Padua had not covered its retreat with a body of Italian cuirassiers who served under his orders. The Germans were thrown by this check into a panic which was the greater from their previous confidence. The discovery of their inferiority, where they had calculated on easy victory, at once completely subdued their courage, and intimidated them from a second encounter; and the Italians, thus taught to despise their ancient masters, learnt also to discard the apprehension of danger from their future attacks. Until the close of the fifteenth century their sense of martial superiority remained unchanged from that hour.

However flattering this trial of arms might have proved to the pride of Italy, if Italy had been united, it was calculated to increase the gloomy forebodings with which Florence had reason to regard the continued success of Gian Galeazzo. Notwithstanding the courageous resistance which the republic had hitherto opposed to his schemes of aggrandizement, his power seemed only to have been confirmed and extended by a vain resistance. After the last pecuniary sacrifices which Florence had cheerfully made to secure the alliance of the emperor and to enlist his cupidity in her cause, his assistance was at an end. A few days after the capture of the duke of Austria, Gian Galeazzo released his prisoner, and it was immediately evident that this act of apparent generosity was not without a sufficient motive. The duke of Austria, after sowing dissensions and distrust in the imperial camp, quitted the army and returned into Germany. His example was contagious where despondency had already succeeded to presumption, and Robert was compelled to retire to Padua and to disband the contingents of the empire. Thus weakened by the desertion of the greater part of his force, he only lingered in Padua with the hope of extorting new subsidies from the Florentines; but that people were weary of paying for services which were sure of never being performed. By the interested offices of the Venetians, who desired the continuance of the war against the duke of Milan, without choosing to contribute to it themselves, or daring openly to provoke the hostility of Gian Galeazzo, the Florentines were indeed persuaded to make one more advance of money to Robert; but finding this supply produced no efficient exertion, they refused farther issues; and the emperor at length withdrew into Germany. (A.D. 1402.)

The whole weight of the war was now to descend upon the Florentines, and their territory was only preserved from being inundated by the Milanese armies, by a new enterprise which delayed the vengeance of Gian Galeazzo. With the design of possessing himself of the signiory of Bologna, he declared war against Giovanni Bentivoglio the tyrant of that city; and inducing the numerous Bolognese exiles to join his ranks, by the hope which he deceitfully held out to them, that he would restore their republic to freedom, he poured his troops into its territory. This attack obliged Bentivoglio to throw himself into the arms of the Florentines, and their forces were immediately sent to his protection. But their alliance could not avert his ruin; and his impatient presumption exposed the Florentine army to an overthrow at Casalecchio, where the Bolognese militia who detested his yoke refused to fight for him. He fled after his defeat to Bologna; the people rose in arms, and delivered the gates to the Milanese troops and their own exiles; and Bentivoglio, after a desperate resistance, was secured, and murdered in prison by order of the Milanese general. It was then seen how well Gian Galeazzo designed to keep his promise to the Bolognese; the forms of their state were restored only that one of his creatures might propose him for signor; his cavalry rode the city; and the republican party were driven again into exile.

The fall of Bologna under her dangerous enemy entailed the last crisis in the fortunes of the Florentine republic. For ten years that free state had maintained an unequal struggle against the power and ambition of the duke of Milan; and had exhausted her strength, and drained her resources by the repetition of unsuccessful efforts. She had no longer allies in the peninsula, or hope of foreign succour; the whole circuit of her frontiers was enclosed by the dependencies of Milan; and Gian Galeazzo, instead of vigorously assailing her territory, stationed his troops with his usual art around it, to cut off all communication with the sea, and with the other states of Italy. By this plan of blockade, he designed at a blow to paralyze the commerce of Florence, to leave the total languor of trade to work its silent and wasting effects, and to await the moment when the enfeebled republic should sink from exhaustion and internal decay. But just at the epoch when Gian Galeazzo seemed about to reach the consummation of his projects, when the prosperity of Florence was sapped at its foundations, and her people were plunged in despair, the days of the tyrant, as if Heaven had interposed for her relief, were already numbered to their close. Gian Galeazzo died suddenly of the pestilence at a castle to which he had retired to escape its contagion, (A.D. 1402.) Thus Florence was unexpectedly delivered; and a verse which was applied to the occasion echoed the public joy through her streets, that the snare was broken and the captives freed.

The death of Gian Galeazzo at once restored the balance of Italy which his successes had destroyed. He left a widow with two sons, Giovanni Maria and Filippo Maria, of whom the eldest was only thirteen years of age. Between these children his last testament divided his ample dominions, with the exception of Pisa and Cremona, which he bequeathed to his natural son Gabriele Maria. The two young princes were committed by his will to the guardianship of the duchess-mother, assisted by a council of regency, of which several of the great captains of mercenaries were members. But if Gian Galeazzo, in leaving the most celebrated condottieri of Italy in the pay of his house, imagined that the fidelity to him which his vigilance and their fears had produced would be transferred to his children, this confidence was strangely opposed to his ordinary political sagacity and foresight, and miserably belied by the event. The tyrant was no sooner dead than the great states, which he had passed his life in enlarging by the dark alternation of perfidy and violence, were seized and rent into pieces by the rapacity and ambition of the men to whose protection he had consigned his boy-heirs.

There can be little to deserve attention or excite interest in the internal commotions of a despotism; and I shall rather relate the result of the dismemberment of the Milanese states, than plunge the reader into a black chaos of rapine, and violence, and cruelties, of perjuries, and treasons, and murder. The duchess-mother—herself a Visconti, and the daughter of Bernabo—was worthy of all her house. Mistaking ferocity for courage, wanton cruelty for masculine vigour, and atrocious perfidy for political skill, she excited universal resistance to her authority; and after provoking an insurrection of the Milanese, was finally seized in 1404 by the party which had usurped the name and authority of her eldest son, and poisoned in prison. In the general dispersion of the elements of government which Gian Galeazzo had established, many of the Lombard cities revolted from Milan; and without one aspiration after freedom, voluntarily surrendered themselves to the descendants of their ancient signors; the original order of petty tyrants whom the Visconti had long dispossessed of their power. Thus Cremona submitted to Ugolino Cavalcabo, Crema to the Benzoni, Placentia to the Scotti, Bergamo to the Suardi, Como to Franchino Rusca. Lodi passed under the dominion of an obscure plebeian; the Beccaria promised to recover their ancient influence in Pavia; and of the generals of Gian Galeazzo, Facino Cane seized the city of Alessandria, Ottobon Terzo occupied Parma, and Pandolfo Malatesta established himself in the signiory of Brescia.

The independent powers of Italy availed themselves of the general ruin which thus appeared to have overtaken the house of Visconti to aggrandize themselves at their expense. Thus Florence, who had been abandoned by all in the hour of her need, easily succeeded, when the danger was past, in forming a powerful confederacy to despoil the heirs of her ancient foe. But she at first procured few immediate advantages for herself. Pope Boniface IX. joined her in a league with a view of recovering the possessions of the church in Romagna; but he had no sooner received the cession of Bologna and Perugia, which gladly exchanged the Milanese tyranny for the milder form of papal government, than he concluded a separate peace with the Milanese regency. In Tuscany the efforts of the Florentines were incessant to restore freedom to the two republics which Gian Galeazzo had enslaved. With their support Sienna recovered her liberty; but Pisa was secured to the bastard Gabriele Maria of Visconti, by the protection which that lord obtained in his new inheritance from the lieutenant who governed for the king of France at Genoa. Florence was compelled by the measures which the French governor adopted for confiscating her merchandize in the Genoese ports, to desist from further enterprises against the signor of Pisa; but she had, within two years after the death of Gian Galeazzo, already perfected the great end of her war against the Visconti. (A.D. 1404.) Her arms reduced the Ghibelin nobles of the Apennines, whose castles overhung her territory, to obedience and subjection; all Tuscany, except Pisa, was delivered from foreign influence; Sienna was free; Bologna and Perugia were wrested from the Milanese yoke. These objects attained, Florence relaxed in her efforts: she indeed still supported those signors who, after the long proscription of the Guelf party in Lombardy, had now revived that faction in the cities under their dominion; but she ceased to act otherwise than as an auxiliary, and left the house of Visconti to struggle with the difficulties by which that family were now sufficiently oppressed.

Amidst the general dissolution of the Milanese power which had followed the death of Gian Galeazzo, the lord of Padua was too enterprising and ambitious, and had too many resentments to gratify against the house of his ancient oppressor, to remain a quiet spectator of the distractions and weakness of Lombardy. The duchess-mother of Milan had desired to obtain his alliance or neutrality by large cessions of territory; but the personal hatred which Jacopo del Verme and others in her council bore to Carrara, had occasioned the rupture of her negotiations, and the invasion of the Milanese states by the lord of

Padua. After some indecisive hostilities, he was invited to undertake an attempt upon Verona. Guglielmo della Scala, son of the last signor of that house, whom Gian Galeazzo had driven from his dominions to close his days miserably, in exile and by poison, now trusted that the moment had arrived for the recovery of his inheritance. He knew that the people of Verona desired to return under the government of his family; he held a correspondence with his partizans in that city; and he induced Carrara, to whose kindness he had been indebted for a subsistence in exile, to aid him in surprising the place. The Paduan army suddenly appeared before Verona, the affection of the citizens seconded their attempt, and the walls were carried by escalade during the night. The eagle of the Scala again rested on the towers of Verona, but amidst the rejoicings which welcomed him to the capital of his fathers, Guglielmo was already seized with a mortal disease. He was so weak that he could not sit on horseback to make his triumphal entry into the city; the fatigue of his inauguration increased his disorder; and he died within a few days. The fall of Verona seemed to the Milanese regency only a preparation for the conquest by the lord of Padua of all the cities beyond the Adige; he had already taken many castles, and laid siege to Vicenza; and in the consciousness of the inability of their own weak and disturbed government to resist his progress, they applied themselves to alarm the jealousy and revive the slumbering hatred of the ancient enemies of his house.

The vindictive oligarchy of Venice had never forgiven the family of Carrara their share in the war of Chiozza, and the ingratitude which had preceded that contest; and though, from temporizing policy, they had indirectly aided Francesco Novello in recovering his throne from the duke of Milan, and had even allowed him formally to reconcile himself with them, they still regarded him with no feelings of amity. Thus, therefore, though they had made few efforts to check the widespreading power of Gian Galeazzo, which really threatened the total subversion of Italian independence, they were easily roused by their long-cherished hatred of Carrara, to believe, or to feign to believe, that the projects of so skilful and warlike a prince must endanger the safety of their state. They were also perhaps prone to suspect that, under the veil of deference to the republic, he doubtless meditated revenge for the misfortunes into which she had plunged his father and himself fifteen years before. If the Venetian rulers had forgotten their habitual dislike and suspicion, Jacopo del Verme, who from his personal enmity to Carrara chose himself to appear before the senate with the Milanese embassy, would have instilled into that body distrust and dread of their enterprising neighbour; and he at least knew how to enlist the ambition of the doge and senate in the Milanese alliance. He offered in the name of the regency of Milan, to cede to Venice all the country, of which Gian Galeazzo had possessed himself, to the eastward of the Adige.

Upon this condition, which at once, in blind hatred to Carrara, gave away to the republic the territory which the attacks of that lord merely endangered, the regency obtained the alliance of the Venetian senate. A governor from Venice immediately arrived at Vicenza; the banner of St. Mark was hung out from the walls; and a summons was sent to Francesco Terzo, the son of the Paduan signer, who commanded the besiegers, to desist from his attack upon a place which now belonged to the republic. The insolent demeanour of the herald who bore the message so exasperated the young chieftain, that he caused or permitted him to be massacred in his presence; and though the eider Carrara himself attempted to preserve his peace with the senate by withdrawing his army from before Vicenza, his submission was vain; and the barbarous violation of the laws of warfare, which his son had authorized, was destined to be severely visited upon all his house. The senate were now resolved on his ruin; their intrigues seduced the youthful signers Della Scala from his alliance; and though Carrara punished their ingratitude by deposing them, the acquisition of the signiory of Verona, which he appropriated to himself, availed him little against the assaults of the puissant republic.

Venice, of all the states of Italy, had most to gain and least to lose from the habitual employment of mercenary troops in the continental wars of the peninsula. Frightful as were the results of this system to other powers, her peculiar situation protected her against the insolence and assaults of these lawless bands, and her commerciàl wealth gave her unbounded resources for their maintenance in her pay. It was an invariable rule of her cautious policy never to admit their dangerous presence within her lagunes; she was secure alike from the disastrous effects of their treasons and of their defeat; and she had every temptation to engage in a warfare in which she only hazarded her treasures. The troops which she now levied for the destruction of Carrara, were of more formidable numbers than had ever been assembled in Lombardy. Her main army of nine thousand cuirassiers under celebrated condottieri was destined for the invasion of the Paduan territory; the lord of Mantua joined her alliance to operate against Verona; and Jacopo del Verme directed another numerous force towards the same quarter. Against all these assaults Carrara could oppose only hit, own unassisted resources; the marquis Nicholas of Este, his son-in-law and sole efficient ally, was compelled after a few useless efforts to leave him to his fate and to make his own peace; and Florence, now occupied only in the pursuit of an enterprise in Tuscany which disgraced her principles, turned a deaf ear to all the solicitations of her old and faithful confederate, and abandoned him, after a weak endeavour to mediate in his favour, to the fury of his merciless enemies. Yet Francesco da Carrara, with his two valiant sons, Francesco Terzo and Giacomo, defended the possessions of his house with a heroism and with talents which might have deserved a happier fortune. Skilfully fortifying the banks of the canals which intersected the low country of Padua, the signor himself with Francesco Terzo guarded this territory like a great fortress, and repulsed the general assaults of the invaders, while Giacomo threw himself into Verona. But the people of that city had no affection for the sway of the Carrara; they revolted, and yielded their signiory by treaty to the Venetians; and Giacomo, whose virtues they respected, and for whose liberty they stipulated, was immediately seized in violation of the treaty, and consigned to the dungeons of Venice, (A.D. 1405.)

Meanwhile misfortune had thickened round the devoted heads of his father and brother. The first range of works which defended the Paduan confines was at length surprised during a violent tempest and carried by assault; a second line behind which the Carrara retired was opened to the invaders by treason; and after a desperate struggle, the Venetians penetrated to the foot of the walls of Padua, and formed the siege of that city. Here they were joined by the army to which Verona had fallen. Behind the ramparts of his capital, Carrara long maintained an unequal conflict against these united hosts, with a resolution which was well seconded by the courage and fidelity of his subjects. But the numerous peasantry, who had sought refuge within the walls with their cattle, fatally overcrowded the place; the confinement of so many men and animals in a narrow compass, together with bad diet and filth, produced their ordinary effects; and a frightful pestilence broke out, which is declared by an eye-witness to have destroyed forty thousand of the defenders. Amidst these horrors Carrara protracted his resistance above seventeen months, constantly deluded with cruel hopes of succour from Florence which were never fulfilled; and he capitulated at last, only when the besiegers had gained one of the gates and forced a part of the city. The Venetian *proveditori*, or commissaries, who, according to the practice of their republic, attended her armies to control the military commanders, declared they had no power to treat with the signor of Padua; but they invited him to deliver the city into their hands, and to proceed to negotiate in person with the senate itself. Upon the faith of a safe conduct, Carrara and his son obeyed their counsel and embarked for Venice. On their arrival in that city they were admitted to an audience of the senate, and threw themselves on their knees before the doge to entreat the mercy of the republic. The doge, raising the suppliants, seated them on either side of his throne, and addressed a discourse to them, in which he recounted the benefits that the republic had at former periods conferred on their house, and reproached them, but without bitterness, with the ingratitude by which they had repaid her. The Carrara replied only by imploring the clemency of the senate; and they were then conducted to the prisons of St. Mark, where they were suffered to see Giacomo, who since his captivity had remained in ignorance of their fate, and little expected to meet them in that abode of misery. The interview between these unhappy relatives could draw tears even from Venetian gaolers.

The implacable hatred of Jacopo del Verme pursued the noble captives to their last hour. While the senate seemed to hesitate on their fate, and had appointed a commission to determine the place of their confinement, he came to Venice, and startled the fears of the council of ten by the emphatic declaration, that, for enemies so dangerous by their valour and restless talents, there was no secure prison but the tomb. This maxim was in perfect accordance with the atrocious policy of that body. They removed the case before their own tribunal, and the signor of Padua was suddenly desired, by the mouth of a friar to prepare for death, (A.D. 1406.) After he had confessed, the priest left him, and two of the council of ten entered his prison, attended by a body of their myrmidons. The indignant prince, who acknowledged no submission to the state of Venice, met his end as fearlessly as he had lived: seizing a wooden stool, the only article of furniture in his dungeon, he rushed upon his murderers, and in the effort to sell his life dearly, was at last overpowered and strangled with the string of a cross-bow. The next day his two brave sons shared the same fate. "Francesco Novello da Carrara," says his biographer and friend, "was of middle stature and well proportioned, though somewhat inclined to corpulency. His complexion was dark, and his countenance rather severe; but his disposition was amiable and merciful, his mind enlightened, his acquirements various, his language elegant, and his courage heroic."

These foul murders were, as it has been truly said, perfectly characteristic of the Venetian government, and would not have been avowedly perpetrated, even in the fifteenth century, by any other state in Europe; and they were followed by a proscription almost equally odious of the younger children of Carrara, who had been placed by their father in safety at Florence, and of the youthful signors Della Scala, They at least had committed no offence against Venice, except that they demanded the restitution of Verona. But the republic dreaded their future hostility; they had been released by Carrara before his own captivity; and the senate now put a price upon their heads. The Della Scala escaped and separated, that they might elude the designs of their enemies, to winder in a long exile and to perish obscurely. Of the two remaining sons of Carrara, one died young a natural death at Florence, but the other, endeavouring thirty years later to recover his father's dominion over Padua, was seized in the abortive attempt and executed at Venice. Thus were extinguished two of the reigning houses of Italy; all their provinces—an extensive territory—had passed under the sceptre of Venice; and the lion of St. Mark was now planted from her lagunes to the Adige, on the towel's of Treviso, Feltro, Belluno, Verona, Vicenza, and Padua.

During the glorious defence of Padua by the ill-fated Carrara, Florence might easily have effected their rescue, if she had remained true to that liberal and virtuous policy, which had constituted her the guardian of the weak against the tyranny of the oppressor; and which, in surveying the dark picture of these faithless and troubled times, still renders her the most interesting object in Italian history. But her citizens at this epoch suffered themselves to be engrossed by a project of selfish ambition, which broke down the line of separation between them and the tyrants of Italy. While their ancient ally the lord of Padua was in his last extremity of distress, they neglected his moving supplications for aid, themselves to pursue their own schemes of vengeance and conquest. When Florence, in the first moment of joy at her deliverance by the death of Gian Galeazzo, laboured to overthrow the authority of the Visconti at Pisa, she was probably as sincere in desiring to restore freedom to that city, as she had proved herself in succouring the people of Sienna. But after Gabriele Maria Visconti, the lord of Pisa, had baffled her designs by committing himself to the protection of the marechal de Boucicault, who commanded for the French king at Genoa, her republican greediness of dominion was suddenly tempted by a secret overture from Boucicault, and her virtue was not proof against his offers. The marechal with difficulty maintained his master's authority over the restless Genoese; he stood in need of more powerful support than the bastard Visconti could afford; and he proposed to the Florentines to sell Pisa to them for 400,000 florins of gold and the promise of their alliance, (A.D. 1405.) Gabriele Maria was himself conscious of his inability to retain his power over Pisa; but he was fearful that Boucicault would usurp the price of his lordship, and he therefore himself entered into negotiations with the Florentines. The Pisans were stung to madness, on discovering that they were about to be sold to their ancient and detested enemies the Florentines; they rose in arras, and driving Visconti from the city, compelled his troops to take refuge in the citadel. But there he maintained himself until he had closed his bargain, and, for 206,000 florins, transferred the signiory of Pisa to the Florentines: he then delivered into the hands of their commissioners the citadel itself and the other castles which he held. Gabriele Maria did not enjoy his reward: he was first plundered of a part of this money by Boucicault, and then of the remainder; and at last was executed at Genoa upon a calumnious charge of treason.

The Florentines shortly lost the citadel which they had purchased at so heavy a price. The Pisans, finding it delivered to a Florentine garrison, pressed the siege of it, which they had already undertaken from the side of their city, with increased vigour; and by the neglect or cowardice of its defenders, it was surprised and immediately razed to the ground. But this transient success only deferred and could not avert the subjugation of the Pisans. The Florentines were inflamed by the disgrace which their arms had suffered, to obstinate resolution and powerful efforts. They haughtily repulsed an embassy which the Pisans sent to remonstrate on the injustice of their aggression, to demand the restitution of their castles, to offer to make good to Florence the sum which she had paid to Gabriele Maria, and to solicit an equitable peace.

As if the iniquitous bargain which they had concluded with Visconti had power to abrogate the natural right of the Pisans to be free, they already addressed them as rebellious subjects; and they immediately made earnest preparation for enforcing their obedience.

It was to no purpose that, to conciliate their enemies, the Pisans, who only asked to govern themselves, recalled to power the exiled faction of the Gambacorti, the partizans of Florence. The rulers and people of that state were not the less sternly resolved on their purpose. The direction of the war was entrusted to ten commissioners, as had become usual with the republic since her contest with the church in the preceding century; and the numerous forces which these ministers had taken into pay were already in movement to close up every avenue to Pisa, and to starve that capital into a surrender, while the minor places in its territory were successively reduced by assault. A few galliots, which the Florentines armed at Genoa, appeared off the mouth of the Arno, to prevent the entrance of supplies from the sea; and so fallen was Pisa, that this petty force maintained the blockade of a city, which had once fitted out her hundred galleys to dispute the dominion of the waves. By land all hope of relief was gradually extinguished. The condottieri, whom the Pisans endeavoured to enrol in their service, were either bought off by gold, or successively intercepted and routed on their approach to the city; and the numerous army of the Florentines, drawing their chain of blockade more closely round the despairing city, at length prevented all introduction of food.

Still the Pisans obstinately defended themselves as became men who fought for all that could dignify life; and even when fatigue and misery and hunger had worn them to the bone, their spirit remained unsubdued. They vainly offered the signiory of their city to Ladislaus king of Naples, and to the duke of Burgundy: the first of these princes engaged to Florence to leave them to their fate, in exchange for the assurance that she would not oppose his occupation of Rome; the second proved too distant or too indifferent to afford them relief. The unhappy citizens, as famine wasted them, endeavoured to banish their useless mouths,—the women, the aged, and the children; but the Florentines mercilessly drove back these sufferers into the place, and had even the cruelty to use violence to them to deter their fellow citizens from a repetition of the attempt to expel them. Thus at last the Pisan granaries were completely emptied; and the wretchedness within the walls became so great, that the people eagerly devoured the weeds that grew in their streets and on the ramparts. But though the citizens with difficulty dragged their emaciated bodies to the post of duty, no word of surrender was heard among them; and when the Gambacorti who governed them, finding further resistance utterly hopeless, capitulated to the Florentines to secure as many advantages as possible for themselves, they were compelled to keep the negotiation a secret from their fellow citizens. They delivered up a gate to the enemy during the night; the besieging army entered; and though the Florentine commissaries immediately introduced supplies of food, and obliged their mercenaries to observe a rare moderation towards the inhabitants, the last elevation of the popular voice in Pisa was to invoke curses on the rulers who had betrayed them. (A.D. 1406.) This conquest of Pisa gave a secure maritime outlet to the Florentine commerce, which had hitherto been dependent on the caprice of neighbouring states; and the prosperity of Florence was thenceforth carried to its highest splendour. Yet in the dispassionate judgment of history, the unjust subjugation of a rival city, which had been but lately free as herself, has left an indelible reproach on her fair fame. The quiet submission of Pisa could be ensured only by the silent depopulation and mortal languor with which she was stricken in her slavery; her majestic edifices became a forsaken solitude; and the contemplative traveller who paces her deserted streets, will even at this hour call to mind the origin of her long decay, and deem the subsequent grandeur of Florence purchased something too dearly.

Since the commencement of the great schism of the church, the papal power had fallen so deeply into contempt or oblivion, that I have scarcely found occasion to notice its precarious existence. But the repeated efforts which, at the period before us, were made to terminate the schism, and their approach to final success, may seem to demand our momentary retrospect and attention to the affairs of the pontificate. Urban VI., to whose intemperate conduct this great division of the church may with safety be ascribed, and whose subsequent reign was no otherwise marked than by ferocious tyranny over his own cardinals, and interference in the revolutions of Naples, terminated his restless life in 1389. The cardinals of his obedience immediately entered into conclave, and elected for his successor Boniface IX. This pontiff after passing many years of his reign under the protection of the Malatesti, lords of Rimini, and seeking to re-establish the papal authority over Romagna, by engaging in the obscure and eternal feuds of that province, was, as we have seen, in some measure enabled to raise the temporal power of his see by the acquisition of Bologna and Perugia after the death of Gian Galeazzo. Rome was also reduced to change her state of mingled independence and anarchy for subjection to his sway; and the severity of his government restrained the independent or turbulent spirit of the people. But, on his decease in 1404, the citizens rose in insurrection under the conduct of the Savelli and Colonna; and it was amidst a wild scene of popular tumult, that the conclave of the Urbanist cardinals raised one of their body to the papal throne by the title of Innocent VII.

The new pope, who was distinguished by the moderation of his character, at first effected an accommodation with the people, and acknowledged their republican freedom. But the intrigues of some of their leaders, and the violence of his own family, produced new troubles; and Ladislaus, king of Naples, who by the secure establishment of his throne had now found leisure to form projects of foreign conquest, insidiously encouraged the Romans in their resistance to the pope, that, by forcing him to abandon the city, he might himself acquire a sovereignty over it. Innocent VII. was compelled to fly before the fury of the populace; and Ladislaus, by the invitation of the Colonna, then entered Rome with a small force, and demanded the signiory of the people. But the citizens had not expelled their pacific sovereign to yield themselves to the yoke of an ambitious monarch. A quarrel between some of the populace and the Neapolitan soldiery swelled into a general engagement; the troops of Ladislaus were worsted; and the king was compelled to evacuate the city, after setting fire to it in several places. His enterprise taught the citizens to desire again the presence of the inoffensive pontiff; he was recalled, and shortly after died; and the election of a new pope, Gregory XII., at Rome, prolonged the duration of the great schism, (A.D. 1406.)

For many years the general voice of Europe had been loudly declared, in reprobating the scandalous division which agitated the church. But the adherence of the leading states of Christendom was so equally balanced between the rival pontiffs of Rome and Avignon, that there appeared no other means of terminating the schism than by inducing both popes to abdicate, and obtaining a new and undisputed election by the union of the cardinals of the two parties. In the endeavour to effect these desirable objects, the court of France, and particularly the university of Paris, had honourably taken the lead. On the death of Clement VII. at Avignon, in 1394, both the kings of France and Aragon, who had adhered to his party, seconded the exertions of the university of Paris in exhorting the Clementine cardinals to abstain from appointing a new pope. But these prelates could not be induced to make such a cession of their pretensions to the opposite faction. While they professed their most earnest desire for a reconciliation on equal terms, and went so far as individually to take a solemn oath to stop at no personal sacrifices, even to the abdication of the papal dignity in case it should devolve upon them, they hastened to assemble in conclave, and raised one of their number, Benedict XIII., to the tiara. Benedict who, until his elevation, had passed for the most moderate man of his party, and who from his previous zeal for the peace of the church, had appeared best fitted for the work of re-union, had no sooner attained the pontifical dignity, than he laboured with ingenious duplicity to perpetuate the dissensions on which his authority rested. It was to no purpose that a French national council withdrew the kingdom from its spiritual allegiance to him; that a French army besieged Avignon; and that he was retained a prisoner in his palace. He repeatedly engaged to abdicate, and as often found some pretext to retract his promise; and after ineffectually abstaining for some years from obedience to either of the rival popes, the French church found it expedient again to recognize the authority of Benedict, though his resignation was not the less importunately demanded.

The hollow negotiations into which, for the sake of appearances, Benedict XIII. was compelled to enter with the pontiff's of the opposite faction, at length however produced more impression than was desired by his crafty policy. Though the cardinals of the other obedience, after the death of Urban VI., had successively placed Boniface IX., Innocent VII., and Gregory XII. in his chair, they were obliged in decency, at the two last of these elections, to impose on themselves the same self-denying oaths in which the prelates of Avignon had set them the example. The increasing indignation of Europe, at the selfish obstinacy which prolonged the scandal of their separation, was so loudly proclaimed after the elevation of Gregory XII., that he found it necessary to invite Benedict XIII. to a mutual abdication for the peace of the church. But there was as little sincerity in his proposal, as in the apparent readiness of Benedict to accept it. The rival pontiff's agreed in rejecting the plan of the French monarch, that each should abdicate in presence of his own college, and that the cardinals of the two obediences should then meet to elect a new pope. Both Gregory and Benedict insisted upon a previous conference, in which their renunciation should take place in presence of the united colleges. The maritime city of Savona in the Genoese territory was named for the scene of this ceremony by mutual consent, and formally yielded by the French king in equal portions for the residence of the two papal courts. But neither pontiff had any intention that the conference should ever take place. Gregory exposed himself by the first evasion, under pretence that, having no naval force, he could not trust himself in a maritime city in the power of his rival, who was escorted by the Genoese galleys; and Benedict, who for some time played his part with more address, not only arrived at the appointed rendezvous, but even made a feint of advancing from thence to meet Gregory, who had proceeded from Rome to Lucca, (A.D. 1407.) But it was no more than a feint; and a servant of Gregory compares the two pontiffs, the one to an aquatic creature who would not quit the coast, and the other to a terrestrial animal who dreaded the water. But the cardinals of the two obediences had been at last seriously roused by the reproaches of Christendom, and were weary of the mutual dissimulation of their masters. The majority of the followers of Gregory first forsook him, and repaired to Pisa (A.D. 1408); most of the opposite party withdrew from the residence of Benedict to Leghorn; the cardinals of Gregory joined them in that town; and the united colleges addressed circular letters, temperately exposing the conduct of Gregory and Benedict, to all the bishops of the two obediences, and inviting the prelates to a general council at Pisa; where the two popes were likewise enjoined to appear before the assembled church of Christ.

Both the pontiffs, on the receipt of this summons, bared their selfish ambition to the world. Benedict, with three cardinals who adhered to him, set sail for Aragon; and Gregory, with four others, withdrew to the protection of the Malatesti of Rimini. The one convoked a council at Perpignan, the other at Ravenna; but these efforts to defeat the intention of the united colleges were unavailing. A numerous body of the prelates of Christendom assembled to meet the cardinals at Pisa, and most of the crowned heads of Europe sent their ambassadors to assist their deliberations. (A.D. 1409.) The council of Pisa, with impartial justice, solemnly deposed both Gregory XII. and Benedict XIII. without deciding on their relative pretensions, and raised the cardinal of Milan to the papal dignity by the title of Alexander V. The first act of the new pope was an endeavour to perfect the peace of the church. For tranquillity of conscience, all nominations to benefices, which had been granted by the rival pontiffs since the commencement of the schism, were confirmed, and all spiritual censures and excommunications annulled. Yet the council of Pisa, so far from healing the schism, only appeared to render it incurable. Spain obstinately maintained her adherence to Benedict XIII.; Naples and some minor states still supported Gregory XII.; and there were now three papal pretenders instead of two. But with the work of this council commenced nevertheless a new ecclesiastical era: the right of the assembled church to depose her rulers had been asserted by a large majority of her representatives; a precedent was established to guide the subsequent and more important council of Constance; and many writers have seen in this epoch the commencement of that long struggle against the absolute dominion of the popedom, for which we are indebted to the final establishment of the Reformation.

The adherence of Ladislaus, king of Naples, to Gregory XII., was occasioned solely by the interested design of prolonging the duration of the schism, and perpetuating the distractions of the papal states. We have formerly traced the character and fortunes of this ambitious monarch to the moment when, at the close of the fourteenth century, he had triumphed against his competitor, Louis of Anjou, and, on the retirement of that prince to Provence, had established his unresisted and arbitrary sway over the kingdom of Naples. From this epoch Ladislaus eagerly meditated schemes of new aggrandizement in the peninsula; but his attention was diverted for some years from Italian affairs, by a similar invitation to that which his father had received from a part of the Hungarian nobility, to ascend their throne. Sigismund, brother of the emperor Wenceslaus, who had been raised to the crown of Hungary by his marriage with the queen Maria, had disgusted the nobles by his debaucheries and cruelty. His person was seized, a general revolt spread through the kingdom, and, when the galleys of Ladislaus appeared on the coast of Dalmatia, Zara and other maritime cities acknowledged his authority. He received the crown of Hungary at Zara; but in the mean time Sigismund had recovered his liberty and the allegiance of the fickle palatines; and Ladislaus, returning to Naples, found it expedient, at the end of several years, to renounce his pretensions to the Hungarian crown. He sold the places which he held in maritime Dalmatia to the Venetians; who thus regained the possessions on those coasts, which their republic had, half a century before, been compelled to cede to Louis of Hungary.

Thus abandoning his transmarine conquests, Ladislaus turned, as we have observed, during the pontificate of Innocent VII., to mingle in the affairs of Rome, and insidiously to foment the troubles of the papal states. He had once failed in endeavouring to occupy the ecclesiastical capital; but the departure of Gregory XII., with the feigned purpose of meeting the rival pope, was too tempting an occasion of seizing upon Rome for Ladislaus to lose. In the year before the assembly of the council of Pisa, he advanced from the Neapolitan frontiers with a formidable army of 12,000 cuirassiers and an equal force of infantry. The Orsini betrayed to him one of the gates of Rome, as the Colonna had done before; the citizens were compelled to capitulate; Perugia was attacked at the same time and induced to surrender; and, under the pretence of acting as the protector of Gregory XII., Ladislaus effected the occupation of the capital and of great part of the ecclesiastical state. But he designed to extend his conquests yet farther; he hoped ultimately to embrace the whole of Italy in his dominion; and, in the magnitude of his ambition, which was as insatiable as his talents were splendid, he even aspired to the imperial crown. In his design to consolidate his power over his new conquests, and to extend his authority towards northern Italy, he imperiously required the Florentines to recognize him for legitimate sovereign of the ecclesiastical states; and he backed the demand by the imposing force of his fine army. But the Florentines had taken part with the council of Pisa, which they had suffered to assemble in their states, and with Alexander V.; they resolved to seat that pontiff in the patrimony of St. Peter; and the army of Ladislaus caused them little dread, since they knew that their gold could readily seduce the condottieri, of whose bands the Neapolitan forces were principally composed.

Having engaged the republic of Sienna in their alliance, the Florentines immediately began to levy a powerful force of mercenaries for the prosecution of the war, which had now become inevitable. The famous company of St. George served in the army of Ladislaus; but their leader Alberic di Barbiano, whom that monarch had created great constable of his kingdom, had lately died, and just before the epoch at which Ladislaus thus lost the services of this great restorer of the military reputation of Italy, he had been compelled, by the condition of the treaty which admitted him into Perugia, to dismiss from his pay a yet more celebrated leader, Braccio di Montone, who was a Perugian exile, and had been educated to arms in the school of St. George. This captain willingly entered into the service of Florence; the republic farther took into her pay Malatesta di Pesaro and other condottieri with their bands; and before the king of Naples could commence his offensive operations, she had assembled two thousand four hundred lances, or seven thousand two hundred cuirassiers. Inferior as was this force to the army of Ladislaus, Braccio di Montone by his able conduct preserved the fortresses of the Florentines and Siennese from falling into the hands of that monarch; he hovered round the invaders, intercepted their convoys, and routed their detachments; and in a short time so straitened their supplies of provisions, that Ladislaus was obliged to retire to Rome.

The Florentines were not satisfied with this first success. While they were providing forces for the defence of their own territory, they had extended the ramifications of their policy with their customary address, and had invited into Italy Louis II. of Anjou, the former competitor of Ladislaus for the Neapolitan crown. They persuaded this prince to renew the pretensions which he founded on the adoption of his father by Joanna; they laboured to revive the Angevin party in Naples; and they induced pope Alexander V., on the arrival of Louis with a body of gens-d'armerie at Pisa, to bestow on him the investiture of that kingdom. The troops of Florence, Sienna, and Bologna were united to the Provençal cavalry; and Louis entered at their head into the ecclesiastical states.

Many of the towns in the patrimony of St. Peter immediately opened their gates to the combined army. Paolo Orsini, who commanded for Ladislaus at Rome with two thousand cuirassiers, was seduced by the gold of Florence; and passing into the pay of the republic, he admitted the allies into the castle of St. Angelo. The possession of Rome was then for some time contested between the combatants; and, although Louis left the army of the league to return to Provence, the Neapolitan troops were finally compelled to evacuate the capital, (A.D. 1410.) Alexander V. was thus established in the possession of the ancient seat of the papacy; but he survived the acquisition only a few months; and the cardinal Balthazar Cossa, a man of ambitious and profligate character, who had exercised a strong influence over the deliberations of the council of Pisa, and whose vices, real or exaggerated, have obtained a disgraceful celebrity in ecclesiastical annals, procured his own succession to the papal chair by the title of John XXIII.

Meanwhile, Louis of Anjou was preparing another expedition into Italy, in which the Florentines designed that he should carry his arms into the Neapolitan dominions. But during the fresh reverses which threatened the power of Ladislaus, he suddenly acquired a new ally. The Genoese, who had long endured the yoke of France with impatience, took advantage of the absence of their governor Boucicault to revolt; and after murdering or expelling all the French who had remained in the city, they restored their republic, and immediately embraced the party of Ladislaus, in opposition to that of France and Anjou. In concert with the Neapolitan galleys, a Genoese squadron encountered the fleet in which Louis with a numerous train of Provençal knights had embarked for Italy, and captured many of his vessels; but the prince himself escaped; and his arrival at Rome was the signal for the advance of the formidable army which Florence, the pope, and Sienna had assembled in that capital. Many of the most celebrated condottieri of Italy served under the banners of this alliance; Braccio di Montone, Paolo Orsini, Angelo della Pergola, and Sforza Attendolo, an adventurer whose descendants were destined to assume a distinguished rank among the sovereigns of the peninsula. But owing to the dissensions of these captains, and the poverty or inactivity of Louis, the campaign against Ladislaus produced no decisive advantage; and the Florentines, finding the whole burthen of the war, which had already cost them immense sums, thrown upon their republic by the utter inability of her allies to meet its expenses, listened to the overtures of Ladislaus. They concluded with him an advantageous peace, in which Sienna was embraced, while John XXIII. and Louis of Anjou continued the war. (A.D. 1411.)

Notwithstanding the defection of Florence and Sienna, the army of Louis of Anjou remained undiminished. Though the gold of the former republic was no longer lavished to gratify their rapacity, the condottieri and their bands preferred serving without pay, but with the prospect of booty, to a total loss of occupation; and the Angevin prince was enabled by their adherence to his fortunes to cross the Neapolitan frontiers at the head of twelve thousand of the bravest cuirassiers of Italy. Ladislaus waited his approach at a place called Rocca Secca, near the river Garigliano, with an army little inferior. But the assault, in which the Angevin prince led his troops, was so impetuous that the cavalry of Ladislaus was completely routed at the first onset: almost all his barons were taken, and even his personal baggage fell into the hands of the conquerors. Their greediness of plunder and avarice of ransom saved the fugitive monarch from the fate of Manfred and Conradin. They were sacking his camp while they ought to have been pressing on his disorderly flight; the mercenary soldiers sold the prisoners their liberty and arms for a few ducats to procure a little money; and Ladislaus finding they did not pursue him, and learning their cupidity, put on a bold countenance. He sent heralds to their camp with supplies of gold, and in a few hours he had ransomed and remounted nearly his whole army. He afterwards declared, that on the first day after his defeat, his person and kingdom were alike in the power of the victors; that on the second, though his person was saved, his kingdom was still at their mercy; but that, on the third, the fruits of their victory had flown. When

Louis of Anjou at last prevailed on his mercenary bands to advance, all the defiles of the Neapolitan frontiers were already securely closed against them by the troops of Laidislaus. Want and sickness soon followed the inactivity to which the invaders were reduced; as the hope of further booty diminished, the mercenaries became ungovernable and mutinous; and Louis was obliged to re-conduct his army to Rome. There he, in weariness and disgust of his enterprise, abandoned it and left Italy for ever; and Ladislaus and John XXIII. alike exhausted by the war, which languished without further circumstances of moment, concluded it in the following summer by the good offices of the Florentines. Ladislaus recognized the authority of the council of Pisa, and submitted to John XXIII. as legitimate pope; and John, in return, paid him 100,000 florins and confirmed to him the investiture of his kingdom, (A.D. 1412.)

The restless and ambitious character of Ladislaus rendered this reconciliation short-lived and ineffectual. Early in the following year, he commissioned Sforza, now in his service, to attack Paolo Orsini, who had established himself in some fiefs of the march of Ancona. With the ostensible purpose of supporting his general in this expedition, which was undertaken with the secret concurrence of the pope, Ladislaus assembled a large army and passed the confines of his kingdom at its head. But on his passage through the ecclesiastical states, he suddenly turned off, and appeared at the gates of Rome; his galleys entered the Tiber; and John XXIII., in consternation at this unexpected treachery, had scarcely time to escape from his capital when an entrance through its walls was betrayed to the troops of Ladislaus. The Neapolitan army entered; and during a sack of several days, Rome experienced all the horrors of barbarian warfare. The perfidious violation of the faith of treaties of which Ladislaus had thus been guilty, his acquisition of Rome, and still more his promise to his army that a yet richer booty awaited them in the pillage of Florence, awakened against him the suspicions and fears of that republic. Her ten commissioners of war were immediately appointed, as if the state were already engaged in hostilities; several condottieri were taken into pay; and preparations were made to oppose the ambitious designs of Ladislaus on a scale proportioned to the power and activity of so dangerous an enemy. But still the Florentine government wished if possible to avoid provoking him to war; and, while they negotiated and temporized, Ladislaus reduced the whole of the patrimony of St. Peter. John XXIII. was now engaged in ecclesiastical affairs which too deeply concerned the very existence of his authority, to leave him time for watching over the preservation of his temporal dominions.

While circumstances seemed to oblige the pope himself to abandon his charge, the Florentines either did not consider themselves bound to engage singly in the defence of the possessions of the church, or they felt their inability to wrest them from the strong arm of Ladislaus. They therefore, in concert with Sienna, signed a new peace with that monarch. But the apparent amity which dictated the treaty thinly veiled the alarming projects of Ladislaus, and the real distrust and suspicion of the republicans. That monarch was now in the zenith of his power: he had removed the northern boundary of his dominions to the confines of Tuscany; he numbered in his service fifteen thousand of the finest gens-d'armerie of Italy; and the establishment of a general tyranny seemed at hand, more extensive and formidable than that with which Gian Galeazzo had threatened the peninsula. Florence in particular, had every thing to dread from a monarch whose power was almost at her gates, and who was at once warlike, ambitious, and unprincipled. But death, which had more than once before so opportunely succoured her, came again to her deliverance; and just as the measures of Ladislaus bore every indication of new aggressions and immediate war, he was suddenly hurried to the grave by a frightful and agonizing disease, the novel symptoms of which were supposed to have been occasioned by his excessive debaucheries. (A.D. 1414.)

The attention of Italy was divided between the change which the death of Ladislaus produced in the condition of a great part of the peninsula, and the approaching convocation of a general council. The anxious expectations of Europe had been completely disappointed by the issue of the council of Pisa. The scandal of the schism had rather been aggravated than repressed; three popes now claimed the obedience of Christendom; and all the disorders and corruptions of the clergy, which had shamefully increased during the long quarrel of the church, were multiplied anew with the number of pretenders to the papal dignity. The simoniacal practices and venality of the divided papacy had forgotten concealment, and exceeded all bounds of decency. The malicious industry with which the organs of the adverse factions bared to the public gaze the vices of their opponents, and the venomous spirit with which they invented atrocious accusations or exaggerated crimes, destroyed every former illusion that had attracted to the Roman pontiffs the blind adoration of mankind. The public and personal character of John XXIII. in particular was assailed with the most odious charges. To provide funds for the war against Ladislaus, he had renewed the sale of indulgences which Boniface IX. had commenced; and the disgust with which this scandalous traffic filled all enlightened and religious minds, was converted into detestation of the pope himself by the assiduous report of his enormous depravity. One universal cry for ecclesiastical reform was raised throughout Europe, and a general council was still in public opinion the favourite remedy for the schism of the papacy, and the flagrant abuses of the church.

The wishes of Christendom were forwarded with active and disinterested zeal, by a monarch, the ordinary qualities of whose character seemed little to promise any virtuous exertion. This was Sigismund of Hungary, who on the death of the emperor Robert in the year 1410, had been raised to the crown of Germany; he was the brother of Wenceslaus, and that feeble monarch, who since his deposition from the imperial throne still reigned over his hereditary states, himself gave him his electoral vote as king of Bohemia. Sigismund was habitually cruel and faithless, and, in his private life, debauched and voluptuous to the last degree. But, in the pursuit of a favourite design, he could evince a constancy and activity of purpose, which no fatigue could tire and no danger appal; and which, standing, on the most famous occasion of his reign, in the place of virtue, has left to his memory a fairer reputation than is otherwise merited by the tenor of his life. In receiving the imperial dignity, he formed the resolution of terminating the schism of the church; and he adhered to it with an inflexible and praiseworthy earnestness, which was strangely contrasted with his general duplicity and selfishness. For some time after his elevation to the throne of the empire, a war in which he was involved with Venice, respecting the possession of the Dalmatian cities sold to her by Ladislaus, delayed the fulfilment of his eager desire both to accomplish his own coronation at Rome, and the assembly of a general council. But, after a lapse of three years, he at length succeeded in concluding a long truce with the Venetian republic, and he then immediately entered Lombardy. (A.D. 1413.) He did not find himself powerful enough to dictate in arms as a master to Italy; and he therefore confined his attention to the affairs of the church.

John XXIII. both apprehended the reproach of Europe, if he should refuse to convoke a council, and was disturbed by the opposite fear of the judgment which such a body might pass on himself. In his negotiations with Sigismund, he dared not oppose its assembly, but he at first insisted that it should take place in some city of Italy. The emperor and the Germans on the other hand, who attributed the disorders of the church to the corruption of the Italian clergy, dreaded the influence which the papal court must exercise over any council held in the peninsula. They, and Europe in general, desired a free assembly to reform the church, as well as to restore its union; and John, after hesitating and betraying much irresolution, had at last the fatal imprudence, for his own interests, to consent that a place beyond the Alps should be chosen for the seat of the council. The pope and the emperor then met in personal conferences in several of the Lombard cities, to perfect the preliminary arrangements; and John XXIII. at length published his bulls to invite the clergy of Christendom to assemble in the imperial city of Constance, (A.D. 1414.)

The famous council of Constance was attended by the emperor and by pope John XXIII. in person; by the ambassadors of almost all Christian princes and states; and, besides the cardinals in obedience to John, by so great a number of episcopal and inferior clergy, and theologians of various nations, that the assembly might with reason arrogate to itself the pretension of representing the civil and ecclesiastical interests of Europe. But the proportion of Italians in the council far exceeded that of other nations; and it might justly be dreaded that, if the suffrages were permitted to reckon by the head, the prelates and others of that country, who were almost universally in the papal interests, would exercise a pernicious influence upon the decisions of the assembled church. It was therefore determined, by the concert of the rest of the council, that the votes should be collected, not by the number of persons, but by nations. Thus four distinct chambers were formed (to which a fifth was afterwards added for Spain) for the Italian, German, French, and English nations; the minor states of Europe being comprehended under one or other of these great divisions. The national chambers deliberated separately upon every proposition; the decision of each body was given as a single voice; and the decrees of the council were regulated by the majority of these national votes.

The first labour of the council was to extinguish the schism, and there appeared no other mode of effecting this great object, than by obliging not only Benedict XIII. and Gregory XII., but John XXIII. also, to resign their pretensions. For, as Spain and a part of Italy rejected the authority of John to adhere to his rivals respectively, the sacrifice of his dignity could alone persuade his opponents to agree in a new choice of the same pope. And though the legitimacy of John's election was not disputed by the greater portion of Europe, the public report of his scandalous vices was readily adopted to justify his deposition. To the demand of the assembled church, that the three papal rivals should equally abdicate their seats, John XXIII. was unwillingly reduced to promise compliance; but he seized the first opportunity of escaping from Constance, in the disguise of a groom; and, retiring to Schaffhausen, found a protector in the duke of Austria. But for the firmness of the emperor, this flight must have been followed by the dissolution of the council. But Sigismund immediately put the duke of Austria under the ban of the empire; all the petty princes and free cities of the neighbouring provinces united in attacking him; and the duke was shortly necessitated to submit to the emperor and the council, and to abandon the pope to his fate. John XXIII. was re-conducted a prisoner to Constance; a process was commenced against him by the council; and, upon loose and general evidence only, articles of accusation were framed against him, which embraced a longer series of atrocious and disgusting crimes, than a whole life of flagitious wickedness could possibly have afforded space to commit. John refused even to see the record of his infamy; he declared his entire resignation to the will of the council; and he was solemnly deposed, and condemned to imprisonment, (A.D. 1415.)

Warned by the fate of John, Gregory XII. who had so obstinately resisted the council of Pisa, but who now found himself abandoned by all his adherents except the lord of Rimini, wisely employed the remains of his authority in descending from his station with some appearance of dignity. His legate arrived at Constance to convene the assembly anew, in order to give it in his name the authority of a council; and, after this vain ceremony, a bull of Gregory was read by which he renounced the pontificate. Sigismund and the council had more difficulty in overcoming the inveterate perverseness of Benedict XIII., and the adherence of Spain to his cause. It was not until the indefatigable emperor had undertaken a long and pacific journey from Constance into Spain, and held a personal conference with the king of Aragon and Benedict at Perpignan, that his efforts were crowned with success. Benedict, indeed, still resisted the wishes of Europe, but the sovereigns of the Spanish peninsula were more accessible to reason. Finding their pontiff deaf to every entreaty to complete the re-union of Christendom, and disgusted by his selfish obstinacy and frantic imbecility, they at length abandoned the dotard. The council of Constance was convoked anew to gratify the pride or scruples of the Spanish church, and to admit her deputies to represent the fifth great nation of Europe; and an unanimous sentence pronounced the deposition of Benedict, and confirmed the work of peace, (A.D. 1417.)

After the remains of the schism had thus been extirpated, Sigismund endeavoured to induce the council to provide for the secure reformation of ecclesiastical abuses, before the election of a new pope to fill the vacant chair of St. Peter. But national dissensions, which had already risen in the assembly, and were artfully fomented by the intrigues of the papal college, increased with alarming violence in every session, and finally defeated the purpose of the emperor. The German and English nations coincided with him; but the Italians, from interested attachment to the power of the papacy, and the French, from jealousy of Sigismund and hatred of the English, ranged themselves on the opposite side, and the Spaniards threw themselves into their scale. Sigismund and his supporters were compelled to yield to this majority; and the council, proceeding to the nomination of a pope, confided the election, upon this solemn occasion, to a double conclave of cardinals and national deputies. The French desired any pontiff but an Italian or a member of the sacred college; but the Germans and English, to oppose their wishes, agreed on this point with the Italians; and the combined interest of these three nations fixed the tiara on the brows of the cardinal Otho Colonna, who assumed the title of Martin V. (A.D. 1418.) The new pontiff speedily defeated the general project of reformation, by treating separately with each nation for the abolition of the ecclesiastical abuses of which they most complained; and he then dissolved the assembly. Thus terminated the great schism of the church, and with it the useful labours of the council of Constance. Of the well-known and execrable condemnation of John Huss and Jerome of Prague, in the early sessions of the council, I have omitted to speak, for the tale of horror has no immediate connexion with Italian history. But the martyrdom of these fathers of the reformed faith, has given an odious character to the council of Constance, and inflicted eternal disgrace upon the principles which governed this celebrated congress of Roman Catholic theologians.

During the period at which our attention has been occupied with the enterprises of Ladislaus of Naples, and the progress and close of the great schism, Lombardy was returning, through a frightful course of suffering, almost to the same condition in which she had been placed in the lifetime of Gian Galeazzo. I have already noticed the anarchy into which that great province was plunged after the decease of the duke of Milan; and, at the epoch of his widow's violent death in prison in 1404, the fortunes of his house had reached their lowest ebb. His eldest son, Giovanni Maria, the new duke of Milan, still a minor, reigned in the capital of Lombardy: his second, Filippo Maria, to whom a part of the province had been bequeathed with the title of count of Pavia, resided in that city. But of the extensive possessions of their parent, the brothers retained only those two places; even in Pavia the Beccaria usurped a paramount authority; and all the other Lombard cities had either revolted to pass under tyrants of their own, or had been seized by the generals of Gian Galeazzo, and converted into lordships for themselves. The whole country was agitated with the struggles of these civic tyrants and ambitious condottieri. The lawless bands of mercenaries who were employed exclusively to decide their quarrels were privileged and steeled in atrocity; and the degraded and wretched people of Lombardy were exposed to every variety of robbery, and torture, and pollution, to gratify the avarice and more brutal passions of the ruffian soldiery.

In the incessant contest of obscure tyrants, which denied to the miserable population of Lombardy any interval of repose, one of the old captains of Gian Galeazzo, Facino Cane, signor of Alessandria, appeared likely to acquire a decided preponderance. His power extended over Novara, Vercelli, and Tortona; the veteran bands which he commanded were numerous and well appointed; and he obliged both the young princes of Milan and Pavia by force of arms, to entrust him with sovereign influence in their councils. If he permitted them to live, it was only because he had no children to whom to bequeath his power. The duke Giovanni Maria had hitherto reserved to himself no other share in the government than to preside at the torture and execution of state criminals. Of all the execrable tyrants produced by the family of Visconti, this was the most madly and wantonly ferocious. His infancy and boyhood had been nursed in atrocities; and as he had advanced towards manhood, he discovered an inherent appetite for blood, and a horrid delight in sporting with the extremities of human agony. His principal diversion was to course the victims of the Milanese tribunals with bloodhounds; and his huntsman, who had fed these dogs with human flesh to accustom them to this royal chase, was his chief favourite. When the prisons of Milan were emptied of prey, Giovanni Maria declared his resolution to avenge the murder of his mother, in which he had himself assisted; and under this plea he successively delivered over Giovanni di Posterla, and many other Ghibelin gentlemen of Milan, to be torn in pieces by his dogs. Even the young son of Posterla was thus inhumanly sacrificed; and when the dogs, perhaps sated with prey, would not fasten on the helpless boy as he knelt for mercy to the duke, the fiendlike huntsman of that prince cut his bowels open with his knife. The reason revolts from the belief of such enormities; yet they are verified by the agreement of several contemporary chroniclers, and history has even preserved the name of the huntsman, Squarcia Giramo, who was the fitting instrument of his master's devilish propensities.

The citizens of Milan might justly prefer the yoke of an ordinary tyrant, to the unrestrained ferocity of this monster of guilt; and when Facino Cane, after completely possessing himself of the government, somewhat in the capacity of regent, was at last known to be seized with a mortal disease, they anticipated the moment with horror when their duke would be freed from his control to reign with redoubled ferocity. The Posterli and other noble families of Milan resolved not tamely to await the renewal of his tyranny; they waylaid him as he was proceeding to mass; they set upon him, and succeeded in ridding the world of his crimes, (A.D. 1412.) A few hours after the assassination of the duke, Facino Cane breathed his last; and Milan seemed abandoned to a new anarchy. The conspirators were disposed to have placed the ducal crown on the head of a bastard of the house of Visconti; but Filippo Maria, the young count of Pavia, evinced unexpected activity and address. He secured the possession of the citadel of Pavia, overawed the Beccaria, and allied himself with the partizans of Facino Cane at Milan. To gain the adherence of the formidable bands of that chief, who were strongly attached to the memory of their general, he offered immediately to espouse his widow, Beatrice Tenda, although she was above twenty years older than himself; and the hasty conclusion of this indecent marriage determined the fidelity of the army of Facino. By their powerful support, Filippo Maria was firmly seated on the ducal throne of Milan; and, though personally unwarlike, he began from the period of his accession gradually to restore the ascendancy of his house in Italy, by the same insidious policy as had been pursued by his father, whom he nearly resembled in character.

When the new duke began his reign, his dominions comprehended only Milan and Pavia, and the four inferior cities over which Facino Cane had established his sway. But the veteran bands of cuirassiers who had served under that condottiere, and were now in the allegiance of Filippo Maria, formed a more numerous and better disciplined force than the signors of Lombardy could oppose to his designs; and he had shortly the penetration or good fortune to discover in his ranks, and to elevate to the supreme command of his army, an adventurer whose splendid abilities and daring courage completely re-established the ascendancy of the Milanese power. This was Francesco Carmagnola, who happened—then a simple cuirassier—to distinguish himself under the eye of the duke, on the only occasion on which Filippo Maria put himself at the head of his army. The prince observed his gallantry and rewarded it by promotion; and from this beginning Carmagnola rapidly rose to be numbered among the greatest captains of Italy. Three years after the accession of Filippo Maria, the operations of Carmagnola began to fill the petty Lombard tyrants with alarm; in the following campaign, he broke the strength of a league which they had formed for their defence, and took Lodi by escalade; and finally, after an obstinate struggle, he reduced numerous cities into subjection to his master, (A.D. 1416.) The lord of Placentia was driven from his possessions; the signor of Lodi was inveigled to Milan by the arts of the duke, treacherously seized, and executed with his son; one of the Beccaria shared the same fate when taken in arms, and another was murdered in prison; and the ruler of Como, despairing of successful resistance, tendered his voluntary submission, (A.D. 1418.)

The first use made by Filippo Maria of the fortune which had thus smiled upon him since his marriage with Beatrice Tenda, was to rid himself of his benefactress. Neither gratitude towards the woman to whom he owed so much, nor respect for her many amiable qualities, could prevail in his vicious nature over his disgust of a connexion in which there existed such a disparity of years. He accused his duchess of an adulterous commerce with a young courtier; the youth was forced by excruciating tortures to avow whatever was desired of him; and he was even induced by the hope of pardon to repeat his shameful confession at the foot of the scaffold. But this weakness could gain him no favour, and he was led to execution with the unhappy Beatrice, from whom the most frightful torments had been unavailing to extract a similar acknowledgment of guilt. In her last moments, she sternly reproached her fellow-sufferer with his base pusillanimity, and died solemnly protesting her innocence, but declaring that the displeasure of Heaven had justly overtaken her for having, by the indecent haste of her union with her murderer, violated the respect which was due to the memory of her first husband.

It is among the mysterious dispensations of a wise Providence that guilt should sometimes be permitted to triumph; and the remorseless destroyer of Beatrice pursued his schemes of ambition with uninterrupted prosperity. The doge of Genoa had joined the league of Lombard signors against the duke of Milan, and, after his successes over these tyrants, Carmagnola invaded the states of that republic. Genoa was no longer under the yoke of France, but she seemed to merit no repose, and to find none but under the dominion of a master. Her people were as usual divided among themselves by the eternal and deadly spirit of faction; and when Carmagnola ravaged her territory in successive campaigns, his army was accompanied by Genoese exiles and assisted by treason. The distracted republic was at the same time engaged in a war with the king of Aragon, who had made a descent upon Corsica; and the alliance of this monarch with Filippo Maria threatened the blockade of Genoa by land and sea. Thus torn by civil war, and assailed by foreign enemies, the doge himself could discover no cessation for the miseries of the state but under the protection of the duke of Milan. He abdicated his power, and under the same conditions, by which the republic had submitted twenty years before to the king of France, consigned the signiory of Genoa to Filippo Maria, (A.D. 1421.) While this acquisition increased the influence and power of the duke of Milan, the few signors who had risen on the death of Gian Galeazzo in the eastern parts of Lombardy, and had hitherto escaped subjugation to Filippo Maria, were easily overthrown by Carmagnola. Besides the chieftains of other petty lordships, Pandolfo Malatesta, signor of Brescia, and Gabrino Fondolo, tyrant of Cremona, were stripped of their possessions. The former was obliged to seek a shelter with his brother at Rimini, the latter was reduced to exchange the lordship of Cremona for a single castle. The marquis of Este was compelled to purchase peace by the cession of Parma; and Francesco Gonzaga, lord of Mantua, was only protected from spoliation by the interference of Venice. That republic, now engaged in extending her dominion over the province of Friuli, had hitherto resisted all the entreaties of her Lombard allies for aid against the formidable power, which even threatened her own continental possessions. But though she had ungratefully abandoned Pandolfo Malatesta, her faithful adherent, who had often commanded her armies, the Mantuan territory was too important a barrier for her provinces, for her to suffer it to be occupied by the duke; and by an amicable treaty which she negotiated with Filippo Maria, she exacted from that prince a guarantee for the states of Gonzaga.

The power of the house of Visconti was now, after twenty years of reverses, triumphantly reestablished in Lombardy; and all the usurpers who had dismembered the principality of Gian Galeazzo, and inflicted so many fresh calamities upon that beautiful country, had been successively hurled from their power. The last enterprise by which Carmagnola crowned the greatness of Filippo Maria, brought his troops into contact with a more formidable enemy than any which they had hitherto encountered, the hardy republicans of the Swiss cantons. The family of Rusca, which had governed at Como, had some pretensions, which they sold to the duke of Milan, over the town of Bellinzona, at the foot of the Alps, where the canton of Uri retained a garrison to guard the passes into their territory. The place was surprised by the Milanese troops, who also seized upon Domo Dossola, and advancing to mount St. Gothard, occupied all the Levantine valley. At another juncture these aggressions would have roused all Switzerland to arms; but the cantons were at this epoch unfortunately agitated by domestic jealousies; their contingents were reluctantly afforded to assist the people of Uri in resenting the injury which they had sustained; and the part only of their force which descended from St. Gothard, consisted but of three thousand infantry, armed with pikes. Yet this small army advanced, without knowing or regarding the strength of their enemies, to offer battle in the field of Arbedo, near Bellinzona, to above double their numbers of the veteran cuirassiers of Italy. The Milanese gensd'armerie commenced the encounter with a furious charge; but their shock was broken against an impenetrable phalanx of pikemen. Four hundred of the Italians were already slain or dismounted, and still the Swiss remained immoveable. Carmagnola then ordered his men-atarms to quit their horses, and charge on foot; and the combat was renewed with obstinate carnage between this invulnerable infantry of cuirassiers and the brave mountaineers. The impervious armour and overwhelming numbers of the Milanese now turned the tide of victory;

but Carmagnola, engaged at the slaughter which had been inflicted on his bands, refused the demand of the republicans for quarter; and the struggle continued with desperation, until the sudden attack of his rearguard, by a foraging detachment of Swiss, induced Carmagnola to draw off his troops, in the supposition that the rest of their army had descended from the mountains. Of the Swiss four hundred men had fallen, of the Italians above three times that number; and their consternation at finding with what an enemy they had to do, was even greater than at the mere amount of their loss. But the Swiss were plunged in dissensions; they abandoned the contest, and suffered many years to elapse before they thought of revenge; and Carmagnola retained possession of the Levantine valley. Thus was the power of Filippo Maria asserted from the Ligurian sea to the summit of mount St. Gothard, and from the frontiers of Piedmont to the confines of the ecclesiastical states, a larger extent of dominion than had fallen to the obedience of any Italian prince since the ruin of the ancient kingdom of the Lombards.

PART II.
Florence—Her prosperity—Aggressions of the duke of Milan—War between Filippo Maria and Florence—Successive defeats of the republic—Venice—Change in her policy—Successful pursuit of continental dominion—Its doubtful advantage—The aid of Venice solicited by the Florentines—Francesco Carmagnola, injuriously treated by Filippo Maria, retires to Venice, and determines her on war—League formed by Florence and Venice—Repeated wars of the two republics against the duke of Milan—Successes of Carmagnola—His victory at Macalo—His reverses—Atrocious ingratitude of Venice to her general—Execution of Carmagnola—Third peace of Ferrara—Splendid acquisitions of Venice—Reign of Joanna II. of Naples—Rivalry of the great condottieri, Sforza Attendolo and Braccio di Montone—Louis III. of Anjou invited by the pope and Sforza to dethrone Joanna—Her adoption of Alfonso of Aragon—War between the Aragonese and Angevin parties—Rupture between the queen and Alfonso—Her substitution of Louis of Anjou for her heir—Death of Sforza and Braccio—Last years and death of Joanna II.—Domestic affairs of Florence—Grandeur of the republic under the Guelf oligarchy—Character of their administration—Revival of the democratical party—Rise of the Medici—Giovanni—And Cosmo—His banishment and triumphant recall—Fall of the oligarchy—Establishment of Cosmo de' Medici in the direction of the state—Disputed succession to the crown of Naples—Contest between Alfonso of Aragon and Regnier of Anjou—Establishment of Alfonso on the Neapolitan throne—Genoa recovers her liberty—New war between the duke of Milan and the republics of Florence and Venice—Rise of Francesco Sforza—Peace of Martinengo—Pontificate of Eugenius IV.—League formed against Francesco Sforza—His gallant defence and reverses—Sforza succoured by Venice and Florence—War of the republics against the duke of Milan—

Death of the duke Filippo Maria—The people of Milan establish a republic—Their numerous enemies—Sforza enters their service—His victories and treachery—He leagues with the Venetians against his employers—Dissensions at Milan—The city besieged by Sforza, declares in his favour—Francesco Sforza, duke of Milan—Rise of the house of Savoy—Its origin—The counts of Maurienne and of Savoy—Commencement of their power in Piedmont—State of that province before the fifteenth century—Piedmont under the dominion of the counts of Savoy—Amadeus VIII., the first duke of his house.

WHEN Filippo Maria, duke of Milan, had reestablished the grandeur of his house, while he inherited the inordinate and perfidious ambition of his father, Florence could scarcely hope for the longer continuance of peace. Since the death of Ladislaus, king of Naples, that republic, leaving Lombardy to its own distractions, had enjoyed nearly ten years of uninterrupted repose and felicity. Under the able and vigorous sway of the Guelf oligarchy, at the head of which the Albizzi indirectly governed in her councils, her states had been protected from all assault or insult. While the rest of Italy was scathed with fire and sword, agriculture flourished in her well-peopled vales; the foreign commerce and wealth of her merchants increased with prodigious activity; and both in the capital itself and in her rural territories, the best evidence of national prosperity was exhibited in a contented and happy population. The rapid aggrandizement of the Milanese power, and the faithless enterprises of Filippo Maria, threatened the first invasion of this tranquil condition; and the Florentines are justly chargeable with want of foresight in suffering that prince, at a time when their strenuous opposition might easily have repressed the growth of his dangerous strength, to renew in his person the alarming ascendancy which his father had acquired over the independence of Italy. The chiefs of the Guelf party, indeed, seem to merit exemption from the reproach of this blindness; for they endeavoured, in 1419, to persuade their republic to afford assistance to Genoa in her struggle against the duke of Milan, and to reject the pacific overtures of Filippo Maria. But the people were not anxious for war; they accused the Guelf aristocracy of restless ambition; and they obliged their rulers to conclude a formal peace with the duke, with whom their state had continued nominally at war ever since the death of his father. By this treaty the Florentines and the duke bound themselves respectively, the former to abstain from interference in the affairs of Lombardy, the other in those of Romagna and Tuscany.

This condition was but imperfectly observed by the duke of Milan from the first moment of its enactment; and he had no sooner firmly planted his throne over Lombardy, than he openly evinced his contempt for his engagement by interfering in the concerns of Bologna. That city, after asserting her freedom during the distractions of the schism, had then passed under the absolute sway of Antonio Galeazzo Bentivoglio, the son of her first tyrant of that name whom she had overthrown; and she had lastly been delivered from the yoke of Antonio, to fall under the papal government. The legate, who commanded in Bologna for the pope, solicited the aid of the duke of Milan in expelling the Bentivogli from their rural fiefs in Romagna; and Filippo Maria not only sent his troops for the purpose into the province, but at the same time, in concert with a Ghibelin party at Forli, seized and garrisoned that lordship. These aggressions were in themselves declarations of war; and the Florentines immediately commenced reprisals, (A.D. 1424.) But they began the hostilities which were thus kindled in Romagna under discouraging and adverse circumstances. The celebrated condottiere, Braccio di Montone, who had formed a principality for himself about Perugia, and was bound by subsidies to serve the Florentines at need with his bands, just at this epoch lost his acquisitions and his life, in a battle against an army which the pope and the sovereigns of Milan and Naples directed against him. The Florentines had fully relied upon him for a general and an army; but the ten of war were now compelled to take various other captains with their bands into pay, and to engage Carlo Malatesta, signer of Rimini, in the supreme command of their forces. But the troops of Milan were every where successful: in the first campaign they surprised the lord of Imola, the ally of Florence, in his city, and afterwards completely routed the Florentine army and made Malatesta himself prisoner near the castle of Zagonara; and in the second year they inflicted on the republic four consecutive defeats, each of which dispersed an army. (A.D. 1425.) To this train of disasters the Florentines opposed that passive but obstinate and elastic courage, which was the enduring virtue of their state. Calmly collecting the wrecks of their mercenary bands, they for the seventh time equipped a new army; and, themselves remaining on the defensive, set in motion every art of negotiation to induce the emperor, the pope, and the Venetians, all of whom were interested in maintaining the equilibrium of Italy, to declare against the duke of Milan. But Sigismund had abundant occupation in Germany; and Martin V. bore a deadly hatred to Florence, for some petty ridicule which he had received from her populace during his residence in the city soon after his elevation to the tiara. It was in the community of interests or ambition between the Venetians and themselves that the Florentines found the alliance which they sought.

Since the commencement of the fifteenth century, the policy of the Venetian republic had taken a new direction. The recovery of the Trevisan March by the Milanese alliance, in her war against the lord of Padua in 1339, had restored to her the small Italian province which she had lost in the war of Chiozza; but it was not until the tempting occasion which was afforded by the offers of the Milanese regency after the death of Gian Galeazzo, that her senate began to indulge in schemes of continental dominion. By the ruin of the houses of Scala and Carrara, the republic came into the possession of a very considerable territory; and from this period a passion for extending her states by new conquests, and for mingling in the wars of Italy, began to prevail in her councils over the ancient policy of the senate:—neutrality in the peninsula, and the pursuit of commercial wealth and aggrandizement in the east. During the minority of the Milanese princes, indeed, her rulers made no attempt to advance her frontier farther into Lombardy; for their attention was occupied for several years with a dangerous war against the emperor Sigismund, which was produced by their purchase of the Dalmatian cities from Ladislaus of Naples. The republic had with difficulty maintained her Italian provinces against the assaults of the emperor, until his eagerness to pacify the church produced a truce. After this accommodation, a sanguinary war, in which Sigismund became engaged with the Bohemian reformers, not only relieved Venice from farther apprehension of his attacks, but enabled her to subjugate the country of Friuli and part of Istria. These provinces had for many centuries acknowledged the temporal sovereignty of the patriarchs of Aquileia; but the reigning prelate paid for his alliance with Sigismund by the loss of his states. The people of Udine, his capital, abandoned him to surrender to Venice; and the republic, by the acquisition of this new territory, secured her continental dominions, and held the passes from Germany into eastern Italy.

Yet the possession of these states on the main land of Italy proved a very questionable advantage to Venice. Since the war of Chiozza, she had recovered, by her purchase from Ladislaus, Zara and other cities on the Dalmatian coast which formerly belonged to her; her maritime colonies in Albania and the Morea had been successfully extended; and her commerce was immense. But after she had acquired a large territory in Italy, she neglected the care of her colonies and her navy, and the interests of her foreign trade,—the true foundations of her power—to engage in the troubled politics and wars of the peninsula. Thus she ruinously expended her resources, which might better have been employed in resisting the Turkish power and upholding her eastern dependencies; and she excited animosities against her in Europe, which were perpetually increasing during the whole of the fifteenth century, until they exploded in the league of Cambray.

When the ambassadors of Florence laboured to unite the Venetian senate in a league with their republic to chastise the ambition and perfidy of Filippo Maria, there were still not wanting in that grave assembly many cautious politicians, and among them the doge Tomaso Mocenigo, to inculcate an adherence to the ancient principles of their state, and the maintenance of neutrality. These pacific counsellors at first succeeded in dissuading the senate from hostilities; but shortly afterwards, on the death of Mocenigo, Francesco Foscari was placed in his chair; and the warlike temper of the new doge realized the dying warning of his predecessor, that his election would bring a contest upon the republic. The Florentines renewed their propositions; and they were now powerfully seconded by the man who had been most instrumental in elevating the pride of their enemy. Francesco Carmagnola had performed too important services for Filippo Maria, to escape the suspicion of so jealous a tyrant. The duke dreaded his popularity with the soldiery, his extraordinary talents, and the influence of the wealth and station which he had himself bestowed upon him. He gradually withdrew all confidence from him, he successively deprived him of his commands, he denied him admission to his presence; and Carmagnola at length indignantly quitted the Milanese dominions, breathing vengeance against his ungrateful master. He first repaired to the duke of Savoy, and revealing to that prince the projects which Filippo Maria had formed for the conquest of his possessions, excited him to arm for his defence. He then traversing Switzerland, to avoid the direct route through the Milanese states, arrived at Venice, and immediately applied himself to instigate the republic to attack Filippo Maria. The picture which he drew before the senate of the treacherous and restless character of the duke, of his secret machinations and dangerous schemes of aggrandizement, determined the wavering councils of the senate. A league was formed between Florence and Venice, by which the two republics bound themselves to maintain at their equal charge 16,000 cuirassiers and 8,000 infantry, and Florence resigned to her ally whatever conquests should be effected in Lombardy. The duke of Savoy, the people of Sienna, the marquis of Este, and the lord of Mantua, successively joined the formidable confederacy; and the allies solemnly declared war against the duke of Milan, (A.D. 1426.)

The operations which followed are interesting only in their results. Carmagnola gratified his revenge by leading the numerous mercenaries of Venice against his former master; victory still attended him; and notwithstanding the opposition of a large Milanese army, under some of the ablest condottieri of the times, he reduced the city of Brescia with its territory in a single campaign. Filippo Maria was seized with a panic at these sudden reverses; and accepting the mediation of the pope, he concluded a peace with his enemies before the close of the year, by which he yielded the conquests of Carmagnola to the Venetians. But he had scarcely signed the treaty when he repented of its terms; his subjects felt the honour of their state put to shame by his concessions; and he was roused by their discontent to resume the struggle in the following year. (A.D. 1427.) Still no better success attended his arms; and Carmagnola advanced to form the siege of Cremona. Around this place—so much had the numerical force of the mercenary armies employed in these Italian wars now increased—nearly seventy thousand combatants were assembled, of whom one half were cavalry; and Filippo Maria for once thought it necessary to encourage his troops by his transient presence. No decisive engagement however occurred at the moment; but, before the end of the campaign, Carmagnola inflicted so complete a route upon the Milanese army, near the village of Macalo upon the Oglio, that 8,000 cuirassiers were made prisoners. This encounter was characterized by some circumstances peculiar to the times. Carmagnola had skilfully posted his army behind a morass, the surface of which, from the dryness of the season, was capable of bearing the weight of infantry. He irritated the enemy to attack him by capturing Macalo before their eyes; but their heavy cavalry had no sooner charged along the causeway intersecting the marshy ground, which he purposely left unguarded, than his infantry assailed them with missiles on both flanks. In attempting to repulse them the Milanese cuirassiers sank into the morass; their column was crowded on the narrow passage, and thrown into confusion; and the infantry of Carmagnola, then venturing among them on the causeway, and stabbing their horses, made prisoners of the dismounted cuirassiers as they lay helpless under the enormous weight of their own impervious armour. We are assured that not a single human life was lost in this encounter; and when the Venetian commissaries on the following morning claimed the numerous prisoners, only a few hundreds were produced. The mercenaries, though ranged under opposite standards, always regarded each other rather as comrades than enemies; the conquerors had released almost all their disarmed captives during the night; and Carmagnola himself gave liberty to the remainder.

After this victory, which Carmagnola was accused by the Venetians of neglecting to improve, all parties except Venice became weary of the burthens of the war (A.D. 1428); and in the following year that republic unwillingly consented to a peace, by which she obtained the cession of Bergamo, and part of the country to the banks of the Adda, in addition to her former conquests; none of her allies obtained any material advantage. The short interval of repose which this pacification afforded to Italy, was broken by the vengeance of Florence for some assistance which the signor of Lucca had given to the duke of Milan. Notwithstanding the state of exhaustion to which the late contests had reduced the resources of the republic, the war against Paolo Guinigi was unanimously resolved upon in her councils, and carried to the gates of Lucca. Guinigi, losing the hope of preserving his power against the assaults of the Florentines, had already entered into a treaty to sell his signiory to them, when the discovery of his negotiation drove his subjects to a successful revolt, (A.D. 1430.) Lucca once more revived as a republic; but Florence refused to grant peace to the state whose tyrant alone she had professed to attack; and a defeat which her army sustained failed in reducing her to moderation. On the contrary, she excited the ambition of the Venetians to a third war against the duke of Milan, who had indirectly assisted the Lucchese; and that republic, in the hope of adding Cremona to her acquisitions, accepted the proposals of Florence, (A.D. 1431.) But in this new contest, the fortune of Carmagnola appeared to have deserted him. He was surprised and defeated; and a fleet of Venetian galleys having ascended the Po to co-operate with him, was soon after attacked and destroyed in his presence by an armament, which Filippo Maria equipped in the same river and manned with Genoese sailors.

The subsequent inactivity to which Carmagnola was reduced by a contagious disorder among his horses, increased the depression of the Venetians; and strengthened the suspicions which they had begun to entertain of the fidelity of their great general, ever since his release of his prisoners after the battle of Macalo. The council of ten had for some time determined on his destruction. He was invited to Venice to confer with the senate on the restoration of peace, and welcomed, both on his route and when he arrived at the capital, with studied and flattering honours. He was introduced into the ducal palace; but his suite were advised to retire, as he would be detained in long conference with the doge and the assembled senate, and it was already late in the day. As soon as the palace was cleared of his attendants, the gates were closed; he was then told that the doge was indisposed, and could not see him until the next morning; and as he crossed the palace court to withdraw, he was suddenly seized. A door which led to his destined prison was opened, and he had only time to exclaim that he was lost, when he was hurled down into his dungeon. A few days afterwards he was put to the torture; and during his sufferings, which were aggravated by a wound received in the service of this detestable oligarchy, a confession of guilt is said to have been extorted from him. No proof, however, was ever adduced against him; and he was conveyed to public execution with a gag over his mouth, as if his murderers could thus stifle the reproach of their enormous ingratitude. He was beheaded between the two pillars which stand before the place of St. Mark. (A.D. 1432.)

After the cruel fate of this illustrious captain, the general war languished during another year, when by the common exhaustion of all parties a new peace was at length concluded at Ferrara. (A.D. 1433.) Lucca remained free; the conquests made since the last pacification were mutually restored; and Filippo Maria conceded to the Florentines the renunciation of his alliances in Tuscany and Romagna. Venice alone retained the acquisitions for which she had been indebted to the valour and ability of Carmagnola. She was now mistress of nine contiguous and valuable provinces in northern Italy: the Dagado—her original territory, a narrow slip of country which skirted the lagunes—the March of Treviso, and the districts of Friuli, Padua, Rovigo, Vicenza, Verona, Bergamo, and Brescia. These territories stretched across Lombardy to the river Adda, beyond which it was fated that the possessions of Venice should, from this period, receive no farther extension.

Before we pursue the course of events further in northern Italy, I must carry the reader back a few years to revert to the history of the southern parts of the peninsula. On the death of Ladislaus, king of Naples, his sister Joanna, as he left no children, had ascended the throne of his kingdom. This princess, who, since the death of her husband, a son of the duke of Austria, had returned to Naples, and who, at the period of her accession to the crown, had already reached her forty-fifth year, was devoid of all mental energy and talent, and the slave of sensual appetites, which seemed to strengthen in intensity as her advancing age increased the shame of indulgence. Throughout her reign she was surrounded by unworthy favourites, in the choice of whom she was determined solely by their personal attractions. Her first minion was Pandolfello Alopo, a young man of five-and-twenty, of low birth, and with the solitary recommendation of a handsome person. The queen lavished honours and power on him; she created him a count and her chamberlain; but his influence could not prevent her from forming a matrimonial alliance, which was importunately pressed upon her by the people, and which she herself felt necessary to the support of her throne. Notwithstanding her notorious dissoluteness, several princes eagerly sought her hand, and she selected from among them James of Bourbon, count of La Marche, with the condition that he should not aspire to the royal dignity. But James was designing and severe; and he had no sooner entered the Neapolitan dominions, than by the support of the nobility, who detested the upstart favourite of Joanna, he assumed the title of king. He was resolved to reign in effect, and to reform the licentious court of the queen; and after celebrating his marriage with her, he immediately caused her minion to be arrested, tortured, and put to a cruel and ignominious death. The confession of the queen's weakness, which was extorted from Pandolfello, was made by James of Bourbon the pretext for subjecting her to a rigid state of durance within her palace; and he seized all the powers of state, and confided them wholly to his French followers.

This severity and preference of foreigners produced their ordinary effects upon the capricious and passionate Neapolitans. The exclusive authority usurped by the French had become generally odious, when the people were strongly excited to indignation and pity by the dejected and careworn appearance of their queen, who, after a year of seclusion, was at last permitted by her husband to be present at an entertainment given to her by a Florentine merchant. The nobles immediately invited the populace to seize the opportunity of delivering their sovereign; the call to arms was eagerly obeyed; and Joanna was rescued from her guards, and conveyed in triumph to one of the royal palaces, (A.D. 1416.) Her husband attempted to take refuge in one of the fortresses of the capital, but he was compelled to submit to the queen; and, after this revolution, Joanna retained him a prisoner for three years, before she was induced by the solicitations of the pope to release him. But the count De La Marche still found himself kept in dependence in her palace; he seized the first occasion of escaping from the capital, and after vainly endeavouring to excite an insurrection in the provinces, he returned to France, and buried his disgust of the world in a Franciscan convent.

Meanwhile Joanna, who could never preserve her freedom from the ascendancy of some favourite, had made the first use of her recovered power to elevate a new minion, Ser Gianni Caraccioli, to the control over her affections which Alopo had formerly enjoyed. Caraccioli however, besides the qualities which rendered him the favoured lover of Joanna, had more prudence than his predecessor, and contrived to gain the good-will of the nobles and people, while he governed in the palace of the queen with despotic sway. The only person who aspired to rival him in authority over the nation, and in the favour of the queen, was the famous condottiere Sforza Attendolo, who had continued in the service of Ladislaus until the death of that monarch, and had been created by him great constable. First treacherously imprisoned by Alopo, and then released by him on the approach of the count De La Marche to confederate against that prince, Sforza had been thrown into chains by James of Bourbon, and narrowly escaped the fate of his associate. The revolution which restored Joanna to power had liberated Sforza also, and reestablished him in his dignity of great constable; and from this period the possession of sovereign influence in the state was disputed between this ambitious captain and Caraccioli. The desire of the feeble queen to rid her favourite of the troublesome opposition of Sforza, gave a new character to the affairs of her kingdom, and connected them in some measure with those of the pontificate.

I have already observed in another place, that the celebrated leader, Braccio di Montone, formed a principality for himself about Perugia. It was amidst the distractions of the papal dominions during the council of Constance, and on the fall of the Neapolitan power immediately after the death of Ladislaus, that this extraordinary man commenced his career of greatness. Himself a noble exile of Perugia, he succeeded, attended by the rest of his banished order, and at the head of veteran bands of adventurers who were devoted to his service, in subjugating his native city after an obstinate resistance. But when he had thus violently established his dominion over Perugia, he at once gained the affections of his subjects by all the qualities of a good sovereign, and attached the people, who passed for the bravest in Italy, to his personal glory by the martial splendour with which he invested their little state. After otherwise extending his possessions, he at last marched against Rome. (A.D. 1417.) On the death of Ladislaus, the ecclesiastical capital had revolted in the name of the pope; but the council of Constance left her almost without a legitimate object of obedience, and Braccio easily took possession of her government with the title of defender of Rome. But he had provoked the hatred of a powerful rival by attacking, during the captivity of Sforza, some fiefs in the patrimony of St. Peter, which

Ladislaus had bestowed upon that general; and Sforza, enraged at this ungenerous conduct from one who had been his ancient companion in arms, eagerly fell into the views of Joanna for his removal from Naples, by leading his own bands, and the forces of the kingdom at her command, against Braccio. He obliged that chieftain by his superior numbers to evacuate Rome; he obeyed the orders of the queen by placing the legate of Martin V. in possession both of that capital, and of the conquests of Ladislaus in the ecclesiastical states; and he passed, by her desire, into the papal service with the army he commanded. In return for these good offices of Joanna, the pope sent two cardinals to Naples to perform, in his name, the ceremony of her coronation; and the queen had besides gained her object in delivering her favourite and herself from the presence of Sforza. That general was now appointed gonfalonier of the church, and prepared to pursue his revenge on Braccio di Montone. He led his troops against his rival to strip him of his principality; but he had to do with a superior genius in the military art. Braccio drew him among the defiles of Romagna, and so completely defeated him, that Sforza, after the capture of about two thousand of his cuirassiers, with difficulty effected his escape to the gates of Viterbo.

The quarrel of Sforza Attendolo and Braccio di Montone had one remarkable consequence. Both these great captains had been educated to arms in the company of St. George, under Alberic di Barbiano; and in their youth they had been sincerely united in the bonds of friendship. But ambition had now severed them; and so great, and so nearly equal was their military character, that the veterans of the school of St. George ranged themselves into opposite factions under their respective banners. This martial rivalry was continued long after the death of the great leaders in whose struggle of fame and ambition it had commenced; it was maintained by the distinguished captains who were formed in their service; and, for above twenty years, the bands, which they had originally created, were almost always arrayed on opposite sides in the wars of the peninsula. Sforza was bred a simple peasant in the village of Cotignola; and though he was invested with considerable fiefs, and with the dignity of great constable in the Neapolitan states, he scarcely rose, to the period of his death, above the doubtful condition of an adventurer. In nobility of birth, in the splendour of his fortunes, and perhaps even in the qualities of command, the personal reputation of Braccio was on the whole superior to that of Sforza; but the greatness of the Perugian signor expired with himself, and the peasant of Cotignola was the ancestor of a ducal dynasty.

On the defeat which Sforza had sustained in his expedition against Braccio, Martin V. applied to the queen of Naples for the means of remounting the army of her great constable. But Caraccioli, who had learnt with joy the discomfiture of Sforza, prevented his mistress from complying with the demand of the pope; and Martin, irritated at her refusal, and disappointed of some hopes which he had entertained that she would adopt his nephew for her heir, shared the indignation of Sforza against the favourite and herself. Their common vengeance prepared a long train of evils for the kingdom of Naples. The nobility of that country were weary of the influence of Caraccioli; Joanna at an advanced age remained without heirs; and circumstances conspired in favouring the dormant pretensions of the house of Anjou to the Neapolitan crown. Secretly encouraging Louis III., the grandson of the adopted heir of the first Joanna, to assert his right of succession to her dominions, the pope reconciled himself with Braccio of Montone; and Sforza, his forces recruited by the subsidies of the Angevin prince, led his army into the Neapolitan states, (A.D. 1420.) When he approached the capital, he sent his baton of command to Joanna, in token of the renunciation of his allegiance; and Louis of Anjou, arriving shortly afterwards from Provence, and disembarking his followers near Naples, joined him at Aversa, and straitened the queen in her residence.

In the critical situation in which Joanna was placed by this invasion, there appeared to herself, or her favourite, no other means of defence than by rendering the reversion of her kingdom the price of foreign assistance. Alfonso, king of Aragon and Sicily, was at this epoch engaged in attempting the conquest of the island of Corsica from the

Genoese; and he was easily tempted to abandon this enterprise by the hope of adding the inheritance of Naples to his possessions, and thus terminating the long separation of the two Sicilies. I have formerly observed that the island of Sicily was, at the close of the fourteenth century, possessed by Martin, son of the king of Aragon, who had married its queen Maria. This union produced no offspring; and on the death of Martin (who had survived his wife) in 1409, his father was suffered to unite Sicily to his crown. Alfonso, by collateral descent, had succeeded to the Aragonese dominions in 1416; and this prince, who was endowed with many brilliant qualities, was now adopted by Joanna as her heir, and shortly dispatched an armament to her aid. His fleet compelled the inferior squadron of Anjou to retire; Louis and Sforza, who were besieging Naples, could not prevent the debarkation of the Aragonese forces; and the fortresses of the capital were consigned to their charge. The war which was thus kindled by the rival pretensions of Aragon and Anjou, was animated in the succeeding year by the presence of Alfonso, and by the entrance into the kingdom of Braccio di Montone, who, attended by his followers, was taken into the service of Joanna, with the title of great constable and prince of Capua, (A.D. 1421.) The contest plunged the state in frightful anarchy, for the nobility, as usual, ranged themselves on opposite sides; but no action of importance was fought. Louis of Anjou was himself without funds to support the army of Sforza, and withdrew to Rome; the pope was weary of contributing to his necessities; and the cause of Alfonso appeared to have gained a decided ascendancy, when a new intrigue in the palace of Joanna, suddenly gave a total change to the posture of affairs.

It appears uncertain whether Alfonso, after delivering Joanna from her enemies, and being publicly recognised as her destined successor, really meditated the anticipation of this inheritance, or was merely unable to brook the insolence of Caraccioli, and resolved to render himself independent of him. But his increasing power, and the occupation of the fortresses of the kingdom by his troops, excited the suspicion and fear of the favourite, who dreaded to receive from his hands the same summary treatment which his predecessor in the queen's affections had experienced from the count De La Marche. He instilled his own apprehensions and jealousy of Alfonso into Joanna; her distrust of her adopted son, which was perceived and returned, daily increased; and she began secretly to negotiate with the Angevin prince who pretended to her crown. By the intervention of the pope, Louis resigned the possession of the places which he held in her kingdom, and Sforza was once more received into the service of the queen. The restoration of this great captain to her favour was attended with a trait of generosity foreign to the perfidious spirit of the age. When Louis of Anjou retired to Rome, Sforza, reduced to the extremity of poverty and distress, suddenly trusted himself with a few unarmed cavaliers in the camp of Braccio, and frankly solicited his rival to aid him by his advice and credit with the queen in re-establishing his fortunes. Braccio was worthy of this reliance on his faith; and the short-lived reconciliation of the two captains was followed by perfect confidence between them. They discussed their respective conduct of past campaigns against each other, as if they had only been engaged in an amicable contest of skill; and it was through the good offices of Braccio, who wished to return to his own principality, that Sforza was re-established in the favour of Joanna. He was not now the less agreeable to the queen and her lover that he favoured the Angevin interest. The mutual animosity between Joanna and Alfonso had already attained such a height that they fortified themselves in different palaces in the capital, and at length an open rupture ensued. Alfonso seized the person of Caraccioli, notwithstanding a safe conduct by which he had induced him to repair to his palace; he besieged Joanna herself in her fortress; and the queen was compelled to summon Sforza, whose troops were quartered in Campania, to her deliverance, (A.D. 1423.) He immediately marched at her command, and encountering the Aragonese troops who obstructed his approach, succeeded, after an obstinate engagement, in annihilating their force. All their captains fell into his hands, and the queen thought the liberty of her minion cheaply purchased in exchange for them.

The deliverance of Joanna and Caraccioli was immediately followed by the queen's revocation of her adoption of Alfonso, and the substitution of Louis III. of Anjou for her heir. When Alfonso found the Angevin faction thus united against him with the party of the queen, by which he had hitherto been supported, he was not long able to maintain his ground in the kingdom; and after vainly endeavouring to induce Braccio di Montone, who was otherwise occupied, to arrive to his support, he yielded before the superior strength of Sforza, and having himself quitted Naples for Aragon, where he was summoned by the affairs of that kingdom, his troops were shortly driven from all the possessions which they held, except one of the castles, of the capital, (A.D. 1424.)

The epoch of the re-establishment of peace in the Neapolitan dominions was marked by the death of the two great rival condottieri. Braccio di Montone, desiring to reduce under his authority the Abruzzos, the government of which Joanna had bestowed upon him, had marched into the province, and laid siege to its capital, Aquila. The people of this city had shut their gates upon him, and resolutely defended themselves. Martin V., who beheld with alarm his increasing power encircling and overawing the states of the church, had induced Joanna to revoke her commission to him, and to promise protection to the besieged; and Sforza, on the departure of Alfonso from Naples, was dispatched to their relief. The rival chiefs were destined to meet in combat no more. Sforza, on arriving at the mouth of the river Pescara, found a body of the enemy posted on the opposite bank. He crossed over with a part of his cavalry and dislodged them; the sea was rising, and he returned to induce the remaining gens-d'armerie to try the dangerous passage; but in attempting to save a page who was canned down the stream, his own horse unfortunately lost his footing, and the hero himself sank into the current. His armour prevented him from swimming; twice his hands appeared above the waves, covered with their iron gauntlets, and vainly clasped in supplication for aid; he was borne down into the ocean, and his corpse was never recovered. It was at this trying moment that Francesco, the celebrated son of Sforza, in the midst of his grief for the loss of his father, displayed all the talent and presence of mind which distinguished him throughout his brilliant career. Though the youngest of his father's captains, he adroitly succeeded in inducing the whole of his fellow-adventurers to take an oath of fidelity to his personal fortunes; and this object accomplished, he easily obtained from Joanna the confirmation of the titles and fiefs of his parent.

Braccio di Montone, forgetting the long enmity of Sforza, and the hostile expedition against himself in which he had lost his life, sincerely deplored his fate. Since his rival could no longer encounter him, it seemed time that he should himself quit the lists, and superstition might anticipate the approach of his own course to its close. The heroes of the fifteenth century were the dupes of judicial astrology; it had been foretold that rivers boded danger to Sforza, and that Braccio should not long survive the death of his opponent; and the accomplishment of the first prediction gave weight to the second. Yet Braccio prepared to encounter the troops of Joanna, of the pope, and of the duke of Milan, with his accustomed courage and skill. Their immense superiority of numbers overwhelmed him; he was defeated, as I have formerly noticed, wounded, and captured. His hurt was not mortal, but his proud spirit rejected all consolation or aid; he never spoke after he was made a prisoner, he refused all sustenance, and in three days after his defeat he expired. His death immediately destroyed the principality which he had formed; but the remains of his bands rallied under Niccolo Piccinino, the ablest of his captains, and passed at first into the service of Florence.

After Alfonso of Aragon and Sicily renounced the contest in southern Italy, Joanna reigned peacefully for about ten years, nor does this long period offer any object worthy of attention. Louis III., acknowledged as her undoubted heir, was satisfied to reside in Calabria, which she assigned to him as a sort of appanage, and where his mild virtues won him the affection of the people. Meanwhile Joanna abandoned herself and her kingdom, without restraint, to the power of Caraccioli; and even when she had passed her sixtieth year she continued, from long habit, to yield to this favourite his original ascendancy over her mind. Caraccioli, however, tyrannized over her feeble spirit even beyond the endurance of womanly love and doating infatuation; and he at length drove her to seek refuge from his imperious humour in the confidence of one of her own sex. This new favourite, the duchess of Suessa, watched the moment when the reproaches of Caraccioli, at the refusal of Joanna to some unreasonable demand, had left her in tears. By her arts she inflamed the weakness of the imbecile old queen to anger against Caraccioli, awakened her apprehensions of his designs, and induced her to permit his arrest. His enemies assassinated him, and obtained an amnesty from the queen, under pretence that he had fallen in resisting the royal order, (A.D. 1432.) This tragedy in the palace of Joanna at first revived the hopes of Alfonso of Aragon, with whom, indeed, Caraccioli himself had lately begun to resume the negotiations of former years. The king now actively pushed his interest with the duchess of Suessa, and by her aid had even obtained from Joanna a secret revocation of her adoption of Louis of Anjou, when he marred his plans by securing the interest of the husband of the duchess, who was detested by his wife. No further steps were taken in favour of Alfonso; and Joanna, on the sudden death of the duke of Anjou, without children, even adopted his brother Regnier. This was her last act, for she died herself shortly after Louis, in her sixty-fifth year, utterly worn out in mind and body, rather by the effects of a life of debauchery than by the usual advances of old age. (A.D. 1435.)

Since the defeat of the Ciompi, and the final establishment, in 1382, of the Guelf oligarchy, under the direction of the house of Albizzi, in sovereign influence over the government of the state, I have scarcely had occasion for notice of the domestic affairs of Florence. But the epoch before us produced a memorable revolution in the republic, which was destined to affect the whole course of her subsequent fortunes. For nearly half a century the triumphant party had swayed her councils with remarkable success abroad, and with few and unimportant interruptions to tranquillity at home. In this period Pisa, Arezzo, Cortona, and other places of inferior note, had passed, either by violence or by the silent progress of dependence as subject allies, under the dominion of the republic; her possessions extended over the half of Tuscany; and the acquisition of the maritime territory of Pisa, and especially of the port of Leghorn, gave a secure and convenient outlet for her foreign commerce. Her manufactures and trade had never been so flourishing; her wealth had increased so prodigiously that her circulating money alone, if its amount has not been exaggerated, exceeded four millions of florins—about two millions sterling; and the superabundance of her riches was elegantly expended in superb architectural embellishment and in the successful cultivation of letters.

As long after the sedition of the Ciompi as the terror endured, with which the memory of that appalling insurrection of the dregs of the populace had filled all the respectable citizens of Florence, the Guelf aristocracy were strongly supported in their proceedings against the democratical party. Their enemies were successively banished; the spirit of the populace and lower citizens had been crushed by defeat; and the Albizzi and the great commoners, their associates, remained the sovereign citizens of the state. The government of this oligarchy was exercised in a very peculiar manner.

Their names did not frequently enter into the lists of gonfaloniers and priors, for, by the mixture of popular election and lottery by which the offices of magistracy were filled, the same persons could only come in by rotation once in two years. But whenever foreign danger threatened the state and the ten of war were to be nominated, the chiefs of the Albizzi were certain to form the majority of that important executive council; and though they did not otherwise appear ostensibly as the rulers of the state, they were generally able, at the biennial replenishing of the bags out of which the names of citizens to hold office were taken, to exclude from election on the new lists all persons hostile to their faction. When this political artifice, this unjust exclusion under the sanction of constitutional forms, failed in effecting the objects of the oligarchy, they did not scruple to have recourse to more open violations of the rights of their opponents. At two different periods—in 1393, when they were alarmed by a conspiracy, and again in 1411—they assembled the parliament of the people, ever disposed to side with the strongest faction; they intimidated the unorganized multitude by their armed adherents; and they obtained the nomination of a temporary dictatorship or *balia*. This was a supreme council of large numbers, into which the oligarchy of course carefully provided that none should be elected but their own partizans. The balia, during the period to which its existence was limited, had the power of naming all magistrates without the process of the lottery, and of banishing suspected persons. It is in the nature of an oligarchy to narrow and restrict the exercise of popular rights; and the ruling faction of Florence were disposed to follow up their second suspension of the constitution, by the establishment of a permanent council of their party, with the right of the initiative voice in every legislative enactment. Thus, if the predominance of their influence had continued, the party of the Albizzi, or Guelf society, from their increasing suspicion and fear of the people, would gradually have deprived them by successive innovations of all share in the government; and would have finished by subjecting the state to an hereditary aristocracy as exclusive, if not as severe and tyrannical, as that of Venice.

The prosperity which Florence had now enjoyed for half a century under the government of the Guelf oligarchy, was principally attributable to the talents and moderation of its leaders. From the fall of the democratical party in 1382, to his own death in 1417, Maso degl' Albizzi was the chief of his house and faction, and the real mover of the republic. He was a profound and vigorous politician, but was just and temperate in personal character. He was surrounded too by friends who were worthy of him; and when he died, Nicola di Uzzano, a man of very similar qualities, undertook the guidance of affairs until Rinaldo degl' Albizzi, the youthful son of Maso, should attain age and experience to occupy the station of his father. As long as Nicola lived, the loss of Maso was supplied to his party and to the state, for both these friends were disposed alike to uphold constitutional liberty: as far at least as was possible consistently with the supremacy of their faction in the republic. But when the oligarchy were deprived by death of the latter of these venerable chiefs, and Rinaldo degl' Albizzi was left alone at the head of his party, the rash and impetuous character of this young leader both disqualified him from the equable government of the state, and yet more from the management of a dangerous struggle with the democratical party, which it was perhaps no longer possible to avoid. (A.D. 1433.)

It was one consequence of the riches which had poured into Florence under the administration of the Albizzi, that the children of many of those who, in the sedition of the Ciompi, had been numbered with the lowest populace, had now risen to wealth and respectability, and indignantly found themselves excluded from political rights. They were easily led to attach themselves to those great families who had formerly advocated the cause of the people; the ancient nobility, too, who had been excluded from the administration of affairs by both factions, united in preference with that which was now oppressed like themselves; and dissensions among the Albizzi had even gradually thrown many of their number into the arms of the same party. The democratical faction had thus altogether become equal to the oligarchy in the wealth, birth, and talents of its adherents, and infinitely superior to that body in numerical strength. But one family, in particular, by the accumulation of its vast commercial wealth, by the mild and cautious demeanour of its chiefs, by their graceful virtues, their humane liberality and princely magnificence, had silently gained the general respect and affection of this party, and now engrossed its absolute direction. This was the celebrated house of the Medici.

The Medici had long ranked at Florence among the principal families of the popolani grandi; and in tracing the foreign and domestic history of the republic during the fourteenth century, I have more than once found occasion to mention their name. In the struggle against the Guelf oligarchy which immediately preceded and followed the insurrection of the Ciompi, Salvestro de' Medici was one of the leaders of the popular faction. Though, owing probably to the moderation of his conduct, he escaped the sentences of death or exile which fell upon his associates, his family were afterwards excluded by the ruling oligarchy from power; and they came from this epoch to be looked upon, throughout the lengthened oppression of the democratical party, as the only stay and support which proscription had left to the popular cause. At the beginning of the fifteenth century, Giovanni de' Ricci, who was only distantly related to Salvestro, was the most distinguished individual of the Medici. During their political reverses, his family had continued the diligent and successful pursuit of commerce; and Giovanni had amassed immense riches, which were graced by an unblemished reputation for commercial integrity. So extensive and honourable were the connexions of his house, that he was known over all Europe as one of the greatest merchants of the age; and his eminence at Florence was supported by his ability, his amiable disposition, and his generous virtues. His evident disinclination to trouble the government of the state, won him the esteem of his political opponents, although he firmly resisted some new encroachments which they attempted upon the rights of the people; and it may be received as a circumstance creditable both to himself and to the liberality of the Albizzi, that we find him several times called to the highest offices of the state, and among them to a seat in the council of the ten of war: an honour which was also bestowed upon his son Cosmo.

The wealth and influence of the Medici were already established; the moderation of Giovanni could not be expected to descend to his heirs. His son Cosmo, who succeeded on his death to his riches and station, inherited his noble and generous qualities, and far surpassed him in talent. But under the veil of prudence, Cosmo concealed an ambition from which his father had been free. The consideration in which he was held by the Venetian republic, his intimacy with Francesco Sforza and other distinguished characters of the peninsula, and the numerous private friends and adherents whom he had acquired by his magnificent generosity in Florence itself, all conspired to render him the first citizen of the republic. He became decidedly the leader of the democratical faction, and in concert with his partizans, began openly to expose the errors of the administration in the conduct of the war against Lucca, the ill success of which had increased the unpopularity of the Albizzi. (A.D. 1430.) The oligarchy were now utterly inferior to their enemies in strength; and yet Rinaldo degl' Albizzi was no sooner left to guide his party without the control of Uzzano, than his impetuosity hastened the crisis of a struggle which, whenever it arrived, could not prove otherwise than ruinous to his faction. The rotation of the lottery gave a gonfalonier and priors to the state who were devoted to the Albizzi, and Rinaldo instigated this signiory to summon Cosmo de' Medici before them, under the pretext that he had been guilty of some malversation in office during his magistracy in the council of war. (A.D. 1433.) Cosmo confiding in his innocence calmly presented himself; he was thrown into prison; and Rinaldo then caused the citizens to be assembled in parliament. His armed followers filled the avenues of the public place; the people were, as usual, intimidated; and a balia was formed of the friends of the Albizzi to deliberate on the fate of Cosmo. A timely bribe to the gonfalonier, or the timidity of the oligarchy, saved the chief of the Medici from an iniquitous sentence of death; but a decree was passed for his banishment for ten years with many of his friends.

Rinaldo, whose procedure had aimed at the life of Cosmo, had vainly goaded his own party to greater violence; the oligarchy now failed altogether in resolution or power. The partizans of Cosmo were not excluded from the new lists of magistracy; and, in about a year, a gonfalonier and priors, all of whom were known to be attached to the cause of the Medici, came by rotation into office. These magistrates retaliated upon the Albizzi the measures which they had adopted. The moderation of Cosmo, in submitting to the injustice of his enemies in preference to plunging his country into civil war, had gained him increased reputation. He had been received in his exile by the republic of Venice with distinguished honours. The first act of the new Florentine signiory, was to obtain the nomination of a balia composed entirely of his friends. By this body Rinaldo, with his whole party, after a fruitless attempt to resist, were banished from the city; and Cosmo was triumphantly recalled. The Guelf oligarchy was completely overthrown; and from this epoch to the close of a long and fortunate life, Cosmo de' Medici exercised a sovereign influence over the affairs of the republic. (A.D. 1434.)

The revolution which gave to Cosmo de' Medici the direction of the Florentine counsels made no change in the foreign relations of the republic. In the same year with his elevation to power, the duke of Milan violated the terms of the last peace of Ferrara, by interfering in a petty sedition in one of the towns of Romagna; and in the new war, by which Florence deemed it necessary to resent this act of bad faith, Venice was still her ally. After some uninteresting hostilities, peace was restored upon the same conditions as before; but the restless temper and incessant projects of Filippo Maria prevented all hope of permanent repose to neighbouring states. A circumstance which arose out of the disputed succession to the throne of Naples, soon involved the two republics in a fresh contest with him.

On the death of Joanna II., Alfonso of Aragon immediately made his claim upon her kingdom. This he primarily founded upon the right which had been transmitted to the house of Aragon by Constance, daughter of Manfred, and, in fact, he already reigned in Sicily as the nearest heir to the house of Swabia, and, through that royal line, to the Norman conquerors of southern Italy—the heroes of the dynasty of Guiscard. These brilliant pretensions were tarnished by the illegitimacy of Manfred, and invalidated by their frequent transmission in the female line from house to house; and although Alfonso laboured to strengthen them by asserting the adoption of Joanna, which he denied that she had possessed the power to revoke, he trusted with more reason to the weight of his arms. The Neapolitans were, for the most part, inclined to have obeyed the testament of Joanna in favour of Regnier of Anjou. But that prince was, unfortunately, at this critical moment for his interests, prisoner to the duke of Burgundy; and Alfonso, landing from Sicily in the Neapolitan states, had already won over many partizans, when a reverse befel him which seemed for ever to wither his hopes. He had laid siege to the city of Gaeta, where the Genoese possessed some commercial establishments, and kept a garrison by desire of the inhabitants. A fleet was fitted out at Genoa to relieve the place, and on the approach of this armament, the chivalrous spirit of Alfonso induced him personally to lead his Catalan sailors to the encounter, (A.D. 1435.) The two fleets met near the island of Ponza, and, notwithstanding the superior numbers of the Catalans and the presence of their king, the standard of Aragon drooped before the banner of St. George. After a long and gallant conflict, the Genoese were completely victorious; the royal galley of Aragon was compelled to strike; and the capture of Alfonso, with his brother and a splendid train of nobles, swelled the pride of the victors.

This naval victory, the most important and glorious that had for a long period been fought in the Mediterranean, produced consequences the most opposite from those which might have been anticipated. The duke of Milan, as sovereign of Genoa, with the design of depriving her of the enjoyment of her triumph, sent an order to her admiral to land the royal prisoner at Savona, from whence Alfonso was immediately conducted to the Milanese court. Filippo Maria, dark and faithless as was his character in many respects, had already proved upon more than one occasion, by his conduct to other prisoners of distinction who had fallen into his hands, that he was not incapable of a generous action. His reception of Alfonso was marked by the most delicate respect; his attentions invited easy converse; and then the graceful accomplishments of the captive monarch—his noble figure, his elegant manners, his classical and sparkling genius—completely charmed his gloomy host into confidence and friendship. Alfonso represented to the duke that the part which, in concert with the eternal hatred of the

Genoese towards the Catalans, he had hitherto taken against him and in favour of the cause of Anjou, was not the true policy for the sovereign of Lombardy; that the French were, of all the neighbours of Italy, the only people to be dreaded; and that, so far from assisting any dynasty of their nation in ascending the Neapolitan throne, the security of his dominions required that he should carefully close the Alps against the intrusion of these dangerous foreigners into the peninsula. Thus the king persuaded Filippo Maria, and with reason, that their mutual interests were clearly identified; he and his nobles were released without ransom and loaded with presents; and when he quitted the capital of the duke, into which he had been conducted a prisoner, a close and lasting alliance had been concluded between them. (A.D. 1436.)

To avoid the necessity of recurring again to the struggle for the Neapolitan crown, I shall in this place briefly relate the issue of the contest between the parties of Aragon and Anjou. On his release from Milan, Alfonso proceeded to Gaeta, which, by the good offices of Filippo Maria, had now declared its adherence to him. Meanwhile Isabella, wife of Regnier, a princess of great spirit, had arrived at Naples to sustain the rights of her captive lord. But she brought with her neither treasures nor soldiers, and though her virtues and prudence endeared her to the Angevin partizans, she supported with difficulty the unequal conflict against the king of Aragon. At the end of about three years, her husband, having effected his ransom, joined her. (A.D. 1438.) He, too, arrived at Naples without money or followers; and, to stay a falling cause, had only courage and generosity of character. These qualities could not prevent the defection of traitors and the selfish desertion of his alliance by the pope; and his possessions were gradually wrested from him, until the city of Naples alone remained in his interest. The people of that capital, however, were still faithful to him, and throughout a long siege were inspired by his presence to endure all the miseries of famine, until the troops of Alfonso entered their city by surprise through a deserted aqueduct. Regnier escaped, but perceiving the hopelessness of a farther struggle, he finally abandoned the kingdom to his rival, and thus left Alfonso to perfect the foundation of the Aragonese dynasty of the Two Sicilies, (A.D. 1442.)

The whole conduct of the duke of Milan, with respect to Alfonso, (to return from this anticipation of the Neapolitan annals,) had excited the greatest indignation at Genoa. Filippo Maria had deprived that capital of the glory of exhibiting a royal captive through her streets; he had afterwards released his prisoner without obtaining for the Genoese any advantage from their victory; and he had allied himself with their enemy. By several injurious actions, the duke had betrayed his suspicion and jealousy of his republican subjects, and his resolution to humiliate them; and their indignation and wounded pride at length burst forth in a furious insurrection. The Milanese garrisons were overpowered and expelled from all the Ligurian territory; and thus Genoa, recovering her liberty, rose again to the rank of an independent state, (A.D. 1435.)

The allied republics of Florence and Venice hailed the re-establishment of the Genoese freedom, as a new curb set upon the ambition of the Milanese duke. They immediately recognized the independence of Genoa, and received her into their alliance and protection, in violation of their existing treaty with the duke, by which they had acknowledged him for signor of that city. This it was which provoked a new war between the confederated republics and Milan. Inflamed with anger at their conduct, and inspired by Rinaldo degl' Albizzi and the Florentine exiles of his party, with the hope of exciting a new revolution in their state, Filippo Maria first made a secret but abortive attempt upon her territories, and afterwards proceeded to more open hostilities, (A.D. 1437.) On the first news that the troops of Milan had begun to act against Florence, Venice put her forces in motion to cause a diversion in favour of her ally, and thus the war was kindled both in Tuscany and Lombardy. I have no intention to trace with minuteness the fluctuating course of this struggle, which continued through several years. The details of the Italian campaigns of the fifteenth century are perhaps more totally devoid of interest, than the military operations of any other age of the world. The tardy movements of the heavy cavalry, of which armies were almost exclusively constituted, and whose advance was arrested by the slightest intrenchment; the feeble results of the hostilities in which such a force could engage; the perpetual treasons, the rapine, the inactivity, by which the condottieri ruined alike their employers and their enemies, and protracted every war in languid indecision; all these circumstances tend to divest the contests of that age of the slightest attraction: while their bloodless character provokes us to ridicule, and deprives the imagination even of the excitement of pity and horror, which the picture of human suffering and destruction might otherwise awaken. The reader will have little cause for regret if I pass over the particulars of these wars to notice only their consequences.

Upon some disagreement regarding the payment of subsidies to Francesco Sforza, which Venice refused, Florence in the second campaign concluded a separate peace with Milan (A.D. 1438); and the Venetians soon found themselves unequal to maintain a continental war unaided, against the whole power of Filippo Maria. Giovanni Francesco, marquis of Mantua, too, deserted their alliance for that of Visconti, and opening a passage to the Milanese troops through his territories into the Venetian provinces, joined them in overrunning the districts of Brescia and Verona. Piccinino, the general of the duke, formed the siege of Brescia, which was heroically defended against him by the Venetian garrison and the inhabitants, notwithstanding his superiority of force, and his numerous artillery. For we may remark as a proof of the increasing use of ordnance against fortresses, that the besiegers employed twenty-four pieces, of which fifteen were bombards, of such a calibre, as to throw stone balls of three hundred pounds' weight. The works of the place were ruined by their fire; and nothing but the fortunate accident by which part of the exterior wall crushed the assailants, instead of choking up the ditch by its fall as expected, saved the defenders. They repulsed the long and furious assault of the

Milanese; and Piccinino, after sustaining a heavy loss, converted the siege into a rigid blockade.

The danger of Brescia, and of all the continental possessions of Venice, awakened the alarm of Florence at the progress of the Milanese arms. Venice applied in her distress to her ancient ally, and a new confederacy was formed between the two republics, (A.D. 1439.) Francesco Sforza was taken with his bands into their joint pay, and placed at the head of their armies; and the talents of this general, and the formidable numbers of the forces ranged under his orders, soon restored the equilibrium of the struggle. On the other side Niccolo Piccinino, with the veteran soldiery of Braccio di Montone, was in the service of Filippo Maria, for whom he commanded in chief. The rival schools of condottieri therefore were ranged against each other, with the plains and defiles of eastern Lombardy for their theatre of combat. They had occupied this field with well balanced success for about three years, when a sudden intrigue of the duke of Milan put a period to the war, and raised Francesco Sforza on the first step of the throne which he was destined to ascend.

Shortly after the death of his father, Sforza had passed with his bands into the pay of Filippo Maria, and had continued to serve him with fidelity and reputation during his three first wars with Venice and Florence. After the conclusion of the third peace of Ferrara, he had led his formidable company into Romagna, and availing himself of the distractions into which the ecclesiastical states were thrown on the death of Martin V., had made an easy and rapid conquest of the March of Ancona and other territories. To purchase his aid against more detested enemies, the new pope, Eugenius IV., was compelled to confirm him in possession of the March, as a fief of the holy see; and, from that epoch, Sforza aspired above the trade of a mere condottiere, to establish himself as an independent prince. Besides his new conquests, he held his father's extensive fiefs in the kingdom of Naples; and he was the chosen leader of a numerous and brilliant gens-d'armerie. He was gifted with consummate political sagacity, and he saw all the splendid opportunities which the state of Italy opened to his ambition. Filippo Maria was without legitimate children, but he had a natural daughter, Bianca; and Sforza perceived the value which her pretensions might acquire, if upheld by the strong arm of a soldier of fortune. He had long obtained from Filippo Maria the promise of her hand; but the suspicious and irresolute duke had alternately retracted and repeated his pledge. While Filippo Maria thus trifled, Sforza strove to impress his future father-in-law, whose timid and faithless character he perfectly understood, with the importance of his alliance. He had therefore passed into the service of the republics against him: but to preserve the possibility of a reconciliation, he had evinced, even in his hostility, a repugnance to carry the war to extremities.

 This artful policy was crowned with success; and Filippo Maria, who was wearied of the war, and found himself oppressed by the insolent demands of his own condottieri, finally turned his eyes upon Sforza to deliver him from the subjection with which he was threatened by his generals. The aspiring and skilful adventurer was besieging the castle of Martinengo for the Venetians; the Milanese commanders had placed him in a very hazardous situation by intercepting his supplies, and shutting up his army between their intrenchments and the castle; and he was already anticipating the fatal moment when he should be starved into a surrender. At this dangerous crisis in his fortunes, he was surprised by a confidential message from Filippo Maria. He was chosen by the duke arbiter of a peace which all the belligerents equally desired; the treaty was signed on the spot; and the restoration of tranquillity was immediately followed by his marriage with Bianca Visconti; who, with youth, beauty, and the greater charm of an amiable mind, brought him for her dowry Cremona and its territory, (A.D. 1441.) By the peace of Martinengo, Filippo Maria acknowledged the freedom of Genoa; but the contending powers generally were established in their former possessions and rights.

 For several years after this pacification, the whole system of Italian politics was closely associated with the personal fortunes of Francesco

Sforza; and the league into which Eugenius IV. now entered for stripping him of his conquests in the ecclesiastical state invites our attention to the affairs of the papacy. Since the elevation of this pontiff to the chair of St. Peter, on the death of Martin V. in 1431, the church had been agitated by dissensions which threatened Europe with the revival of the great schism. By a decree passed at Constance, it had been provided that general councils should be convoked at regular intervals. Martin V. dreaded the repetition of such assemblies beyond the Alps; and he had therefore endeavoured to hold them in Italy, where he could more easily influence their deliberations. But the party in the church, whose object it was to reform the abuses of papal authority, as eagerly desired a transalpine congress; and Martin was compelled by the wishes of Europe to appoint the city of Basle for the seat of a future council. The period assigned for its convocation had arrived in the first year of the pontificate of Eugenius IV.; and after the pope, who anticipated the republican tone of its discussions, had vainly endeavoured to transfer its session to an Italian city, a long and obstinate contest arose between him and the assembled representatives of Christendom. In the course of this struggle, the council of Basle proceeded, in 1439, to the extremity of deposing Eugenius, and electing Amadeus, a retired duke of Savoy, to fill his chair. But their intemperate spirit disgusted the powers of Europe; their partizans gradually deserted them; and the schism which they had raised quietly expired, with no other consequence than to throw the plan of restraining the papal power by periodical councils into discredit and disuse.

    I pass lightly over the transactions at the council of Basle, for they have little connexion with our subject. The only influence of the dispute between Eugenius and that assembly, upon the affairs of Italy, was to increase the disorders into which the temporal dominions of the church were thrown by the violence and incapacity of the pope, Martin V. had recovered and left the papal states under the authority of the holy see; he had governed them with ability; and his care to aggrandize his family, the Colonna, was the greatest reproach which attached to his fame as a sovereign. But Eugenius IV. had no sooner succeeded him, than the perverse and vicious qualities of this pope produced new troubles and anarchy. Besides his contest with the council of Basle and the Hussites of Germany, he was at the same time, or in rapid succession, at war against the Colonna, against the citizens of Rome, against Sforza and other condottieri, against Alfonso of Aragon, and, in concert with Venice and Florence, against the duke of Milan. Over the Colonna he prevailed; but the people of Rome, who were driven by his exactions to revolt in 1438, compelled him to seek a refuge at Florence, and once more conjured up the fleeting image of a republic. By ceding the March of Ancona to Sforza, he procured the powerful aid of that chieftain against other invaders, and recovered great part of his remaining states; and after having first endeavoured by arms, on the death of Joanna II., to seize upon Naples as a lapsed fief of the holy see, and then seconded the partizans of Regnier against Alfonso, he shortly after the peace of Martinengo unscrupulously deserted the Angevin prince, to pursue a new scheme of ambition and treachery.

Although Eugenius IV. was indebted to Sforza for the recovery of his temporal dominion in Romagna, it had not been without the greatest reluctance that he was compelled to erect the March of Ancona into an independent fief for that great condottiere. Gratitude for the services of Sforza, who had faithfully fulfilled his engagement to him, was a feeling foreign to the selfish nature of this pope; and he now eagerly entered into a proposal for despoiling the general, whom he had created gonfalonier of the church, of all his possessions in the March. Sforza had yet more powerful enemies than Eugenius IV. In the affairs of Naples he had followed his father's politics, and continued his attachment to the house of Anjou; he was the declared partizan of Regnier; and Alfonso naturally returned his enmity. To pursue his plans more freely in northern Italy, Sforza had, however, concluded a truce with the Aragonese monarch for his fiefs in Campania and the Abruzzos; but Alfonso had, notwithstanding, treacherously taken advantage of his absence to attack these possessions. As soon as Sforza was liberated by the peace of Martinengo to direct his attention southward, he put his troops in motion to chastise the perfidy of Alfonso, to succour Regnier of Anjou—then in the height of his distress at Naples—and to defend his father's great fiefs in the kingdom. But the moment had arrived when it behoved him to look to his own safety alone. Alfonso, alarmed at his approach, sent pressing entreaties to his ally the duke of Milan, to dissuade his son-in-law from succouring Regnier; and Filippo Maria, who might have accomplished this object amicably by his personal influence, preferred to effect it through the ruin of his daughter's husband. Although he had bestowed the hand of Bianca upon Sforza, his capricious and jealous temper deterred him from reposing his confidence on so aspiring a son-in-law, and filled him, on the contrary, with hatred and suspicion of him. It shamed his pride that circumstances had reduced him to mingle the blood of the Visconti with that of a peasant; and he could see only in the hero Sforza an upstart to disgrace his dynasty as a successor, or to hurl him from his throne as a rival. On the application of Alfonso, he did not attempt to dissuade Sforza from his expedition against that monarch: but he dispatched Niccolo Piccinino with a formidable body of gens-d'armerie into Romagna; he wrote to Eugenius IV. that the time was come for his recovery of the March of Ancona; and he offered him the services of his general and his troops for the purpose. The pope was at once seduced by self-interest to accept the proposal; and it was for this that he basely sacrificed the man who had served him, that he deserted the Angevin prince whose cause he had espoused, and that he accomplished the ruin of Regnier by diverting the arms of Sforza to his own defence.

The valiant son of the peasant of Cotignola now found himself the devoted object of a hostile league, which embraced three of the greatest powers of Italy; the pope, the king of Naples, and the duke of Milan. Assailed as he was from all quarters, he defended the fortunes, to which his own and his father's adventurous courage and talents had raised him, with admirable spirit. He showed a front to his various enemies wherever they appeared, he repeatedly fought and defeated them in detail, his master-mind and his presence seemed to be given simultaneously to every point of danger. But his resources were too unequal to those of his oppressors, to render it possible for him to maintain so continued and adverse a struggle. He had full occasion to discover the difference between making war as a condottiere in the pay of others, and being reduced to defend his own possessions: and the progress of the war palpably betrayed the weakness of the little military monarchy which he had founded. The country was devoured by his own soldiery, and ravaged by the enemy: the contributions, by which he ruined his people, were still utterly insufficient to maintain his troops; and his subjects, bound to him by no hereditary affection or ties of honour and patriotism, every where revolted. In less than four years he was completely stripped of every fief in the Neapolitan territories, and of the whole of the March of Ancona. At one period, indeed, some remorse appeared to have seized Filippo Maria for his oppression of his son-in-law, and his interference arrested the fall of Sforza. (A.D. 1446.) But this interval of compunction was shortly succeeded by a new paroxysm of suspicion and enmity; and the duke was himself the mover of a new league against Sforza, which completed his spoliation. His enemies seemed resolved to leave him no spot whereon to repose his weary head. Alfonso and the pope had already wrested from him all that he had possessed in central and southern Italy; and the parent of his wife now endeavoured to perfect his ruin, and to seize upon his only remaining territory of Cremona, which he had himself assigned to him for the dowry of Bianca. But this attempt at length determined the republics of Florence and Venice to arm against Filippo Maria, and gave to Sforza, at least, the means of supporting his bands in employment.

The republics of Venice and Florence were not ignorant that the maintenance of the balance of Italy, against the alliance of the king of Naples and the duke of Milan, required that Sforza should be supported; and they were aware that even their own safety would be compromised by his destruction. Besides the very large sums which the personal friendship of Cosmo de' Medici contributed to the wants of Sforza from his private purse, the republics had from time to time assisted the general with considerable subsidies, and ineffectually employed their good offices in his behalf. But from one cause or other they had too long delayed to declare openly in his favour, until Filippo Maria, by his attack upon Cremona, violated the peace of Martinengo, which they had expressly guaranteed. They then armed with vigour, and war was again kindled in Lombardy. Besides dispatching succours to Sforza, who still hovered about the March of Ancona, the allied republics successfully undertook for him the relief of Cremona. At Casal Maggiore, between that city and Parma, the Venetian generalissimo gained so complete a victory over the Milanese forces, that all the country from the Adda to the Oglio, with its fortresses, at once submitted to the conqueror. The Venetian army even carried their ravages to the gates of Milan; and Filippo Maria, trembling within his capital, once more changed his inconstant politics. The war had been occasioned solely by his hatred of his son-in-law, and his determination to ruin him. Yet it was to Sforza himself that he now recurred for protection. He implored him to defend the destined inheritance of his wife against his own ally. It was far from the design of Sforza that the ambitious republic should wrest from Filippo Maria provinces which he hoped himself to possess; and he had already listened to the overtures of his father-in-law, when the Venetian senate, who suspected his fidelity, commissioned their general to surprise and occupy his city of Cremona. The attempt failed by the vigilance of the governor, and this abortive perfidy at once determined Sforza to accept the proposals of his father-in-law. He actively commenced preparations for opening the campaign in his cause; but the duke was still unable to divest himself of suspicious fear and jealous dislike of him. He wavered, and ordered him not to enter his dominions; and it was not until the enemy had penetrated within three miles of Milan, that he finally summoned him, without reservation, to his aid. Sforza immediately concentrated his army, and commenced his march from Romagna into Lombardy. He had just reached the village of Cotignola, from whence he derived his origin, when the intelligence was brought to him, that Filippo Maria, whose health had long been declining, had suddenly expired of dysentery, (A.D. 1447.)

The death of the duke Filippo Maria Visconti, the last sovereign of his house, seemed the commencement of a new era in the condition of Milan, and of all central Lombardy. The council of his ministers, which assembled immediately after his death, was agitated by different interests. Sforza was not without his partizans, who advocated the natural succession of the husband of Bianca to the states of her father; but the principal leaders of the school of Braccio, among whom the two sons of Niccolo Piccinino had now, since his death, acquired most influence, were adverse to the elevation of the chieftain of the rival military faction. They declared in the council against Sforza, and in favour of Alfonso, king of the Sicilies, in virtue of a real or pretended testament of the late duke; and their influence prevailed. A lieutenant of Alfonso, who had conducted a small auxiliary force into Lombardy, was admitted into the citadel and the castle of Milan, and the banner of his sovereign was displayed from their ramparts. But the nobles and principal citizens of Milan, who had so long been oppressed by a race of tyrants, were not disposed to bow their necks to a new yoke, at the will of a council of ministers. They called the people to arms, they barricaded the streets of the capital, and blockaded the citadel and castle. The citizens of Milan were then assembled in a general parliament; and a republican constitution was framed under a supreme executive council to be renewed, like that of Florence, every two months. The few troops of Alfonso, separated by many hundred miles from the armies of their monarch, were shortly terrified into a surrender of the fortresses which they held. The government of the people was established in the capital; and the condottieri, who had served the ducal state under Filippo Maria, generally engaged their fidelity to the new republic.

The people of Milan, however, had not succeeded to the power of their late duke. The authority of their republic was scarcely acknowledged beyond their own walls: almost every city of the duchy claimed an equal right with the capital to govern itself; Pavia, Tortona, Parma, and other towns, erected themselves into republics; and all Lombardy was filled with revolt and anarchy. Meanwhile numerous foreign enemies threatened the new government of the capital. Though the hostility of Florence had subsided into indifference, the Venetians eagerly extended their conquests in central Lombardy. The duke of Savoy, the marquis of Montferrat, the Genoese, and the marquis of Este, assailed the possessions of Filippo Maria, on opposite frontiers, by intrigues or by arms; the duke of Orleans, who owed his birth to the marriage of his father with Valentine Visconti, daughter of Gian Galeazzo, declared his right to the dominions of his uncle; and, finally, Alfonso, king of the Sicilies, threatened the assertion of his pretensions. Thus oppressed and menaced from every quarter, the new Milanese republic, distrustful of the projects of Francesco Sforza, yet dreading his open assaults, could discover no better policy than to avert his hostility by taking him into pay, and employing his formidable bands against other enemies.

On the death of Filippo Maria, Sforza, who had first lost all his states, except Cremona, by the enmity of that prince, and then forfeited the alliance of the Venetians to reconcile himself with him, had nothing left but his personal fame and talents, the command of veteran bands, and a very questionable claim to inherit the states of his father-in-law. He therefore gladly accepted the offer of the Milanese government to take him into their pay, upon the same conditions, and for the defence of the same country, as he had agreed upon with the late duke. But Sforza had in no degree laid aside his hopes and projects of acquiring the ducal crown. In entering the service of the new republic, he had still the same end in view; and he steadily continued the pursuit of a faithless policy, which, with self-interest for its only spring of action, disregarded every law of morality, and shamelessly violated the most solemn obligation of oaths. His whole conduct was a practical illustration of those detestable principles which Machiavel has embodied into his celebrated treatise; and yet the man, who might have afforded the model after which the great Florentine sketched the character of his prince, had a fairer and a higher fame than almost any of the distinguished personages of the same age and country. He was the private friend of Cosmo de' Medici, and of several princes of the houses of Este, and Gonzaga, and Montefeltro, whose protection of letters and art shed a brilliant lustre over their times and themselves. Sforza was at least equal to these, his illustrious associates in virtue; he was faithful, devoted, and liberal in his private affections. With what indignation and disgust must we then contemplate the political morality of an age, which taught the hero, of elevated mind and generous feeling, to know no other disgrace than that of failure in the struggle of injustice and duplicity!

Francesco Sforza had no sooner united his veteran bands to the old gens-d'armerie of Filippo Maria than he every where turned the tide of success. The new republic of Parma was terrified by his approach to submit to that of Milan; the people of Pavia and Tortona, to the great jealousy of the Milanese, bestowed the sovereignty of their cities on Sforza himself; and the French force, which was acting for the duke of Orleans in western Lombardy, was totally defeated; though not without a previous carnage, so unusual in these bloodless wars, as to strike the Italian conquerors with terrific impressions of the ferocity of these ultramontane enemies. Meanwhile the Venetians, since their victory at Casal Maggiore, had spread their conquering troops over so extensive a tract of country, that they were unable to assemble in force at any single point, and this dispersion had all the consequences of a defeat. Sforza, after other successes, sat down before Placentia, then, next to Milan, the largest city in Lombardy. His artillery laid the walls open with a rapidity which gave an earnest of a total change in the relations of the science of attack and defence; and, notwithstanding the obstinate resistance of a numerous garrison, his troops, to the surprise of the age, entered the place through the breach, by a general assault. This important blow was followed, in the next campaign, by the recovery of many castles which the Venetians had conquered on the Adda; by the capture and destruction of the whole of a large fleet which they had sent up the Po, and by the total rout of their army at Caravaggio. (A.D. 1448.)

Francesco Sforza was conscious that he now approached the goal of his ambition: he had recovered the possessions of Milan from the hands of the Venetians, and invaded their provinces: he had hitherto succeeded, by the arts of his numerous agents at Milan, in exciting clamour against proposals for a peace, which was equally desirable for that republic and for Venice; and he had sufficiently humiliated the Venetians. He perceived that the termination of hostilities was at hand; he dreaded a pacification between the belligerents; and he saw that the time had arrived for preventing it, and accomplishing his purposes, by changing his party. Notwithstanding the suspicions of the Milanese government, he had, with consummate address, veiled the real extent of his designs; and he now, one-and-thirty days only after his victory at Caravaggio, secretly concluded a treaty with the Venetians, by which he agreed to evacuate their territory, and make some cessions to them, and they engaged, in return, to assist him in ascending the throne of Filippo Maria, He then assembled his troops: he declared to them that the Milanese republic had ungratefully resolved to deprive him of Pavia and Cremona, and to rob them of the fruits of their victories; and he proclaimed his schemes of vengeance, and his new alliance with Venice. His mercenary bands needed little incentive to any enterprise of which booty was to be the reward: and he led them, in concert with a Venetian force, against the state whose pay they were receiving.

The permanent revival of a republic in the centre of Lombardy might have fortified and upheld the cause of freedom in the peninsula; and a just and enlightened policy should have impelled both Florence and Venice to support the new liberties of the Milanese. But Florence was influenced by the private partiality of Cosmo de Medici, and secretly favoured the projects of Sforza; and Venice was swayed by selfish ambition to league against the rising commonwealth. The first emotion of the public mind at Milan, at the defection of Sforza, was indignation at his perfidy; the next feeling was the necessity of vigorous preparation for resisting his detestable yoke. The rulers of the people garrisoned their fortresses, they levied a numerous militia, and equipped them with muskets; and this arm, which had yet been little used, at first struck terror into their enemies. But experience had now betrayed the imperfection of the means of defence, which the fortresses of the times could oppose to the assaults of artillery. The garrisons of the Milanese were rapidly reduced; while, notwithstanding the panic created by the novel employment of small fire-arms, their defective construction would admit only of a tardy discharge, and was neither assisted by the modern invention of the bayonet or the use of the puissant pike. The Milanese generals dared not lead their undisciplined militia against a veteran gens-d'armerie; and the army of Sforza, approaching the capital, invested it by a rigid blockade. (A.D. 1449.)

Meanwhile the people of Milan had evinced their unfitness for the enjoyment of freedom. Ages of subjection to the tyranny of the Visconti had long extinguished the spirit that had once inspired their ancestors of Legnano. The late revolution failed in developing the energies of any master-mind, and guided by no leaders worthy of the crisis, they were torn by furious dissensions and plunged in intestine commotion. Although Venice, repenting of her share in the aggrandizement of Sforza, and expecting no farther advantage from his alliance, now made peace with the Milanese republic, and even began to act hostilely against her former confederate, her succour came too late to avert the ruin of the new commonwealth. Sforza pursued the siege of Milan with unshaken determination; his skilful operations prevented any attempt for the relief of the city; and the numerous populace, after enduring all the horrors of famine, were at last driven to revolt against their rulers. The gates of Milan were thrown open, and Sforza, whose name had lately been breathed only with execration, was welcomed to the capital of his principality by the acclamations of the inconstant and joyful multitude. The whole states of Filippo Maria immediately submitted to his authority; and his coronation was celebrated with royal magnificence. The Florentines sent an embassy of their most distinguished citizens to congratulate him on his accession; and the states of Italy in general acknowledged the title of the new duke of Milan. Francesco Sforza had thus attained the summit of grandeur, which his bold and unscrupulous ambition had projected. No subsequent reverses were to cloud the splendour of his own fortunes; and he could not penetrate the veil of futurity to discover that the toil, and danger, and perfidy by which he had dearly founded the aggrandizement of his descendants, were to produce only for them a gloomy consummation of misery and crime.

The importance of a new power, which had gradually been increasing on the western frontiers of the Milanese states, takes its date from the beginning of the fifteenth century; and I may conveniently append to the present chapter some account of the rise of a dynasty, which had already established over Piedmont a sovereignty destined to endure to our times. The origin of the house of Savoy is buried in obscurity; and the history of the part of Italy over which its authority was gradually extended, has been far less successfully explored than that of any other province of the peninsula. Muratori, the most indefatigable and learned of Italian antiquaries, is repeatedly compelled to acknowledge that the mode in which the transalpine chieftains of Savoy superseded the great feudatories of Susa and Ivrea has baffled his inquiry; and the affairs of Piedmont in the middle ages have neither been developed, like those of Lombardy and Tuscany, by numerous contemporary chroniclers, nor very frequently illustrated by modern research. But if we know little of the annals of Piedmont, and of the early memoirs of its present sovereigns, we have probably not much to regret. There is in no degree reason to attribute to this part of our subject the same interest with the long tragedy of Lombardy, the maritime glories of Venice, or the magnanimous spirit and intellectual splendour of Florence.

The house of Savoy derives its descent from the counts of Maurienne, a petty lordship in the Savoyard valley, which is watered by the little river of Arc. If their genealogist Guichenon be correct, the first of these chieftains was a German prince of the imperial line of Saxony, who, at the end of the tenth century, obtained his fief by service to Rodolph III., king of Burgundy. About a hundred years later, Otho, the fourth in descent from this founder of his line, married the daughter of the last marquis of Susa, and is supposed to have inherited great part of his possessions. From this period the counts of Maurienne began gradually to extend their sovereignty over all Savoy; and, at the end of the eleventh century, may perhaps also with safety be dated the first foundation of their power on the Italian side of the Alps. Here their elevation was long repressed by the jealousy of the civic states of Piedmont, and by the rivalry of the great chieftains of the province, the principal of whom were the marquisses of Montferrat and Saluzzo. These princes, and the counts of Savoy themselves, subjugated or swallowed up inferior lordships, and engrossed most of the rural territories of Piedmont. Turin, Asti, Vercelli, and other cities of the province, which appear in the twelfth century to have gained a republican freedom, much in the same manner as those of Lombardy, fell also like them in the following age, by the effects of their vicious dissensions. In the factions of the thirteenth century, the counts of Savoy mingled in Italian politics as favourers of the imperial interests and of the Ghibelin party. In the beginning of this age they seized, under the imperial banner, upon Turin their future capital. The citizens, however, did not tamely submit to their yoke; they frequently revolted; and they even defeated the count Boniface I. and took him prisoner. After a long series of alternate resistance and submission, it was not until about the middle of the fourteenth century, that the people of Turin and other Piedmontese cities finally reposed, from the incessant struggles of faction, in obedience to the counts of Savoy.

Under Amadeus VI., whose long reign of thirty-nine years terminated in 1383, the Italian states of the counts of Savoy assumed a regular consolidation. Amadeus, who acquired the sirname of the Comte-Verd, from the colour of his arms, was one of the greatest characters of his house. Besides receiving the voluntary submission of the cities of Piedmont, he obliged all the petty signers of the province to acknowledge his sovereignty; he obtained from Louis I. of Anjou, as count of Provence, the renunciation of his claims over Piedmont, in return for the aid which he gave that prince in his Neapolitan expedition; and the house of Savoy now acquired a decided preponderance over the marquisates of Montferrat and Saluzzo. The fortunate reign of the Comte-Verd prepared the entrance of his family among the crowned heads of Europe. His son's life was short; but his grandson, Amadeus VIII., after a tranquil minority, found himself, at the opening of the fifteenth century, possessor of Savoy and of almost all Piedmont. To his transalpine dominions he annexed by purchase the county of Geneva; and, on the side of Lombardy, he made considerable acquisitions of territory on the dismemberment of the Milanese states after the death of Gian Galeazzo, and during the troubled reign of Filippo Maria. The possessions of Amadeus VIII. were also swelled by the extinction of collateral branches of his family. A century and a half earlier, the power of the house of Savoy had been checked in its growth by a division of its territory among three brothers and their heirs; but Amadeus VIII. now became the sole representative of his dynasty. The simple title of count was no longer suitable either to his dignity or the extent of his dominion; and he obtained from the emperor Sigismund letters patent, which elevated his states into an imperial duchy. The policy was simple and enlightened, which taught the new duke of Savoy, as an Italian prince, to regard the alliance of Florence and Venice as a protection against the superior force of the Visconti, and as a barrier against aggression from Germany; and he profited by the successes of the republics against Filippo Maria. It was this Amadeus VIII., the first duke of Savoy, who, after retiring, on the death of his wife, from the world in grief or disgust, was seduced by the council of Basle to accept a disputed tiara, and to endure its aggravated cares for about nine years; when he himself convoked a council to witness his resignation of a wearisome dignity, and withdrew again to the retirement in which he died. His son Louis, who had succeeded to the duchy of Savoy on his abdication, and whose reign continued beyond the middle of the century, was a prince of inferior qualities, (A.D. 1439.) But he increased his possessions after the death of Filippo Maria of Milan, by first opposing Sforza in his war with the Milanese republic, and then obtaining from that prince before his final success, a considerable cession of territory, as the price of his alliance. The dukes of Savoy thenceforth were to mingle in all the political combinations of the peninsula; but we shall not discover any farther important increase to their power for several ages, for their decided ascendancy over the destiny of Italy was the work of later times. They have risen with her fall, and triumphed in her disgrace; and the consummation of their royal ambition has been coeval with the bitterest years of her servitude.

CHAPTER VII. FROM THE MIDDLE OF THE FIFTEENTH CENTURY TO THE ENTRANCE INTO ITALY OF CHARLES VIII., KING OF FRANCE, a.d. 1450—1494.

PART I.
Change in the system of Italian alliances, on the accession of Francesco Sforza to the Milanese throne—League of Alfonso of Naples and Venice against the duke of Milan and Florence—General war in Italy—Capture of Constantinople by the Turks—Consternation and danger of Italy—Peace of Lodi—Quadruple league of Naples, Milan, Florence, and Venice—Pontificate of Nicholas V.—Abortive conspiracy of Stefano Porcari—Incessant troubles and revolutions of Genoa—War of Alfonso of Naples against the republic—His death and character—Unpopularity of his son Ferdinand—The barons of Naples offer their crown to the house of Anjou—Obstinate civil war in their kingdom between the parties of Anjou and Aragon—Share of other Italian powers in the contest—Final triumph of Ferdinand—General repose of Italy—Affairs of Venice—Story of the Foscari—Institution of the inquisitors of state—Danger of Venice from the growth of the Ottoman power—War between the republic and the Turks—Crusade projected by pope Pius II. against the infidels—His death—Pope Paul II.—Conquest of Negropont by the Turks—Alarm of Italy—League against the infidels—Its abortive results—Entrance of the Turks into Italy—Close of the war between Venice and the Ottomans—The Genoese lose their possessions in the Black Sea—Acquisition of Cyprus by the Venetians.

THE elevation of Francesco Sforza to the ducal throne of Milan changed the whole system of Italian alliances. Alfonso of Aragon had been bound by the ties of interest, if not of personal regard and gratitude, to Filippo Maria; and during the lifetime of that duke, a firm and intimate union had subsisted between Naples and Milan; while, on the other hand, the republics of Florence and Venice had been driven, by the restless designs of Filippo Maria, to coalesce against him for their mutual defence, and for the maintenance of the political balance of Italy, (A.D. 1450.) But the accession of Sforza to the crown of the Visconti placed these four leading powers of the peninsula, Naples, Milan, Florence, and Venice, in new and opposite relations to each other. Alfonso still regarded Sforza only as the partizan of the house of Anjou, and, consequently, as his personal enemy. In depriving him of his fiefs in the kingdom of Naples, he felt that he had given him reason to cherish feelings of exasperation and vengeance on his new throne; and he desired to anticipate him in the contest of mutual injuries.

The connexion between Florence and Venice was as much severed, as that between Milan and Naples. The paramount influence of Cosmo de'

Medici—the warm personal friend of Sforza—over the counsels of Florence, had thrown that republic completely into the party of the new duke, and occasioned her to form a close alliance with Milan. But Venice was still bent upon schemes of continental aggrandizement in Lombardy, and enraged at her sister republic for having thwarted her purposes, by privately aiding Sforza with subsidies. She saw in that prince a far more dangerous neighbour and formidable antagonist than his predecessors, and divided her enmity almost equally between him and Florence, who had favoured his elevation. The king of Naples had but lately been at war with both the republics. By some aggressions in Tuscany in 1447, he had provoked the Florentines to a contest, with the languid and uninteresting operations of which I have not thought it necessary to occupy the attention of the reader; and some commercial disputes had also led to naval hostilities between the Venetians and his subjects. Both these unimportant wars were terminated by negotiation at the period before us; and Alfonso discovered not only a ready means of reconciliation with the Venetians, but a desirable occasion of confederating with them, in the animosity which they bore to his enemy Sforza and to the Florentines.

Since the entrance of Sforza into Milan, the hostile operations, which the Venetians had carried on against him, seemed to have expired in the common exhaustion of the combatants, and under the dreadful ravages of a pestilence which broke out in Lombardy. But an offensive league was now formed by the king of Naples and the Venetians against the duke of Milan and the Florentines. The contracting parties endeavoured to engage the secondary states of the peninsula in their alliance; and Louis, duke of Savoy, and the marquis of Montferrat, were easily induced, by the hope of new acquisitions, to join the confederates against Sforza. (A.D. 1451.) Both the reigning families of Este and Gonzaga were, at this epoch, more honourably distinguished by their passion for literature and art, and by the intellectual splendour with which they invested their courts, than by the share which they took in Italian politics. Borso, of Este, who had just succeeded his brother, the marquis Lionel, in the states of Ferrara and Modena, steadily maintained his neutrality; but Louis III., marquis of Mantua, embraced the alliance of Sforza. Notwithstanding the Venetian intrigues, the communities of Sienna and Bologna also, remained firm in the alliance of Florence; and that republic, now perceiving the hostile temper of Venice, seriously prepared for war, and cemented an alliance, offensive and defensive, with the duke of Milan.

While the league between the king of Naples and the Venetians was thus exciting a general war in Italy, and developing the political affections of her various states, the commencement of hostilities was for a short time retarded by the entrance into Lombardy of the emperor Frederic III. To receive the crown of the empire at Rome, appeared to be the only object of Frederic, an insignificant and feeble prince. He arrived in Italy without an army, he quitted it immediately after his coronation; and as the last Italian expedition of the emperor Sigismund had absolutely produced not a single occurrence worthy of notice, beyond the sale of the dignity of marquis to the family of Gonzaga, so this visit of Frederic deserves to be remembered only as the occasion on which the ducal crown was conferred on the house of Este. Frederic III. invested the marquis Borso with the title of duke of Modena and Reggio. These states were regarded as fiefs of the empire; but that of Ferrara was supposed to be held of the holy see; and it was not until nineteen years later, that this most ancient possession of the house of Este, and the capital of their dominions, was erected by pope Paul II. into a duchy in their favour.

Just as Frederic III. was withdrawing from Italy after the ceremonial of his coronation, the senate of Venice declared war against the duke of Milan; and shortly afterwards the king of Naples commenced hostilities against the republic of Florence. Both Tuscany and Lombardy immediately became the theatre of warlike operations, (A.D. 1452.) Into the former province, Alfonso dispatched an army to attack the Florentines under the command of his natural son Ferdinand, and entrusted the guidance of this prince, whom he destined for his successor, to Federigo di Montefeltro, count of Urbino in Romagna, one of the most able warriors and accomplished characters of his age. But, from whatever cause, the campaign in Tuscany produced little fruit. The army of Ferdinand was unaccompanied by artillery, and the whole Neapolitan strength was vainly consumed in the siege of a few petty Florentine castles. The operations in Lombardy were not more decisive. Sforza, attacked on opposite frontiers by the troops of Savoy and Montferrat, and by the Venetians, opposed his enemies with an equality of force which balanced the fortune of the contest; and, as usual, in the inglorious warfare of the times, we meet with a total dearth of all interest. The second year of the war was equally barren in events of importance; and, although the armies employed in Lombardy were so numerous, that nearly 40,000 cuirassiers were brought into the field, not a single action of consequence was fought, (A.D. 1453.) The Florentines succeeded by their negotiations and subsidies in inducing old Regnier of Anjou, the former rival of Alfonso of Naples, to lead an army across the Alps to reinforce Sforza in Lombardy; but the impetuous chivalry of France were soon wearied of the systematic protraction of Italian hostilities; and, after a service of a few months, the followers of Regnier, who himself shared their impatience, induced him to reconduct them to their country.

The indecisive character and ruinous expenditure of the war had already moderated the animosity of the contending powers of Italy, when the intelligence of the fall of Constantinople, before the arms of Mahomet II., struck consternation into Europe, and excited general remorse for the callous neglect, which had abandoned to destruction the most ancient empire of Christendom. The sentiment of religious sympathy for the fate of the vanquished Greeks was combined with horror at the merciless butcheries of their infidel conquerors, and with appalling presages of the universal dominion of the Turks. To the powers of Italy the danger was imminent: the empire of the crescent was established at the eastern gates of Europe, and seemed already to menace and overshadow the peninsula with impending ruin. A congress was summoned to meet at Rome under the presidency of the pope, Nicholas V.; and all the belligerent states eagerly expressed their desire for the restoration of peace, that their united forces might be directed against the general enemy, (A.D. 1454.) But when their deputies had assembled, it was soon manifested by their exaggerated pretensions, how weak was the sense of common peril, or the generous desire of delivering the eastern Christians, when opposed to the selfishness of individual interests. The pope himself is accused of having endeavoured to perpetuate the quarrel of the Italian states, whose distractions prevented their interference with the repose of his own dominions; and it became altogether evident that no accommodation could be wrought at the congress. But Florence nevertheless had no particular object in continuing the war; and two at least of the other contending parties sincerely desired a pacification. Sforza had reached the highest point of his ambition; his excellent sense taught him that he had no farther aggrandizement to expect; and he was intent only upon bequeathing to his dynasty the secure possession of the Milanese states. Himself originally a condottiere, he was perfectly versed in the treacherous principles which actuated the mercenary leaders and their bands; and the experience of his own successful projects was in itself an alarming warning of the danger which he, as a prince, might in turn incur from the faithless ambition of these adventurers. Peace could alone preserve his resources from their rapacity, and enable him to dispense with their services, and to crush the fatal system by which they existed. Venice was at length awakened, by the successes of Mahomet II., to a conviction of the perilous condition in which her scattered dependencies in the east were placed by the terrific growth of the Turkish power. The late operations in Lombardy left besides little hope to the republic of farther acquisitions on the continent of Italy.

The pacific inclinations of Sforza were, under these circumstances, shared by the Venetian senate: negotiations were secretly opened, and Italy was suddenly surprised by the conclusion of a peace at Lodi between Venice and Milan, to which the other belligerents were invited to accede. The terms of the treaty provided only for some inconsiderable regulations of territory; and the minor powers, respectively in hostility to the two states, were easily compelled to submit to the equitable conditions imposed on them. Florence herself not only assented cheerfully to the pacification, but signed a defensive league with Milan and Venice for the maintenance of the public repose. The king of Naples, alone, indignant that, as the principal monarch of the peninsula, he had not been consulted in the negotiations at Lodi, and still desirous of obliging Florence to reimburse him for the charges of the war, for some time delayed his acquiescence in the general peace. But the signature of the new alliance of Milan and the two republics shook his resolution; and he had, besides, an important object to gain by accepting its intentions. He had no legitimate offspring, and the kingdoms to which he had succeeded by regular inheritance would necessarily devolve on a collateral branch of the Aragonese dynasty; but the crown of Naples, which he had acquired by his own ability and courage, he was desirous of leaving to his natural son Ferdinand. By interchanging with the leading states of Italy a mutual obligation of defence, he farther looked to obtain an implied recognition of the rights of Ferdinand to his succession on the Neapolitan throne. He, therefore, at length yielded his accession to the peace of Lodi; and, under the guarantee of the pope, a quadruple league was then formed between the sovereigns of Naples and Milan, and the republics of Florence and Venice, for the preservation of tranquillity in Italy.

The sovereign pontiff who mingled in the negotiations was, as I have before mentioned, Nicholas V. (A.D. 1455.) The reign of this pope, who had succeeded Eugenius IV., in 1447, is, however, chiefly remarkable for his zealous patronage of letters, and as the era of the last abortive effort for the establishment of republican freedom in the ancient capital of the universe. Nicholas V. was the son of an obscure physician of Sarzana, and, while only himself a poor priest, had displayed an ardent passion for the recovery of the relics of classical literature. His industrious learning and talents procured for him the friendship of

Cosmo de' Medici, and excited the attention of his ecclesiastical superiors. After a long service in inferior stations, Eugenius IV. attached him to his person; and he then rose, in twelve months, to the highest dignities of the church. On the death of Eugenius, at Rome, one of those sudden and capricious accidents, which have so often determined the votes of the conclave, elevated the new cardinal to the chair of St. Peter; and, by the influence of his personal character, his reign was shortly signalized by the extinction of the schism caused by the council of Basle. He persuaded the anti-pope, Amadeus of Savoy, to resign his pretensions to the tiara, and admitted him, with the cardinals of his creation, into the sacred college. During a pontificate of eight years, Nicholas proved himself a splendid and munificent patron of learning. The papal court was crowded with men of letters, who were fostered by his bounty; the Vatican library was founded, and above five thousand ancient manuscripts were collected by his care; and a greater number of the Greek classics were translated into Latin by his command, during the brief remnant of his life, than in the five centuries which had preceded his elevation. His patronage of the arts was not less distinguished: the venerable monuments of the capital were preserved and cherished by his enthusiastic admiration; the sacred edifices of Rome and of the other cities of his states were repaired and embellished; and the erection of many superb structures, at once attested his magnificent spirit and the purity of his taste.

The political administration of Nicholas V. was not calculated to support the fair fame of his intellectual qualities. His arbitrary measures, and the cruelties into which he was hurried, by his fears of popular commotion, have fastened upon his memory a reproach of mingled tyranny and weakness, for which a palliation will vainly be sought, either in his mere restoration of the volumes of antiquity, or in the splendour of his architectural works. Notwithstanding the insurrection of 1433, by which the citizens of Rome had compelled Eugenius IV. to seek safety in flight, and effected a transient revival of their republican institutions, they had shortly fallen again under the tyrannical authority of that pontiff; and, at the epoch of his death, they found themselves absolutely divested of all the privileges of freemen. The interregnum, which necessarily preceded the election of his successor, appeared a favourable occasion for the assertion of their public rights. It was in an assembly of the citizens, at this juncture, that Stefano Porcari, a Roman, of noble birth and spotless character, first raised himself to notice, by his ardent aspirations after freedom. His mind was heated by the writings of Petrarch, and perhaps by the desire of emulating the career of Rienzi, whose vivid imagination and impassioned eloquence seemed, in some measure, to have descended upon him. But his exertions proved less fortunate or powerful than those of the celebrated tribune. He eagerly exposed, before his assembled fellow-citizens, the degradation of their state; he endeavoured to fire them by the exclamation, that there was no enslaved and petty community so abject, as not to watch the moment of a tyrant's death to deliver themselves from bondage; and he exhorted his countrymen to seize the opportunity of imposing a constitutional charter upon the future pope. But all his efforts to rouse the Roman people to a kindred spirit with his own were unavailing; they produced no resolution in the assembly; and, as their only result, Porcari was denounced to the new pontiff as a dangerous character. The suspicion already excited against him was strengthened by the continuance of his projects for the establishment of liberty at Rome: and his interference at some public games, in a slight riot, to which he strove to give a political object, furnished the cause for a papal sentence against him of exile to Bologna.

Nicholas V., whose life of personal servitude had taught him only the despotic relation between master and dependent, was resolved to exact from his subjects an obedience as unlimited as that which he had himself been accustomed to yield to his superiors. But if the arbitrary principles which thus regulated his government were to be maintained, his banishment of Porcari was apparently a lenient sentence. Yet it only provoked the continued prosecution of the designs which had occasioned it. In his exile, Porcari brooded over the disgraceful submission of the city of his birth—the once mighty capital of antiquity—to the yoke of a slothful priesthood; and his distempered fancy blinded him to the truth, that the hour for restoring the fallen majesty of Rome was for ever past. He imprudently formed a conspiracy, which was equally extravagant and hopeless. His intentions, says Macchiavel, coldly, might be commended by some, but his judgment must be censured by all. He secretly returned to Rome; and, in concert with his nephew and a few bold associates, who shared his enthusiasm, and whom he had summoned to meet him at his own house, prepared to seize the persons of the pope and cardinals, and to use them as hostages for obtaining the surrender of the city gates and the castle of St. Angelo. But, even while Porcari was deliberating with the conspirators, he was betrayed. The senator of Rome, receiving notice of an unusual assemblage at the house of the exile, surrounded it with his soldiery. The conspirators were attacked and overpowered; some of them escaped, but Porcari himself was taken on the spot, and the pope condemned him to death, without even the formality of a trial. Together with nine of his associates, he was hanged, in less than twenty-four hours after his capture, from the battlements of St. Angelo: and thus miserably perished the last of the champions of Roman liberty,—the victims of the illusions of ancient glory.

Nicholas V. was persuaded that the conspirators had desired his life, and he became from this period at once as timid and ferocious as he had before been confiding and mild. The punishment of Porcari was followed by continual and iniquitous executions, (A.D. 1454.) As many of the conspirators who had taken refuge in other states as the pope could induce the different governments to deliver up to him, were put to death; and several other persons suffered capitally, who were either wholly innocent, or upon whom no more than the bare suspicion had fallen of a distant implication in the late plot. Yet amidst these sanguinary proceedings, Nicholas bore a mind ill at peace with itself; he did not very long survive the reign of terror which he had established;

and in his last days he wept bitterly, while he declared that he had found no man to approach him with the language of truth. (A.D. 1455.) He was succeeded on the papal throne by the cardinal Alfonso Borgia, a Spaniard of advanced age, who assumed the title of Calixtus III. By the elevation of his family, this pontiff prepared an infamous celebrity for their name, and rendered the extinction of the last spark of freedom at Rome nearly coeval with the establishment of the most odious race of her tyrants.

Though the peace of Lodi and the quadruple league which followed had the happy effects of tranquillizing Italy in general, no respite from suffering was yielded by these treaties to one of the few surviving republics of the peninsula. Ever since the Genoese had thrown off the yoke of Filippo Maria of Milan in 1435, their state had been for twenty years one restless and furious volcano of incessant political convulsions. During this period, as indeed throughout the whole of the fourteenth and fifteenth centuries, the revolutions of Genoa were so numerous and rapid, the alternate triumph and overthrow of parties so transient and hurried, and the consequences of these oscillations of faction so utterly evanescent, that I shall avoid the unprofitable attempt to burthen the mind of the reader with a crowd of vicissitudes, which it would be useless, if it were not also impossible, for the memory to retain. Such details must in themselves occupy whole chapters, while they would scarcely deserve our attention; and I shall therefore pass them over with a few general notices of their prominent characteristics.

There is perhaps little difficulty in ascribing to the influence of an ill-balanced aristocracy the origin of those disorders which, for nearly two centuries, may be said to have fatally distinguished Genoa as the unhappiest republic within the experience of all history. The rivalry of the four leading houses of the old nobility had originally inoculated the people with the virulent spirit of factious hatred. The subsequent exclusion of the ancient aristocracy from the privileges of government, had only made way for the rise of opulent and powerful families of great commoners; and the fierce struggles of these new leaders, with the old nobles, and with each other, still farther habituated the mass of the citizens to eternal commotion and bloodshed, and made the thirst of license and change their dominant passion. There is no record in the annals of the world of a series of civil wars and revolutions, at once so sanguinary, lengthened, and ceaseless, as those which were fought in the commercial streets and narrow territory of Genoa. If the citizens, in moments of exhaustion and weariness, sighed for repose from the fearful uproar of faction, they knew no better resource than to seek for tranquillity under the yoke of a foreign master. If the shame of slavery, or their impatience of firm and regular government roused them to reassert their independence, it became still the independence of anarchy. The people had no sooner established a faction in power, than they at once abandoned its support to bestow their affections on its opponents; and these again were only raised to be in turn the sport of the popular inconstancy. No principle, no lasting political attachments, no regard for the safety of the state, actuated either the turbulent people or their rulers. The insatiable love of \revolution was their only intelligible motive; a bold intolerance of servitude their only approach to virtue. Thus, though they frequently surrendered themselves to the sovereignty of France or of Milan, they never tamely endured the arbitrary authority of a prince; and they vigorously cast off their chains, as often as they had imprudently invited their galling imposition.

At the epoch before us, Genoa was oppressed both by her usual dissensions at home, and by foreign assaults and reverses. The great plebeian families of the Fregosi and Adorni were desperately contending for the supremacy; and we find them alternately in banishment, and occupying the ducal chair and the national councils. So superior was the influence which they divided to the power of the old nobility, and of the rest of their own order, that the four ancient families of the Spinola, the Doria, the Fieschi, and the Grimaldi, as well as the Guarci and other distinguished commoners, were either content to range themselves under the respective banners of these arrogant rivals, or reduced to exercise a secondary influence in the state. The

Adorni and their adherents formed altogether perhaps the weaker party. They were at this juncture in banishment, and as interminable civil wars had taught an unsuccessful faction to see no guilt or shame in alliance with the enemies of their country, the exiles raised their arms against Genoa in concert with Alfonso of Naples. In addition to the distress which the rancorous hostility of that monarch entailed on the republic, she was a severe sufferer by the fall of the eastern empire to the Turks. Her flourishing and invaluable colony of Pera had, almost without succour from the parent state, and without resistance, followed the fate of Constantinople. After this heavy loss, the isle of Chio and Caffa, with her other possessions in the Levant and Black Sea, were in imminent danger; and still the strength of the republic was consumed in intestine discord. The rulers of Genoa were conscious of the peril in which these transmarine possessions were placed by foreign attacks and their own neglect. Yet either dreading that amidst the troubles of the state, they should want the means of protecting its foreign dependencies, or as if desirous of being released from all other care than the pursuit of factious quarrels, they consigned the sovereignty of all their colonies to the bank of St. George. That celebrated company of state creditors which had been incorporated in 1407, and the councils of which, by a singular and happy fortune, were never agitated by the national madness of party, was certainly better qualified for the trust than the ephemeral chiefs of the republic itself.

Alfonso of Naples, besides the hereditary hatred which always reigned between the Genoese and his Catalan subjects, bore an irreconcileable enmity to that people. He had never forgiven them their support of the Angevin party in the civil wars of Naples, nor the affront of his naval defeat at Ponza, and subsequent captivity. Though, therefore, he had been for a short time at peace with their republic, it was only while the Adorni were in power, and flattered his pride by the annual payment of an honorary tribute. His connexion with that family and party had been formed during their exile and rebellion against their country; and when they were again expelled from Genoa, Alfonso gratified his animosity against their fellow citizens, under the show of protection to them. In signing the quadruple league of 1455, he had extorted a concession from the other contracting parties, that Genoa under the Fregosi should be excluded from the general guarantee of pacification; and in the same year he attacked the coasts of the divided and exhausted state, while the exiled party acted in concert with his fleets. This desultory and harassing warfare by land and sea continued during three years. The Genoese vainly sought aid in Italy against the attacks of Alfonso; for the powers of the league were restricted from assisting them by the condition which they had weakly permitted the king of Naples to annex to their treaty with him. The doge, Piero Fregoso, at length applied to Charles VII., king of France, for protection; and to that monarch, upon the same terms which had been made with his father in 1396, was the signiory of Genoa formally consigned, (A.D. 1458.)

The doge was sensible that the sufferings of continued warfare had rendered his authority odious to his countrymen; but in therefore voluntarily resigning his station, he resolved not to yield a victory to the king of Naples; and the French sovereign was required to choose for his lieutenant at Genoa the hereditary enemy of Alfonso. This was John, titular duke of Calabria, son of his ancient rival, Regnier of Anjou. The Angevin prince arrived to assume his new command, with ten galleys and a body of French troops. But his appearance in Italy only induced Alfonso to push his operations against the Genoese in a more systematic and determined manner than he had hitherto done. He fitted out a numerous fleet, which formed the blockade of their capital; he disembarked the flower of the Neapolitan troops in their territory; and their numerous exiles at the same time descended from the Ligurian mountains, and laid siege to the city. But while John of Anjou with his followers and the citizens were courageously awaiting an assault, the operations of the war before Genoa were suddenly suspended by intelligence of the death of Alfonso. The besieging armament at once dispersed. The Catalan and Neapolitan forces returned to the ports of their respective kingdoms, and the exiles to their mountains; and Genoa was left, less to the repose of victory than to the miseries of exhaustion and pestilence.

Alfonso, king of Aragon, Catalonia, Valencia, the Balearic Isles, and Sardinia, and of Naples and Sicily, owed less of the splendour which surrounded his throne to these extensive possessions, than to the force of his personal character. He was an able captain, and an active and skilful statesman; and, in an age when the sovereigns of Italy rivalled each other in the protection of literature, far surpassed them all in his real love of learning, his passionate enthusiasm for antiquity, and his magnificent patronage of genius. These mental virtues were graced in him by all the dazzling accomplishments of chivalry: by a captivating affability and seductive eloquence, by a romantic tenderness for the softer sex, and by the frank dignity and heroic courage of knighthood. His court of Naples, which he chose for his residence above any of his patrimonial states, was the school of letters, and the scene of architectural grandeur and sumptuous pageantry. A high-minded and generous prince, Alfonso in many respects well merited the sirname of the Magnanimous, with which his lettered contemporaries delighted to honour him, and to repay his unbounded liberality; but this and all his fair qualities were too nearly allied to defects. His Neapolitan subjects, charmed with his confidence in their love and with the flattering preference which induced him to reside among them, overlooked the lavish profusion that obliged him to load them with taxes; but his restless ambition, and more than one act of bad faith into which it betrayed him, did not deserve the same easy judgment. Still his few vices should in candour be ascribed rather to the influence of the times of violence and treachery in which he lived, than to his own noble nature. His virtues would claim admiration in any age, and, in the fifteenth century, he was the greatest and most amiable monarch of Europe.

The affection which the Neapolitans bore to this distinguished sovereign was not transferred to his only son Ferdinand, for whom, notwithstanding the illegitimacy of his birth, Alfonso had earnestly laboured to procure their allegiance. As he had no lawful issue, the rules of inheritance and equity consigned all his patrimonial crowns to his brother, the king of Navarre; but the right of the regular Aragonese dynasty to the kingdom of Naples—his personal acquisition—appeared more questionable, and it was the darling object of his life to secure its throne for his son. Besides the indirect guarantee of the quadruple league, he had been careful to obtain from successive popes, as feudal superiors of the Neapolitan crown, a formal settlement in favour of Ferdinand. The decision of the parliament of the kingdom,—a better title—had ratified his intentions; and when he died, the right of his son to succeed him appeared established by the consent of his feudal chief and his people, and guaranteed by all the states of the Italian peninsula.

But the dark and perfidious temper of Ferdinand was little calculated to interest either his father's subjects or allies in his behalf. Alfonso had scarcely breathed his last, when the principal Neapolitan barons, who had acquired a perfect acquaintance with the character of Ferdinand, began secretly to plot against his pretensions. They offered their allegiance first to the new king of Aragon, and, on receiving discouragement from him, to the house of Anjou. Regnier, the ancient rival of Alfonso, was still in existence, but his son John was nearer at hand in the exercise of the government of Genoa, and it was to him that the malcontents addressed themselves. John of Anjou eagerly accepted their offer; the Genoese engaged to assist him with their forces; and he endeavoured by negotiation to obtain the support of the other Italian powers in his enterprise. Both Regnier and his son were more or less known throughout Italy, and the uprightness and simplicity of character, which advantageously contrasted them both with Ferdinand, made a general impression in their favour. Notwithstanding the obligations of the quadruple league, Florence assisted the duke John with presents, and Venice evinced an inclination to befriend him. Sforza alone, who never lost sight of the pretensions of the duke of Orleans to the Milanese throne, remained true to his sound policy of preventing the establishment of any French dynasty in Italy. He declared his resolution firmly to maintain his existing alliance, and prepared for the vigorous support of Ferdinand. His negotiations were even more serviceable to that prince than his arms. By his earnest representations to his friend Cosmo de' Medici and to the Venetians, of the danger which threatened all Italy if the French, already in possession of Genoa and Asti, should be suffered to place a prince of their nation on the throne of Naples, he obtained from both the republics of Florence and Venice a sincere and common declaration of neutrality in the contest between the parties of Anjou and Aragon.

With still greater success, Sforza had already converted the threatened hostility of the papacy against Ferdinand into an earnest resolution to defend him. Immediately on Alfonso's death, Calixtus III., in contempt of the repeated sanction given by his predecessors to Ferdinand's succession, pronounced the fief of Naples to have lapsed to the holy see; but the years of the feeble old pontiff ill suited the schemes of selfish ambition which dictated this breach of decency and faith. He followed Alfonso to the grave in little more than a month, and was succeeded by the celebrated Æneas Silvius Piccolomini, one of the most learned men and enlightened statesmen of his times. With the new pontiff, who assumed the title of Pius II., Sforza made the support of Ferdinand the condition of his alliance; and he so impressed him with the conviction that the aggrandizement of the French in Italy must reduce the holy see to an absolute dependence on them, that Pius, whose foresight was as clear as that of the Milanese prince, saw all his danger, and immediately devoted himself to the Aragonese cause as his own.

Meanwhile John of Anjou, nothing discouraged by the opposition of Sforza, was not the less resolved to accept the overtures of the Neapolitan barons. In concert with Ferdinand, the duke of Milan endeavoured to find sufficient occupation for the Angevin prince at Genoa. Piero Fregoso, the late doge, upon some disgust at the conduct of the French, had retired into Lombardy, where Sforza now assisted him in levying troops to act against John. With the co-operation of the galleys of Ferdinand, Fregoso invaded Liguria, and attacked Genoa by land and sea. (A.D. 1459.) But no success attended his operations; the Genoese remained attached to their governor; and, in a second expedition, Fregoso himself was killed in an ineffectual assault. John of Anjou, thus relieved of all apprehensions for the safety of the city, set sail with a Genoese and Provençal armament for the coast of Naples; where he had no sooner displayed his standard, than Orsini, prince of Tarento, the most powerful noble of the realm, the dukes of Suessa and Sora, and other great feudatories, openly declared for him. Their rebellion broke forth in all quarters against Ferdinand; his adherents and troops were every where routed; and many of the principal places in the kingdom opened their gates to the French prince. Forces from all parts of Italy now poured into the Neapolitan states. The duke of Milan sent his two brothers with an army to the succour of Ferdinand, and the troops of Pius II. passed the frontier in the same cause: while, on the other hand, Jacopo Piccinino, the surviving son of Niccolo, led his bands from a predatory warfare in Romagna to enter the Angevin service; and numbers of the veteran adventurers of Italy gladly enrolled themselves under this distinguished captain,—the last who remained of the great condottieri of former years, (A.D. 1460.)

While the Milanese army was opposed to this celebrated commander in the Abruzzos, Ferdinand forming his junction with the papal forces, advanced against the duke John of Anjou, who was about to lay siege to Nola. That prince retired at his approach to some strong country about Sarno, where, near the castle of that name, Ferdinand surprised his camp during the night. But the victorious soldiery dispersed to plunder, and the Angevin captains, rallying their troops and falling in turn upon their assailants during the disorder of a pillage, put them to a total rout. Nearly the whole army of Ferdinand was captured, and he escaped himself with difficulty from the field. Three weeks later, a battle was fought at San Fabbiato in the Abruzzos, between Piccinino and the

Milanese army. At the close of a combat of unusual slaughter and desperation for these Italian wars, Piccinino first drew off his troops; but the heavier loss of the Milanese had all the effects of a complete defeat.

By these brilliant successes, the kingdom was left almost wholly in the hands of the Angevin party, and it may seem strange how John of Anjou failed of an ultimate triumph. But the usual fate of his house in their Neapolitan contests still overtook him. The prince of Tarento, whose niece was married to Ferdinand, suffered himself to be moved by her supplications, notwithstanding his aversion for the character of her husband. He relaxed in his exertions in the Angevin cause, and finally deserted it; and he is accused of having neutralized the effects of the late successes by his perfidious counsels, which the duke John blindly followed. Thus he induced him to consume in the siege of some petty towns the remainder of the summer, which should have been employed in the reduction of the capital itself. But the zeal and activity with which Sforza remounted his worsted troops, and fed the Neapolitan war with men and money and artillery, had yet greater influence upon its decision. Encouraged by his powerful succours, the Aragonese party recovered from their panic, and, early in the following year, a new revolution at Genoa more than counterbalanced all their reverses in the kingdom, (A.D. 1461.)

After the departure of the duke of Anjou from that city, several causes had contributed gradually, as usual, to disgust the people with their foreign rulers. The old nobles and the plebeians had violent and constant altercations in the councils of the state on the distribution of the public burthens, from which the aristocracy claimed an exemption, though their pressure was aggravated by the exhaustion left by civil discords and pestilence, and by the Neapolitan war. The French governor sided with the nobles in these disputes, and thus imprudently attracted the discontent of the people towards his own authority. A furious insurrection arose; and the great plebeian parties of the Adorni and Fregosi, agreeing for once in common hatred against the foreigners, and succoured by the duke of Milan, together expelled the French from the city. It was to no purpose that old Regnier of Anjou arrived with a fleet and army from Provence, and disembarked his troops to attempt the recovery of the place. The Genoese, with the aid of Sforza, repulsed their assaults, and routed them with such severe slaughter, that nearly 3000 French were killed, or drowned in attempting to escape to their vessels.

This revolution of Genoa was a cruel blow to the Angevin party. It deprived them of the alliance, the fleets, and the subsidies of that republic, and of a ready point of intermediate support from France. The resources of Regnier himself were completely exhausted, his son could no longer maintain the advantages which he had gained, and in the next campaign the fortunes of Ferdinand acquired a decided preponderance, (A.D. 1462.) Forming a junction with the Milanese army, he inflicted a signal defeat upon the Angevins near the castle of Orsaria, and from this period entered on a series of brilliant successes, which were unchecked by a single reverse of any consequence. The prince of Tarento, perceiving that the affairs of the house of Anjou were becoming desperate, and that their resources were utterly expended, was the first to abandon the duke John, and hastened the reconciliation with Ferdinand, which he had for some time been secretly negotiating. His defection was soon followed by that of Jacopo Piccinino, who went over to the standard of the Aragonese prince with all his army, (A.D. 1463.) The cities and the barons of the Angevin party, one by one, imitated the same example; and John of Anjou, whom they had so eagerly invited into their kingdom, finding himself abandoned by fortune, betrayed by his friends, and destitute of the means of continuing the contest, at last yielded the game to his triumphant adversary. After a personal deliberation between him and his father Regnier, who himself brought his son a reinforcement of a few galleys to the Neapolitan coast, the two princes of Anjou resolved to shed no more blood in a ruined cause; and at once setting sail for France, left the long-contested throne of Naples to the quiet possession of Ferdinand, (A.D. 1464.)

Peace had already been restored in Romagna by the submission to the pope of the family of the Malatesti, who had been in arms against him in the Angevin alliance; and only one event was wanting to terminate in all Italy the troubles which the disputed succession of Alfonso of Naples had created. Genoa was again torn by the furious dissensions and civil wars of the Fregosi and Adorni, who had begun to combat in the streets, even at the moment when they were engaged in common in expelling the French. The Fregosi prevailed, but it was only themselves to separate into opposite parties, and to deliver over the republic to sedition, rapine, and anarchy; until the weary state, with the usual alternation of its fortunes, was prepared to sink from these turbulent horrors into the repose of slavery. Meanwhile Francesco Sforza was weaving his intrigues to secure so valuable a dominion for himself. By seducing all the exiles and malcontents to his interest, the old nobles, the party of the Adorni, and even some of the Fregosi, and by advancing the Milanese troops towards Genoa, he succeeded in overturning the ruling faction. The sovereignty of the state was immediately deferred to him, upon the same conditions which had too often been accepted and broken by foreign masters; and in submission to the duke of Milan, Genoa shared the general pacification of the peninsula.

For several years after the war of the Neapolitan succession, the peace of Italy was little interrupted by internal hostilities. The appalling progress of the Turkish dominion filled all the states of the peninsula with well-founded apprehensions for their common safety, and in some measure checked their disposition for mutual violence and injury. In the arduous struggle to repel the advance of the infidel arms, which threatened the total subjugation of Europe, Venice was, by her position, her commercial relations, and her numerous dependencies in the Grecian seas, of all the Christian powers first exposed to the storms of Ottoman war, and most deeply interested in the issue of the contest.

She therefore naturally had by far the greatest share in hostilities which excited the anxious attention, and might influence the fate of the whole peninsula; and if we except a few domestic revolutions, almost all that is important in Italian history for a considerable period after the settlement of Ferdinand on the throne of Naples, is to be found in the Venetian annals.

Before we offer a general notice of the foreign affairs of the republic during these years, we may pause to relate one of those dark episodes which mark the fearful despotism and phlegmatic cruelty of her government, and throw so peculiar and sombre a colouring over her domestic history. At the epoch when the peace of Lodi terminated the long continental warfare of Venice, the ducal chair was still filled by that Francesco Foscari, against whose passion for war his grave predecessor had cautioned the senate. The prediction of Mocenigo had been fulfilled: for above thirty years the ambition of Foscari to signalize his reign by conquests in Italy, had plunged the republic in incessant hostility; and the splendour of the dominion which she established in Lombardy was balanced by the ills of war and pestilence, the exhaustion of her treasures, and the neglect of her transmarine interests. But the continental aggrandizement of the state veiled the real decay by which it was dearly purchased: and Foscari, whose personal activity and talents had guided the warlike counsels of the republic, acquired a dazzling reputation and enjoyed a greater credit than almost any of his predecessors. The influence and glory of the doge were alone sufficient to excite the watchful jealousy of the council of ten; a knowledge of his ambitious character had increased their distrust and suspicion; and they had only awaited the opportunity to punish the chief magistrate of their state for his popularity and fame. If the desire of elevating his family had once inflamed Foscari, his pride had already been quenched in domestic sorrows, and chilled by age. He had lost three sons, the successive hopes of his house; only a fourth, Jacopo, survived: and it was by the infliction of frightful miseries on him, that the council of ten, with cold and stern malignity, seized the occasion of embittering the last years of his father.

Upon a secret accusation of having, contrary to law, received presents of jewels from Filippo Maria of Milan, Jacopo Foscari was, in 1445, dragged before the council of ten. In the presence of that tribunal, at which his unhappy parent was compelled to preside, (such was the refinement of Venetian cruelty,) he was tortured into an avowal of the charge, and then condemned, by a sentence which the doge was obliged to pronounce from his own lips, to an eternal banishment from the city. For five years after this, Jacopo Foscari lived tranquilly in his exile at Treviso, until, in 1450, one of the council of ten was assassinated. From his causes of hatred to that body, for their oppression of his father and himself, and from the accidental presence of his servant at Venice, Jacopo was suspected of the murder. He was brought to the capital, and again put to the question before the council. But the roost frightful torments could wring no confession from him; the doge was still the agonized spectator of his sufferings, and still they were prolonged by his inhuman tyrants to an extent which unsettled the reason of the victim. He was now sent to a distant banishment in the colonies; and the real author of the assassination, with which he had been charged, was discovered, by a dying confession.

The innocence, the fearful wretchedness of Jacopo Foscari made no impression on his enemies; his longing fits for home became a madness; and finding that all hope of restoration to his family was past, he contrived, in the wildness of his despair, a means of at least embracing them before he died. He wrote from his exile to Sforza, imploring his interference with the senate; and knowing that this application to a foreign prince would in itself be construed into a crime, he purposely suffered the letter to fall into the hands of the spies who surrounded him. It was forwarded to the council of ten, and Jacopo, as he had expected, was immediately summoned a prisoner to Venice. For the third time was he tortured before the eyes of his father; the touching declaration that he had written the letter merely to gain a last sight of his aged parents and his wife, moved not the compassion of his enemies; and his frame was mangled and dislocated anew. In this state, his distracted family were permitted to visit him in prison, and his heart thus received its last, its sad satisfaction. The sentence of banishment was confirmed with increased severity, but his eternal release from earthly oppressors was at hand; and his agonised limbs had scarcely dragged over the shore of his exile, when exhausted nature sighed forth her pain—and he died.

The unhappy doge had twice solicited permission to abdicate a dignity which had proved so fatal to his family and to himself, and by the resignation of which he hoped to satiate the hatred of his enemies, and to stop the persecution of his son. But the council of ten had as often forcibly retained him on the throne. He was now eighty-six years of age, and after the death of Jacopo, oppressed with years and grief, was no longer capable of discharging the vain ceremonial of his office. But his enemies could not suffer him to die in peace. Among them the most implacable was Jacopo Loredano, who bore an hereditary enmity to the house of Foscari, and attributed to Francesco—apparently without any proof—the sudden death of his father and uncle. At the instigation of this bitter foe, who was now chief of the council of ten, it was resolved by that tribunal to finish the humiliation of the doge, whose abdication they had before refused to accept. They now required him to resign his dignity; but an oath which they had themselves extorted from him forbade him to do so; and they then passed a sentence of deposition against him. They would have induced him to leave the palace of government privately; but he insisted on quitting it by the same great staircase on which, thirty-four years before, he had solemnly been installed in his dignity, (A.D. 1457.) Leaning on his staff, the old man descended from the palace, amidst the indignant sympathy of the assembled multitude, and retired to his private house: but his heart was broken. The sound of the great bell of St. Mark, which tolled to announce the election of his successor, struck on his ear as a death-knell. His agitation produced the rupture of a blood-vessel and instantaneous suffocation. The people had dared to regret his fate; and we may learn their feeling and the tyranny of their rulers, from a decree of the council of ten, which forbade them, on pain of death, to speak of the affair of Francesco Foscari.

So much, indeed, had the suspicious temper of the Venetian government increased, that the council of ten now appeared too numerous a body for the purposes of vigilance, secrecy, and severity; and by a decree of the great council in 1454, a permanent committee was selected from among the ten of three inquisitors of state, whose despotic authority was to be paramount over even that of their colleagues. The inquisitors of state rendered no account whatever of their magistracy. Their public power over the state was unbounded, their secret jurisdiction universal. Their sentences were restrained by no forms, and their executions so buried in oblivion, that even the blood which they shed was without a trace. The lives of their own colleagues were left at their disposal; unanimity only was required for their decisions; but two of them might appoint an extraordinary inquisitor, to assist in the trial of the third if requisite. So mysterious was the administration of this detestable tribunal, and so deep the awe which it inspired almost to the last days of the republic, that the learned Venetian who, in the middle of the last century, accurately traced the civil history of his country, appears to tremble when he declares that it is the duty of a good citizen to preserve a sacred respect for so illustrious a magistracy, and to abstain from attempting to penetrate, still more to divulge, that which it was their pleasure to clothe in obscurity.

After the tragic fate of the Foscari, Venice enjoyed for a considerable time a respite from the long wars which had attended the administration of Francesco. But the Turks were meanwhile constantly advancing their conquests towards the eastern frontiers of Italy; and the petty states which had existed in Macedon, and from thence towards Albania and the Morea, successively fell before their arms. In the terror created by the extinction of the eastern empire, the

Venetians, whose foreign possessions might next dread the assaults of Mahomet II., had thought less of resistance than of submission to that mighty conqueror. After the capture of Constantinople, they had hastened to ransom their merchants who had fallen into his hands in that city, and to conclude with him a treaty of peace and amity, by which their commercial subjects were permitted to continue in his capital under the government of one of their own magistrates. But every year had since increased the danger of the republic; and the Turkish power had at length penetrated within a day's journey of her Italian frontiers, and yet nearer to her maritime possessions in the Morea, when, on the refusal of one of her governors in that peninsula to deliver up a slave, who had robbed the treasury of the pacha of Athens, the infidels seized upon her city of Argos. (A.D. 1463.) The republic was not without hopes of inducing the Greeks throughout the Morea to rise against the Turkish yoke; and her senate resolved to embark in an arduous warfare, which had perhaps become inevitable, but which in its-protracted course was destined to yield only exhaustion and defeat. The expedition of land and naval forces, which the senate fitted out, was at first successful in over-running the Morea, and fortifying the isthmus of Corinth with an immense rampart; but on the approach of a large Turkish army, the republican general shamefully abandoned the easy defence of this bulwark, and the Venetians were driven into their maritime fortresses, (A.D. 1464.)

The war between the Venetians and the Turks re-animated the zeal of the pope, Pius II., who since his promotion to the tiara had seriously designed a crusade against the infidels, and who was now relieved from the anxiety which the Neapolitan succession had occasioned to him. The aged pontiff ardently engaged in the effort to rouse the nations of Christendom to deliver their brethren in faith from the Musulman yoke; and with a pious sincerity which we must at least admire, resolved himself to embark in the perils of the sacred expedition. He induced the celebrated Albanian hero, George Castriot or Scanderberg, who had for twenty years valiantly defended the mountains of Epirus against the assaults of the Turks, to resume the war against them. He invited all Christians who desired to assume the cross to meet him at Ancona; and he proceeded himself to that port, whither immense numbers of adventurers and persons of the lowest classes had repaired at his summons, but without money, or arms, or provisions. But the princes of the Italian peninsula, as well as of the rest of Europe, did not share the enthusiasm of their spiritual chief; their zeal was limited to empty professions; and the Venetians alone at length sent their galleys to convoy the crusaders, who had already separated in discouragement. Pius II. lived only to reach the destined place of embarkation. A violent disorder, aggravated by disappointment and grief, terminated his life. The new pope Paul II., whose persecution of letters has given him a disgraceful celebrity, in no respect shared the spirit of his predecessor. Though he assembled a diet of ambassadors from the Italian powers to deliberate on the prosecution of the sacred war, all parties were now alike insincere in the cause. The vicinity of the Turks, from whom Italy was only separated by a narrow branch of the sea, could not unite them in the common defence; and Venice was abandoned to sustain alone all the burthens of the war into which she had entered.

For some years after the death of Pius II., the contest between the republic and the infidels was maintained without any decisive result, either among the islands of the Grecian Archipelago, or on the coasts of the Morea. In that peninsula, the Venetians defended themselves with difficulty; or if they attempted any offensive operation, it was only to subject the unhappy Greeks to the alternate ravages of their armies and of the Turks. And in the Levant, also, the naval superiority of the republic was evinced only in a course of devastation and piracy, which obliged her natural allies to make common cause with the Musulmans. But at length Mahomet II. prepared for the more vigorous prosecution of the war. An immense army was collected at Constantinople, together with the most powerful fleet with which the Musulmans had ever put to sea. This mighty armament, which, in the exaggerations of the Latins, is variously stated from one hundred thousand to three hundred thousand men and four hundred vessels, was directed, by land and sea, along the Thracian coast towards Greece, by the ancient route of Xerxes; and its object was the conquest of the island of Negropont, the most important of all the Venetian possessions in the Archipelago, (A.D. 1470.) The Venetian force in the island was small, and the inferior strength of the squadron, which was dispatched to its relief, was rendered more conspicuous by the incapacity or cowardice of its admiral. Mahomet II. commanded his army in person; he passed the narrow strait, from the mainland of Greece to the island, by a bridge of boats which his fleet established; the Venetian troops were massacred after a desperate resistance and a feeble attempt of the squadron to succour them; and Negropont remained in the hands of the Turks.

The fall of Negropont created a general panic throughout Italy. Hitherto the Venetians had appeared masters of the seas, and as long as their naval superiority lasted, the waters of the Mediterranean formed an impassable barrier for the Ottomans. But the sudden creation of an overpowering Turkish marine revealed to Italy that her shores were open to the assaults of the fierce conqueror, who had sworn to destroy the throne of Christendom. Paul II., who had hitherto intrigued only to trouble the internal repose of the peninsula, was now terrified into earnest endeavours to unite its powers against the Turks; and he readily induced all the Italian states to renew the quadruple league of 1455 for their common defence, (A.D. 1471.) The pope died soon afterwards, and was succeeded by Sixtus IV.; but his views were pursued; and a respectable armament, fitted out in the papal states, joined the Venetian admiral at the same time with a Neapolitan squadron of like force, which was dispatched by Ferdinand. The combined Christian fleet numbered nearly one hundred great galleys; and the Venetian admiral Mocenigo, to whom the supreme command was deferred, had resolved to divert the war from the Grecian islands to the continent of Asia Minor. The Turkish navy did not attempt to leave the Dardanelles to oppose him; and the Asiatic coast was horribly ravaged by the allies in a predatory contest, which fell alike on the

Christian and Turkish inhabitants. But except the pillage and destruction of Smyrna, the war produced nothing worthy of notice; the sovereign of Persia, who allied himself with the enemies of his faith, was defeated by Mahomet II.; and after the ill success of this diversion, the naval efforts of the Italians, which had produced no adequate return for an immense expenditure, gradually expired.

Meanwhile the war in Albania and in the Morea was prosecuted with various success; but there is nothing to interest us in its obscure details or distant connexion with our immediate subject. The appearance of the Turks in Italy itself is more worthy of notice. It was in 1472 that, after having rapidly traversed Carniola, their cavalry penetrated for the first time into Friuli. Their object was only plunder; but this earnest of future invasions excited appalling apprehensions; and, five years afterwards, these were idealized by a second and more serious expedition of the pacha of Bosnia into the same province, (A.D. 1477.) The Venetians had been careful to fortify their whole eastern frontier with intrenchments, but they were surprised by the unexpected advance of the pacha. The Venetian troops were defeated; and the infidels, spreading themselves over the plains between the Isonzo and the Tagliamento, even passed the latter of these rivers, and filled the whole country with flames, which were visible by night from the towers of Venice itself. That capital was struck with consternation; the inhabitants, with those of the districts of Padua, Verona, and Vicenza, were called out to arms; but the infidels again retired, without attempting to establish themselves in the territory of the republic. (A.D. 1478.) In the following year, the pacha of Bosnia once more appeared on the banks of the Isonzo; but the Venetians were better prepared to receive him. Their numerous troops remained quietly behind their intrenchments, and the Turks were compelled to retreat, without having effected an entrance into Friuli. But the repetition of these attacks, the difficulty with which the contest was maintained in Albania, and the desertion of the cause by all other Christian powers, taught the Venetian senate that peace could alone save their republic from destruction. They were, therefore, glad to obtain from Mahomet II. upon his own terms, a pacification for which they had long endeavoured to negotiate. The city of Scutari and the part of Albania which, since the death of Scanderberg, the Venetians had occupied and defended, were ceded to the sultan, together with the important island of Negropont, and an annual tribute in lieu of duties upon Venetian merchandize. But all other conquests were mutually restored, and thus terminated fifteen years of the most arduous warfare in which the republic had ever been engaged, (A.D. 1479.)

While Venice was thus contending with difficulty against the Ottoman power for the preservation of her colonies, Genoa, with less vigour and fortune, had lost the whole of her possessions and influence in the Black Sea. With the sceptre of Constantinople, the Turks had acquired the key of the Euxine; the Genoese could no longer communicate by sea with their great colony of Caffa, except at the pleasure of the sultan; and it was easy to foresee that Mahomet II. would not permit them long to retain so valuable a dependency. Upon the occasion of some petty quarrel with the colonists of Caffa, the Tartar governor of the Crimea besieged the place, and invited the cooperation of the sultan, (A.D. 1475.) The Turkish fleet appeared before the port, and easily effected a breach in the walls; the colonists were reduced to capitulate; and the last vestige of the Genoese power in the Euxine was thus destroyed. The misfortunes of the Genoese were without a counterpoise; but the reverses of Venice in the late war were balanced by the acquisition of the large and beautiful island of Cyprus.

Ever since the conquest of Cyprus by our Richard Cœur-de-Lion, and his gift of its crown to Guy of Lusignan, the descendants of that chieftain had preserved his inheritance with the kingly title. But a disputed succession and a civil war in 1439, entailed ruin on the dynasty of Lusignan. After a contest between the legitimate daughter, and James, the natural son of the late king, in which the latter prevailed, the Venetians bestowed on him their protection and the hand of Catherine Cornaro, a young lady of noble family, who was solemnly declared the adopted daughter of the republic. The new king of Cyprus, who had thus contracted the singular relation of son-in-law to the Venetian state, fulfilled its duties with fidelity and deference. But he died after only a short reign; and the republic immediately acted as the natural guardian of his widow and posthumous child. The Cypriots, however, were not disposed to accept of the insidious protection of a foreign state; and, during the absence of the Venetian fleet, they rebelled against the queen, and deprived her of the charge of her infant son. On his return, Mocenigo, the Venetian admiral, saw the importance of the crisis. He collected a strong body of land forces from the republican colonies; he awed the islanders into submission, and occupied their fortresses with his troops; and from this epoch Cyprus may be numbered among the possessions of Venice. The infant son of James of Lusignan and Catherine Cornaro died; the republic faithlessly removed to Venice some natural children on whom, in default of legitimate issue, James had settled the succession; and, in 1489, the Venetian government at length wholly threw off the mask and completed their perfidious usurpation, by obliging the adopted daughter of their state to abdicate her kingdom. Catherine Cornaro had enjoyed no more than the shadow of royalty under the authority of the delegated counsellors of the Venetian senate: but that body were still fearful of her attempting to render herself independent by a second marriage; and after obtaining her solemn act of resignation in favour of the republic, they withdrew her from the island, and assigned her for life a castle and a revenue in their Lombard states.

PART II.
Domestic affairs of Florence—Government of Cosmo de' Medici—His death and character—Piero de' Medici—Struggles against his authority—Final establishment of the sovereign influence of the Medici—Death of Piero—Lorenzo and Giuliano de' Medici—Conspiracy of the Pazzi—Pope Sixtus IV.—His share in the plot—Murder of Giuliano de' Medici—Overthrow of the conspirators—Lorenzo de' Medici, sole ruler of Florence—State of the Milanese duchy—Death of Francesco Sforza—Reign of his son, Galeazzo Maria—His crimes and violent death—Minority of his son, Gian Galeazzo—Continued persecution of Lorenzo de' Medici by Sixtus IV.—Unjust war against Florence undertaken by that pope and the king of Naples—their intrigues to deprive the Florentines of the Milanese alliance—Ludovico Sforza usurps the government of Milan in the name of the young duke—Progress of the war against Florence—

Disasters of that state—Discontent of the people—Mission to the king of Naples generously hazarded by Lorenzo de' Medici—He persuades Ferdinand to conclude peace with Florence—The condition of that state still critical—Landing of a Turkish army near Otranto—Universal terror of Italy—Peace granted by the pope to Florence—Abrupt termination of the Turkish enterprize—Renewed ambition of Sixtus IV.—His league with Venice to despoil the House of Este—New war thus excited in Italy—Its progress—Peace of Bagnolo—Death of Sixtus IV.—Pope Innocent VIII.—His quarrel with the king of Naples—Discontent of the Neapolitan nobles against Ferdinand—Their revolt, supported by the pope—Alliance of Florence and Milan with Ferdinand—General war in Italy—Bloodless encounter at Lamentana—Innocent terrified into peace—Subsequent cruelties of Ferdinand against his barons—War of Sarzana between Genoa and Florence—Genoa relapses under the yoke of Milan—General repose of Italy—Last years of Lorenzo de' Medici—His final destruction of Florentine liberty—The honour of the state sacrificed to save him from bankruptcy—His death—Estimate of the character of Lorenzo de' Medici—Prognostics of a new era in the political condition of Europe—Selfish and vicious characters of the rulers of Italy—Pope Alexander VI.—Attempt of Ludovico Sforza to form a league for the protection of Italy against foreigners frustrated by the vanity of Piero de' Medici—Alarm of Sforza at the disposition of the king of Naples to protect his nephew, Gian Galeazzo—He invites Charles VIII., of France, into Italy—Claims of Charles to the crown of Naples—His treaty with Ludovico Sforza—Preparations of Ferdinand of Naples for defence—His death—Alfonso II. of Naples pursues his father's measures—Commencement of hostilities—Entrance of Charles VIII. into Italy.

HAVING arrived at the close of the arduous struggle of Venice against the Turkish power, our attention is recalled to the internal affairs of Italy. Among these, the domestic condition of Florence still forms the most interesting object; and we must take up the history of that republic from the revolution of 1434, which summoned Cosmo de' Medici from exile to exercise a supreme control over the government of the state. With that triumph of the house of Medici, commenced the last act in the great drama of Florentine liberty, of which the descendants of Cosmo were to complete the destruction. Hitherto Florence had endured all the storms of political violence: she had been exposed to the dangerous enterprises of foreign tyrants, and constantly agitated by the fierce contests of her own implacable factions; but she had never rested in subjection to the will of a single master. If the administration of the Guelf oligarchy had been partial and arbitrary, it was still in principle republican. The Albizzi and their friends had, in general, respected the forms of the constitution, and, under their sway, hope still remained for the ultimate preservation of the commonwealth.

But with the elevation of the Medici, the general spirit of party was overruled by blind devotion to the hereditary chiefs of a single great family. The Medici had numerous dependents and clients; but the event proved that they had no political equals in their party: no corrivals in their own counsels of sufficient weight and authority to divide their power and check their influence. They were lords among retainers, and both their own ambition, and the subserviency of their adherents, could have no other tendency than to establish a monarchical government. The prudence and insidious moderation which singularly distinguished that family, their vast wealth, and even their generous virtues, rendered them the most dangerous enemies which a republic could cherish in her bosom; and the fall of Florence under their sway is a memorable example, how much more to be dreaded by a free state is the union of popular affection in a single house, than all the oscillations and divisions of party.

The establishment of Cosmo de' Medici in power, was followed by numerous acts of tyranny. The balia formed of his adherents passed sentences of exile upon all the leaders of the fallen oligarchy, and upon a great number of the principal persons of Florence, whose attachment to that body rendered them objects of dread or even of suspicion. Several citizens were also put to death; and for about twenty years, by six successive renewals of the balia, the functions of the constitution were kept in continued suspension. At length, in 1455, the regular mode of drawing magistrates was suffered to revive under the scrutiny of the partizans of the Medici. It would seem that even this tardy and imperfect restoration of the public rights, was produced only by the jealousy which some of the friends of Cosmo began to entertain of his exclusive authority. He himself was not averse from an occasion of showing them how absolutely their influence depended upon his will. The popular magistracy was no sooner restored amidst transports of public joy, than the men who had usurped all the offices of state under the sanction of Cosmo, found themselves objects of attack to the new administration and of contempt to their fellow-citizens. They were shortly glad to apply themselves to Cosmo to obtain a new balia. To punish them, he at first rejected their supplications, and even traversed an unsuccessful effort which they made to carry the measure without him. Having thus increased their humiliation, and exposed to them their own weakness, Cosmo then thought it time to prevent freedom from rearing its head. He no longer opposed the wishes of his friends to create a balia, but he was careful to throw on them the reproach of the usurpation which was necessary to the maintenance of his own sovereign influence. He left to Luca Pitti, a man of wealth and presumptuous character, the care of convening a parliament, without himself appearing to participate in the design. The assembly was, as usual, overawed by an armed force, which occupied the avenues to the public place; the nomination of a balia, entirely in the Medicean interest, was assented to by the surprised and trembling people; and torture, exile, and death fell upon some of the citizens who had betrayed most attachment to popular liberty. (A.D. 1458.)

Cosmo was now at an advanced age, the infirmities of which were aggravated by severe paroxysms of gout; and he gradually withdrew from public affairs, to pass most of his time at his country seat in the lettered society which he loved. Luca Pitti profited by the retreat of his chief to raise himself. It was he, and no longer Cosmo, who seemed the leader of the dominant party. He openly made a sale of his favour and protection from justice to replenish his exhausted coffers, and to enable him to finish the superb palace which he, notwithstanding, was still obliged to leave incomplete; and which, becoming in after times the residence of the grand dukes of Florence, only preserved his name to commemorate his impotent vanity. Cosmo was disgusted at the conduct of his followers in supporting the tyranny of this man; but he was daily more disinclined from interference in politics by his great age; and he was finally broken in spirit by the death of his second son, on whose character he had fondly rested his hopes for the future grandeur of his house. He survived this heavy affliction only a year, and died regretted alike by numerous friends, whom he had loaded with benefits, and by his enemies, who had learnt to anticipate with dread the tyranny of his party when no longer restrained by his moderation. (A.D. 1464.)

If we reject the fulsome adulation which the numerous men of letters, who were cherished by the bounty of the Medici, lavished on all their house, and which has been absurdly echoed in later times, we must still agree with a severer judge than these flatterers and their copyists, that Cosmo de' Medici was the greatest citizen who ever raised himself to authority in a republic. With a more durable power, and a happier fortune than Pericles, he governed the Athens of the middle ages with uninterrupted success for thirty years, and enriched her with all the wonders of art. This too was done, not at the public charge, but at his own cost; and still the simplicity of his habits, and the careful pursuit of his commercial profession, enabled him to reserve a portion of his immense wealth for the splendid patronage of learning and learned men. He was a warm friend and a generous patron, an able merchant, and one of the most skilful and penetrating statesmen of his times; while his taste in art, and judgment in letters, shed a pleasing lustre over his more essential qualities. But, as the citizen of a free state, his character had the disgraceful stain, which brands the reputation of all his descendants. He preferred the personal indulgence of a selfish ambition to the true grandeur and happiness of Florence; and the free suffrage of history will hesitate to confirm to his memory that glorious title of father of his country, which was inscribed on his tomb by the republic whose independence he had ruined.

Cosmo de' Medici left only one son, Piero, whose inferiority in talents, and constitutional infirmity of health, seemed little calculated to maintain the ascendancy of his house. But it was a convincing proof how firmly Cosmo had planted the foundations of an hereditary influence, that notwithstanding the bodily ailments which appeared to incapacitate Piero from the direction of public affairs, he was enabled successfully to assume his father's authority over the counsels of the state. The ancient partizans of Cosmo, who, in his declining years, had occupied the government under Luca Pitti, were resolved not to admit the control of Pieri. The majority of them were actuated by jealousy and selfish ambition, a few by more praiseworthy motives. One of these men, Neroni Diotisalvo, by giving Piero the treacherous advice to withdraw his property from a commerce which his health precluded him from superintending, led him to ruin many of his Florentine debtors by requiring payment of loans which his father had advanced to them. He thus converted many clients into enemies, before he discovered the snare in time to prevent the decay of his influence.

Piero displayed more ability in the struggle which was now carried on in the public councils, between his numerous creatures and the faction which had withdrawn from his house. On the expiration of the last balia, some of that party endeavoured to avail themselves of the restoration of the constitutional magistracy to deliver the state from his influence, but their projects were overruled by his adherents; and they then formed a conspiracy to effect their purposes by violence. With this view they secretly collected an armed force, and obtained the promise of support from the duke of Modena. Piero, however, penetrating their plans, evinced an unexpected activity. He procured the aid of troops from the duke of Milan, and from Giovanni Bentivoglio who governed at Bologna, to watch the motions of the Modenese force; and, attended by his son Lorenzo, he repaired in a litter from his country seat, at which he was usually detained by his infirmities, to Florence, where his partizans had assembled a great number of armed men in his palace. Meanwhile he had succeeded by his intrigues in winning over Luca Pitti to his party. That ambitious citizen, whose talents were very unequal to the station to which he had aspired, was seduced by a hollow overture of a matrimonial alliance with the Medici, to desert his party; and his associates, intimidated by his defection, suffered the moment to escape for an appeal to arms. They were reduced to consent to an accommodation by the interference of the existing signiory. After this, Piero only dissembled until the rotation of magistracy left the direction of the state in the hands of men subservient to his interests; and he then threw off the mask. (A.D. 1466.) A parliament of the people was assembled, the public place was filled with soldiery devoted to the Medici, and a new balia was nominated of the creatures of Piero. A considerable number of the citizens of note who had shown themselves hostile to his authority were banished; and Luca Pitti, who had betrayed them, was only exempted from the same sentence, to drag out the rest of his days amidst the universal contempt of all parties.

By this revolution the authority of the Medici over Florence might be considered as finally established, and Piero remained the acknowledged ruler of the state. By successive sentences of banishment since the triumph of Cosmo in 1434, Italy had been filled with Florentine exiles of adverse parties. Their common misfortunes produced a reconciliation among them, and they succeeded in instigating Venice and some of the minor powers to support their cause. Piero, on the other hand, confirmed the alliance of Florence with Milan and Naples (A.D. 1467); and a general war seemed thus kindled in the peninsula, which the pope, Paul II., sedulously strove to foment. But after an uninteresting campaign, a pacification was concluded between the contending powers, without any stipulation in behalf of the Florentine outlaws. This short war afforded the government of the Medici a pretext for new acts of proscription and severity. The administration of justice was openly prostituted to purposes of oppression and venality; and Piero, oppressed by his bodily sufferings, and disgusted with the tyrannical conduct of his own followers, closed his life in retirement, amidst factious excesses which his increasing infirmities had denied him the power to repress, (A.D. 1469.)

Piero de' Medici left two sons, of whom the eldest, Lorenzo, was only twenty-one years of age; Giuliano, the second, was five years younger. Notwithstanding their extreme youth, the brothers were invited by their friends to assume the supreme authority of the state. The men who, under Piero, had engrossed the offices of administration, and whose tyranny had provoked his dying indignation, were not without the ambition of ruling in their own names. But they felt that it was far easier to maintain a power cemented by time, than to elevate a new one, and they preferred the abuses of a factious government, by which they hoped to continue to profit under the nominal supremacy of the young Medici, to the love of their country, or even to the desire of personal independence. They therefore hastened to offer their professions of respect to Lorenzo and Giuliano, as the sole rulers of Florence. The brothers received the charge of the state with modesty and prudence. Lorenzo, who acted for his brother, did not at first assume to himself the conduct of affairs, but left the real administration of the republic in the hands of the same party which had hitherto held it. Divided between the studies and the tastes of youth, the brothers were constantly either surrounded in their palace by all the men who were most distinguished in Florence for literature and art, or occupied in charming the populace with brilliant festivals. Meanwhile the public peace was for several years wholly undisturbed, except by two seditions at Prato and Volterra, which were easily quelled. As he advanced in manhood, however, Lorenzo gradually drew to himself and his brother the exclusive and arbitrary conduct of affairs. For nearly nine years the two Medici had enjoyed their splendid distinction and tranquil fortune, when their dream of intellectual pleasure and political security was suddenly broken by the explosion of a fearful conspiracy.

Among the great families who had hitherto lived in amity with the Medici, were the Pazzi of the Val d'Arno. (A.D. 1478.) Originally noble, this powerful house had shared the general exclusion of their order from political rights, until Cosmo de' Medici, who felt the necessity of strengthening himself by the alliance of the old aristocracy, had obtained a decree for their admission into the class of commoners. Adopting the habits, when they began to share the privileges of their fellow-citizens, the Pazzi entered into commerce. Their bank became one of the most celebrated in Italy; and they rivalled the Medici in wealth, while they excelled them in their illustrious descent. Cosmo, to secure their friendship by the ties of blood, had bestowed his granddaughter, the sister of Lorenzo, in marriage upon one of this distinguished family; but Lorenzo himself, entertaining an extreme jealousy of their greatness, had pursued a very opposite policy. Giovanni de' Pazzi, one of the brothers of his sister's husband, had married the only child of an opulent citizen, who died intestate; and Lorenzo, to prevent the son-in-law from aggrandizing himself by the immense wealth that should thus have devolved upon his wife, caused a law to be passed, by which nephews were preferred to daughters in succession to the inheritance of an intestate. This law was iniquitously gifted with a retrospective force; and thus Giovanni de' Pazzi was deprived, as Lorenzo designed, of the property of his father-in-law, who had not thought it necessary to make a will to secure it to his only child. Lorenzo followed up this injury by the careful exclusion of all the Pazzi, except his brother-in-law Guglielmo, from those offices of dignity in the state, to which their rank and influence entitled them to aspire. He thus filled the whole family with natural indignation; and the eldest brother of Guglielmo, Francesco de' Pazzi, a man of bold and violent temper, withdrew from Florence to Rome (where the Pazzi had established a branch of their firm) to escape from the pride of the Medici, which his own arrogance ill enabled him to brook. The pope, Sixtus IV., shared his enmity to the Medici; he deprived them of the office of bankers to the holy see, which they had hitherto held, to bestow it upon Francesco; and the common feeling, which animated the pontiff and his new agent, soon led to frequent intercourse between them, and to dangerous machinations against the rulers of Florence.

Sixtus IV. had been raised to the papal throne in 1471, on the death of Paul II., whose reign had only been distinguished by his persecution of the literary men of Rome, and by his repeated, though ineffectual efforts, to disturb the tranquillity of Italy. The pontificate of Sixtus was entirely devoted to the scandalous aggrandizement of his numerous nephews, or illegitimate sons; whose equivocal relationship to him, and luxurious extravagance, increased the indecency of their sudden exaltation from obscurity to enormous wealth and possessions. To form principalities for these individuals, Sixtus had filled Romagna with troubles; and had occasioned the Medici to feel justly alarmed for the peace of the peninsula. They had therefore afforded assistance to the signer of Castello, and other Romagnal chieftains, against the attacks of the papal family; and, observing the formation of a close alliance between Ferdinand, king of Naples, and the pope, they had, in 1474, united Florence in a league with the duke of Milan and the Venetian republic, to maintain the repose of northern Italy. The opposition which the Medici had thus raised to the aggrandizement of his family, had inflamed the pope with violent resentment against them; and, together with one of his nephews, the count Girolamo Riario, he readily embarked with Francesco de' Pazzi in an atrocious plot for their destruction. As the result of an open insurrection at Florence appeared hopeless, it was resolved to have recourse to assassination. Francesco Salviati, archbishop of Pisa, who had some causes of personal animosity against the Medici, eagerly engaged in the undertaking; and Francesco de' Pazzi repaired to Florence to mature the scheme. There he succeeded in inducing his uncle Jacopo de' Pazzi, the chief of his house, with others of his relations, to enter the conspiracy; which was also embraced by Jacopo Salviati, brother of the archbishop, by a son of the celebrated historian Poggio Bracciolini, and by several ecclesiastics and adherents of the Pazzi.

The design of the conspirators was to assassinate both the brothers, Lorenzo and Giuliano, at the same instant; for the murder of one would, otherwise, only have the effect of putting the other upon his guard. The pope therefore wrote to the cardinal Riario, nephew of count Girolamo, a youth of only eighteen years of age, whom he had just admitted into the sacred college, and who was then studying at the university of Pisa, to desire him to obey whatever directions he should receive from the archbishop of Pisa; and Salviati, accordingly, carried him to a seat of the Pazzi, near Florence. The conspirators knew that the new cardinal must be welcomed with public entertainments, at which they hoped that the Medici might be found present together, and dispatched while unsuspicious of danger. Jacopo de' Pazzi gave a fete, to which both the brothers were accordingly invited: Lorenzo, however, alone came, for

Giuliano was indisposed. But Lorenzo, as had been foreseen, made sumptuous preparations to receive the cardinal at his villa at Fiesole; and there the conspirators fully resolved to execute their purpose. The entertainment took place, but still Giuliano was absent; and the Pazzi, thus again disappointed, and despairing of securing the presence of the younger Medici at a second festival to be given by his brother, resolved to defer their enterprise no longer than the following Sunday, when the cardinal was to be present at high mass at the cathedral of Florence;— an occasion on which it was thought that neither of the Medici could, with decency, absent himself. There it was determined that, in the midst of the most solemn offices of religion, the crime of assassination should be perpetrated; that the elevation of the host, as the kneeling victims bowed their heads, should be the signal of murder; and that, at the moment of the sacrifice, the archbishop Salviati and others should seize the palace of the signiory, while Jacopo de' Pazzi was to raise the city by the cry of liberty. Francesco de' Pazzi charged himself, together with Bernardo Bandini, a daring and devoted partizan of his house, with the assassination of Giuliano. Giovan Battista Montesecco, a condottiere in the papal service, had boldly engaged with his single hand to dispatch Lorenzo, while he understood that the murder was to take place at a festival. But when Montesecco found that it was before the altar of God that it was intended he should shed the blood of a man, whose hospitality he had enjoyed, his courage failed him. The soldier declared that he dared not add sacrilege to murder and perfidy; and his office was committed to two ecclesiastics, who had not the same scruples.

When the appointed morning arrived, the cardinal Riario and Lorenzo de' Medici were already at the cathedral; the church was rapidly filling with people, and still Giuliano de' Medici did not appear. The conspirators began to dread another disappointment, and Francesco de' Pazzi and Bernardo Bandini left the cathedral to seek for him, and to persuade him that his absence would be invidiously remarked. Every feeling which revolts at murder and treachery is strengthened, when we learn the terms of familiarity on which these men had just been living with him whom they were luring to death. They passed their arms round his waist, as if to draw him in playful violence towards the church, but in reality to feel whether he had put on his cuirass, which he wore with habitual timidity under his garments. But Giuliano was indisposed; he had discarded his armour; and so unsuspicious was he at that hour of impending evil, that he even left at home the dagger which usually hung at his side. As he entered the church, and approached the altar, the two conspirators kept close to him; the two priestly assassins had also fixed themselves in the throng beside Lorenzo; and when the host was raised, and every knee was bending in adoration, Bandini struck his dagger into the breast of Giuliano. The victim staggered and fell, and Francesco de' Pazzi threw himself upon him with such blind fury, that besides inflicting on him several blows with his dagger, the least a death, he grievously wounded himself in the thigh. At the same moment, the two priests attacked Lorenzo. One of them struck at his throat, but missed his aim; and the blow, which only slightly grazed Medici in the neck, merely startled him to his defence. Rapidly throwing his cloak about his left arm for a shield, he drew his sword, and courageously defended himself until his attendants came to his aid. The priests then lost courage and fled: but Bandini, his dagger reeking with the blood of Giuliano, now endeavoured to rush upon Lorenzo, and stabbed one of his train to the heart, who interposed to defend him, Lorenzo, however, was by this time surrounded by his friends, who hastily sought refuge with him in the sacristy, and closed its brazen doors. Meanwhile the whole church was filled with consternation; and the first moment of surprise and alarm had no sooner passed, than the friends of the Medici collected from all quarters, and conveyed Lorenzo in safety to his palace.

During this scene in the cathedral, the archbishop Salviati, with a strong band of conspirators, attempted, as had been concerted, to seize the palace of the signiory and the persons of the magistrates. After filling the outer apartments with his followers, the archbishop obtained by his rank an easy admission to the presence of the gonfalonier and priors who were sitting. But instead of immediately attacking them, he hesitated, and his manner betrayed so much confusion, that the suspicion of the gonfalonier being excited, he rushed from the hall and assembled the guards and servants of the palace. The doors were secured, and the conspirators were furiously assaulted by the magistrates and their attendants with such motley weapons and instruments as the furniture of the palace afforded. Dispersed and intimidated, they made but a feeble resistance, and were all either slaughtered on the spot, hurled from the windows, or made prisoners. Jacopo de' Pazzi, followed by a troop of soldiery, attempted to succour them, after an abortive effort to excite the citizens to revolt by crying liberty through the streets. But the magistrates held the palace until numerous citizens came to their aid, and Jacopo, seeing that the game was lost, fled into the country.

The fate of most of the conspirators was not long delayed. The archbishop Salviati was hanged from a window of the public palace, even in his prelatical robes. Francesco de' Pazzi, who, exhausted by loss of blood from his self-inflicted wound, had been obliged to confine himself to his uncle's house, was dragged from his bed, and suspended from the same place of execution. Jacopo himself, being discovered and arrested in the country by the peasantry, was brought into the city a few days afterwards, and similarly executed, with another of his nephews, whose knowledge of the conspiracy was his only crime, for he had refused to engage in it, and the whole of the devoted family of the Pazzi were condemned to exile, except Guglielmo, the brother-in-law of Lorenzo. The priests who had attacked Lorenzo, the condottiere Montesecco, and above seventy inferior persons besides, suffered death; and even Bernardo Bandini, though he escaped for a time to Constantinople, paid the forfeit of his crimes; for Lorenzo had sufficient influence with Mahomet II. to cause him to be seized and sent to Florence for execution. The young cardinal Riario, rather an instrument than an accomplice in the conspiracy, was with difficulty saved by

Lorenzo from being torn to pieces by the fury of the Florentine mob; but his attendants were mercilessly butchered by them.

The conspiracy of the Pazzi strikingly displayed the absoluteness of the Medicean dominion over the will and affections of the people of Florence. So far from showing any disposition to join the Pazzi in revolt, the populace were filled with grief and fury at the murder of Giuliano, and at the peril in which Lorenzo had stood. They had flown to arms to defend the Medici, and they paraded Florence for whole days to commit every outrage upon the dead bodies of the conspirators which still defiled the streets. The cry of "Palle! Palle!"—the armorial device of the Medici—continually resounded through the city; and the memory of the tragedy wherein Giuliano had fallen, was always associated in the public mind with a deepened and affectionate interest for the safety of Lorenzo, and with an attachment to his person which lasted to his death.

When Sixtus IV. found that the conspiracy of the Pazzi had failed, he immediately followed up the flagitious part which he had taken in that plot, by disturbing all Italy with the more open pursuit of his implacable resentment against Lorenzo de' Medici. But before we observe the continued effects of the fierce and unholy spirit by which this pontiff disgraced the assumed sanctity of his office, we may pause for a few moments to notice the condition of the Milanese duchy. Francesco Sforza, whose enlightened policy and good government as a sovereign had almost atoned for the perfidious career through which he had reached his throne, survived the war of the Neapolitan succession only two years. At the moment of his death, his eldest legitimate son, Galeazzo Maria, was in France at the head of an army, with which he had sent him to assist Louis XI. in the civil wars of that kingdom, (A.D. 1466.) But the quiet possession of the ducal states was secured to Galcazzo Maria, by the wise measures of his mother Bianca Visconti; and hastening his return, he assumed the crown without opposition. Though not without ability, the new duke had few qualities in common with his father. He indeed faithfully preserved his alliance with

Florence, and maintained vigorous order in his dominions. But he was vain and arrogant, pusillanimous and cruel; and in the detestable vices of his private life, he closely resembled that race of odious tyrants, the Visconti, from whom he was descended in the maternal line. In the first years of his reign, he repaid the affection and prudent counsels of his amiable mother, Bianca, with base ingratitude. He obliged her to quit his court, and such was the opinion which he had already taught his subjects to conceive of his wickedness, that her sudden death was universally attributed to poison administered by his orders.

The subsequent conduct of Galeazzo Maria might well countenance the belief of even so revolting a crime. While he revelled with ferocious delight in the infliction of frightful cruelties upon all who fell under his displeasure, his debaucheries were attended with circumstances of intolerable outrage, and carried shame and desolation into the principal houses of Milan. Not contented with forcibly tearing wives and daughters from their homes, he gloried in obliging their natural protectors to become the instruments of their dishonour. The discarded objects of his brutality were then abandoned to his guards, and the last insult of the tyrant was to make a public boast and a derision of their misery. For ten years his degraded subjects had endured his atrocities, when a young man of noble family, Girolamo Olgiato, whose beloved sister had fallen a sacrifice to the passions of this monster, resolved to rid the earth of his crimes. His design was embraced by two other kindred spirits, who shared his injuries or his detestation of an insupportable tyranny. As Galeazzo Maria was moving in his ducal state through the church of St. Stefano during a public festival, the three conspirators suddenly approached him, and together stuck their daggers at the same instant into his body. (A.D. 1476.) The tyrant fell dead on the spot; but the abject crowd which filled the church wanted courage to protect their deliverers. The accomplices of Girolamo were killed by the guards of the duke in attempting to fly; and though the youth himself escaped at the moment to his home, his parent refused him the shelter which a friend afforded. He was shortly discovered and executed, after enduring frightful tortures with unshaken constancy, and a firm conviction of the justice of his cause.

It had doubtless been the hope of the conspirators, that the people would seize the moment of their liberation from tyranny by the death of Galeazzo to establish a republican constitution. But the Milanese proved that the debasing influence of a long servitude had disqualified them for the assertion of the common rights of humanity. While the ducal government was paralyzed by the sudden fate of the tyrant, they made not the slightest effort to strike for freedom; and Gian Galeazzo, the son of the late duke, a boy of eight years of age, was suffered peaceably to succeed him. The duchess Bonne of Savoy, the widow of Galeazzo Maria, took the reins of government for her child, and all the states of Italy assured her by their ambassadors of friendship and protection. The regency of Bonne deservedly acquired the reputation of prudence and justice; but her station was one of exceeding difficulty, for her husband had left several brothers of dangerous character. The youngest of the five uncles of the infant duke refused to trouble the duchess-mother; but the four others, Sforza, who held the dignity of duke of Bari by the gift of the king of Naples, Ludovico, surnamed the Moor, Ottaviano, and Ascanio, leagued to usurp all the authority of the state. Galeazzo Maria, who knew their restless ambition, had removed them from his court, but immediately after his death they hastened to Milan; and, to overthrow the government of Bonne, laboured to revive the old quarrel of the Guelfs and Ghibelins by declaring themselves the supporters of the latter faction. But the administration of the duchess-mother was firmly sustained by a man of talents and probity, Cecco Simoneta, who after justly acquiring the confidence of Francesco Sforza, had served his son Galeazzo with equal fidelity, and by his abilities and virtue had neutralized many of the caprices and extravagancies of that execrable tyrant.

Simoneta was now the chief minister and chosen counsellor of the duchess-mother, and it would have been well for herself and her son, if she had never swerved from his guidance. After a vain attempt to conciliate the uncles of the young duke, by admitting the leaders of the faction which they had revived into the council of regency, Simoneta found that they were still plotting against the duchess and himself. Penetrating their designs, he caused some of their accomplices to be arrested, and the brothers then flew to arms, and endeavoured to excite an insurrection in the capital against the minister. But none of the citizens joined them; they were compelled to retire from Milan, and one of them, Ottaviano, perished on his retreat in attempting to swim across the Adda. Through the influence of Simoneta, the three survivors with their principal adherents were sentenced (A.D. 1477), by a decree of the council of regency, to a banishment in which they still remained in the following year, when the hostilities which the pope excited in the peninsula gave them but too favourable an occasion for renewing their machinations.

As Sixtus IV., in his rage at the failure of the conspiracy of the Pazzi, threw off the mask and declared himself overtly against Lorenzo de' Medici, he did not even attempt an exculpation of his notorious share in that plot. But affecting indignation and horror at the outrage offered to the church in the ignominious death of the archbishop of Pisa, he immediately declared Florence excommunicated if her citizens should fail to deliver up Lorenzo and all the perpetrators of that act to the vengeance of the ecclesiastical tribunals. At the same time he published an alliance which he had already formed against the Medici with Ferdinand of Naples, and with Sienna; for that republic, too, had some petty causes of hostility to Florence. War was now declared by the league against Lorenzo; the Florentine territory was invaded by their troops, and the pope reiterated spiritual fulminations in support of his temporal arms.

The Florentine government vainly endeavoured to deprecate the violence of the pontiff, by acknowledging their fault in having themselves put to death the archbishop and the priests his accomplices, who were subject only to ecclesiastical jurisdiction; but finding this submission without effect, they had recourse to more energetic measures for the protection of their state. Preparing vigorously for the defence of their frontiers, they addressed themselves at the same time to most of the powers of Italy and of Europe; they represented the iniquitous conduct of the pope, and they convoked at Florence a synod of the Tuscan clergy to appeal to a general council against his tyranny and spiritual sentences. These proceedings were not without their weight. The king of France and other princes remonstrated in a high tone with the pope against the prosecution of an unjust war; and though the Venetians, whose contest with the Turks was not yet concluded, abstained from actively engaging in the impending hostilities, the Milanese regency firmly resolved to support the cause of Lorenzo de' Medici, and the duke of Ferrara undertook the personal command of the Florentine forces.

Sixtus IV., however, was not the less strongly bent on his purposes, and his league with Ferdinand of Naples rendered him still very superior in strength to Lorenzo de' Medici and his allies. The pope gave the command of the numerous forces which he levied among the Romagnol signers to Federigo of Urbino, whom he had some years before raised to the ducal dignity; and Alfonso duke of Calabria, son of king Ferdinand, joining that celebrated captain with a Neapolitan army, the confederates gained several successes against the Florentine troops under the duke of Ferrara, who proved himself either faithless to the cause which he had embraced, or destitute of military skill. Meanwhile Sixtus and Ferdinand bestirred themselves to deprive the Florentines of the powerful aid of Milan. By their intrigues they induced the Adorni, who governed Genoa under the Milanese regency, to throw off that yoke; and a numerous army, which the duchess Bonne dispatched into Liguria to support the authority of her son, was defeated by the Genoese with signal disgrace. Though a new revolution afterwards placed the Fregosi at the head of the government of Genoa, the continued independence of that state was equally destructive to the Milanese authority, and therefore injurious to the interests of Lorenzo de' Medici and his country.

The pope now applied himself to persuade yet more dangerous enemies than the Genoese to attack the duchess-regent of Milan. By the machinations of his legate and princely emissaries, he played upon the simple devotion of the Swiss, and animated their religious and warlike spirit in his service against Milan: as if the contest into which his criminal passions had hurried him had been the cause of God. A large body of the Swiss invaded Lombardy, and though they made but one desultory campaign, this short expedition not only augmented the reputation of their prowess in Italy by a defeat which they gave the Milanese army, but embarrassed the counsels of the duchess, and effectually diverted her resources from the succour of Florence. The storm which threatened the government of Bonne from the Alps had scarcely been calmed by the prudent negotiations of her minister Simoneta, when the uncles of the young duke of Milan, in the alliance of the pope, and attended by some Genoese troops, entered Lombardy from their exile, (A.D. 1479.) The eldest was now dead, not without suspicion of having been poisoned by his brother Ludovico the Moor, who succeeded him in his duchy of Bari. On the appearance of the Sforza in the Milanese states, they declared that they only came to deliver their young nephew and his mother herself from the authority of Simoneta; and under this pretence they took possession of a great number of the strong places of Lombardy, which opened their gates to them. The court of Bonne was at the time agitated by cabals against her minister; and at the persuasion of his enemies, she had the weakness to enter into an accommodation with Ludovico, and to invite him to Milan.

When Simoneta learnt the determination of the duchess, he declared to her that the part which she had taken would entail destruction on him and the loss of power to her. Ludovico had scarcely entered the capital, when the prophecy of her veteran and faithful counsellor began its fulfilment. Almost the first act of Ludovico was to cause Simoneta to be arrested, with the principal persons who were attached to his party. After lingering for nearly a year in prison, where he was treated with frightful barbarity, the old minister was finally beheaded, and Ludovico then declared his nephew Gian Galeazzo, though only twelve years old, of sufficient age to assume the reins of government for himself. This was merely to afford a plea for the removal of the duchess from power; many of her counsellors were imprisoned, plundered, and exiled, and she was thus driven by mortification and insults to withdraw from the capital. From this epoch Ludovico the Moor, with the air of directing the judgment of the young duke, usurped in his name all the authority of the state, and became in fact the sovereign of his nephew's dominions. His alliance with the pope and with Ferdinand of Naples had placed him in opposition to Florence, and that state might thenceforth expect to number Milan among her enemies.

Meanwhile the progress of the war in Tuscany had been for two years exceedingly unfavourable to Florence. Lorenzo de' Medici, though absolutely directing the affairs of that state, as if he had been her legitimate sovereign, did not show himself at the head of her armies. His absence from the field was probably occasioned by his consciousness that he had neither experience nor talent for military command; but the want of some controlling authority in the Florentine camp was fatally evinced. The duke of Ferrara and the chieftains of inferior rank serving with their bands in Florentine pay, despised the interference of the republican commissaries who attended their movements. They consumed the resources of the state, and passed the season for active operations in violent disagreements among themselves; while the confederates, under the dukes of Calabria and Urbino, ravaged or conquered great part of the Florentine territory. Lorenzo de' Medici, in the midst of these reverses, did not, however, lose courage. He actively and successfully negotiated for the assistance of Venice, now delivered from her Turkish war; and in concert with that republic, he planned the revival of the Angevin pretensions upon Naples. Though the Venetians still hung back from becoming principals in the war, their ambassadors, together with those of Florence, made overtures to Regnier II., duke of Lorraine, on whom the Angevin rights had devolved through the female line; and that prince eagerly listened to their proposals.

But the people of Florence did not share the spirit of their leader. Their state was exhausted and desolated, their commerce was almost destroyed, and their burthens were hourly becoming more ruinous, in the support of an unfortunate war; which had been undertaken and endured, not to protect the true interests of Florence, but for the personal safety of the individual who governed them. They began openly to manifest their disgust and discontent; and Lorenzo, after the alarming experience of two disastrous campaigns and the loss of the Milanese alliance, had to dread the change of the popular affection and the overthrow of his own authority. Some decisive step became necessary on his part, when the inaction of a truce, which was unexpectedly proposed by the duke of Calabria, gave the people a dangerous leisure to brood over their distresses. The cessation of hostilities, however, more fortunately afforded him an opening for the adoption of a measure, than which there appeared no other resource, while it was in itself both wise and generous. He resolved to proceed immediately to Naples, and to commit himself into the hands of king Ferdinand, though his avowed enemy, with the hope of discovering how that monarch was secretly affected, and of persuading him of the impolicy of continuing a war, the prolongation of which could gratify only the rancour of the pontiff, or his desire of aggrandizing his family.

This enterprise was not without its imminent danger from the faithless temper of Ferdinand; but Lorenzo probably judged, with the penetration and foresight which marked his character, that the interests of that prince would render him favourable to a pacification. By voluntarily absenting himself from Florence, he would both convince the world that he was not the tyrant of his country, who feared to trust himself among enemies under the simple guarantee of the rights of an ambassador; and that, if necessary, he was prepared to make a noble devotion of his safety and life to the interests of his fellow-citizens, who had suffered so much in his personal cause. He accordingly quitted Florence, and being provided with formal authority to treat in the name of the republic with the king, passed by sea to Naples, where he was received with distinguished honours.

Ferdinand had entered into the war against Lorenzo de' Medici merely from the ordinary motives of ambition, and not, like Sixtus, for the indulgence of personal animosity. He therefore desired to pursue the contest no longer than suited his political interests, and these seemed now to demand peace. His son, the duke of Calabria, during his campaigns in Tuscany, had acquired so decided an ascendancy in the factions of Sienna, that he hoped to establish his sovereign authority over that stormy commonwealth. Since the revolt of Genoa from Milan, that republic also had fallen much into dependance upon Naples; and the revolution in the Milanese government had been the means of extending the same influence into Lombardy. To pursue his intrigues in these several quarters, and to strengthen a growing power, the repose of a peace was necessary to Ferdinand. No object remained to induce him to continue the war; and he was therefore the more disposed to listen to the overtures of Lorenzo, whose attractive qualities perhaps gained upon his personal regard, and whose suggestions had certainly more weight upon his fears. Lorenzo reminded the king of the danger to which his throne was exposed from the claims of the house of Anjou: that it was easier for the Florentines to revenge themselves against their enemies, by calling in a French prince who pretended to the crown of Naples, than it would be to protect Italy afterwards from the consequences of thus introducing a foreign power to mingle in her quarrels; and that the common interests of the Florentines and of Ferdinand himself should teach them to prefer a faithful alliance with each other to a senseless war between their states. These considerations were not new to the king, and made a strong impression upon him. But he detained Lorenzo at his court, to observe whether his removal from Florence produced any revolution there. Finding that state, on the contrary, continue its tranquil obedience to the Medicean party even in the absence of its chief, Ferdinand signed a peace with him as the ambassador of his republic, restored all his conquests, and interchanged a mutual guarantee of dominion, upon the simple condition that his son should be taken into Florentine pay, with an annual stipend of 60,000 florins. This treaty adjusted, Lorenzo hastened his return to Florence, where the grateful joy and increased affection of the people enthusiastically greeted him, on the successful termination of his mission, as the benefactor and saviour of his country.

But peace with Ferdinand did not release Florence from more than one cause of anxiety. The pope was still obstinately resolved to pursue Lorenzo de' Medici to destruction by the continuance of the war; and the duke of Calabria, instead of withdrawing the Neapolitan troops from Tuscany, remained at Sienna, weaving his toils about that republic, and still menacing the surrounding country. But just when Lorenzo had most reason to dread an approaching crisis, an event suddenly occurred which paralyzed all Italy with terror, induced the pope at once in his panic to abandon the indulgence of his rancour, and obliged the duke of Calabria to evacuate Sienna and to march to the defence of his father's dominions. This was the debarkation near Otranto of a formidable Turkish army. Mahomet II., who was still living, and who claimed the provinces of southern Italy as ancient dependencies of the sceptre of Constantinople, seriously meditated the subjugation of all Italy; and his enterprise against Otranto was only intended as a prelude to more extensive plans of conquest. In undertaking it he was instigated by the Venetians, who in their jealousy of the late reconciliation between Lorenzo de' Medici and Ferdinand of Naples, did not hesitate to concert the ruin of the latter, even at the hazard of delivering the whole peninsula into the hands of the infidels.

It is difficult, in the modern decay of the Ottoman power, to conceive the fear and horror which, during the fifteenth century, its gigantic and rapid growth produced throughout Christendom. Sixtus IV., to whose distempered apprehension the Turks seemed already at the gates of Rome, addressed bulls to all Christian princes, and especially to the powers of Italy, earnestly exhorting them to peace among themselves and common war against the infidels. In his terror, he set them the example by voluntarily offering to accept the submission of the Florentines, which he had hitherto so obstinately refused. A solemn embassy was accordingly sent to him of some of the principal citizens of Florence, who threw themselves at his feet, confessed that their state had sinned against the church, and implored his pardon. The haughty pontiff in reply reproached them in violent terms for their disobedience to the holy see, but concluded by granting them absolution, removing the interdict from their city, and agreeing to equitable terms of peace.

The Turks, on their landing near Otranto, had immediately laid siege to that important city, and as the place was unprepared for defence, they in a few days, notwithstanding the gallant resistance of the people, entered it by the breach, and made a horrible massacre of the inhabitants. But immediately after this success, Mahomet II. recalled the main force of the expedition, leaving a strong garrison of above seven thousand men in Otranto. The duke of Calabria, being hastily summoned by his father with his army from Tuscany, and joined by numerous reinforcements, laid siege to the Turkish garrison by land and sea. The infidels had, however, already assembled a powerful armament with 25,000 troops on the opposite shores of the Adriatic to relieve Otranto, and pursue their conquests in Italy, when an abrupt termination was put to their designs by the death of Mahomet II., and the civil war which broke out between his sons. (A.D. 1481.) Despairing of succour during this distracted state of the Ottoman empire, the Turkish garrison of Otranto capitulated upon honourable terms, which were however immediately violated.

The death of Mahomet II., the fierce conqueror of Constantinople, was hailed by all the Italian powers, as a deliverance from the greatest peril to which Christendom had ever been exposed. Accordingly the pope was no sooner thus released from the dismay which had so violently agitated him, than he immediately laboured to disturb the repose that Italy had only just begun to enjoy since the late war. Thenceforth he gave the reins to his ambition of aggrandizing his favourite nephew Girolamo Riario, count of Imola, to gratify whose interests and passions he had already so long embroiled the peninsula. Sixtus IV. now found a spirit which responded to his own in the councils of Venice. That ambitious republic was also freed from alarm of the Turkish power; and grasping at an extension of her territory towards Tuscany, she eagerly listened to the proposals of Sixtus and his nephew to despoil the house of Este and partition its states. The Venetians easily made an occasion of quarrel with Ercole, the reigning duke of Ferrara; and the pope joined them in a declaration of war, without even troubling himself to find a plea for this aggression. (A.D. 1482.) Several of the minor signors of Italy joined this league of the pope and the Venetians; but the king of Naples, the duke of Milan, the marquis of Mantua, and the Florentines, could not tamely suffer the spoliation of the Ferrarese dominions to enrich the papal family, and more especially the Venetians, who were already so powerful. These four powers, with other lesser states, therefore formed a counter-league for the defence of the duke of Ferrara; and thus Italy was agitated from one extremity to the other by a general war which commenced in all quarters.

We shall find no temptation to follow the events of this contest, in which, as most of the parties were rather lukewarm allies than principals, the operations of their mercenary armies were even more languid and indecisive than was usual in that age. The duke of Ferrara, notwithstanding the imposing array of his protectors, was the chief sufferer, since his enemies invaded and dismembered his states with much more zeal than his friends defended them. His ruin seemed hourly advancing, his protectors were gradually abandoning him, and all was prosperity with the league of the pope and the Venetians, when Sixtus, upon some sudden and unexplained caprice—whether jealous of the republic, offended at slights evinced by her senate to his nephew, or tempted by secret offers from the king of Naples—destroyed the work of his own hands, and signed a peace with Ferdinand, by which he guaranteed to the house of Este the integrity of its dominions. Notwithstanding the defection of Sixtus, the Venetians still resolved to pursue their conquests (A.D. 1483); and though the pope now placed himself at the head of the league for the defence of the duke of Ferrara, and excommunicated his late allies, they fearlessly prepared to resist him, and to support the war against all the powers of Italy. They trusted perhaps as much to the speedy separation of a confederacy composed of such discordant and various materials, as to their own resources; and though the league gained some trifling advantages, such success brought no relief to the duchy of Ferrara, which was exhausted alike by the presence of invaders and defenders. In effect, the league soon approached its dissolution. The allies grew weary of the war; the duke of Ferrara must be ruined by its continuance; and Venice alone was obstinately resolved upon pressing it, or at least retaining a part of her conquests.

Under these circumstances a peace was at last accommodated by negotiation between the Venetians and Ludovico Sforza, the real sovereign of Milan. By this treaty, which was afterwards ratified by the ambassadors of the other belligerents at Bagnolo, the Venetians were left in possession of a considerable extent of territory about Rovigo, at the expense of the house of Este. The interests of several of the weaker powers, as well as of the duke of Ferrara, were more or less sacrificed to those of the stronger; but the pope was more dissatisfied than any of the other allies, for the peace offered no acquisitions to his nephew. He refused to confirm its stipulations; but he was now incapable of opposing resistance to them. He had already been alarmingly attacked by gout in the stomach, and the intelligence of this treaty is said to have thrown him into a paroxysm of passion, which hastened his dissolution, (A.D. 1484.) During his whole pontificate the sole objects of Sixtus IV. had been to aggrandize his worthless relatives, and to gratify his fierce animosities, at the expense of every upright principle and duty. To accomplish these ends he had shrunk from no crime; he had felt no compunction in devastating the peninsula with injustice and bloodshed; and his last emotion was regret that he was compelled to leave Italy at peace.

The individual of their body whom the cardinals in conclave now seated in the vacant chair of St. Peter, was in character and habits very different from the late pontiff. Innocent VIII. was as indolent and feeble in spirit, as Sixtus IV. had been active and turbulent. Like his predecessor, indeed, the new pope was surrounded by relatives, for whose interests he was ready to make any sacrifice of the public good. Seven children were the results of his various amours; and forgetting the decent practice of his church, which might have taught him by frequent examples to disguise the claims of these objects upon his paternal affection under the plea of mere consanguinity, he introduced a novel scandal into the papacy by openly acknowledging them all. But neither Innocent nor his children were of a restless and enterprising temperament. They did not disturb Italy by their crimes like Sixtus and his family; and debauchery, extortion, and unblushing venality remained the only reproaches of the papal court. Innocent himself was a well-intentioned man; but he was constantly governed by unworthy favourites, to whom he permitted every irregularity; and his domestic administration was sullied by the vices of his dependents.

Innocent VIII. had been indebted for his first elevation in the church to the patronage of Ferdinand of Naples, and that monarch naturally expected to find in him a faithful adherent. But experience had shown that the popes were seldom remarkable for gratitude to the early founders of their fortunes, and more frequently desirous of making their former masters feel that the relations of dependence were reversed. Immediately after his accession to the tiara. Innocent began to assume a haughty tone towards his old patron, and demanded the payment of the feudal tribute from the Neapolitan kingdom to the holy see, with which Sixtus IV. had dispensed. As the breach which this demand created gradually widened, the ambition of the pope was seduced by the state of the Neapolitan kingdom, to attempt the total overthrow of the Aragonese dynasty. Ferdinand had always been deservedly unpopular with his subjects. Besides the general rigour and cruelty of his government, his reign had been distinguished by many acts of bad faith and perfidy. After his triumph over John of Anjou, he had violated the solemn obligation of oaths to ruin the barons who had supported that prince. He had seized the duke of Suessa, imprisoned him, and despoiled him of his states; he had inveigled into his power the celebrated condottiere Jacopo Piccinino, and caused him to be murdered in his dungeon; and after striking terror into the nobles by these iniquitous proceedings, he had bruised their power with a rod of iron, and equally oppressed them and the rest of his people. The general disaffection produced by his tyranny was increased by the character of his eldest son. If the Neapolitans justly feared and detested the relentless and arbitrary temper of their reigning monarch, they had still more reason to anticipate with abhorrence the rule of his successor. Alfonso, duke of Calabria, had already shown himself more tyrannical and cruel in his nature than his father, and thoroughly vicious in all his propensities. The resentment of the nobles was aggravated to the highest pitch by the violences which he committed in the royal name, and they negotiated with Innocent VIII. to obtain his aid against their princes, engaging to place their kingdom, already a fief of the holy see, under his immediate authority. The pope eagerly countenanced their discontent; and an act of treachery attempted by the duke of Calabria shortly gave him a feasible occasion for commencing hostilities against Ferdinand.

The city of Aquila, though contained within the Neapolitan dominions, had long enjoyed a municipal independence, which the duke now violated by seizing the principal citizen-noble of the place, and treacherously introducing his troops within its walls, (A.D. 1485.) The magistracy, after vain remonstrances with Alfonso, excited their fellow-citizens to rise in arms; the soldiery of the duke were either slain or expelled; and the people of Aquila then implored the papal protection. Innocent immediately sent a body of troops to their defence; and most of the Neapolitan great feudatories and barons, now secure of his support, at the same time assembled in a general congress at Melfi, and raised the standard of revolt. The count of Sarno and Antonio Petrucci, two of

Ferdinand's own ministers, who had reason to dread the future oppression of the duke of Calabria, secretly entered into a correspondence with the insurgents, and the rebellion rapidly spread throughout the kingdom. To give more effect to the confederacy of the Neapolitan nobles, the pope endeavoured to gain the co-operation of Venice. But that republic, averse from engaging in new hostilities, yet, since the war of Ferrara, cherishing her enmity against the king of Naples, adopted a middle course. Her senate declined the alliance of the pope, but suffered their general Roberto di San Severino to engage in the papal service with thirty-two squadrons of their mercenary cavalry.

In his distress, Ferdinand formally applied to Florence and Milan for the succours which those states were bound by treaty to afford him. But to the consideration of Lorenzo de' Medici the king might lay some personal claim, and it was particularly to him that his solicitations were addressed. Lorenzo had lived on terms of amity with the pope ever since his accession: but he was not the less averse from seeing the papacy aggrandized by the extension of its temporal influence in southern Italy, and by the fall of Ferdinand; and he was sensible of the advantages which might accrue to his family from the alliance of that monarch. He therefore earnestly engaged Florence in support of the king of Naples and in opposition to Innocent VIII.; and Ludovico Sforza, from similar motives of policy, threw the weight of Milan into the same scale.

None of the contending parties or their allies were thoroughly prepared for war; and Ferdinand, who conducted his affairs with remarkable skill, endeavoured to temporize with his barons by an affected moderation, which, although they utterly distrusted him, was not without its profit for his cause. Retaining only an army of observation to keep the insurgents in check without attacking them, he dispatched his chief force under the duke of Calabria into the states of the church, to unite with the Florentine and Milanese contingents, and to combat San Severino and the papal troops before they could arrive to the support of the Neapolitan barons. After a considerable interval of inaction, the two armies of the duke and of San Severino, met at the bridge of Lamentana. (A.D. 1486.) So ridiculous had Italian warfare become, that, during an encounter of several hours between the hostile array of cuirassiers, not a single soldier was either killed or wounded; but as the army of the duke of Calabria at last pushed their opponents off the field and took some prisoners, this bloodless contest had all the effects of a victory for the Neapolitan prince, who immediately began to approach towards Rome.

Although Innocent VIII. had ambitiously involved himself in the design to overthrow the king of Naples, he had neither energy nor talents for the successful conduct of a project of such magnitude and difficulty. He suffered himself to be thrown into consternation by the first reverse; and Lorenzo de' Medici, seizing the auspicious moment for his ally, easily succeeded in terrifying the imbecile pope into the abandonment of his schemes, by insisting to him on the danger of his position, Ferdinand the Catholic and Isabella, the sovereigns of the united kingdoms of Aragon and Castile, who now for the first time began to interfere in the politics of Italy, also exhorted Innocent to peace, and offered their good offices for concluding the war. Having inherited the crown of Sicily with that of Aragon, Ferdinand the Catholic had an immediate interest in promoting the repose of Italy for the security of his insular dominions, while he was engaged with his queen in the conquest of Granada. By the mediation of the Spanish sovereigns and the exertions of Lorenzo de' Medici, a treaty was concluded at Rome between the pope and Ferdinand of Naples, by which the king agreed to all the demands of Innocent: to pay the disputed tribute to the holy see with all its arrears, to pardon the rebel barons, to suffer them to dwell unmolested in their castles and domains, and to acknowledge both them and the community of Aquila as immediate feudatories of the pope.

But it was farthest from the intentions of the perfidious Ferdinand to observe any of these conditions. As soon as he found that peace was secured, he immediately imprisoned the count of Sarno and Antonio Petrucci, and under pretence that they had not been included by name in the provisions of the treaty, confiscated their property and put them to a cruel death. For a short time after this alarming earnest of his spirit, he continued to observe some respect for the barons who had confederated, until having assured himself that the pope was no longer prepared to resist him, or to afford them protection, he seized upon Aquila and expelled the papal garrison. He next caused many of the principal barons who had been in arms against him to be arrested and massacred in prison; and having by these atrocities delivered himself from the fear of his nobles, he finally threw off all deference for the pope himself, refused to discharge the tribute which he had promised, and arrogated to himself the nomination of ecclesiastical benefices in his dominions. Innocent dared neither to show at the moment any resentment at these insults, nor at the audacious murder of adherents, whom he was solemnly bound to protect. Three years afterwards he was induced, by the hope of assistance from France, to declare war anew against Ferdinand; but finding the French sovereign not in readiness to support him, all his hostility was confined to the promulgation of a few bulls, and closed by a new treaty; which renewed the promise of tribute like the last, and was similarly violated by Ferdinand.

After the conclusion of the Neapolitan war, the repose of Italy was scarcely disturbed for eight years, until the too famous invasion of the French, which occasioned the ruin of her independence and grandeur. The peace of Rome had, however, left one partial quarrel undecided. This was a dispute between Florence and Genoa, for the possession of the town of Sarzana on the confines of their states, which one of the Fregosi had seized, after the Florentines had acquired the place by purchase from his family. Conscious of his inability to preserve it, however, Agostino Fregoso had surrendered the sovereignty of the town to the great Genoese bank of St. George; and Lorenzo de' Medici, after an ineffectual endeavour to obtain the cession of the place by negotiation, resolved to assert the Florentine rights by arms. A petty war had thus been produced between the two republics, and some hostilities had taken place; until the more important contest in support of Ferdinand of Naples suspended the assaults of the Florentines. The treaty of Rome had now, however, left Lorenzo de' Medici at liberty to direct the forces of Florence against Sarzana, which was besieged and taken, (A.D. 1487.) The war had a far more disastrous issue to the Genoese, than the loss of this object of dispute. The pretence of mediating between the belligerents, afforded the crafty Ludovico Sforza an occasion of carrying his intrigues into the bosom of that inconstant republic. He engaged the doge, the cardinal Paolo Fregoso, by bestowing a lady of the house of Sforza in marriage upon his natural son, to place the state under the sovereignty of Milan. But though this new connexion of Fregoso filled his fellow-citizens with suspicion of his designs and produced an insurrection, the party of the Adorni, which prevailed over the doge and his adherents after a furious conflict, fell precisely into the measure of which Fregoso had been suspected. The ambassadors of Ludovico the Moor were permitted to mediate between the hostile factions; an accommodation was effected, by which the cardinal doge abdicated the supreme authority for a pension; and an Adorno assumed the government of Genoa as lieutenant of the duke of Milan, (A.D. 1488.)

After the war of Sarzana was extinguished by the capture of that place, the government of Lorenzo de' Medici at Florence was materially disturbed neither by foreign nor domestic troubles; and during the short residue of his life, the tranquillity of his administration was favoured by the general repose of Italy. The reputation of his personal talents and virtues, yet more than his station as the powerful ruler of Florence, certainly gave him a great and honourable influence in the political counsels of the peninsula. He had essentially proved his power to serve the king of Naples; and if motives of gratitude were incapable of actuating so odious a tyrant, he had at least commanded his respect. Venice was disposed for peace; the power of Ludovico Sforza at Milan was yet sufficiently precarious to induce him to court the friendship of Florence for that duchy; and the inclination of the remaining great power of Italy—the popedom—was of course wholly regulated by the character of the reigning pontiff. It was over the feeble mind of Innocent that the superior genius of Lorenzo de' Medici had acquired its most important ascendancy. Feeling his own weakness, the pope, after the peace of Rome, had surrendered himself almost implicitly to the guidance of Lorenzo. If the disgraceful abandonment of the Neapolitan barons by Innocent, and his pusillanimous submission to the insults of Ferdinand, are to be attributed to Medici, his interested counsels redounded as little to his own honour as to that of the pope. Yet, on the other hand, the moderation with which Lorenzo interposed in the affairs of Romagna, deservedly procured for him a high reputation for wisdom and justice, and were exceedingly advantageous to Innocent, in securing the tranquil obedience of the turbulent and faithless signors of that province to him as their feudal superior.

Lorenzo found his account in rendering these services to the pope, for he thus, and by giving one of his daughters in marriage to the eldest of Innocent's natural sons, prepared the way for the ecclesiastical grandeur of his family. The gratitude of Innocent VIII. laid the first step for the elevation of the house of Medici to the highest honours of the Roman church. At the ambitious solicitation of Lorenzo, the pope scandalized the religious sense of the age by bestowing the dignity of cardinal upon his second son, Giovanni de' Medici, then a boy of only thirteen years of age. The pope evinced his shame of this prostitution of his authority, for he laid an obligation upon the boy-cardinal not to assume the insignia and functions of his new dignity for three years longer; and still Giovanni, who afterwards, under the celebrated title of Leo X., was to shed increased lustre over the lettered name of Medici, was, on entering the consistory at the age of sixteen years, the youngest man who had ever sat in the papal college, (A.D. 1489.)

While Lorenzo de' Medici was thus extending the power of his family by his external connexions, he was labouring with equal solicitude to consolidate his government, and to perpetuate the authority of his house over Florence. In the ambitious pursuit of these objects, he might perhaps deceive himself with the excuse, that he was only providing for the tranquillity of the state, and silence the inward reproaches of conscience and patriotism by appealing to the general equity of his administration. Yet, to the memory of Lorenzo de' Medici must the shame be attached, of having completed the utter min of that noble fabric of Florentine liberty, which Cosmo and his son had but too successfully dilapidated. It was after his return from his dangerous mission to Ferdinand of Naples in 1480, that he availed himself of the grateful enthusiasm of his fellow-citizens in his favour, to deprive them of the last remains of their ancient constitution. To avoid, the inconvenient remonstrances of a popular magistracy, he resolved to put an end to its authority. By the operation of a balia, the usual instrument of usurpation at Florence, he abolished the two regular legislative councils of the republic, the consiglio di popolo, and the consiglio di commune; and committed the functions of these democratical bodies to a permanent senate of seventy persons devoted to his will. The gonfaloniers and priors of arts were thenceforth to be nominated by this assembly; and though these phantoms of ancient liberty were still retained to fill the void which the total suppression of their offices would have occasioned, and to delude the people with the forms of their old republic, they were only suffered to pass idly through the vain ceremonial of the hour. At length even this illusion was insolently exposed to the public eye. (A.D. 1489.) A gonfalonier in retiring from office had, in conjunction with the priors, his colleagues in the signiory, ventured, without consulting Lorenzo, to admonish some of the inferior magistrates for a neglect of duty. For this legitimate exercise of authority, the gonfalonier was himself fined; "for it was considered," says Ammirato, "audacious that he had acted without the sanction of the prince of the government"—a title now first recognized in the once free republic of Florence.

The interests of this prince were a superior, the dignity of the state a minor consideration. The commercial firm of the Medici had still continued its operations, notwithstanding the political grandeur of that house. But in thus incongruously mingling the functions of the prince and the merchant, Lorenzo had been unable to superintend his private affairs, and they had fallen into total ruin. His factors in the different capitals of Europe ridiculously aped the style and expenditure of royal ministers; and their mismanagement and extravagance completed the consequences of his own neglect. The moment arrived when his banks could no longer fulfil their obligations; the state was required to extricate him from his embarrassments; and so overwhelming had these become, notwithstanding the immense capital left by Cosmo, that, to save his grandson from the disgrace of bankruptcy, the public faith and credit were shamelessly violated. (A.D. 1490.) The interest of the national debt was diminished, several pious foundations were suppressed, and the state currency was received in taxes below its circulating value, to be re-issued by the government at its full rate. The bankruptcy of Lorenzo being thus averted by that of his country, he withdrew his capital from employment in a ruinous commerce, and invested it in immense landed estates.

After these transactions, there is nothing either in the history of Florence, or of that of Italy in general, to demand notice, until the death of Lorenzo himself. This event was hastened by constitutional disorders, which appear to have been hereditary in his family, and which finally carried him to a premature grave, at the early age of forty-four years, (A.D. 1492.) His death, which was followed almost immediately by that of Innocent VIII., occurred at a fortunate moment for his glory. New and mightier actors were about to enter on the theatre of Italian politics; an epoch of gigantic ambition and signal revolutions was approaching; and the general settlement of the European kingdoms was only to prepare the desolation of the peninsula by the quarrels of foreigners. Not all the political sagacity and foresight which were attributed to Lorenzo de' Medici, could have diverted the storm that was gathering over his country, and he must have survived only to have been crushed at last in the collision of more overwhelming powers, or to have witnessed the final degradation and misery of Italy.

The character of this celebrated man, who is still known by the surname of the Magnificent, has been so variously stated by literary and political partiality, that it is not easy to gather an unbiassed estimate of his virtues and merits. On the one hand, it has been strangely maintained, that his attachment to Italian liberty was as distinguished and sincere as his love of letters; and, on the other, the warm advocates of freedom, in natural indignation at his final and selfish destruction of the fairest among the republics of the peninsula, have perhaps not always been just to his many real excellencies. It must at least be our endeavour to weigh these opposite opinions in the balance of historical evidence. If we judge the personal qualities of Lorenzo de' Medici by the standard of his times, we shall find that few of his contemporaries equalled him in the moral beauty of his private life, and that not one of the Italian statesmen of that age can be compared to him in his personal exemption from flagrant and revolting crime. His mental recreations were chaste and ennobling; he was affectionate and faithful to his numerous friends, munificent and courteous in his general disposition, and exemplary in all the domestic relations. In his political dealings he was neither profligate nor regardless of oaths, nor cruel and blood-thirsty, nor habitually perfidious. For, as no distinct charge of murder or treachery has ever been credibly established against him, the few vague imputations of guilt which he could not escape, are contradicted by the whole recorded tenor of his conduct, and should in equity be ascribed only to the dreadful frequency of such crimes; to which, in his age and country, it was believed that no politician could scruple to have recourse.

The private character, then, of Lorenzo de' Medici might, even in our happier times, still be deemed unsullied and noble: he is only further to be considered, with reference to his public life, as the statesman and the protector of learning and genius. Of him in this last capacity, it may seem scarcely within my province to speak; yet in noticing generally the versatility and extent of his literary talents and attainments, his pure and exquisite taste for the arts, the enthusiasm of his intellectual spirit, and his splendid patronage of philosophers, scholars, and poets, of painters, architects, and sculptors,—it is here that we must rest his true glory; that of having honourably associated his name with the most brilliant epoch in the literary history of Italy. Hence it is that Lorenzo de' Medici has merited the admiration of centuries; and his panegyrists have done neither wisely nor justly in labouring to claim for him a more universal pre-eminence, as the unerring holder of the political balance of Italy, and the disinterested promoter of the happiness of Florence. In these respects his reputation has been, I think, grossly over-rated, and his fame in a great measure undeservedly bestowed. That he was an active, a prudent, and an acute politician, is certain. A tone of moderation and justice pervaded his transactions with foreign powers, and repaid him in the general estimation which it secured to him, and even in the ultimate success that it unquestionably favoured. His ambition was great, but it rarely exceeded his prudence; and his thirst of power was not the mere blind avarice of dominion. There is no doubt that the brilliancy of his talents, and the public opinion of his equity, obtained for him, in the latter part of his life, a remarkable ascendancy in most of the cabinets of Italy; and therefore his eulogists have taken occasion to describe him as the balance-point of the Italian potentates, whose affairs he kept in such nice equilibrium as to prevent the preponderance of any particular state. But, as Sismondi has justly remarked, there is really no sufficient evidence of this incessant action and controlling watchfulness of Lorenzo over all the motions of the states of the peninsula.

With still less foundation has it been pretended that the idea of the balance of power originated in his capacious mind. But it would be very difficult to prove to demonstration that Lorenzo even steadily pursued the system ascribed to him; and we should look in vain for its results, either in his habitual maintenance of defensive alliances for the security of the weaker states, or in any other of his negotiations. But this being as it may, it must at least be evident to every one who has bestowed the commonest attention upon the history of Florence, that, for full a century before the government of Lorenzo, the theory of the balance of power had been distinctly understood in her councils, and put into practice in her alliances. Hence the hatred with which she inspired all the tyrants of Italy; hence her usual protection of the weak against the oppressor, her frequent coalitions with the minor powers of the peninsula, her extensive negotiations, by which, whenever Italy itself contained no hope of succour, she penetrated into all the courts of Europe. The enemies and precursors of Cosmo in the Florentine administration, the Guelf oligarchy, were the earlier movers of a system, which so far from originating in his family, rather fell into decay under their selfish policy.

I use this term of selfish policy advisedly, for it was the distinguishing characteristic of all the Medici; and that it actuated Lorenzo in his public administration, to the exclusion of every opposing principle of duty to his country, and of every ennobling sentiment of patriotism, is the merited reproach of his life. To his personal security and ambition he sacrificed the few remains of Florentine freedom which his ancestors had spared: to the aggrandizement of his family, and the extension of their influence, all his negotiations and alliances were directed. The lustre of his private virtues would secure him from being numbered with the contemporary tyrants of Italy,—with Galeazzo and Ludovico Sforza, with Sixtus and with Ferdinand; but it is only as the enlightened patron of letters and art, that his memory is entitled to unqualified admiration.

The tranquillity of Florence and of Italy was not broken immediately after the death of Lorenzo de' Medici; and Piero, the eldest of his three sons, took possession, without difficulty, of his arbitrary power. But, amidst the repose of the peninsula, the general aspect of Europe every where bore indications that a new era was opening in the history of mankind; that a train of political combinations was rapidly forming, more extensive and grand in their objects, and more formidable and overwhelming in their probable results, than any which the world had hitherto known. All the monarchies of Europe, after the long anarchy of the feudal ages, had subsided into internal order, and were prepared, by the consolidation of their energies, for the vigorous trial of their relative forces. France, after the death of Louis XI., and during the minority of his son, had acquired a new attitude of grandeur and strength under the glorious administration of a regency; and the young sovereign, Charles VIII., on assuming the reins of government at this epoch, found himself the powerful master of a great and well-organized kingdom. The whole of the Spanish peninsula, by the conquest of Granada, was united under one dynasty; and Ferdinand, the Catholic, had already planted the vast foundations of that empire, of which his wily policy meditated the extension from Sicily to the continent of Italy. Our own island had passed under the severe and vigorous sceptre of the Tudors; and the house of Austria, by the matrimonial acquisition of the Netherlands, had arrived at an increase of dominion, which gave a dangerous preponderance to its influence, under Maximilian, the son and successor in the imperial dignity of Frederic III.

Thus, on every side, the rulers of Italy beheld the consolidation of gigantic powers, which menaced their country with impending destruction. As long as they were divided among themselves by their miserable animosities, they could not fail to perceive that their general position was one of weakness and danger. A mutual sacrifice of jarring interests, a common oblivion of petty dissensions, and a federal league of all their monarchies and republics, could alone preserve the national independence of Italy; and such an association, formed with sincerity, and maintained with good faith, would be abundantly sufficient for their protection from every effort of foreign ambition. But the treacherous and selfish spirit of their politicians rendered them incapable of founding their safety on the basis of integrity. The pre-eminence of Italy over the rest of Europe in all the arts of civilization and refinement, was not graced by public and private virtue; and we may reflect with profit, but we cannot observe with surprise, that her greatness was extinguished by her vices.

The destiny of Italy was often influenced by the character of the sovereign pontiffs; and the successor, whom the conclave gave to Innocent VIII. at this critical juncture was the most detestable of mankind. This was the cardinal Roderigo Borgia, who, under the pontifical title of Alexander VI., was to load the Romish church with its consummation of infamy. Ludovico Sforza was rendered peculiarly sensible, by the proximity of the Milanese duchy to the Alps, of the danger to which Italy was exposed from the ambition of foreigners. An alliance, which had been established in 1480, still subsisted between him and the king of Naples, the duke of Ferrara, and the Florentines; and he endeavoured to induce the rulers of those states to convince the world, by a joint embassy to the new pope, that they were determined to maintain their league for the defence of the peninsula. Such a measure might have induced Alexander VI. and the Venetians to unite in the same cause; but Piero de' Medici, who was utterly destitute of his father's prudence and enlightened policy, was led by his pride and vanity to repulse the overtures of Ludovico, and to attach himself exclusively to the king of Naples, by whose aid he hoped to convert his authority over Florence into a declared despotism under a princely title. Meanwhile, he had been rapidly consuming the inheritance of his father's popularity, and had already betrayed the jealous and tyrannical spirit which might be expected to guide his administration, by banishing his two cousins (descended from the brother of the great Cosmo) from Florence, upon some capricious suspicion.

The Milanese usurper soon became alarmed at the intimate connexion between Medici and Ferdinand. Though his nephew, Gian Galeazzo, had now attained the full age of manhood, Ludovico still continued entirely to exclude him from the government which, ever since his boyish years, he had exercised in his name. The young duke was feeble and imbecile in character; but he had married the daughter of the duke of Calabria; and the proud and courageous spirit of the Neapolitan princess ill-brooked Ludovico's usurpation of her husband's rights. She appealed to the protection of her grandfather Ferdinand;

and the consequent demand of the Neapolitan king, that the young duke should be put in immediate possession of his legitimate authority, increased the distrust of Ludovico at the negotiation between Ferdinand and Piero de' Medici. He endeavoured to secure his own power, by persuading the pope, the Venetians, and the duke of Ferrara, to enter with him into a league, as a counterpoise to the union of Naples and Florence; but still apprehending the insufficiency of this measure for his protection, he addressed himself to Charles VIII. of France, and sealed the ruin of Italian independence by inviting that monarch into the peninsula, (A.D. 1493.)

The ancient pretensions of the house of Anjou to the sovereignty of Naples had now merged, as far at least as the force of testaments could transfer them, into the French crown. By the premature death of that John of Anjou, who had sustained the claims of his family against Ferdinand of Naples, his father Regnier was left without male issue. But the daughter of Regnier had therefore legally conveyed the Angevin rights to her son, another Regnier, duke of Lorraine. Her marriage into a hostile family was, however, so disagreeable to her father, that, to the prejudice of his grandson, he bequeathed his county of Provence, and his pretensions over Naples, to a count of Maine, his nephew; who finally, on his death-bed, transferred all his possessions and rights to his cousin, Louis XI., king of France. Louis immediately seized upon Provence, notwithstanding the better title of Regnier of Lorraine; but the prudent and crafty monarch was not seduced to attempt the dangerous assertion of the more splendid but barren part of the Angevin inheritance. The inconsiderate vanity and weak ambition of Charles VIII. prepared him to enter with avidity on an enterprise from which his father had wisely abstained; and when Ludovico Sforza solicited him to assert his claim upon the crown of Naples, he was easily tempted to engage in an enterprise which was favoured by the prosperity, and might be supported by the resources, of his own kingdom. A treaty was speedily adjusted, by which Sforza bound himself to assist the French king in the conquest of Naples, and Charles guaranteed to the Milanese usurper the possession of his authority. Thus far Ludovico Sforza seemed to approach the consummation of his design, to place the ducal crown of Milan on his own head. But the very means which he employed for the attainment of his bad purposes brought with them the punishment of his guilt. He forgot, in his eagerness to render the French the instruments of his ambition, that a prince of their nation was a competitor for the states which he was himself unjustly labouring to retain; that the duke of Orleans, by his descent from Valentine Visconti, claimed the ancient dominions of her family, by a prior and more legitimate title than the house of Sforza.

As soon as Charles VIII. resolved to attempt the conquest of Naples, he abandoned every other consideration, and hastened to sacrifice the real interests of his own kingdom in the pursuit of this chimerical enterprise. He was at open war with our Henry VII., and with Maximilian, king of the Romans, and on bad terms with Ferdinand and Isabella of Spain. To all these sovereigns he made most improvident concessions, to bind them by treaty not to disturb his expedition into Italy or the peace of France in his absence. At the same time, to conciliate the favour of Christian Europe for his attack upon Naples, he solemnly and publicly declared that, after the assertion of his just rights, it was his ultimate design to carry his arms from Italy against the empire of the Turkish infidels.

When intelligence of the hostile designs of Charles VIII. reached the old king of Naples, he exerted every effort of skilful negotiation to avert the storm, or to strengthen his power of resisting it. But the presumptuous monarch of France haughtily rejected every attempt to compromise his claims; and Ludovico Sforza, who had staked his fate upon a dangerous alliance, had gone too far to retract. To all the friendly overtures of Ferdinand, to all his representations of the ruinous consequences of suffering a foreign power to enter the peninsula, Ludovico returned only deceitful professions, which were merely intended to gain time and to ward off an attack, until he should be supported by the arrival of the French. The Venetians, too, who secretly desired the humiliation of the Neapolitan dynasty, determined, with a narrow policy, to shelter themselves under a neutrality, and to watch the progress of events. Ferdinand succeeded, however, in winning over Alexander VI. to his alliance, by bestowing the hand of his granddaughter, a natural child of Alfonso, upon one of the pope's sons, and by making other sacrifices to the ambition of the papal family; and he drew his connexion still closer with Piero de' Medici. He then resolutely armed to resist his enemies; but he was not destined to encounter the storm which menaced his house, and he suddenly died at the advanced age of seventy years, in the midst of his active and vigorous measures for defence, (A.D. 1494.)

Ferdinand was succeeded by his eldest son, Alfonso II., who, inheriting some portion of his ability, surpassed him, as I have formerly observed, in all the darker qualities of his character, and by his tyrannical and cruel conduct had long rendered himself universally odious. The authority of the new king, however, was recognized by his subjects without opposition; and he immediately confirmed his father's alliances and pursued his warlike preparations. As it was uncertain whether the French would attempt the invasion of Italy by land or sea, Alfonso sent a powerful fleet under his brother, don Frederic, to the coast of Liguria; and at the same time dispatched his youthful son, don Ferdinand, with an army into Romagna, to form his junction with the papal and Florentine auxiliaries. Meanwhile, Charles VIII. had caused his cousin and presumptive heir, the duke of Orleans, to pass by sea with a French squadron to Genoa; where, by the aid of his treasures, a magnificent naval armament was already in forward preparation, while a body of Swiss troops, which had been levied in French pay in the cantons, joined the Milanese forces in the same city. On the arrival of the fleet of Alfonso off the Ligurian coast, some unimportant hostilities ensued, in which the Neapolitans were for the most part unsuccessful. In the mean time, the French troops were pouring into Lombardy from the defiles of the Alps; and still young Ferdinand of Naples was restrained by his counsellors from advancing into the Milanese states to attack them in detail, and endeavour to excite a revolt against Ludovico Sforza; until it was learnt, too late, in his camp, that Charles VIII. had himself passed the mountains, and descended into Italy at the head of his army.

CHAPTER VIII. FROM THE INVASION OF CHARLES VIII. TO THE SUBJECTION OF ITALY TO THE EMPEROR CHARLES V., a.d. 1494-1530.

PART I.
Unopposed march of Charles VIII.—The Milanese crown assumed by Ludovico Sforza on the death of his nephew—Entrance of the French army into Tuscany—Disaffection of the Florentines against Piero de' Medici—His abject submission to Charles VIII.—Expulsion of the Medici from Florence—The Pisans permitted by Charles VIII. to throw off the yoke of Florence—Advance of Charles VIII. towards Rome—Terror and submission of Alexander VI.—Entrance of Charles into Rome—Amount and composition of his army—Dismay of Alfonso II. of Naples at the approach of the French—His abdication and flight—Ferdinand II. king of Naples—His vain efforts to defend his throne—He retires to Ischia—Conquest of Naples by Charles VIII.—Imprudent security of the French monarch—Alarm of the Italian powers at his success—League of Venice against him—Danger of his situation—He resolves to return to France with a part of his army—Narrative of his march—Battle of Fornova—Glorious victory of Charles VIII. over the Italian league—He concludes peace with Milan, and repasses the Alps into France—Ferdinand II. attacks the French troops in Naples, and recovers that kingdom—His death—Frederic, king of Naples—War of Pisa for the maintenance of her freedom against Florence—Share of other powers in the contest—General truce in Europe—Singular state of Florence at this epoch—Rise of the fanatic Savonarola—He acquires a prodigious ascendancy over the people—His despotic authority in the state—Curious occasion of his fall—Charles VIII. of France succeeded by Louis XII.—Claims of Louis upon the crown of Milan, as well as that of Naples—Conquest of the Milanese duchy by the French—Captivity and end of Ludovico Sforza—Crimes of pope Alexander VI. and his son Cæsar Borgia—Condition of Romagna—Conquest of that province by Cæsar Borgia—Designs of Louis XII. upon Naples—His treaty with Ferdinand, the Catholic, for the partition of that kingdom—Iniquity of this alliance—Conquest of Naples by the French and Spaniards—Fate of Frederic of Naples—Extinction of the Aragonese dynasty of Naples—Quarrel of the French and Spaniards over their spoil—Battles of Cerignoles and of the Garigliano Expulsion of the French from Naples—Truce between France and Spain—Establishment of the long dominion of Spain over Naples—Continued atrocities and success of Cæsar Borgia—Death of Alexander VI.—Reverses of Borgia—Pope Julius II.—Fall of Cæsar Borgia—Story of his end—Repose and servitude of Italy—Julius II. re-establishes the papal power in Romagna—Transient war of Maximilian, emperor-elect, against France and Venice—Continued struggle of the Pisans against the Florentine yoke—Their valiant resistance—Final subjugation of their city—Review of the condition and policy of Venice—Her late war with the Turks—The hatred of numerous enemies provoked by her continental aggrandizement—General coalition in Europe against her—League of Cambray—Presumptuous confidence of the republic—Commencement of hostilities—Battle of Aignadello—Total defeat of the Venetians—Their continental provinces rapidly overrun by the confederates—Abject despair of the Venetians—The league gradually dissolved by their submission—Julius II. reconciled with them—Revival of the fortunes of Venice—Recapture of Padua—Fruitless siege of that city by the confederates under the emperor Maximilian—Re-establishment of the Venetian affairs.

THE entrance of Charles VIII. into Italy might easily have been prevented, notwithstanding the disunion of the peninsula, if the powers who held the passes of the western Alps had steadily resolved to close them against his march. But unhappily for the Italians, both the duchy of Savoy and the marquisate of Montferrat were at this epoch suffering from the disorders of minorities and the weakness of female government. Charles was welcomed into Piedmont with distinguished honours by the princesses who exercised the regencies of these states; and, after finding a magnificent reception in his passage through Turin and Casal, he arrived at Pavia, where he was met by Ludovico Sforza, and supplied with the subsidies and resources of Milan. It was in the castle of Pavia that the ill-fated young duke of Milan was retained with his duchess and children. His health had for some time shown alarming symptoms of decay; and his perfidious uncle had scarcely accompanied Charles on his continued march as far as Parma, when he was recalled by the intelligence of his death. The mysterious illness of Gian Galeazzo, and his dissolution at a period that accorded so perfectly with the machinations of his uncle, created deep and general suspicion that Ludovico had caused a slow poison to be administered to him. The character of the Moor but too well justified the belief of his guilt; and partly on the plea that the infancy of Gian Galeazzo's children rendered their succession inadvisable at such a difficult crisis, partly by virtue of an imperial investiture which he had already gained for himself in secret from Maximilian, Ludovico Sforza assumed the ducal crown of Milan.

Meanwhile, Charles VIII., turning aside to the south-west from Parma, had passed into Tuscany through the Apennines, without opposition, by the route of Pontremoli. When the French army here entered the narrow territory between the mountains and the sea, their march through this difficult and barren country might have been arrested at every mile by a far inferior force. But while the whole Neapolitan army under prince Ferdinand was stationed on the eastern side of the Apennines to defend the entrance into Romagna, no effectual steps had been taken by their allies to oppose the invaders in Tuscany. The pope and the Florentines had undertaken to guard the frontiers of that province: but Alexander VI. was sufficiently occupied in the Roman state by an insurrection of the Colonna, the allies of France; and Piero de' Medici, whose incapacity was now signally displayed, had neglected all measures of safety.

As the French approached, the Florentines no longer concealed the indignation which their ruler had already excited by his vain and insolent deportment, so different from the moderation of demeanour which his family had in general cautiously preserved. The people of Florence had always been attached to French alliances; Piero de' Medici had engaged them in a quarrel to which they seemed strangers; and their discontent was openly expressed at his rashness in provoking a danger which he wanted either the energy or the strength to repel. Amidst his terror at the popular fermentation, and the foreign hostility which threatened his power, Piero forgot the difference in situation and character between his father and himself, and resolved to imitate the conduct of Lorenzo, who had averted his destruction by committing himself, in his celebrated mission to Naples, into the hands of an enemy. He hastened to the French camp, and threw himself at the feet of Charles. But his submission was received by the haughty monarch with cold contempt, and accepted only upon the most disgraceful conditions. Though the Florentines had no army in the field, they held the fortresses of Sarzana and Pietra Santa—the keys of the narrow and mountainous district into which the French had entered. For the invaders to reduce these strong places by force would consume precious time, to leave them behind in the hands of enemies would be most dangerous; and Charles insisted that the two fortresses, together with Pisa and other minor posts, should be instantly surrendered to him. Piero had the weakness to cause a compliance with these demands, and thus sealed his own ruin. Returning immediately afterwards to Florence, he found the whole city roused to fury by his unauthorized and pusillanimous sacrifice of the public honour. He was denied admission into the palace of the signiory; he was incapable of any courageous effort to assert his authority; and after his brother, the cardinal Giovanni, with more spirit had vainly endeavoured to assemble the partizans of his family, by traversing the streets with the once animating cry of Palle! Palle! the Medici were compelled to retire from Florence. The gates were closed after them, and Piero completed the measure of his imbecility by withdrawing to Venice instead of returning to the French king, who, for his own purposes, would in all probability have supported his authority against the people.

On the expulsion of the Medici from Florence, the republican government revived, and the signiory sent ambassadors to Charles VIII., to establish amicable relations with him. The French monarch, who was still advancing, had meanwhile passed through Lucca, where he was received by that republic with submission, and entered Pisa. At the solicitation of the people of that city, he permitted them to throw off the Florentine yoke. The magistrates and soldiery of the sovereign republic were expelled, the Pisans re-established their ancient state, and Charles, leaving a French garrison in one of the citadels of the place, pursued his route to Florence, and made his triumphal entry into that capital at the head of his troops. The Florentines had hitherto found little reason for satisfaction at the conduct of the king; and though they received him amicably within their walls, he affected at first to treat them as a conquered people. He hesitated whether he should not restore the Medici; he made most extravagant proposals as the price of his friendship; and though the firmness displayed by the signiory in their negotiations with him had the effect of moderating his demands, he finally extorted large subsidies, in return for the conclusion of the treaty, by which he tacitly acknowledged the independence of the republic. He then hastened his march to the south by Sienna. That turbulent republic, like Lucca, seemed, amidst the collision of mightier interests, to have shrunken into utter insignificance. Charles took unresisted possession of her fortresses, expelled the civic guard of her magistrates, left a garrison within her walls, and proceeded with his army towards Rome.

Finding his line of defence in Romagna turned by the unopposed march of the French through Tuscany, prince Ferdinand of Naples had now retired with his army upon Rome. The sire d'Aubigny, a prince of the house of Stuart, in the service of France, who had been opposed to him with the first troops that had entered Italy and the Milanese forces, at the same time joined Charles VIII. before Florence; and the chieftains of Romagna began to tender their submission to the French monarch. The approach of the whole invading army towards the ecclesiastical capital threw Alexander VI. into the utmost irresolution and dismay. He at first, in concert with don Ferdinand, thought of defending the immense circuit of Rome; but when Charles VIII. had crossed the Tiber above the city, his courage forsook him. He consented to receive the French army into the capital, and the Neapolitan prince was compelled hastily to evacuate it, and to continue his retreat to his own frontiers.

In making his entrance into Rome, the French king sedulously strove to display the amount and warlike array of his troops; and we possess, in the account of a contemporary, a curious picture of the astonishment and imposing effects which were produced upon the Italians, by the novel equipment and composition of this transalpine host. The enumeration is worth repeating, for it illustrates the progress of the military art, and may serve to explain the nature of some striking changes which warfare was now undergoing. The vanguard of the French army in entering Rome, was formed of Swiss and German infantry, of whom Charles had about eight thousand in his pay. The discomfiture into which the phalanx of Swiss pikemen had more than once thrown the Austrian and Burgundian chivalry, and the experience of the Swiss valour in transient incursions into the Milanese states, had raised the military reputation of the hardy natives of the cantons throughout Europe, and at length, in the fifteenth century, brought infantry into repute. But it is particularly from the fatal wars of foreigners in Italy, which commenced at the crisis before us, that we may date the revival of the tactical principles of antiquity, the employment of infantry as the true nerve of armies:—a practice which has always since prevailed, and which must continue wherever war rises into a science. The Swiss and German bands of Charles VIII. Were ranged into regular battalions; and these were clothed in uniforms of various colours, and marched by beat of drum under their respective standards. They were armed with pikes and halberds, ten feet in length, and among every thousand were mingled an hundred musqueteers. Their leaders were distinguished by the waving plumes of their crested helmets; the front ranks of the soldiery, too, wore casques and cuirasses; but the rest were without defensive armour. After these brave and disciplined bands, marched the Gascon crossbow-men, of whom, and other inferior infantry, there were in all about fourteen thousand. They were followed again by the gens-d'armerie, the gallant chivalry of France, in complete casings of steel, and armed, like the Italian cuirassiers, with the ponderous lance. Of this heavy horse the French army mustered some three thousand; with twice that number of attendant lighter cavalry, equipped with helmet and cuirass, with the demi-lance and the long bow. A train of artillery, such as had hitherto never been seen, completed this formidable array. The French had already wrought remarkable improvements in their ordnance. Their gun-carriages on two wheels were fastened for travelling to limbers, much in the present form; and their train numbered thirty-four pieces of large brass cannon; besides others of smaller descriptions, the culverins and falconets of the times. Around the king's person were his household bands: Scottish and native archers, and squadrons of guards splendidly appointed and composed entirely of the flower of the French nobility. Charles was attended by several cardinals at variance with the pope, by the Colonna and a crowd of other Italian captains, and by a brilliant train of the great feudatories of his crown. It was only three hours after noon when the French army began to file into Rome, and the entrance of different troops continued without intermission until long after night-fall. The torch light which glanced on the arms, and partially developed the dark masses of the soldiery, threw a wild and lurid character over the scene, and added to its stern grandeur.

It was from the castle of St. Angelo, to which the pope had retired, that he treated with the French king, (A.D. 1495.) The conditions of peace were soon adjusted, by which Charles swore to respect the spiritual authority of the pontiff, and to receive him for his ally; and Alexander, on his part, promised, on the demand of the king, to deliver to him fortresses and hostages, as the only sure pledges of his faith. Charles remained nearly a month at Rome, while his troops were forming on the frontiers of Naples to enter that kingdom in two bodies by the Abruzzos and the Terra di Lavoro. In the mean time, at the Neapolitan court, all was confusion and panic. Alfonso II., who, vicious and cruel as he was, had formerly, in the wars of Italy and in that against the Turkish invasion at Otranto, gained a great reputation for courage and military talent, was now completely overcome by his terror of the invaders and the alarms of a guilty conscience. He saw, or fancied, his subjects preparing to satiate upon his person their vengeance for the long train of cruelties of which, during his father's reign, he had been the author or active instrument. By day, the execration of the populace, who rejoiced in the approach of the French as bringing deliverance from his odious sway, resounded under the windows of his palace: by night, in dreams or waking apparitions, the figures of his murdered barons seemed to flit before him, and weighed down his troubled and coward spirit. Thus distracted by apprehensions, and torn by remorse, after shutting himself up in one of the fortresses of Naples, he resolved to fly from his kingdom, as if he could escape from himself. On the same day on which Charles VIII. quitted Rome, Alfonso precipitately abdicated in favour of his son Ferdinand; and embarking with his treasures on board his galleys, sailed to Sicily, where his cousin Ferdinand the Catholic gave him an asylum. The short residue of his life was passed among priests in penance and religious observances, and he died before the close of the same year.

The flight of Alfonso II. left his son Ferdinand only the ruins of a throne. The young monarch himself deserved to be popular; and having, just before his father's abdication, returned to Naples, leaving his army on the frontiers, his presence calmed the public agitation, and he took possession of his crown without opposition. If he had begun to reign earlier, his amiable and courageous qualities might perhaps have fixed the affections of his people, and animated their enthusiasm in his cause; but it was now too late. When he hastened to resume the command of his troops in the impregnable position in which he had placed them at San Germano, near the river Garigliano, he found them already conquered by their fears. The French had taken by assault two castles on the frontiers, the walls of which their powerful artillery had laid open in a few hours; and they had put the whole garrisons to the sword. The ferocity with which the French carried on hostilities, so different from their own languid and bloodless operations, at first struck inconceivable horror and affright into the Italians. The Neapolitan soldiery could not be persuaded to face their terrible enemies; and they retired in disorder to Capua on the mere appearance of the French vanguard. Almost all the towns of the kingdom, too, either from terror at the invaders, from ancient attachment to the Angevin pretensions, or from disaffection to the house of Aragon, began to show symptoms of revolt; and from Capua, where he had laboured to arrest the flight of his army, Ferdinand II. was summoned to Naples to quell an insurrection of the populace. His presence had again an instantaneous effect in appeasing the capital; but the short interval of his forced separation from his army was sufficient to complete the subversion of his throne. The condottieri in his pay, and at their head the marshal Gian Giacomo Trivulzio—who became afterwards so celebrated in the Italian wars, and never sullied his fame by a second treason—treated with Charles VIII., and went over with their bands to his standard.

This shameful defection consummated the triumph of the French monarch. When Ferdinand returned from the capital, he found the few troops who still adhered to him in full retreat, Capua in revolt, the banners of France floating over her walls, and her gates closed against him by the inhabitants. He sorrowfully retraced his route to Naples; but the news of his reverses had arrived before him. The populace of the capital were once more in commotion; he had reason to apprehend that the mercenaries who still remained in his pay designed to deliver him to the enemy; and perceiving that farther resistance was hopeless, he abandoned the continent, and, embarking with his family, sought refuge in the neighbouring little island of Ischia. The French army were already at the gates of Naples, and, on the following day, Charles VIII. made his proud entry into his new capital. The whole kingdom, with the exception of a few maritime places, submitted with thoughtless joy to his authority; almost all the Neapolitan nobility hastened to tender to him their allegiance; and the terror which had preceded his arms spread even to the opposite shores of the Adriatic. The Turks seeing the standards of France every where displayed over the Neapolitan towns, and anticipating the immediate passage of Charles VIII. into Epirus, were stricken with such a panic that they abandoned their fortresses on that coast, as if the dreaded conqueror of Naples had already assailed them with resistless might.

After his easy triumph, the reckless and imprudent sovereign of France reposed in his new kingdom, as if no reflection on the inconstancy of fortune could trouble his career of vanity and pleasure. Not only he, but his whole court and army, abandoned themselves to all the enjoyments of sense which a delicious climate, a country overflowing with luxuries, and a voluptuous capital, could afford. Charles was completely engrossed in the celebration of festivals and tournaments, and the pursuit of licentious gallantry. No thought was given to the prosecution of the war against the Turks, which had been so ostentatiously announced to Christendom to sanction the expedition into Italy. The security of the real objects of the French invasion was equally neglected. No attempt was made to disturb Ferdinand II. in his retreat at Ischia; all the offices and fiefs of the crown were wrested from the Neapolitans to be bestowed on Frenchmen; and there was scarcely a native nobleman who was not deprived of some dignity or possession, and insulted by the undisguised arrogance of Charles and his courtiers. French officers filled the provinces and oppressed the people in their avidity to amass money; and the rejoicings with which the Neapolitans had welcomed the advance of the invaders and the overthrow of the Aragonese dynasty, were rapidly converted into detestation of their new masters. But Charles VIII. continued still unsuspicious of an approaching reverse, when he was suddenly roused from his dream of conquest by intelligence from the historian Philip de Comines, his ambassador at Venice, of the formation of a powerful league against him in northern Italy.

When their first consternation at the rapid success of the French invasion had somewhat subsided, the Italian states had full leisure to perceive the bitter fruits of their disunion, in the subjugation which threatened the whole peninsula. No single power of Italy was equal to cope with the French; but it was seen that the expulsion of the invaders, who had been so rashly invited into the country, might easily be effected by a confederacy. The duke Ludovico of Milan, who had himself prepared the storm of French war, had already discovered that he had most to dread from its ravages. The duke of Orleans, who had been left in Lombardy by Charles VIII. in his city of Asti, began openly to assert his pretensions to the Milanese duchy; and while Charles himself showed a disposition to countenance the personal enemies of Ludovico, he refused him the investiture of a Neapolitan principality which he had promised. The duke therefore earnestly applied himself to engage Venice in a league against the French king.

That republic was already filled with alarm at the aggrandizement of Charles, and sensible of the impolicy of preserving the neutrality which she had originally professed. Maximilian, king of the Romans and emperor-elect, and Ferdinand the Catholic, shared her disquietude. The one, besides an old enmity against the king of France, was stung in his pride and ambition by the fear that Charles VIII. aspired to the imperial dignity; the other trembled for the safety of his kingdom of

Sicily from the vicinity of the French, and could not behold with indifference the overthrow of an Aragonese dynasty, and the expulsion of his cousin Ferdinand of Naples from a throne which had added lustre and dignity to his own house. Negotiations were secretly opened at Venice between the republic and the ambassadors of Maximilian and of Spain and Milan; and a league was solemnly concluded by these four powers. The purposes for which it was formed were declared to be the maintenance of the authority of the holy see, the protection of the liberties of Italy and of the respective rights of the confederates, and the common defence of Christendom against the Turks. But the publication of these ostensible objects scarcely concealed that the real designs and secret engagements of the league were directed against Charles VIII. The pope himself was at least an accessory to it, and the other powers of Italy were invited to enter it. But the duke of Ferrara professed to maintain a neutrality, and the Florentines, little satisfaction as the conduct of the French monarch had afforded them, remained faithful to their alliance with him.

Notwithstanding the secresy of the Venetian negotiations, Philip de Comines,—who has left us so animated a narrative of the reign of Louis XI., and of this expedition of Charles,—had already, by his vigilance, long penetrated the extent of his master's danger, and apprized him of the storm which was gathering. But the presumptuous and improvident monarch was not the better prepared for his defence, and the promulgation of the league of Venice broke over him like a thunder-stroke. The peril of his situation was great, and promised to become hourly more alarming. A Spanish armament had arrived in Sicily under the famous Gonsalvo da Cordova, whose name itself was already formidable, from his exploits in the war of Granada. The Venetians and the duke of Milan were actively hastening their warlike preparations; and while the contemplated junction of the German bands of Maximilian with their forces in Lombardy threatened' to intercept the communications of Charles VIII. with France, the republican fleets menaced the coasts of Naples. In the general discontent of that kingdom, the people began every where to show their reviving affection for the Aragonese dynasty. Otranto opened her gates to don Frederic, the uncle of Ferdinand II., and, in concert with some Spanish troops who landed from Sicily, that prince shortly gathered considerable strength in Apulia.

Amidst these increasing difficulties, there appeared to Charles VIII. and his counsellors no prospect of safety but in a return to France; for which indeed his nobility and the whole army, with the restless temper of their nation, had for some time begun to sigh with impatience. But, notwithstanding the immense treasures expended by Charles at Genoa and in France for the equipment of a naval armament, his fleet had so wasted by neglect and the accidents of the ocean, that he had not a sufficient number of vessels left to transport his army by sea. He had therefore no alternative but to retrace his former route through Italy. Still, unwilling entirely to abandon his easy conquests, he imprudently resolved to leave a force behind him for their defence. He thus uselessly divided and weakened his army, as if a part of it could guard what the whole were too weak to preserve. He named for his viceroy the duke Gilbert de Montpensier, a prince of courage, but of talents very unequal to the importance and difficulties of such a command; and he placed under his orders several of his ablest captains, with a moiety of his gens-d'armerie, three thousand Swiss infantry, and a large body of Gascons. Having made these dispositions, the king, with the remainder of his army, set out for Rome on his homeward route.

Alexander VI. had, almost immediately after the passage of Charles VIII. through the papal states on his advance to Naples, shown an inclination to violate his treaty with the king. He had refused to put the invaders in possession of Spoleto, one of the promised fortresses; and his son, the cardinal Cæsar Borgia, found means to escape from the French camp, in which he had consented to reside, under the title of papal legate, but in reality as a hostage. Subsequently, Alexander had joined the league of Venice; but he was still averse from openly commencing a war, as long as his states were exposed to the ravages of the French. Charles, on his part, was in no condition to provoke hostilities; and though the pope, rejecting his entreaties to afford him an amicable conference, retired from Rome at his approach, he passed through the ecclesiastical capital in a peaceful manner, and continued his march with his army towards Tuscany.

On his arrival in that province, he did not conduct himself with more prudence than he had hitherto done, and made several unnecessary delays; though Comines, who joined him at Sienna, apprized him that the Venetians and the duke of Milan were rapidly assembling an army of forty thousand men on his route, at the entrance from Tuscany into Lombardy. He consumed several days at Sienna in regulating the troubled state of that city, and weakened himself by leaving a garrison there, which was in a short time expelled in a new commotion. With the same want of judgment, he suffered his march to be arrested by the affairs of Pisa. On the one hand, he was urged by the Florentines to restore that city to them, as he had promised; and on the other, the Pisans, shrinking with horror from falling again under the yoke which they had thrown off with his connivance, implored him not to abandon them to their former tyrants. The distress of this unhappy people excited so much sympathy among the French nobles and soldiery, that Charles, assailed by importunities on all sides, wavered and hesitated, and took no other measures than to leave more troops in the Pisan fortresses. Before his final breach of engagement with the Florentines in this respect, his countenance of Piero de' Medici, who was now in his camp, converted the patience, with which they had hitherto endured his injurious proceedings against them, into violent suspicion and alarm. They vigorously prepared for their defence, and the dangerous spirit which they evinced induced the king to turn aside from their city on his route.

Meanwhile, hostilities had already been commenced in Lombardy by the duke of Orleans, who having, at Asti, received reinforcements from France, surprised the Milanese city of Novara. But he was immediately himself besieged in that fortress by a superior force of the duke of

Milan; and Charles VIII. yet lingered idly in Tuscany, until the main army, levied by that prince and the Venetians, had enjoyed full opportunity to assemble about Parma. Thus, when the French army, now reduced to no more than nine thousand regular troops, and encumbered with a numerous artillery, which was transported with extreme difficulty through the Apennines, had descended from those mountains into Lombardy, they found the confederates, of four times their number, encamped in the plains below the village of Fornova, under the command of the marquis of Mantua. On the following day the French king, after an ineffectual endeavour to obtain a free passage into his own dominions by negotiation, was attacked on his march by the Italian army. The gens-d'armerie of the confederates, led by the marquis of Mantua himself, made a gallant assault; but instead of throwing the whole of their superior force at once into action, they held back their strong reserves, as usual in the Italian combats. Their light cavalry and infantry, in place of supporting them, fell at the same time to plunder the baggage of the enemy; and the French, who compensated for their vast inferiority in numbers by their superior valour and impetuous tactics, gained a brilliant victory. They lost only two hundred men, but the Italians above three thousand: for the conquerors, who gave no quarter in the pursuit, made dreadful havoc among the fugitive infantry.

After this shameful defeat, the Italian army, though still very superior in numerical amount, only harassed the French rear, and never regained courage to hazard a second general attack; and Charles VIII. continued his march through Lombardy into Piedmont. At Asti and Turin his wearied troops at last found repose, after enduring continued privations and hardships, without abandoning a single piece of artillery. But, in the mean time, the French troops, who were shut up in Novara under the duke of Orleans, were cut off from all communication with their countrymen. While Charles was immersed in pleasures at Turin, the whole confederate army which had been defeated at Fornova, joined the Milanese forces before Novara. Though the duke of Orleans had nearly eight thousand good troops, they were without magazines, and were shortly reduced to the last extremity of want. When Charles was at length awakened to their distress, it was too late to attempt their relief against the numerous army which, reinforced by many thousand German mercenaries, now surrounded them. The king, therefore, saw no other resource, than to detach the duke of Milan from the confederacy by the cession of Novara. Upon this condition, Ludovico signed a peace with the French monarch, which the Venetians did not care to oppose. The duke of Orleans and his followers being thus liberated, Charles VIII. finally recrossed the Alps into his own dominions.

While the French king was thus abandoning the peninsula, the situation of the army which he had left at Naples had already become desperate. Ferdinand II., aware of the general discontent of the Neapolitans against their French invaders, had quitted his retreat at Ischia, and seconded by Gonsalvo da Cordova and a body of Spanish gens-d'armerie, landed from Sicily in Calabria, where he soon formed an army; while the Venetian fleet began to attack the French on the coast of the Adriatic, and defection multiplied against them in all quarters. Although, therefore, the sire d'Aubigny inflicted an utter defeat on Ferdinand and Gonsalvo at Seminara, this success could not establish the French affairs. The king, retiring into Sicily, was shortly in a condition to resume the offensive, and to appear with a Spanish squadron off Naples itself, close to which—on the day after that on which the battle of Fornova was fought in upper Italy—he was encouraged by his partizans to attempt a landing, notwithstanding the presence of the French viceroy with a small army. Montpensier issued from the walls to oppose him; and the Neapolitans immediately rose in arms, received the squadron of Ferdinand into their port, and welcomed the return of the king with transports of joy.

Montpensier made an obstinate and valiant struggle to maintain himself in the fortresses and in part of the city itself; but being surrounded and straitened for food by the Neapolitans, he was at length compelled, after a siege of three months, to capitulate at the moment when De Precy, one of the French captains, after defeating a detachment of Ferdinand's army, was advancing to his relief. During a suspension of hostilities, the viceroy, however, violated his faith and escaped from his blockade; and though Ferdinand II. had recovered his capital, the whole French force, cooperating together in the provinces, supported an unequal contest for some time longer. But deserted as they were by their inconstant and selfish monarch, who, after his return to France, made no serious effort to relieve or reinforce them, they were at once assailed by Ferdinand himself, by the Spaniards under Gonsalvo, and by the Venetian army; the succour of which was afforded to the Neapolitan monarch, in exchange for his subsidies and the pledge of Otranto and other towns. Thus the viceroy, whose army daily wasted by desertion, disease, and the sword, was at last surrounded for the second time, and shut up in his position at Atella in the Basilicate; where the increasing force of the enemy, continued losses, and want of food, reduced the French to despair, and finally obliged Montpensier to sign a convention for his evacuation of the kingdom. The French troops were to be transported to their own country; but as some of their garrisons in other quarters still held out, Ferdinand made this a pretext for delaying the execution of the treaty. The troops who had capitulated were detained in an unhealthy situation, where a pestilence, breaking out among them, swept off four thousand out of five, with Montpensier himself, (A.D. 1496.)

Ferdinand II. had enjoyed the recovery of his crown only one short month, when he was suddenly carried to the grave in the flower of his age. As he left no children, his uncle Frederic ascended the throne, and immediately devoted his exertions to cement the public peace and the union of all parties, by his amiable moderation and by his forgiveness of the opponents of his house. Receiving the submission of the few remaining garrisons of the French, he hastened to dispatch the sad wreck of their gallant army to their own shores, and thus was the whole kingdom cleared of its invaders. The captains left by Charles VIII. in

Tuscany had, some time before, sold the fortresses which they held to the Pisans, to Genoa, and to Lucca; and altogether the last vestige of the French conquests had now disappeared. Such was the fruitless issue of the rash expedition which, to gratify only his vanity and wanton ambition, Charles VIII. had undertaken without reflection and conducted without wisdom; but which yet, by its imposing circumstances and its occurrence at the opening of a new era in the political constitution of Europe, has given to his character a brilliant though unmerited reputation for energy and heroism.

The close of this expedition of the French monarch, destined as it was to plant the seeds of new wars, and revolutions, and calamities for Italy, left at the moment only one open quarrel undecided: the struggle of Pisa for the preservation of her liberties against the iron yoke of Florence. But even the petty war, thus kindled between the two cities, was sufficient to throw all Italy into flames. The duke of Milan and the Venetians took the Pisans under their protection, and sent troops to their support. Maximilian, the emperor-elect, too, was induced to join these powers in an expedition into Tuscany for the same purpose, which he undertook and abandoned alike, after an unsuccessful siege of Leghorn, with the inconstancy and levity that belonged to his character. All this desultory warfare was conducted with the languor of the old Italian tactics, and marked by a total want of interesting circumstances; and the contest still lingered in indecision, when it was at last suspended by an armistice between Charles VIII. and Ferdinand and Isabella of Spain. Since the Aragonese dynasty had recovered the throne of Naples, and the troops of Charles VIII. had been expelled from that kingdom, neither the French nor Spanish monarchs had a sufficient motive for pursuing the hostilities in which they were still engaged on the Pyrennean frontier; and they therefore concluded a truce which, extending to Italy and embracing their allies respectively, gave a brief season of repose to the wearied people of the peninsula, (A.D. 1497.)

During the troubles excited in Italy by the expedition of Charles VIII., the internal condition of Florence afforded a singular and striking example of the power of religious enthusiasm. Since the expulsion of Piero de' Medici, the political councils of that republic had been almost wholly swayed by the influence of a fanatic of extraordinary character. This was the famous Girolamo Savonarola, a Dominican friar of noble birth, who, though a native of Ferrara, had established himself at Florence in a convent of his order, during the lifetime of Lorenzo de' Medici. As a preacher he was then already distinguished by the sanctity of his demeanour, his impassioned eloquence, and his vehement calls to repentance. He declared himself the chosen minister of the Almighty to denounce the wickedness of the age and the scandalous corruptions of the church of Christ, and to foretel the chastisements of the Divine wrath. He soon gained a prodigious ascendency over the minds of his hearers; and he began, even before the death of Lorenzo, to show that his designs were political as well as religious. During the imprudent administration of Piero his boldness increased; he thundered from the pulpit against temporal usurpation, as well as against ecclesiastical abuses and individual sins; and his addresses to the immense assemblages of his auditors were not more sermons, than violent exhortations to the assertion of democratical rights. The terror excited by his fearful predictions combined with his political harangues to form a numerous party, who were equally distinguished by their devotional austerity and their zeal for liberty; and the spirit with which he animated his disciples contributed not a little to the expulsion of the Medici.

After that event, all the families exiled in the sixty years, during which the dominion of the Medici had lasted, were restored to their rights; and among them the collateral branch of his own house which Piero had driven into banishment. Florence was now divided into three parties; and of these the strongest was that of the *Frateschi* or *Piagnoni*, the monastics or penitents, of which Savonarola was the despotic leader; and it contained not only the majority of the lower people, but a great number of citizens of wealth and family, among whom Francesco Valori and Paol' Antonio Soderini were the most conspicuous. This faction was violently opposed by an association of great families, which acquired the name of the *Compagnacci* or libertines, and desiring to replace the authority of the Medici by an oligarchy, denounced the friar upon all occasions as a false prophet and factious impostor. The discomfited adherents of the Medici, the *Bigi*, or the grey, as they were called, from the obscurity in which they were compelled to hold themselves, formed the third and weakest faction. But the partizans of Savonarola bore down all opposition; and I shall not stop to relate the uninteresting changes in the form of administration which left the real guidance of the republic in the hands of the friar.

The fanatical madness, with which he filled the great mass of the citizens, had however one singular effect in determining the bias of the republic in political transactions. He had ventured to prophecy that Charles VIII. was destined to be the divine instrument in reforming the church; and to the general confidence in his predictions, is to be attributed the patient continuance of the Florentines in the alliance of that monarch under his injurious treatment of them, and even after they had been compelled to close their gates against him. After the return of Charles into France, a conspiracy, formed by the adherents of the Medici to re-establish the authority of Piero, betrayed the real ambition and lust of worldly power, which lurked under the wild enthusiasm or daring imposture of Savonarola. To secure the execution of the conspirators, who had alarmed the fears of his party, he countenanced the violation of a law which had been previously enacted at his own suggestion. This desertion of his principles, together with the failure of his prophecies on the divine mission of Charles, and the miraculous assistance which his arms were to receive, shook the credit of Savonarola; but his ruin was hastened by an opposing spirit of fanaticism, as strange as that which he had himself excited.

In his denunciations of the crimes of the church, Savonarola had not feared to expose the scandalous life of the pope himself. Alexander VI., who trembled at the dangerous example offered by his public reproaches, was rendered his implacable foe. He excommunicated him as a heretic, and allying himself with the enemies of the friar, stirred up the rival monastic order to preach against him. An obstinate contest thus commenced at Florence, into which the Franciscans and Dominicans eagerly entered against each other, as if the honour of their respective rules were staked on the quarrel. To prove the truth of the doctrines of Savonarola, one of his disciples and brethren, a Dominican friar, challenged any individual among his opponents to pass with him through a flaming pile. A Franciscan was found insane enough to submit to the test; and to such a pitch of excitement was all Florence roused in the question, that the fearful contest was made a business of state. The flames were kindled before the signiory and an immense concourse of the people; but when the champions appeared, Savonarola insisted that his brother should bear the consecrated host with him when he entered the fire. The Franciscans immediately seized the occasion to exclaim in horror against so sacrilegious a proposal; but Savonarola was inflexible, and the day closed while the point was yet in dispute. But the populace were furious with disappointment at the loss of the horrible spectacle which they had anticipated; they revolted at 'the impious desire of Savonarola to commit their Saviour to the flames; and in that hour the dominion of the friar ended. His enemies availed themselves of the popular ferment to lead the mob to attack the house of Francesco Valori, his chief adherent; and that citizen and his wife were immediately murdered, and their residence consumed to ashes. Savonarola himself, abandoned by the people, was then seized with two friars, his most devoted disciples; and their fate need scarcely be told. The pope was suffered to appoint a commission to try the three for heresy; and his vengeance was glutted by their committal to the flames. The government of Florence then passed into the hands of the political opponents of Savonarola:—the faction of the Compagnacci. (A.D. 1498.)

At the expiration of the general truce which had prevailed in Italy, the Florentines, who were obstinately bent on reducing Pisa to her former obedience, eagerly renewed hostilities against that state; and the Pisans continued to defend their new liberty with equal resolution. Both the Venetians and the duke of Milan had assisted them, with the interested view of finally acquiring the sovereignty of their city. But the Pisans reposed confidence in the former alone; and Ludovico, finding his own perfidious designs impracticable, and dreading the success of the Venetians, whose troops were freely admitted into the Pisan fortresses, changed his crooked policy and allied himself with the Florentines. But while the operations of this war were still pursued with indecisive fortune, and had only the effect, by their enormous charges, of exhausting the resources both of Venice and Florence, the attention of Italy was attracted to the progress of far more important events. Charles VIII. of France, dying suddenly of apoplexy, had been succeeded, as he left no children, by his distant cousin, the duke of Orleans, (A.D. 1498.) This prince, who ascended the throne under the title of Louis XII., was neither remarkable for ability nor strength of character; but he possessed some fair qualities, and in every way excited more esteem and respect than his predecessor. His claim upon the crown of Milan, as well as that of Naples, rendered him also an object of much more anxious regard and apprehension for the Italians; and he was not slow in evincing his resolution to support his pretensions by arms. By descent from his grandmother, Valentine Visconti, he maintained his right to the inheritance of her house; and questionable as was his title, it seemed at least superior to that by which the family of Sforza held the Milanese duchy.

The situation of the duke Ludovico of Milan offered facilities for dethroning him, which availed the French king more than all his appeals to the laws of succession. Odious as was the Moor to his subjects by his usurpation, his perfidious character, and the suspicious circumstances of his nephew's death, he had now, in the war of Pisa, rendered Venice his enemy. That ambitious and vindictive republic readily engaged in the views of Louis XII. She hastened to free herself from the burthensome and unprofitable charge of the Pisan war, by referring the settlement of her differences, and those of Pisa, with Florence, to the arbitration of the duke of Ferrara. Though the Pisans indignantly refused to submit to the decision pronounced by that prince, that they should be guaranteed in municipal rights under the government of Florence, the Venetians deserted them to their fate, to follow their own schemes of vengeance and aggrandizement. They concluded a treaty with Louis XII., by which they bound themselves, in return for the promised cession of Cremona, and a part of the Milanese territory, to co-operate with him in conquering the whole duchy, by an invasion simultaneous with his own. Meanwhile Louis had already secured the aid of the pope, both in obtaining a divorce which he desired, and in his designs upon Italy. He engaged to assist Cæsar Borgia, the pope's son, in spoiling the Romagnol signors, and in thus founding a principality for himself; and he bestowed the French title of duke of Valentinois upon that cardinal, who publicly abjured his priestly vows, that he might throw off every shackle which could impede a career of abandoned ambition.

Ludovico the Moor was now about to reap the just fruits of a life of usurpation and perfidy. Assailed by enemies of overwhelming power, he vainly looked around for protection. The monarchs of Germany and Spain had deserted him: the former was now engrossed in a furious war with the Swiss; the latter had just concluded an amicable treaty with Louis XII., without making stipulations in favour of any of the Italian powers. Of these, Florence was in the friendship of France; and though Frederic, king of Naples, whose cause was common with that of Ludovico, promised to afford him assistance, so utterly exhausted was his kingdom that he was absolutely unable thus to provide for his own security. The only aid obtained by Ludovico Sforza, who, though forsaken by all, did not abandon himself, was from the enemies of Christendom. He prevailed on the Turkish sultan, who dreaded the coalition of France with Venice, to make a diversion in his favour by attacking that republic; and the Milanese usurper himself assembled two considerable armies for the defence of his states on their eastern and western frontiers. But these measures could not avert his downfall; and all his preparations for resistance had scarcely power to delay the moment of its completion.

The alliances and arrangements of Louis being settled, his forces began to pass the Alps, and assembled in the friendly territory of Piedmont, (A.D. 1499.) They consisted of 1600 lances, making with their attendant array 9600 cavalry, for the full equipment of a lance was now six horses; of 5000 Swiss, 4000 Gascons, and 4000 other French infantry. The king confided the command of this army to the marshal Gian Giacomo Trivulzio, together with the sire d'Aubigny and the count de Ligny; and while the Venetians at the same time made their invasion from the opposite frontier, these leaders entered the Milanese duchy, and completed its conquest in the short space of twenty days. For when the French army, with their customary vigour and ferocity, had earned the fortress of Annona by assault, and put the garrison to the sword, this execution struck such a terror into the Milanese soldiery, that they dared not show face to the invaders. Their general, from cowardice or treachery, set them the example of flight; the whole army dispersed; all the Milanese towns hastened to offer their submission; and the French entered the capital in triumph. The Milanese people were oppressed with taxes, and disaffected to the usurpation of Ludovico. They every where received the French with transports of joy; their duke, perceiving resistance hopeless at the moment, hastily retired through the mountains into Germany with a considerable treasure; and Louis XII. only followed his army into Italy to take formal possession of his new duchy.

Louis had scarcely terminated a residence of a few weeks at Milan before the people, finding that their condition was not materially improved under the French dominion, passed from the elation of false hope to sudden disappointment and murmurs.

Between the alternations of rival despotisms, there can seldom be cause for a lasting preference; and this change in the disposition of the Milanese is less a proof of any inconstancy in themselves, than of the inveterate miseries of their lot. On the return of Louis XII. to France, the government of Trivulzio, whom he left as his lieutenant, increased in oppression; and when Ludovico Sforza, who had employed his treasures in levying an army of Burgundian and Swiss mercenaries, re-entered his duchy at their head, he found an universal revolution of popular affection in his favour, (A.D. 1500.) He was received with bursts of enthusiasm, and advancing with celerity, took possession of Milan; from whence Trivulzio, leaving a garrison in the citadel, was compelled to retire with precipitation to Novara, to await reinforcements from France.

But the final ruin of the Moor was as rapid as his success. The Swiss, formerly so renowned for their pure morals and simple good faith, had been corrupted by their constant employment in these mercenary wars. Rendered insolent by the high reputation of their military prowess, and greedy of gain, and utterly debauched by high pay and unbridled licence, they were now capable of sullying their glory by an odious treason. Their bands in the service of Ludovico, finding his treasures exhausted, mutinied, and finished by betraying his person into the hands of the French army. He was sent to France, where he miserably ended his days, after ten years of solitary and rigorous imprisonment. He had placed his own children in safety at the court of Maximilian; but the infant son of his deceased nephew Gian Galeazzo, and many of his near relatives, were made prisoners as well as himself; and the captivity of almost all the descendants of the great Sforza seemed to confirm Louis XII. in the possession of the ducal throne of Milan.

While great part of Lombardy was thus passing under the dominion of the French king, Cæsar Borgia was successfully engaged in that scheme of ambition in Romagna, which Louis XII. was bound by his engagement with him, and with his father Alexander VI., to support. The design was to form a principality for Borgia by the destruction of the Romagnol signors, who, in no more than nominal obedience to the papacy, divided the possession of that province with a few petty civic communities. The object of the papal family was pursued through a course of atrocious perfidy, for which language would afford no term; if its development in the celebrated treatise of a contemporary had not stamped it in eternal infamy with the name of the writer, who could find nothing to reprehend in Cæsar Borgia. A Macchiavelian policy had doubtless long prevailed in Italy, and was only perfected by Alexander and his apostate son; but in the various enormity of their private lives, these pests of mankind had seldom, if ever, been equalled. Poison and the dagger were their habitual instruments for the removal of enemies; their public and flagitious debaucheries I shall not describe; on their yet more horrible and secret depravity I dare not dilate. Of one of their execrable passions Lucrezia Borgia, the daughter of Alexander, was the guilty object. Her eldest brother was sacrificed by the hand of Cæsar to the gratification of an incestuous jealousy; and she was at once the paramour of her father, and of his surviving son.

Romagna, in which Casar Borgia was to conduct the troubled scene of his ambition, had indeed for ages, with the papal territory in general, been the perpetual theatre of violence and horrors. Amidst the constant desolation of the wars in which its petty princes were engaged, it was impossible for their vassals to pursue the arts of peaceful life. They found no security but in castellated villages; their agriculture was only a hurried labour; and after the harvest which they snatched with difficulty, no traces of cultivation remained. The modern sterility and deadly climate of some of these regions were prepared during ages of ferocity; and this was particularly the case in the Campagna di Roma, which was ravaged by the eternal feuds of the Orsini and Colonna. If a fortalice was surprised or carried by assault, it was burnt to the earth and its inhabitants murdered. Its dependant district was abandoned; the pestilential airs of the desert then spread over it; and their malignant influence forbade the return of population. The people of Romagna were made warlike by the incessant hostilities, and desperately wicked by the evil government and character of their signors. These chieftains, the feudatories of the holy see, were taught from their boyhood to pursue war as their vocation. They formed their vassals into bands of gens-d'armerie, more or less numerous, at the head of which they alternately carried on their hostilities against each other, or passed as sovereign-condottieri into the service of the richer powers of the peninsula. The numerous little capitals of their states were carefully fortified; and their palaces were at once embellished by the elegances of literature and art, and defiled with many a deed of gloomy horror. For, of such things was the Italian mind capable, that these princes, the patrons of learned men, of poets, and of sculptors, were yet too frequently monsters of guilt. Their political annals are deeply imbued in perfidy, and blood, and hereditary revenge: the records of their houses are varied only by the assassinations and the incestuous commerce of the nearest relatives.

When Borgia, with the aid of 1800 French cavalry and 4000 Swiss pikemen detached from the army of Milan, and with some condottieri and their bands in his personal service, began to attack these princes, it was proved by his father's conduct and his own, as the cardinal Albornoz had once proved before, how even the Romagnol treachery, which had been for ages proverbial, could be surpassed by the superior perfidy of churchmen. Borgia first attacked and reduced the city and lordship of Imola. Forli was next assailed, and taken by a furious assault of the Swiss, after an heroic defence by its widowed countess. The ancient houses of the Manfredi and Malatesti at Faenza and at Rimini, and a branch of the Sforza at Pesaro, were destined for the next ruin. The lords of Rimini and Pesaro abandoned their capitals and fled from their states; but Astorre III. de' Manfredi, the youthful signor of Faenza, made a protracted and vigorous resistance; and at length capitulated only upon condition that he should be free to go where he would. But Borgia detained him in his camp, under the friendly pretext of making him his pupil in the military art, and in a few days sent him to Rome. There, after having been the victim of the horrible debauchery either of Alexander or of Borgia himself, the boy-prince was strangled, with his natural brother.

The fall of Faenza completed the conquest of Romagna. (A.D. 1501.) Louis XII. had declared that he should regard as a personal injury any opposition to the duke of Valentinois; and, so great was the dread now inspired by the French power, that none of the Italian states had, after this, dared to assist the chieftains of the province. Even Venice had formally withdrawn the protection which she was engaged by treaty to afford to the princes of Rimini and Faenza. Romagna was now, therefore, erected by Alexander VI. into a papal duchy for his son; and Cæsar Borgia joined this new title to his dukedom of Valentinois. He endeavoured to cement his power by pursuing the exiled families of the deposed chieftains with assassination and poison; but he laboured with skilful and selfish policy to win the affections of his new subjects by the establishment of order and justice. Some rigorous examples were necessary; and he designedly chose for his lieutenant a man of severe and obdurate character, Ramiro d'Orco, who soon converted the long and frightful anarchy of Romagna into a state of regular government. But many were the sanguinary executions before this salutary revolution was achieved; and Borgia, from whose plans it was farthest that the horrible severity of this administration should be attributed to his directions, no sooner found order introduced into his new duchy, and cruelty no longer requisite, than he perfidiously ended by directing the execution of d'Orco himself, and exposing his body to glut the vengeance of the people. The peaceful submission of Romagna was, however, far from satisfying the bad ambition of Borgia. He extended his faithless intrigues into Tuscany, and had already begun to trouble the republics of that province, and Florence in particular, by declaring himself in arms the protector of the exiled Medici; when he was compelled by his engagements to suspend the prosecution of his own subordinate projects of aggrandizement, to second those of. Louis XII., and, with his forces, to attend the army of that monarch in a new expedition for the conquest of Naples.

If Louis XII. had been contented with the acquisition and temperate government of Milan, he might perhaps have habituated his new subjects to his authority; and by confirming his influence over the intermediate states of Savoy and Montferrat, might have firmly connected his Italian conquests with his native dominions. But the same ambition which had intoxicated the youthful vanity and inexperience of Charles VIII., seduced his better judgment and maturer years. From the situation of his affairs, he was certainly better entitled than his predecessor to calculate on a successful issue to his invasion of Naples. His Milanese dominions gave him strong points of support; he was in strict alliance with the pope and with Venice; and, while the other Italian powers trembled before him, his opponent, Frederic, king of Naples, without treasures or an army, his fortresses in ruins, his arsenals empty, and his kingdom desolated by the last war, was absolutely destitute of all means of defence. Yet Louis XII. still wavered in indecision: he doubted his power of conquering Naples much less than his strength to preserve the acquisition; for he dreaded the opposition of the sovereigns of Spain, and knew the ease with which they might succour their relative Frederic from Sicily, as they had done Ferdinand II. before. He did not, therefore, finally undertake his scheme of conquest, until he discovered that Ferdinand the Catholic was restrained by no scruples from sharing the spoil with him. That monarch pretended that Alfonso the Magnanimous had not possessed the right to alienate the kingdom of Naples from the legitimate branch of the Aragonese dynasty; and that therefore he was himself the lawful heir of that monarch to its throne. But as Louis XII. had also rival pretensions through the house of Anjou, Ferdinand proposed to compromise their respective claims by a division of the kingdom. The French sovereign eagerly closed with the hollow proposal: the capital, the Terra di Lavoro, and the Abruzzos, were assigned to Louis XII. with the usual style of king of Jerusalem and Naples; and Ferdinand the Catholic agreed to content himself with Apulia and Calabria, and the title of duke of these two provinces, to be held, like the kingdom, by investiture from the pope.

This treaty of partition, by which in itself Ferdinand the Catholic proposed to spoil his near relative and ally, was attended with circumstances of yet deeper and more atrocious perfidy. It was agreed that, while the French army openly advanced against Naples, the Spanish troops should gain possession of the fortresses of the kingdom, under pretence of co-operating with Frederic to repulse the invaders. Ferdinand the Catholic, professing his usual zeal in the cause of religion, fitted out a strong expedition at Malaga under Gonsalvo da Cordova to attack the Turks; and he caused his general and troops, after a few operations against the infidels, to winter in Sicily without exciting suspicion of his real designs. As the French invasion became certain, Ferdinand, under the guise of protection, offered his cousin this army for his defence, and thus induced his unsuspecting relative to invite his betrayers into his dominions.

Meanwhile the French army was approaching. (A.D. 1501.) It was led by d'Aubigny, and consisted of 6000 cavalry, with 4000 Swiss and 6000 Gascon and other French infantry. Cæsar Borgia and his contingents swelled this force; and at Genoa—which had followed the fate of the Milanese duchy, and was under French government—a strong squadron was equipped which co-operated with d'Aubigny and carried 6000 land forces. The Neapolitan king had left nothing neglected to oppose the invaders; but all his exertions could not assemble a sufficient native force to resist them, and his sole hope was reposed on Gonsalvo and his army. This general, who executed his master's projects with a perfidy which well emulated that of the royal hypocrite, dissembled to the last moment, and occupied many of the Neapolitan fortresses with Spanish troops, under pretence of strengthening the positions of his army. But when the French had at length passed the Neapolitan frontiers, he threw off the mask, and avowed his shameless commission, which the pope had already sanctioned, to partition the kingdom with the general of Louis XII.

This accumulation of aggression and treachery Frederic could not hope to withstand. He was compelled to retire from the frontiers to Naples, whither the French, after being admitted by treachery into Capua, and making a horrible massacre there, rapidly followed him. The unfortunate king had no alternative but to abandon to them his capital and its citadels; and he was permitted by capitulation to retire to Ischia. There, considering a farther struggle utterly hopeless, he in his rash indignation against the perfidy of his relative Ferdinand, made his choice to throw himself upon the generosity of the natural rival of his house. He obtained a safe conduct to proceed to France; where Louis XII., touched with his confidence, assigned him the title of duke of Anjou with a liberal revenue. But it was accompanied by the condition that he should never more quit Finance, and a guard was placed upon him, at once to watch over his safety and to prevent his escape. His eldest son, whom he had posted at Tarento, soon after surrendered that city to the Spaniards, upon the solemn oath of their general that he should be allowed to retire whither he pleased; but he was, notwithstanding, seized by Gonsalvo and sent a prisoner to Spain, where he survived to the middle of the sixteenth century, and died without issue. Frederic himself ended his days in France three years after his retirement; and both his other sons, who had accompanied him to that kingdom, died young without leaving children. Thus terminated the branch of the Aragonese dynasty, which had reigned at Naples for sixty-five years.

The object of the iniquitous alliance, between Louis XII. and Ferdinand the Catholic, had no sooner been effected by the submission of the kingdom of Naples to their arms, than the victors quarrelled over the spoil. The division of the conquered country had not been accurately defined by the partition treaty; and instead of attempting to regulate it by an equitable accommodation, the sovereigns of France and Spain left their generals to decide their differences by arms. Though they were neither of them prepared for war, hostilities commenced between their troops. (A.D. 1502.) The French were at first the stronger party; and the duke de Nemours, whom Louis had appointed his viceroy, gained several advantages in the first campaign; while Gonsalvo, who was left by his master without reinforcements, with difficulty maintained himself in a corner of the kingdom. But his brilliant military talents compensated, for the want of every other resource; and early in the following year Ferdinand began to support him with vigour, (A.D. 1503.) The superior genius of Gonsalvo then turned the tide of success; and while Ferdinand amused the French king with hollow negotiations for peace, and thus prevented him from succouring the duke de Nemours, the incapacity of that commander hastened the ruin of the French affairs. Near the castle of Cerignoles in Apulia, the two armies came to a general encounter; and in this decisive battle the French were totally defeated. Nemours himself was killed, and the whole kingdom at once submitted to the conquerors, with the exception of Gaeta and two or three other fortresses, in which the remains of the French army were immediately besieged. Gonsalvo entered Naples in triumph, and the nobles and people with their accustomed facility took the oaths of allegiance to their new sovereign.

Louis XII., finding himself the dupe of Ferdinand, resolved not to resign so easily the possession of the Neapolitan kingdom; and a new and formidable French army of 10,000 cavalry and 18,000 infantry assembled in Lombardy, and passed into southern Italy. They found Gonsalvo posted to receive them with a much inferior force behind the river Garigliano. But there, amidst a series of harassing operations under the autumnal rains, the disagreements of the French leaders, and the insubordination of their troops, were disadvantageously opposed to the admirable conduct of Gonsalvo and the patient valour of the Spanish infantry, which was now growing deservedly famous. Daily acquiring the superiority, Gonsalvo at last forced the passage of the Garigliano, and inflicted so total a rout upon the retreating French, that after the loss of baggage and artillery, the remnant of their army capitulated with permission to retire to France. Piero de' Medici had been a wanderer in the French camp; and in the attempt to escape after this defeat on the Garigliano, he perished miserably in that river by the sinking of his overloaded boat.

On this loss of a second army, Louis XII., who already feared for the safety of his Milanese duchy, gave up the war of Naples in despair. Resuming his negotiations with the Spanish monarch, he hastened to terminate the contest by a truce for three years; leaving the kingdom of Naples in the hands of the Spaniards, and providing in other respects for the general repose of Italy. Thus was the long dominion of the monarchs of Spain over the Neapolitan states introduced by the conquests of Gonsalvo da Cordova. When that general was first sent into Sicily, in 1495, he was invested, in the usual strain of Spanish hyperbole, with the rank of Great Captain of the petty army which he conducted; but this title became lastingly associated with his name in a more honourable sense, (A.D. 1504.) The perfidy which disgraced his exploits must for ever destroy our admiration of the man: but to the memory of the soldier it would be unjust to deny, that his heroic courage, his splendid fortunes, and his rare military genius, well merited the homage awarded to him by his own age in the emphatic appellation of the Great Captain. The services which he had performed were too important not to provoke the ingratitude of the suspicious Ferdinand. In visiting his new Italian dominions two years after their conquest, that monarch loaded Gonsalvo, his viceroy, with dignities and honours; but he would no longer leave him to govern at Naples, and he carried the hero with him to Spain, and enviously plunged him into an obscurity in which he closed his days.

While Louis XII. was reaping the just fruits of his unprincipled alliance with Ferdinand, and had discovered too late the imprudence of having himself given the first footing to so crafty and powerful a rival in the kingdom of Naples, all central Italy was successively agitated by the restless ambition of Cæsar Borgia, and the results of his faithless projects. On his return to Romagna, after the conquest of Naples by the French, he was not satisfied with the quiet possession of that duchy, but meditated the extension of his power over the rest of the papal states:

over the March of Ancona, and the provinces immediately surrounding the capital. He had designs upon the states of Urbino and Camerino; and he compassed the seizure of both by treachery and murder. Under pretence of executing a papal sentence against the lord of Camerino, he required the duke of Urbino, as a vassal of the church, to afford him the loan of his troops and artillery; and when that prince had unsuspiciously obeyed, and left himself without the means of resistance, Borgia poured an army into the duchy, and seizing its defenceless places, obliged the duke to fly for his life to the court of Mantua. He then inveigled the signer of Camerino, with two of his sons, to friendly conference, and caused the three to be immediately strangled.

After the success of these flagitious enterprises, Cæsar Borgia, still with the aid of the French, proceeded to weave his toils against the remaining vassals of the church, though they were most of them in his own service as condottieri. But these captains, the Orsini, who held vast fiefs about Rome, the Vitelli, lords of Città di Castello, the Bentivogli of Bologna, and other signers, penetrated his treachery and discovered their danger, in time to withdraw their bands from his service, and to enter into a formidable coalition against him. They defeated some of his troops, and their measures already threatened his destruction, when he succeeded in lulling them into security by his inaction. No man ever knew how to betray, under the mask of moderation and frankness, so well as Borgia; and, notwithstanding his notorious ill faith, such was his consummate dissimulation, that it deceived even these wily Romagnol signers. He confessed that he was indebted to their services for his past successes; he made no secret of his earnest desire to be reconciled with them, and he offered them extremely advantageous terms. By these means he induced them to conclude a peace with him; and even so regained their confidence, that they entered again into his service. But meanwhile he had been otherwise secretly augmenting his forces, and preparing his schemes of vengeance; and having lured two of the Orsini, and the signers of Fermo and Castello under his banners at Sinigaglia, he suddenly had them seized. Their troops were simultaneously attacked in their quarters, and the four condottieri themselves were strangled. Alexander VI. at the same time arrested the cardinal Orsini, and caused him to be poisoned in prison; and Borgia, amidst the general horror inspired by his character, then easily possessed himself of the fiefs of the signers whom he had murdered or terrified into flight.

The views of Borgia were not confined to the states of the church, and his machinations and hostile acts in Tuscany had already caused serious alarm to the Florentines in particular. The deference of Borgia for the French king, and the alliance between that monarch and the Florentines, had hitherto formed a protection for their republic. But the French affairs were now declining in southern Italy; and as success began to abandon their arms in the war of Naples against the Spaniards, Borgia, of whose policy fidelity to a ruined cause formed no part, assumed an audacious tone with his former allies, and even entered into secret negotiations with Gonsalvo and the Spanish court. While Louis XII. was making his last effort to re-establish his power at Naples, Borgia was left free to consummate his schemes of tyranny against the Tuscan states, and even aspired to hold the balance between France and Spain. But in the midst of his daring projects, and lofty aspirations, his fall was already at hand. At a supper given by the pope to the cardinal di Corneto, with the intention of poisoning that prelate, the wine which contained the fatal mixture was given by mistake to Alexander himself, and to his son, as well as to the cardinal. The two latter of the three, after enduring frightful agonies, slowly recovered, by strength of constitution and medical treatment, from the effects of the poison; but the pope himself sank under its violence, and fell, the victim of his own wickedness;—a fitting close for a life of infamy and execrable crimes.

The death of Alexander VI. proved the ruin of his son. Borgia had calculated and provided against the consequences of such an event to his own power, whenever it should occur; but he had not anticipated that he should himself be reduced, at the same moment, to the brink of the grave. While he lay dangerously ill, protected by his troops, in the palace of the Vatican, the surviving chieftains of the Orsini appeared in arms in Rome itself and in its provinces. The families of the other signers, whom he had latterly deposed or murdered, simultaneously entered into their states and recovered them; and these powers, immediately afterwards uniting their forces to those of the Orsini, attacked and totally routed his army. Borgia, who was still ill, found a refuge in the castle of St. Angelo; but, with this defeat, fell the pride of his blood-stained and detestable ambition. The Venetians, no longer restrained from assailing him by the interference of France, and freed from the pressure of a Turkish war which had lately occupied them, sent their troops into Romagna, and seized many fortresses; other places in the province revolted in favour of the families of their ancient chieftains, whom Borgia had dispossessed; and a new pope finally compelled the fallen tyrant to surrender to him the poor remains of his possessions.

The death of Alexander VI. occurred at the moment when the French army was advancing to Naples through the ecclesiastical states; and the opposite parties in the conclave, dreading the consequences of a protracted interregnum, at so troubled a juncture, and yet equally unwilling to yield to their adversaries, agreed to nominate a pope whose infirmities must insure his speedy dissolution. The object of this choice, Pius III., reigned scarcely a month; and before his death the cardinal Giuliano della Rovere, nephew of Sixtus IV., had time to secure a majority of suffrages in the papal college, by allying himself with Cæsar Borgia. The cardinal Giuliano had long lived in exile from Rome at the French court, and in open hostility with Alexander VI. and his son; but Borgia, in the imminent dangers which surrounded him, thought to secure the protection of his ancient foe, by rendering him important services. The suffrages of several cardinals, who still remained in the interest of Borgia, turned the balance in the conclave, and seated the nephew of Sixtus IV. in the papal chair. The new pope, who assumed the title of Julius II., deluded Borgia by his reputation for sincerity; and that man, who had never kept faith with any one, reposed in strange security upon the promises and gratitude of the violent enemy of his house. He was yet undeceived, when Julius II. suddenly seized his person at Ostia, and detained him a prisoner, until he had purchased his freedom by ordering the delivery of his remaining fortresses to the papal troops. He was then suffered to depart, and repaired to Naples, where Gonsalvo da Cordova had promised him an asylum. But on his arrival there, just before the signature of the three years' truce between France and Spain, Gonsalvo required the pleasure of his master respecting him, and by his command treacherously arrested and sent him a prisoner to Spain.

Thus was this monster of ferocious perfidy himself at length the victim of wanton ill-faith and cruelty. Ferdinand the Catholic, whom he had never offended, designed him to linger, and to find a tomb in his dungeon. But Cæsar Borgia, who had so long troubled Italy, and outraged humanity with his ambition and crimes, found at last a grave, too honourable for a life stained with the commission of every atrocity. He escaped from his prison after a short captivity, and found protection from the king of Navarre, whose sister he had formerly married; and instigating that sovereign to a war with the Spaniards, terminated as the general of his troops, and on the field of battle, his turbulent and flagitious career, (A.D. 1507.)

In the universal joy of the Italians at the season of repose afforded to them by the truce between the monarchs of France and Spain, they might endeavour to banish every thought of the humiliation which had now overtaken their country. But it was evident that Italy had surrendered herself to receive the law from foreigners: that she was henceforth to bleed, not for her own independence, but in their quarrels, and to rest from her struggles, not in the pride of victory and the enjoyment of well-earned rights, but at the pleasure only of her masters, and in the shame of servitude. The signature of a treaty of peace at Blois, which followed the truce between Louis XII. and Ferdinand long before its expiration, confirmed the tranquillity of the peninsula. For nearly five years Italy slumbered on her chains; startled only by the report of perpetual and hollow negotiations, and dangerous projects among the foreign arbiters of her destiny; and undisturbed, except by some partial hostilities, which I shall notice and dismiss in few words.

The first of these, in point of time, was the reestablishment of the authority of the church over great part of Romagna, after the fall of Cæsar Borgia. The new pope, Julius II., overawed the Venetians by his menaces to cede to him many of the places which they had seized in that province, but others they persisted in retaining; and their obstinacy inflamed Julius with a secret resentment, which was one day destined to burst forth with fearful violence against their republic. After the recovery of minor Romagnol fiefs, several of which he retained under the immediate government of the church, the active and warlike pontiffs, who headed his own troops, led them against Bologna, to wrest that city from its signer, Giovanni Bentivoglio, and to reduce it to its ancient dependence upon the papacy. He was completely successful: Bentivoglio was obliged to fly; his capital was taken under the government of the church (A.D. 1506); and though Julius granted the inhabitants a municipal constitution, Bologna ceased from that period, except for one short interval of commotion, to be numbered among the independent cities of Italy. Perugia was at the same time, on the submission of its signor, placed under papal government, with liberal privileges, (A.D. 1507.)

The next circumstance that engaged the attention of Italy was the revolt of Genoa, which had hitherto given obedience to Louis XII., as if that fallen republic had become a component part of his duchy of Milan. But the insurrection of the Genoese, first against their nobles, and afterwards against Louis on his supporting that order, presents no interesting features to detain us in our approach to more important objects. For the French king having assembled an army in his Milanese dominions, and led his troops in person against Genoa, the terrified people, after a few feeble attempts to resist, quickly surrendered at discretion; and Louis punished their rebellion, as he doubtless termed it, with exemplary severity. Neither shall I stop to relate the particulars of a transient war which Maximilian, king of the Romans, directed against Venice and the Milanese possessions of France. (A.D. 1508.) This contest, which was marked only on his part by a few desultory and ill-conducted operations, served again to exhibit to general contempt the insignificant power, the inconstancy of purpose, and the characteristic levity of the emperor-elect. But this war was more important in the passions which it left to rankle, than in its consequences at the moment. Maximilian, who was compelled to leave all his Istrian ports (which Venice had captured) in the hands of that republic, remained deeply humiliated by the disgraceful termination of the enterprises, to which he had been provoked by mere wanton ambition. Louis XII., on his part, professed violent indignation, that Venice would not continue the war to gratify purposes altogether foreign to her quarrel and to her interests. Thus a common exasperation against the republic animated her discomfited enemy, and her offended ally.

Throughout the repose of Italy, thus chequered only by occasional alarms, the war of Florence and Pisa had still remained an open wound. For above fourteen years, the Pisans had vigorously defended their recovered freedom. Protected and deserted in turn by all the states of the peninsula, and by the more commanding powers of France, Spain, and the empire; their prosperity blasted by a long servitude, their resources exhausted, their territory ravaged, and their city besieged; they had still warded off the yoke, which the stronger republic endeavoured to rivet once more on their necks. The vicissitudes which their unhappy city suffered in the struggle, were not perhaps marked by any very striking circumstances; or at least none of her surviving sons had the courage to paint the horrors of her agony and fall, and we know them only in the general relation of her adversaries. We can therefore have no pleasure in imitating the prolixity of the great Florentine historian on a theme which might have had greater attractions in the more rude and simple narrative of some Pisan chronicler.

It is, however, evident, in the pages of Guicciardini, that the resistance of Pisa was worthy rather of the most brilliant period of her ancient glories, than of her long decay and expiring struggles. When every foreign power had abandoned the Pisans, and the superior forces of the Florentines had entirely blockaded their city, and reduced them to the last stages of want, the sovereigns of France and Spain set a price upon their misery. These monarchs refused to permit the Florentines to perfect their conquest, until they had each been paid for their consent; the former 100,000, and the latter 50,000 florins. The Florentines were then suffered to complete the work of subjugation, (A.D. 1509.) The Pisans capitulated, and were certainly treated with liberality by the victors; but when their city thus passed again under the dominion of Florence, all the inhabitants who were distinguished by birth, wealth, or courage, disdaining their chains, preferred independence, even in exile, to voluntary submission and servitude. They emigrated in great numbers to Lucca, to Sardinia, and to Sicily; while the bolder spirits among them entered into the French service, and, in the licence of camps and the excitement of glory, found some consolation for the loss of their country and civil rights, and the ruin of their fortunes.

At the moment when the Florentines were left to complete the reduction of Pisa, the principal powers of Italy were engaged in a project of far greater importance and magnitude; and before the surrender of that city, almost the whole force of Europe was already in action, to overwhelm the great maritime republic of the peninsula. Since Italy had become a prey to the invasion of foreigners, the boasted wisdom of Venice had been but poorly manifested. It was little to the credit of her ancient prudence, that she had been blinded to the fatal consequences of suffering strangers to gain the mastery in Lombardy and Naples, and to overshadow the peninsula with their malignant influence. Actuated solely by a narrow and shortsighted policy, she had made no lasting and consistent efforts to preserve the independence of Italy; and she had even been seduced by her grasping desire of continental dominion, to share the spoil with enemies, whom she had herself the greatest reasons to dread. After aiding Louis XII. in his conquest of the Milanese duchy, she was, indeed, for some time deprived of the means of resisting the danger which she had provoked. While that prince and Ferdinand of Spain were completing their iniquitous partition of Naples, and struggling for the possession of their prey, she was assailed by the arms of the Turks, and reduced to confine her attention to the resistance of their dreaded power.

The disputed causes of this dangerous war, which broke out in 1499, it is of little moment to notice. Partly at the instigation of Ludovico Sforza, partly with the restless spirit of conquest which distinguished the Ottoman empire in that age, the sultan, Bajazet II., turned his whole power by land and sea against the Venetian possessions in Istria, Dalmatia, and the continent and islands of Greece. The republic was not equal to the successful maintenance of the contest against his gigantic strength; and though the pope, the kings of Spain, France, and Portugal, and the knights of Jerusalem from their stronghold of Rhodes, successively joined their squadrons to her naval armaments against the infidels, these occasional and partial succours failed in giving a favourable turn to the war. Without any decisive event, the republic, in 1503, by the sacrifice of St. Maura and some possessions in the Morea, rejoiced to conclude a peace with the Porte, which was destined to last above thirty years.

The conduct pursued by the Venetians in Italy, after this pacification, ripened the general animosity and envy against them, of which the seeds had long been sown by their successful career of continental aggrandizement. By their usurpations in Romagna, they had provoked the hatred of that most haughty and ambitious of pontiffs, Julius II. The issue of the war in which they had engaged with Louis XII. against Maximilian left both those sovereigns their enemies; and, while their retention of the maritime Neapolitan fortresses, which they had received in pledge from Ferdinand II., gave the king of Spain, as the present possessor of southern Italy, an object to gain, by uniting with their other enemies, several of the minor Italian princes had ancient grievances to revenge upon them.

To the various causes of animosity, just or otherwise, which influenced all these powers, is to be attributed their union in the most comprehensive political scheme of ambition and vengeance which Europe had yet witnessed. Several preparatory negotiations were carried on at different periods amongst the pope and the sovereigns of Germany, France, and Spain; and at length Margaret, duchess dowager of Savoy, daughter of Maximilian, and governess of the Low Countries,—a princess in whose character was united all the strength of mind of a man, with the fine tact and dexterity of her sex,—and the cardinal of Amboise, minister of Louis XII., met on the part of the emperor-elect and the French king, in the city of Cambray, under pretence of regulating some affairs of the duchy of Gueldres. An ambassador of Ferdinand also attended in the same city, but Margaret and the cardinal deliberated in secret without any assistants; and the general league of Europe, to dismember the territories of the most ancient state of the universe, was definitely arranged between a priest and a woman, (A.D. 1508.) The celebrated league of Cambray, as regulated by these negotiator, provided, besides minor stipulations, that Venice should be compelled, by the combined attack of the confederates, to restore to the pope all the possessions which she had ever usurped in Romagna: to Maximilian, Padua, Verona, and Vicenza, to which he pretended as imperial fiefs, and Friuli and the Trevisan March, which he claimed as duke of Austria: to Louis XII., Brescia, Bergamo, Cremona, and all the ancient dependencies of the Milanese duchy, which the republic had at different periods conquered from the Visconti: to Ferdinand of Spain, the maritime places which she retained in his kingdom of Naples; and, to the sovereigns of Ferrara and Mantua, whatever had in former times belonged to their houses. In a word, the accomplishment of the objects proposed by the confederacy would have the effect of reducing again the Italian possessions of Venice to her lagunes, and to the narrow strip of the mainland—the Dogado—which bordered on those waters, and had anciently formed the only continental possession of the republic. Almost all the princes of Europe were thus immediately interested in the design to crush the power and humiliate the pride of the arrogant queen of the Adriatic; and that the number of her puissant enemies might be equalled only by the extent of Christian Europe, distant powers, such as England, who had no pretensions to make to her spoils, were yet solicited to swell the confederation.

When the Venetians discovered the existence of the league of Cambray, which was as long as possible cautiously veiled from their penetration, the council of ten manifested a presumption and rash imprudence strangely at variance with the usual character of their government. The pope, of whose ultimate policy the expulsion of every foreign power from Italy was the dearest object, dreaded that the success of the league would augment the influence of strangers over the peninsula. He therefore made overtures to the Venetians for a reconciliation, before he would ratify the treaty; but the council of ten madly refused to detach him from the league by the cession of the disputed Romagnol fiefs, and the storm then burst upon their heads. The vigour with which the republic immediately prepared for war at least gave a consistency to her confidence. Though she failed in an endeavour to seduce Maximilian from the league, and to prevail upon the king of England and the Turkish sultan to make diversions in her favour, she remained unshaken in purpose. Her commercial wealth, which the progress of the Portuguese discoveries and trade in the East Indies had not yet had time to undermine, was judiciously employed in levying for her defence one of the most brilliant and numerous armies which Italy had ever seen; and a formidable naval armament was at the same time fitted out to cooperate with the land forces, wherever it might be possible. But in the midst of these active preparations, the state was troubled by several calamities, which struck terror into the superstitious, as so many omens of the approaching destruction of the republic. The fine arsenal of Venice was nearly consumed by a dreadful conflagration; the fortress of Brescia was fired by a stroke of lightning, and its walls laid open by an explosion which followed; a bark laden with treasure foundered on its passage to Ravenna; and the most precious archives of the state were destroyed by the accidental burning or fall of the building which contained them.

The king of France was the foremost of the confederates in attacking the republic; and as soon as his operations commenced, and while the tempest of war was gathering against Venice from all quarters, the pope struck that devoted state with the spiritual weapons of excommunication and interdict, (A.D. 1509.) The army, which was led by Louis XII. in person, and suffered to pass the Adda without opposition, consisted of 12,000 gensd'armerie and attendant cavalry, with an array of infantry, Swiss, French, and Italian, which has been variously stated under 20,000 men. The principal force of the Venetians was ranged against the French king in the Ghiara d'Adda, with orders to remain on the defensive. The captain-general of the republic, Nicolo Orsini, count of Pitigliano, a leader of distinguished reputation, was disposed by his character to follow his instructions and avoid any decisive encounter; but Bartolommeo d'Alviano, the second in command, who did not yield to him in martial fame, was as bold and impetuous as the other was cautious and deliberate. Near the village of Aignadello, d'Alviano with the rear-guard of the retreating Venetians came in contact with the advance of the French. He at first repulsed their attacks; but in so doing suffered himself to be entangled with the whole invading army, while Pitigliano, with the main body of the Venetians, was still pursuing his march. When a general engagement had thus become inevitable, Pitigliano was too distant, or in the onset neglected, to afford his second in command effectual support; and after an obstinate struggle, in which d'Alviano displayed extraordinary courage, and was wounded and made prisoner, the Venetians were totally routed. Pitigliano escaped with his gens-d'armerie, but all his artillery fell into the hands of the conquerors; and such was the ferocity which had now succeeded in these wars to the bloodless combats of the last century, that above ten thousand men were left dead on the field, of whom by far the greatest number were Italians.

Louis XII. followed up his success with a rapidity and skill which did more credit to his military talents than the mere issue of the battle itself. Caravaggio, Bergamo, Brescia, Crema, Cremona, and other towns, immediately opened their gates on his hasty advance; and disaffection to the republic was not wanting to aid him among the nobles of most of these places. Peschiera alone attempted to stand an assault; and the king with an execrable cruelty, from the reproach of which his character had in general been free, caused the brave governor and his son to be hanged from the battlements. At the same time with these operations, the papal troops successfully invaded the Romagnol possessions of Venice; and the duke of Ferrara and the marquis of Mantua from opposite quarters took the field, and seized upon the territories to which they laid claim. The imperialists entered unresisted into Friuli and Istria, and continuing to advance, received the submission of Verona, Vicenza, and Padua; while the Spaniards laid siege to the Venetian garrisons on the Neapolitan coasts. The wreck of the Venetian army under Pitigliano had meanwhile been reduced by panic and desertion to the most deplorable condition. Flying before the victors, that general was obliged, by the terror of his troops, to abandon the whole Terra Firma, and to seek shelter on the shore of the lagunes at Mestre; and, of all the Venetian dependencies, Treviso alone retained sufficient fidelity and courage to close her gates and defend her walls against the invaders.

The calamities which followed the fatal battle of Aignadello in such thick succession, had changed the presumption of the Venetians into abject despair. The ancient and vaunted constancy of their senate sank at once into a despondency and terror, as new in the annals of their republic as the rash imprudence which had preceded these reverses. They vainly endeavoured to propitiate Maximilian, by evacuating the territories which he claimed. They strove to detach the king of Spain from the league, by withdrawing their troops from the maritime fortresses of Calabria. They pursued the same plan in Romagna, by voluntarily surrendering the strong fortress of Ravenna, and all that they still possessed in that province, to Julius II. Formally absolving their continental subjects from their allegiance, they shut themselves up in their capital, and preparing for its defence, thought only of preserving by their maritime forces the existence of their state within the impregnable lagunes. This strange and pusillanimous abandonment of all the objects, for which the republic had, for more than a century, been eagerly contending, was often afterwards regarded—so easy had it become for the Venetian government to maintain its long established reputation for profound and mysterious policy—as a stroke of consummate wisdom and foresight. The senate, interested as that body was in strengthening an illusion so calculated to augment the respect of its subjects and of the world, gladly lent itself to the general belief, and boasted the success of a deep and premeditated scheme. But the circumstances which, at the time, attended the prostration of the republic before her enemies, contradict this assumption, and bore all the marks of an excessive, and assuredly a well-founded terror. For the Venetian army was completely disorganized; all the resources of the state began to fail under a prodigious expenditure; the continental provinces were invaded at every point; and in every city the old factions of the Guelfs and Ghibelins revived with the hope of revolution.

This sudden submission to calamities, which appears to have been prompted only by despair, had certainly, however, all the consequences that could have attended the most admirable policy. The king of Spain, contented with the evacuation of the Neapolitan ports by Venice, had no longer an object in pursuing the ruin of the republic to aggrandize France and the empire. Louis XII., on his part, regarding the war as terminated by his conquests, and impatient to revisit France, disbanded his army and quitted Italy. And while Julius II., by the surrender of the Romagnol places, had acquired the political advantages which he sought, his personal arrogance was flattered by the humiliation and contrition of the republic, who dispatched an embassy of her most distinguished citizens to implore his mercy and pardon. Having thus succeeded in his primary design of humbling the Venetians, Julius II. began to direct his attention to a plan yet dearer to his imagination, and more worthy of his enterprising genius; the expulsion of every foreign power from the peninsula. Secretly animated by this purpose, he would no longer refuse to accept the submission of the Venetians; and he began to show a favour towards them, which in a few months terminated in a complete reconciliation.

Meanwhile the first gleam of success dawned upon the Venetians. In the insolence of the French and the brutality of the German soldiery, the inhabitants of the conquered provinces had soon cause to contrast their state under the Venetians, with what it had become under foreigners, and to deplore the change. The French army was disbanded, the Spanish and papal powers had silently withdrawn from the contest; and a ray of hope broke in upon the counsels of the Venetians, when the senate perceived that the distrust, or coldness, or alienation of the allies, had left Maximilian single-handed to contend with them. The wonted courage, the energy, and the wisdom of the government at once revived; they strained every nerve, and spared no pecuniary sacrifices, to recruit and re-organize their army; and they had already prepared to act offensively, when, by the aid of the people of Padua, that city was surprised by a body of their troops, and the German garrison compelled to fly. From the day on which this important place was recovered, may be dated the revival of the republic; and it was long commemorated accordingly at Venice. The Venetian army immediately advanced; the territory of Padua followed the fate of the city; and these successes were strengthened by the surprise and capture of the marquis of Mantua, who had imprudently exposed himself with a small force on the Veronese frontiers.

Maximilian had hitherto himself made few efforts, and profited only by the exertions of his allies; but the loss of Padua stung him with shame and fear at the consequences of his own negligence. He hastened the tardy assembly of his army; and being joined by a body of French gens-d'armerie, and numerous auxiliaries of the different members of the league, he laid siege to Padua, with an army of near forty thousand men of various nations, and an immense train of two hundred pieces of cannon. The Venetians had thrown their whole army into Padua to defend the immense circuit of its walls; they had sedulously improved and augmented its fortifications; and the young nobles of Venice were suffered to vie with each other in repairing to the scene of danger, to share in the peril and glory of the defence. The artillery of the besiegers effected several breaches in the works; and Maximilian made repeated efforts to carry the place by a general assault. To stimulate the rival courage of his German, and French, and Spanish troops, the emperor assigned different points of attack to each nation; but the obstinate resolution of the defenders prevailed over all these attempts; and Maximilian was finally compelled to raise the siege, to dismiss his auxiliaries, and to retire into Germany, with signal loss of military reputation.

The issue of this expedition of Maximilian confirmed the re-establishment of the Venetian affairs. The republic, pursuing her offensive operations, rapidly recovered a considerable part of her Lombard territory. She was now even sufficiently strong to attempt vengeance against the duke of Ferrara, by invading his states and penetrating to his capital; and though her forces sustained a severe defeat in this enterprise, the duke, at the end of the eventful campaign which had threatened the annihilation of Venice, was but too happy to screen himself from farther assaults by the mediation of the pope. I need not describe the indecisive operations of the following year, in which the exertions of the Venetian arms still balanced the event against the united forces of the French and imperialists; but the designs of Julius II. now gave a new character to the political and military relations of the peninsula. (A.D. 1510.)

PART II.
Resolution of Julius II. to expel the French from Italy—First hostilities—Abortive council of Pisa, summoned by Louis XII. and the emperor against the pope—The holy league formed by Julius II. against the French—Distress of Louis XII.—General war in Italy—Exploits of Gaston

de Foix—Sanguinary battle of Ravenna—Victory of the French—Death of Gaston de Foix—The fortune of the French in Italy perishes with him—Their expulsion from the peninsula—The freedom of Genoa restored—Maximilian Sforza placed on the throne of Milan—Disunion of the powers of the holy league—Death of Julius II.—Pope Leo X.—Retrospect of Florentine affairs since the expulsion of the Medici—Restoration of that family—Servitude of the state—Affairs of Italy during the pontificate of Leo X.—Last enterprise of Louis XII. of France—His reconciliation with the papacy, and death—The accession of Francis I. to the French crown introduces a period of more comprehensive policy and warfare in Europe—Impossibility of tracing its vicissitudes with minuteness in this work—General sketch of its events—Conquest of the Milanese duchy by Francis I.—Deposition of Maximilian Sforza—Death of Ferdinand the Catholic—Succession of his grandson Charles to the Spanish dominions—General peace in Italy—Competition of Charles of Spain and Francis I. for the imperial crown—Alliance of the pope and the emperor Charles V. against Francis I.—Conquest of the Milanese duchy by the confederates—Death of Leo X.—Continued and unsuccessful enterprises of Francis I. in Italy—Francesco Sforza, duke of Milan—Pope Adrian VI.—Pope Clement VII.—Disastrous consequences of the battle of Pavia to Italy—Charles V. all-powerful in the peninsula—Attempt of the Italian powers to resist his yoke—Treachery of the marquis of Pescara—General league of Italy for the recovery of independence—Its impotent results—Fatal misconduct and vacillation of Clement VII.—Sack of Rome by the Imperialists—Condition of Genoa—Fortunes and character of Andrea Doria—He restores the republic, under the protection of Charles V.—His magnanimous patriotism—Desertion of the Italian league by Clement VII. and Francis I., by the treaty of Barcelona and peace of Cambray—Final subjection of Italy to the emperor Charles V.—Last struggle of the Florentine republic—The Medici—Their second expulsion from Florence—Renewal of the republican constitution—Resolution of the Florentines to maintain their liberties against the emperor and the Medici—Their gallant and protracted defence—Fall of Florence—Alessandro de' Medici, first duke of Florence—Extinction of the republic.

IN the resolution, which Julius II. had formed, to clear Italy of her foreign masters, that enterprising pontiff determined that the storm should first fall upon the French. With the violence which distinguished his character, he had conceived a personal animosity against Louis XII., which was aggravated by several trivial disagreements; and he eagerly sought an occasion for a rupture with him. (A.D. 1510.) The constancy with which Alfonso, duke of Ferrara, adhered to the French alliance, diverted a portion of his indignation against that prince; and upon some pretexts of the disobedience of Alfonso to the holy see, he thundered an excommunication against him, and against all who should protect him. At the same time that the papal troops invaded the state of Ferrara, the pope stirred up enemies in all quarters against the king of France; and Louis XII., notwithstanding the superstitious scruples which sensibly affected him, at engaging in hostilities against the supreme head of the church, found himself reduced in his own defence to repel the aggressions of the restless pontiff, and to protect his faithful confederate. His troops were soon called upon to combat the warlike pope in person; for Julius, now exciting the Venetians to attack the prince whom he had before protected, induced them to enter the Ferrarese territory in concert with the papal forces, and himself directed the operations of the combined army. At the siege of Mirandola, the pope, in the depth of winter, visited the trenches and urged the fire of the batteries; and not contented with shocking all religious minds by this scandalous spectacle, his impatience to take possession of the place as a conqueror was so great, that, on its capitulation, he entered the fortress by the breach, in preference to waiting until the gates could be unclosed, and the intrenchments which defended them levelled for his passage, (A.D. 1511.) This success was soon more than counterbalanced. The old marshal Trivulzio being now placed by Louis XII. at the head of the French army in Italy, rapidly advanced with a strong force towards Bologna, where the pope was then residing. Julius was compelled to fly for safety to Ravenna, and from thence to Rome; Bologna was captured by the French; and the papal army was totally routed in its neighbourhood.

If Louis XII. had suffered his general to use his advantage, he might have dictated peace to Julius II. under the walls of Rome. But in the midst of his successes, the pious monarch, at the reflection that he was combating the church, was troubled with continual horror and remorse. He forbade Trivulzio from following up his victory; he ordered him to withdraw his troops into the Milanese territory; and he declared that, though he was conscious of having committed no fault, he was ready to humble himself before the pope, and to demand pardon of his holiness, so that he might but obtain peace. But finding all his pacific overtures lost upon the inflexible Julius, he at last, in concert with the emperor-elect, ventured upon a measure which had long occupied their deliberations. This was to assemble a general council of the church, and to summon the pope before it, by their own authority and that of a few disaffected cardinals, who had seceded from the court of Julius II. By this expedient, Louis strove to quiet his own vain scruples of conscience, and to destroy the formidable power of his enemy, by depriving him of his sacred character. But the attempt failed miserably. The mockery of a council, which was convened to meet at Pisa, was supported only by the presence of the French and imperial commissioners, of four rebellious cardinals, and of a few other prelates; and Louis XII. himself, instead of supporting his own work with vigour, betrayed his irresolution and weakness by his eagerness still to negotiate with the pontiff. Julius well knew his superstitious timidity, and availed himself of it. He summoned a council to meet by his legitimate authority at the Lateran; he laid all places which should give shelter to the schismatic council, and all princes who should support the assembly, under a general interdict and excommunication; and he finally succeeded in giving a consolidation and consistency to his plans, by the formation of a regular league against the French.

Hitherto Ferdinand the Catholic had of late been occupied in the prosecution of some conquests against the Moors in Africa; but his attention was now recalled to the affairs of Italy. A rupture with France suited his views in other quarters, and after addressing remonstrances to Louis XII. with his usual hypocrisy against the sin of combating the ecclesiastical chief of Christendom, he thought himself at liberty to enter into a hostile confederacy against his ancient ally. A treaty was signed at Rome between the pope, the king of Spain, and the Venetians, under the prostituted title of the holy league. Its objects were declared to be, the maintenance of union in the church, which was menaced with a division by the schismatic council of Pisa; the recovery of Bologna and other ecclesiastical fiefs—meaning those of the duke of Ferrara—for the papacy; and the expulsion from Italy of all who should oppose these designs:—that is to say, of the king of France.

At the same time, the pope endeavoured to raise other enemies against Louis XII. His hopes were directed both towards England and Switzerland. Over the vain pride and inexperience of the English king, his influence and that of Ferdinand prevailed; and Henry VIII., joining the league, created by his arms in France a powerful diversion in its favour. With the Swiss, Louis XII. had imprudently embroiled himself; and the pope, on the other hand, acquired so great an influence over those devout republicans, that after having already induced them to make one desultory invasion of the Milanese duchy, he now engaged them in a second. This expedition, although undertaken with formidable numbers, terminated, it is true, like the first. After penetrating to the gates of Milan, the Swiss suddenly withdrew to their mountains, either moved by caprice, or the difficulties of their enterprise, or, as is most probable, bribed by the French: for the venality and treachery of their mercenary bands had now exceeded all shame, and their only object in war was to extort money alike from their employers and their enemies. Notwithstanding the abortive issue of their descent into the Milanese duchy, the ancient terror of their arms had contributed to increase the distresses which surrounded the French. Louis XII., oppressed by so many enemies, was left without one efficient ally. While the other great powers of Europe were arrayed against him, the emperor-elect was only in name his confederate: Maximilian, indeed, desired the continuance of the war, but he was in no way disposed to share its burthens. In Italy the duke of Ferrara, who alone remained faithful to France, was himself rather in need of protection, than capable of affording assistance. All the other states of the peninsula, who were not actively engaged in the holy league,—the marquis of Mantua, and the Tuscan republics of Florence, Sienna, and Lucca,—endeavoured to secure their safety by a policy suited to their weakness. They observed a cautious and silent neutrality, as if they were desirous of burying their very existence in obscurity.

When Julius II. found himself supported by the puissant league which he had formed, he pursued the refractory cardinals, and the council of Pisa and its adherents, with unqualified violence. As the thunders of the Vatican fell upon the schismatic assembly, the Italian clergy generally hastened to disclaim all connexion with its proceedings;

and the cardinals who were to open its session, publicly reviled by the Pisan mob, and with difficulty protected by a French escort, were compelled to fly from the city, and to seek refuge at Milan, where the popular contempt still awaited them. But the contest between the French king and the holy league remained to be decided by other arms than the bulls and excommunications of the pope. It was late in the year before hostilities commenced by the advance into Romagna of the papal and Spanish armies, under the command of the viceroy of Naples, don Raymond de Cardona; while the Venetian forces began to act vigorously in eastern Lombardy. But the superior strength of the league was more than counterbalanced by the extraordinary abilities of the young hero, who now began to appear at the head of the French armies. This was the famous Gaston de Foix, duke of Nemours, and nephew of Louis XII., who, after having already, at the early age of twenty-two years, given brilliant indications of courage and military talents, was at this juncture entrusted with the supreme command of his countrymen in Italy, and won by his splendid achievements in a few short months, an immortality of martial glory.

Gaston de Foix commenced his quick series of triumphs by leading his army from the Ferrarese duchy to the relief of Bologna, to which the confederates under don Raymond de Cardona had laid siege in the beginning of the new year. (A.D. 1512.) The allies, to avoid an engagement upon unfavourable terms, were compelled to retreat before him; but the intelligence, that the Venetians from another quarter had entered the city of Brescia by surprise, and were pressing the siege of its citadel, summoned him into eastern Lombardy. He flew with incredible celerity to repel this new danger. Violating the neutral territory of Mantua, to gain the direct line to Brescia, he traversed it with his gens-d'armerie so rapidly, that he marched fifty Italian miles in one day. He fell upon the Venetians, and cut to pieces two large bodies of their forces on his route; and reaching Brescia in time to save its citadel, he inflicted a total defeat upon the republican array in the streets of the city itself. The battle was obstinate, and the carnage terrific; the citizens valiantly supported the Venetians; and eight thousand persons had perished in an indiscriminate massacre before their resistance ceased. For several days Brescia was given over to all the horrors which could follow an assault; and Gaston de Foix stained his victory alike by the atrocities which he permitted, and by the subsequent execution of a Brescian noble and his sons, who had supported the Venetian cause.

The victory of the young Nemours restored the ascendancy of the French affairs in eastern Lombardy; and having received reinforcements from France, he marched again by command of his sovereign into Romagna, for the purpose of obliging the pope by a decisive battle to listen to terms of accommodation. Under the walls of Ravenna, the contending armies closed in the most obstinate and sanguinary encounter of the age. Gaston de Foix had under his orders a numerous gens-d'armerie, 5000 landsknechts or German foot, 5000 Gascon, and 8000 other French and Italian infantry, besides the contingent and the fine artillery of the duke of Ferrara. The papal and Spanish forces under don Raymond de Cardona numbered rather a larger force of cavalry; their infantry were only 10,000, but of these 7000 were the famous Spanish bands under Pietro Navarro, and the remainder Italians. The viceroy of Naples had orders to avoid a battle; but Nemours, by besieging Ravenna, drew him to intrench his army in the vicinity of that place for its protection, and then boldly attacked him. After a murderous cannonade on both sides, in which the assailants at first suffered most, the gens-d'armerie of the confederates, who were not covered, like the infantry, by their intrenchments, were at length so galled in flank by the artillery of the duke of Ferrara, that they impatiently sallied from their lines. The Spanish infantry followed to their support, and the battle became general throughout the field. After a long and furious struggle, the brilliant gensd'armerie of France overpowered the cavalry of the allies, and compelling them to seek safety in flight, fell upon the Spanish foot. Those gallant bands had already inflicted dreadful havoc among the German landsknechts, as immovable, but not so dexterous in the management of arms as themselves; and now, pressed and assailed on all sides, they yet maintained their array, and slowly retired, still repulsing their enemies, until they were suffered to continue their retreat unmolested. Of the two small armies, ten thousand men, at the very lowest computation, lay dead on the field; of whom two-thirds were of the allies. The day was decidedly with the French; the baggage, the artillery, and many standards of the confederates remained in their hands; together with the papal legate, the cardinal Giovanni de' Medici, and all the leaders of the defeated army, except the viceroy, who fled too soon for his fame. But the French had sustained an irreparable loss. Their youthful hero, Gaston de Foix, fell in the arms of victory, in a last charge against the Spanish bands. So dazzling had been his brief career, that he can scarcely be said to have died prematurely: he had sullied his exploits by a ferocity which even surpassed the usual reproach of the age; but if, in admiration of his transcendent talents, we could forget—what never should be forgotten—their misapplication to the misery and destruction of his species, he might be pronounced to have already attained the summit of human glory.

If Gaston de Foix had survived his victory at Ravenna still to animate the enthusiasm of his followers, there was nothing to oppose his march to Rome and to Naples, or to prevent him from giving law to the pope in one capital, and re-establishing the authority of his sovereign in the other. But with the invincible young hero perished the fortunes of the French in Italy. Notwithstanding the consternation with which the battle of Ravenna filled the powers of the holy league, and the immediate submission of great part of Romagna to the conquerors, the victory of the French proved more fatal to themselves than to their enemies. Besides the duke of Nemours, they had lost all their favourite captains, and the flower of their soldiery. The sieur de La Palisse, who succeeded De Foix in the command, could neither inspire the remnant of his array with the same confidence, nor repress the disorders, and weariness, and disgust, which now reigned in their camp. To aggravate the losses of the battle, Louis XII. was not only unable to send reinforcements into Italy, but compelled by his war with England and with Ferdinand on the Pyrennean frontiers, to recall part of his forces into France.

Under these circumstances, Julius 11. was the first of the confederates to recover from his alarm, and to resume his wonted activity and spirit. He hastened another expedition of the Swiss into the Milanese duchy, which he had already projected; he induced the emperor-elect to confirm a truce with the Venetians, to which he had bribed his avarice or necessities; and it soon became evident that the battle of Ravenna had prepared the way for the total expulsion of the French from the peninsula. La Palisse, on the rumoured approach of the Swiss, was obliged to evacuate Romagna, and to retire into the Milanese duchy to provide for its defence. The Spanish and papal forces therefore again advanced into Romagna, and recovered many places; the Swiss descended from their mountains to the formidable number of 20,000 foot, and joined the Venetian army; and at this critical juncture, the artful negotiations of Ferdinand of Spain induced the emperor-elect to enter the holy league, and to co-operate in raising to the ducal throne of Milan his namesake, Maximilian Sforza, son of Ludovico the Moor, and cousin of his empress, who had long resided at his court. The French were utterly unable to resist the accumulation of hostility, which now overwhelmed their weakened and disorganized forces. They were driven through the Milanese duchy, as the Swiss and Venetians advanced, without even the power to offer a battle. Their retreat was harassed by the inhabitants, who took a fearful vengeance upon their detachments and stragglers for their past tyranny; and they did not consider themselves in safety until they had reached the confines of France. The surrender of Bologna, and the few other garrisons which the retreating army had left in Lombardy, alone remained to complete the expulsion of the French from Italy.

This catastrophe of course produced an immediate change in the aspect of the peninsula. The pope at once recovered Bologna, and other cities and territories in Romagna; and the duke of Ferrara was compelled to repair to Rome, and to submit to his mercy. By his good offices, Julius gave liberty to his native city, Genoa, where one of the Fregosi, amidst the acclamations of the people, was proclaimed doge of the reviving republic. Maximilian Sforza was introduced with great solemnity into Milan, and took possession of that duchy; and these arrangements might appear to offer an earnest of future tranquillity, since they were the work of a general alliance of the church and the empire, the Swiss and the Italian powers. But the holy league experienced the fate of all such confederacies. Its members agreed no longer, when their common object had been accomplished. The pope, the great mover of the league, was the first to impair its work. He dismembered Parma and Placentia from the Milanese duchy, under pretence that they were ancient fiefs of the church; he was bent upon stripping the house of Este of the duchy of Ferrara; and Alfonso with difficulty escaped from detention at Rome, to put himself upon the defensive. At the same time, the hostility which Julius evinced towards the Spaniards, betrayed that the completion of his projects aimed at the expulsion of all foreign powers from Italy. It was on the Swiss, on whom he had bestowed the title of defenders of the church, and who, in giving Maximilian Sforza possession of the Milanese duchy, had exacted enormous contributions for their services, that he principally relied for assistance. The young duke of Milan had already subjects of complaint against the pontiff; and the rival pretensions of the emperor and the Venetians in Lombardy, threatened new disturbances. Thus the powers of the league were all distracted by various and opposite interests; nor was Louis XII. himself disposed to renounce, without farther efforts, the possession of his Milanese dominions. Amidst the numerous and contradictory negotiations with which all Europe was filled by the rapid dissolution of the holy league, Julius II. was, notwithstanding his advanced age, still the great agitator. But his own days were fast ebbing to their close; and after a short illness, death overtook him in the vigour of his active intellect, while he was yet eagerly occupied in his great object of clearing the peninsula of the influence of foreign princes: or, as he was accustomed to term it, of driving the barbarians out of Italy.

The incessant troubles created by the turbulent ambition, the violence, and the warlike temper of Julius II., rendered the wish general in the Roman conclave, that his successor should resemble him as little as possible. This desire produced the election of the cardinal Giovanni de' Medici, the second son of Lorenzo the Magnificent, who was already known by that love of letters, which has often since obtained for his memory, under his pontifical title of Leo X., an exaggerated reputation. This celebrated pontiff, in whose person the Medici thus attained the supreme dignity in the church, had already contributed by his address to the revival of the fortunes of his family; and their restoration to sovereign power at Florence, which had almost immediately preceded the death of Julius II., was in a great measure prepared by his prudence and conciliation.

Since the war of Pisa, Florence had sunk into a repose which had more of exhaustion than of real security or strength. Evidently attached to the French cause, yet fearful of openly and vigorously assisting it, the republic, from the timidity of her rulers, had fallen into insignificance and obscurity. But as her inclinations were known, she had only neglected to support her ally, Louis XII., without being able to propitiate his enemies. Since the first entrance of the French into Italy, the mightier combatants who crowded the political stage might naturally displace powers of inferior physical strength, from the station which they had previously occupied; and the unwarlike and commercial republic of Florence would necessarily, perhaps, sink into a state of the second order. In contrasting the glorious influence which Florence had maintained over Italy in earlier times, with her nullity at the epoch before us, we should doubtless err in attributing the disgraceful change, as some writers have done, exclusively to the effects of her long submission to the Medici, rather than to the great revolution which had already taken place in the aspect of Europe. But there can, I think, be little doubt that the protracted dictatorship of that family had completely ruined the springs of republican energy; and that in its consequences, even when the yoke was shaken off, it was proved to have extinguished the passive courage, and the energy which had once animated all classes of citizens in the maintenance of the freedom and political station of their commonwealth. If the party of the Albizzi had continued to guide the counsels of the republic, they might not have been able altogether to avert the fate of Italy, or the decline of Florentine power. But under their vigorous administration, the political importance of the republic would never have dwindled into contempt; or, if to fall was inevitable, she would have fallen gloriously in the struggle for Italian independence.

On the expulsion of the Medici, the Florentines had rejected alike their ancient mode of appointing magistrates by lottery, and an attempt made by the aristocratical party, through the agency of a balia, to commit the election of the signiory to an oligarchy of twenty *accoppiatori* or commissioners. The triumph of the democratical faction under Savonarola had been followed by the establishment of a general sovereign council; in which every individual, who could prove that his family had for three generations enjoyed the rights of citizenship, was entitled to a seat. To this body, which was composed of about eighteen hundred citizens, was confided the election of the magistracy. The signiory was still changed every two months; until, after the death of Savonarola, and amidst the troubles of Italy, it was found or imagined that this perpetual rotation of administration gave a dangerous instability to the government of the republic. In 1502, therefore, a gonfalonier or president of the state was chosen for life with limited powers.

The person selected for this office was Piero Soderini, a man of good intentions but of weak character. It was under his temporizing government that Florence had remained, to the epoch of the late expulsion of the French from Italy; and in this lapse of ten years, his want of energy had gradually lost him the popular affection and provoked opposition to his sway. On the other hand, since the death of

Piero de' Medici, the cardinal Giovanni had succeeded, by his moderation and his sedulous protection of Florentines at the papal court, in effacing the animosity which the violent character of his brother had excited. Thus, when the viceroy of Naples, after the expulsion of the French from Italy, entered Tuscany with a small Spanish army, attended by the Medici, a strong party in Florence were already prepared to restore the exiled family of their ancient rulers to power. The gonfalonier was seized by a body of conspirators and deposed; he was conducted from the city without personal violence; and after eighteen years of banishment the Medici re-entered Florence as her masters. The functions of the general council were suppressed, and the government was entrusted to a perpetual balia of between sixty and seventy members, all creatures of the Medici, and named by them exclusively.

Over this narrow and disgraceful oligarchy, which continued to administer the Florentine affairs until the last and temporary expulsion of the Medici in 1527, that family ruled with despotic sway. Their house, when thus restored to power, was represented by the cardinal Giovanni and Giuliano, surviving sons of Lorenzo the Magnificent, and by their nephew, Lorenzo II., the son of their deceased elder brother; and they were attended by Giulio, natural son of that brother of Lorenzo de' Medici, who fell in the conspiracy of the Pazzi. This illegitimate cousin of the cardinal Giovanni was one day like him to ascend the papal chair, and to assume the title of Clement VII. The triumph of the Medici was not followed by any signal acts of severity until the discovery of an abortive conspiracy against them; which is remarkable only as the celebrated Macchiavelli, who had been secretary of the republic, was a sharer in the plot. Upon him and others, the creatures of the Medici, after subjecting them to horrible tortures, passed sentences of banishment; but Leo X., on succeeding to the tiara, commenced his reign by an act of clemency to his countrymen, and procured an amnesty for all the conspirators.

The dissolution of the holy league was followed, almost immediately after the accession of Leo X., by new hostilities in Lombardy. Louis XII. and the Venetians once more allied themselves for the partition of the Milanese states; and a French army, crossing the Alps, invaded the duchy from the one side, while the republican forces attacked it on the other. But the Swiss thought their national honour engaged in the defence of Lombardy. The cantons poured their infantry into Italy to protect Maximilian Sforza; and these hardy bands, unassisted by cavalry, completely defeated the invading army near Novara, and put the French chivalry to so disgraceful a rout, that this body, notwithstanding their ancient reputation for gallantry, precipitately abandoned the duchy and evacuated Italy without once daring to rein in their flight. After this new reverse of the French arms, the Swiss remained inactive in Lombardy; but the Spanish and papal forces fell upon the Venetian territories. Neither Leo X. nor Ferdinand of Spain, indeed, had declared war against the Venetians; but the Spanish viceroy was compelled to seek subsistence and employment for his army, and the confederates under his orders acted against Venice as auxiliaries of the emperor-elect, whose old quarrel with the republic was still open. But no great event marked the issue of the campaign; and a pacification between the papacy and the French king, which was effected before the close of the year, narrowed the circle of hostility.

Louis XII., besides being wearied by a course of disasters, was sincerely desirous of reconciling himself with the church. He formally renounced the support of the schismatic council of Pisa, whose seat had been transferred to Lyons; and after this act Leo X., who had no longer any object in opposing him, not only accepted his submission, but engaged the Swiss cantons to conclude their differences with him. The plans which the pope had secretly formed for the aggrandizement of his family appeared likely to convert his peace with Louis into a close alliance, (A.D. 1514.) He induced his brother to leave the government of Florence in the hands of their nephew Lorenzo; and he designed to recompense Giuliano, by forming a principality for him of Parma and

Placentia, which Julius II. had annexed to the holy see, or even by raising him to the throne of Naples at the expense of Ferdinand of Spain. In these projects he was encouraged to expect the assistance of France and of Venice; when the sudden death of Louis XII. disconcerted his negotiations, and put a check upon the schemes of Medicean ambition. (A.D. 1515.)

With the accession to the French throne of the celebrated prince who followed Louis XII., may be said to commence the last period of that struggle, wherein Italy was destined to survive the total extinction of national independence and honour: a struggle wherein she was hurled from the splendid distinction which she had occupied in the middle ages, and buried in the abyss of degradation from which she has never since risen. Hitherto it has been my endeavour to detail with some minuteness the shifting vicissitudes of her brilliant though troubled fortunes; for until the period at which we have now arrived, the seal had not been finally set upon the fate, which doomed her to be no more than the prize of ambition for the great rival powers of Europe. But after the accession of Francis I. to the French crown, and the subsequent union of Spain and the empire under Charles V., Italy became the arena of the gigantic contest, in which these puissant monarchs contended for the mastery. Hitherto Italian history had been distinctive and national: it was now for fifteen years to be inseparably blended with the general affairs of Europe; to be in itself but the memorial of servitude and misery, and attractive and important only as embraced in the comprehensive rivalry of the houses of France and Austria. In tracing the annals of Italy to the busy opening of the sixteenth century, I might hope to present the general English reader with circumstances which have been but partially told in our language; but I cannot pretend, within the limits necessarily imposed on this work, to describe at large the extensive political combinations and warfare which, after agitating all Europe, left Italy in subjection to the emperor Charles V. Nor would any desirable object be gained by the attempt to repeat the story of events, with which every historical student may be presumed to be familiar: since they are to be found in the pages of one of our most popular and elegant writers. The remainder of the present chapter, then, will be occupied rather with an abstract, or general view of the leading vicissitudes of Italy during the period to which it is devoted, than to any elaborate narrative of events.

The chivalric gallantry and ambition of Francis I., which inspired him, almost immediately after his succession to the throne of Louis XII., with the design to retrieve the disgraces of the French arms, and to assert the title of his dynasty to the Milanese crown, was the first circumstance which entailed a new series of disasters upon Italy. His defeat of the Swiss, in the sanguinary and well-contested field of Marignano, put a period to the protection which the brave infantry of the cantons had afforded to Maximilian Sforza; and the submission of that feeble prince, (who exchanged his ducal throne for a pension and a retreat in France,) the alliance of Venice, and the terror of Leo X., all seemed to promise the lasting establishment of the French monarch in the Milanese duchy. The death of Ferdinand the Catholic, early in the following year, put his power at rest from the machinations of that wily and perfidious enemy of his throne; and the abortive issue of a formidable expedition, which the emperor Maximilian led into Italy against the French and Venetian confederacy, and concluded with his usual levity, confirmed the security of Francis, (A.D. 1516.) The measure with which the young heir of the Spanish crown commenced his reign, however insincere his moderation, gave under these circumstances an unusual period of repose to the peninsula. The amicable treaty of Noyon, concluded by Charles with the French king, was almost immediately followed by a pacification between his grandfather, the emperor Maximilian, and Venice, (A.D. 1517.) The republic recovered the entire possession of her continental provinces; and thus terminated the fierce and ruinous wars into which she had been plunged by the league of Cambray. But though Venice had escaped from the destruction which menaced her, her strength was already sapped at its vitals; and to her latest hour she never recovered the exhaustion of her resources, and the gradual decay of her commerce and wealth, which had been simultaneous with that perilous contest. The conquest of Egypt by the Turks had already destroyed her lucrative connexion with Alexandria and the Red Sea; and the spice trade with the east, which the Portuguese now carried on, since their discovery of the passage to India round the Cape of Good Hope, invaded the rich monopoly, which her merchants had previously engrossed through the ports of the Levant.

The death of the old emperor Maximilian, and the competition of his grandson Charles, and of Francis I., for the imperial dignity, after four years of peace, threatened interruption to the deep tranquillity of Italy, (A.D. 1519.) But two years passed after the election of Charles to the throne of the empire, before the flames of war were again lighted up in the peninsula. In espousing a side in the quarrel between Francis and Charles, Leo X. could no longer be actuated by motives of family ambition. Both his brother Giuliano, and his nephew Lorenzo, were now dead, without male issue from their marriages. No legitimate heir remained of the race of the great Cosmo; and though the pope chose rather to consign the sovereignty of Florence to his bastard cousin, the cardinal Giulio, than to restore to his injured country her independence and republican rights, the desire of aggrandizing his house, which had engrossed him during the lifetime of his brother and nephew, had necessarily expired with them. But Leo was still instigated by personal vanity and ambition; he was envious of the reputation which Julius II. had acquired by the extension of the papal dominions; and he desired to imitate that warlike pontiff, without possessing either his activity or political ability. After balancing between the great rival monarchs, he finally embraced the party of the emperor. Upon condition that Parma and Placentia should be re-annexed to the holy see, he engaged with Charles to establish Francesco Sforza, brother of Maximilian, and second son of the Moor, in the rest of the Milanese dominions, and to assist in expelling the French from Italy.

The weakness to which Francis abandoned his forces in the Milanese duchy, the misconduct of the sieur de Lautrec, the French viceroy, who commanded them, and the discontent with which his oppressive government had filled the people, all seconded the operations of the combined imperial and papal army. The confederates were gladly admitted into Milan, and almost all the other cities of the duchy; and the French troops were compelled to retire for safety into the territory of the Venetians, who continued faithful to their alliance with Francis I. Parma and Placentia thus fell, as had been agreed, into the hands of the pope; but Leo X. only survived long enough to receive the first tidings of these successes, and to close his life and pontificate with the apparent accomplishment of his ambitious views. He died suddenly, (A.D. 1521,) not without some suspicion of poison; and his decease for a time paralyzed the spirit of the confederacy between the papacy and the empire. In the mediocrity of his political character, there was indeed little to have rendered the abrupt dissolution of Leo X. an event of any importance at a less critical juncture; and his pontificate would have been remarkable only for the voluptuous profusion of his court, the scandalous sale of indulgences to recruit his exhausted coffers, and the consequent rise of the reformation: if his protection, partial as it was, of letters and art had not obtained for his memory a brilliant distinction in literary history.

In the disorder into which the imperial and papal confederacy was thrown by the death of Leo X., the French might easily have recovered possession of the Milanese duchy. But a fatality seemed always to attend their operations in Italy. The scandalous negligence of Francis I., and the wasteful dissipation of his resources, left his general Lautrec without the means of supporting an army; and though that commander was joined in the next campaign by a numerous levy of Swiss infantry, and enabled to approach Milan at their head, his want of money soon entailed fresh ruin on the French affairs, (A.D. 1522.) His mercenaries becoming mutinous at receiving no pay, obliged him to attack the imperialists under great disadvantages in their strong position at

Bicocca; and, notwithstanding the valour by which the Swiss endeavoured to justify their own rashness, they were defeated with terrific slaughter. After this overthrow, the French were once more compelled to evacuate Italy; and Francesco Sforza was seated on the throne of Milan.

The obstinacy with which, notwithstanding every reverse, Francis I. still persisted in the resolution to support his pretensions to that duchy, induced the new pope Adrian VI., after vainly labouring for the restoration of peace to Christendom, to embrace the alliance of the emperor. The little dependence which the Venetians found it possible to repose upon so imprudent and reckless a monarch as Francis, and their fear of being abandoned to support the burthen of a contest against the emperor, led them also to change their party, and to form engagements with Charles for the maintenance of Sforza in the Milanese duchy, (A.D. 1523.) A league was therefore concluded between their republic, the emperor, the pope, the king of England, the duke of Milan, and other Italian powers, for the repose of Italy and its defence against Francis I. This powerful coalition could not deter the French sovereign from persevering in his designs. He assembled a numerous army for a new invasion of the peninsula; and as he was prevented, by suddenly discovering the conspiracy of the constable of Bourbon against his throne, from leading his forces in person, he dispatched them into Lombardy under his favourite, the admiral Bonnivet. (A.D. 1524.) The absolute want of ability in that courtier, whose counsels were to involve his master in yet more signal calamities, produced the destruction of the fine army which he commanded; and his rout at Biagrassa closed this invasion like all the similar expeditions which had preceded it.

These ill-conducted and unfortunate enterprises of the French, and the repeated successes of the imperial arms, were silently riveting the chains of Italy. Charles V. was already all-powerful in the peninsula. He held the kingdom of Naples as a portion of his vast hereditary dominions; from Spain he drew the finest troops of the age; from his imperial authority in Germany, and from the states of his brother, the archduke of Austria, whose frontiers joined those of Italy, he derived an imposing power and warlike resources; and his bands held military occupation of Lombardy, and oppressed that beautiful country with all the horrors which an ill-paid and ferocious soldiery could inflict. At this appalling epoch for the independence and happiness of Italy, the administration of the holy see, which had always exercised so paramount, and often so fatal an influence, on the fortunes of the peninsula, fell into the hands of the pontiff, whose imbecile and fluctuating policy was to hasten the ruin of his country, and to overwhelm the capital of Christendom with an accumulation of horrors.

On the death of Leo X., an accident in the conclave had raised Adrian VI. to the tiara; and after the brief reign of this pontiff, which lasted not quite two years, the influence of the Medicean party in the sacred college placed Clement VII. (Giulio de' Medici) in the vacant chair of St. Peter. The foreign birth of Adrian VI., his stern contempt for the arts, his austerity and bigotry, and even his monastic virtues, had all rendered him an object of hatred and ridicule to the corrupt and polished Italians. The simplicity of his personal character, and his ignorance of political affairs, had alike disqualified him for the office, which might have graced his station, of protecting the liberties of the peninsula. But Clement VII., who succeeded him while the expedition of Bonnivet was yet in progress, was still less calculated to avert the impending ruin of Italy; and his misconduct aggravated the evils, for which the virtuous qualities of Adrian might at least have obtained a partial alleviation.

It was before the close of the same year with the discomfiture of Bonnivet, that Francis I. entered Lombardy at the head of a brilliant army, and commenced that fatal expedition which terminated with his captivity. While the fortune of his enterprise hung in suspense, both Clement VII. and the Venetians withdrew from supporting Charles V. in a contest, the successful issue of which, experience had proved, must confirm the servitude of Italy. The fears of the pope and the republic were the same: their desire was equal to effect a general pacification while the strength of the contending powers was still balanced; and both the Venetians, and Clement in the name of his see and of the Florentine state, signed a pacific treaty with the French king. If the pope at this juncture had sincerely joined Venice and the other native powers of the peninsula, as was proposed to him, in an armed neutrality, such a coalition might have dictated peace to the belligerents, and might yet have saved the cause of Italian independence. But the imbecility, the irresolution, and the avarice of Clement VII. rendered him incapable of a vigorous and enlightened policy. He hesitated and wavered, and suffered the struggle to proceed, which could only leave the peninsula at the mercy of the conqueror.

It is not my intention to relate the vicissitudes of the eventful campaign in Lombardy, which closed with the famous battle of Pavia and the captivity of the French monarch. On that disastrous day, the sun of Italian independence was finally quenched in foreign blood; and from that hour, the emperor Charles V. secured the mastery of the peninsula almost as completely as if he had annexed to his diadems of the empire and of Naples, the iron crown of Lombardy, the keys of St. Peter, and the sceptre of the Adriatic. The consternation of all the Italian powers was extreme; and their first endeavour was to form a general league for common defence; which, but a few months before, might have had an effectual and glorious result. But Clement VII., ever irresolute and vacillating, instead of vigorously uniting with the Venetians and the worsted French, suffered himself still to be amused by the imperial generals with faithless negotiations, and even concluded a separate treaty and a new alliance with their master.

These commanders, imagining that they had thus no longer to fear a general league of the Italians, abandoned themselves without restraint to the indulgence of intolerable insolence and extortion. They thus at last drove the pope, who had already lost so many more promising occasions, to enter into a secret confederacy with the Venetians. The allies negotiated for the support of the king of England and the Swiss; and they obtained from Louise, mother of the captive monarch of France and regent of his kingdom, a promise to renounce the French pretensions upon Milan, and to maintain Francesco Sforza on his throne. That prince was suffered by the tyranny of the imperial generals, who occupied his duchy with their troops, to enjoy only the shadow of sovereignty; and as soon as he found that he might expect the support of France, he in secret gladly entered into the league between the pope and the Venetians. The confederates observed with pleasure that the greater part of the imperial army in Lombardy was already disbanded. Lannoy, the viceroy of Naples, had conveyed his royal captive to Spain, and the constable of Bourbon had followed him. The weakness of the imperial forces, and the absence of these commanders, were favourable to the views of the powers of the league; but they founded their hopes of success yet more upon the disgust with which the famous marquis of Pescara, who was left in command of the imperialists in Italy, was at this epoch known to be filled at the partiality of Charles V. for Lannoy.

Pescara, himself a Neapolitan nobleman, could not, it was imagined, be insensible to the degradation of Italy. His present temper of mind appeared likely to incline him to adopt any proposal of vengeance against the emperor; and so great was the estimation of his talents and influence, that the pope did not consider that, in offering the marquis the investiture of the kingdom of Naples, he should be rewarding his patriotism or stimulating his ambition and vengeance too highly. The agent of the allies, in this delicate negotiation, was Girolamo Morone, chancellor of the Milanese duchy, who had, by his consummate abilities for political intrigue, rendered the court of his master, Sforza, the focus of the confederacy. To this man, Pescara listened with deep and anxious attention, while he gradually unfolded the able projects of the confederates, and showed that the aid of the marquis, in dispersing the Spanish troops in quarters where they might be destroyed in detail, was alone necessary to the accomplishment of their schemes. Pescara finally embraced the cause of his country, but embraced it only to betray. Whether he had merely listened to the proposals of the allies to communicate them to Charles as he afterwards pretended; or whether, after engaging with sincerity in the Italian league, he was induced to abandon it from despair of its success; his treachery, either to his master or to his country, was alike certain and disgraceful. After some delay, he made known the whole intrigue to the emperor, drew Morone to his quarters at Novara and arrested him, seized upon all the strong places in the Milanese duchy which the Spanish troops did not already occupy, and blockaded the duke Francesco himself in the castle of his capital. Pescara was already stricken with a mortal disorder before he had accomplished this iniquity, and he shortly died. His military exploits had been great; but their renown cannot extenuate the infamy, which brands his memory as the betrayer of his country.

Even after the discovery of Pescara's treachery, the wavering pontiff still hesitated to commit himself by hostilities, until he found, on the release of Francis I. from captivity, that the French monarch breathed vengeance against Charles V., and was resolved to evade the execution of the treaty which he had concluded with the emperor at Madrid. Then assured of the support of Francis and the countenance of Henry VIII., the pope at last took his decision. The long-desired league for Italian independence was finally adjusted: to oblige the emperor to restore the Milanese duchy to Sforza, and to deliver up the sons of Francis whom he held as hostages, were declared to be the objects of the contracting parties. Besides the foreign powers, the pope, the state of Florence, the Venetian republic, and the duke of Milan, were the principal confederates; and as the pontiff placed himself at their head, they gave to their alliance the title of the Holy League, (A.D. 1526.)

But the struggle was vain against the destiny of Italy; or rather the hour was arrived, in which the want of energy and real union in her governments, the extinction of all courage and military spirit in the mass of her people, the vices and cowardice, alike of her rulers and subjects, were to fill up the measure of her degradation and calamities. Numerous armies were indeed assembled by the Italian powers, but these were bodies without soul. They were neither warmed by the sense of honour, nor stung by the dread of intolerable shame: neither animated by a generous devotion in their country's cause, nor steeled by her wrongs to desperation and vengeance. The magnitude of the crisis could not rouse their generals to vigorous operations: the soldiery, if they fought at all, fought only with the indifference of mercenaries. The disgrace of the result must be branded, in truth, on the moral degeneracy into which the nation had already sunk; but there were also various secondary causes for the failure. Francis I., whose reverses had now superadded a distrust in his own fortunes to the natural defects of his character, to his indecision and negligence, his abandonment to pleasure, and his aversion for business. Francis I. shamefully deserted the support of his allies. The duke of Urbino, the general of the Venetians, whose rank obtained for him the supreme command of the confederates, though not destitute of military talents, was, of all men, from his timid and cautious and indecisive character, least calculated to conduct the operations of a league, whose strength mouldered while he delayed. Although his forces were far superior to those of the imperialists in Lombardy, he suffered them to continue the siege of the castle of Milan, in which Sforza was still shut up. He gave time for the constable of Bourbon to arrive with reinforcements from Spain, and to assume the command of the enemy; and while he remained inactive in sight of Milan, the unfortunate duke was obliged to capitulate for the evacuation of his capital.

But the irresolution and misconduct of the pope were even more conspicuous than the military errors of the confederates; and his infatuation completed the ruin of their cause. Terrified at the ill success of the league, and weary of the contest, he suffered himself to be deluded into negotiations for peace by the agents of Charles V., until his enemy, the cardinal Pompeo Colonna, with the forces of his powerful house, surprised him in his capital, and obliged him to capitulate for a separate truce. His defection paralyzed the league; and their affairs were not improved when, as soon as his imminent danger was past, he imprudently resumed hostilities, only to be a second time lulled into security by a new suspension of arms between his troops and those of the viceroy of Naples. He disbanded his forces, and not even the advance of Bourbon towards Rome with his army from Lombardy,—equally formidable for their numbers, their ferocity, and their licentious contempt of all authority,—could rouse him to a sense of his danger.

Bourbon had been left by the emperor, whose finances were always in disorder, absolutely destitute of all means of supporting the numerous forces which served under the imperial standard: German, Spanish, and Italian,—for Italians were ever to be found in arras against their national cause. He was compelled to lead them to find subsistence in the papal territories; and, on their repeated mutinies for want of pay, could appease them only, by offering to their passions the riches and sack of Rome. The duke of Urbino followed him at a distance with the confederate army, and either from his habitual timidity, or his hatred of the house of Medici, made not an effort to succour the pope. It was to no purpose that the viceroy of Naples informed Bourbon of the new suspension of arms which he had concluded with the pope. The constable was perhaps unwilling, he was certainly unable, to arrest the advance of his lawless host; and he led them, in the last hour of his disgraceful career, to the assault of the venerable capital of Christendom. I may draw a veil over the horrors that followed: the immensity of human wickedness and human suffering, the fearful and protracted reign of lust, and rapine, and blood, (A.D. 1527.) Never had Rome, in her prostration before the barbarians of the north, in the long retribution for her ancient tyranny over the universe, endured such extremity of woe, as agonized her wretched population on this dreadful and memorable occasion. Amidst such a scene, the captivity of the imbecile pontiff was the lightest of calamities, which his own incapacity had eminently provoked. After vainly seeking refuge in the castle of St. Angelo, he was compelled to deliver himself a prisoner to the imperial arms.

The horrible sack of Rome, and yet more the captivity of the father of the church, excited universal indignation in Europe; wherever the new religious opinions had not yet penetrated. Upon this occasion, at least, Francis I. was roused to vigorous exertion, as well by policy as by mistaken piety, in the endeavour to rescue the pope from the hands of Charles V. Henry VIII. shared his zeal and his alarm at the progress of the imperial power, and engaged by treaty to assist him with subsidies. Italy was chosen for the theatre of their combined efforts; and Lautrec once more crossed the Alps at the head of a powerful French army, and began to co-operate actively with the Venetians in Lombardy. The duke of Ferrara and the marquis of Mantua joined the confederacy against the imperialists; and the Florentines, though on the news of the capture of the pope they had risen against the Medicean yoke, and expelled the cardinals who governed their state for Clement VII., also earnestly embraced the French alliance. Thus the Florentines entered the league, whose object it was to procure freedom for the pope, their immediate enemy; but, with the restoration of their republic, had appeared also their ancient and enthusiastic attachment to a French connexion. They justly regarded the emperor as the most dangerous foe to the liberties of Italy; and they were hurried away alike by dread of his designs, and by the indulgence of their old affections, to declare against him and in favour of his rival. Thus they imprudently, as we say at least after the event, lost the only opportunity which the unhappy circumstances of the times afforded of saving some wrecks of freedom, by at once throwing themselves into the arms of the emperor, and committing their cause to his protection and generosity.

While the operations of the allies were proceeding favourably in Lombardy, they solemnly published the renewal of their league. It now embraced the kings of France and England, the republics of Venice and Florence, the dukes of Milan and Ferrara, and the marquis of Mantua; and these contracting parties declared the captive pope the head of their confederacy. Their arms might easily have recovered for Francesco Sforza the possession of his whole duchy, for the imperialists at Milan were now in very small force; but Lautrec had his master's commands not to bring the war in Lombardy to a conclusion; lest the Venetians and Sforza, having no farther reason to fear the emperor, should relax in their efforts. He therefore, alleging his orders for the immediate deliverance of the pope, led his army towards southern Italy. He had scarcely entered the papal territories when Clement, who had already signed an agreement with imperial commissioners for his ransom, escaped from his prison on the day preceding that on which he was to be set at liberty, and arrived at the French camp. But dismayed and humiliated by his misfortunes, the feeble pontiff in recovering his freedom, was prepared to renounce all his former projects, and desirous only of peace; although he did not refuse the support of the confederacy.

The object for which he had entered the papal dominions being concluded by the release of Clement VII., Lautrec now passed on to attempt the conquest of the kingdom of Naples, (A.D. 1528.) On his approach, the imperial generals with difficulty prevailed on their troops to quit Rome; where they had remained inactive for ten months, and prolonged the unspeakable horrors of the first sack. A fearful pestilence which, to deepen the calamities of Italy, was now spreading over the land, had already borne its destroying vengeance among this ruffian soldiery; and before their evacuation of Rome, above half their numbers had been swept off by its ravages, and by other disorders, the effects of intemperance and debauchery. The enfeebled remains of the imperialists were pursued by Lautrec at the head of his flourishing array; almost the whole kingdom of Naples, impatient to throw off the Spanish yoke, declared for the French; the forces of Charles V. were shut up in the capital; and while the combined fleets of France, and Venice, and Genoa, successively appeared off the harbour and intercepted all supplies, Lautrec with his superior army commenced a rigid blockade by land.

But Lautrec suffered the siege of Naples to linger in indecision, until it terminated by a total change in the relative condition of the combatants. His troops being encamped during the sultry season in the environs of the capital, which are at such periods always unhealthy, were attacked by violent sickness. Some of their prisoners communicated to them the pestilence which had been so destructive at Rome; and while the imperialists recovered health and confidence, contagious and epidemic diseases made fearful havoc among the besiegers, and plunged them into discouragement and misery, which were aggravated as usual by the neglect of their sovereign to their pecuniary necessities. In this critical position of affairs, the imprudence of Francis, by provoking the defection of the hero of Genoa, the famous admiral Andrea Doria, brought despair and destruction on the French army.

In the vicissitudes of the long wars, which had desolated Italy since the first entrance of the French, Genoa, so fallen from her ancient glories during the whole of the fifteenth century, had generally shared the ignominious fortunes of the Milanese duchy. As the French and their enemies prevailed in turn, her political condition had miserably oscillated under foreign sovereignty, between the alternate preponderance of adverse and implacable factions. Latterly, she had groaned under imperial tyranny until, during the temporary success of the confederates, and by the aid of Doria, the faction of the Fregosi and the French dominion were re-established within her walls. Doria, whose name has eclipsed or enhanced the earlier splendour of his illustrious house, had been bred to the sea like his noble ancestors, and had early entered the naval service of France. Although he had passed little of his life in his native city, his anxiety for her liberties and prosperity was not the less enthusiastic. He had created a numerous squadron which followed his personal fortunes; and his indignation at the wrongs sustained by Genoa, in the sack and pillage which had attended the triumph of the imperialists in 1522, rendered him the most dreaded enemy on the ocean of the Spanish name. Animated by hatred to common enemies, he had hitherto served the French cause with fidelity and zeal; but his honest sincerity had provoked the rancorous dislike of the courtiers of Francis I., and that monarch was filled by their arts with suspicion and distrust of him. His valuable counsel was treated with slight and neglect; his eminent services were repaid by insult and ingratitude. These private affronts he keenly felt as a high-spirited and honourable man; but his animosity against the imperialists might have stifled his sense of personal injury, if he had not had abundant reason to perceive that it was the purpose of Francis I. to regard his country, not as an independent republic, but as a conquered and subject city. As the term of his engagement with that monarch was about to expire, he boldly demanded justice for his country and himself. Francis replied by dispatching an officer to supersede him in the command of the French fleet, and even to seize his person and his own galleys. Doria honourably delivered up the French vessels; but he declared that, for his galleys, they were his own to do with as he would. With this force he withdrew; and the French admiral dared not molest his retreat. He immediately concluded a negotiation with Charles V. His principal demand was the freedom of his native city; and the emperor, who knew the value of his services, received them upon his own terms, and in the issue faithfully observed his engagements.

The first operation of Doria was to return with relief and protection for the imperial army to Naples, which he had before blockaded. On his arrival, the French, who had lost their naval superiority by his defection, were, in addition to the former horrors of pestilence, now reduced to all the calamities of want. They were in their turn besieged in their camp; Lautrec himself sank under the weight of mental agony and bodily disease; and on his death, the miserable remains of the French army were reduced to a disgraceful capitulation. After this success, Doria immediately sailed for Genoa. The French garrison in that city were weak; the people hailed their noble deliverer with gratitude and support; their tyrants were obliged to capitulate; and the republic of Genoa revived.

It was now in the power of Doria to have rendered himself the master of his country; for the emperor, who loved not the name of freedom, offered to invest him with the title of prince of Genoa, and to maintain him in the sovereignty of that state. But the proposal served only to display the magnanimity of the hero, and to confirm his true greatness. He refused to raise himself upon the ruin of his country. He insisted upon the accomplishment of the imperial promise to recognise the liberties of the republic. He completely pacified her factions, which had hitherto seemed implacable; and so disinterested was his patriotism, so noble his ambition, that he declined the office of doge, because he deemed its useful exercise incompatible with his continuance in the imperial service, by which he hoped to preserve the protection of Charles for his fellow-citizens. Well did he merit, even to the close of a long and honourable life, the titles which their gratitude inscribed on his statue: the best of citizens, the successful champion, and the restorer of public liberty.

Doria had at least obtained a municipal independence for his native city: he could not control the fate of Italy, or defer the hour of her servitude. The destruction of one French army before Naples, and the surprise and dispersion of a second in Lombardy, which almost immediately followed, put a term to the hopes of Francis I. Broken in spirit, and exhausted in resources by an unvaried train of disasters, he thought no longer of retrieving his disgraces by arms; to obtain the release of his children, he scrupled not to desert his allies and to forfeit his honour. The pope, equally unscrupulous and yet more eager for peace, anticipated him in the desertion of the Italian confederacy. He found a pacific disposition in the emperor which seconded his own. Charles had many reasons for desiring a pacification which he could dictate as a conqueror: the embarrassment and exhaustion of his finances; the alarming progress of the reformation in Germany; the danger which menaced that country from the power of the Turks, who had already overrun Hungary. To detach Clement VII. from the number of his enemies, he granted him the most favourable terms; his principal stipulation was to reduce Florence again under the yoke of the Medici; and for this and other objects, the pope, by the treaty of Barcelona, was content to betray Italy to the imperial yoke. (A.D. 1529.) But the monstrous perfidy and baseness of the French king, almost immediately afterwards, diverted the reproaches and indignation of Italy from the lighter dishonour of the impotent and faithless pontiff. By the peace which Francis concluded with the emperor at Cambray, he abandoned all his confederates, at the moment when he was urging them to persevere in hostilities, by earnest promises of continued support. He stipulated nothing in favour of the Venetians, or of the dukes of Milan and Ferrara; nothing for the Florentines, who had provoked the imperial vengeance by his alliance; nothing for the French adherents in the Neapolitan kingdom, who had incurred the penalties of rebellion by their attachment to his cause.

After having triumphed as much by his negotiations as his arms, Charles V. at length appeared in person in Italy, with the imposing power and the pride of a victor. Doria with his galleys escorted him from Spain; strong reinforcements for his Italian army attended or awaited him; and their junction with the imperialists already in the peninsula, formed a numerous and brilliant assemblage of veteran troops. The powers of Italy were prostrate before him; but the situation of his affairs in Germany imposed on him a moderation which was foreign to his severe and haughty temper. He granted peace to the Venetians, and the duke of Ferrara, on tolerable conditions; he pardoned Francesco Sforza, and permitted him the possession of the Milanese duchy; he received the dukes of Savoy and Urbino, and the marquises of Montferrat and Mantua with indulgence, and raised the last of these princes to the ducal dignity; he treated Sienna and Lucca, which had long been devoted to the imperial party, with favour; and upon the republic of Genoa in particular, he conferred several privileges, through consideration for Doria, whom he loaded with distinction. But all these acts spoke only the good pleasure of a master, who had no longer any thing to dread from conquered and terrified subjects. Venice, though she preserved her territories, felt her weakness, and the decay of her resources, and trembled before him; the pope was yet more powerless; the kingdom of the Two Sicilies was his; the dukes of Milan, Savoy, Ferrara, Mantua, Urbino, and other petty princes, the republics of Genoa, Sienna, and Lucca, were conscious that they existed only by his sufferance. Thus the coronation of Charles V., which the pope performed at Bologna, was a galling and too certain type of the servitude of Italy (A.D. 1530); and when the emperor, after that ceremony, passed into Germany, he had perfected a despotism, the security of which left him no cause for future inquietude.

The fatal corruption of the Italian mind had too long and too well prepared the nation for servitude; and in the vivid recollection of suffering during so many years of cruel warfare, the people were ready to hail any pacification with transports of joy. The repose which Charles V. bestowed upon Italy, while he rivetted the yoke on her degenerate sons, was therefore received with universal acclamations of gratitude and delight. One city alone spurned the general humiliation, and nobly preferred to cling to the last hopes of independence, rather than to share in a peace, which was to be obtained only by an ignominious submission. Florence, the most illustrious of the Italian republics of the middle ages, the bright exemplar of their generous passion for freedom, their early civilization and commerce, and their intellectual splendour,—Florence alone, amidst the degradation of Italy, was awakened to the magnanimous spirit of former times. Originally, after having resisted for centuries all the efforts of tyranny, she had surrendered herself, not to open oppression or foreign violence, but to the abuse of popular affection, and to the seductive arts and insidious virtues of a republican family. After having long yielded almost unconsciously to the absolute dominion of that family, she had twice roused herself, and shaken off their authority; and now, in the extreme hour of Italian shame, amidst the mouldered ruins of Italian liberty, she seemed to revive by the memory of her ancient greatness, for one dauntless, though expiring struggle. As she had surpassed all her sister states in wealth, and power, and elegant refinement, so it became her to survive their rivalry, and to perish the latest:—to gather the robe of republican virtue around her, and to fall the last victim in that cause, of which she had once been the guardian and firmest support.

The death of Leo X. had extinguished the legitimate male posterity of Cosmo de' Medici; and there remained only three bastards of his house, whose dubious title to the name which they bore increased the shame of submission to their sovereignty. These were Guilio de' Medici (Clement VII.,) and two youths, Alessandro and Ippolito, the reputed sons, the former of Lorenzo (son of Piero II.), and the latter of Giuliano (youngest brother of Leo X.). When Clement VII. ascended the papal chair, he displayed more attachment to imaginary family interests, than to the welfare of his country; and though the blood of Alessandro and Ippolito was even more impure or suspicious than his own, he chose to identify their elevation with the continued grandeur of the Medici. It was therefore that he designed for them the sovereignty of Florence, and appointed a regency of three cardinals to govern for them during their minority. When the Florentines had succeeded, during his own captivity, in banishing this Medicean regency without bloodshed, he still adhered, as to a darling passion, to the hope of again reducing Florence under his despotic authority, and transmitting its sovereignty to his destined heirs. Thus, in betraying Italy to Charles V. by the treaty of Barcelona, he made that object his principal condition. Ippolito, one of his cousins, he had placed in the church, and bestowed on him a cardinal's hat. The temporal dignity of the Medici was therefore represented by the other, Alessandro, alone; and it was for him that the emperor engaged to reserve the sovereignty of Florence, and the hand of his own natural daughter.

On the recovery of their independence, the Florentines had re-established their republican constitution pretty much as it had existed before the restoration of the Medici in 1512. It was vested ill a general council of the citizens, who elected the gonfalonier and signiory: the supreme magistrate was now to hold his office, not for life, but for one year only; the signiory was changed every three months. With liberty revived the spirit of faction, from the baleful effects of which it would seem that no republic can ever hope to escape. Florence had again her aristocratical and popular parties; nor were there wanting in her counsels some remains of the religious fanaticism that had formerly distinguished the followers of Savonarola, of whom a few were yet living. The secret adherents of the Medici, too, were not inactive; and, as the crisis grew more alarming, their numbers were swelled by the accession of all those whose prudence or timidity was greater than their patriotism. But the mass of the citizens were sincere and zealous in the resolution to maintain their newly-recovered rights, and prepared to evince it by the endurance of every privation and danger. Thus, although abandoned by all their allies, they firmly rejected every proposal of submission either to the emperor or the pope; and though Andrea Doria, who eagerly desired to save their liberties from total ruin, offered, before the treaty of Barcelona, to secure them the protection of Charles V. by his mediation, they finally refused to quit the alliance of France, or to accept any compromise with the emperor.

Their courage was shortly put to the severest trial, and their pledge of constancy was nobly redeemed even by the unhappy issue of the struggle.

Abandoned by France and by Italy, assailed by the united forces of the empire and the church, the kingdoms of Spain and of Naples, this people, heretofore so unwarlike, surprised the world by a gallant, a protracted, and a skilful defence. A new military spirit seemed at once kindled in them by the justice of their cause, and even by the appalling desolation in which they were left. Deprived of all hope of foreign succour, they resolved to place their sole dependence on a national militia. The population of their capital and territory were armed and enrolled into regular battalions; the property of individuals was cheerfully sacrificed to the public good; their defences were improved and augmented; and the immortal Michelangiolo, who was charged with the office of director-general of the fortifications of Florence, consecrated his sublime genius to the noblest, the best of purposes, the service of his suffering country.

The public courage only rose as the storm of war burst upon the state. The imperial army, which had annihilated the French before

Naples, entered Tuscany under the prince of Orange. The same general who, after the death of Bourbon, had commanded at Rome, and the remains of the same ferocious bands, which had sacked his capital and held him captive, were thus now instigated by Clement VII. to accomplish his vengeance against his native city; and the force of this invading army was soon augmented, by the junction of the other imperial troops in Italy, to forty thousand men. Yet against the vastly superior numbers of this veteran army, composed of the finest troops of the age, the newly-levied militia of Florence, aided only by a few condottieri and their bands, maintained an obstinate contest for above twelve months, and more than once balanced the fortune of the war. After reducing the surrounding territory, the imperialists penetrated to the walls of Florence, and surrounded the city on all sides with their intrenchments. But they were repulsed in an attempt to carry the defences by escalade; they were compelled to convert the siege into a blockade; and they were harassed, and they suffered many losses, as well by the frequent and vigorous sallies of the defenders, as by the active and desultory operations of Florentine partizans from without. In one of these encounters at Gavinana, the prince of Orange himself was slain; but his death was more than counterbalanced by the fall in the same action of the most gallant and enterprising leader of the Florentines, Francesco Ferrucci, and the destruction of the detachment which he had commanded. The imperialists had not, however, purchased their victory without an immense carnage; and their main army was already thrown into such discouragement by the death of their commander, that a general assault upon their lines before Florence might at this crisis have won the deliverance of the city. The signiory perceiving the importance of the juncture, sent orders to their captain-general, Malatesta Baglioni, lord of Perugia, to issue with their whole force and attack the imperial camp. But treason had already sealed the fate of the unhappy republic. Baglioni had for some time been in treaty with the enemy; and the moment was arrived when the traitor could find associates in the city. A pestilence, after assailing the besieging army, had been communicated from their camp to the city; its terrors were augmented by the dread of approaching famine; and when Baglioni refused obedience to the commands of the signiory to make a last and desperate effort against the besiegers, he was seconded by the secret adherents of the Medici, and by all who were wearied of privation and suffering and terrified at the threatened accumulation of evils. Supported by these men, Baglioni, to his and their eternal infamy, delivered one of the bastions of the city to the imperial troops; and Florence was lost.

From the extremity of misery, from a civil war in the streets, a fruitless aggravation of carnage, and a frightful pillage by the foreign soldiery, Florence was saved by the submission of the signiory to inevitable fortune. They obtained for their country an honourable capitulation; but conditions are of little avail, when they are conceded by sovereigns without faith, and afterwards appealed to by men without power. In the name of his master and of the emperor, the papal commissioner granted a general amnesty to the citizens, and guaranteed the preservation of Florentine liberty under such a modified constitution as should subsequently be determined. But the treaty was scarcely dry before it was shamelessly violated; and by a refinement of insult and mockery of faith, the constitutional forms of the republic were the instruments chosen for its destruction. The papal commissioner had no sooner entered the city with the emigrants of the Medicean faction, than he obliged the signiory to summon a parliament of the people. By foreign halberds, the mass of the citizens were either beaten back from the public place or deterred from attending. A few hundreds of the Medicean partizans and of the lower populace were alone suffered to enter, and by the breath of this pretended assemblage of the people, a balia was formed of the creatures of the Medici. Then torture, exile, or death fell upon the principal champions of liberty; more than one whom the sword of the executioner was suffered to spare, perished in prison by poison or hunger; and before the prolonged balia resigned their functions, they had declared Alessandro de' Medici the first duke of Florence, and formally suppressed even the name of the republic.

CHAPTER IX. STATE OF ITALY DURING THE REMAINDER OF THE SIXTEENTH CENTURY, a.d. 1530-1600.

Insignificance of Italian history after the subjugation of the peninsula by Charles V.—General affairs of Italy after that epoch until the peace of Chateau Cambresis: a period of frequent wars—The limits and existence of the Italian states regulated by the treaty of Chateau Cambresis—Italy ceases to be the theatre of European contest, and remains undisturbed by wars to the close of the sixteenth century—Oppression and misery of her people—Particular and domestic fortunes of the different Italian states during all this period—Naples and Milan—Oppressive character and ruinous influence of the Spanish administration in those states—Repeated and vain attempts to establish the Spanish inquisition in them—The popedom—Decline of its splendour—Succession of pontiffs—Paul IV.—Change introduced by him in the objects of papal policy—The popes the persecutors of the reformed faith—Maladministration of their own states—Brief interval of vigorous government—Sixtus V.—Grandeur of his character—Rise of the ducal house of Parma—Pietro Luigi Farnése, son of pope Paul III., the first duke—His assassination—Reverses of Ottavio, his son and successor—The grandeur of the house of Farnése established by Alessandro, the famous prince of Parma—Ferrara and Modena—Extinction of the legitimate line of Este—Ferrara annexed to the holy see—Decay of that capital and duchy—The seat of the house of Este transferred to Modena—Mantua—Annexation of Montferrat to that duchy—Savoy—Unfortunate reign of duke Charles III.—Spoliation of his states—His son, Emmanuel Philibert, restores the fortunes of his house—His glorious and pacific reign— Charles Emmanuel I.—Succeeds in closing the gates of Italy against the French—Tuscany—Government of Florence after the extinction of the republic—Alessandro de' Medici, the first duke or doge—His tyranny and excesses—His assassination by his cousin Lorenzino—Cosmo de' Medici, his successor, triumphs over the last effort of the republican exiles, and treats them with merciless cruelty—He acquires the sovereignty of Sienna—Fall of that republic—Cosmo I. created grand-duke of Tuscany—Fearful tragedy in his family—His son, the grand-duke Francesco—His atrocious system of assassinations—His marriage with Bianco Capello, "daughter of the Venetian republic"—Romantic story of that lady—The grand-duke and his duchess poisoned by his brother, the cardinal Ferdinando—Reign of Ferdinando, grand-duke of Tuscany—Lucca—Establishment of the oligarchy of that republic—Genoa—Aristocratical constitution promoted by Andrea Doria—Popular discontents—Conspiracy of Fiesco—Its successful execution rendered abortive by the death of its leader—Final consolidation of the Genoese oligarchy—Venice—Unimpaired vigour of her oligarchical despotism, and internal tranquillity of the state—Decay of the foreign power of the republic—Neutrality wisely observed by her senate but twice interrupted during this period by Turkish wars—The first of these concluded by the loss of several colonies—The second a yet more ruinous struggle—Conquest of Cypress by the Turks—League of Christian powers with Venice against the infidels—Great battle of Lepanto—That victory of the league entirely without fruits—Peace purchased by Venice with the loss of Cyprus.

WITH her subjection to the emperor Charles V. the national existence of Italy may be said to have terminated; and from this epoch, until she was roused from the lethargy of three centuries, only to suffer anew in the gigantic revolutions of our times, and to become again the prize of foreign tyrants, her history is almost a blank. The fall of her independence was coeval with the decline of honourable energy and social virtue in her people; and the extinction of all interest in their history is simultaneous with the completion of their moral and political degradation. In conducting the subject of these volumes to its conclusion,—that is, to the moment at which the French revolution burst upon the astonished world,—our course will be rapid and our notices general.

Fallen from her rank amongst the nations of Europe, Italy ceased to mingle in their political combinations. Her greatest provinces were immediately subject to strangers; her petty sovereigns, and her few surviving republics, ignobly followed in the train of foreign negotiation and foreign conquest. Except the insignificant vicissitudes of her native dynasties, we shall find scarcely any thing in her languid annals and protracted servitude to arrest our attention; for even though her two principal maritime republics,—their glories faded and their ancient importance extinguished,—were still suffered to preserve the remnants of sovereignty, their fate only attracts our curiosity from the associations of the past, and their condition cannot otherwise excite our interest, than as we should contemplate the venerable but dilapidated ruins of antiquity. Such is the poverty of Italian history, in the remainder of the sixteenth, in the whole of the seventeenth, and in the eighteenth century, until the commencement of the wars of the French revolution, that we shall find no difficulty in compressing the events of these three long periods into the same number of chapters. In each, a few pages will suffice to describe the general political aspect of the peninsula: whatever is worth narrating in the particular and domestic fortunes of individual states, may afterwards be told briefly, under an equal number of separate heads.

The first circumstance, after the peace of Cambray, which interrupted the ignominious repose of Italy, was the renewal of hostilities between Francis I. and the emperor. During the expedition of Charles V. against Tunis, the French monarch availed himself of the distraction of the imperial strength to commence his offensive operations. His troops broke into the territories of the duke of Savoy, against whom he had some causes of dissatisfaction, and easily wrested all Savoy, and the greater part of Piedmont, from that feeble prince; while the imperialists took possession of the remainder of his states, under pretence of defending them. (A.D. 1535.) Meanwhile the death of Francesco Sforza, who left no posterity, revived the long wars for the possession of the Milanese state. On the one hand, Francis I., alleging that he had only ceded that duchy to Sforza and his descendants, insisted that his rights returned to him in full force by the decease of that prince without issue: on the other, Charles V. anticipated his designs by seizing the duchy as a lapsed fief of the empire.

Francis I., after some hollow negotiations with his crafty rival, once more staked the decision of his pretensions on a trial of arms. Lombardy became again the theatre of furious contests between the French and imperialists; but the usual fortunes of Francis still pursued him; and although his troops inflicted a sanguinary defeat on their opponents in the battle of Cerisolles, the fruits of their victory were lost by the necessity, under which the French monarch was placed, of turning his strength to the defence of the northern frontiers of his own kingdom, (A.D. 1544.) The peace of Crespi, in the same year, left Charles in possession of Lombardy; and though Francis still retained part of the dominions of the duke of Savoy, the despotic authority of his rival over Italy remained unshaken.

The tranquillity restored to the peninsula by the peace of Crespi was not materially disturbed for several years. This period was indeed signalized by the abortive conspiracy of Fiesco at Genoa, and earlier by the separation of Parma and Placentia from the papal dominions, and their erection into a sovereign duchy. These territories, which originally formed part of the Milanese states, had first been annexed to the holy see by the conquests of Julius II.; they had frequently changed masters in the subsequent convulsions of Italy; and their possession had finally been confirmed to the papacy by the consent of Francesco Sforza. By the subserviency of the sacred college, the reigning pontiff Paul III., of the family of Farnése, was suffered to detach these valuable dependencies from the holy see, and to bestow them upon his son with the ducal dignity, (A.D. 1545.) But neither the trifling change which was wrought in the divisions of Lombardy, by the creation of the duchy of Parma and Placentia, nor the dangerous conspiracy of Fiesco, affected the general aspect and the quietude of Italy, (A.D. 1547.)

Shortly after the death of pope Paul III., however, the determination of the emperor to spoil his family, obliged Ottavio Farnése, the reigning duke of Parma, to throw himself into the arms of Henry II., the new monarch of France; and thus a new war was kindled in Lombardy and Piedmont, in which the French appeared, as the defenders of Ottavio, against the forces of Charles V. and of the new pope, Julius III. (A.D. 1551.) The war of Parma produced no memorable event, until it was extended into Tuscany by the revolt of Sienna against the grievous oppression of the Spanish garrison, which the people had themselves introduced to curb the tyranny of the aristocratical faction of their republic. After expelling their Spanish masters, the Siennese invited the aid of the French for the maintenance of their liberties against the emperor, (A.D. 1552.) The war in Tuscany was marked by some alternations of success, but the French were finally expelled from that province; and after an obstinate siege and a gallant defence of ten months, Sienna was reduced by the imperial arms. (A.D. 1555.)

When, in the same year with this event, the emperor Charles V. executed the extraordinary resolution of abdicating his throne, and resigning his immense possessions to his son Philip II., the flames of war which had raged in Europe with such intense violence during the greater part of his long reign, seemed already expiring in their embers. But they were re-kindled in Italy, almost immediately after the accession of Philip II., by the fierce passions of Paul IV., a rash and violent pontiff. In his indignation at the opposition which Charles V. had raised against his election, and moreover to gratify the ambition of his family, Paul IV. had already instigated Henry II. of France to join him in a league to ruin the imperial power in Italy; and he now, in concert with the French monarch, directed against Philip II. the hostile measures which he had prepared against his father. Philip II., that most odious of tyrants, whose atrocious cruelty and imbecile superstition may divide the judgment of mankind between execration and contempt, shrank with horror from the impiety of combatting the pontiff, whom he had regarded as the vicegerent of God upon earth. He therefore vainly exhausted every resource of negotiation, before he was reconciled by the opinion of the Spanish ecclesiastics, whom he anxiously consulted, to the lawfulness of engaging in such a contest. At length he was prevailed upon to suffer the duke of Alva to lead the veteran Spanish bands from the kingdom of Naples into the papal territories. The advance of Alva to the gates of Rome, however, struck consternation into the sacred college; and the haughty and obstinate pontiff was compelled by the terror of his cardinals to conclude a truce with the Spanish general, which he immediately broke on learning the approach of a superior French army under the duke de Guise, (A.D. 1556.)

This celebrated captain of France, to whom the project was confided of conquering the kingdom of Naples from the Spaniards was, however, able to accomplish nothing in Italy, which accorded with his past and subsequent fame. Crossing the Alps at the head of 20,000 men, he penetrated, without meeting any resistance, through Lombardy and Tuscany to the ecclesiastical capital, (A.D. 1557.) If he could effect the reduction of the kingdom of Naples, it was imagined that the Spanish provinces in northern Italy must fall of themselves; and having, therefore, left the Milanese duchy unassailed behind him, he passed on from Rome to the banks of the Garigliano, where he found Alva posted with an inferior force to oppose him. The wily caution of the Spanish general and the patient valour of his troops disconcerted the impetuosity of the French and the military skill of their gallant leader; and disease had already begun to make fearful havoc in the ranks of the invaders, when Guise was recalled, by the victory of the Spaniards at

St. Quentin, to defend the frontiers of France. He suddenly evacuated Italy with his army; and Paul IV. was abandoned to the mercy of the Spaniards. But such was now the superstitious veneration which they shared with or had imbibed from their monarch, that Paul IV. had little to fear from their success. After having reduced the pontiff to extremities, the proud Alva prostrated himself at his feet; in the name of his master and nation, abjectly implored absolution and pardon; and poured out the expression of repentance for having resisted and punished his aggressions.

The efforts of the French and Spanish arms were now wholly diverted to the frontiers of the Netherlands; and the future invasion or repose of Italy was to be decided by the operations of the war in that quarter. The question was determined by the well-balanced forces of the combatants, and the consequent desire which both the French and Spanish monarchs now entertained to terminate their differences; and the Italians, who had long forgotten the hope, and had ceased to deserve the possession of independence, were at least fortunate in escaping from a renewal of former horrors. The treaty, which was shortly concluded at Chateau 'Cambresis, appeared to terminate the long rivalry of the French and Spanish monarchies, and reestablished the peace of Europe, almost all the states of which were parties to it, as the allies either of Henry or of Philip, (A.D. 1559.) But in its consequences to Italy, this famous treaty was particularly important. To detach the duke of Parma from the French interest during the late war, Philip had already restored to him the part of his states which Charles V. had formerly seized: to confirm the fidelity of Cosmo I., afterwards grand-duke of Tuscany, he had assigned Sienna to the sceptre of the Medici, and retained only in Tuscany the small maritime district which was destined to form a Spanish province, under the title of Lo stato d'egli Presidi—the state of the garrisons. The general pacification confirmed these cessions of Philip: it also restored to the house of Savoy the greater part of its possessions, which the French and Spanish kings engaged to evacuate; and it left the kingdom of Naples and the duchy of Milan under the recognised sovereignty of Spain.

Thus the treaty of Chateau Cambresis may be considered to have finally regulated the limits and the existence of those Italian principalities and provinces which, under despotic government, whether native or foreign, had embraced almost the whole surface of the peninsula; and it left only the shadow of republican freedom to Venice, Genoa, Lucca, and—if it be worth naming—to the petty community of San Marino in the ecclesiastical states. But this same pacification is yet more remarkable, as the era from which Italy ceased to be the theatre of contention between the monarchs of Spain and Germany and France, in their struggle for the mastery of continental Europe. Other regions were now to be scathed by their ambition, and other countries were to succeed to that inheritance of warfare and all its calamities, of which Italy had reaped, and was yet to reap, only the bitterest fruits.

From the epoch of the treaty of Chateau Cambresis to the close of the sixteenth century, Italy remained, in one sense, in profound and uninterrupted peace. During this long period of forty-one years, her provinces were neither troubled by a single invasion of foreign armies, nor by any hostilities of importance between her own feeble and nerveless powers. But this half century presented, nevertheless, any thing rather than the aspect of public happiness and prosperity. Her wretched people enjoyed none of the real blessings of peace. Subject either to the oppressive yoke of their native despots, or to the more general influence of the arch-tyrant of Spain, they were abandoned to all the exactions of arbitrary government, and compelled to lavish their blood in foreign wars and in quarrels not their own. While France, torn by religious and civil dissensions, sank for a time from her political station among the powers of the continent, and was no longer capable of affording protection or exciting jealousy, Philip II. was left free to indulge in the peninsula all the obdurate tyranny of his nature. He was neither constrained to practise moderation by the danger of foreign interference, nor checked in his despotism by the fear of provoking a resistance which must be hopeless. The popes were interested in supporting his career of bigotry and religious persecution, the other powers of Italy crouched before him in abject submission. To feed the religious wars, in which he embarked as a principal or an accessary, in the endeavour to crush the protestant cause in France, in the Low Countries, and in Germany, he drained Italy of her resources in money and in men.

The ruinous consumption of treasure, the fearful waste of human life, in these distant and iniquitous wars, demanded a perpetual renovation; and still Italy was the victim of fresh sacrifices to the insatiable demon of destruction. The Italians, it is true, were taught in these foreign contests to resume their post among the military of Europe. Their generals and their soldiery aspired to rival the old Spanish bands in martial glory, in talents, and in courage; and from being associated in the same ranks, became identified with them in reputation and character. But in recovering the qualities of soldiership in foreign service, they learnt not to employ their energies for the defence and the honour of their country. If the sacrifice of all the Italian blood which was shed in foreign quarrel had revived a national spirit, it would not have been expended too dearly. But while the Italian soldiery fought with the courage of freemen, they continued the slaves of a despot, and while the Italian youth were consumed in transalpine warfare, their suffering country groaned under an iron yoke, and was abandoned a prey to the unresisted assaults of the infidels. Her coasts, left without troops or defences in fortifications and shipping, were insulted and ravaged by the constant descents of the corsairs of Turkey and Barbary. Her maritime villages were burnt, her maritime population dragged off into slavery; and her tyrants, while they denied the people the power of defending themselves, were unable or careless also to afford them protection and safety.

Such then were the principal events of universal concern in Italy, and such was the general condition of the peninsula, from its subjugation by Charles V. to the conclusion of the sixteenth century. To detail the oppression and the miseries of the people at more length, would only be to present a vain and endless repetition of the same picture of debasement and suffering. In proceeding to offer a series of rapid sketches of the distinct and internal vicissitudes which befel the various divisions of the peninsula during the same period, I shall therefore dismiss the ungrateful subject of national humiliation and wretchedness; and shall only attempt to render a brief abstract of the leading occurrences which influenced the fortunes, and of the revolutions which changed the aspect, of the principal Italian states until the close of the century. In this manner, I shall trace in succession the fate of the Spanish dominions of Naples and Milan; the temporal relations of the popedom; the rise of the ducal house of Parma; the domestic affairs of the other Italian duchies of Ferrara and Modena, of Mantua, of Savoy, and of Tuscany; and the republican annals of Genoa and Venice.

By the possession of the states of Naples and Milan in continental Italy, the immediate sovereignty of Spain, besides its extension to the insular kingdoms of Sicily and Sardinia, was established over the fairest portion of the peninsula. In all these dependencies, sufficient in themselves by their population, and the advantages of position and fertility with which nature has blessed them, to have constituted a powerful monarchy, the influence of the Spanish administration was fatally displayed. During the seventy years embraced in this chapter, the government of the viceroys of Naples exhibited all the evils which intolerable impositions, and a total ignorance of the most simple principles of political economy, could inflict upon a people. The researches of Giannone have led him to the declaration, that it is perfectly incredible what enormous sums were continually extorted from the unhappy Neapolitans, by the fourteen viceroys and lieutenants, who successively governed the kingdom during the long reign of Philip II. But the blind oppression exercised by these men, and their gross errors of policy, were even more mischievous than their own mere rapacity, or the craving demands of the court of Madrid. Their absurd and iniquitous monopolies paralyzed commerce, and even produced repeated famines in the midst of abundance; their tyranny systematically debased the nobility, and laboured to extirpate the last remains of popular energy; and their government, nerveless against foreign enemies and native banditti, was formidable only to its own peaceable subjects. The whole interior of the kingdom was infested by troops of robbers, who defied the arm of justice; and the sea-coasts were left so destitute of defence that, during the wars of Charles V. and his son against the Ottoman Porte, they were perpetually ravaged by the Turkish and Algerine fleets. In these frightful incursions, which were conducted successively during the greater part of the sixteenth century, by the famous corsairs Home and Hayradin Barbarossa, by Dragut Rayz, and by two kings of Algiers, whom the Italians call Piali and Ulucciali, whole cities and districts were desolated, and their inhabitants torn away into hopeless captivity. The sister kingdom of Sicily was a prey to the same internal misgovernment and disorders, the same ravages, and the same misery.

Meanwhile the Spanish governors of the Milanese duchy emulated the mal-administration of the viceroys of Naples; and the fortune of central Lombardy was superior only to that of the Sicilies, as its inland territory presented no points of access for the infidel pirates. From the death of Francesco Sforza in 1535, Milan became a Spanish province: for notwithstanding his faithless negotiations with the French monarchs, it never entered into the serious purpose of Charles V. to part with so valuable an acquisition, still less to transfer it to his enemies; and the peace of Château Cambresis formally consigned it, as we have seen, to the Spanish monarchy. Even the withering influence of such a despotism as that of Philip II., succeeding to the desolation of long and ruinous wars, could not wholly destroy the obstinate fertility of the Lombard plains; but the manufactures and commerce, which had once caused them to overflow with an exuberance of wealth and population, utterly perished under the weight of impositions, in the invention of which infatuation and tyranny combined to extinguish every germ of industrious excitement.

While the people of Naples and Milan in general tamely submitted to these various and cruel inflictions of mis-government, it is singular and worthy of remark, that they boldly and steadily opposed one project of the Spanish court. There had seemed no limits to their endurance, until their oppressors laboured to establish the inquisition in Italy on the same footing as in Spain; and then the nobles and the people firmly agreed in determining to resist this aggravation of their sufferings: the union of temporal and spiritual oppression, the frightful consummation of a twofold despotism. It was, as has been observed by several writers, curious to find this resistance in a people at once so abject and so superstitious as the Neapolitans; but besides sharing in the universal horror excited in Europe by the atrocious cruelties of the Spanish inquisition, the Neapolitans were shocked in their religious feelings, and they considered their national honour outraged by the accusation of heresy, which was implied in the attempt to introduce that bloody tribunal into their kingdom. Under their Aragonese kings, the exercise in Naples of the inquisition, which was always of a much milder character in Italy than in Spain, had not been permitted to the papal authority; and when the Neapolitans submitted to Ferdinand the Catholic, so strong was the apprehension excited by their knowledge of the execrable system of ecclesiastical tyranny which he had cemented in Spain, that they extorted from Gonsalvo da Cordova, in the name of his master, a solemn promise that there should never be inquisition nor inquisitor within their kingdom. Ferdinand, who was some years later inflamed by his bigotry to violate this engagement, found such a ferment created by the attempt that, after sending over inquisitors from Spain, he finally resolved, rather than encounter the risk of losing the kingdom altogether, to renounce his design, and to confirm the promise of Gonsalvo.

But, before the middle of the sixteenth century, the alarming progress of the reformation, and the discovery that the new opinions had penetrated into Italy, occasioned the emperor Charles V. to resume the project which his predecessor had abandoned; and in 1547 he wrote to the viceroy of Naples, don Pedro di Toledo, desiring him to use his utmost endeavour peaceably to introduce the inquisition into that kingdom. Toledo executed his commands with great art; and secretly moving the pope to promulgate a brief for the occasion, he pretended that the measure emanated neither from his master nor himself, but from the zeal of his holiness for the purity of religion. But the publication of the papal instrument neither blinded the people, nor diverted their fury from its real authors. The edict itself was torn down by the populace from the doors of the cathedral of Naples; and such was the general indignation and horror of all classes of the inhabitants at its tendency, that the whole capital arose in arms. The Spanish troops in the city were furiously attacked, and obliged, after much slaughter, to shut themselves up with the viceroy in the castles; the Neapolitans organized a regular provisional government, and levied forces for their defence; and they resolved to render obedience to don Pedro no longer. But at the same time, they endeavoured cautiously to avoid the appearance of rebellion against their sovereign; and they dispatched the prince of Salerno, and a deputy from the commons to Charles, as their ambassadors, firmly to remonstrate against the establishment of the inquisition. The statement which the viceroy transmitted to his master of the spirit of the people was more effectual in promoting their cause; and the emperor, after much blood had already been shed on both sides, found it prudent to lay aside all thoughts of persevering in his design. But he nevertheless assumed his usual high tone of authority; he insisted that the Neapolitans should unconditionally deliver up their arms, before he would declare his pleasure; and though, after their obedience to this command, he deputed the viceroy to give his promise that there should be no inquisition, he fined their city heavily, he excepted thirty-six nobles and others among the popular leaders from the general pardon, and he caused several of this number to be cruelly put to death. No farther open attempt was, however, made during the sixteenth century, to introduce the inquisition into Naples; and though Philip II. eagerly desired it, such violent and alarming remonstrances from the citizens of the capital followed the bare rumour of his intentions, that he was induced to deny that he had ever entertained them.

But the views of Philip II. were more openly betrayed at Milan; and his designs, in which ferocious bigotry, mingled with a detestable policy of state, were still encountered with the same resolution, which at Naples had formed so singular a contrast with the slavish submission of the people on other occasions. In the Milanese duchy the Italian inquisition was already established; but its operations did not satisfy the relentless and gloomy severity of Philip, and in 1663 he obtained a bull from the pope, which authorized the re-modelling of that tribunal on the Spanish plan. The people of the duchy, however, prepared to resist the innovation with arms in their hands; and their governor, the duke of Sessa, who fortunately was a man of moderate and prudent character, observing their exasperation, succeeded in dissuading his sovereign from prosecuting the measure, before it had produced the same scenes of commotion and bloodshed, which had occurred sixteen years before at Naples.

During the middle ages, the Roman pontiffs had usually shown themselves the enemies of Italian liberty and happiness; and their political ambition and personal vices had finally hastened the ruin of Italian independence. Yet such were the natural fruits of their selfish and iniquitous policy, that the subjugation of the peninsula to foreign dominion may be numbered among the immediate causes of the decline of the papal power. After the fatal blow which the reformation gave to the ecclesiastical authority of the popes over the half of Europe, the holy see was necessarily shorn of much of its ancient lustre. But the overwhelming influence of the Spanish sovereigns was as destructive to the temporal grandeur of the popedom in Italy, as the reformation proved to its spiritual despotism in other countries. The vain efforts of the impotent successors of Gregory VII. and Innocent III. to repress the growth of the protestant faith in the sixteenth century, belong to the ecclesiastical history of Europe; our business is only to regard the popes as Italian sovereigns; and, in this capacity, they rapidly sank almost to an equality with the other subjugated powers of the peninsula.

As, by the treaty of Barcelona between Charles V. and Clement VII., the holy see had recovered its territorial possessions, the decay of the papacy might not be immediately perceptible; and the pontificate of Paul III., who succeeded Clement in 1534, was marked by the same system of family aggrandizement, which had been the exclusive and darling policy of former popes. But Paul III. was the last of those ambitious pontiffs, who devoted the intrigues of the Roman court to the elevation of their relatives to sovereign power, and who were suffered to dismember the states of the church in favour of their own families. Julius III., who, on his death in 1549, was raised to the papal chair, was engrossed only in personal pleasures, and by his love of pomp and sensual indulgence recalled the image of the voluptuous court of Leo X., without its tasteful magnificence and lettered splendour. He terminated his career of debauchery in 1555: and after a brief interval of a month, in which an ephemeral pope, Marcellus II., was elected and died, his tiara descended upon the brows of an ecclesiastic of widely opposite character, the cardinal Giovan Piero Caraffa.

This pontiff, who assumed the title of Paul IV., entered on his station with the haughty notions of its prerogatives, which were natural to his austere and impetuous spirit. Hence his efforts in concert with France, unsuccessful as they proved, to overthrow the Spanish greatness, that he might extricate the popedom from the galling state of dependance to which the absolute ascendancy of that power in Italy had reduced it. Paul IV. is remarkable as the last pontiff who embarked in a contest, which had now become hopeless, and as the first who, giving a new direction to the policy of the holy see, employed all the influence, the arts, and the resources of the Roman church, against the protestant cause. He had, during the pontificate of Paul III., already made himself conspicuous for his persecuting zeal. He had been the principal agent in the establishment of the inquisition at Rome, and had himself filled the office of grand inquisitor. He seated himself in the chair of St. Peter with the detestable spirit of that vocation; and the character of his pontificate responded to the violence of his temper. His mantle descended upon a long series of his successors. Pius IV., who replaced him on his death in 1559; Pius V., who received the tiara in the following year; Gregory XIII., who was elected in 1572, and died in 1585; Sixtus V., who next reigned until 1590; Urban VII., Gregory XIV., and Innocent IX., who each filled the papal chair only a few mouths; and Clement VIII., whose pontificate commenced in 1592 and extended beyond the close of the century: all pursued the same political and religious system. Resigning the hope, and perhaps the desire, of reestablishing the independence of their see, they maintained an intimate and obsequious alliance with the royal bigot of Spain; they seconded his furious persecution of the protestant faith; they fed the civil wars of the Low Countries, of France, and of Germany; and their atrocious machinations against the throne of our famous maiden queen were unceasing. In the sincerity of their zeal, the purity of their private lives, and their abandonment of family ambition, their career was perhaps less flagitious than that of their precursors in earlier ages; but they were the active instigators of all the calamities of Europe, during the last half of the sixteenth century.

In Italy, the administration of all these popes deserves principally to be noticed, for their successful efforts to crush the germs of the reformed religion. These had been thickly sown among the votaries of literature in the peninsula; but the mass of the Italian people were either too indifferent or too deeply buried in error and abject superstition to be roused to the generous and anxious pursuit of eternal truth: and the Roman inquisition was readily suffered to quench the spirit of inquiry in the blood of men, whose opinions were unsupported by the sympathy of their nation. The civil government of the popes was as fatal to the prosperity of their own states as their ecclesiastical measures were to the repose and happiness of the world. As in the

Spanish provinces, ruinous monopolies extinguished industry and banished population; whole tracts of country, that had once been distinguished for fertility, were abandoned to the malaria of the desert and to eternal sterility; the Musulman corsairs were suffered to ravage the coasts; and hordes, and even armies, of banditti infested the interior.

During one short period only, the reign of disorder was suspended in the papal territories; and one only among the popes whom I have enumerated relieved the disgrace of his share in the work of religious persecution, by the stern virtues of his temporal administration. Sixtus V. brought from the vilest origin a natural dignity of address which graced a crown, a vigour of mind that might have fitted him to wield the sceptre of the universe, and intellectual tastes that seemed to belong to a milder character and to fairer times. During his pontificate of five years, he suppressed robbery in his states, and created a strong and vigilant police; he united impartial justice with despotic severity; he embellished Rome with many superb monuments of art; and he accumulated an immense treasure by oppressive exactions. We may doubt whether he merited most the admiration or the hatred of his subjects; but the pontiffs who had preceded and who followed him deserved only their hatred. After his death, the public disorders revived without mitigation; the domestic annals of the papacy resumed their insignificance; and the annexation of Ferrara to the dominion of the holy see, which I shall presently notice, was the only occurrence that relieved their monotony until the opening of the seventeenth century.

From considering the temporal affairs of the popedom, we naturally turn to observe the rise of the ducal line of Farnése at Parma, which sprang from a papal stock. I have remarked that Paul III. was the last of those ambitious popes who rendered the interests of the holy see subordinate to the aggrandizement of their families. The designs of Paul, himself the representative of the noble Roman house of Farnése, were ultimately successful; since, although partially defeated during his life, they led to the establishment of his descendants on the throne of

Parma and Placentia for nearly two hundred years. I have already mentioned that he gained the consent of the sacred college to alienate those states from the holy see in 1545, that he might erect them into a duchy for his natural son, Pietro Luigi Farnése; and the emperor Charles V. had already some years before, to secure the support of the papacy against France, bestowed the hand of his natural daughter Margaret, widow of Alessandro de' Medici, upon Ottavio, son of Pietro Luigi, and grandson of Paul III. Notwithstanding this measure, Charles V. was not subsequently, however, the more disposed to confirm to the house of Farnése the investiture of their new possessions, which he claimed as part of the Milanese duchy; and he soon evinced no friendly disposition towards his own son-in-law, Ottavio.

Pietro Luigi, the first duke of Parma, proved himself, by his extortions, his cruelties, and his debaucheries, scarcely less detestable than any of the ancient tyrants of Lombardy. He thus provoked a conspiracy and insurrection of the nobles of Placentia, where he resided; and he was assassinated by them at that place in 1547, after a reign of only two years. The city was immediately seized in the imperial name by Gonzaga, governor of Milan, who, if he did not instigate it, was at least privy to their design; and Paul III., besides his grief at the death of a son whom, notwithstanding his atrocious vices, he tenderly loved, suffered an aggravation of sorrow by the loss of so valuable a possession. To deter the emperor from appropriating Parma also to himself, he could devise no other expedient than altogether to retract his grant from his family, and to reoccupy that city for the holy see, whose rights he conceived that the emperor would not venture to invade. Ottavio Farnése thus found himself deprived of one part of his inheritance by the treachery of his father-in-law, the emperor, and of the remainder by the hazardous policy of his grandfather, the pope. The death of Paul, which shortly followed, seemed at first to complete the ruin of his fortunes; but that event, on the contrary, curiously paved the way for their revival. By the numerous creations of cardinals, which Paul III. had made during his long pontificate, he had filled the sacred college with his relatives and creatures; and the Farnése party, who after his death still commanded a majority in the conclave, by raising Julius III. to the tiara, obtained the restitution of Parma to Ottavio from the gratitude of the new pope.

The prosperity of the ducal house of Farnése was not yet securely established. The emperor still retained Placentia, and Julius III. soon forgot the services of that family. In 1551, the pope leagued with Charles V. to deprive the duke Ottavio of the fief which he had restored to him. Farnése was thus reduced, as we have seen, to place himself under the protection of the French; and this measure, and the indecisive war which followed, became his salvation. He still preserved his throne when Charles V. terminated his reign; and one of the first acts of Philip II., when Italy was menaced by the invasion of the duke de Guise, was to win him over from the French alliance, and to secure his gratitude, by yielding Placentia again to him. But a Spanish garrison was still left in the citadel of that place; and it was only the brilliant military career of Alessandro Farnése, the celebrated prince of Parma, son of duke Ottavio, which finally consummated the greatness of his family. Entering the service of Philip II., Alessandro gradually won the respect and favour of that gloomy monarch; and at length, in 1585, as a reward for his achievements, the Spanish troops were withdrawn from his father's territories. The duke Ottavio closed his life in the following year; but Alessandro never took possession of his throne. He died at the head of the Spanish armies in the Low Countries in 1592; and his son Ranuccio quietly commenced his reign over the duchy of Parma and Placentia, under the double protection of the holy see and the monarchy of Spain.

The loss which the papal states sustained, by the alienation of Parma and Placentia, was repaired, before the end of the sixteenth century, by the acquisition of a duchy little inferior in extent to those territories:— that of Ferrara. After the death, in 1534, of its duke Alfonso I., who, during the fatal wars of Italy, had sustained so many reverses by the hostility of successive pontiffs, there is little to interest us in the annals of the house of Este. The long reign of Ercole II., the successor of Alfonso, which extended to the year 1559, was remarkable only for his unimportant share in the wars anterior to the peace of Chateau Cambresis, and for the abject submission to Philip II., with which he was finally permitted to expiate his attachment to the French interests. His son Alfonso II., the obsequious servant of Spain, has acquired his only distinction,—an odious celebrity in literary history,—by his persecution of the unhappy Tasso. With the death of this feeble prince without issue in 1597, terminated the legitimate Italian branch of the ancient and illustrious line of Este. But there remained an illegitimate representative of his house, whom he designed for his successor; don Cesare da Este, the grandson of Alfonso I. by a natural son of that duke. The inheritance of Ferrara and Modena had passed in the preceding century to bastards, without opposition from the popes, the feudal superiors of the former duchy. But the imbecile character of don Cesare now encouraged the reigning pontiff, Clement VIII., to declare that all the ecclesiastical fiefs of the house of Este reverted, of right, to the holy see on the extinction of the legitimate line. The papal troops, on the death of Alfonso II., invaded the Ferrarese state; and Cesare suffered himself to be terrified by then approach into an ignominious and formal surrender of that duchy to the holy see. By the indifference of the emperor Rodolph II., he was permitted to retain the investiture of the remaining possessions of his ancestors: the duchies of Modena and Reggio, over which, as imperial and not papal fiefs, the pope could not decently assert any right.

In passing beneath the papal yoke, the duchy of Ferrara which, under the government of the house of Este, had been one of the most fertile provinces of Italy, soon became a desert and marshy waste. The capital itself lost its industrious population and commercial riches; its architectural magnificence crumbled into ruins; and its modern aspect retains no trace of that splendid court, in which literature and art repaid the fostering protection of its sovereigns by reflecting lustre on their heads. Modena, to which the seat of the house of Este was transferred, flourished by the decay of Ferrara, and assumed a new air of industry, and wealth, and elegance.

The contemporary annals of the houses of Este and Gonzaga are equally barren of interest; and the only occurrence in the fortunes of the dukes of Mantua, which I am called upon to notice in the period before us, is the annexation of the territory of Montferrat to their patrimonial inheritance. On the death of the last marquis of Montferrat without male heirs, in 1533, Federigo II. of Mantua claimed his states in right of his duchess, the eldest sister of the deceased prince. Montferrat was decidedly a feminine fief; but the emperor Charles V., who had seized the marquisate, suffered three years to elapse before he was induced to recognise the just pretensions of Gonzaga, and to bestow the investiture upon him. But in 1536 Federigo at last united its coronet to his ducal crown; and from this epoch to the end of the century, no vicissitude either of good or evil varied the obscure and sluggish rule of that prince and his successors over Mantua and Montferrat.

The fortunes of the house of Savoy were not so monotonous and equable. From the decease of Louis, the second duke of that family, who had survived, as I have formerly observed, beyond the middle of the fifteenth century, (to 1465,) there is little to merit attention in the affairs of Savoy and Piedmont, until his sceptre fell into the hands of his unfortunate descendant, Charles III. During this period of forty years, six princes, almost all of insignificant character, successively wore the ducal crown, without illustrating their names or aggrandizing their power by any remarkable achievement. But the reign of Charles III., which commenced in 1504, introduced a new era of humiliation and calamities for his dynasty and his people. For thirty years after his accession, in the long wars of Italy, he was permitted to preserve an inglorious neutrality; for which, during the gigantic contest between the houses of France and Austria at least, he was principally indebted to his common relationship with both the rival monarchs. Louise of Savoy, mother of Francis I., was his own sister; and the empress of Charles V. was the sister of his duchess, Beatrice of Portugal. The contending forces of his nephew and his brother-in-law alternately traversed his states; but these sovereigns seemed for several years by mutual consent to abstain from ravaging them, or from reducing him to take a decisive part in their quarrel.

But some injurious demands of Francis I. upon the Savoyard territories, in his mother's name and his own, gradually alienated Charles III. from his connexion with that monarch, and prepared the way for the rupture and the French invasion which, in 1535, deprived the house of Savoy of almost all its dominions From this epoch, for twenty-five years, with few intervals of repose, Piedmont. became the principal theatre of war between the French and imperialists, and was successively devasted by both parties with frightful violence, as the balance of victory inclined to either cause. Spoiled alike by his two relatives, by the open enemy and the selfish ally, Charles III. was equally ruined by the success of the one and the other. The imperialists seized and retained whatever they could save or wrest from the French; and to augment the misfortunes of the duke, the valuable city of Geneva, which had long acknowledged the sovereignty of his house, embraced the reformed faith, spurned his efforts to restrain its exercise, and throwing off the yoke of Savoy for ever, established her republican independence, (A.D. 1535.) Of all the states of his ancestors, Nice was almost the sole possession which remained to him; and his relief of that city, which was besieged by land and sea in 1543 by the combined forces of the French and the Turks, was the only successful enterprise of his life.

On the death of this unfortunate prince in 1553, there remained to his only son and successor, Emmanuel Philibert, little more than the ducal title and his own good sword. Preceding the famous prince of Parma in a similar career of military glory, he had entered the Spanish service, and by his eminent talents so won the confidence of Charles V. that he was entrusted, at the early age of twenty-five years, with the supreme command in the Low Countries; and his subsequent victory at St. Quentin prepared the way for the re-establishment of his house. The peace of Chateau Cambresis, which his successes enabled Philip II. in some measure to dictate to France, restored to him the greater part of the dominions which Francis I. had wrested from his father; but the French were still permitted to retain Turin and several other important places in Piedmont, while the ingratitude of Philip II. withheld from him Vercelli and Asti.

When the new duke of Savoy took possession of his states, he found the whole country in ruins: agriculture abandoned, commerce and finances destroyed, cities depopulated, and foreign garrisons bristling in the heart of his territories. In the general anarchy, the nobles had forgotten obedience and assumed a petty independence; and the people were borne down by long wars and foreign oppression, and broken in spirit: their ancient attachment to their sovereigns was succeeded by indifference, their national feelings were extinguished in their private miseries. But in their prince was fortunately blended all the pacific wisdom of the consummate statesman, with the more dazzling qualities of the hero; and if Amadeus VIII., the first duke of Savoy, was the founder of the grandeur of his house, to Emmanuel Philibert belongs the superior reputation of having retrieved its fall, and restored and augmented its power. Renouncing the vain passion for martial glory, he laboured incessantly for twenty years after the partial restitution of his states to preserve them in peace, to consolidate their union and strength, and to secure them against future assaults. Nor were his efforts unsuccessful. His reign was disturbed by no hostilities; his dominions recovered their prosperity, his subjects enjoyed the blessings of justice and order; and if his power was absolute, it was at least exerted for the welfare of a people who had forgotten, or who had never learnt to be free, and whose contentment was disturbed by few aspirations after liberty. The first care of the duke was sedulously to repair and improve the fortresses of Savoy and Piedmont, and to increase their number; his next project was to create a militia in both those provinces, by which he obtained a well-disciplined national infantry of twenty thousand men, and raised the people in their own estimation; and, finally, during the civil distractions of France, he adroitly succeeded, in 1562 and 1574, in obtaining from Francis II. and Henry III. the cession of all the places in Piedmont, which had been unjustly withheld from him.

The dominions of the house of Savoy were now recovered; their strength was increased, and their consolidation perfected. Emmanuel Philibert passed the residue of his reign in encouraging agriculture, in promoting commerce and the useful arts, in improving his revenues, and in patronising learning. He revived the university of Turin and founded several endowments; by his exertions the silkworm and mulberry were introduced into Piedmont, and shortly produced large returns of wealth; other manufactures were also established; and an active maritime trade was opened at Nice. When this enlightened prince and benefactor of his country terminated his life in 1580, in the vigour of intellect, and at the age of only fifty-two years, the possession of the marquisate of Saluzzo was alone wanting to complete the security of his dominions, and to exclude the French altogether from Italy.

With a less pacific temper and with more rashness, his son and successor, Charles Emmanuel I., devoted his reign to the attainment of that object. In 1548, on the extinction of the sovereign branch of the family of Saluzzo, Henry II. of France had taken possession of this marquisate and annexed it, by a very doubtful title, to his dominions as a lapsed fief of his crown. Emmanuel Philibert had seen, with well-founded inquietude, the French monarchs still possessed of a territory, by which they commanded the gates of Italy; and his son found the furious civil wars, which were now consuming the strength of France, too favourable an occasion to be lost for asserting the plausible claim of his house to the reversion of the marquisate of Saluzzo. He accordingly possessed himself with ease of that territory in 1588. He afterwards also, in concert with Philip II., engaged in the war against Henry IV., and was included in the peace of Virvins in 1598. But three years intervened between that treaty and the final settlement of his differences with Henry IV. for the possession of the contested marquisate; and it was not until after the opening of the seventeenth century that the French monarch ceded that territory to him in exchange for the county of Bresse in Savoy. Henry IV. thus consented to close against himself the passes of the Alps; and the dukes of Savoy, by the loss of a part of their ultramontane possessions, became more exclusively Italian sovereigns. From this epoch, also, Italy ceased to apprehend the renewal of those invasions from France, which had been attended with so many horrors, and associated with all the shame and the suffering of the people of the peninsula.

The last of the ducal dynasties of the peninsula, whose elevation and fortunes demand notice at the period before us, is that of Tuscany; and we have now rapidly to follow the train of events, by which a single despotism overspread the fair face of that province: the cradle of Italian poesy, the strong hold of Italian independence, the brilliant theatre of freedom, of literature, and of the arts, before the kindred elements of political and intellectual greatness were buried in a common ruin. In the last chapter, we have observed the extinction of the Florentine republic; the composition of a balia of the creatures of pope Clement VII.; and the appointment by that body of Alessandro de' Medici to an absolute and hereditary authority over the fallen state, with the title of doge or duke. An oligarchical senate of forty-eight persons, and a larger council of the same character, all the members of which were nominated for life, were at the same time created, to supply the vain image of constitutional government; but Alessandro was the despot of Florence.

The imperial pleasure confirmed his authority; and he secured his power by the ordinary means of a tyrant, conscious of the detestation of his subjects. He maintained a large body of foreign mercenaries; he erected a citadel in Florence to curb the disaffection of the people; and he indulged himself and his myrmidons in the commission, against the domestic peace of families and the rights of the community, of every crime which could add poignant insult to the usual evils of oppression. His intolerable excesses multiplied the number of exiles of the principal families of Florence, with whom the other states of Italy were now filled; and many even of those men, who had basely laboured to elevate his house upon the ruins of their country's liberty, found it impossible to exist under the tyranny which was the work of their own hands. An ineffectual appeal was made to the emperor, after the death of Clement VII., to induce him to withdraw his protection from his unworthy and odious creature. Besides Filippo Strozzi, the representative of that ancient family, and the most wealthy private individual in Europe, the Ridolfi, the Salviati and others, names once among the most illustrious in the Florentine republic, joined in this remonstrance; and even the cardinal Ippolito de' Medici united his exertions against his infamous cousin. But Alessandro succeeded in removing the cardinal by poison; and when Charles V. admitted the duke and his enemies to a public hearing at Naples in 1536, he was induced by his hatred of the republican cause, and his knowledge of the partiality of the Florentines towards France, not only to confirm his protection to Alessandro, but to fulfil the promise which he had formerly given to Clement VII., by bestowing on him the hand of his natural daughter.

By this conduct of the emperor, the Florentines lost all hope of deliverance from their execrable tyrant; but an act of private treachery procured for them that relief which was denied by the justice or commiseration of the arbiter of Italy. Lorenzino de' Medici, the representative of the collateral branch of that family, (which descended from the brother of the great Cosmo,) a young man of considerable intellectual acquirements, but of abandoned morals, was the bosom companion of the duke, and the minister of his infamous debaucheries. Whatever were his secret motives,—whether, as the next heir of Alessandro, he hoped to succeed to his power, or was really stimulated by the desire of immortalizing himself as the deliverer of his country,— he resolved to assassinate the duke.

Under pretence of having secured for him an assignation with a lady of great beauty, a married woman, and a near relative of his own, he induced Alessandro to quit the palace one night, and to repair unattended and disguised to his house. There, in a private and remote apartment, he left him, apparently for the purpose of escorting the lady to the spot; but while the duke, who had thrown himself on a couch, was unsuspiciously awaiting his return, he suddenly re-entered the room, followed by an assassin, and plunged a dagger into the bosom of the libertine prince, (A.D. 1537.) The wound was mortal, but Alessandro nevertheless made a desperate struggle with his murderer, until, as they grappled on the couch, the attendant of Lorenzino deliberately completed the deed of horror, by cutting the throat of the duke. The plan of Lorenzino had been laid with such secrecy and ability, that the murder was accomplished without alarm; but he had no sooner dispatched his victim than, losing all presence of mind, he neither attempted to proclaim the death of the tyrant, and to raise the city by the cry of liberty, nor to possess himself of the vacant government. He precipitately fled from the city, and joined the exiles at Venice; and before, in their surprise, they could take effectual measures for availing themselves of his act, the opportunity for restoring the republic was lost.

By the Florentine exiles, and by all the lovers of extinguished freedom in the peninsula, the assassination of the tyrant of Florence was applauded in unmeasured terms, as an act of the highest republican virtue; and Lorenzino de' Medici himself was eulogized and sung as a new Brutus, the saviour of I his country. Some modern writers also have not been ashamed to hesitate between praise and reprobation of this deed. But its atrocious perfidy is fitted to create only the sentiment of unmingled abhorrence; and the acknowledged previous depravity of Lorenzino forbids us from attributing even the incentive of a mistaken principle of duty, to the corrupted sensualist, and the base pander of another's lusts. There is nothing more dangerous to acknowledge, or more improbable in itself, than the compatibility of political virtue with personal iniquity; nor should the pure cause of freedom ever be sullied by association with a crime, at which every better feeling of our nature revolts.

Except in her deliverance from his personal excesses, Florence derived no advantage from the murder of the duke Alessandro. The leading members of the oligarchical senate, among whom the historian Guicciardini had acted too conspicuous a part for his own fair fame, were conscious of having provoked the hatred of their fellow-citizens, and dreaded the re-establishment of a popular government. They conducted themselves with great ability; they secured the city, with the soldiery of the late tyrant, before they permitted the news of his death to transpire; and they raised to the supreme power the youthful Cosmo de' Medici: son of Giovanni, the celebrated captain of the black bands, and after Lorenzino, next representative of the collateral branch of the sovereign house.

This young man was living in retirement near Florence; and Guicciardini and his party, judging of him only by his inexperience, doubted not that they should be permitted to engross all the powers of government in his name. But in this expectation they were bitterly mistaken. Cosmo was no sooner installed in his new dignity than, with equal ambition and dissimulation and energy, he determined to rule without them. His election was confirmed by the emperor, who placed garrisons in the Florentine fortresses, under pretence of supporting him; and when the exiles made a last and generous effort in arms to recover freedom for their country, with the aid of Francis I., they were utterly defeated by the imperial forces in the service of Cosmo, and the greater number of them fell into his power. They experienced no mercy: all who were most illustrious by their personal characters, and the names which they bore, were consigned to the rack and the sword of the executioner; and Filippo Strozzi, the most distinguished among them, whose fate was longest in suspense, perished the last of these victims in the cause of Florentine liberty. (A.D. 1538.)

The first cruel triumph of Cosmo was over his enemies; his next, a worthy consummation of ingratitude, was the expulsion of his friends, the artificers of his power. He dismissed them from all offices of authority, successively to terminate their lives in mortification and disgrace. Having thus removed every obstacle to his solitary despotism, Cosmo devoted the long residue of his life to the extension of his dominions. He never was able to free his throne from the chains with which Charles V. and his son continued to encircle it; for it was by foreign protection alone that he maintained his usurpation against the general hatred of his subjects. But he persevered in the objects of his base ambition, until all Tuscany, except the republic of Lucca, and the province of the Spanish garrisons, was consigned to his government. His most important acquisition was the state of Sienna. For the reduction of that republic, after its revolt against Spanish oppression, and its alliance with France, Charles V. was principally indebted to the skilful exertions of the duke, and the army which he created; though Cosmo never himself appeared at the head of his troops. Charles V. however retained the possession which Cosmo had won; and it was only in 1557, two years after this successful and iniquitous war, that Philip II. resigned to his dependant the prize of Sienna. The annals of that ferocious and turbulent republic offer, perhaps, few such splendid and deeply attractive associations, as those which bind our interest and sympathy to the fortunes of Florence; but the last struggle of Sienna, a struggle of hopeless and desperate heroism against foreign oppressors, at least merits an honourable record, and ennobles the last days of her commonwealth.

Cosmo I. had hitherto reigned under no other character, than the ambiguous one of chief or prince of the Florentine state. But twelve years after his acquisition of Sienna, he at length prevailed on pope Pius V. to bestow on him the title of grand-duke of Tuscany, (A.D. 1569.) His right to this new dignity was, however, for some time contested by the other Italian princes; and it was only in 1575 that an imperial investiture to the same effect, granted to his son by Maximilian II., secured the universal recognition of the Medici among the sovereign houses of Europe. The reign of Cosmo had been sullied by numerous acts of atrocious cruelty, ingratitude, and perfidy, which were poorly relieved by his passionate taste for literature and art. There is sometimes retribution on earth, even for successful crime: a fearful domestic tragedy embittered the latter years of Cosmo, and thickened the gloom of that self-bereavement in which he had left himself, by spurning his early friends and supporters from his side. Two of his sons perished under circumstances of such mystery and shame, that their fate was sedulously enveloped in an obscurity which the public eye never entirely penetrated. But it was believed that one of them, don Giovanni, fell by the hand of his brother, and that the miserable father sternly revenged his death by plunging his dagger in the heart of the guilty fratricide, don Garcias;—even in the arms of his other parent, Eleonora di Toledo, who sank into her grave under this accumulation of horrors.

On the death of Cosmo I., he was succeeded by his eldest son Francesco: a prince who, without his talents, inherited his perfidious cruelty, and was the slave of licentious passions, to which he had himself been a stranger, (A.D. 1575.) The discovery in 1578 of a last conspiracy of the partizans of liberty at Florence, to overthrow an usurpation which no lapse of time could legalize, gave occasion to display all the merciless spirit of the grand-duke. A great number of persons were executed; nor was the appetite of Francesco for blood thus satiated. Against the distinguished exiles who, having in 1537 escaped the fate of Filippo Strozzi and his associates, still survived, and to whom Catherine de' Medici had given refuge at the French court, the grand-duke employed a regular system of extermination. He took the most expert Italian assassins into his pay, and sent them to his ambassador at Paris. To aid the work of the dagger, he supplied that agent of murder with subtle poisons, of which, under pretence of making chemical experiments, Cosmo I. had established a manufacture in his palace; and he set a price of four thousand ducats upon the head of each of the enemies of his house. It was in vain that the wretched exiles, discovering their danger by the assassination of the first victim of this infernal plot, dispersed from Paris, and endeavoured to bury themselves in remote provinces of France and other countries. The emissaries of the grand-duke, rendered indefatigable by avarice, were successful in dogging their flight; and permitted them neither escape nor repose until the last of them had passed from a violent death into the quiet of the grave.

The only remaining event of importance in the reign of Francesco was his marriage with Bianca Capello, celebrated for her adoption by the republic of Venice. The whole story of this lady is a romance; but a romance rounded with a tale of murder, (A.D. 1579.) The daughter of a nobleman of Venice, she had inspired a young Florentine with an ardent attachment which, imagining him to be a man of birth, she had suffered herself to return. On discovering his humble station, she implored him not to complete the ruin of their common fortunes by persisting in his suit. But she could not refuse him a last adieu and a nocturnal assignation; and on attempting to regain her father's palace, she found the gates already closed. The first imprudence led to a greater; she threw herself into a gondola with her lover, accompanied him to Florence, and there married him. Thenceforth she lived in obscurity, until the duke Francesco saw her by chance, was inflamed with a violent passion by her beauty, and made his intention to reconcile her with her family the pretext of frequent visits. Her husband was invited to court, loaded with advancement—and assassinated. The grand-duke then shortly became a widower. He retained Bianca in his palace, and sent ambassadors to Venice to demand her hand; and the senate, desirous to honour the future grand-duchess with a fitting preparation for a throne, adopted her by the title of "daughter of the Venetian republic." Her marriage with the grand-duke was then concluded; but not without the violent opposition of his brother, the cardinal Ferdinando. After some years, however, the indignation of the cardinal, at the unworthy alliance of his house with the dissolute child of a Venetian noble, appeared to have subsided; he was reconciled with the ducal pair, and invited them to a banquet; but it was only to administer poison to them both. (A.D. 1587.)

Ferdinando de' Medici, on succeeding to the crown, which he had compassed by treachery and fratricide, abjured his priestly vows, that he might be at liberty to marry. But, notwithstanding his personal depravity, he was not without eminent talents for government. He assiduously promoted commerce and maritime enterprise among his subjects; and he aspired to deliver his throne of Tuscany from a long and oppressive dependence on the Spanish monarchy. With this view, he concluded and maintained a close alliance with Henry IV. of France; but, after the treaty with Savoy, by which that monarch, at the opening of the new century, excluded himself from communication with Italy, the grand-duke of Tuscany necessarily fell again under the Spanish yoke, from which he had laboured to extricate his dominions.

Though one state of Tuscany continued, during the whole of the sixteenth century, to enjoy the forms of a free constitution, such was the insignificance in which its fortunes were plunged, that, in the annals of the times, we are scarcely reminded of its existence. The solitary republic of Lucca founded the best hope of escape from utter subjugation in an obscurity from which she only once emerged. For shelter against the secret machinations and open assaults of Cosmo I., her rulers, feeling their weakness, had recourse to intrigues in the imperial councils, and succeeded, by enormous bribes to the ministers of Charles V., in obtaining the protection of that monarch. From this epoch a few uninteresting domestic convulsions alone varied her condition. In the struggle between the aristocratical and democratical factions in her councils, the former finally prevailed, and in 1556 obtained the enactment of a law, (called the Legge Martiniana, from its author, the gonfalonier Martino Bernardino,) which indirectly, but securely, restricted eligibility for all offices of state within narrow limits, and thus established at Lucca, as the closing of the great council had anciently at Venice, a sovereign and hereditary oligarchy.

In the condition of Italy under a number of petty despotisms, an oligarchical government was perhaps the only form under which a republic could still preserve its existence. The fierce independence of a democracy could ill amalgamate with the mingled pride and servility of the tyrants of the peninsula, who were themselves little more than the slaves of a foreign potentate. Of the only three republics of the middle ages which were still permitted to survive, Venice needed no change to assimilate her mockery of a free constitution with the spirit of the age; the new institutions of Lucca were a milder conformity with a similar system; and even the stormy commonwealth of Genoa had already subsided into obedience to an organized and sovereign aristocracy. When Andrea Doria restored the political existence of his republic, he laboured, doubtless with the zeal and discretion of true patriotism, to establish, in concert with his friends, the best constitution of which the times were susceptible. To prevent the revival of those feuds, which had inflicted such cruel wounds upon the public happiness, the very names of the Adorni and Fregosi were suppressed, and those families were incorporated into others. With similar views, the laws were repealed which excluded the old nobility from offices of magistracy; and a curious arrangement was adopted to admit all the families of any consideration in Genoa, with equal rights within the same circle of aristocracy.

It had always been customary for the powerful Genoese houses to augment their strength by adopting inferior families, who assumed their names and arms, and in return for protection, engaged in all their quarrels. This ancient practice, the nurse of faction, was now rendered conducive to a better object. Twenty-eight houses, or *alberghi*, as they were termed, were named, in one or other of which all citizens of substance and of ancient republican descent were admitted without distinction of parties: care being taken to mingle Guelfs and Ghibelins, nobles and plebeians, partizans of the Adorni, and adherents of the Fregosi, in every albergo. Thus was created a sovereign aristocracy, which formally raised to the rank of a gentleman every landed proprietor in the maritime territory of Liguria, and every citizen of Genoa, who could prove the purity of his republican ancestry, and was in a condition to contribute to the necessities of the state. In this new order by hereditary right, was vested exclusively the government of the republic; and every gentleman took his seat by rotation in the grand council of four hundred, which was renewed annually. The grand council elected a senate of a hundred members, also for one year; and a new doge and signiory of eight were similarly chosen every two years, with other magistrates.

This constitution of 1528, which, at the moment when the very existence of the republic was threatened with dissolution, fixed its independence and gave a great number of citizens a share in the government, was at first received with transports of joy. It covered ancient dissensions with oblivion, and for nearly twenty years gave uninterrupted repose to Genoa. But in the process of time, new causes of dissatisfaction arose. The lower people found themselves excluded from all share in the national representation, and desired again to exchange their subjection to the aristocracy, for the old popular system, even with all its attendant convulsions and anarchy. Nor were there wanting some restless and turbulent spirits, to whom the dependence of the republic upon the emperor, and the great influence of Doria and his family, were galling and obnoxious. The talents and virtues of Andrea himself commanded admiration and love; his tried disinterestedness and generous devotion to his country's rights were above all suspicion. But as he advanced in years, his domestic affections fondly centred in a grand-nephew, Giannettino Doria, whom he designed for his heir, and made it his passion to indulge and aggrandize. As Andrea's infirmities increased, he entrusted Giannettino with the command of his galleys in the imperial service, and suffered him gradually to assume that ascendancy in the councils of the state, which he had himself deservedly enjoyed. He was unconscious how little his grand-nephew's character resembled his own; but the Genoese observed with gloomy forebodings the ambition and arrogance of that young man; and the aristocracy, in particular, were stung by his overbearing insolence and dangerous pretensions.

While increasing jealousy and suspicion were rankling in the public mind, a young nobleman, who, under many qualities which secured the popular esteem, concealed an audacious and inordinate ambition, was encouraged by the discontent of the people to attempt the destruction of the aristocracy, of the Doria, and of the Spanish authority over the republic. (A.D. 1547.) This was the famous Giovanni Ludovico de' Fieschi, count of Lavagna. Inheriting the ancient enmity of his noble house towards that of Doria, he was particularly wounded in his pride by the presumption of Giannettino, in endeavouring to convert his great-uncle's influence into an hereditary dignity; and he thought the first rank in the state not an object of too difficult attainment for his own illustrious birth and daring aspirations. Assuring himself secretly of the future support of France, of the pope, Paul III., and of his son the duke of Parma, against the imperial vengeance, he induced many citizens of the old popular party to embrace and second his design.

The immediate and sanguinary purpose of this desperate conspiracy was to assassinate the Doria and to seize the city; and Fiesco, under pretence of fitting out some galleys, which he had procured from the pope, to cruise at his own cost against the Turkish infidels, introduced a body of his retainers and of hired soldiery within the walls. Privately assembling this armed force with the band of conspirators in his palace, he invited all the citizens, whom he considered most disaffected to the government, to an evening entertainment. When his company had entered, and the doors were closed and guarded, he then communicated his project to the astonished assembly; and setting before them in a passionate harangue the danger in which the republic stood from the power of the Doria and the protection accorded to them by the emperor, he demanded for his undertaking a co-operation, which none of his guests, surrounded as they were by his armed retainers, dared to refuse. Those among them who disapproved of the enterprise, were yet constrained to engage in it; and in the dead of night, Fiesco sallied at their head into the slumbering city. With one detachment, he himself undertook the attack of the harbour, in which Doria's galleys lay dismantled; while his brothers and other leaders were entrusted with the seizure of the different gates and strongholds of the city. In a short time every assault had succeeded; all Genoa was filled with tumult and uproar; and at the cry of "Fiesco and liberty!" many of the populace, to whom the leader and his cause were alike dear, rose in arms and joined the insurgents. The palace of the Doria was without the walls; but Giannettino, roused by the tumult, hastened to the city, and met his death at one of the gates, which was already in the hands of the conspirators. The aged Andrea, then finding that all was lost, took horse, infirm as he was, and sought safety by flight into the country.

The triumph of Fiesco now seemed to have reached its consummation; but he was already beyond its enjoyment. Even at the moment when all opposition had ceased, and he prepared to quit the harbour and to rejoin his victorious companions in the city, a plank, on which he was hastily passing from the shore to a galley, overturned and precipitated him in his heavy armour into the sea—to rise no more. When his fate was known, his followers immediately lost courage; and instead of taking possession of the palace of government as conquerors, they began to treat for mercy with the few assembled senators. An amnesty was granted to them; the Fieschi withdrew from the city; and before morning tranquillity reigned again in Genoa. The old Doria, in the course of the day, re-entered the capital amidst the joyful acclamations of the citizens; and if he could forget the tragical death of his beloved nephew and the ebullition of factious ingratitude, no farther calamity shaded the residue of a life, which was prolonged to the age of ninety-four; and for above thirteen years after this solitary and brief interruption in his fortunate and glorious career.

After the death of this illustrious patriot in 1560, Genoa was troubled both by foreign disasters and intestine dissensions. In 1564, Corsica revolted from her yoke; and it was not without a dangerous struggle of four years, that that valuable dependency was again secured to the republic. During this crisis, too, in 1566, the isle of Scio, which the Genoese family of Giustiniani held of their country as a kind of fief, was conquered by the Turks. But such reverses affected the happiness of Genoa less than the progress of discord within her walls, both in the councils of the aristocracy, and between that order and the dependant people. The latter had an eternal source of discontent in their exclusion from political rights: the former were split into factions by the jealousy between the ancient nobility and their new associates in the aristocracy, whose rights were ill defined. The quarrel of the privileged orders rose to such a height that, at length the mediation of the pope, the emperor, and the king of Spain was accepted, as the only mode of averting a civil war.

By the arbitration of these powers, the constitution of Genoa was once more modified. The new nobles were placed on an exact equality with the old in the sovereign aristocracy; the institution of the alberghi was suppressed; and every family resumed its original name. But the interests of the mass of the people were entirely sacrificed; and the consolidation of an hereditary aristocracy finally confirmed the limitation of all political rights within the pale of that order. The strength of old associations and manners, the force of public opinion, and the long habits of a democracy, had still however some effect upon the laws of the republic. It was provided that ten new citizens might annually be admitted into the noble and privileged body. The persons who received such prerogatives and honours ceased, indeed, thenceforth to belong to the people: they shared the interests and adopted the feelings of the order into which they were received. But, as some of the old aristocratical families became extinct, and others dwindled in numbers, this practice of recruiting from the popular ranks alone prevented the Genoese oligarchy from becoming as narrow, exclusive, and oppressive, as that of Venice itself.

The government of Venice, that stem and imposing edifice of antiquity, seemed meanwhile to have suffered no dilapidation from the shock of centuries. Frowning over the gay and splendid bosom of the Adriatic, it stood like a feudal donjon; its massive grandeur deepened in gloom, not impaired, by the ravages of time; its form alike unchanged and unchangeable. But if this fabric of real despotism, which had been erected for the pretended security of republican freedom, was not even menaced by domestic assaults, its outworks were no longer proof against foreign hostility. No decay of the Venetian power was indeed perceptible in the severity and oppression of the oligarchy towards its own subjects; and the whole of the period before us was undistinguished by the slightest vicissitude in the internal government and affairs of the state. But before the peace of Cambray, the progress of maritime discovery had diverted the commerce of the world, which Venice had once engrossed, into other channels; the conduits of her wealth and prosperity were dried up; and long wars had aggravated her losses and consumed her treasures. Her senate wisely laboured to veil the hopeless exhaustion of her resources, and the decline of her strength, under the guise of moderation and neutrality; and their efforts were so successful in concealing the weakness and languor of her fallen condition, that Venice may be said to have preserved the reputation of her ancient grandeur in Christian Europe, for nearly two centuries after its real extinction.

But the colonial possessions of the republic were exposed to attacks from a quarter, in which ancient impressions had less influence, and present weakness was more palpably exhibited. The Ottoman power had not yet passed its zenith; the eastern dependencies of Venice were tempting spoils for the ambition and cupidity of the sultans; and twice, during the last seventy years of the sixteenth century, was the republic forcibly dragged from the repose and oblivion, in which the senate studiously enveloped her, to suffer an unequal collision with the gigantic masses and furious energy of the Turkish power. Two unfortunate and cruel wars with the Porte broke the long intervals of her monotonous tranquillity; and these are, for the greater part of a century, the only occurrences in Venetian history to require our brief notice.

Into the first of these contests, Venice was forced in 1537, during the scandalous alliance of Francis I. with Solyman the Magnificent against the imperial power. The French monarch vainly endeavoured to persuade the republic to confederate with him and with the infidels; the sultan was determined to oblige her at all hazards to abandon her posture of neutrality; and his injurious and hostile proceedings, instead of terrifying her into making common cause with him, naturally drove her to throw herself into the arms of the imperial party. After some accidental affrays at sea had widened the rupture into an open war, a large Turkish armament was directed against Corfu, and horribly devastated that island, but without attempting its reduction. The naval forces of Venice, which were inferior in numbers to those of Solyman, could not prevent this disaster; but, in the following year, a formal league was signed between the emperor, the pope, and the Venetians, against their common and infidel enemies, (A.D. 1538.) This confederacy might have sufficed to chastise the ambitious spirit of the Turks; but Charles V., who had concluded a truce with France, was now solicitous only to leave the burthens of the war upon Venice, to use her resources and husband his own, and to obtain better terms for himself through her sacrifices. Doria, his admiral, was restrained from all vigorous action; and finding their colonies wrested from them in successive campaigns, while the galleys of their imperial ally were either altogether withheld from joining their fleet, or permitted to make only a few vain demonstrations, the Venetians at length resolved no longer to support a struggle, the whole weight of which fell hopelessly on themselves. They sought and obtained a separate peace, by leaving in the hands of the victorious Turks the islands of Palmos, Cesina, Nio, Stampalia, and Pares in the Archipelago, and the strong towns of Napoli and Malvagia, which the republic had still possessed in the Morea. (A.D. 1540.)

By the cessation of the Turkish projects against the colonies of Venice, just thirty years of profound peace were permitted to the republic, between the conclusion of this unfortunate war, and the second and yet more ruinous struggle. But at length the sultan Selim II., after making immense preparations in his arsenals, offered the senate the insulting alternative of encountering the resistless might of his arms, or of surrendering to his sceptre the island of Cyprus, where he pretended that an asylum was afforded to the corsairs who plundered his subjects. The republic, stricken as she was with mortal languor, could only return one answer to the insolent demand, which would rob her of her fairest possession; and a furious war immediately commenced. A Turkish army, exceeding 50,000 men at the lowest computation, was promptly disembarked on the coast of Cyprus, with a formidable train of artillery; while 150 galleys protected and aided the operations of this numerous force.

The Venetian troops in Cyprus had numbered only three thousand men, and even this inadequate garrison was now thinned by disease: the native militia was contemptible, the peasantry were ill affected, and the island contained only two fortresses. Yet the sieges of both these places, of the capital Nicosia and of Famagosta, were signalized by two of the finest defences on record. The whole relation, indeed, of this war of Cyprus is full of that intense interest, which the unshrinking heroism of inferior strength, the despair and the unhappy fate of the brave, can never cease to command. But the numerous details of the struggle would carry us beyond our limits, and I proceed at once to the result. The whole island was overrun, and Nicosia reduced in the first campaign; and Famagosta yielded to exhaustion and famine in the following year, after thousands of the infidels had fallen in sanguinary and ineffectual assaults before the open breaches of the place. Its capitulation completed the conquest of Cyprus by the Turks, and was immediately violated by the inhuman torture and murder of Marc' Antonio Bragadino, the governor of the fortress, who had covered himself with glory in its defence.

When the Turks disembarked their formidable array in Cyprus, the Venetians by extraordinary efforts had fitted out a naval armament of near a hundred galleys, and great vessels:—a force not unworthy of the prouder days of their republic. But even this fleet was far outnumbered by that of the enemy; and the senate dared not provoke the risk of an encounter. All their attempts to assist the gallant defenders of their most precious colony had therefore been limited to the hasty introduction of a few reinforcements into Famagosta, during the temporary absence of the main squadron of the Turks. Meanwhile, however, the senate were earnestly engaged in soliciting the powers of Europe to form a league with their republic, in a cause which was in some measure that of all Christendom. But of the nations of the cross, they could at first induce only the pope and other Italian powers to afford them the feeble succour of a few galleys; and when Philip II. of Spain was, after some delay, instigated by mingled fanaticism and self-interest to engage in the support of the republic, his selfish caution paralyzed the exertions of the league, as that of his father had done in the preceding war. The orders of Philip to his admiral, to whom the chief command of the allied fleets was yielded, prevented any vigorous measure until Cyprus had already fallen. But at length don Juan of Austria, natural brother of Philip, was permitted by that monarch to assume the office of generalissimo of the Christian league; and the impetuosity of this young prince could not be restrained to accord with the sluggish policy of the Spanish court. The Turkish fleet, now swollen to the enormous force of two hundred and fifty galleys, and other vessels of war, had already appeared in the Ionian sea; the Christian armament of equal strength was concentrated off Corfu.

At length, in the gulf of Lepanto, near the ancient promontory of Actium,—famous for the only naval battle, says Daru, which ever decided the fate of an empire—the banners of the cross and the crescent floated over five hundred decks, in the most gigantic and sanguinary naval encounter, which any age of the world had yet seen. (A.D. 1571.) Along the whole extent of the vast hostile lines of four miles, the day was long and furiously contested; the ancient names of the Venetian oligarchy were once more emblazoned in glorious achievement; the ancient maritime valour of the republic seemed once again to rekindle in all its lustre, for this last and expiring effort. The triumph of the Christian alliance was complete, and the chief honours of the victory were due to the Venetians. Thirty thousand Turks were slain; near two hundred of their vessels were captured, sunk, stranded, or burnt: and the conquerors purchased their brilliant success with the lives of five thousand of their bravest.

Strange as it should seem, the victory of Lepanto was a barren triumph. The confederates immediately separated, and returned to their ports to enjoy their useless laurels, and to repair their losses. No farther operations were attempted after the destruction of the Turkish fleet; and the Venetians found the deplorable exhaustion of their overstrained energies the only fruits of their success. The Turks covered the Grecian seas with a new armament before the following summer, scarcely inferior in strength to that which they had lost; and the confederates having vainly endeavoured to bring them to action, dispersed, after a short and insignificant campaign. The Venetians had more reason to dread the desertion of their allies, and the total consumption of their resources, than to hope for any ultimate advantage from the war. The Turks equally desired repose, but were resolved not to part with their acquisition; and the republic, by leaving them in possession of Cyprus, finally obtained a peace, (A.D. 1573.) By thus submitting to the loss of a subject kingdom,—a loss cruelly aggravated by its shame—the discrowned queen of the Adriatic was suffered to sink again into the languid slumber, which endured beyond the close of the sixteenth century.

CHAPTER X. STATE OF ITALY DURING THE SEVENTEENTH CENTURY, a.d. 1600-1700.

PART I.

General aspect of Italy in the seventeenth century—Confirmed degradation of the people—Total corruption of Italian manners—Cecisbeism—The unimportant political fortunes of the peninsula during this century; best described in noticing the affairs of its states under separate heads—The Spanish provinces of Italy—Milan and Sardinia—Naples—Rapacious oppression and mal-administration of the Spanish government in that kingdom—General discontent of the people—Singular and abortive conspiracy of the monastic orders in Calabria—The Neapolitans driven to revolt by want and misery—Furious insurrection of the populace of the capital, headed by the fisherman Masaniello—Fearful power of that demagogue—The viceroy compelled to yield to the insurgents—He obtains the assassination of Masaniello—The aggravated perfidy of the Spaniards produces new bloodshed and successful revolt—The Neapolitans determine to erect a republic—Divisions among the people—Termination of the insurrection—The Spanish despotism re-established with signal cruelty, and maintained to the end of the century—Sicily—Its fate similar to that of the sister kingdom of Naples—Ineffectual insurrection at Palermo—More serious revolt of Messina—The Spanish governor expelled—The Messinese declare Louis XIV. of France king of Sicily—Progress of the contest of Messina between France and Spain—Louis XIV. basely and cruelly deserts the Messinese—Their accumulated miseries—Merciless punishment of their revolt by the Spanish government—Decay of Messina—The popedom—Succession of pontiffs—Paul V.—His abortive attempts to revive the ancient pretensions of the holy see—Urban VIII.—War of the Barberini—The duchy of Urbino annexed to the papacy; and the fiefs of Castro and Ronciglione also—Alexander VII.—Quarrel respecting the privileges of the French embassy at Rome—Insolent pretensions of Louis XIV., maintained by the humiliation of the holy see—Innocent XI.—The dignity of the papacy again violated by Louis XIV.—The French king at length relaxes in his pretensions—Unimportant pontificates of the successors of Innocent XI.—Parma.—Reigns of the dukes Ranuccio I., Odoard, and Ranuccio II.—Sloth and hereditary corpulence of the princes of Farnése—Approaching extinction of their line—Modena—Reigns of Cesare. Alfonso III , Francesco I., Alfonso IV., Francesco II., and Rinaldo of Este—Mantua—General war caused by the disputed succession to that duchy—Disgraceful reign and abandoned character of Ferdinand Charles, the last duke—Tuscany—Reign of the archduke Ferdinando I.—His encouragement of commercial industry in his states—He founds the prosperity of Leghorn, and amasses immense treasures—His son, Cosmo II., pursues his enlightened policy—Ferdinando II.—The treasury drained by furnishing subsidies to the house of Austria—Extinction of the political importance of Tuscany—Reign of Cosmo III.—Florence the seat of gloomy superstition.

THE general aspect of Italy during the whole course of the seventeenth century, remained unchanged by any signal revolution. The period which had already elapsed between the extinction of national and civil independence and the opening of the period before us, had sufficed to establish the permanency of the several despotic governments of the peninsula, and to regulate the limits of their various states and provinces. If we except some popular commotions in Naples and Sicily, the struggle between the oppressed and the oppressor had wholly ceased. Servitude had become the heirloom of the people; and they bowed their necks unresistingly and from habit to the grievous yoke which their fathers had borne before them. Their tyrants, domestic and foreign, revelled or slumbered on their thrones. The Italian princes of the seventeenth century were more voluptuous and effeminate, but perhaps were less ferocious and sanguinary than the ancient Visconti, the Scala, the Carrara, the Gonzaga. But the condition of their subjects was not the less degraded. Their sceptres had broken every mouldering relic of freedom; and their dynasties, unmolested in their seats, were left (I except that of Savoy) to that quiet and gradual extinction which was ensured by the progress of mental and corporeal degeneracy: the hereditary consequences of slothful and bloated intemperance. The seventeenth century, however, saw untroubled to its close the reign of several ducal houses, which were to become extinct in the following age.

Compared with that of the preceding century, the history of Italy at this period may appear less deeply tinged with national crime, and humiliation, and misery; for the expiring throes of political vitality had been followed by the stillness of death. But, as a distinguished writer has well remarked, we should greatly err if, in observing that history is little more than the record of human calamity, we should conclude that the times over which it is silent are necessarily less characterized by misfortune. History can seldom penetrate into the recesses of society, can rarely observe the shipwreck of domestic peace, and the destruction of private virtue. The happiness and the wretchedness of families equally escape its cognizance. But we know that, in the country and in the times which now engage our attention, the frightful corruption of manners and morality had sapped the most sacred relations of life. The influence of the Spanish sovereignty over a great part of the peninsula had made way for the introduction of many Castilian prejudices; and these were fatally engrafted on the vices of a people already too prone to licentious gallantry. The merchant-noble of the Italian republics had been taught to see no degradation in commerce; and some of the numerous members of his house were always engaged in pursuits which increased the wealth and consequence of their family. But the haughty cavalier of Spain viewed the exercise of such plebeian industry with bitter contempt. The Spanish military inundated the peninsula; and the growth of Spanish sentiment was encouraged by the Italian princes. They induced their courtiers to withdraw their capitals from commerce, that they might invest them in estates, which descended to their eldest sons, the representatives of their families; and the younger branches of every noble house were condemned to patrician indolence, poverty, and celibacy. It was to recompense these younger sons, thus sacrificed to family pride, and for ever debarred from forming matrimonial connexions, that the strange and demoralizing office of the *cecisbeo*, or *cavaliere servente*, was instituted: an office which, under the guise of romantic politeness, and fostered by the dissolute example of the Italian princes and their courts, thinly veiled the universal privilege of adultery.

This pernicious and execrable fashion poisoned the sweet fountain of domestic happiness and confidence at its sources. The wife was no longer the intimate of her husband's heart, the faithful partner of his joys and cares. The eternal presence of the licensed paramour blasted his peace; and the emotions of paternal love were converted into distracting doubts or baleful indifference. The degraded parent, husband, son, fled from the pollution which reigned within his own dwelling, himself to plunge into a similar vortex of corruption. All the social ties were loosened: need we demand of history if public happiness could reside in that land, where private morality had perished?

In attempting to bring the unimportant fortunes of Italy during the seventeenth century into a general point of view, we should find considerable and needless difficulty, (A.D. 1607.) In the beginning of the century, a quarrel between the popedom and Venice appeared likely to kindle a general war in the peninsula; but the difference was terminated by negotiation, (A.D. 1627.) Twenty years later, the disputed succession of the duchy of Mantua created more lasting troubles, and involved all Lombardy in hostilities; in which the imperialists, the Spaniards, the French, and the troops of Savoy, once more mingled on the ancient theatre of so many sanguinary wars and calamitous devastations. But this uninteresting struggle, if not marked by less cruelty and rapine towards the inhabitants of the country, was pursued with less destructive vigour and activity than in the preceding century; nor were the French arms attended by those violent alternations of success and failure which had formerly inflicted such woes upon the peninsula. From the epoch at which Henry IV. excluded himself from Italy by the Savoyard treaty, until the ambitious designs of cardinal Richelieu involved France in the support of the pretensions of the Grisons over the Valteline country against Spain, the French standards had not been displayed beyond the Alps. But from the moment at which the celebrated minister of Louis XIII. engaged in this enterprise, until the peace of the Pyrenees, the incessant contest of the French and Spanish monarchies, in which the dukes of Savoy and other Italian powers variously embarked, was continually extended to the frontiers of Piedmont and Lombardy.

The arms of the combatants, however, seldom penetrated beyond the northern limits of Italy; and their rivalry, which held such a fatal influence on the peace of other parts of the European continent, can scarcely be said to have materially affected the national affairs of the peninsula. Meanwhile, the few brief and petty internal hostilities which arose and terminated among the Italian princes, were of still less general consequence and interest. The subsequent gigantic wars into which Louis XIV., by his insatiable lust of conquest, forced the great powers of Europe, were little felt in Italy until the close of the century; except in the territories of the dukes of Savoy. Thus, altogether, instead of endeavouring to trace the history of Italy during the seventeenth century as one integral and undivided subject, it will be more convenient still to consider the few important events in the contemporary annals of her different provinces as really appertaining, without much connexion, to distinct and separate states; and the affairs of these I shall notice nearly in the same order as in the last chapter.

The immediate dominion of the Spanish monarchy over great part of Italy, lasted during the whole of the seventeenth century. Naples, Sicily, Milan, and Sardinia, were exposed alike to the oppression of the Spanish court, and to the inherent vices of its administration. Its grievous exactions were rendered more ruinous by the injudicious and absurd manner of their infliction; by the private rapacity of the viceroys, and the peculation of their officers. Its despotism was aggravated by all the wantonness of power, and all the contemptuous insolence of pride. But of these four subject states, the two last, Milan and Sardinia, suffered in silence; and except that the Lombard duchy was almost incessantly a prey to warfare and ravages, from which the insular kingdom was exempted, a common obscurity and total dearth of all interest equally pervade the annals of both. But the fortunes of the two kingdoms of Naples and Sicily were more remarkable from the violent efforts of the people, ill conducted and unsuccessful though these were, to shake off the intolerable yoke of Spain.

To describe the state of the viceroyalty of Naples in the seventeenth century, I need only repeat and strengthen the picture drawn in the last chapter. For, as the decline of the Spanish monarchy, which had already commenced in the reign of Philip II., continued rapidly progressive under his successors, the third and fourth Philip, and the feeble Charles II., so the necessities of the Spanish government became more pressing, and its demands more rapacious and exorbitant. Of the revenue of about six millions of gold ducats, which the viceroys extorted from the kingdom, less than one million and a half covered the whole public charge, civil and military, of the country; and after all their own embezzlements and those of their subalterns, they sent yearly to Spain more than four millions, no part of which ever returned. Thus was the kingdom perpetually drained of wealth, which nothing but the lavish abundance of nature in that most fertile of regions could in any degree have renovated. But even the luxuriant opulence of Naples could neither satisfy the avarice of the court of Madrid, nor protect the people from misery and want under a government, whose impositions increased with the public exhaustion, and were multiplied with equal infatuation and wickedness upon the common necessaries of life. In this manner, duties were established upon flesh, fish, oil, and even upon flour and bread; and the people found themselves crushed under taxation, to pay the debts and to feed the armies of Spain. Their wealth and their youth were alike drawn out of their country, in quarrels altogether foreign to the national interests: in the unfortunate and mismanaged wars of the Spanish court in Lombardy and Catalonia, in the Low Countries and Germany. Meanwhile, as during the last century, the interior of the kingdom was almost always infested with banditti, rendered daring and reckless of crime by their numbers and the defenceless state of society; and so ill guarded were the sea-coasts, that the Turkish pirates made habitual descents during the whole course of the century, ravaged the country, attacked villages and even cities, and carried off the people into slavery.

It cannot excite our surprise, that the evils of the Spanish administration filled the Neapolitans with discontent and indignation: we may only wonder, that any people could be found abject enough to submit to a government, at once so oppressive and feeble. The first decided attempt to throw off the foreign yoke had its origin among an order, in which such a spirit might least be anticipated. In the last year of the sixteenth century, Tommaso Campanella, a Dominican friar, had on account, says Giannone, of his wicked life and the suspicion of infidelity, incurred the rigours of the Roman inquisition. On his release he laboured, in revenge for the treatment which he had received at Rome, to induce the brethren of his own order, the Augustins, and the Franciscans, to excite a religious and political revolution in Calabria. He acquired among them the same reputation for sanctity and prophetic illumination, which Savonarola had gained at Florence a hundred years before. He secretly inveighed against the Spanish tyranny; he declared that he was appointed by the Almighty to overthrow it, and to establish a republic in its place; and he succeeded in enlisting the monastic orders and several bishops of Calabria in the cause. By their exhortations, a multitude of the people and banditti of the province were roused to second him; and his design was embraced by great numbers of the provincial barons, whose names the historian declares that he suppresses from regard to their descendants. Campanella relied likewise on the assistance of the Turks in the meditated insurrection. But the secret of so extensive a conspiracy could not be preserved; the government got notice of it before it was ripe for execution; and Campanella and his chief priestly associates, with other conspirators, were adroitly arrested. Many of them were put to death under circumstances of atrocious cruelty; but Campanella himself, in the extremity of his torments, had the consummate address to render his confessions so perplexed and incoherent, that he was regarded as a madman, and sentenced only to perpetual imprisonment; from which he contrived at length to escape. He fled to France, and peaceably ended his life many years afterwards at Paris.

After the suppression of this conspiracy, Naples was frequently agitated at different intervals by commotions, into which the lower people were driven by misery and want. These partial ebullitions of popular discontent were not, however, marked by any very serious character until the middle of the century; when the tyranny of the vice-regal government, and the disorders and wretchedness of the kingdom, reached their consummation. The Spanish resources of taxation had been exhausted on the ordinary articles of consumption; the poor of the capital and kingdom had been successively compelled to forego the use of meat and bread by heavy duties; and the abundant fruits of their happy climate remained almost their sole means of support. The duke d'Arcos, who was then viceroy, could find no other expedient to meet the still craving demands of his court, upon a country already drained of its life-blood, than to impose a tax upon this last supply of food; and his measure roused the famishing people to desperation.

An accidental affray in the market of Naples swelled into a general insurrection of the populace of the capital; and an obscure and bold individual from the dregs of the people immediately rose to the head of the insurgents. Tommaso Aniello, better known under the name of Masaniello, a native of Amalfi and servant of a fisherman, had received an affront from the officers of the customs, and sought an occasion of gratifying his lurking vengeance. Seizing the moment when the popular exasperation was at its height, he led the rioters to the attack and demolition of the custom-house. The flames of insurrection at once spread with uncontrollable violence; the palace of the viceroy was pillaged; and d'Arcos himself was driven for refuge to one of the castles of Naples. The infuriated populace murdered many of the nobles, burnt the houses of all who were obnoxious to them, and filled the whole capital with flames and blood. Their youthful idol Masaniello, tattered and half naked, with a scaffold for his throne and the sword for his sceptre, commanded every where with absolute sway. Backed by 150,000 men, rudely armed in various ways, and all dreadful in their long smothered ferocity, their leader (I use the forcible language of a great native historian) killed with a nod and set fire with a look; for to what place soever he beckoned, heads were struck off and houses set in flames.

The viceroy, terrified into virtue at these excesses, which the long oppression of his court and his own tyranny had provoked, and finding the insurrection spreading through the provinces, consented to all the demands of Masaniello and his followers. By a treaty which he concluded with the insurgents, he solemnly promised the repeal of all the taxes imposed since the time of Charles V., and engaged that no new duties should thenceforth be levied; he guaranteed the ancient and long violated privileges of parliament: and he bound himself by oath to an act of oblivion. A short interval of calm was thus gained; but the perfidious viceroy employed it only in gratifying the vanity of Masaniello by caresses and entertainments; until, having caused a potion to be administered to him in his wine at a banquet, he succeeded in unsettling his reason. The demagogue then by his extravagancies and cruelties lost the affection of the people; and d'Arcos easily procured his assassination by some of his own followers.

The viceroy had no sooner thus deprived the people of their young leader, whose native talents had rendered him truly formidable, than he immediately showed a determination to break all the articles of his compact. But the people, penetrating his treachery, flew again to arms; and the insurrection burst forth in the capital and provinces with more sanguinary fury than before. Again d'Arcos dissembled; and again the deluded people had laid down their arms; when, on the appearance of a Spanish fleet before Naples, the citadels and shipping suddenly opened a tremendous cannonade on the city; and at the same moment, some thousand Spanish infantry disembarked, and commenced a general massacre in the streets. The Neapolitans were confounded and panic-stricken at this aggravated perfidy; but they were a hundred times more numerous than the handful of troops which assailed them. When they recovered from their first consternation, they attacked their enemies in every street; and after a frightful carnage on both sides, the Spaniards were driven either into the fortresses, or the sea.

After this conflict, the people, who, since the death of Masaniello, had fallen under the influence of Gennaro Annese, a soldier of mean birth, resolved fiercely and fearlessly to throw off the Spanish yoke altogether. It chanced that Henry, duke de Guise, who by maternal descent from the second line of Anjou, had some hereditary pretensions to the Neapolitan crown, was at this juncture at Rome on his private business; and to him the insurgents applied, with the offer of constituting him their captain-general. At the same time, they resolved to erect Naples into a republic under his presidency; and the duke, a high-spirited prince, hastened to assume a command, which opened so many glorious prospects of ambition. The contest with the Spanish viceroy, his fortresses, and squadron, was then resumed with new bloodshed, and with indecisive results. But though the Neapolitans had hailed the name of a republic with rapture, they were, of all people, by their inconsistency and irresolution, least qualified for such a form of government. In this insurrection, they had for some time professed obedience to the king of Spain, while they were resisting his arms; and even now they wavered, and were divided among themselves. On the one hand, the duke de Guise, outraged by their excesses, and grasping perhaps at the establishment of an arbitrary power in his own person, began to exercise an odious authority, and showed himself intolerant of the influence of Annese: on the other, that leader of the people was irritated at finding himself deprived of all command. In his jealousy of Guise, he basely resolved to betray his countrymen to the Spaniards; and in the temporary absence of the duke, who had left the city with a small force to protect the introduction of some supplies, he opened the gates to the enemy, (A.D. 1648.) The Spanish troops re-entered the capital; the abject multitude received them with acclamations; and De Guise himself, in endeavouring to effect his flight, was made prisoner, and sent to Spain, in one of whose gloomy dungeons he mourned for some years the vanity of his ambition.

Thus, in a few hours, was the Spanish yoke again fixed on the necks of the prostrate Neapolitans; and it was rivetted more firmly and grievously than ever. As soon as their submission is secured, almost all the men who had taken a prominent share in the insurrection, and who had been promised pardon, were seized, and under various pretences of their having meditated new troubles, were either publicly or privately executed. The traitor Gennaro Annese himself shared the same fate:—a worthy example, that neither the faith of oaths, nor the memory of eminent services, are securities against the jealousy and vengeance of despotism. That despotism had no longer any thing to fear from the degraded people, who had returned under its iron sceptre. The miseries of Naples could not increase; but they were not diminished until the death of Charles II., and the extinction of the Austrian dynasty of Spain, in the last year of the century.

The sister kingdom of Sicily had long shared the lot of Naples, in all the distresses which the tyrannical and impolitic government of Spain could inflict upon the people. The Sicilians were only more fortunate than their continental neighbours, as the inferior wealth and resources of their island rendered them a less inviting prey to the insatiable necessities of Spain, to the drain of her wars, and the rapacity of her ministers. But even in Sicily, which by the excellence of its soil for raising corn seems intended to be the granary of Italy, the Spanish government succeeded in creating artificial dearth, and squalid penury; and in the natural seat of abundance, the people were often without bread to eat. Their misery goaded them at length nearly to the commission of the same excesses as those which have just been described at Naples. A few months earlier than the revolt under Masaniello, the lower orders rose at Palermo, chose for their leader one Guiseppe d'Alessi, a person of as low condition as the Neapolitan demagogue, and under his orders put their viceroy, the marquis de Los Velos, to flight. But this insurrection at Palermo was less serious than that of Naples, and after passing through similar stages, was more easily quelled. The Sicilian viceroy, like d'Arcos, did not scruple at premeditated violation of the solemnity of oaths. Like him, he swore to grant the people all their demands, and a total amnesty; and yet, after perfidiously obtaining the assassination of the popular leader, he caused the inhabitants to be slaughtered in the streets, their chiefs to be hanged, and the burthens which he had been forced to remove, to be laid on again.

This detestable admixture of perfidy and sanguinary violence bent the spirit of the Palermitans to the yoke, and Sicily relapsed into the tameness of suffering for above twenty-seven years; until this tranquillity was broken, during the general war in Europe, which preceded the treaty of Nimeguen, by a new and more dangerous insurrection. The city of Messina had, until this epoch, in some measure enjoyed a republican constitution, and was governed by a senate of its own, under the presidency only of a Spanish lieutenant, with very limited powers. This freedom of the city had ensured its prosperity: its population amounted to sixty thousand souls, its commerce flourished, and its wealth rivalled the dreams of avarice. The Neapolitan historian asserts that the privileges of the people had rendered them insolent; but there is more reason to believe that the Spanish government looked with a jealous and unfriendly eye upon a happy independence, which was calculated to fill their other Sicilian subjects with bitter repinings at the gloomy contrast of their own wretched slavery. Several differences with successive viceroys regarding their privileges, had inspired the citizens of Messina with discontent; and at length they rose in open rebellion against their Spanish governor, don Diego di Soria, and expelled him from the city. (A.D. 1674.) Despairing of defending their rights without assistance, against the whole power of the Spanish monarchy, they had then recourse to Louis XIV., and tempted him with the offer of the sovereignty of their city, and the eventual union of their whole island with the French dominions. Louis eagerly closed with a proposal, which opened at least an advantageous diversion in his war against Spain. He was proclaimed king of Sicily at Messina, and immediately dispatched a small squadron to take possession of the city in his name.

The arrival of this force was succeeded early in the following year, by that of a more formidable French fleet, under the duke de Vivonne; and the Messinese, being encouraged by these succours, rejected all the Spanish offers of indemnity and accommodation. On the other hand, the court of Madrid being roused to exertion by the danger of losing the whole island, had fitted out a strong armament to secure its preservation, and the recovery of Messina; and a Dutch fleet under the famous De Ruyter arrived in the Mediterranean to co-operate with the Spanish forces. The war in Sicily was prosecuted with fury on both sides for nearly four years; and several sanguinary battles were fought off the coast, between the combined fleets and that of France. In all of these the French had the advantage: in one, the gallant De Ruyter fell; and in another, the French, under Vivonne and Du Quesne, with inferior force, attacked the Dutch and Spanish squadrons of twenty-seven sail of the line, nineteen galleys, and several fire-ships at anchor, under the guns of Palermo, and gained a complete victory. This success placed Messina in security; and might have enabled both Naples and Sicily to throw off the onerous dominion of Spain. But the spiritless and subjugated people evinced no disposition to rise against their oppressors; and all the efforts of the French eventually failed in extending the authority of their monarch beyond the walls of Messina.

The French king had lost the hope of possessing himself of all Sicily, and was already weary of supporting the Messinese, when the conferences for a general peace were opened at Nimeguen. There, dictating as a conqueror, he might at least have stipulated for the ancient rights of the Messinese, and insisted upon an amnesty for the brave citizens, who, relying on the sacred obligation of protection, had utterly provoked the vengeance of their Spanish governors by placing themselves under his sceptre. But, that his pride might not suffer by a formal evacuation of the city as a condition of the approaching peace, he basely preferred the gratification of this absurd punctilio to the real preservation of honour, and the common dictates of humanity. His troops were secretly ordered to abandon Messina before the signature of peace; and so precipitate was their embarkation, that the wretched inhabitants, stricken with sudden terror at their impending fate, despairing of pardon from their former governors, and hopeless of successful resistance against them, had only a few hours to choose between exile and anticipated death, (A.D. 1678.) Seven thousand of them hurried on board the French fleet, without having time to secure even their money or portable articles, and the French commander, fearing that his Vessels would be overcrowded, sailed from the harbour; while two thousand more of the fugitives yet remained on the beach with outstretched arms, in the last agonies of despair, vainly imploring him with piercing cries not to abandon them to their merciless enemies. The condition of the Messinese who fled for refuge to France, and of those who remained in the city, differed little in the event. Louis XIV., after affording the former an asylum for scarcely more than one short year, inhumanly chased them in the last stage of destitution from his dominions. About five hundred of them, rashly venturing to return to their country, under the faith of Spanish passports, were seized on their arrival at Messina, and either executed or condemned to the galleys. Many others, even of the highest rank, were reduced to beg their bread over Europe, or to congregate in bands, and rob on the highways; and the miserable remnant, plunged into the abyss of desperation, passed into Turkey, and fearfully consummated their wretchedness by the renunciation of their faith. Their brethren, who had not quitted Messina, had meanwhile at first been deluded with the hope of pardon by the Spanish viceroy of Sicily. But the amnesty which he published was revoked by special orders from Madrid; and all, who had been in any way conspicuous in the insurrection, were either put to death or banished. Messina was deprived of all its privileges; the town-house was razed to the ground; and on the spot was erected a galling monument of the degradation of the city:—a pyramid surmounted by the statue of the king of Spain, cast with the metal of the great bell which had formerly summoned the people to their free parliaments. The purposes of Spanish tyranny were accomplished; the population of Messina had dwindled from sixty to eleven thousand persons; and the obedience of the city was ensured by a desolation from which it has never since risen to its ancient prosperity.

Thus were the annals of Naples and Sicily distinguished only, during the seventeenth century, by paroxysms of popular suffering. The condition of central Italy was more obscure and tranquil; for the maladministration of its rulers did not occasion the same resistance. Yet if the papal government was less decidedly tyrannical and rapacious than that of Spain, the evils, which had become inherent in it during preceding ages, remained undiminished and incurable; and agricultural and commercial industry was permanently banished from the Roman states. Meanwhile the succession of the pontiffs was marked by few circumstances to arrest our attention. To Clement VIII., who reigned at the opening of the century, succeeded, in 1605, Leo XI. of the family of Medici, who survived his election only a few weeks; and on his death the cardinal Camillo Borghese was raised to the tiara by the title of Paul V. Filled with extravagant and exploded opinions of the authority of the holy see, Paul V. signalized the commencement of his pontificate by the impotent attempt to revive those pretensions of the papal jurisdiction and supremacy over the powers of the earth, which, in the dark ages, had inundated Italy and the empire with blood. He thus involved the papacy in disputes with several of the catholic governments of Europe, and in a serious difference with Venice in particular, which will find a more appropriate notice in the affairs of that republic. After his merited defeat on this occasion, he cautiously avoided to compromise his authority by the repetition of any similar efforts; and during the remainder of his pontificate of sixteen years, his only cares were to embellish the ecclesiastical capital, and to enrich his nephews with vast estates in the Roman patrimony, which thus became the hereditary possessions of the family of Borghese.

Paul V., on his death in 1621, was succeeded by Gregory XV., whose insignificant pontificate filled only two years; and in 1623 the conclave placed the cardinal Maffeo Barberini in the chair of St. Peter, under the name of Urban VIII. This pope, during a reign of twenty-one years, was wholly under the guidance of his two nephews, the cardinal Antonio, and Taddeo Barberini, prefect of Rome. These ambitious relatives were not satisfied with the riches which he heaped upon them+; and their project of acquiring for their family the Roman duchies of Castro and Ronciglione, fiefs held of the church by the house of Farnése, involved the papacy in a war with Parma. Odoard Farnése, the reigning duke of Parma, had contracted immense debts to charitable foundations at Rome, of which he neglected to pay even the interest. He thus afforded Taddeo Barberini, as prefect of that capital, a pretext for summoning him before the apostolic chamber; and on his contemptuous neglect of the citation, the Barberini obtained an order for sequestrating his Roman fiefs. The duke of Parma had recourse to arms for his defence; the pope excommunicated him; and hostilities commenced between him and Taddeo, who acted as general of the Church, (A.D. 1641.) But this war of the Barberini, as it has been named,—the only strictly Italian contest of the century,—produced no decisive result. It was invested with a ridiculous character by the cowardice of Taddeo and the papal troops, who, to the number of eighteen thousand, fled before a handful of cavalry under the duke Odoard. After this disgraceful check, the Barberini were but too happy to obtain a suspension of arms; and the war was shortly terminated by a treaty, which left the combatants in their original state, (A.D. 1644.)

Urban VIII., or rather his nephews, had thus failed in gaining possession of the fiefs of Castro and Ronciglione; but the pope had succeeded, some years before, in securing to the holy see a much more important acquisition, which he did not venture to appropriate to his family. This was the duchy of Urbino, which had remained under the sovereignty of the family of Rovere since the beginning of the sixteenth century, when Julius II. had induced the last prince of the line of Montefeltro to adopt his nephew for a successor. The house of Rovere had for one hundred and twenty years maintained the intellectual splendour of the little court of Urbino, the most polished in Italy; but Urban VIII. persuaded the aged duke, Francesco Maria, who had no male heirs, to abdicate his sovereignty in favour of the Church, (A.D. 1626.) The duchy of Urbino was annexed to the Roman states; and the industry and prosperity, for which it had been remarkable under its own princes, immediately withered.

Urban VIII. was succeeded in 1644 by Innocent X., who revived with more success the pretensions of the holy see to the fiefs of Castro and Ronciglione. The unliquidated debts of the house of Farnése were still the pretext for the seizure of these possessions; but the papal officers were expelled from Castro, and the bishop, whom Innocent had installed in that see, was murdered by order of the minister of Ranuccio II., duke of Parma. The pope was so highly exasperated by these acts, that he directed his whole force against Castro; the Parmesan troops were repulsed in the attempt to succour the place; and when famine had compelled it to surrender, the pope, confounding the innocent inhabitants with the perpetrators of the assassination, caused the city to be razed to its foundations, and a pyramid to be erected on the ruins commemorative of his vengeance, (A.D. 1649.) The restitution of these fiefs to the house of Parma was made a condition of the peace of the Pyrenees; but Alexander VII., who succeeded Innocent X. in 1656, contrived, after many negotiations, to obtain permission to hold them in pledge, until Ranuccio II. should discharge the debts of his crown. By the failure of the duke to satisfy this engagement, the disputed states remained finally annexed to the popedom.

The pontificate of Alexander VII. proved, however, an epoch of grievous humiliation for the pride of the holy see. In 1660, an affray was occasioned at Rome through the privileges arrogantly claimed by the French ambassadors, of protecting all the quarter of the city near their residence from the usual operations of justice; and Louis XIV. determined, in the insolence of his power, to support a pretension which would be intolerable to the meanest court in Europe. He sent the duke de Crequi as his ambassador to Rome, with a numerous and well-armed retinue, to brave the pope in his own capital. De Crequi took formal military possession of a certain number of streets near the palace of his embassy, according to the extent over which the right of asylum had been permitted by usage to his predecessors. He placed guards throughout this circuit, as if it had been one of his master's fortresses; and the papal government, anxious to avoid a rupture with the haughty monarch of France, overlooked the usurpation. But every effort to preserve peace was ineffectual against the resolution which had been taken on the opposite side to provoke some open quarrel. The duke de Crequi's people made it their occupation to outrage the police of Rome, and to insult the Corsican guard of the pope. Still, even these excesses of the French were tolerated by Alexander, until they rose to such a height that the peaceful citizens dared no longer to pass through the streets by night. At length the Corsican guard were goaded into a fray with the followers of the embassy, which brought matters to the crisis desired by Louis. While the Corsicans were violently irritated by the death of one of their comrades in the broil, they happened to meet the carriage of the duchess de Crequi: they fired upon and killed two of her attendants; and the duke immediately quitted Rome, as if his master had received in his person an unprovoked and mortal affront.

Alexander VII. soon found that Louis XIV. was resolved to avail himself of the most serious colouring which could be given to this affair. The king expelled the pope's nuncio from France; he seized upon Avignon and its papal dependencies; and he assembled an army in Provence, which crossed the Alps to take satisfaction in Rome itself. The pope at first showed an inclination to assert the common rights of every crown with becoming spirit; and he endeavoured to engage several catholic princes to protect the dignity of the holy see. But none of the great powers were in a condition at that juncture to undertake his defence. His own temporal strength was quite unequal to a struggle with France; the spiritual arms of the Vatican had now fallen into contempt; and he had the bitter mortification of being obliged to submit to the terms of accommodation which Louis XIV. imperiously dictated. The principal of these were, the banishment of all the persons who had taken a part in the insult offered to the train of the French ambassador; the suppression of the Corsican guard; the erection of a column, even in Rome, with a legend to proclaim the injury and its reparation; and, finally, the mission of one of the pope's own family to Paris to make his apologies, (A.D. 1664.) All these humiliating conditions were subscribed to, and rigorously enforced. Hitherto the papal legates had appeared at the courts of Europe only to give laws and impose contributions: the cardinal Chigi, the nephew of Alexander VII., was the first ecclesiastic dispatched in that character to any monarch, to demand pardon for the holy see.

Alexander VII. did not survive this memorable epoch of degradation for the papacy above three years. He was succeeded in 1667 by Clement IX., who wore the triple crown only two years, and was replaced in 1669 by Clement X. The unimportant reign of this pope occupied seven years, and closed in 1676. The pontificate of his successor, Innocent XI., was more remarkable for the renewal of the quarrel respecting the privileges of the French embassy. To terminate the flagrant abuses which these privileges engendered, Innocent published a decree that no foreign minister should thenceforth be accredited at the papal court, until he had expressly renounced every pretension of the kind. This reasonable provision was admitted without opposition by all the catholic monarchs, except Louis XIV.: but he alone refused to recognise its justice; and on the death of the duke d'Estrées, his ambassador at Rome, he sent the marquis de Lavardin to succeed him, and to enforce the maintenance of the old privileges. For this purpose, Lavardin was attended by a body of eight hundred armed men; and the sovereignty of the pope was again insolently braved in his own capital. The guards of Lavardin violently excluded the papal police from all access to the quarter of the city which they occupied; and Innocent at length excommunicated the ambassador. This proceeding would at Paris have excited only ridicule; but in Rome the outraged pride of the court, and the prejudices which still enveloped the ancient throne of papal supremacy and superstition, excluded Lavardin from the pale of society; and he found the solitude in which he was left so irksome, that he at last petitioned to be recalled.

The pontificate of Innocent XI. terminated in 1690; and it was not until three years after his death, that Louis XIV. was at length persuaded to desist from the assertion of a pretended right, which could have no other object than to gratify his pride at the expense of multiplying crime and anarchy, in the chosen seat of the religion which he professed. This was the last event in the papal annals of the seventeenth century, which deserves to be recorded. We have already found the reigns of several of the popes entirely barren of circumstance; and after that of Innocent XI., I should be altogether at a loss how to bestow a single comment upon the obscure pontificates of his three next successors: of Alexander VIII., who died in 1692; of Innocent XII.; and of Clement XI., who was placed in the chair of St. Peter in the last year of the century.

The two contests with the popedom, which the house of Farnése maintained for the possession of the fiefs of Castro and Ronciglione, were almost the only remarkable circumstances in the annals of the duchy of Parma during this century. Ranuccio I., the son of the hero Alessandro Farnése, who wore the ducal crown at its commencement, resembled his father in no quality but mere courage. His long reign was distinguished only for its habitual tyranny and avarice; and for the wanton cruelty with which he caused a great number of his nobility and other subjects to be put to death in 1612, that he might confiscate their property under the charge of a conspiracy, which appears to have had no real existence. He was succeeded in 1622 by his son, Odoard, whose misplaced confidence in his military talents plunged his subjects into many calamities. Vainly imagining that the martial virtues of his grandfather Alessandro were hereditary in his person, he eagerly sought occasions of entering on a career of activity and distinction in the field, for which his egotistical presumption and his excessive corpulence equally disqualified him. By engaging, in 1635, in the war between France and Spain in northern Italy, as the ally of the former power, he exposed his states to cruel ravages; and though, in the subsequent war of the Barberini, he was indebted to the misconduct of the papal army for the preservation of his fiefs, that contest did not terminate until he had consumed the resources of his duchy by his prodigality and ignorance.

The death of Odoard in 1646, relieved his subjects from the apprehension of a continuance of similar evils from his restless temper; and the mild and indolent character of his son Ranuccio II., seemed to promise an era of greater tranquillity. But Ranuccio was always governed by unworthy favourites, who oppressed his people; and it was one of these ministers, whose violence, as we have seen, provoked the destruction of Castro, and entailed the loss of its dependencies on the duchy of Parma. The long and feeble reign of Ranuccio II., thus marked only by disgrace, was a fitting prelude to the extinction of the sovereignty and existence of the house of Farnése. Buried in slothful indulgence and lethargy, the members of the ducal family were oppressed with hereditary obesity, which shortened their lives. Ranuccio II. himself survived to the year 1694; but he might already anticipate the approaching failure of the male line of his dynasty. Odoard, the eldest of his sons, had died before him of suffocation, the consequence of corpulence; the two others, don Francesco and don Vincente, who were destined successively to ascend the throne after him, resembled their brother in their diseased constitutions; and the probability that these princes would die without issue, rendered their niece, Elisabetta Farnése, daughter of Odoard, sole presumptive heiress of the states of her family.

Of the dukes of Parma, whose reigns filled the seventeenth century, not one deserved either the love of his people or the respect of posterity. The contemporary annals of the princes of Este were graced by more ability and virtue. But the reduction of the dominion of those sovereigns to the narrow limits of the duchies of Modena and Reggio, diminished the consequence which their ancestors had enjoyed in Italy during the preceding century, before the seizure of Ferrara by the Roman see. Don Cesare of Este, whose weakness had submitted to this spoliation, reigned until the year 1628. His subjects of Modena forgave him a pusillanimity which had rendered their city the elegant seat of his beneficent reign. His son, Alfonso III., who succeeded him, was stricken with such wondrous affliction for the death of his wife, only a few months after his accession to the ducal crown, that he abdicated his throne, and retired into a Capuchin convent in the Tyrol. On this event, his son Francesco I. assumed his sceptre in 1629, and reigned nearly thirty years. Joining in the wars of the times in upper Italy between France and Spain, and alternately espousing their opposite causes, Francesco I. acquired the reputation of one of the ablest captains of his age, as he was also one of the best sovereigns. His skilful conduct and policy in these unimportant contests were rewarded by the extension of his territories; and in 1636, the little principality of Correggio (more famous in the annals of art than of war) was annexed to his imperial fiefs. Neither the short reign of his son and successor, Alfonso IV., which commenced in 1658 and ended in 1662, nor that of his grandson, Francesco II., which began with a feeble minority, and terminated after a protracted administration of the same character, demand our particular notice; and in 1694, the cardinal Rinaldo, son of the first Francesco, succeeded his nephew, and entered upon a reign which was reserved for signal calamities in the first years of the new century.

In the affairs of Parma and Modena, during the century before us, there is scarcely any thing to invite our attention; but the fortunes of Mantua, so obscure in the preceding age, were rendered somewhat remarkable in this, by the wars which the disputed succession to its sovereignty occasioned. The reign of Vincente I., who, having succeeded to the ducal crowns of Mantua and Montferrat in 1587, still wore them at the opening of the seventeenth century, and that of his successor Francesco IV., were equally obscure and unimportant. But, on the death of Francesco, in 1612, some troubles arose, from the pretensions which the duke of Savoy advanced anew over the state of Montferrat. It was not until after several years, that negotiations terminated the indecisive hostilities which were thus occasioned, and in which Spain interfered directly against the duke of Savoy, while France more indirectly assisted him. By the treaty of Asti in 1615, and of Madrid in 1617, the duke of Savoy engaged to leave Montferrat to the house of Gonzaga, until the emperor should decide on his claims. The last duke of Mantua, Francesco IV., had left only a daughter: but, as Montferrat was a feminine fief, that state descended to her; while her father's two brothers, Ferdinando and Vincente II., reigned successively over Mantua without leaving issue. On the death of the latter of these two princes, both of whom shortened their days by their infamous debaucheries, the direct male line of the ducal house of Gonzaga became extinct; and the right of succession to the Mantuan duchy devolved on a collateral branch, descended from a younger son of the duke Federigo II., who had died in 1540. This part of the family of Gonzaga was established in France, in possession of the first honours of nobility, and was now represented by Charles, duke de Nevers. By sending his son, the duke de Rethel, to Mantua in the last illness of Vincente II., Charles not only secured the succession to that duchy, which he might lawfully claim, but re-annexed Montferrat to its diadem. For, on the very same night on which Vincente II. expired, the duke de Rethel received the hand of Maria, the daughter of Francesco IV., and heiress of Montferrat; and the right of inheritance to all the states of the ducal line, thus centered in the branch of Nevers.

The new ducal house of Gonzaga did not commence its sovereignty over Mantua and Montferrat without violent opposition. The duke of Savoy renewed his claim upon the latter province; and Cesare Gonzaga, duke of Guastalla, the representative of a distant branch of that family, made pretensions to the duchy of Mantua, (A.D. 1627.) At the same time, the Spanish government thought to take advantage of a disputed succession, for the purpose of annexing the Mantuan to the Milanese states; and the emperor Ferdinand II. placed the duke de Nevers under the ban of the empire, for having taken possession of its dependant fiefs, without waiting for a formal investiture at its hands. The objects of Ferdinand were evidently to revive the imperial jurisdiction in Italy, and to enrich the Spanish dynasty of his family by the acquisition of these states. To promote these combined plans of the house of Austria, an imperial army crossed the Alps, and surprised the city of Mantua, which was sacked with merciless ferocity. (A.D. 1630.) At the same time, the duke of Savoy concluded a treaty with Spain, for the partition of Montferrat; and the new duke of Mantua seemed likely to be dispossessed of the whole of his dominions. But fortunately for him, it was at this juncture that cardinal Richelieu had entered on his famous design of humbling the power and ambition of both the Spanish and German dynasties of the house of Austria; and a French army under Louis XIII. in person forcing the pass of Susa, crossed the Alps to support the Gonzaga of Nevers against all their enemies. I pass over the uninteresting details of the general war, which was thus kinded in northern Italy by the Mantuan succession. When Richelieu himself appeared on the theatre of contest, at the head of a formidable French army, all resistance was hopeless; and his success shortly produced an accommodation between the belligerents in the peninsula, by which the emperor was compelled to bestow the disputed investiture of Mantua and Montferrat upon Charles of Nevers. (A.D. 1631.)

This prince, who thenceforth reigned at Mantua under the title of Charles I., retained that duchy without farther opposition. But in 1635 he was drawn, by the memory of the eminent services which France had rendered him, into an alliance with that power against Spain, in the new war which broke out between the rival dynasties of Bourbon and Austria. Such a connexion could serve, however, only to destroy the repose, and endanger the safety of his duchies. Neither Charles I. nor his son Charles II., who succeeded him in 1637, could prevent Montferrat from being perpetually overrun and ravaged by the contending armies of France, Spain, the empire, and Savoy: and the Mantuan dukes almost abandoned every effort to retain the possession of that province until, after being for above twenty years the seat of warfare and desolation, it was at length restored to Charles II. by the general peace of the Pyrenees.

Charles II. died in 1665; and his son Ferdinand Charles commenced the long and disgraceful reign, with which the sovereignty and race of the Gonzaga were to terminate early in the next century. This prince, more dissolute, more insensible of dishonour, more deeply buried in grovelling vice, than almost any of his predecessors, was worthy of being the last of a family which, since its elevation to the tyranny of Mantua, had, during four centuries of sovereignty, relieved its career of blood and debauchery by few examples of true greatness and virtue. To gratify his extravagance, and indulge in his low and vicious excesses, Ferdinand Charles crushed his people under grievous taxation. To raise fresh supplies, which his exhausted states could no longer afford, he shamelessly in 1680 sold Casal, the capital of Montferrat, to Louis XIV., who immediately occupied the place with twelve thousand men under his general Catinat. The sums which the duke thus raised, either by extortion from his oppressed subjects, or from this disgraceful transaction, were dissipated in abandoned pleasures in the carnivals of Venice, among a people who openly evinced their contempt for him, and whose sovereign oligarchy passed a decree, forbidding any of their noble body from mingling in his society.

From the affairs of Mantua, we may pass to those of Tuscany; but the transition is attended with little augmentation of interest. A common dearth of attraction marks the annals of most of the despotisms of Italy; and when Tuscany descended to the rank of a duchy, her pre-eminence of splendour survived only in the past, and her modern story sank into the same ignominious obscurity with that of Parma and Modena, and Mantua. We are reminded only of the existence of the solitary republic which survived in this quarter of Italy, to wonder how Lucca escaped subjugation to the power, whose dominions encircled and hemmed in her narrow territory; and we are permitted to contemplate her ancient republican rivals, Florence, Sienna, and Pisa, only as the capital, and the provincial cities of the ducal sovereigns of Tuscany. Of these princes of the house of Medici, four reigned successively during the seventeenth century. At its commencement, the ducal crown was worn by Ferdinando I., whose personal vices and political talents have been already noticed. After the failure of his project to throw off the Spanish yoke, his efforts were exclusively devoted to the encouragement of commerce and maritime industry among his subjects; and the enlightened measures, to which he was prompted by a thorough knowledge of the science of government, and a keen perception of his own interests, were rewarded with signal success. To attract the trade of the Mediterranean to the shores of Tuscany, he made choice of the castle of Leghorn for the seat of a free port. He improved the natural advantages of its harbour, which had already excited the attention of some of his predecessors, by several grand and useful works; he invested the town which rose on the site, with liberal privileges; and from this epoch, Leghorn continued to flourish, until it attained the mercantile prosperity and opulence, which have rendered it one of the first maritime cities of the peninsula. The skilful policy, which Ferdinando I. pursued in this and other respects, produced a rapid influx of wealth into his states; and before his death, which occurred in 1609, he had amassed immense treasures.

Several of the first princes of the ducal house of Medici seemed to have inherited some portion of that commercial ability, by which their merchant ancestors had founded the grandeur of their house; and they profited by the contempt or ignorance, which precluded other Italian princes from rivalling them in the cultivation of the same pursuits. Cosmo II., the son and successor of Ferdinando, imitated his example with even more earnest zeal, and with more brilliant success. But on his death, in 1621, the minority of his son Ferdinando II. destroyed the transient prosperity of the ducal government. The rich treasury of the two preceding dukes was drained in furnishing troops and subsidies to Spain and Austria; and Ferdinando, who was left under the guardianship of his grandmother and mother, was only released from female tutelage on attaining the age of manhood, to exhibit during his long reign all the enfeebling consequences of such an education. His character was mild, peaceable, and benevolent; and his administration responded to his personal qualities. From this epoch, the political importance of Tuscany entirely ceased; the state was stricken with moral paralysis; and lethargy and indolence became the only characteristics of the government and the people.

Ferdinando II., however, was not destitute of talents; and the enthusiasm with which the grand-duke and his brother promoted the cultivation of science, at least protected his inactive reign from the reproach of utter insignificance. But his son, Cosmo III., who ascended his throne in 1670, reigned with a weakness, which was relieved by no intellectual tastes. Unhappy and suspicious in his temper, his life was embittered by domestic disagreements with his duchess; fanatical and bigotted, he was constantly surrounded and governed by monks; and at the close of the seventeenth century, Florence, once the throne of literature, the fair and splendid seat of all the arts which can embellish and illumine life, was converted into the temple of gloomy superstition and hypocrisy.

PART II.
Savoy—General character of its princes and their government—Charles Emmanuel I.—His share, during the remainder of his reign, in the wars of France and Spain in northern Italy—Disastrous consequences of his overweening ambition—His death—Victor Amadeus I.—Tyrannical ascendancy of the French in Piedmont throughout his short reign—Calamitous minority of his son, Charles Emmanuel II.—Civil war in Savoy and Piedmont, aggravated by the interference of France and Spain—Charles Emmanuel II. does not recover all his states until the peace of the Pyrenees—The remainder of his reign unimportant—Victor Amadeus II.—His early indications of consummate political talents—His opposition to the designs of Louis XIV. of France—He joins the league of Augsburg—War in Piedmont, sustained by Victor Amadeus and his allies against the French—Fortitude and activity of the duke—He concludes a separate peace, and compels a general recognition of the neutrality of Italy—His power prodigiously augmented—Genoa—Differences of the republic with the house of Savoy—Exclusive character of the Genoese sovereign oligarchy—Mutual hatred between that body and the unprivileged orders—Conspiracy of Giulio Cesare Vachero—Its detection and punishment—Difference between the republic and France provoked by the arrogance of Louis XIV.—Cruel bombardment of Genoa by the French—The senate compelled, by this barbarous outrage, to make submission to the tyrant—Venice—Partial recovery of her ancient activity and vigour during this century—Quarrel between the republic and pope Paul V.—The senate always distinguished for their resistance to ecclesiastical encroachments—Universal religious toleration a maxim of their policy—Intolerable pretensions of Paul V. steadily opposed by the Venetian government—Papal sentence of excommunication and interdict passed against the republic—Firm resistance of the senate to its operations—Desire of the pope to have recourse to temporal arms—He is compelled to renounce his pretensions to procure an accommodation—Signal triumph of the republic—Its good effects for catholic Europe—Energy of the Venetian senate in maintaining their sovereignty over the Adriatic—The Uscochi—Origin of those pirates of Dalmatia—Their incessant and bold depredations in the gulf—The Austrian government protect them—Serious resolution at length formed by Venice to chastise them—Consequent war with the house of Austria—Alliance of the republic with Savoy and the seven United provinces—Conclusion of the war—The objects of Venice attained by the dispersion of the Uscochi and the assertion of her dominion over the Adriatic—Exasperation of Spain against the republic—Story of the famous conspiracy attributed to the Spanish ambassador, for the destruction of Venice—Share of Venice in the other Italian wars of this century against the house of Austria; terminated by the peace of Chierasco—Remarkable recognition of her dominion over the Adriatic—Little connexion between the affairs of Venice and of the other Italian states during the remainder of the century—Unprovoked attack of the Turks upon the republic-Long and disastrous war of Candia marked by many glorious naval achievements of the Venetian arms—Heroic and sanguinary defence of Candia—Peace obtained by the republic by the cession of that island—New war of Venice, in concert with the empire, against the infidels—Victorious and brilliant career of the republican arms—Conquest of the Morea—The republic exhausted by her efforts—Peace of Carlowitz—The Morea retained by Venice.

WHILE the other ducal thrones of Italy were thus for the most part filled only by slothful voluptuaries, that of Savoy seemed reserved for a succession of sovereigns, whose fearless activity and political talents constantly placed their characters in brilliant contrast with the indolence and imbecility of their despicable contemporaries. The house of Savoy owes its progressive and successful elevation, from petty foundations to regal dignity, more to the personal abilities of its chiefs, than perhaps any other royal family in Europe. Its long line of princes is very thickly studded with able captains and skilful statesmen, who were the artificers of their own greatness, and who gradually raised for their descendants the fabric of a monarchy. This fabric, indeed, was erected merely for a strong-hold of arbitrary power; and it rose in strength and increased in durability, as the ruins of Italian freedom crumbled around it. Its completion bore the same date with the destruction of whatever might excite our sympathy and merit our interest in Italian history; and the repair of its dilapidated power is not among the least evils, which the peninsula has endured in these days. The career of the dynasty of Savoy is adorned, therefore, with little moral beauty, and associated with few recollections, on which the mind can dwell with satisfaction. Yet, in comparison with other despotisms, the government of the house of Savoy merits the distinction, until our own times at least, of mildness and paternal affection towards its subjects. The race of its sovereigns has produced no monsters of tyranny and blood; and if many of them were unscrupulous in their political transactions with foreign states, history has not to reproach them with the vicious excesses of their domestic administration.

When the seventeenth century opened, the sceptre of Piedmont and Savoy was wielded, as we have formerly seen, by the duke Charles Emmanuel I., who, by his treaty with Henry IV. of France in the year 1601, exchanged his Savoyard county of Bresse for the Italian marquisate of Saluzzo. By this arrangement, Charles Emmanuel sacrificed a fertile province to acquire a barren and rocky territory; but he excluded the French from an easy access into Piedmont, and strengthened his Italian frontier. By consolidating his states, he gained a considerable advance towards the future independence of his family; and the superiority of his policy over that of Henry IV. in this transaction, occasioned the remark of a contemporary, that the French king had bargained like a pedlar, and the Savoyard duke like a king.

From this epoch, the house of Savoy became almost exclusively an Italian power, and its princes, to use the language of one of their historians, thenceforth viewed the remains of their transmontane possessions, only as a nobleman, moving in the splendour of a court, regards the ancient and neglected fief, from which he derives his title. Charles Emmanuel found that the improvement effected in the geographical posture of his states immediately increased his importance; and his alliance was courted both by France and Spain. But during the remainder of his long reign, his own restless and overweening ambition, and the natural difficulties of his situation, placed as he was with inferior strength between two mighty rivals, entailed many calamities on his dominions. He made an unsuccessful attempt in 1602 to surprise Geneva by an escalade in the night, and after a disgraceful repulse concluded a peace, which recognised the independence of that republic. Ten years later, he endeavoured, as we have seen, to wrest Montferrat from the house of Gonzaga; but being violently opposed by Spain, and weakly supported by France, he was compelled, after several years of hostilities, to submit his claim to the decision of the emperor:—or, in other words, to abandon it altogether. Such checks to his ambition were, however, of little importance, in comparison with the reverses consequent upon the share which he took in the war of the Mantuan succession, (A.D. 1628.)

In that contest he was induced, by the hope of partitioning Montferrat with the Spaniards, to unite with them against the new duke of Mantua and the French his supporters; and he suffered heavily in this alliance. When Louis XIII., at the head of a gallant army, forced the strong pass of Susa against the duke and his troops, and overran all Piedmont, Charles Emmanuel was compelled to purchase the deliverance of his states by signing a separate peace, and leaving the fortress of Susa as a pledge in the hands of the conquerors. They insisted farther that he should act offensively against his former allies; but Louis XIII. and his great minister Richelieu were no sooner recalled into France by the war against the protestants, than the versatile duke, resenting their tyranny, immediately resumed his league with Spain.

The possession of Susa rendered the French masters of the gates of the Savoyard dominions; and as soon as Richelieu had triumphantly concluded the war against the Huguenots, he returned to the Alps. He was invested by his master with a supreme military command, which disgraced his priestly functions; and he poured the forces of France again into Piedmont. The strong city of Pignerol was reduced in a few days; many other fortresses were captured and razed to their foundations; all Savoy was conquered by the French king in person; and above half of Piedmont was seized by his forces under the warlike cardinal. Amidst so many cruel reverses, oppressed by the overwhelming strength of his enemies, and abandoned by his Spanish allies, who made no vigorous efforts to arrest the progress of the French, Charles Emmanuel suddenly breathed his last, after a reign of fifty years, (A.D. 1630.) He was regarded by his contemporaries as a consummate politician and an accomplished captain. The praise of generalship may be accorded him; but the glare of talent which dazzled his times has vanished, and the admirable politician appears only as a restless intriguer.

Victor Amadeus I., his eldest son and successor, was the husband of Christina, daughter of Henry IV. of France, and therefore disposed to ally himself with her country. Almost immediately after his accession to the ducal crown, he entered into negotiations with Richelieu, which terminated in a truce. In the following year, the general peace, which concluded the war with the Mantuan succession, was signed at Chierasco. (A.D. 1631.) By this treaty, the new duke of Savoy recovered all his dominions except Pignerol, which he was compelled to cede to the French; who, although Richelieu restored Susa to Victor Amadeus, thus retained possession of the passes of the Alps by Briançon and the valley of Exilles. Victor Amadeus was not inferior to his father either in courage or abilities; but he was not equally restless and intriguing. Submitting to circumstances beyond his control, he endured the ascendancy which France had acquired over his states, and the yet more galling pride of Richelieu, with temper and prudence. To the close of his short reign, he maintained with good faith a close alliance with Louis XIII.; which indeed it was scarcely optional with him to have rejected, and which, in 1634, involved him, as an auxiliary, in a new war undertaken by Richelieu against the house of Austria.

The death of Victor Amadeus in 1637, while this contest was yet raging, was the prelude to still heavier calamities for his house and his subjects, than either had known for nearly a century. He left two infant sons, the eldest of whom dying almost immediately after him, the succession devolved upon the other, Charles Emmanuel II., a boy of four years of age. By his testament, Victor Amadeus committed the regency of his states, and the care of his children, to his duchess Christina. The government of that princess was in the outset assailed by the secret machinations of Richelieu, and by the open hostility of the brothers of her late husband. Richelieu designed to imprison the sister, and to despoil the nephew of his own master; and he would have annexed their states to the French monarchy, under the plea that the care of the young prince and the regency of his duchy belonged of right to Louis XIII., as his maternal uncle. When the vigilance of Christina defeated the intention of the cardinal to surprise her at Vercelli, the sister of Louis XIII. had still to endure all the despotic insolence of her brother's minister. The conduct of her husband's relations left her however no alternative, but, by submission to Richelieu, to purchase the aid of the French against them.

Both the brothers of Victor Amadeus, the cardinal Maurice, and prince Thomas (founder of the branch of Savoy-Carignan), had quarrelled with the late duke, and withdrawn from his court to embrace the party of his enemies; the one entered the service of the emperor, the other that of the king of Spain in the low countries. On the death of Victor Amadeus, they returned to Piedmont only to trouble the administration of Christina by themselves laying claim to the regency; and at length, on her resisting their pretensions, they openly asserted them in arms. The two princes were supported by the house of Austria; the duchess-regent was protected by France; and the whole country of Savoy and Piedmont was at once plunged into the aggravated horrors of foreign and civil war. (A.D. 1639.) In the first year of this unhappy contest, the capital was delivered into the hands of prince Thomas by his partizans; and the regent, escaping with difficulty on this surprise into the citadel of Turin, was compelled to consign the defence of that fortress to the French, who treacherously retained the deposit for eighteen years. In like manner, they acquired possession of several important places; the Spaniards on their part became masters of others; and while the regent and her brothers-in-law were vainly contending for the government of Piedmont, they were betrayed alike by the ill faith and designing ambition of their respective protectors.

A reconciliation in the ducal family was at length effected by the tardy discovery that mutual injuries could terminate only in common ruin. The two princes deserted the party of Spain, and succeeded in recovering for their house most of the fortresses which they had aided the Spaniards in reducing. The duchess-mother retained the regency; and the princes were gratified with the same appanages by which she had originally offered to purchase their friendship. Still the French remained all-powerful in Piedmont; and if death had not interrupted the projects of Richelieu, it is probable that the ducal house of Savoy would have been utterly sacrificed to his skilful and unprincipled policy, and that its dominions would have been permanently annexed to the monarchy of France. Even under the government of his more pacific successor, Mazarin, it was not until the year 1657 that the French garrison was withdrawn from the citadel of Turin; and this act of justice was only extorted from that minister as the price of his niece's marriage into the ducal family of Savoy. The exhaustion of Spain, and the internal troubles of France, had totally prevented the active prosecution in northern Italy of the long war between those powers. But the embers of hostility were not wholly extinguished in Piedmont until the peace of the Pyrenees, by which Charles Emmanuel II. recovered all his duchy except Pignerol and its Alpine passes, and these the French still retained, (A.D. 1659)

The termination of the minority of Charles Emmanuel II. in 1648, had put an end to the intrigues of his uncles. But the duke continued to submit to the ambitious and able control of his mother until her death; and his subsequent reign was in no respect brilliant His states, however, after the treaty of the Pyrenees, enjoyed a long interval of repose; and though the early close of his life in 1675 subjected them to another minority, it proved neither turbulent nor calamitous, as his own had done. His son, the celebrated Victor Amadeus II., was only nine years old when he nominally commenced his reign under the regency of his mother. This princess, a daughter of the French house of Nemours, had all the ambition without the talents which had distinguished the duchess Christina. Surrounded by French favourites and by the partizans of that nation, she was wholly subservient to the will of Louis XIV.; and Victor Amadeus, on attaining the age of manhood, gave the first indications of the consummate political ability for which he became afterwards so famous, by his decent address in dispossessing his reluctant parent and her faction of all influence in public affairs, without having recourse to actual violence, (A.D. 1689.)

The policy of the duke soon excited the suspicion of Louis XIV.; and after exhausting all the resources of negotiation and intrigue for some years, to gain him over to his purpose of wresting Milan from the Spaniards, the French monarch resolved to disarm him. But Victor Amadeus penetrated his designs, and anticipated their execution. He was too good a politician, and too sensible of his own weakness, not to discover that, if he consented to open a free passage to Louis XIV. through his dominions, and to aid him in effecting the conquest of Lombardy, he should speedily be despoiled in his turn, and reduced to the rank of a vassal of the French crown. He therefore acceded to the league of Augsburg between the empire, England, Spain, and Holland; and his subjects eagerly seconded him in his resolution rather to encounter the dangers of a contest with the gigantic power of France, than to submit without a struggle to the imperious and humiliating demands of Louis. (A.D. 1090.)

The commencement of the war in Piedmont was marked by a torrent of misfortune, which might have overwhelmed a prince of less fortitude than Victor Amadeus with sudden despair. Although he was joined by a Spanish army at the opening of hostilities, the French, who commanded the gates of Italy by the possession of Pignerol, had already assembled in force in Piedmont. They were led by Catinat, who deserves to be mentioned among the most accomplished and scientific captains of his own or of any age; and the superior abilities of this great commander triumphed over the military talents of the young duke. At the battle of Stafarda in the first campaign, the allies were totally defeated; and great part both of Savoy and Piedmont was almost immediately afterwards reduced by the conquerors. Victor Amadeus was however undismayed; he continued the war with energy and skill; and the support of his allies and his own activity had the effect of balancing the fortune of the contest. Penetrating into France, he was even enabled to retaliate upon his enemies by this diversion, for the ravage of his dominions; and although Catinat, in the fourth campaign, inflicted at Marsaglia upon the Piedmontese, Austrian and Spanish armies under the duke in person and the famous prince Eugene, a yet more calamitous and memorable defeat than that at Stafarda, the allies speedily recovered from this disaster.

But it comes not within my purpose to repeat the often told tale of military operations, which belong to the general history of Europe. After six years of incessant warfare, Victor Amadeus was still in an attitude to render his neutrality an important object for France to gain, and one which he had himself every reason to desire. So that it could be attained with advantage to himself, he was little scrupulous in abandoning his allies; and the conditions which he extorted from Louis XIV. had all the results of victory. By the separate peace concluded between France and Savoy at Turin, Louis XIV. abandoned the possession of Pignerol and restored all his conquests in Savoy and Piedmont; but the most material stipulation of the treaty was the neutrality of all Italy, to which the contracting parties equally bound themselves to oblige all other powers to accede, (A.D. 1696.) To enforce this article, Victor Amadeus did not hesitate to join his arms to those of France against his former allies; and the entrance of his forces, in conjunction with the army of Catinat, into the Milanese territories, immediately compelled the emperor and the king of Spain to consent to a suspension of arms in the peninsula.

The allies of Victor Amadeus might justly reproach him with a desertion of their cause, and perhaps even with the aggravation of perfidy; but he deserved the gratitude of Italy, if not for his selfish policy, at least for its fruits. In closing the gates of his own frontiers, he had skilfully provided also for the repose of the peninsula and its evacuation by the French. All Italy regarded him as a liberator; the security of his own dominions was effected; and his power and consequence were prodigiously augmented. Thus, by establishing the independence of his states, he prepared the claim of his house to the assumption of the royal title among the powers of Europe, to which he elevated it in the beginning of the new century.

The increasing power of the sovereigns of Piedmont was a foreboding of evil for the only republic of the middle ages, which had partially escaped the storms of despotism in that quarter of Italy; and Genoa had already gained, during the seventeenth century, sufficient experience of the dangers of her vicinity, to the princes of the house of Savoy. In the Grison war between France and the house of Austria, the republic was involved by her dependence upon Spain; and the share which she took in the contest enabled the duke of Savoy, then in alliance with France, to draw down the weight of the French arms upon her. Besides being actuated by the usual rapacity of his ambition, with the hope of annexing the Genoese territory to his states, Charles Emmanuel I. had several causes of offence against the republic. Her rulers had before given assistance to the Spaniards against him; they had attempted to controul him in the purchase of the fief of Zucarel from the family of Carretto; and the populace of Genoa had insulted him by defacing his portrait in their city during the excesses of a riot. He therefore pointed out Genoa to his allies for an easy and important conquest; and while he overran the Ligurian country, a French army of 30,000 men under the constable de Lesdiguieres advanced to the siege of the republican capital. Though the Genoese were unprovided against this sudden attack, they were animated by the brave spirit, and the eloquence of one of their fellow-citizens, a member of the illustrious house of Doria, to oppose a firm resistance to the besiegers; and their gallant defence of the city was converted into a triumph, at the moment when they were reduced to extremity, (A.D. 1625.) A powerful Spanish armament, equipped with unusual vigour, arrived to their succour from Naples and Milan; the French were compelled to raise the siege; and the peace, which shortly followed these hostilities, served only to cover the duke of Savoy with the disgrace of merited failure, in his designs against the existence of the republic.

The secret hostility which Charles Emmanuel cherished against Genoa, menaced her, a few years later, with more imminent perils; since the revengeful spirit of the duke was associated with the discontent of a large party in the republic. I have formerly noticed the constitution of the sovereign oligarchy of Genoa, and its tendency, by the extinction of some noble houses, and the reduction of numbers in others, to narrow the circle of political rights. The surviving body, meanwhile, were sparing in the use of the law, which authorized them to admit ten new families annually to a share in their privileges of sovereignty. The senate either began to elude it altogether, or applied it only to childless or aged individuals. Thus, before the middle of the seventeenth century, the number of persons whose names appeared in the libro d'oro—the golden volume of privileged nobility—had dwindled to about seven hundred. A law was then passed, by which the whole of these exclusive proprietors of the rights of citizenship thenceforth took their seats in the great council, on reaching the age of manhood, instead of entering it by rotation, as had formerly been the practice, when the republic was represented by a more comprehensive aristocracy.

While the arrogance and the individual importance of the members of the oligarchy were increased in proportion to this diminution in their numbers, another class, that of the unprivileged aristocracy of birth and wealth, had multiplied in the state. Many ancient houses, possessors of rural fiefs in Liguria, and invested with titles of nobility, had been originally omitted in the roll of citizenship; many other families of newer pretensions had since acquired riches and distinction by commercial industry, and other accidents of fortune; and the union of all these constituted an order, which rivalled the oligarchy in the usual sources of pride, and far outweighed them in numbers. Affected superiority and contempt on the one hand, and mortification and envy on the other, produced reciprocal hatred between these branches of the Genoese aristocracy; and their divisions inspired the duke of Savoy with the hope of plunging the state into an anarchy, by which he might profit.

Pursuing his master's views, the ambassador of Charles Emmanuel at Genoa, selected a wealthy merchant of the unprivileged aristocracy, Giulio Cesare Vachero, for the agitator and leader of a conspiracy to overthrow the oligarchical constitution. (A.D. 1628.) Vachero, although engaged in the occupation of commerce, aspired to move in the sphere of nobility. His immense riches, his numerous retinue, his splendid establishment, rivalled the magnificence of the Fregosi, the Adorni, the popolani grandi of other days. He always appeared armed and in martial costume,—the characteristics of the gentleman of the times; he was surrounded by bravos; and he unscrupulously employed these desperate men in the atrocious gratification of his pride and his vengeance. He found sufficient occupation for their poniards in the numerous petty affronts, which the privileged nobles delighted to heap on a person of his condition. Vachero was stung to the soul by all the scorn and disdain which the highly-born affect for upstart and unwarranted pretensions: by the contemptuous denial of the courtesy of a passing salutation, the supercilious stare, the provoking smile of derision, the taunting inuendo, the jest, the sneer. Every one of these slights or insults offered to himself or his wife was washed out in the blood of the noble offenders.

But all these covert assassinations could not satiate the revengeful spirit, and heal the rankling irritation of Vachero; and he was easily instigated by the arts of the Savoyard ambassador to organize a plot, and to place himself at its head, for the destruction of the oligarchy. He knew that his discontent was shared by all the citizens like himself, whose names had not been admitted into the libro d'oro; and he reckoned on the co-operation of very many of the feudal signors of Liguria, whose ancient houses had never been inserted in that register, and who found their consequence eclipsed in the city, by their detested and more fortunate rivals of the oligarchy. He readily induced a numerous party to embrace his design; he secretly increased the force of his retainers and bravos; and he lavished immense sums among the lower people, to secure their fidelity without intrusting them with his plans. The day was already named for the attack of the palace of government: it was determined to overpower the foreign guard; to cast the senators from the windows; to massacre all the individuals embraced in the privileged order; to change the constitution of the republic; and finally, to invest Vachero with the supreme authority of the state, by the title of doge, and under the protection of the duke of Savoy. But at the moment when the conspiracy was ripe for execution, it was betrayed to the government by a retainer of Vachero, who had been appointed to act a subordinate share in it. Vachero himself, and a few other leading personages in the plot, were secured before the alarm was given to the rest, who immediately fled. The guilt of Vachero and his accomplices was clearly established; the proofs against them were even supported by the conduct of the duke of Savoy, who openly avowed himself the protector of their enterprise; and notwithstanding his arrogant threat of revenging their punishment upon the republic, the senate did not hesitate to order their immediate execution.

The insolent menaces of Charles Emmanuel were vain; and the firmness of the Genoese government produced no material consequences. During the distractions which closed his own reign, and which, filling that of his son, extended through the minority of his grandsons, the republic remained undisturbed by the aggressions of the house of Savoy. In this long period of above forty years, the repose of Genoa was disturbed neither by any other foreign hostilities, nor by intestine commotions. (A.D. 1072.) A second war, which at length broke out between the republic and the duchy of Savoy, during the reign of Charles Emmanuel II., scarcely merits our notice, for its circumstances and its conclusion were alike insignificant; and during the remainder of the seventeenth century, the Genoese oligarchy were only startled from their dream of pride and security by a single event:—the most humiliating, until our own times at least, in the long annals of their republic.

When Louis XIV. became master of Casal by purchase from the duke of Mantua he demanded of the republic of Genoa permission to establish a depot at the port of Savona, for the free supply of salt to the inhabitants of his new city, and the transit of warlike stores and recruits for his garrison. The Genoese government were sufficiently acquainted with the character of the French monarch, to anticipate that their compliance with this demand would terminate in his appropriating the port of Savona altogether to himself; and cautiously exerting the option of refusal which they unquestionably possessed, they eluded the application. With equal right and more boldness, they fitted out a few galleys to guard their coasts against any surprise, and to protect their revenue on salt. Louis imperiously required them to disarm this squadron; and then, driven beyond all the limits of endurance, and justly incensed at such an insult upon the independence of the republic, the senate treated the summons with contempt.

But the oligarchy of Genoa had not sufficiently measured the weakness of their state, or the implacable and unbounded pride of the powerful tyrant. A French armament of fourteen sail of the line, with a long train of frigates, galleys and bomb ketches, suddenly appeared before Genoa, and a furious bombardment of three days, in which fifty thousand shells and carcases are said to have been thrown into the place, reduced to a heap of ruins half the numerous and magnificent palaces, which had obtained for Genoa the appellation of THE PROUD. The senate were compelled to save the remains of their capital from total destruction by an unqualified submission; and the terms dictated by the arrogance of the French monarch, obliged the doge and four of the principal senators, to repair in their robes of state to Paris, to sue for pardon and to supplicate his clemency. The epithets of glory have often been prostituted on the character of Louis XIV., by those who are easily dazzled with the glare of false splendour; but of all the wholesale outrages upon humanity which disgraced the detestable ambition of that heartless destroyer of his species, this unprovoked assault upon a defenceless people, merely to gratify his insatiable vanity, was—if we except the horrible devastation of the Palatinate—the most barbarous and wanton.

While Genoa was either wholly subservient to the influence of Spain, with difficulty repulsing the machinations of the princes of Savoy, or enduring all the insulting arrogance of France; her ancient rival was holding her political course with more pretensions to independence and dignity. Throughout the age before us, Venice seemed roused to the exertion of the few remains of her ancient spirit and strength. Starting with renewed vigour from the languor and obscurity of the preceding century, the republic evinced a proud resolution to maintain her prescriptive rights, and even in some measure aspired to assert the lost independence of Italy. Her efforts in this latter respect, indeed, deserve to be mentioned, rather for the courage which dictated them, than for their results. The relative force of the states of Europe had too essentially changed, the commercial foundations of her own prosperity were too irretrievably ruined, to render it possible that she should rear her head again above other powers of the second order, or become the protectress and successful champion of the peninsula. But, in the seventeenth century, the annals of Venice were at least not stained with disgrace. Even her losses, in a protracted and unequal contest with the Turks, were redeemed from shame by many brilliant acts of heroism in her unavailing defence; and the unfortunate issue of one war was balanced by the happier results of a second. But it was in the assertion of some of her long recognised pretensions, that the firmness of the republic was conspicuous, and her success unalloyed.

The first of the struggles, in which Venice was called upon to engage in this century, was produced, soon after its opening, by that violent attempt of pope Paul V., to which I have before alluded, to revive the monstrous and exploded doctrine of the papal jurisdiction and supremacy over the temporal affairs of the world, (A.D. 1605.) The Venetians had, even in the dark ages, been remarkable for their freedom from the trammels of superstition, and consistent in repelling the encroachments of ecclesiastical power. Upon no occasion would the senate either permit the publication or execution of any papal decree in their territories, until it had received their previous sanction; or suffer an appeal to the court of Rome from any of their subjects, except by their own authority, and through the ambassador of the republic. The jurisdiction of the council of ten was as despotic and final over the Venetian clergy, as over all other classes in the state; and while ecclesiastics were rigidly excluded from all interference in political affairs, and from the exercise of any civil functions, the right of the secular tribunals to judge them in every case not purely spiritual was a principle, from which the government never departed either in theory or practice. Of all the extravagant privileges claimed by the Romish church for its militia, the exemption of the ecclesiastical body from taxation (unless as the immediate act of the popes) was the only one recognized by the Venetian government; and to annul this immunity was a project which had more than once been entertained.

With a spirit similar to that which retained the clergy under due subjection, universal religious toleration was a steady maxim of the Venetian senate. The public and peaceable worship of the Musulman, the Jew, the Greek, the Armenian, had always been equally permitted in the republican dominions; and in latter times even the protestant sects had met in the capital and provinces with a like indulgence. The iniquitous principles of the oligarchical administration forbid us from attributing to its conduct in these respects any higher or more enlightened motive, than the interested and necessary policy of a commercial state. But it is a striking proof of the ability and stern vigilance of this government, that, notwithstanding its universal toleration and rejection of ecclesiastical control, no pretence was left for the popes to impugn its zealous fidelity to the Romish church; and that, at a time when all Europe was convulsed by the struggle of religious opinions, Venice alone could receive into her corrupted bosom the elements of discord, without shaking the foundations of her established faith, or sustaining the slightest shock to her habitual tranquillity.

The fierce temper with which Paul V. seated himself on the papal throne, and the systematic determination of the Venetian senate to submit to no ecclesiastical usurpations, could not fail to bring the republic into collision with so rash and violent a pontiff. Accordingly Paul V. had scarcely commenced his reign, when he conceived offence at the refusal of the senate to provoke a war with the Turks, by assisting the Hungarians at his command with subsidies against the infidels. His dissatisfaction with the republic was increased by her obstinacy in levying duty upon all merchandize entering the papal ports in the Adriatic:—a matter in which, assuredly, religion was in nowise interested; and it reached its height when the senate passed a law, or rather revived an old one, forbidding the further alienation of immoveable property in favour of religious foundations; which indeed, even in their states, were already possessed of overgrown wealth.

At this juncture the council of ten, acting upon its established principle of subjecting priests to secular jurisdiction, caused two ecclesiastics, a canon of Vicenza, named Sarraceno, and an abbot of Nervesa, to be successively arrested and thrown into prison, to await their trials for offences with which they were charged. Their alleged crimes were of the blackest enormity: rape in the one case; assassination, poisonings, and parricide in the other. The pope, as if the rights of the church had been violently outraged by these arrests, summoned the doge and senate to deliver over the two priests to the spiritual arm, on pain of excommunication; and he seized the occasion to demand, under the same penalty, the repeal of the existing regulations against the increase of ecclesiastical edifices and property. But the doge and senate, positively refusing to retract their measures, treated the papal menaces with the contempt which they deserved; and Paul V. then struck them, their capital, and their whole republic with excommunication and interdict, (A.D. 1606.)

The Venetian government endured his anathemas, so appalling to the votaries of superstition, with unshaken firmness. In reply to the papal denunciations of the divine wrath against the republic, they successfully published repeated and forcible appeals to the justice of their cause, and to the common sense of the world. The general sentiment of catholic Europe responded to their arguments; and their own subjects, filled with indignation at the unprovoked sentence against the state, zealously seconded their spirit. In private the doge had not hesitated to hold out to the papal nuncio an alarming threat, that the perseverance of his holiness in violent measures would impel the republic to dissolve her connexion altogether with the Roman see; and the open procedure of the senate was scarcely less bold. On pain of death, all parochial ministers and monks in the Venetian states were commanded to pay no regard to the interdict, and to continue to perform the offices of religion as usual. The secular clergy yielded implicit obedience to the decree, and when the Jesuits, Capuchins, and other monastic orders, endeavoured to qualify their allegiance, between the pope and the republic, by making a reservation against the performance of mass, they were immediately deprived of their possessions, and expelled from the Venetian territories.

The pope, finding his spiritual weapons ineffectual against the constancy of the Venetians, showed an inclination to have recourse to temporal arms. He levied troops, and endeavoured to engage Philip III. of Spain and other princes in the support of his authority. At the same time, both the Spanish monarch and Henry IV. of France, the ally of the republic, began to interest themselves in a quarrel, which nearly concerned all catholic powers, and threatened Europe with commotion. In reality, both sovereigns aspired to the honour of being the arbiter of the difference. But the feint of arming to second the pope, by which Philip III. hoped to terrify the republic into submitting to his mediation, had only the effect of determining the senate to prefer the interposition of his rival; and Henry IV. became the zealous negotiator between the pope and the republic.

Paul V. discovered at length that Spain had no serious resolution to support him by arms, and that, without the application of a force which he could not command, it was vain to expect submission from so inflexible a body as the Venetian oligarchy. He was therefore reduced to the most humiliating compromise of his boasted dignity. (A.D. 1607.) Without obtaining a single concession on the point in dispute, he was obliged to revoke his spiritual sentences. The doge and senate would not even receive an absolution; they refused to alter their decree against the alienation of property in favour of the church; and though they consigned the two imprisoned ecclesiastics to the disposal of Henry IV., they accompanied this act with a formal declaration, that was intended only as a voluntary mark of their respect for that monarch their ally, and to be in no degree construed into an abandonment of their right and practice of subjecting their clergy to secular jurisdiction. Even their deference for Henry IV. could not prevail over their resentment and suspicion of the banished Jesuits: they peremptorily refused to reinstate that order in its possessions; and it was not until after the middle of the century, that the Jesuits obtained admission again into the states of the republic. Thus, with the signal triumph of Venice, terminated a struggle, happily a bloodless one, which was not less remarkable for the firmness of the republic, than important for its general effects in crushing the pretensions of papal tyranny. For its issue may assuredly be regarded as having relieved all Roman Catholic states from future dread of excommunication and interdict:—and therefore from the danger of spiritual engines, impotent in themselves, and formidable only when unresisted.

With the same unyielding spirit which characterized their resistance to papal and ecclesiastical usurpation, the Venetian senate resolved to tolerate no infringement upon the tyrannical pretension of their own republic to the despotic sovereignty of the Adriatic gulf. Before the contest with Paul V., their state had already been seriously incommoded by the piracies of the Uscochi. This community, originally formed of Christian inhabitants of Dalmatia and Croatia, had been driven, in the sixteenth century, by the perpetual Turkish invasions of their provinces, to the fastness of Clissa, whence they successfully retaliated upon their infidel foes by incursions into the Ottoman territories. At length, overpowered by the Turks, and dispersed from their stronghold, these Uscochi, or refugees, as their name implies in the Dalmatian tongue, were collected by Ferdinand, archduke of Austria (afterwards emperor), and established in the maritime town of Segna to guard that post against the Turks. In their new station, which, on the land side, was protected from access by mountains and forests, while numerous islets and intricate shallows rendered it difficult of approach from the sea, the Uscochi betook themselves to piracy; and, for above seventy years, their light and swift barks boldly infested the Adriatic with impunity. Their first attacks were directed against the infidels; but irritated by the interference of the Venetians, who, as sovereigns of the gulf, found themselves compelled by the complaints and threats of the Porte to punish their freebooting enterprizes, they began to extend their depredations to the commerce of the republic.

It was to little purpose that the senate called upon the Austrian government to restrain its lawless subjects: their representations were either eluded altogether, or failed in obtaining any effectual satisfaction. The Uscochi, a fearless and desperate band, recruited by outlaws and men of abandoned lives, became more audacious by the connivance of Austria; and the republic was obliged to maintain a small squadron constantly at sea to protect her commerce against them. At length, after having recourse alternately, for above half a century, to fruitless negotiations with Austria, and insufficient attempts to chastise the pirates, the republic seriously determined to put an end to their vexatious hostilities and increasing insolence. The capture of a Venetian galley and the massacre of its crew in 1615, and an irruption of the Uscochi into Istria, brought affairs to a crisis. The Austrian government, then directed by the archduke Ferdinand of Styria, instead of giving satisfaction for these outrages, demanded the free navigation of the Adriatic for its vessels; and the senate found an appeal to arms the only mode of preserving its efficient sovereignty over the gulf. The Venetian troops made reprisals on the Austrian territory; and an open war commenced between the archduke and the republic.

This contest was soon associated, by the interference of Spain, with the hostilities then carried on between that monarchy and the duke of Savoy in northern Italy respecting Montferrat. For protection against the enmity of the two branches of the house of Austria, Venice united herself with Savoy, and largely subsidized that state. She even sought more distant allies; and a league offensive and defensive was signed between her and the seven united provinces. Notwithstanding the difference of religious faith which, in that age, constituted in itself a principle of political hostility, the two republics found a bond of union stronger than this repulsion, in their common reasons for opposing the Spanish power. They engaged to afford each other a reciprocal assistance in money, vessels, or men, whenever menaced with attack; and in fulfilment of this treaty, a strong body of Dutch troops arrived in the Adriatic. Before the disembarkation of this force, the Venetians had already gained some advantages in the Austrian provinces on the coasts of the gulf; and the archduke was induced by the appearance of the Dutch, and his projects in Germany, to open negotiations for a general peace in northern Italy.

The same treaty terminated the wars of the house of Austria respecting Montferrat and the Uscochi. Ferdinand of Austria gave security for the dispersion of the pirates, whom he had protected; and thus the Venetian republic was finally delivered from the vexatious and lawless depredations of these freebooters, who had so long annoyed her commerce and harassed her subjects, (A.D. 1617.) It does not appear that the force of this singular race of pirates, who had thus risen into historical notice, ever exceeded a thousand men; but their extraordinary hardihood and ferocity, their incessant enterprises and activity, their inaccessible position, and the connivance of Austria, had rendered them formidable enemies. Their depredations, and the constant expense of petty armaments against them, were estimated to have cost the Venetians in thirty years a loss of more than 20,000,000 of gold ducats; and no less a question than the security of the dominion of the republic over the Adriatic was decided by the war against them.

Although Spain and Venice had not been regularly at war, the tyrannical ascendancy exercised by the Spanish court over the affairs of Italy, occasioned the Venetians to regard that power with particular apprehension and enmity; and the spirit shown by the senate in the late contest had filled the Spanish government with implacable hatred towards the republic. By her alliances and her whole procedure, Venice had declared against the house of Austria, and betrayed her disposition to curb the alarming and overspreading authority of both its branches in the peninsula. The haughty ministers of Philip III. secretly nourished projects of vengeance against the state, which had dared to manifest a systematic hostility to the Spanish dominion; and they are accused, even in apparent peace, of having regarded the republic as an enemy whom it behoved them to destroy. At the epoch of the conclusion of the war relative to Montferrat and the Uscochi, the duke d'Ossuna was viceroy of Naples, don Pedro di Toledo governor of Milan, and the marquis of Bedemar ambassador at Venice from the court of Madrid. To the hostility entertained against the republic by these three ministers, the two former of whom governed the Italian possessions of Spain with almost regal independence, has usually been attributed the formation, with the connivance of the court of Madrid, of one of the most atrocious and deep-laid conspiracies on record. The real character of this mysterious transaction must ever remain among the unsolved problems of history; for even the circumstances, which were partially suffered by the council of ten to transpire, were so imperfectly explained, and so liable to suspicion from the habitual iniquity of their policy, as to have given rise to a thousand various and contradictory versions of the same events. Of these I shall attempt to collect only such as are scarcely open to doubt.

The Venetians had no reason to hope that the exasperation of the Spanish government, at the part which they had taken in the late war in Italy, would die away with the termination of hostilities; and it appeared to the world a consequence of the enmity of the court of Madrid towards the republic, that the duke d'Ossuna, the viceroy of Naples, continued his warlike equipments in that kingdom with undiminished activity, notwithstanding the signature of peace, (A.D. 1618.) The viceroy, indeed, pretended that his naval armaments were designed against the infidels; and when the court of Madrid recalled the royal Spanish fleet from the coasts of Italy, the duke d'Ossuna sent the Neapolitan squadron to sea under a flag emblazoned with his own family arms. But it was difficult to suppose either, that a viceroy dared to hoist his personal standard unsanctioned by his sovereign, and would be suffered to engage in a private war against the Ottoman empire, or that he would require for that purpose the charts of the Venetian lagunes, and the flat-bottomed vessels fitted for their navigation, which he busily collected. The republic accordingly manifested serious alarm, and sedulously prepared for defence.

Affairs were in this state, when one morning several strangers were found suspended from the gibbets of the square of St. Mark. The public consternation increased when, on the following dawn, other bodies were also found hanging on the same fatal spot, also of strangers. It was at the same time whispered that numerous arrests had filled the dungeons of the council of ten with some hundreds of criminals; and there was too certain proof that many persons had been privately drowned in the canals of Venice. To these fearful indications that the state had been alarmed by some extraordinary danger, the terrors of which were magnified by their obscurity, were shortly added further rumours that several foreigners serving in the fleet had been poniarded, hanged, or cast into the sea. The city was then filled with the most alarming reports: that a conspiracy of long duration had been discovered; that its object was to massacre the nobility, to destroy the republic, to deliver the whole capital to flames and pillage; that the Spanish ambassador was the mover of the horrible plot. Venice was filled with indignation and terror; yet the impenetrable council of ten preserved the most profound silence, neither confirming nor contradicting the general belief. The life of the marquis of Bedemar was violently threatened by the populace; he retired from Venice; the senate received a new ambassador from Spain without any signs of displeasure; and, finally, it was not until five months after the executions, that the government commanded solemn thanksgiving to be offered up to the Almighty for the preservation of the state from the dangers which had threatened its existence.

Of the extent of these dangers nothing was ever certainly known; but amongst the persons executed the most conspicuous was ascertained to be a French naval captain of high reputation for ability and courage in his vocation, Jacques Pierre, who, after a life passed in enterprises of a doubtful or piratical character, had apparently deserted the service of the viceroy of Naples to embrace that of the republic. This man, and a brother adventurer, one Langlade, who had been employed in the arsenal in the construction of petards and other fireworks, were absent from Venice with the fleet when the other executions took place; and they were suddenly put to death while on this service. Two other French captains named Regnault and Bouslart, with numerous foreigners, principally of the same nation, who had lately been taken into the republican service, were privately tortured and executed in various ways in the capital; and altogether two hundred and sixty officers and other military adventurers are stated to have perished by the hands of the executioner for their alleged share in the conspiracy. The vengeance or shocking policy of the council of ten proceeded yet farther; and so careful were that body to bury every trace of this inexplicable affair in the deepest oblivion, that Antoine Jaffier, also a French captain, and other informers, who had revealed the existence of a plot, though at first rewarded, were all in the sequel either known to have met a violent death, or mysteriously disappeared altogether. Of the three Spanish ministers, to whom it has been customary to assign the origin of the conspiracy, the two principal were distinguished by opposite fates. The marquis of Bedemar, after the termination of his embassy, found signal political advancement, and finished by obtaining a cardinal's hat, by the interest of his court with the holy see. But the duke d'Ossuna, after being removed from his viceroyalty, was disgraced on suspicion of having designed to renounce his allegiance, and to place the crown of Naples on his own head; and he died in prison.

Whether the safety of Venice had really been endangered or not by the machinations of Spain, the measures of that power were observed by the senate with a watchful and jealous eye; and, for many years, the policy of the republic was constantly employed in endeavours to counteract the projects of the house of Austria. In 1619, the Venetians perceived with violent alarm that the court of Madrid, under pretence of protecting the catholics of the Valteline against their rulers, the protestants of the Grison confederation, was labouring to acquire the possession of that valley, which by connecting the Milanese states with the Tyrol, would cement the dominions of the Spanish and German dynasties of the Austrian family. The establishment of this easy communication was particularly dangerous for the Venetians; because it would envelope their states, from the Lisonzo to the Po, with an unbroken chain of hostile posts, and would intercept all direct intercourse with Savoy and the territories of France. The senate eagerly therefore negotiated the league between these two last powers and their republic, which, in 1623, was followed by the Grison war against the house of Austria. This contest produced little satisfactory fruits for the Venetians; and it did not terminate before the Grisons, though they recovered their sovereignty over the Valteline, had themselves embraced the party of Spain.

The Grison war had not closed, when Venice was drawn, by her systematic opposition to the Spanish power, into a more important quarrel:—that of the Mantuan succession, in which she of course espoused the cause of the Gonzaga of Nevers. In this struggle the republic, who sent an army of 20,000 men into the field on her Lombard frontiers, experienced nothing but disgrace; and the senate were but too happy to find their states left, by the peace of Chierasco in 1631, precisely in the same situation as before the war; while the prince whom they had supported remained seated on the throne of Mantua. This pacification reconciled the republic with the house of Austria, and terminated her share in the Italian wars of the seventeenth century. Her efforts to promote the deliverance of the peninsula from the Spanish power, can scarcely be said to have met with success; nor was the rapid decline of that monarchy, which had already commenced, hastened, perhaps, by her hostility. But she had displayed remarkable energy in the policy of her counsels; and the recovery of her own particular independence was at least triumphantly effected. So completely were her pretensions to the sovereignty of the Adriatic maintained that, when, in the year 1630, just before the conclusion of the Mantuan war, a princess of the Spanish dynasty wished to pass by sea from Naples to Trieste, to espouse the son of the emperor, the senate refused to allow the Spanish squadron to escort her, as an infringement upon their right of excluding every foreign armament from the gulf; but they gallantly offered their own fleet for her service. The Spanish government at first rejected the offer; but the Venetians, says Giannone, boldly declared that, if the Spaniards were resolved to prefer a trial of force to their friendly proposal, the infanta must fight her way to her wedding through fire and smoke. The haughty court of Madrid was compelled to yield; and the Venetian admiral, Antonio Pisani, then gave the princess a convoy in splendid bearing to Trieste with a squadron of light galleys.

Throughout the remainder of the seventeenth century, the affairs of Venice had little connexion with those of the other Italian states; and in tracing the annals of the republic, our attention is wholly diverted to the eastern theatre of her struggles against the Ottoman power. It was a sudden and overwhelming aggression, which first broke the long interval of peace between the Turkish and Venetian governments. Under pretence of taking vengeance upon the knights of Malta, for the capture of some Turkish vessels, the Porte fitted out an enormous expedition; and three hundred and forty-eight galleys and other vessels of war, with an immense number of transports, having on board a land-force of 50,000 men, issued from the Dardanelles with the ostensible design of attacking the strong-hold of the order of St. John. (A.D. 1645.) But instead of making sail for Malta, the fleet of the sultan steered for the shores of Candia; and unexpectedly, and without any provocation, the Turkish army disembarked on that island. The Venetians, although the senate had conceived some uneasiness on the real destination of the Ottoman expedition, were little prepared for resistance; but they defended themselves against this faithless surprise with remarkable courage, and even with desperation. During a long war of twenty-five years, the most ruinous which they had ever sustained against the infidels, the Venetian senate and all classes of their subjects displayed a zealous energy and a fortitude, worthy of the best days of their republic. But the resources of Venice were no longer what they had been in the early ages of her prosperity; and although the empire of the sultans had declined from the meridian of its power, the contest was still too disproportionate between the fanatical and warlike myriads of Turkey and the limited forces of a maritime state. The Venetians, perhaps, could not withdraw from the unequal conflict with honour; but the prudent senate might easily foresee its disastrous result.

The first important operation of the Turkish army in Candia was the siege of Canea, one of the principal cities of the island. Before the end of the first campaign, the assailants had entered that place by capitulation; but so gallant was the defence that, although the garrison was composed only of two or three thousand native militia, twenty thousand Turks are said to have fallen before the walls. Meanwhile at Venice, all orders had rivalled each other in devotion and pecuniary sacrifices to preserve the most valuable colony of the state; and notwithstanding the apathy of Spain, the disorders of France and the empire, and other causes, which deprived the republic of the efficient support of Christendom against a common enemy, the senate were able to reinforce the garrisons of Candia, and to oppose a powerful fleet to the infidels. The naval force of the republic was still indeed very inferior in numbers to that of the Moslems; but this inferiority was compensated by the advantages of skill and disciplined courage; and throughout the war the offensive operations of the Venetians on the waves, strikingly displayed their superiority in maritime science and conduct. For many successive years, the Venetian squadrons assumed and triumphantly maintained their station, during the seasons of active operations, at the mouth of the Dardanelles, and blockaded the straits and the port of Constantinople. The Musulmans constantly endeavoured with furious perseverance to remove the shame of their confinement by an inferior force; but they were almost always defeated. The naval trophies of Venice were swelled by many brilliant victories, but by five in particular: in 1649 near Smyrna; in 1651 near Pares; in 1655 at the passage of the Dardanelles; and, in the two following years, at the same place. In these encounters, the exploits of the patrician families of Morosini, of Grimani, of Mocenigo, emulated the glorious deeds of their illustrious ancestors; and their successes gave temporary possession to the republic of some ports in Dalmatia, and of several islands in the Archipelago.

But, notwithstanding the devotion and courage of the Venetians on their own element, and their desperate resistance in the fortresses of Candia, the war in that island was draining the life-blood of the republic, without affording one rational hope of ultimate success. The vigilance of the Venetian squadrons could not prevent the Turks from feeding their army in Candia with desultory and perpetual reinforcements of Janissaries and other troops from the neighbouring shores of the Morea; and whenever tempests, or exhaustion, or the overwhelming strength of the Ottoman armaments, compelled the republican fleet to retire into port, the numbers of the invading army were swollen by fresh thousands. The exhaustless stream of the Ottoman population was directed with unceasing flow towards the scene of contest: the Porte was contented to purchase the acquisition of Candia by the sacrifice of hecatombs of human victims. To raise new resources, the Venetian senate were reduced to the humiliating expedient of offering the dignity of admission into their body, and the highest offices of state, to public sale: to obtain the continued means of succouring Candia, they implored the aid of all the powers of Europe. As the contest became more desperate, their entreaties met with general attention; and almost every Christian state afforded them a few reinforcements. But these were never simultaneous or numerous; and though they arrested the progress of the infidels, they only protracted the calamitous struggle.

In 1648 the Turkish army had penetrated to the walls of Candia, the capital of the island; and for twenty years they kept that city in a continued state of siege. But it was only in the year 1666, that the assaults of the infidels attained their consummation of vigour, by the debarkation of reinforcements which raised their army to 70,000 men, and on the arrival of Achmet Kiupergli, the famous Ottoman vizier, to assume in person the direction of their irresistible force. This able commander was opposed by a leader in no respect inferior to him,

Francesco Morosini, captain-general of the Venetians; and thenceforth the defence of Candia was signalized by prodigies of desperate valour, which exceed all belief. But we, in these days, are surprised to find that the Turks, in the direction of their approaches, and the employment of an immense battering train, showed a far superior skill to that of the Christians. The details of the siege of Candia belong to the history of the military art; but the general reader will best imagine the obstinacy of the defence from the fact that, in six months, the combatants exchanged thirty-two general assaults and seventeen furious sallies; that above six hundred mines were sprung; and that four thousand Christians and twenty thousand Musulmans perished in the ditches and trenches of the place.

The most numerous and the last reinforcement received by the Venetians was six thousand French troops, despatched by Louis XIV. under the dukes of Beaufort and Navailles. The characteristic rashness of their nation induced these commanders, contrary to the advice of Morosini, to hazard an imprudent sortie, in which they were totally defeated, and the former of these noblemen slain. After this disaster, no entreaty of Morosini could prevent the duke de Navailles from abandoning the defence of the city, with a precipitation as great as that which had provoked the calamity. The French re-embarked; the other auxiliaries followed their example; and Morosini was left with a handful of Venetians among a mass of blackened and untenable ruins. Thus deserted, after a glorious though hopeless resistance which has immortalized his name, Francesco Morosini ventured on his sole responsibility to conclude a treaty of peace with the vizier, which the Venetian senate, notwithstanding their jealousy of such unauthorized acts in their officers, rejoiced to confirm. The whole island of Candia, except two or three ports, was surrendered to the Turks; the republic preserved her other possessions in the Levant; and the war was thus terminated by the event of a siege, in the long course of which the incredible number of 120,000 Turks and 30,000 Christians are declared to have perished, (A.D. 1669.)

Notwithstanding the unfortunate issue of this war, the Venetian republic had not come off without honour from an unequal struggle, which had been signalized by ten naval victories, and by one of the most stubborn and brilliant defences recorded in history. Although, therefore, a prodigious expenditure of blood and treasure had utterly drained the resources of the republic, her courage was unsubdued, and her pride was even augmented by the events of the contest. The successes of the infidels had inspired less terror than indignant impatience and thirst of revenge; and the senate watched in secret for the first favourable occasion of retaliating upon the Musulmans. After the Venetian strength had been repaired by fifteen years of uninterrupted repose and prosperous industry, this occasion of vengeance was found, in the war which the Porte had declared against the empire in 1682. An offensive league was signed between the emperor, the king of Poland, the czar of Muscovy, and the Venetians. The principal stipulation of this alliance was, that each party should be guaranteed in the possession of its future conquests from the infidels; and the republic immediately fitted out a squadron of twenty-four sail of the line, and about fifty galleys, (A.D. 1684.)

There appeared but one man at Venice worthy of the chief command: that Francesco Morosini, who had so gallantly defended Candia, and whom the senate and people had rewarded with the most flagrant ingratitude. A strange and wanton accusation of cowardice was too palpably belied by every event of his public life, to be persisted in, even by the envy which his eminent reputation had provoked, and by the malignity that commonly waits upon public services, where they have been unfortunate. But a second and unprovoked charge of malversation had been followed by imprisonment. Still, however, devoting himself to his country's cause, and forgetting his private injuries, Morosini shamed his enemies by a noble revenge; and, once more at the head of the Venetian armaments, he led them to a brilliant career of victory. The chief force of the Ottoman empire was diverted to the Austrian war; and the vigorous efforts of the republican armies were feebly or unsuccessfully resisted by the divided strength of the Musulmans. In the first naval campaign, the mouth of the; Adriatic was secured by the reduction of the island of St. Maura, one of the keys of the gulf; and the neighbouring continent of Greece was invaded. In three years more, Morosini consummated his bold design of wresting the whole of the Morea from the infidels. In the course of the operations in that peninsula, the count of Königsmarck, a Swedish officer who was entrusted with the command of the Venetian land forces under the captain-general, inflicted two signal defeats in the field upon the Turkish armies. Modon, Argos, and Napoli di Romania, the capital of the Morea, successively fell after regular sieges; the capture of Corinth completed the conquest of the peninsula; and Morosini, pursuing his triumphs beyond the isthmus, finally planted the banner of St. Mark upon the smoking ruins of Athens. (A.D. 1687.)

After this uninterrupted course of victory, the republican arms were checked by an unsuccessful descent upon Negropont; where a pestilence broke out in the camp of the besiegers, and carried off, among other victims, the count of Königsmarck, who had greatly distinguished himself in the preceding campaigns, (A.D. 1688.) The abandonment of this enterprise was followed by an equally fruitless invasion of Candia; and by another expedition against the island of Scio, which was won and lost in the course of twelve months. A naval defeat occasioned this reverse; and though the superiority of the Venetian marine was afterwards redeemed by three successive victories over the Ottoman fleets, these encounters were all indecisive in their immediate consequences. At length, however, the republic found an honourable repose for her overstrained energies, which had been but too deeply impaired and exhausted by the length, and even by the victorious activity of the war. By the treaty of Carlowitz, which the republic, in concert with the empire, concluded with the Ottoman Porte, Venice retained all her conquests in the Morea (including Corinth and its isthmus), the islands of Egina and St. Maura, and some Dalmatian fortresses which she had captured; and she restored Athens and her remaining acquisitions on the Grecian continent, (A.D. 1699.)

Francesco Morosini did not survive to witness the glorious termination of the war, in which his achievements had repaired the disastrous issue of his earlier services. After the conquest of the Morea, the tardy gratitude of his country in some degree atoned for the treatment which he had suffered. He was raised by acclamation, on the first vacancy, to the ducal throne; and the jealous senate, with a rare and merited confidence, united the continued command of their armies with his new and more illustrious office of doge. He sank under age, infirmities, and fatigue, in his seventy-sixth year, while still exercising his functions of captain-general in the Morea with unremitted zeal; and with him perished the last of the patrician heroes of Venice.

CHAPTER XI. STATE OF ITALY DURING THE EIGHTEENTH CENTURY, UNTIL THE COMMENCEMENT OF THE WARS OF THE FRENCH REVOLUTION, a.d. 1700-1789.

PART I.
Death of Charles II. of Spain—Extinction of the Spanish branch of the house of Austria—Long influence of that event on the state of Italy—The disposal of the Italian provinces, regulated at the absolute will of foreign cabinets—Abject condition and confirmed degradation of the people—General sketch of the shifting aspect of the peninsula, until the peace of Aix-la-Chapelle—War of the Spanish succession—The authority of Philip V. recognized in the Spanish provinces of Italy—The Bourbon cause at first supported by Victor Amadeus II. of Savoy—His defection entails the ruin of the Bourbon interests in the peninsula—Battle of Turin—Evacuation of all Italy by the French-Neutrality of most of the Italian powers in this war—Ferdinand Charles, duke of Mantua, ruined by the reverses of his French allies—Extinction of the house of Gonzaga—Peace of Utrecht—Montferrat acquired by Victor Amadeus; and Sicily also, with the regal title—Naples, Sardinia, Milan, &c. assigned to the empire—Short period of repose for Italy, interrupted by the ambition of cardinal Alberoni, and of the Spanish court—War of the quadruple alliance—Issue of the contest—The kingdom of Sardinia (in exchange for Sicily) permanently assigned to the house of Savoy—The crowns of the Two Sicilies reunited under the empire—Peace of Italy for thirteen years—Extinction of the ducal house of Farnése at Parma—Their duchy inherited by don Carlos of Spain—Italy made the theatre of the war of the Polish election—Conquest of the Sicilies by the Spaniards—The crowns of those kingdoms received by the infant don Carlos—Peace of Vienna—Death of the emperor Charles VI.—The furious war of the Austrian succession fills Italy with rapine and havoc—Active share taken in this war by Charles Emmanuel III., king of Sardinia—His skilful and artful policy—Sanguinary campaigns in northern Italy—Peace of Aix-la-Chapelle—The independence of Italy an object of that treaty—Its abortive results upon a people without patriotism or virtue—Total insignificance of Italian history during the long peace between the treaty of Aix-la-Chapelle and the French revolution—Domestic fortunes, &c. of the different Italian states in the eighteenth century—Little separate notice required for those of Lucca—Milan and Mantua—Parma and Placentia—Naples and Sicily—Reign of the infant don Carlos over those kingdoms—His laudable efforts to promote their welfare—His errors—Succession of don Carlos to the Spanish crown (Charles III.)—Reign of Ferdinand IV. over the Sicilies—His minority—His neglected education—His marriage—Authority engrossed by the young queen—Rise of her favourite Acton—His unlimited influence.

THE last year of the seventeenth century was marked by an event which too surely foreboded the convulsion of Europe to its centre; and when the new age rose upon Italy, the political horizon of the peninsula was already darkened by the gathering tempest. The death of Charles II. of Spain extinguished the branch of the Austrian dynasty, whose sceptre had so long bruised the fairest provinces of Italy; and the people of

Naples and Milan, of Sicily and Sardinia, with mingled hope and anxiety, might anticipate either the amelioration of their fortune, or the aggravation of their miseries' by the contention of foreign pretenders. The succession to the vast states of the Spanish monarchy involved momentous political consequences for all the leading powers of Europe; but for the Italians the question was invested with fearful importance. It was vitally connected with their public and private happiness, with their future prosperity and virtue, with all the associations by which the nature of a government can influence the condition and the character of a people. Accordingly the dissolution of the gigantic fabric of despotism, which Charles V. had cemented, was felt in Italy, not only during the first shock of the war of the Spanish succession: it affected the general aspect of the peninsula, by the perpetual transfer of her states through foreign masters, for nearly half a century; and it was not until the peace of Aix-la-Chapelle, in 1748, that the assignment of her provinces was finally adjusted by the arbiters of Europe.

During this long period, the voice of the Italian, people was never heard in the European cabinets whose deliberations regulated their fate. Neither their wishes nor their interests, neither their affections nor even their most just and natural rights, were ever once regarded. To satisfy the conflicting pretensions of the royal houses of France, Spain, and Germany, to place the political system of Europe in that nice equilibrium, which had become the favourite and exclusive object of the politicians of the eighteenth century, Italy was treated as a common spoil for the wholesale plunderers of the earth. The loveliest region of the universe was degraded into a general property for barter. Its beautiful provinces were carved and parcelled out by the sword and the law of expediency: torn into fragments to glut the craving ambition of the portionless children of monarchs: cast into the balance to adjust the scales of dominion, and to equipoise empires.

The power which the rulers of other nations thus exerted of rendering Italy, by universal consent, the sport and prey of their political game, could never indeed have been acquired, if her people had not already invited wrong and contempt by their spiritless degeneracy. But the vices, produced or deepened by the demoralizing consequences of tyranny, are no excuse for the perpetuity of oppression; and the statesmen of Europe, who made a mockery of Italian rights and independence, are heavily chargeable with having confirmed and completed the debasement of Italian character. During the eighteenth century, successive generations were habituated to see themselves repeatedly transferred, like the slave-population of an American estate, with the soil to which they were attached. All affection for their governors, all pride in their country, all desire of distinction by manly arts, was necessarily extinguished in their bosoms.

If such be a correct picture of the condition and character to which the Italians had been reduced, there can be little either to interest or profit in the detailed study of this part of their history; except in the general moral which may be drawn from their fate. Over the last division of the present work we shall have even fewer temptations to linger than over the annals of the two preceding centuries; and altogether abandoning the wish or the design to observe with minuteness the particular events of successive years, we shall pass with accelerated rapidity through the brief remainder of our subject. The wars of which Italy was the scene in the first half of the eighteenth century, resembled those which had ravaged the peninsula in the age of Charles V.; in so far as they belonged to the individual history of other nations, or to the general history of Europe, rather than merely to that of the unhappy country which formed only the arena of foreign contests. To other and more voluminous works must it therefore be left to describe the operations of the European wars of the eighteenth century: it will be sufficient in this place if we briefly collect and observe their consequences upon the political divisions and the dynasties of Italy.

On the death of Charles II. of Spain, the publication of his unexpected testament, in favour of the second of the grandsons of Louis XIV. disconcerted all the projects of the European powers; who had already twice, during the last years of the feeble monarch, divided his vast dominions in anticipation among various claimants. When Louis XIV. resolved to support the title of his grandson to the inheritance of all the Spanish empire, he found at first no difficulty in securing the obedience of its Italian dependencies to Philip V. By directions from the Junta of regency, constituted at Madrid to await the arrival of the new king, the viceroys and governors of Naples, Milan, Sicily, Sardinia, and the state of the Tuscan garrisons, quietly placed all these kingdoms and provinces under the authority of Philip V. For the defence of these new Italian acquisitions of the house of Bourbon, Louis XIV. depended principally upon the aid of Victor Amadeus II. of Savoy, whose two daughters were now married to his grandsons: the one to the duke of Burgundy the presumptive heir of the French crown, the other to the new monarch of Spain.

When, with the formation of the grand alliance between the empire, England, and Holland, against the house of Bourbon, the famous war of the Spanish succession commenced, the imperial arms made no serious impression upon Italy, as long as the duke of Savoy remained faithful to the French interest. But with Victor Amadeus, the ties of blood had far less influence than the dictates of selfish ambition. The extension of his dominions was the darling object of all his policy; and he was not slow to discover that, if the issue of the war should leave Philip V. in possession of the Milanese, he must resign all prospect of swelling his own territories, thus compressed between the states of the two branches of the Bourbon dynasty. With the hope perhaps of terrifying that house into the cession of Lombardy to him in exchange for Savoy, he entered into negotiations with the imperialists. But Louis XIV., apprehending his defection, ordered the duke de Vendome, his general in northern Italy, to disarm the Savoyard contingent serving in his army; and Victor Amadeus, on the promise of large subsidies from England, and of some territorial advantages from the emperor, immediately changed his party, and joined the grand alliance, (A.D. 1703.)

The defection of Victor Amadeus caused in the sequel the ruin of the French and Spanish affairs in the peninsula. The first consequences of his unscrupulous policy were, however, sufficiently disastrous to his own interests. All Savoy was conquered by the French; and Susa, Pignerol, and other fortresses of Piedmont, were likewise immediately reduced by their arms. In the following campaigns, after a course of uninterrupted successes over the Austrian and Savoyard forces, the duke de Vendome overran all Piedmont; and he finally laid siege to Victor Amadeus himself in his capital, with a formidable army of one hundred battalions of infantry and sixty squadrons of cavalry. This was the great crisis in the fortunes of the Italian war, and of the house of Savoy. Vendôme was vainly recalled from Piedmont to stem the victorious career of the British arms under Marlborough on the northern frontiers of France; and at this inauspicious moment for the French cause, Victor Amadeus, who had escaped with some cavalry from Turin, united himself with prince Eugene, who, after receiving powerful reinforcements from Germany, was advancing to his relief. The French commanders imprudently awaited the approach of the allies in their lines before Turin; their army was totally defeated; and the loss of 20,000 men was followed by the necessity of evacuating all Italy, (A.D. 1706.) The kingdom of Naples, which had been drained of troops to reinforce the French army of Lombardy, was invaded by an Austrian corps; and the authority of the archduke Charles, the brother of the emperor, and the rival of Philip V. in the Spanish succession, was peaceably recognized in the capital and provinces, (A.D. 1707.) All Lombardy and Piedmont were at the same time abandoned by the French under a convention signed at Milan; and the battle of Turin may be said to have terminated the war of the succession in Italy; for the peninsula remained untroubled by any farther hostilities of moment until the peace of Utrecht.

Most of the native governments of the peninsula had endeavoured, by a strict and cautious neutrality, to avert the storm of war from their frontiers. The republic of Venice, the popedom, the grand-duchy of Tuscany, and other inferior states, sought only to avoid entanglement in a quarrel, from the issue of which their rulers had nothing to hope and every thing to dread. But all their efforts and protestations could not wholly prevent the occasional violation of their territories by the belligerents. They succeeded generally, indeed, in purchasing, by submission to insult and outrage, a safety which, however inglorious, was perhaps best suited to their weakness, and preferable to the certainty of greater evils. Besides the duke of Savoy, two only among the Italian sovereigns ventured to adopt a more perilous course; and the engagements of these princes with the great rival powers were attended with common misery to their subjects, but with very opposite results for themselves. Rinaldo of Este, duke of Modena and Reggio, embracing the imperial party, had been driven from his states and obliged to take refuge in the papal dominions, during the successes of the French. His conquered duchies suffered all the usual inflictions of military rapine and insolence; but they were restored to him on their evacuation by the French.

On the other hand, Ferdinand Charles, the dissolute and contemptible duke of Mantua, had suffered himself to be seduced by the gold of Louis XIV. to admit a French garrison into his capital; and on the triumph of the imperialists, after the battle of Turin, Louis abandoned him, by the convention of Milan, to the mercy of the conquerors. An imperial sentence, passed against him at Vienna, had already declared him, as a feudatory of the empire, to have incurred the forfeiture of rebellion and felony by his alliance with the French king. His states were confiscated; Montferrat was assigned to the duke of Savoy; Mantua was annexed to the Milanese province; and Ferdinand Charles, after wandering through the Venetian provinces, a miserable pensioner of France, died in the following year. As he left no children, the sovereign line of the Gonzaga of Mantua terminated in his person, (A.D. 1708.) A junior branch of his house continued to reign over the petty principality of Guastalla, but was not suffered to succeed to his forfeited states; and the failure of that collateral line, a few years before the peace of Aix-la-Chapelle, completed the extinction of the family of Gonzaga.

The peace of Utrecht regulated the destiny of Italy; and though the new emperor Charles VI. refused at the time to accede to its provisions, the treaty of Rastadt, which he concluded in the following year with Louis XIV., made no change in any of those terms of the former pacification which related to the disposal of the Italian provinces. (A.D. 1713.) Besides cessions from France, which secured all the passes of the Alps, the duke of Savoy had acquired Montferrat and other territories, the promised reward of his alliance with the empire; and the union of these new possessions, which intersected Piedmont, with that great province and Savoy, completed the consolidation and security of his continental power. But Victor Amadeus gained a more brilliant, if not a more important accession of dominion. The island of Sicily was reserved for his share of the spoils of the old Spanish monarchy; and the acquisition of the insular kingdom entitled him to encircle his brows with the regal crown. The Bourbon sovereign of Spain was suffered to retain none of the Italian provinces. At the same time that he abandoned Sicily to Victor Amadeus, he yielded to the German branch of the house of Austria the remainder of the Spanish dominions in Italy. His former rival, the archduke Charles, thus annexed to the imperial and Austrian crowns (to which he had lately succeeded by the death of his brother Joseph) those of Naples and Sardinia, with the provinces of Milan, Mantua, and the Tuscan garrisons.

It was by the ambitious intrigues of an Italian princess and an Italian priest, that the repose of the peninsula was first disturbed, only four years after this pacification. Giulio Alberoni, the son of a peasant, and originally a poor curate near Parma, had risen by his talents and artful spirit to the office of first minister of Spain. Philip V., on the death of his queen Maria Louisa of Savoy, had espoused the princess Elisabetta Farnése; and Alberoni, by means of this marriage, of which he was regarded as the author, enjoyed the favour of the new queen, and acquired an absolute ascendancy over the feeble mind of her husband. His first object was to obtain a cardinal's hat for himself; and being indulged with that honour by the pope, the next and more comprehensive scheme of his ambition was to signalize his public administration. To his energetic and audacious conceptions, it seemed not too gigantic or arduous an undertaking to recover for the Spanish monarchy all its ancient possessions and power in Italy, which had been totally lost by the peace of Utrecht. He duped the wily Victor Amadeus, and enlisted him in his views, by the promise of the Milanese provinces in exchange for Sicily; and the disgust, which the stem and haughty insolence of the imperial government had already excited in the peninsula, rendered the pope, the grand-duke of Tuscany, and other Italian princes, not adverse to the designs of the Spanish minister.

But the great powers of Europe looked with far different eyes upon his inquiet ambition. The personal interests and feelings of the duke of Orleans, who now governed France during the minority of Louis XV., placed him in opposition to Philip V.; and the duke discovered a plot laid by Alberoni, through the Spanish ambassador at Paris, to deprive him of the regency of France, to which the cardinal persuaded his master to assert his claim as the nearest relative of Louis XV. The intrigues held with the Scottish Jacobites by Alberoni, who had formed a chimerical scheme of placing the Pretender on the throne of Great Britain, and thus securing a new and grateful ally for Spain, rendered George I. as jealous as the duke of Orleans of the designs of the court of Madrid. For their mutual protection against the machinations of Alberoni, the British monarch and the French regent negotiated a defensive league between Great Britain, France, and Holland, which, by the accession of the emperor to its objects, shortly swelled into the famous quadruple alliance, (A.D. 1718.)

Besides the provision of the contracting parties for their mutual defence, the quadruple alliance laboured at once to provide for the continued repose of Italy, and to gratify the ambition both of the family of Austria and of the Spanish house of Bourbon. Although Parma and Placentia were not feminine fiefs, the approaching extinction of the male line of Farnése gave Elisabetta the best subsisting claim to the succession of her uncle's states. To the grand-duchy of Tuscany she had also pretensions by maternal descent, after the failure of the male ducal line of Medici; which, like that of Farnése, seemed to be fast approaching its termination. As, therefore, the children of the young queen were excluded from the expectation of ascending the Spanish throne, which the sons of Philip by his first marriage were of course destined to inherit, the idea was conceived of forming an establishment in Italy for don Carlos her firstborn; and the quadruple alliance provided that the young prince should be guaranteed in the succession both of Parma and Placentia, and of Tuscany, on the death of the last princes of the Farnése and Medicean dynasties. It was to reconcile the emperor to this admission of a Spanish prince into Italy, that Sicily was assigned to him in exchange for Sardinia. The weaker powers and the people were alone sacrificed. While the princes of Parma and Tuscany were compelled to endure the cruel mortification of seeing foreign statesmen dispose by anticipation of their inheritance, during their own lives, and without their option; and while, with a far more flagrant usurpation of natural rights, the will of their subjects was as little consulted; it was resolved to compel Victor Amadeus to receive, as an equivalent for his new kingdom of Sicily, that of Sardinia, which boasted not a third part of either its population or general value.

The provisions of the quadruple alliance were haughtily rejected by Alberoni, who had already entered on the active prosecution of his designs upon the Italian provinces. Having hitherto endeavoured, during his short administration, to recruit the exhausted strength of Spain, he now plunged that monarch headlong into a new contest, with such forces as had been regained in four years of peace; and his vigorous, but overwrought direction of the resources of the state, seemed at first to justify his presumption. A body of eight thousand Spaniards were disembarked on the island of Sardinia, and at once wrested that kingdom from the feeble garrisons of the imperialists, (A.D. 1717.) In the following year, a large Spanish fleet of sixty vessels of war, convoying thirty-five thousand landforces, appeared in the Mediterranean; and notwithstanding the previous negotiations of

Alberoni with Victor Amadeus, Sicily was the first object of attack. Against this perfidious surprise, the Savoyard prince was in no condition to defend his new kingdom; and though his viceroy at first endeavoured to resist the progress of the Spanish arras, Victor Amadeus, sensible of his weakness and inability to afford the necessary succours for preserving so distant a possession, made a merit of necessity, and assented to the provisions of the quadruple alliance, (A.D. 1718.) Withdrawing his troops from the contest, he assumed the title of king of Sardinia, though he yet possessed not a foot of territory in that island.

Meanwhile the powers of the quadruple alliance, finding all negotiations hopeless, had begun to act vigorously against the Spanish forces. Even before the open declaration of war, to which England and France had now recourse to reduce the court of Spain to abandon its designs, Sir George Byng, the British admiral in the Mediterranean, had not hesitated to attack the Spanish fleet, which he completely annihilated off the Sicilian coast. This disaster overthrew all the magnificent projects of Alberoni. The British admiral poured the imperial troops from the Italian continent into Sicily; and the Spaniards rapidly lost ground, and made overtures for evacuating the island. The enterprises of the court of Madrid were equally unfortunate in other quarters; and Philip V. at last discovering the impracticability of Alberoni's schemes, sacrificed his minister to the jealousy of the European powers, and acceded to the terms of the quadruple alliance, (A.D. 1719.) Victor Amadeus was placed in possession of the kingdom of Sardinia, which his house have retained ever since this epoch with the regal title. The cupidity of the emperor was satisfied by the reunion of the crowns of the Two Sicilies in his favour; and the ambitious maternal anxiety of the Spanish queen was allayed, by the promised reversion of the states of the Medici and of her own family to the infant don Carlos (A.D. 1720.)

For thirteen years after the conclusion of the war of the quadruple alliance, Italy was left in profound and uninterrupted repose. The first half of the eighteenth century was completely the age of political chicanery; and the intricate negotiations, which engrossed the attention and only served to expose the laborious insincerity of the statesmen of Europe, seemed to be ever threatening new troubles. But the treaties, which followed that of the quadruple alliance in thick succession for many years, had no other effect in Italy than to secure the Parmesan succession to the infant don Carlos of Spain. It was observed in the last chapter that Francesco and Antonio, the two surviving sons of the duke Ranuccio II. of Parma and Placentia, who died in 1694, had both inherited the diseased and enormous corpulence of their family. Neither of them had issue; the duke Francesco terminated his reign and life in 1727; and Antonio his successor survived him only four years. The death of the youngest of her uncles realized the ambitious hopes, which Elisabetta Farnése had cherished of conveying the states of her own house to her son. (A.D. 1731.) The male line of Farnése having thus become extinct, the youthful don Carlos, with a body of Spanish troops, was quietly put in possession of the duchies of Parma and Placentia, and reluctantly acknowledged by the last prince of the Medici, as his destined successor in the grand-duchy of Tuscany.

The final settlement of the Parmesan and Tuscan succession seemed to eradicate the seeds of hostilities in Italy; but it had become the unhappy fortune of that country to follow captive in the train of foreign negotiation, and to suffer and to bleed for the most distant broils of her foreign masters. Only two years had elapsed after the elevation of the Spanish prince to the ducal throne of Parma, when Italy was suddenly chosen as the field for the decision of a quarrel, which had originated in the disputed election of a king of Poland. Upon this occasion, the two branches of the Bourbon dynasty united in the same league against the house of Austria, and resolved to attack its possessions in Italy. Charles Emmanuel III., the new king of Sardinia, joined their formidable confederacy; and the imperial strength in the peninsula was crushed under its weight.

While Charles Emmanuel, at the head of the French and Piedmontese troops, easily conquered the whole Milanese states in a short time; the Spaniards at Parma, being delivered of all apprehension for the issue of the war in Lombardy, found themselves at liberty to divert their views to the south. A Spanish army of 30,000 men disembarked in the peninsula under the duke di Montemar, and joined don Carlos; and that young prince, at the age of seventeen, assuming the nominal command in chief of the forces of Spain in Italy, led them to attempt the conquest of the Sicilies. The duke di Montemar, who guided his military operations, gained for him a complete and decisive victory at Bitonto in Apulia over the feeble imperial army, which was entrusted with the defence of southern Italy. The opposition of language, and manners, and character, between the Germans and Italians, rendered the cold sullen tyranny of Austria peculiarly hateful to the volatile Neapolitans; and they eagerly threw off a yoke, to which time had not yet habituated them. The capital had already opened its gates before the battle of Bitonto; and the provinces hastened to offer a ready submission to the conquerors. The Sicilians imitated the example of their continental neighbours; and at Naples and Palermo don Carlos received the crowns of the Two Sicilies, (A.D. 1735.) For the facility with which the Spaniards had effected these conquests, they were principally indebted to the powerful operations of the French in Lombardy, and to the vigour with which the armies of Louis XV. pressed those of the emperor in Germany, and prevented him from dispatching sufficient succours to his Italian dependencies. The court of Madrid now began to cherish again the hope of recovering the whole of the Italian provinces, which the Spanish monarchy had lost by the peace of Utrecht; and the duke di Montemar conducted his army into Lombardy to unite with the French and Piedmontese in completing the expulsion of the Austrians from the peninsula. But the emperor, discouraged by so many reverses, made overtures of peace; and the French cabinet was not disposed to indulge the ambition of Spain with farther acquisitions. Negotiations for a general peace were opened, to which Philip V. was compelled to accede; and at length the confirmation of the preliminaries by the peace of Vienna once more changed the aspect of Italy. The crowns of Naples and Sicily were secured to don Carlos. The provinces of Milan and Mantua were left to the emperor; the duchies of Parma and Placentia were annexed to his Lombard possessions, to recompense him in some measure for the loss of the Sicilies; and the extinction of the house of Medici by the death of the grand-duke Giovan Gastone, while the negotiations were yet pending, completed a new arrangement for the succession of Tuscany. Francis, duke of Lorraine, who had lately received the hand of Maria Theresa, the eldest daughter and heiress of the emperor, took possession of the grand-duchy, in exchange for his hereditary states; and Charles VI. was gratified by this favourable provision for his son-in-law and destined successor in the imperial dignity. Finally, the king of Sardinia, in lieu of the ambitious hopes with which he had been amused of possessing all the Milanese duchy, was obliged to content himself with the acquisition of the valuable districts of Tortona and Novara.

This general accommodation among the arbiters of Italy procured only a brief interval of repose for the degraded people of the peninsula, before they were exposed to far greater evils, than those which they had suffered in the short course of the late war. The emperor Charles VI. died only two years after the confirmation of the peace of Vienna; and the very powers, who by that treaty had guaranteed the famous pragmatic sanction—or act by which the emperor was allowed to settle his hereditary states, as he had no son, upon his daughter Maria Theresa—conspired to rob her of those dominions. The furious war of the Austrian succession which followed, filled Italy during seven years with rapine and havoc. In the year after the death of Charles VI., a Spanish army under the duke di Montemar, disembarked on the Tuscan coast to attempt farther conquests in Italy; and although these troops arrived to attack the territories of his consort, the new grand-duke was obliged to affect a neutrality and to permit their free passage through his dominions. On the other hand, the king of the Sicilies, who desired to aid his father's forces in their operations, was equally compelled to sign a neutrality, by the appearance of a British squadron in the bay of Naples, and the threatened bombardment of that city. This humiliation, to which the exposed situation of his capital reduced him, did not, however, prevent the Neapolitan monarch at a later period from taking part in the war. But his engagement in the contest had only the effect of drawing the Austrian arms into southern Italy, and inflicting the ravages of a licentious soldiery upon the neutral states of the Church and the frontiers of Naples, (A.D. 1742.)

But northern Italy was the constant theatre of far more destructive hostilities; and the Italian sovereign, who acted the most conspicuous part in the general war of Europe, was Charles Emmanuel III., the king of Sardinia. That active and politic prince, pursuing the skilful but selfish and unscrupulous system of aggrandizement, which had become habitual to the Savoyard dynasty, made a traffic of his alliance to the highest bidder. He first offered to join the confederated Bourbons; but the court of Spain could not be induced to purchase his adherence by promising him an adequate share of the Milanese states, which the Spaniards were confident of regaining. Charles Emmanuel therefore deserted the Bourbon alliance to range himself in the party of Maria Theresa. But it was not until he had extorted new cessions of territory from that princess in Lombardy, and large subsidies from our country which protected her, that he entered seriously and vigorously into the war, as the auxiliary of Austria and England. As soon as Charles Emmanuel began to declare himself against the Bourbon cause, his states became immediately the prey of invasion. Although the Spanish dynasty pretended to lay claim to the whole succession of the house of Austria, the real motive which actuated the court of Madrid in these wars, was the ambition of the queen of Spain, Elisabetta Farnése, to obtain an establishment in Italy for another of her sons, the infant don Philip; and that prince, leading a Spanish army from the Pyrenees through the south of France, over-ran and occupied all Savoy, which was mercilessly pillaged by his troops. But don Philip was unable to penetrate into Piedmont; and meanwhile the duke di Montemar, with the Spanish army already in Italy, had been opposed successfully by the Austrians and Piedmontese on the opposite frontiers of Lombardy.

But Charles Emmanuel, even after he had formally pledged himself to England and Austria, was perpetually carrying on secret and separate negotiations with the Bourbons; and it was only because he could not obtain all the terms which he demanded of them, and because he was also as suspicious of their ill-faith as he was conscious of his own, that he maintained his alliances unchanged to the end of the war. (A.D. 1743.) His states were almost constantly the theatre of hostilities, equally destructive to his subjects, whether success or failure alternately attended his career. Yet he displayed activity and skill and courage, scarcely inferior to the brilliant qualities which had distinguished his father Victor Amadeus. When, however, the infant don Philip had been joined by the prince de Conti with 20,000 men, all the efforts of the Sardinian monarch, though he headed his troops in person, could not resist the desperate valour of the French and Spanish confederates; who, forcing the tremendous passes of the Alps broke triumphantly into Piedmont, and for some time swept over its plains as conquerors, (A.D. 1744.) But reinforced by the Austrians, Charles Emmanuel, before the end of the same campaign, turned the tide of fortune, and obliged the allies to retire for the winter into France. They still retained possession of the duchy of Savoy, and crushed the inhabitants under every species of oppression.

In the following year, Genoa declared for the Bourbon confederation; and the Spanish and French forces under don Philip, being thus at liberty to form a junction in the territories of that republic with the second Spanish army from Naples, the king of Sardinia and the Austrians were utterly unable to resist their immense superiority of numbers, (A.D. 1745.) In this campaign, Parma and Placentia were reduced by the duke of Modena, the ally of France and Spain; Turin was menaced with bombardment; Tortona fell to the Bourbon arms; Pavia was carried by assault; and don Philip, penetrating into the heart of

Lombardy, closed the operations of the year by his victorious entry into Milan. But such were the sudden vicissitudes of this sanguinary war, that the brilliant successes of the Spanish prince were shortly rendered nugatory by a growing misunderstanding between the courts of Paris and Madrid, and by the arrival of large reinforcements for the Austrian army in the peninsula, (A.D. 1746.) Don Philip lost, in less than another year, all that he had acquired in the preceding campaign. He was driven out of Milan; he was obliged to evacuate all Lombardy; and the French and Spanish forces were finally compelled, by the increasing strength of the Austrians, to re-cross the Alps, and to make their retreat into France. The king of Sardinia and his allies carried the war into Provence, without meeting with much success; and the French in their turn endeavoured once more to penetrate into Piedmont. But while that quarter of Italy was threatened with new ravages, the peninsula was saved from farther miseries by the signature of the peace of Aix-la-Chapelle. (A.D. 1748.)

One of the declared purposes of the European powers in their assembled congress, was to give independence to Italy; and if that object could have been attained without the restoration of ancient freedom, and the revival of national virtue among the Italians, the provisions of the treaty of Aix-la-Chapelle would have been wise and equitable. The Austrians were permitted to retain only Milan and Mantua; and all other foreign powers consented to exclude themselves from the peninsula. The grand-duke, Francis of Lorraine, now become emperor, engaged to resign Tuscany to a younger branch of his imperial house. The throne of the Two Sicilies was confirmed to don Carlos and his heirs, to form a distinct and independent branch of the Spanish house of Bourbon; and the duchies of Parma and Placentia were elevated anew into a sovereign state in favour of don Philip, who thus became the founder of a third dynasty of the same family. The king of Sardinia received some farther accessions of territory, which were detached from the duchy of Milan; and all the other native powers of Italy remained, or were re-established in their former condition.

Thus was Italy, after two centuries of prostration under the yoke of other nations, relieved from the long oppression of foreigners. A small portion only of her territory remained subject to the empire; and all the rest of the peninsula was divided among a few independent governments. But after the peace of Aix-la-Chapelle, Italy was still as little constituted as before to command the respect or the fear of the world. Her people for the most part cherished no attachment for rulers, to whom they were indebted neither for benefits nor happiness; in whose success they could feel no community of interest, and whose aggrandizement could reflect no glory on themselves. The condition of Italy after the nominal restoration of her independence, offers, as a philosophical writer has well remarked, a striking lesson of political experience. The powers of Europe, after having in some measure annihilated a great nation, were at length awakened to a sense of the injury which they had inflicted upon humanity, and upon the general political system of the world. They laboured sincerely to repair the work of destruction: there was nothing which they did not restore to Italy, except, what they could not restore, the extinguished energies and dignity of the people. Forty years of profound peace succeeded to their attempt; and these were only forty years of effeminacy, weakness, and corruption:—a memorable example to statesmen, that the mere act of their will can neither renovate a degraded nation, nor replenish its weight in the political balance; and that national independence is a vain boon, where the people are not interested in its preservation, and where no institutions revive the spirit of honour, and the honest excitement of freedom.

During these forty years of languid peace—from the treaty of Aix-la-Chapelle to the epoch of the French revolution—the general history of Italy presents not a single circumstance for our observation; and it only remains for us to pass in rapid review the few domestic occurrences of any moment in the different Italian states of the eighteenth century. The affairs of the Sicilies, of the popedom, of the states of the house of Savoy, of the duchies of Tuscany and Modena, and of the republics of

Genoa and Venice, may each require a brief notice. But the obscure or tranquil fortunes of Lucca, of the Milanese and Mantuan provinces, and of the duchy of Parma and Placentia, would scarcely merit a separate place in this enumeration. The Lucchese oligarchy continued to exist undisturbed and ingloriously. The ancient duchies of Milan and Mantua, after the middle of the century, rapidly recovered from the perpetual ravages of the war of the Austrian succession; and the government of the imperial house of Lorraine (of that day at least) deserved the praise of lenity and justice, in comparison with the previous oppression of the Spanish administration. By the dismemberment of a great part of its dependent territories in favour of the house of Savoy, the city of Milan itself was shorn of much of the wealth and population which had belonged to the capital of Lombardy. But the provinces, of which it remained the seat of government, were raised by their own admirable fertility, and the new influence of a more enlightened policy in their governors, to considerable prosperity; and when the French revolution violently interrupted the work of peace, the Lombard dominions of Austria, the only part of Italy under foreign government, gave some hope of improvement in literature, science, and public spirit, and formed certainly the most flourishing division of the peninsula.

The duchies of Parma and Placentia, which had once more been separated from that of Milan to form the independent appendage of a Spanish prince relapsed into the deep oblivion from which the dispute for their possession had alone drawn them. Don Philip reigned until the year 1765; and his son and successor, Don Ferdinand, occupied his throne beyond the period assigned to this work. The administration of both these princes was, in a political sense, marked by no important event; but the literary and scientific tastes of Don Philip entitled him to be mentioned with respect, and shed some beneficial influence on his ducal states.

The transition of the crowns of Naples and Sicily, from the extinguished Spanish branch of the house of Austria to the collateral line of Germany, and from that dynasty again to a junior member of the Spanish Bourbons, has already been noticed; and we take up the annals of the Sicilies from the epoch only, at which the infant don Carlos was confirmed in the possession of their throne by the treaty of Vienna. This sovereign, who reigned at Naples under the title of Charles VII., but who is better known by his later designation of Charles III. of Spain, governed southern Italy for above twenty-one years. The general reputation of his character has perhaps been much over-rated; but, as the monarch of the Sicilies, he undoubtedly laboured to promote the welfare of his kingdom. The war of the Spanish succession paralyzed all his efforts during the first half of his reign; but after the restoration of tranquillity in 1748, he devoted himself zealously and exclusively to the pacific work of improvement. He was well seconded by the virtuous intentions, if not by the limited talents, of his minister Tanucci. The principal error of both proceeded from their ignorance of the first principles of finance; and the cultivated mind and theoretical knowledge of Tanucci fitted him less for the active conduct of affairs, than for the station of professor of law, from which the king had raised him to his friendship and confidence. It has been objected as a second mistake of Charles or his minister that the system of government which they adopted contemplated only the continuance of peace, and contained no provision against the possibility of war. No attempt was made either to kindle a martial spirit in the people, or to rouse them to the power of defending themselves from foreign aggression and insult. The army, the fortifications, and all warlike establishments were suffered to fall into utter decay; and the military force of the kingdom, which was nominally fixed at thirty thousand men, was kept so incomplete that it rarely exceeded half that number. The only security for the preservation of honourable peace at home was forgotten in a system, which neglected the means of commanding respect abroad; but Charles occupied himself, as if he indulged the delusive hope of maintaining his subjects in eternal tranquillity. He studiously embellished his capital; and the useful public works—harbours, aqueducts, canals, and national granaries—which preserve the memory of his reign, are magnificent and numerous.

The laudable exertions of Charles were but just beginning to produce beneficial effects, when he was summoned by the death of his elder brother, Ferdinand VI. of Spain, who left no children, to assume the crown of that kingdom, (A.D. 1759.) According to the spirit of the peace of Aix-la-Chapelle, his next brother, don Philip, duke of Parma, should have succeeded to the vacant throne of the Sicilies; but Charles III. was permitted to place one of his own younger sons in the seat which he had just quitted. His eldest son betrayed such marks of hopeless idiotcy that it was necessary to set him altogether aside from the succession to any part of his dominions; the inheritance of the Spanish throne was reserved for the second, who afterwards reigned under the title of Charles IV.; and it was to the third that the sceptre of the Sicilies was assigned. This prince, who under the name of Ferdinand IV. of Naples and Sicily has continued to reign to these times, was then a boy of nine years of age. Charles appointed a Neapolitan council of regency to govern in his son's name; but the marquis Tanucci remained the real dictator of the public administration; and the new monarch of Spain continued to exercise a decisive influence over the councils of the Two Sicilies during the whole of his son's minority, and even for some time after its expiration. It was by the act of Tanucci, and in conjunction with the policy of Charles, that the Jesuits were expelled from the Two Sicilies and from Spain at the same epoch; that the ancient usurpations of the holy see were boldly repressed; and that the progress of other useful reforms was zealously forwarded.

It was the most fatal negligence of Charles III., and the lasting misfortune of his son, that the education of Ferdinand IV. was entrusted to the prince di San Nicandro, a man utterly destitute of ability or knowledge. The young monarch, who was not deficient in natural capacity, was thus permitted to remain in the grossest ignorance. The sports of the field were the only occupation and amusement of his youth; and the character of his subsequent reign was deplorably influenced by the idleness and distaste for public affairs, in which he had been suffered to grow up. The marriage of Ferdinand, with the princess Caroline of Austria, put a term to the ascendancy of Charles III. over the Neapolitan counsels. His faithful servant Tanucci lost his authority in the administration; some years afterwards he was finally disgraced; and the ambitious consort of Ferdinand, having gained an absolute sway over the mind of her feeble husband, engrossed the direction of the state. Her assumption of the reins of sovereignty was followed by the rise of a minion, who acquired as decided an influence over her spirit, as she already exercised over that of the king. This was the famous Acton, a low Irish adventurer, who, after occupying some station in the French marine, passed into Tuscany, and was received into the service of the grand duke. He had the good fortune to distinguish himself in an expedition against the pirates of Barbary; and thenceforth his elevation was astonishingly rapid. He became known to the queen, and was entrusted with the direction of the Neapolitan navy. Still young, and gifted with consummate address, he won the personal favour of Caroline; he governed while he seemed implicitly to obey her; and without any higher qualifications, or any knowledge beyond the narrow circle of his profession, he was successively raised to the office of minister of war and of foreign affairs. The whole power of government centered in his person; and Acton was the real sovereign of the Sicilies, when the corrupt court and the misgoverned state encountered the universal shock of the French revolution.

PART II.
The popedom—State of the papal power and dominions in the eighteenth century—Universal revolt of Europe against the papal authority—Succession of pontiffs—Benedict XIV. (Lambertini)—His enlightened and amiable spirit—Clement XIV. (Ganganelli)—His virtues and accomplishments—Suppression of the Jesuits—Pius VI.—Unimportant commencement of his calamitous pontificate—States of the house of Savoy—Their continual aggrandizement—Victor Amadeus II.—His admirable domestic administration—His abdication—His vain attempt to resume his crown—Revolting ingratitude of his son—His death—Reign of Charles Emmanuel III.—Wisdom of his government—Victor Amadeus III.—Tuscany—Sombre reign of the grand-duke Cosmo III. de' Medici—His vain efforts to perpetuate the existence of his house—His death—Giovan Gastone, the last duke of his line—Reckless dissipation of his reign—His

death—Extinction of the sovereign line of Medici—The grand-duchy under the house of Lorraine—Government of the emperor Francis I.—Beneficent reign of Peter Leopold of Lorraine—His numerous reforms—Prosperity of the grand-duchy—He quits it to assume the imperial crown—Ingratitude of the Tuscans—Total cessation of the work of improvement—Modena—Continued decline of the house of Este—Long and calamitous reigns of the dukes Rinaldo, Francesco III., and Ercole III.—Approaching extinction of their line—Genoa—Share of the republic in the war of the Austrian succession—The city basely surrendered to the Austrians by the senate—Intolerable insolence and exactions of the conquerors—General insurrection of the lower people against their foreign tyrants—The Austrians driven with loss and disgrace from the city—Heroic constancy of the people—The oligarchy suffered to revive—Affairs of Corsica—The people of that island driven to revolt by the tyranny of Genoa—Long struggle of Genoa to recover her dominions—Adventures of Theodore de Neuhoff, the ephemeral king of Corsica—The senate of Genoa obtains the aid of France—A republic established in Corsica—Government of Paschal Paoli—The sovereignty of Corsica ceded to Louis XV. by the Genoese senate—Conquest of the island by the French—Venice—Weakness and final decay of the republic—Forced neutrality of the state in the wars of Europe—Re-conquest of the Morea by the Turks—Peace of Passarowitz—Venice falls into utter oblivion—Relaxation of vigour in the Venetian despotism—Frightful licentiousness of private manners in Venice—Conclusion.

THE papal history of the eighteenth century is marked by few circumstances of importance or interest. But the succession of pontiffs during this age is adorned with examples of moral excellence and even of intellectual accomplishments, which would have done honour to any of the temporal thrones of the world. The spectacle of personal worth in a Lambertini or a Ganganelli might almost reconcile the mind to the existence of an authority, which in their hands seemed to offer some atonement to insulted credulity for the usurpation and imposture of its foundations. But all the efforts of pontiffs, who were worthy in themselves of respect and esteem, could not correct the inherent vices of the ecclesiastical government, or arrest the fearful and rapid progress of desolation and decay in their states. In their relations with temporal powers, the popes were no longer permitted to domineer over the consciences of princes and the superstitious fears of their people. The most bigotted nations began to spurn the degradation of blind submission to the holy see; and the universal revolt of catholic Europe against the pretensions of papal jurisdiction had, for the interests of the popedom, all the fatal results of a new Reformation. In the eighteenth century, the successors of the Gregories and the Innocents of the olden time might deplore the causes, which had released the human mind from the trammels of superstition, and taught it to burst from the thraldom of their ancient influence. But they had at least penetration to discern the total change of circumstances; and, in general, they accommodated their measures with discretion and wisdom to the fallen fortunes of their see.

Pope Clement XI. who, as I observed in the last chapter, was placed in the chair of St. Peter in the last year of the seventeenth century, occupied his seat for twenty-one years. The proceedings against the Jansenists, to which he was in a great measure inveigled or compelled to give his reluctant consent, belong only to the history of France; but the share which he was obliged to take in those religious disputes, was the circumstance that most embittered the happiness of his long pontificate. In Italy, too, the war of the Spanish succession filled him for several years with perpetual disquietude; and the strict neutrality, of which his weakness dictated the necessity, and which he wished to observe with scrupulous impartiality between the great rival powers, could not shield his states from pillage and his dignity from outrage. Each of the candidates for the Spanish throne reproached him that he favoured the other; and the Austrians, by the commission of every excess in the papal territories, after their victory at Turin, compelled him to annul the recognition of Philip V. as king of Spain, which the French had extorted from him, and to substitute the name of the archduke Charles in its place.

The death of Clement XI. in 1721, was followed by the elevation of Innocent XIII., whose unimportant pontificate lasted only three years; and, in 1724, Benedict XIII. was raised to the tiara. The name of this pope has acquired the reproach of fanaticism and superstition, by his publication of the ridiculous legend of Gregory VII.; and the blind confidence which he placed in the infamous cardinal Coscia, exposed the Roman people to the intolerable rapacity and venality of that avaricious minister and his subaltern extortioners. Yet in personal conduct, Benedict XIII. was pious, meek, and charitable; and it was his advanced age and infirmities, rather than natural deficiency of understanding, which his subjects had cause to deplore. His successor Clement XII., who replaced him in 1730, and reigned ten years, was of very opposite character. He belonged rather to the class of popes who, in the two preceding centuries, had sacrificed their tranquillity in the vain endeavour to repress the growth of religious independence, than to that of the pacific pontiffs who immediately preceded and followed him. He successively embroiled himself with the courts of Portugal, France, Austria, and Spain; and he showed so little disposition to resign any of the absolute prerogatives of his see, that his pontificate was consumed in eternal and ineffectual contention. The European powers evinced an utter disregard for the assumed sanctity of his station; and at the close of the war of the Polish election, the Austrian army violated the neutrality of his states, and lived at free quarters in the provinces of Romagna and Ferrara; while the Spaniards and Neapolitans plundered the environs of Rome and the patrimony of St. Peter. The papal subjects, notwithstanding the neutrality of his holiness, were thus exposed to all the ravages of war.

It was on the death of Clement XII. in 1740, that Prospero Lambertini, the most enlightened and virtuous of the Roman pontiffs, was raised to the tiara under the title of Benedict XIV. This amiable man has been justly characterized as the first pope, who knew how to resign with dignity the extravagant pretensions of the holy see. He immediately accommodated all the disputes, in which his predecessor had involved the papacy; he endeavoured to establish a wise economy in the administration of his states; and he acquired, by his tolerant and unassuming spirit, the esteem and veneration of all Europe. Yet the influence of his personal character, and the purity of his intentions, could not protect his subjects from insult and suffering, during the sanguinary war of the Austrian succession. But after the peace of Aix-la-Chapelle, his efforts were unceasing to repair the ravages caused by the unprovoked violation of his neutrality; and his people had reason to deem his life too short, when it terminated in 1758.

The successor of Lambertini did not emulate his moderation. Clement XIII. evinced a laudable desire for the reform of manners, and for the correction of the clergy. But his zeal for the defence of the Roman Catholic faith was mingled with the rash and selfish design of re-establishing the papal power; and he was far from possessing the talents, the address, the persuasive manner, or even the firmness of Benedict XIV. He engaged, as Clement XII. had done, in fatal disputes with the Catholic princes, which only exhibited to contempt the imbecility of his spiritual authority; and like that pontiff he exposed himself and his dignity to cruel humiliations. He died in 1769, and it required all the conciliating policy of another Lambertini to calm the irritation, which his injudicious violence had excited among the great powers of Europe. The cardinal Lorenzo Ganganelli, who was placed at this critical juncture in the chair of St. Peter, under the title of Clement XIV., was eminently qualified for the difficult task of allaying the ferment, which his imprudent predecessor had provoked; and his wise and moderate conduct soon healed all the divisions of the Roman Catholic church. Regular, but unostentatious in all the exercises of devotion; simple and unaffected in his manners; intellectual and philosophical in his tastes; humanity and temperance were the favourite virtues of this celebrated pontiff. He had cultivated them in the cell of a monastery; they did not forsake him on his throne; and they deserve the place which the chisel of Canova has assigned to them on his tomb. Of his own zeal for the arts, the foundation of the Capitoline Museum is a noble monument; but the most memorable political and ecclesiastical act of his reign was the suppression of the order of Jesuits. Before his elevation to the tiara, he had pledged himself to the courts of France, Spain, and the Two Sicilies, for the execution of this remarkable measure; and the later assent of the empress-queen Maria Theresa left him no excuse for delaying its consummation, (A.D. 1773.) The reluctance which he evinced to perform his promise, did not proceed from any affection to the proscribed order; but from personal apprehension of their vengeance. This solitary weakness of his elevated mind hastened him to the grave. After the act of suppression, he was haunted by perpetual fear of poison; his frame sank under the horrors of a diseased imagination; and he died of the effects of terror, acting upon a constitution already enfeebled by study and application to business. He was himself persuaded that he had been poisoned by the Jesuits; and the general hatred, which was entertained at the time against the suppressed body, caused the accusation to be loudly echoed. But the charge was contradicted by the report of his physicians, and seems to have been wholly groundless. The long pontificate of Pius VI., who succeeded him in 1775, will not merit attention in this place; for the sufferings and humiliation of that unhappy and well-meaning pontiff—the victim of foreign tyranny—belong to a later period than is embraced in the present work.

During the first half of the eighteenth century, we have seen the power of the house of Savoy continually increased by the military and political talents of its princes, and by the consummate art, with which they accommodated their alliances in the wars of Europe to the selfish gratification of their personal ambition and interest. Victor Amadeus II. betrayed his ultimate views, when he compared Italy to an artichoke, which must be eaten leaf by leaf; and his son pursued his designs with similar fortune, and with equal or even superior address. Thus, at the peace of Utrecht, the acquisition of Montferrat and other important territories consolidated their continental states; and though Sicily was lost in the war of the quadruple alliance, the possession of Sardinia with the regal title was still no contemptible prize for the descendants of the counts of Maurienne. Thus, too, the issue of the war of 1733 added one considerable fragment of the Milanese duchy to Piedmont; and the peace of Aix-la-Chapelle tore another large district from the Austrian provinces of Italy, and gave the kings of Sardinia the line of the Tesino and of lake Maggiore for their eastern frontier.

The able administration, by which Victor Amadeus II. and his son laboured to improve the resources of their states, was as remarkable as their energy and courage in the work of aggrandizement. After the peace of Utrecht, the former of those princes employed the sixteen remaining years of his long reign in strengthening his fortresses and army; in encouraging the progress of learning and intelligence among his subjects; in simplifying the administration of justice; and in fostering agriculture, commerce, and manufactures: particularly those in Piedmont of silk and cloths. Victor Amadeus had received from nature a passionate love of system, and a remarkable capacity for detail. The equalization of the land-tax, which he commenced in his dominions, has often been cited as a model of financial arrangement. His wise measures in other respects had already doubled his revenues, without oppressing his people; and we may applaud the general principle, without inquiring into the particular policy, which stripped the feudatories of Savoy and Piedmont of their exclusive privileges, and subjected the noble order to the same burthens as the other classes of his subjects.

The protracted and brilliant career of Victor Amadeus had enchained the attention of Europe: the close of his life might exhibit to contempt the mockery of human ambition. In some unexplained fit of caprice, the old monarch resolved to abdicate the regal crown and the throne of those dominions, which it had been the pride and labour of his years to acquire, to extend, and to improve. In an assembly of the ministers of state, the great functionaries of justice, and all the principal nobles of Sardinia, Savoy, and Piedmont, he solemnly resigned his authority, and transferred the allegiance of his subjects to his son Charles Emmanuel; and reserving to himself only an income suitable for a provincial nobleman, he chose for the place of his retirement, the half-ruined castle of Chamberry, the ancient capital of the duchy of Savoy, (A.D. 1730.) He was accompanied to this retreat by a lady, the widow of the count di San Sebastiano, who had long privately been his mistress, and whom, having lately married, he now created marchioness of Spino.

But he had scarcely lived a year in this seclusion, before he became completely weary of a repose, so different from all the tenor of his past life, and so unnatural to his restless spirit. His mind was irritated by the discovery—a discovery which history might have revealed to him earlier—that a monarch who dethrones himself offers only an allurement for ingratitude and neglect. His discontent was inflamed by the aspiring suggestions of his wife, who still cherished the hope of sharing a throne; and after removing to the castle of Moncalieri near Turin, he made a rash effort to resume the reins of government. But his subjects remembered only his inquiet enterprises and his despotic temper, and forgot the later benefits of his reign. When he privately appeared at the gates of his capital, they were closed against him; and when his son, with a spirit which resembled his own, shamefully preferred the dictates of ambition to those of nature, no arm was raised to defend him. He returned in despair to Moncalieri; he was outrageously torn from his bed in the dead of night, and hurried half-naked into rigorous imprisonment at Rivoli; and his wife shared a similar fate, and was at first separated from him. His son resisted his pressing solicitations for an interview, and never afterwards saw him. He was permitted to return to Moncalieri; and he died there, still in confinement, in the following year:—an example of the inextinguishable lust of power, and the victim of detestable filial ingratitude. (A.D. 1732.)

The active and warlike career of Charles Emmanuel III., until the peace of Aix-la-Chapelle gave final security and repose to his states, has been already noticed in the general affairs of Italy. After that pacification of Europe, he reigned in uninterrupted tranquillity for twenty-five years; and however the mind may revolt from his conduct as a son, we are bound to acknowledge that Charles Emmanuel III. was a great general, a great politician, a great and even a good king. After the termination of hostilities in 1748, he rivalled and surpassed his father in the wisdom of his administration. So much had the power of his house already increased before his last war, that at its commencement, fifteen days only after the declaration of hostilities, he was able to take the field at the head of an army of 40,000 of his native troops, highly disciplined, and abundantly supplied with a train of artillery and pontoons, and all the materiel of scientific warfare. The leisure of his after years was employed in the admirable construction of a chain of Alpine fortresses, which might have proved an impregnable frontier for his states and for all Italy against the invasion of the French revolutionary armies; if those beautiful works had been defended with the same skill which constructed them; or if the son of Charles Emmanuel had inherited his unconquerable spirit and his eminent talents.

Nor were the labours of this active monarch confined to martial objects. He perfected the equalization of the land-tax and the compilation of laws, which his father had commenced: he built many splendid edifices of civil architecture; and he extended an enlightened and generous protection to men of science and letters. On his death, he was succeeded by his son Victor Amadeus III., a prince of inferior capacity; but who deserves to be mentioned with respect for his encouragement of literature and art, and his efforts to turn the pacific commencement of his reign to profit, by embellishing his states, and bestowing on them a variety of useful establishments, (A.D. 1773.) Thus passed the first twenty-six years of his reign: the storm of foreign war which clouded the evening of his life belongs not to our present subject.

In the fortunes of the grand-duchy of Tuscany, during the age embraced in this chapter, we have already noticed the prominent circumstance:—the extinction of the sovereign line of the Medici, and the assignment of their throne to a younger branch of the imperial house of Lorraine. The sombre reign of the grand-duke Cosmo III., during which Florence became the seat of fanatical superstition, may be said to have prepared the annihilation of his family. His unhappy disposition seemed to shed a withering influence upon whatever he attempted. Miserable in his own matrimonial connexion, he was destined to inflict the curse of sterility upon every marriage which he anxiously negotiated to perpetuate the existence of his house. He caused his two sons to marry: they had neither of them children, and the second separated from his wife. He gave his only daughter to the elector-palatine: she bore that prince no issue. Then, foreseeing with bitter certainty the extinction of his own posterity, but still clinging to the hope of preserving at least the duration of his family, he induced his brother, the cardinal Francesco Maria de' Medici, to abjure his vow of celibacy, and at an advanced age to espouse a princess of Gonzaga: but this marriage was not more fortunate than the others. Thus disappointed in every design of prolonging the existence of a dynasty, whose years were already inevitably numbered to their close, Cosmo III. sank into the tomb; but not before he had survived all the male heirs of his family, except his second son, Giovan Gastone.

That prince, who succeeded him, was oppressed with infirmities, which confined him almost habitually to his couch. His life had hitherto been overclouded with gloom and wearisome disgust by the austere and morose temper of his father, and by the hypocritical sanctity which Cosmo had brought into vogue at his court. The first care of Giovan Gastone on his deliverance from the constraint in which he had lived beyond the age of fifty years, was to plunge headlong into the opposite extremes of extravagance and folly. His bed was surrounded by buffoons and flatterers, by rapacious menials, and low-born favourites, who, so that they but amused his vacant idleness, and beguiled him of the recollection of his infirmities, enjoyed the impunity to dilapidate and consume his finances by every species of embezzlement. Reckless of the future, and desirous only of closing his ears against the humiliating report of that diplomatic contest for his succession which filled all the courts of Europe, he thought not of the miseries and wrongs of his people. He set no bounds to his profusion and the dissipation of their wealth; and when he died, his reign had inflicted many deep wounds on the natural prosperity of Tuscany, (A.D. 1737.) The death of his sister, a few years afterwards, completed the extinction of the sovereign house of Medici. A distant collateral branch of the same original stock descended from one of the ancestors of the great Cosmo, was left to survive even to these times; but no claim to the inheritance of the ducal house was ever recognized in its members.

Francis of Lorraine, the consort of Maria Theresa of Austria, to whom this inheritance was assigned by the peace of Vienna, naturally resided little in Tuscany, and his elevation to the imperial crown seemed to consign the grand-duchy to the long administration of foreign viceroys. But the governors chosen by Francis were men of ability and virtue, who strove to ameliorate the condition of the people (A.D. 1765); and on the death of the emperor Francis, his will, in consonance with the spirit of the peace of Aix-la-Chapelle, gave to Tuscany a sovereign of its own. This was his second son, Peter Leopold, to whom he bequeathed the grand-duchy, while his eldest, Joseph II., succeeded to his imperial crown.

Leopold was only eighteen years of age, when he commenced a reign, which exhibited to admiration the rare spectacle of a patriot and a philosopher on the throne. It may be true, as it has been asserted, that his actions were not always free from the taint of error and selfishness; for where are human motives to be found of unalloyed purity? But that the ultimate and the dearest object of his heart was to render his people happy, it is impossible to doubt. Among a multitude of useful labours, he fostered science and art; he encouraged agriculture, by bringing neglected lands into cultivation, by dividing them into a great number of little properties, subject only to an easy rent, and by giving every cultivator a security and an interest in the produce of the soil; he promoted commerce by destroying all restrictions; and he left the people to raise in their own way the moderate supplies by which his economy enabled him to support the administration, and to discharge the public debt of the nation. He disbanded his army as a pernicious and useless expense in a feeble state; and he trusted the safety of his person, at all times and under all circumstances, to the affection of a people with whom he often mingled unknown, that he might observe their character and learn their wants. His reforms extended through the ecclesiastical establishment, the departments of state, the execution of the laws, and even through the manners of his subjects. And yet nothing was done rashly or in haste. He was a sincere friend to religion, but his zeal did not prevent him from introducing a commutation of tithes, and subjecting church lands to the general burthens of the state. He banished the inquisition, and reduced the number of monks and nuns, by restraining the facility with which the monastic vows had irrevocably been sealed. He opened the offices of state to all ranks; he threw down all exclusions and forms of absurd etiquette in his court; and he introduced a perfect equality in judicial rights. Finally, he simplified the forms of justice; he abolished torture, corporeal mutilation, the pain of death, and the confiscation of property; and yet he knew how to diminish crime, and to render assassination unknown in his dominions.

Such were the acts by which this great and good prince left his practical virtues to speak by their results. The defects of his character—for nature is not perfect, and history therefore cannot be a panegyric—were too anxious a desire of interference in the minor details of government, and too arbitrary a spirit in the enforcement of his favourite measures. He ardently desired the happiness of his subjects, but he resolved that they must be happy after his own ideas; and in his zeal to watch over the integrity of his ministers, he descended to the meanness of placing spies upon their actions, and gaining secret access to their papers by the use of false keys. His people were wearied of his vigilance, even in their own cause; and the machinations of the priesthood, and the depraved morals of the nation, often leagued to oppose his most salutary reforms. Thus when, after successfully devoting himself for twenty-five years to promote the prosperity of Tuscany, he was called to the imperial throne by the death of his brother Joseph II., he had too much reason to complain of the insensibility and ingratitude which secretly rejoiced at his removal. On taking possession of the Austrian states, in the year after the period to which this work is limited, he transferred the crown of Tuscany to his second son, Ferdinand Joseph. The total cessation of improvement in the state which he quitted, might then afford one more proof how fragile is the prosperity which the beat administered despotism can confer;

how short-lived the public rights which depend on the duration of one man's virtues and power, and which are neither guarded by the spirit of the people, nor secured by a free constitution against the malice or accidents of tyranny.

The languid annals of the duchy of Modena during the eighteenth century, will demand even less of our notice, than those of Tuscany; since while they offer only a similar spectacle of the decay, and final extinction of an ancient dynasty, their monotonous tale of public calamity is relieved by no fair interval of prosperity. I have mentioned that the duke Rinaldo of Este, who occupied the throne of Modena and Reggio when the new century commenced, entailed frightful misery upon his people by taking part in the war of the Spanish succession against the Bourbons. His subjects were horribly pillaged and ill-treated by the French during their successes: but the battle of Turin reinstated Rinaldo in his duchies; and the emperor, four years after the peace of Utrecht, rewarded his fidelity by selling to him the investiture of a third little duchy:—that of Mirandola, of which Charles VI. had deprived the noble house of Pico by confiscation. This accession of territory was, however, no recompense to the subjects of Rinaldo for their sufferings; and they smarted by a repetition of foreign oppression for his attachment to the house of Austria. In the war of the Polish election, Rinaldo, who had now attained a great age, was a second time obliged to fly, and to abandon his states to the French and Spanish armies; by the peace of Vienna he was a second time reinstated in his capital; and he soon after died there. (A.D. 1737.)

His son, Francesco III., who succeeded him, aggravated the misfortunes of his subjects by the display of a more warlike temper, of some talents for military command, and of more ambition for personal distinction. He was thus induced (reversing his father's politics) to take an active part in the war of the Austrian succession against Maria Theresa; and he was driven from his territories by her troops, and those of the king of Sardinia. While he was obliged, with his little army, to share the fortune of the Bourbon standards, his states being overrun for the third time in fifty years, were devastated and pillaged; and his people were crushed under the weight of enormous contributions. The peace of Aix-la-Chapelle at length restored his states to him, ruined by the depredations of the Austrians and Piedmontese, who had occupied them for several years; and he increased the general misery by his own exactions and ill-regulated measures of finance. His reign was protracted to forty-three years, and he died at a very advanced age; but his patronage of Muratori and Tiraboschi,—both his subjects, and the most learned among the modern Italians—is the only circumstance which reflects any honour upon his otherwise inglorious and oppressive administration. (A.D. 1780.)

Francesco III. was succeeded by his son, Ercole III., who was already in the evening of life when he assumed the ducal crown. It was the declining fortune of the house of Este to be represented by old men; and avarice is too often the vice of age. The two last dukes had been deservedly reproached with their exactions; and yet their rapacity might be remembered by their subjects for liberality and self-denial, in comparison with the grasping extortions of Ercole III. The miser-prince thus accumulated an immense treasure which, when the hour of foreign danger arrived, instead of serving for his defence, only excited the cupidity, and provoked the assaults of enemies. Ercole III. gave his only daughter in marriage to one of the Austrian archdukes; he had neither son nor male heirs; and before the convulsion of the French revolution shook him from his seat, he might already foresee the approaching and inevitable extinction of his line.

The fortunes of the house of Este flowed in a parallel channel with those of Italy:—a stream, fierce and turbulent in emerging from its dark and far remote source; sparkling, resplendent and beauteous in its onward tide: languid, cold, and sunless in its later course; and finally losing itself, silent and unnoticed, in the ocean of time. The marquises of Este displayed the blazonry of their nobility in the fields of Italy, long before the names of the Scala, the Carrara, the Gonzaga, the Visconti, the Medici, had broken forth from obscurity; and their descendants survived to witness the extinction of all these rival houses, and to perish the latest of the native dynasties of Italy. The story of the house of Este is connected, indeed, with the Italian annals, not by the support, but the destruction of Italian freedom; and the stern judgment of history will see little to applaud in the political career of its princes. But to the scholar, the enthusiast of poesy, the passionate votary of art, the court of Ferrara is classic ground; the very names of the lettered princes of Este, unworthy patrons of brighter spirits though they were, are a talisman for awakening sweet recollections; and it is impossible to follow the last of this race of ancient lineage and high associations to their ignoble tomb without some degree of interest, perhaps even of regret.

Having brought down the annals of the various monarchies and principalities of the peninsula to the appointed period, and traced the fate of all the native Italian dynasties to their extinction; it only remains for us to devote our concluding pages to the affairs of those two ancient and rival states, which still preserved the vain image of republican government. Genoa and Venice still existed, and their existence was associated to the world with the memory of their departed glories: when kingdoms were their subject provinces, and foreign capitals their factories; when their sons fiercely struggled for the mastery of the waves, and the spoils of the east were poured into their laps for the dowries of their daughters. Genoa and Venice still existed; but they existed only in their monuments of extinguished greatness, and veiled their imbecility only under the lengthening shadows of names that had once been mighty.

Genoa, anciently the throne of a bold and untameable democracy, insolent as brave, and licentious as free, had long become the quiet seat of a staid and imperturbable oligarchy. Severe and odious to the people, that sovereign body had bruised the head of the commonalty too effectually to dread any ebullition of the public hatred. During the first half of the eighteenth century, no event of interest or importance had marked the foreign relations of the republic,—except the insurrection of

Corsica, which I shall presently notice; and no domestic transaction disturbed the repose and inglorious oblivion which the senate desired for themselves and their state. In observing the nullity of the Genoese annals, which throughout this epoch offer no facts to merit our attention, it might have been imagined that all patriotism, all feeling against the stings of shame and tyranny, was utterly deadened and blunted in the people. But suddenly their domestic was exchanged for a foreign despotism; they were galled to the quick and goaded to desperation by brutal oppression; and then, in the midst of their degradation and decay, they proved that there had yet slumbered in their bosoms more than a spark of the generous fire, which had animated their forefathers. They charmed the attention and admiration of Europe by the last expiring and glorious burst of that hereditary spirit, once turbulent indeed, but nobly intolerant of servitude, and which two centuries of debasement had not been able utterly to extinguish.

In the war of the Austrian succession, the Genoese senate had been induced to join the Bourbon arms, because the king of Sardinia had espoused the opposite cause of Maria Theresa, and they dreaded his being permitted to seize the marquisate of Finale, to which they had some pretensions. The position of their republic rendered their alliance very acceptable to the French and Spaniards; and the empress-queen and Charles Emmanuel were enraged at their hostility in a commensurate degree. The efforts of the Genoese materially contributed to the success of the confederate Bourbons in the campaign of 1745; and the reverses of the following year left them exposed singly to all the vengeance of their exasperated enemies. The French and Spanish forces evacuated Italy, and retired, as we have seen, into Provence; they deserted Genoa to her fate; and while the Austrians and Piedmontese, their pursuers, appeared at the gates of the city, a British squadron blockaded the port. Terrified at their danger, the pusillanimous senate had no other thought than to capitulate; and the marquis Botta Adorno, the Austrian general, was suffered to take possession of the gates, without being even required to respect the honour; and independence of the state or the property of the people. The senate engaged to surrender their troops as prisoners of war; to deliver up all the artillery and warlike stores of the republic; to send the doge and six of their body to Vienna to implore the pardon of the empress-queen; and to place four other senators in the hands of the Austrian general, as hostages for the fulfilment of these disgraceful conditions.

Botta Adorno was no sooner admitted into the city with 15,000 men, while the remainder of the Austrian and Piedmontese army encamped in the Genoese territory, than he began to take the most insulting and oppressive advantage of his success and of the pusillanimity of the senate. His exactions, and the rapine and insolence of his troops, exceeded all bounds; and yet they fell short of the tyrannical and revengeful commands of his court. In less than three months, he extorted contributions to the amount of 24,000,000 florins; lie suffered his troops to commit the most brutal excesses among the citizens and peasantry; and he exiled many of the nobles. It was in vain that the senate strained every effort to satisfy his exorbitant demands: that the ancient national bank of St. George was drained of its treasures; that the church plate and the valuables of private persons were put in requisition; that the degraded government toiled to discover fresh means of appeasing their foreign tyrants. The Austrian general and his troops multiplied their rapacities and their insults; until, swallowing up property and outraging every feeling of humanity, they left the miserable people literally nothing but life to lose. The indignant passions of the Genoese were thus naturally heated to the last stage of desperation; and it required but the slightest collision to fill Genoa with the flames of insurrection.

At this juncture, a faint gleam of hope might break upon the goaded and suffering people, who still possessed courage to merit a better government than their degenerate oligarchy. The main Austrian and Piedmontese army passed on after their retreating opponents into Provence; Botta began to dispatch part of the artillery from the arsenal, to assist them in the siege of Antibes, and a petty accident in the streets produced a general insurrection. In the removal of a mortar its carriage broke down, a crowd was collected, an Austrian officer insolently struck a Genoese with his cane, who refused to assist in extricating the gun, and the long smothered hatred burst forth. The man boldly wounded the petty tyrant; the populace immediately assailed the Austrian party with a shower of stones; and the whole body of the lower people flew to arms. The numerous German garrison, confounded by the sudden revolt, attacked on all sides, entangled in the narrow streets of Genoa, and crushed under missiles from the housetops and windows, were overpowered and routed in detail. Their commanders, like themselves, were seized with a panic terror; the strength of the insurgents increased during the night, and every massive palace of Genoa was converted by the people into a citadel. In less than twenty-four hours, the Austrians were driven with disgrace from the city, with the loss of eight thousand men and all their artillery and matériel, and finally, they were compelled to evacuate the whole republican territory. The gates of Genoa and the passes of the mountains were occupied and guarded by the citizens and peasantry; and the independence of the republic revived.

This glorious assertion of freedom deserves to be recorded as the work alone of the lower people of Genoa and its rural dependencies. Some few of the senators, indeed, had bravely directed the operations of the citizens, after the insurrection became general, but their body collectively had for some time neither the energy to assume the military guidance of the state, nor the courage openly to support the desperate resolution of their subjects. Even after the Austrians were finally expelled, and the populace had bristled the ramparts with artillery, and armed themselves from the arsenals, the oligarchy endeavoured to disclaim to the council of state at Vienna all share in the insurrection, and it was only when they discovered that the Austrian government breathed nothing but vengeance, that they were driven to share the desperation of the people. They then solicited and obtained succours by sea from France, and several thousand French troops, under the duke de Boufflers, were introduced into Genoa to aid the citizens in the defence of the place, (A.D. 1747.) Thus, when the numerous Austrian and Piedmontese army, which had retired from Provence, forced the mountain passes and sat down before the walls, the courage of the Genoese and their allies set the formidable strength of their besiegers at defiance, and repelled all their attempts. When money was wanted, the ladies of Genoa voluntarily consigned their jewels to the public coffers; when provisions became scarce, the inhabitants endured hunger without a murmur; and though their fate was for some time doubtful, their resolution never slackened. At length they were relieved by a French army, which compelled their enemies to raise the siege; and in the following year the peace of Aix-la-Chapelle confirmed the recovered independence of the republic. But nobly and generously as the Genoese had saved their country, the fruits of the struggle were reaped only by the contemptible government whose cowardice had betrayed them: and the brave people, with miserable infatuation, suffered the feeble oligarchy again to rear its baleful head, and to lord it over their legitimate rights.

After this tale of heroism in the people of Genoa, we must turn to contemplate the continued fruits of misgovernment in their rulers. The senate had wanted vigour to defend themselves and their republic; and their own oppression of the only colony which had remained to the state, was as grievous as that which they would tamely have endured from their own foreign tyrants. Sixteen years before the surrender of Genoa, the people of Corsica had been driven by the intolerable exactions of Pinelli, the commissary-general of the republic, and her other officers, into a general insurrection against her yoke. The insurgents, under a popular leader named Pompiliani, reduced Bastia and other places of importance; and the Genoese senate, finding their own forces inadequate to repress the universal revolt, were obliged to have recourse to the emperor Charles VI. (A.D. 1730.) The Austrian troops filled Corsica with flames and bloodshed: but they had failed in subduing the stubborn courage of the half-civilized islanders, when the emperor recalled them to defend his own Italian dominions in the war of the Polish election; and the Genoese forces were then reduced to shut themselves up in their maritime garrisons.

From that epoch, the war of Corsica was an open wound which continually drained the strength of Genoa. The senate vainly endeavoured, alternately by arms, by negotiations, and by the most atrocious perfidy, to recover their authority. But against open hostilities the Corsicans were more than a match for their old masters; and every repetition of treachery only increased their exasperation, and their hatred of the Genoese yoke. At length the condition of Corsica tempted the wild ambition of a poor German baron, Theodore de Neuhoff, who had wandered an adventurer through several of the European courts. This man conceived the bold idea of making himself king of Corsica; and one of the strangest caprices of fortune realized his aspirations. From Genoa itself, he opened a correspondence with some of the principal Corsican insurgents. He impudently boasted of his influence with most of the crowned heads of Europe; the simple Corsicans were easily duped; and when he appeared in the island with a few followers and some arms which he had inveigled the regency of Tunis to lend him, the islanders flocked to his standard. He was crowned with a wreath of laurel instead of a jewelled diadem, under the title of Theodore I.; he formed a court; instituted an order of knighthood; and for some time aped the part of royalty with ridiculous success. (A.D. 1736.) His adventures might fill volumes; but his indigence broke the vain dream of ambition; and after quitting his kingdom and roaming over Europe in fruitless efforts to raise supplies equal to his designs, he at last died a beggar in London.

Meanwhile the senate of Genoa, hopeless of reducing the Corsicans without foreign aid, had recourse to the king of France. Louis XV. for many years afforded them succours of men and money: but the former served only to give the French power a footing in the island; and the immense debts contracted by the republic to the French monarchy, contributed still more to prepare the way for the loss of a colony, in which every effort failed to re-establish an authority deservedly hated by the islanders. The war of the Austrian succession obliged the French to withdraw their auxiliary forces from Corsica, as a preceding contest had compelled Charles VI. to discontinue his aid to the Genoese. A native republican government was established in the island; the Genoese, again assisted at intervals by France, continued their efforts; and the struggle proceeded for many years, until the celebrated Paschal Paoli at length appeared at the head of his countrymen. Though his reputation has been much exaggerated, Paoli wanted neither courage nor enlightened views to qualify him for his arduous situation. But when the French, after the close of the seven years' war, mingled again in the affairs of Corsica, first as mediators, and afterwards as hostile invaders; the difficulties which surrounded his administration, and divisions among the Corsicans themselves, rendered it, perhaps, impossible for him to avert the destruction of his government and the subjugation of the island.

The senate of Genoa, convinced of the hopelessness of recovering the dominion of their revolted colony, finally resolved to cede to Louis XV. the sovereignty which they could not retain. (A.D. 1768.) The French monarch gladly accepted so valuable an acquisition, as an indemnity for the immense sums which he had lent to the Genoese; and he caused himself to be proclaimed king of Corsica. Paoli and his islanders, although surprised, made an obstinate resistance to this usurpation; and Louis XV. expended much of the blood and treasure of his subjects in maintaining it. His troops were at the end of two campaigns even driven into the maritime fortresses. But at length the court of France seriously resolved on the reduction of the island; and the debarkation of a formidable French army decided the contest in two months. The timid, the wavering, the disaffected, deserted the cause of their country; Paoli was compelled to expatriate himself; and the Corsicans generally took the oaths of allegiance to Louis XV.

The decline of Genoa had at least been relieved by one transient and brilliant example of popular courage: the last age of the Venetian republic presented only the silent and unbroken progress of corruption, and the irretrievable decay of political energies. After the close of the seventeenth century, Venice fell into utter oblivion and contempt; and her senate, whose successful maxim it had long been to conceal the weakness of their state under the appearance of a wise moderation, could no more disguise the secret of their impotence. The important conquest of the Morea, for which they had been indebted to the splendid abilities of Francesco Morosini, and to the temporary distraction of the Porte in its war with the empire, was absolutely the last worthy achievement of the republican arms; and the overstrained efforts, by which it was dearly purchased, served only to hasten the moment of incurable exhaustion. The senate were more than ever, therefore, reduced to shun all participation in the contests of other powers; and they were prepared to endure every insult rather than endanger the precarious existence of their state by vain appeals to hostilities.

In the war of the Spanish succession, the senate persisted in refusing to take any part; and they contented themselves with the endeavour to inspire respect for their neutrality, by forming an army of about 20,000 men in their Lombard provinces, and putting their fortresses into a state of defence. But when the French and imperialists in northern Italy alternately violated their territory in the most flagrant manner, the senate appeared insensible to these insults. Their spiritless forbearance was canned yet farther. The emperor fitted out some vessels of war at Trieste: a petty French squadron, penetrating to the head of the Adriatic, made captures of Austrian and Venetian shipping employed in transporting supplies to the imperial armies in Lombardy, and even burnt an imperial man-of-war in the Venetian port of Malamocco: and still these repeated infringements of the boasted sovereignty of the gulf, and of the dignity of the republic, were patiently endured.

By submitting to these degradations, the senate maintained their inglorious neutrality to the end of the war; but peace was scarcely restored in Christian Europe, when their republic was assailed by a new and inevitable danger. They witnessed its approach with a blindness paralleled only by the insensibility which they had just exhibited: or rather, perhaps, they were still paralyzed by the same timidity, which had become habitual, to neglect every means of defence. The rumour of active and gigantic preparations in the arsenals of Constantinople could not rouse them to look to the security of their eastern dependencies; and when the sultan Selim III. suddenly broke the peace of Carlowitz without provocation, and directed a formidable armament by land and sea against the Morea, the Venetian troops in that peninsula did not exceed eight thousand men. The Turkish army, of ten times that force, broke through the isthmus of Corinth; that city and all the other fortresses of the Morea, which had been slowly won by the Venetians at the expense of so much blood and treasure, were able to make no effectual resistance, and in one short month the whole of the peninsula was conquered by the infidels. (A.D. 1714.) The alliance of the emperor with the Venetians diverted the efforts of the Turks, and saved the Dalmatian provinces of the republic from following the fate of the Morea. But in the third year of the war, a new and powerful Turkish armament made a descent upon Corfu, (A.D. 1716.) Notwithstanding the gallant defence of the governor, the famous Saxon count de Schullembourg, who had entered the Venetian service, that island must have fallen, if the Turks had not been terrified by the reverses of their arms in Hungary, into a voluntary abandonment of their enterprise. It was with little effect that the feeble Venetian fleet was joined, as in former contests against the infidels, by a few galleys of the pope, the grand-duke of Tuscany, and the order of Malta, and received the partial aid of small Spanish and Portuguese squadrons: it was to little purpose that the republican navy showed some remains of its ancient spirit, (A.D. 1717.) Two obstinate and indecisive combats could not retrieve the fallen fortunes of Venice; and the senate were compelled to accept the terms of the peace of Passarowitz, by which the emperor preserved his own conquests at the expense of his ally. (A.D. 1718.) Venice was obliged to abandon the Morea to the Porte; and the same treaty finally adjusted the limits of her frontiers and those of the Ottoman empire. Of all her eastern dependencies, she now preserved only the seven Ionian islands, the coast of Dalmatia and part of Albania; and these, with her lagunes, and her continental provinces in Italy and Istria, composed her territories:—an extent of dominion which might still have given power and commanded respect, if the administration of the republic had not already been diseased and corrupt at its vitals.

From this epoch, Venice fell from her place in history. Reduced to a passive and sluggish existence, her name ceased to be mingled in the political discussions, the alliances, and the wars of the other states of Europe. Her commerce was annihilated; her manufactures dwindled so miserably that, in one branch alone, that of cloths, the annual fabrication fell from one hundred and twenty to five thousand pieces; her revenues did not supply the expenses of her rapacious administration; and before the close of her career, her national debt had increased to 48,000,000 of ducats. Her naval force shrank to eight or ten sail of the line, a few frigates, and four galleys; and while she remained neutral and powerless, her claim to the sovereignty of the Adriatic was contemptuously violated in every maritime war of the European powers. In like manner, her Italian dominions were insulted with impunity throughout the first half of the century, whenever Lombardy was the theatre of hostilities. About twelve thousand Italian, Sclavonian, and other adventurers constituted her only military force; and from a debased and heterogeneous population of above 3,000,000 souls, her government drew no means of public defence.

This hopeless decay of political resources was accompanied by the reign of venality, peculation, and negligence in the provinces, and the palpable decline of vigour in the domestic administration of the capital. Whether this relaxation in severity in the government was itself the cause of the national weakness; or whether it was by that weakness that the oligarchy were taught to feel the necessity of conciliating the popular affection; the gloomy tyranny of Venice lost much of its energy during the eighteenth century. Originally constituted as it had been to restrain the power of the doge, to humble the pride even of the aristocracy from which it annually sprang, and to crush the license of popular spirit, the removal of its pressure was calculated to loosen all the bonds of order in the vitiated state. Four times during the last half of the century was it attempted in the great council to abolish the jurisdiction and existence of the council of ten and of the inquisitors of state; and though the project as often failed by the want of union among the nobles, the boldness with which it was repeatedly introduced, and the moderation with which the standing tyranny used its victory, equally betrayed that the national sloth and imbecility had stricken even the most active and merciless of despotisms. Debauched, unprincipled, and needy, the aristocracy had desired the annihilation of every check upon their embezzlements and vices: the degraded people hailed their self-inflicted defeat in these attempts with satisfaction, and rejoiced that a despotism yet remained, which reduced the nobles to a common slavery with themselves.

The inactivity of that despotism was seized by all classes as a privilege for unbounded licentiousness and depravity of morals. Dissoluteness of private life had, indeed, ever been permitted by the council of ten, to corrupt the public mind, and to divert its attention from affairs of state. The tyrants of Venice had trusted perhaps to their own energy, to supply the place of virtue and its attendant patriotism in the people. But their own vigour had fled; and the depravity of all classes had remained to increase with frightful intensity. It was then in vain that the government endeavoured to stem the tide of corruption in a city, where patricians presided at the public gambling tables in their robes of magistracy; where the miserable children of prostitution were employed by the police to ruin men whose wealth might render them dangerous; where the laws protected the contracts by which mothers unblushingly made a traffic of their daughters' honour; and where, by the facility of divorce, the ecclesiastical court was besieged at the same moment with nine hundred petitions for the privilege of legalized adultery .

Such was Venice, when the wild deluge of the French revolution swept her from the political map of the world. But we are not called upon in this place to observe the total extinction of her political existence; nor to contemplate the final ruin of that government, which for thirteen hundred years had resisted all the convulsions of time. Yet he who has lingered over her chequered annals, will quit them at the epoch before us with a melancholy interest; for he will see only in her miserable fall the consummation of the long tragedy of Italy. And among a free, and happy, and intellectual people, that tragedy will speak with a deep-fraught and awful application. By Englishmen it should never be forgotten, that it is only the abuse of the choicest bounty of Heaven, which has brought a moral desolation upon the fairest land of the universe: that it is because the gifted ancestors of the Italian people consumed their inheritance of freedom in wanton and licentious riot; because they recklessly gave the reins to their untamed and fatal passions; above all, because, in the early cultivation and refinement of intellect, they forgot to associate it with virtue, and presumptuously neglected to hallow it by religion, that their descendants have come to this thing:—that they have been abandoned to the scorn and oppression of the despots of Europe, and have become a bye-word of mingled contempt and pity to the more fortunate nations of the universe.

Made in the USA
Lexington, KY
18 January 2015